# Predictive HR Analytics

# Predictive HR Analytics
## Mastering the HR metric

Martin R Edwards and
Kirsten Edwards

LONDON  PHILADELPHIA  NEW DELHI

**Publisher's note**

Every possible effort has been made to ensure that the information contained in this book is accurate at the time of going to press, and the publisher and authors cannot accept responsibility for any errors or omissions, however caused. No responsibility for loss or damage occasioned to any person acting, or refraining from action, as a result of the material in this publication can be accepted by the editor, the publisher or the authors.

First published in Great Britain and the United States in 2016 by Kogan Page Limited

Apart from any fair dealing for the purposes of research or private study, or criticism or review, as permitted under the Copyright, Designs and Patents Act 1988, this publication may only be reproduced, stored or transmitted, in any form or by any means, with the prior permission in writing of the publishers, or in the case of reprographic reproduction in accordance with the terms and licences issued by the CLA. Enquiries concerning reproduction outside these terms should be sent to the publishers at the undermentioned addresses:

2nd Floor, 45 Gee Street
London EC1V 3RS
United Kingdom
www.koganpage.com

1518 Walnut Street, Suite 900
Philadelphia PA 19102
USA

4737/23 Ansari Road
Daryaganj
New Delhi 110002
India

© Martin R Edwards and Kirsten Edwards, 2016

The right of Martin R Edwards and Kirsten Edwards to be identified as the authors of this work has been asserted by them in accordance with the Copyright, Designs and Patents Act 1988.

ISBN      978 0 7494 7391 4
E-ISBN  978 0 7494 7392 1

**British Library Cataloguing-in-Publication Data**

A CIP record for this book is available from the British Library.

**Library of Congress Cataloging-in-Publication Data**

Names: Edwards, Martin R., author. | Edwards, Kirsten.
Title: Predictive HR analytics : mastering the HR metric / Martin R. Edwards, Kirsten Edwards.
Description: London ; Philadelphia : Kogan Page, [2016] | Includes bibliographical references and index.
Identifiers: LCCN 2015050726 (print) | LCCN 2016004035 (ebook) | ISBN 9780749473914 (paperback) | ISBN 9780749473921 (ebook)
Subjects: LCSH: Personnel management–Statistical methods. | BISAC: BUSINESS & ECONOMICS / Human Resources & Personnel Management. | BUSINESS & ECONOMICS / Organizational Development.
Classification: LCC HF5549 .E4155 2016 (print) | LCC HF5549 (ebook) | DDC 658.3001/5195–dc23
LC record available at http://lccn.loc.gov/2015050726

Typeset by Graphicraft Limited, Hong Kong
Print production managed by Jellyfish
Printed and bound by CPI Group (UK) Ltd, Croydon, CR0 4YY

# CONTENTS

*Preface* xi
*Acknowledgements* xiv

## 01 Understanding HR analytics 1

Predictive HR analytics defined 2
Understanding the need (and business case) for mastering and utilizing predictive HR analytic techniques 2
Human capital data storage and 'big (HR) data' manipulation 3
Predictors, prediction and predictive modelling 4
Current state of HR analytic professional and academic training 5
Business applications of modelling 7
HR analytics and HR people strategy 7
Becoming a persuasive HR function 8
References 8
Further reading 9

## 02 HR information systems and data 10

Information sources 11
Analysis software options 13
Using SPSS 15
Preparing the data 21
Big data 53
References 56

## 03 Analysis strategies 57

From descriptive reports to predictive analytics 57
Statistical significance 59
Data integrity 61
Types of data 62
Categorical variable types 62
Continuous variable types 64
Using group/team-level or individual-level data 66
Dependent variables and independent variables 66
Your toolkit: types of statistical tests 68
Statistical tests for categorical data (binary, nominal, ordinal) 75
Statistical tests for continuous/interval-level data 85
Factor analysis and reliability analysis 103
What you will need 106

Summary  106
References  107

## 04 Case study 1: Diversity analytics  108

Equality, diversity and inclusion  108
Approaches to measuring and managing D&I  109
Example 1: gender and job grade analysis using frequency tables and chi square  111
Example 2a: exploring ethnic diversity across teams using descriptive statistics  122
Example 2b: comparing ethnicity and gender across two functions in an organization using the independent samples t-test  128
Example 3: using multiple linear regression to model and predict ethnic diversity variation across teams  135
Testing the impact of diversity: interacting diversity categories in predictive modelling  141
A final note  143
References  143

## 05 Case study 2: Employee attitude surveys – engagement and workforce perceptions  144

What is employee engagement?  145
How do we measure employee engagement?  147
Interrogating the measures  150
Conceptual explanation of factor analysis  153
Example 1: two constructs – exploratory factor analysis  158
Reliability analysis  165
Example 2: reliability analysis on a four-item engagement scale  166
Example 3: reliability and factor testing with group-level engagement data  170
Analysis and outcomes  174
Example 4: using the independent samples t-test to determine differences in engagement levels  177
Example 5: using multiple regression to predict team-level engagement  183
Actions and business context  188
References  189

## 06 Case study 3: Predicting employee turnover  190

Employee turnover and why it is such an important part of HR management information  190
Descriptive turnover analysis as a day-to-day activity  192

Measuring turnover at individual or team level   192
Exploring differences in both individual and team-level turnover   193
Example 1a: using frequency tables to explore regional differences in staff turnover   194
Example 1b: using chi-square analysis to explore regional differences in individual staff turnover   198
Example 2: using one-way ANOVA to analyse team-level turnover by country   203
Example 3: predicting individual turnover   217
Example 4: predicting team turnover   226
Modelling the costs of turnover and the business case for action   231
Summary   235
References   235

## 07   Case study 4: Predicting employee performance   237

What can we measure to indicate performance?   238
What methods might we use?   239
Practical examples using multiple linear regression to predict performance   240
Ethical considerations caveat in performance data analysis   282
Considering the possible range of performance analytic models   283
References   284

## 08   Case study 5: Recruitment and selection analytics   285

Reliability and validity of selection methods   286
Human bias in recruitment selection   287
Example 1: consistency of gender and BAME proportions in the applicant pool   287
Example 2: investigating the influence of gender and BAME on shortlisting and offers made   290
Validating selection techniques as predictors of performance   302
Example 3: predicting performance from selection data using multiple linear regression   307
Example 4: predicting turnover from selection data – validating selection techniques by predicting turnover   310
Further considerations   317
References   318

## 09  Case study 6: Monitoring the impact of interventions  319

Tracking the impact of interventions  319
Example 1: stress before and after intervention  325
Example 2: stress before and after intervention by gender  330
Example 3: value-change initiative  336
Example 4: value-change initiative by department  344
Example 5: supermarket checkout training intervention  352
Example 6: supermarket checkout training course – Redux  359
Evidence-based practice and responsible investment  363
References  364

## 10  Business applications: Scenario modelling and business cases  365

Predictive modelling scenarios  366
Example 1: customer reinvestment  367
Example 2: modelling the potential impact of a training programme  373
Obtaining individual values for the outcomes of our predictive models  382
Example 3: predicting the likelihood of leaving  383
Making graduate selection decisions with evidence obtained from previous performance data  390
Example 4: constructing the business case for investment in an induction day  394
Example 5: using predictive models to help make a selection decision in graduate recruitment  398
Example 6: which candidate might be a 'flight risk'?  406
Further consideration on the use of evidence-based recommendations in selection  410
References  411

## 11  More advanced HR analytic techniques  412

Mediation processes  414
Moderation and interaction analysis  416
Multi-level linear modelling  421
Curvilinear relationships  423
Structural equation models  427
Growth models  427
Latent class analysis  430
Response surface methodology and polynomial regression analysis  431
The SPSS syntax interface  435
References  436

## 12 Reflection on HR analytics: Usage, ethics and limitations 437

HR analytics as a scientific discipline 437
The metric becomes the behaviour driver: Institutionalized Metric-Oriented Behaviour (IMOB) 439
Balanced scorecard of metrics 441
What is the analytic sample? 441
The missing group 443
The missing factor 444
Carving time and space to be rigorous and thorough 445
Be sceptical and interrogate the results 445
The importance of quality data and measures 446
Taking ethical considerations seriously 447
Ethical standards for the HR analytics team 450
The metric and the data are linked to human beings 451
References 452

*Index* 453

---

Supporting resources to accompany this book are available at the following url. (Please scroll to the bottom of the page and complete the form to access the resources.)

**www.koganpage.com/PHRA**

*To Lily and Max*

# PREFACE

## Who this book is for

This book is for anyone working in the human resource (HR) function, anyone working in a management information (MI) function, anyone who is studying HR, management or business analytics, and anyone who has to make decisions about people in an organizational context.

## Why we wrote this book

We decided to write this book because we saw a need for a straightforward how-to book to help people carry out some basic statistical analysis on the data available in organizations; analysis that can really unlock the enormous potential that exists in finding patterns and relationships between key pieces of information held about people and teams.

Martin began his journey into statistics and analytics when studying for an undergraduate degree in psychology. Subsequently, after an MSc in Industrial Relations and Personnel Management, Martin spent a number of years in HR consultancy, then completed a PhD at King's College London. Since 2002 Martin has taught statistics to business BSc students, MSc and PhD students at the King's School of Management and Business. He soon realized the need for this book after running some predictive HR analytics training sessions for a number of MI teams (there seemed to be a lack of application of any statistical methods to what HR MI teams tended to do; thus the real 'predictive value' of statistical analysis was not being realized).

Kirsten has loved mathematics ever since her parents bought her a 'Little Professor' handheld maths game at the age of four. From then on, she willingly relinquished any chance of being cool by proudly representing her high school in mathematics competitions in Australia in the 1980s, and whilst studying for her BSc in Mathematics spent much of her time tutoring schoolchildren who had difficulty with maths.

After her first graduate job at the Queensland TAB where she developed sales forecasting models and wrote uninteresting manuals for database systems (amongst other things such as helping novice gamblers to place bets on Melbourne Cup Day), Kirsten branched out into consulting and spent seven years at IBM (and various subsidiaries) and three years at Capgemini Consulting, working with organizations in North America, Europe and Asia. Whilst at Capgemini she completed an MSc in Human Resource Management and Organizational Analysis when she began to fully appreciate the potential of two worlds colliding – statistics and HR. She then went on to spend six years in the HR function at the Royal Bank of Scotland before returning to consulting again. Kirsten saw a need for this book to help others make the most of the information they have, help the HR function to claim further credibility in strategic organizational decision making and perhaps to relieve the anxiety felt by some when it comes to statistics.

Little Professor

# DIY

The key difference that this book has over other books on predictive HR analytics is that we show you how to actually run analyses with different types of HR-related data and we also guide you through the statistical models required for each type of analysis. Furthermore, we also show you how to run the analysis with SPSS. Whilst there are books on the market that discuss HR analytics, and there are also books out there that show people how to run statistical analysis with SPSS, no other book combines both of these. This book could be used by anyone who wants to learn statistical analysis techniques, and we use applied HR data here. It is not designed to be *just* a statistics book, but we go through the statistical procedures in enough depth for the reader not to need to buy a stats book as well (until they get a bit more advanced). However, this book is likely to be the most useful for people who want to get some experience running statistical models with HR data. This could be students on an HR master's degree or it could be MI practitioners who want some guidance on how to apply statistical models to their HR data.

## How to use this book

The structure of this book includes a brief introduction in Chapter 1 to the field of predictive HR analytics, where we set out how and why the analytic methods used in this book are different from the kind of activity that HR functions and MI teams currently undertake as a norm.

In Chapter 2 we discuss the nature of HR data and demonstrate how to convert HR data into a workable form to analyse with SPSS. We also explain why we use SPSS as a software package example.

Chapter 3 is really a reference section; it discusses the aim of statistical models, inferential statistics and significance. It then goes on to describe and outline the statistical analytic techniques used in this book; it sets out when certain analytic tests should be used in what context.

Chapters 4–9 are all case study 'meat and bones' chapters: Chapter 4 – diversity analysis; Chapter 5 – employee attitude and engagement data; Chapter 6 – employee turnover analysis; Chapter 7 – predicting employee performance; Chapter 8 – recruitment and selection analysis; and Chapter 9 – evaluating the impact of interventions. In each of these chapters we give a brief introduction to the issues and topic areas and demonstrate a number of ways that HR-related data can be analysed/modelled in each case. We supply example data sets to be used in each chapter and walk the analyst through how to run a range of possible analytic models in each case. Importantly we show how to interpret the statistical results and highlight some '*snapshot hidden gems*' that the analytic techniques expose in each case. The example data sets can be found at **www.koganpage.com/PHRA**.

Chapter 10 discusses and introduces a range of different more advanced analytic techniques that we do not cover but feel it is important for the budding analyst to get a conceptual understanding of their potential.

Chapter 11 is all about applying the predictive models to try and get the most out of the analysis in terms of 'predictive modelling'. Here we give examples of the true potential that predictive HR analytics can bring to an organization. Finally, we end the book on a reflective note: the journey of HR analytics is fraught with obstacles and potential sticky problems – this chapter encourages the analyst to reflect and think critically about the predictive HR analytic project, with the aim of ensuring that the analyst does not carry out HR analytics without considering the limitations and ethical challenges that the activity raises.

By the end of the book the HR analyst should have gained considerable experience of applying statistical models to HR data and should be ready to use their analytic capabilities and set sail into their own organization's ocean of people-related data. *Bon voyage*!

# ACKNOWLEDGEMENTS

There are several people we would like to thank in the creation of this book and it would be difficult to mention them all.

Very special thanks go to our reviewers, Katie Field, Kate Averre, Kim Hoque and Mike Clinton. Your collective insight greatly improved the book's academic rigour and professional application.

Thanks also go to some of Kirsten's previous colleagues for answering odd questions at random intervals on a plethora of things over the course of the last 12 months. This includes Helen Young, Sarah Mayhew, Mike McGowan and David Carnegie. Martin would like to specifically thank David, Riccardo, Jon and Mike at King's, all of whom showed enough encouragement to get the project underway!

We would also like to thank the individuals at Kogan Page for their guidance and support. In particular we would like to thank Katy Hamilton for supporting the project from the beginning and helping us get our ideas off the ground, Lucy Carter for her support and encouragement and finally Philippa Fiszzon and Amanda Dackombe for helping us get things over the line at the end.

We would also like to thank all the individuals who have kindly provided a testimonial for the book.

# Understanding HR analytics

**01**

> Arguably the most practical tool and greatest potential for organizational management is the emergence of predictive analytics.
>
> **FITZ-ENZ AND MATTOX II (2014)**

> Analytics present a tremendous opportunity to help organizations understand what they don't yet know... By identifying trends and patterns, HR professionals and management teams can make better strategic decisions about the workforce challenges that they may soon face.
>
> **HUSELID (2014)**

Much has been written and said about HR analytics over recent years and we are now seeing a number of books (eg Fitz-enz and Mattox II, 2014; Sesil, 2013; Smith, 2013) being published that can help inquisitive HR professionals (and HR students) begin to understand what predictive HR analytics might involve. As the above quotes demonstrate, some very influential HR thinkers are making impressive claims as to the potential that the application of HR analytics could bring to businesses. However, the reality is that even though many HR professionals may have a conceptual understanding of what HR analytics might involve, very few people have the relevant competencies to be able to actually carry out truly 'predictive' HR analytics. This book aims to help people develop these competencies and begin to demystify what may (for many) currently be hidden behind the 'magic curtain' of HR analytics; the book hopes to metaphorically pull back both curtains and give potential analysts the tools to tie them securely to the wall. Before we go on to discuss and help demystify HR analytics it is important to define our terms and set out our stall as to what we mean by 'predictive HR analytics'.

## Predictive HR analytics defined

We define 'predictive HR analytics' as: the systematic application of predictive modelling using inferential statistics to existing HR people-related data in order to inform judgements about possible causal factors driving key HR-related performance indicators.

Put simply, we take the sophisticated statistics and quantitative analyses techniques that scientists use to predict things (such as what may cause heart disease or what might help to cure cancer) and apply them to the information we hold about people in organizations. This enables us to test statistical models and predict things such as what might drive high performance or what might cause an employee to leave the organization. Furthermore, where appropriate, we can also then apply these predictive models to make tangible predictions about particular results or outcomes (eg employee or organizational behaviour) that we might expect to find given certain conditions.

Being able to apply predictive statistical models to HR-related data requires some knowledge of statistics and the capability (and experience) to understand and interpret meaning behind results that analyses are telling us. At the moment (as discussed in various places within this book) very few HR functions actually utilize statistical analytical techniques that are available to them. More often than not, whilst HR metrics and HR analytics teams do (at the moment) process and report on vast amounts of people-related data, very few apply statistical techniques that enable predictive inferences to be made.

## Understanding the need (and business case) for mastering and utilizing predictive HR analytic techniques

HR information and management information (MI) teams currently spend considerable time and effort producing descriptive report after descriptive report – monitoring them, comparing them across geographical boundaries and over time periods, but often doing very little else with the report other than producing it – again and again. Descriptive HR reports usually produced by MI teams will generally only present a picture or 'snapshot' of what is occurring in the organization at that particular time. Whilst there is little doubt that these reports are useful to the business in ensuring that managers understand what is going on within the organization, there is a real limit to what these reports can tell us. Descriptive reports do very little more than describe what is happening; they lack the capability to help understand and account for *why* things are happening in the organization. Furthermore, when running these reports, the analysts generally fail to interrogate the data fully for other possible explanatory factors (which can help clarify why something might be happening). They also tend to fail to test or check the degree to which their data might be robust and valid. Furthermore, descriptive reports do not in any way help us to make predictions about what we might find in the future. It is this ability that differentiates predictive HR analytics from the analysis currently carried out by the majority of HR MI teams.

Experts such as Bersin (2012) outline the importance of using predictive analytics to help organizations predict and understand the performance of a person (or indeed a group of people) based on available historical data. Once that sufficient people-related data has been collected over time, it is then possible to analyse patterns and trends based on this historical data. As quoted in the epigraph to this chapter, in 2014 Huselid argued: 'Analytics present a tremendous opportunity to help organizations understand what they don't yet know... By identifying trends and patterns, HR professionals and management teams can make better strategic decisions about the workforce challenges that they may soon face.' Predictive HR analytics therefore offers the opportunity to help model and analyse historical data and interrogate patterns in order to help understand causal factors and do exactly what Bersin and Huselid are suggesting is important.

Knowing what has happened in our organization and having evidence for why things have happened, in particular what the drivers are of certain behaviours within our organization, will undoubtedly help us to make better decisions. For example, if we can identify predictors of things like high performance, productivity increases, staff retention, higher employee and team engagement, then this information gives managers a good steer as to what strategic activities to invest in to help lever important employee outcomes.

## Human capital data storage and 'big (HR) data' manipulation

To be able to realize the potential of predictive HR analytics all of us are reliant upon what current and historical data is available. Predictive HR analytics relies completely on good data; we cannot look for patterns in data when the available data is limited and sketchy. Thus the success of HR analytics is completely reliant on the availability of good people-related information. As we discuss in Chapter 2, increasingly HR functions are not necessarily faced with the problem of there being a lack of data available – they are often faced with the problem that there is too much data to know what to do with. Much has been talked about in the popular and practitioner press about 'big data' (we discuss this in Chapter 2). Thus a challenge often faced by an HR analytics team is what to do with all the people-related HR data that is available. Once we have sufficient HR-related data, one of the biggest challenges is getting that data into the right format for analysis (we walk through an example of this in Chapter 2).

Useful HR-related data is made up of many different types of information and might include the following:

- skills and qualifications;
- measures of particular competencies;
- training attended;
- levels of employee engagement;
- customer satisfaction data;
- performance appraisal records;
- pay, bonus and remuneration data.

It takes time and considerable manipulation of data files to make sure that the models run are appropriate to the type of data available, so Chapter 2 talks more about systems and data, and Chapter 3 will help you to determine which models to run for which circumstance. Ultimately, the data available (and the data that is missing) is the key determining factor on what kind of analysis can be carried out and what business questions can be answered. The other important factor is respect for the 'head space' required to be able to fully engage with the data, the analysis, and what it all means for the organization.

# Predictors, prediction and predictive modelling

By definition, central to the idea of 'predictive' HR analytics is that something can be 'predicted'. One of the critiques sometimes posed at predictive HR analytics is that the 'predictive' part is very rarely realized. Obviously, if the future was known by an organization then this would be extremely useful and managers would be able to make strategic decisions in order to exploit it. Presumably this is one of the reasons why 'predictive analytics' as a term has become so popular. However, in terms of analytics, there are a number of ways that we can use the term 'predictive' and it is worth distinguishing this at the start so that we can be comfortable with our use of the term in this book (and indeed the title of the book!).

One of the ways that we (and others) use the term 'prediction' is related to the idea of identifying 'predictors' or potential 'causal' factors that help explain why a particular feature or measure shows variation (eg why performance levels vary amongst employees). As we explain in Chapter 3, some of the analytic techniques that we use aim to explore relationships between many different types of data (or variables) in order to identify 'predictors' of some important HR outcome (such as employee performance or staff turnover). This type of analysis is used to identify trends and relationships between multiple factors with the hope of obtaining information that suggests the possible causes of variation in the phenomenon that we are hoping to predict. Assuming that we find a range of significant features of our people-related data where variation is associated (in a unique way) with an increase or decrease in what we hope to account for, we can say that we have found potential 'predictors'. In this context one can also refer to these predictors as potential 'drivers' of our outcome. Importantly, the use of the word 'predictors' here implies that we seek out and have found potential 'causes' of variation on the feature we are trying to predict (see Chapter 12 for our discussion of causality and challenges of assuming that relationships found in data imply 'causality'). Almost all of our case study chapters (Chapters 4–9) utilize analytics that relate to this form of the word 'prediction'.

A second use of the term in the context of 'predictive HR analytics' is the use of 'predictive modelling'. Here, we take features and findings of our analysis (for example, where we identify a series of factors that were related to variations in staff productivity or sales), then we apply our model to help demonstrate or 'predict' what would happen to our key outcome variable (eg staff productivity or sales) if we could do something to change or adjust the key drivers that we have identified. We demonstrate this use of the word 'prediction' in Chapter 10.

Finally, a third use of the term 'prediction' that we can use in the context of 'predictive HR analytics' is that we can translate the findings from our 'predictive models' where we identified 'predictors' of variation in our particular outcome variable (eg staff productivity or sales) and use the resulting model to 'predict' how current or future employees (or teams) may behave (eg staff productivity or sales) in the future. We also demonstrate this use of the word 'prediction' in Chapter 10 where we show how, through identifying patterns and trends in existing data, you can apply a particular algorithm to newly collected information so as to provide evidence-based predictions of possible future behaviour that can help managers to make a decision.

Importantly, this book can help provide a 'walk-through' and demonstrate to students of HR analytics how they can apply statistics in order to fully utilize all aspects of the promise that the term 'predictive HR analytics' implies.

# Current state of HR analytic professional and academic training

At the time of writing, the majority of HR functions do not have the core capabilities to carry out predictive HR analytics activities. Certainly the vast majority of people who enter the HR profession (in the UK at least) do not have the required skills to be able to carry out any sophisticated predictive HR analytics. Having taught statistics and HRM to many hundreds of HR master's degree students over more than a decade, it is clear to Martin that many HR students can get to master's level training without having had any formal statistics training. There are always exceptions, of course, and the exceptions are often those who have learnt statistics at undergraduate degree level when they have come from a traditional discipline such as economics, mathematics or psychology, which have statistics as a substantial part of the degree content. Within many countries, even when students have come from a business or management degree, such students can often sidestep statistics (almost) completely. In addition to this, many HR professionals move into HR without formal academic training and are unlikely to have had any formal training in statistics.

If we take the UK as an example and we look at the competency requirements for membership into the Chartered Institute of Personnel and Development (CIPD), even with advanced-level module expectations there is very little requirement that candidates develop numerical abilities (let alone statistical abilities). At the time of writing, the requirement for statistical or numerical knowledge in advanced-level HR training with the CIPD is found in only one of the six learning outcomes, relating to employee engagement – and that quantitative learning outcome is an optional one (and thus can be avoided by those who see HR as a 'safe haven' from numbers). Interestingly, although this learning outcome is optional, the requirement does refer to what seems to be quite a rigorous statistical competence. The module requires the candidate to: 'design and undertake an analysis of relationships, causal or correlational, between level of employee engagement and organizational performance, measured by both process efficiencies and corporate outcomes'. This expectation is, however, undermined by the degree to which it is completely unrealistic to expect this of students who are learning this module – mainly because to achieve this the candidate will already need to have an advanced level of statistical training, especially for the 'causal' piece. If they do not, then their involvement with this particular learning outcome will be highly superficial.

The crucial point here is that reference to the necessity of developing statistical competence is either ambiguous or completely optional in the CIPD advanced-level syllabus, making it easy for HR students to succeed in getting through an advanced-level HR qualification without actually having built capabilities with quantitative analytic techniques. A cursory glance at the required capabilities and other HR professional bodies that one can find in other countries such as the AHRI (Australia), SHRM (United States), HRPA (Canada) and NIPM (India) tells a similar story.

Whether the individual is an HR generalist, a specialist in one particular area (such as talent, diversity or engagement), or the head of HR for a large multinational organization, the need to identify and understand trends and patterns, to take bias and gut instinct out of decision making, and to predict organizational challenges is something that will set them apart in becoming a credible, high-performing HR professional in a persuasive HR function helping an organization to be successful. This competence gap needs to be addressed if the HR profession is to fully exploit the opportunities that Huselid is alluding to in the quote at the beginning of this chapter.

Importantly, one of the key aims of this book is to help educate HR students and practitioners so as to help have a positive impact on the profession as a whole by adding to the quantitative literacy of people within it. Of course, in trying to achieve this aim, we will always be confronted with the phenomenon of many people having an automatic 'off switch' when it comes to statistics. This is no doubt why books out there have titles such as *Statistics for people who think they hate statistics* and *Statistics without tears*, etc. We argue, and truly believe, that having a strong quantitative analytic capability and knowledge of statistics will provide a firm foundation for any HR professional. Thus, mastering the HR metric by learning to carry out predictive HR analytics will fundamentally strengthen the skillset of the profession.

## Business applications of modelling

Almost all of the analyses presented in this book will have significant business implications and application; sometimes this is obvious and sometimes this requires a careful consideration of the results of the models tested. One of the things that the HR analytics team will need to be able to do, as a matter of course, is to be able to translate analysis findings to potential business applications. We discuss this in Chapter 10 where we give some examples of translating our predictive models to specific applications. However, we only touch the surface of presenting examples of ways in which the analytics in this book could be translated to specific business applications. Importantly, any HR analytics team should instil a mentality of always looking to answer the 'So what?' question (one that they will inevitably be asked when presenting their analytic results). The analytics team need to be always on the lookout for how their findings could be translated to useful practice knowledge, and whether any particular knowledge gained can help to strengthen and steer the organization's people strategy.

## HR analytics and HR people strategy

In learning and applying the methods outlined in this book, it should become obvious to the analytics team that it is possible to use analytical models to help steer, adjust and even drive business strategy. Ultimately the analytics approaches recommended can provide evidence-based pointers for practice and can help take some emotion and gut instinct out of 'people' decision making. Methods such as those described in all of the case study chapters should be able to help highlight key strategic factors to focus on when dividing a people strategy plan, and the methods outlined in Chapter 9 (monitoring the impact of people interventions) will assist the HR function in tracking and monitoring the success of their people plan (proving opportunities for reflection and adjustment to the plan). We discuss how to use predictive models to improve performance, turnover and hiring decisions – essential areas of HR on which the success of the function is measured. Hopefully the methods discussed in this book will assist HR analytics teams and their organizations to make sound, evidence-based people decisions that will help the organization to prosper – and, in doing so, value the HR function.

## Becoming a persuasive HR function

*The development of HR's strategic role has been an evolution...*
*The next step in the evolution is for HR professionals, and particularly senior HR professionals, to develop what we call analytic literacy.*

**HUSELID AND BECKER (2005: 279).**

As you work through this book, you will begin to understand the opportunities that can open up for answering business questions, even those that have not been asked yet! We believe that this 'analytic literacy' will help transform the HR function. An HR function that fully utilizes predictive HR analytics capabilities will be more credible because the function will be able to present robust 'hard' evidence to show that it has a good understanding of what makes its people tick, along with knowledge of who is likely to perform well, who is likely to leave, which parts of the organization are showing race or gender bias, which candidates are likely to be successful in the organization, and which interventions had a significant impact on the organization and which did not. The function will be able to carry out substantial 'what if' scenario modelling to help build solid business cases that help the organization to make decisions around whether particular investments are likely to be worthwhile, and what the return on those investments are likely to be.

By systematically going through this book and the exercises provided, any developing HR analytics team should have increased their capabilities and learnt many things that will help them to become *Masters of the HR Metric*.

## References

Bersin, J (2012) The HR Measurement Framework, Bersin and Associates Research Report, November

Fitz-enz, J and Mattox II, J R (2014) *Predictive Analytics for Human Resources*, Wiley, New Jersey

Huselid, M A and Becker, B E (2005) 'Improving Human Resources' Analytical Literacy: Lessons from Moneyball', in D Ulrich, M Losey and S Meisinger (Eds), *Future of Human Resource Management*, John Wiley and Sons, New York

Huselid, M (2014) [accessed 30 November 2015] The Corporate Mirror, *D'Amore-McKim School of Business* [Online] http://www.damoremckimleadersatworkblog.com/corporate-mirror-looking-big-data-analytics-workforce-management/#sthash.4qx5y7F3.dpuf

Sesil, J C (2013) *Applying Advanced Analytics to HR Management Decision: Methods for selection, developing incentives and improving collaboration*, Pearson, New Jersey

Smith, T (2013) *HR Analytics: The what, why and how...*, CreateSpace Independent Publishing Platform

## Further reading

CIPD [accessed 30 November 2015] Talent Analytics and Big Data – The Challenge for HR [Online] http://www.cipd.co.uk/hr-resources/research/talent-analytics-big-data.aspx

Holley, N [accessed 30 November 2015] Big Data and HR: The Henley Centre for HR Excellence, *Henley Business School* [Online] http://www.henley.ac.uk/html/hwss/files/Henley-Centre-for-HR-Excellence-Big-Data-Research-paper.pdf

IBM [accessed 30 November 2015] Analytics: The New Path to Value, *IBM and MIT Sloan Review* [Online] http://www-935.ibm.com/services/uk/gbs/pdf/Analytics_The_new_path_to_value.pdf

KPMG [accessed 30 November 2015] People are the Real Number: HR Analytics has Come of Age [Online] https://www.kpmg.com/GR/en/IssuesAndInsights/ArticlesPublications/Documents/workforce-analytics-download.pdf

# HR information systems and data     02

We hope that Chapter 1 has given you a good understanding of the benefits that predictive HR analytics techniques can bring to an organization. Before we get into the actual analysis piece, it is worth taking time out to understand the lay of the land. What type of data do you have in the organization already: what illuminating nuggets of information may be hidden on a spreadsheet in a colleague's personal folder, or the sales database, or the learning and development (L&D) records that could all tell a story when the pieces come together?

To illustrate with a simple example, looking at the customer satisfaction survey results alone can provide some useful information about how our customers feel about our customer-facing staff. It is difficult, though, to determine prescriptive action that should be taken from customer satisfaction survey results by themselves. If the results are poor overall, we may issue a guidance paper to all customer-facing staff. If, however, the data is linked to L&D team records, we might find that staff who attended a relationship management course in the previous quarter obtain the best customer service results. Or if we link it to our client profile information, we might find that it is our ethnic minority clients in branches outside major cities that are our most dissatisfied, suggesting that we may need to provide some unconscious bias or diversity awareness training. The more relevant information we have linked, the better chance we have of understanding the big picture of what is actually going on, which in turn means the better chance we have of correctly diagnosing a problem and prescribing a solution that will work – we don't want to spend time and money putting a plaster cast on the entire foot if all that is broken is the middle toe.

In this chapter, we look at:

- information source examples: what you are likely to find and where;
- the software: a short review of analytics software packages;
- using SPSS: becoming familiar with the SPSS environment;
- preparing the data: what the data looks like, getting it into SPSS and preparing it for analysis;
- big data: what it is and why it is valuable to organizations.

While it would be impossible to list all of the possible information sources in all organizations, the next section looks at what many organizations are likely to have and may give you ideas on where to look.

# Information sources

The information available in the form of data to be analysed will vary greatly depending on the type of organization. In this book, we look not only at the data typically managed by an HR department, but also important customer satisfaction and operational data that is key to running a successful organization. The key is not to be limited by what is immediately available in the HR department, even if you are in an HR role. It is when the information is expanded, linked together and analysed with rigorous statistical techniques that we find what is truly happening in our organization. Some examples of the types of data we consider in this book are outlined in Table 2.1.

By linking data sources and thinking broadly across the whole organization, we are able to model organizational patterns of behaviour and link HR and people-management practices directly with revenue and efficiency. In order to link and analyse the information available with ease, we need to use a statistical analysis package, of which there are many available on the market.

**TABLE 2.1** Information source examples

| Information Source | Description | Example |
| --- | --- | --- |
| HR database (such as SAP or Oracle) | Information describing the employee across a wide range of people-management activities, including employee personal details, performance, diversity data, promotion information. | Age, gender, education level, role, salary, performance ratings, disabilities, tenure, sickness absence, leaver information, country location, team leader, etc. |
| Employee attitude survey data (often stored in survey programmes and exported to Excel) | Survey results from annual employee attitude surveys. Either managed in-house or with an external survey provider organization. Typically containing employee engagement data. The information will depend purely on the questions asked in the survey; however, the examples to the right will give an idea of what can be included. Further information on employee engagement and survey data can be found in Chapter 5 (employee attitude surveys – engagement and workforce perceptions). | Job-strain level, employee engagement, job satisfaction, person–organization fit and perceptions of justice. |

**TABLE 2.1** *continued*

| Information Source | Description | Example |
|---|---|---|
| Customer satisfaction survey data (often stored in survey programmes and exported to Excel) | Often run by marketing or sales functions, customer satisfaction survey data often provides extremely useful information about customer preferences and, when linked to employee profile and operational data, can help organizations to identify how changes to employee skills and behaviours, as well as any operational or process changes, can have a direct impact on the customer experience. Further information on employee engagement and survey data can be found in the employee engagement case study in Chapter 5. | Customer ratings on specific services, branches and customer-facing employees, customer loyalty, customer preferences, customer satisfaction, likelihood of further business. |
| Sales performance data | Information usually owned by the sales function, recording details of sales performance and revenues. This information is key to determining organizational revenues and the success or otherwise of salespeople and teams in meeting targets. When linked with employee data and operational information it can also help determine the conditions under which salespeople and teams are more likely to succeed or, put another way, what individual or team characteristics tend to make for a more positive bottom line. | Average monthly sales, number of new customers introduced, meeting or not meeting target, individual or team daily, weekly or monthly sales. |
| Operational performance data | Information or data measuring the successful running of the business. Usually referring to efficiency. | Supermarket scan rates, call-centre call durations, average number of calls dropped out, average number of queries resolved on first contact, time taken to onboard a new customer, etc. |

# Analysis software options

There is no shortage of statistical software programs and, because many of them are prohibitively expensive for individual users, the one you use is likely to be determined by the organization you are currently involved with. The good news is that there is lots of overlap between the packages, and the analyses generally produce the same core output; once you learn one, it is relatively straightforward to transfer those skills to another system. So although in this book we only use SPSS for our examples, the skills you learn and the analytic methods we take you through may be applied in most other systems. Here are a few of the common analysis software systems that you are likely to encounter and some details according to an online review by a stats expert (Kane, 2012).

## *SPSS*

SPSS is a very user-friendly statistical package (which is the main reason we use SPSS in our examples in this book) with a graphical user interface and a point-and-click menu for running procedures. It is relatively easy to learn and, although it does have the option for coding syntax for the more advanced user, it is the clear leader of all the statistical software packages in its ability to run many complex procedures by using the mouse and menus alone. Although SPSS does not cover all statistical procedures, it does cover what is required by 95 per cent of users (and each new version seems to have more and more options). SPSS is the best package for being able to transfer output to other formats for reports. Although it can sometimes be slow at processing very large amounts of data, SPSS is good for extracting subsets of smaller data for analysis and the process to do this is relatively simple to learn. Once you have the data loaded into SPSS, a great benefit is the ease at which it is possible to manipulate that data (eg to relabel and create new variables, etc).

## *Minitab*

Minitab also has a user-friendly menu-based user interface for running procedures and has been noted as the simplest package to learn. Like SPSS, Minitab enables users to do most analysis procedures without having to understand the coding syntax. It does not cover all statistical procedures, but does cover what is required by 95 per cent of users. In terms of manipulating data, once the data is in Minitab, it can sometimes be difficult to change (Kane, 2012). It can also be difficult to transfer output to other formats for inclusion in reports.

### Stata

Although Stata does have some menus, it is primarily command-line driven and hence takes a bit longer to master. Stata does offer a more comprehensive range of statistical procedures and is often used by economists. It is quite good at being able to manipulate data once it is in the system; however, the user will need to learn the command-line interface systems in the first instance. On the negative side, it can be difficult to transfer data and output to other formats for reports (Kane, 2012).

### SAS

SAS is primarily a command-line-driven package with relatively few menu-driven procedures. For this reason it can take some time to master. It is a very powerful package and offers a more comprehensive range of statistical procedures than the others discussed here. It is also the leader in being able to handle large amounts of data, which could be pertinent depending on the type of organization, and particularly relevant considering the section on 'big data' later in this chapter. It is also possible to extract small subsets of large data quickly. Finally, it can also be difficult in SAS to transfer output to other formats for reports (Kane, 2012).

### R

Possibly the most exciting thing about R is that it is free. R is command-line syntax driven, which requires a fair amount of learning time in the first instance; it does have a menu-driven user interface as well but this is rather limited. The limited nature of the user interface, however, does mean that it is far more difficult to learn than SPSS or Minitab – you have to learn a programming syntax language. R is one of the leading packages when it comes to the range of statistical procedures offered; however, it is worth noting that 95 per cent of most users of statistical software packages – and arguably 100 per cent of HR analytics professionals – could get what they need from packages such as SPSS and Minitab, which are far more user friendly. Deep analysis of output often requires further commands and the user needs to know what they are looking for. Kane (2012) also notes the graphical output that R produces to 'pretty much blow away anything that seems feasible in other packages'. While it is said to have the best data importation facility of all the packages, it is said to struggle with very large data sets (Kane, 2012). Finally, it requires command-line edits in order to manipulate the data once it has been imported. Definitely one for the experts!

## JASP

A new software package to definitely look out for is JASP. Although at the time of writing this book, the JASP program is still in development stage, early versions show this to have the potential to be a game changer in 'point and click' user interface statistical software packages. Like R, the developers intend to make this freely available. Definitely one to watch!

None of the packages outlined here, however, produce high-quality graphs. So if you are looking to put your report into an executive or board paper, one option is to put the data into a charting package at the end. There are a lot of packages on the market to do this; some recommended by Kane (2012) are SigmaPlot, Grapher, MagicPlot and ThreeDify Excel Grapher.

# Using SPSS

Although there are many statistical software packages available on the market, for the case studies outlined in this book we have decided to use SPSS. Why? Largely because it is the one we have most experience in; it is also one of the most 'user friendly'. If your university or organization uses different software, don't worry, you will still find the case studies and analysis useful – indeed the analytic methods outlined in Chapter 3 are the same regardless of the software. If, in our case study example, we recommend a particular form of analysis and discuss results, a user familiar with another program should be able to translate these examples to another package with relative ease. Importantly, the output should be the same across all packages. Also, once you get to know one statistical software package, it is much easier for you to learn a second one – because you are essentially trying to do the same thing. It is the work beforehand – knowing which test or which procedure to run – that is where the real skill comes in. Chapter 3 (Analysis strategies) will walk you through the steps in determining which statistical test to use in which situation. It is also worth noting that the screenshots and menu commands used in this book are based on SPSS version 20.0 (Mac).

The first thing you will notice about SPSS is that it has two windows: the data view and the variable view.

## The SPSS data view

The SPSS data view has a similar appearance to a Microsoft Excel spreadsheet. You can either enter the data manually or import it from another source. This is the screen where you can view and edit the raw data (see Figure 2.1).

**FIGURE 2.1**

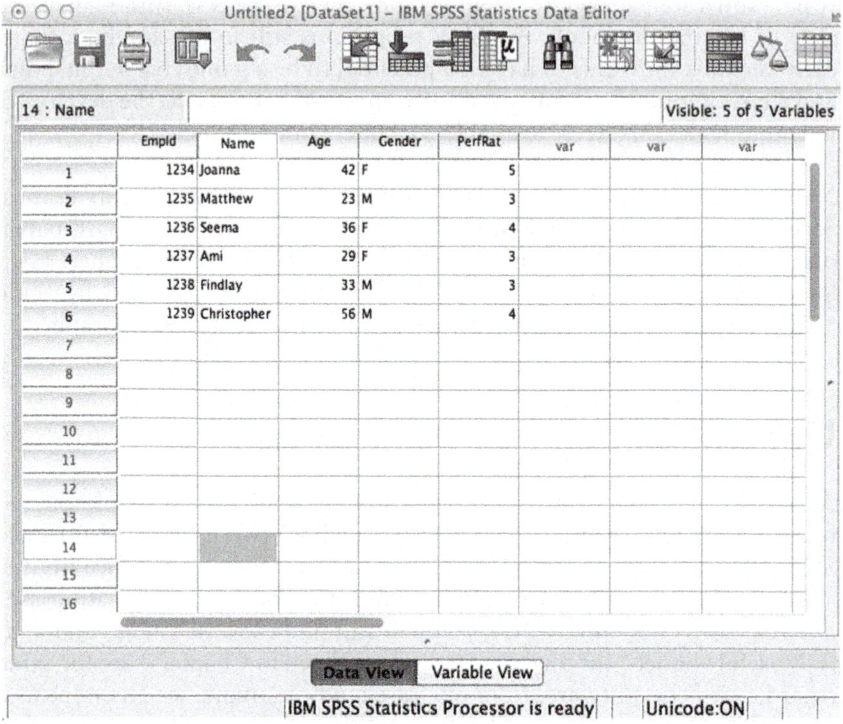
Untitled2 [DataSet1] - IBM SPSS Statistics Data Editor
14 : Name
Visible: 5 of 5 Variables
EmpId Name Age Gender PerfRat var var var
1 1234 Joanna 42 F 5
2 1235 Matthew 23 M 3
3 1236 Seema 36 F 4
4 1237 Ami 29 F 3
5 1238 Findlay 33 M 3
6 1239 Christopher 56 M 4
Data View
Variable View
IBM SPSS Statistics Processor is ready
Unicode:ON

In the data view, we have the following key pieces of information:

- Each row is a 'case', which for much of the work we do in HR analytics would be an employee (or possibly another object entity such as a team if the data set represents team-level data). When the data is linked to individuals, you could think of each row as storing all information on each employee.
- Each column is a 'variable', which represents a characteristic or attribute of the employee, such as age, gender or performance rating.
- Each cell is then a value. It shows the value of the variable for the case, or the value of the attribute for the employee: for example, 42 years old, female, with a performance rating of 5.

So, in many examples in HR analytics, there will typically be one row for each employee.

Helpfully, data can be cut and pasted to and from SPSS and Microsoft Word or Excel.

## The SPSS variable view

We talk about the different types of variables in detail in Chapter 3, but for now we can just focus on setting up the names and characteristics of the variables. As for the names of the variables, we can think of these names as the column headings in the data (similar to Excel). Just as we are able to format the cells in a spreadsheet to be a number, currency, date, text, etc, we can also set the variable attributes in SPSS; we do this in the 'variable view' (see Figure 2.2).

When you switch to the variable view (by clicking on the 'Variable View' tab at the bottom of the screen; see Figure 2.2) you will see that this view shows us all the variables and their attributes. Here each row represents a variable, and each column is a variable attribute. In the variable view we can add, delete and modify variables. When we add a variable, the attributes we need to set and how this is done are outlined below.

### Variable name

The variable 'Name' cell (see Figure 2.2) is where you enter the name of the variable: you simply type this into the cell. SPSS can be a bit picky about the variable names so you may find that you type in a name you are happy with only to be asked to change it. If you keep to the following basic rules, though, you will be okay in most cases:

- Make sure each variable name is unique. This makes sense – we would get confused about which one you were talking about if you had duplication.
- Do not have any spaces in the variable name.
- Stick with the alphabet. If you do use numbers and symbols, make sure they are not the first character.

### Type

The variable 'Type' cell (see Figure 2.2) is where you enter the data type of the variable, similar to in Microsoft Excel where you select whether the cell is a date or a number, etc. Once you click on the Type cell in the variable view you will see the box presented in Figure 2.3.

In most cases in HR analytics, you will be working with numbers ('Numeric') as in the values for a variable measure such as 'age' (eg 46, 55, etc), or text values such as the variable 'employee first name' (eg Joe, Mary, Bob), or a date, such as 'start date' (eg 24/07/2015). It is important to set these up in the variable view before entering any data.

### Width

In the variable 'Width' cell (see Figure 2.2) you simply enter the number of characters used to display the data. A 'Numeric' will default to 8 and a 'String' will default to 16.

FIGURE 2.2

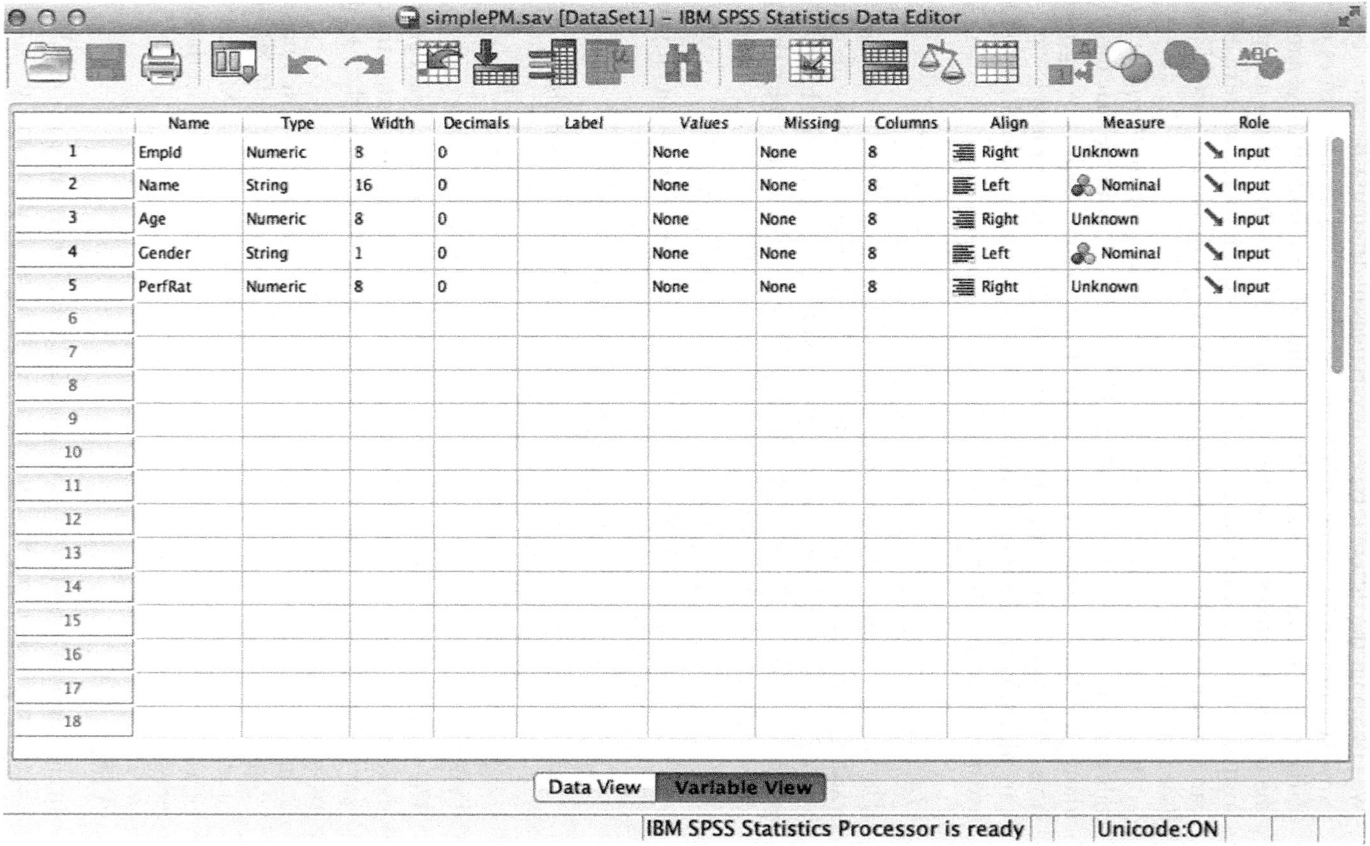
simplePM.sav [DataSet1] – IBM SPSS Statistics Data Editor
Name Type Width Decimals Label Values Missing Columns Align Measure Role
1 EmpId Numeric 8 0 None None 8 Right Unknown Input
2 Name String 16 0 None None 8 Left Nominal Input
3 Age Numeric 8 0 None None 8 Right Unknown Input
4 Gender String 1 0 None None 8 Left Nominal Input
5 PerfRat Numeric 8 0 None None 8 Right Unknown Input
6
7
8
9
10
11
12
13
14
15
16
17
18
Data View
Variable View
IBM SPSS Statistics Processor is ready
Unicode:ON

## FIGURE 2.3

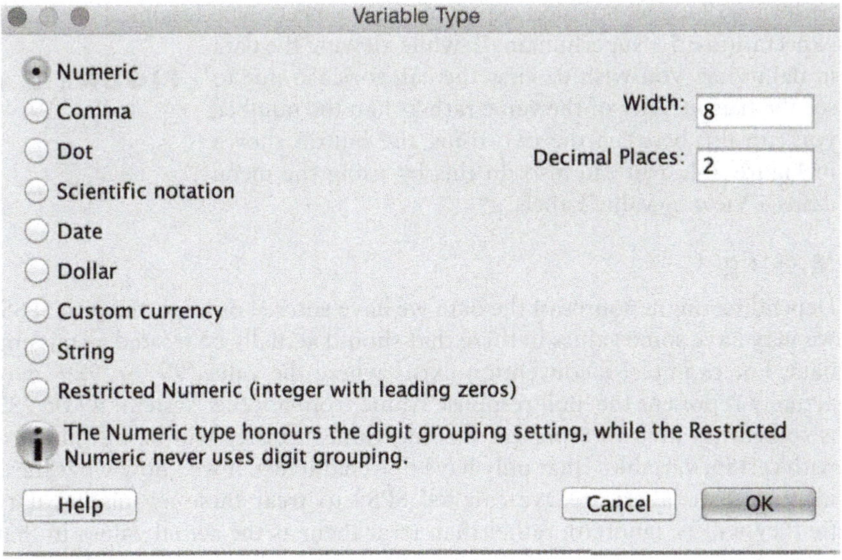

```
Variable Type

● Numeric
○ Comma                           Width: 8
○ Dot                             Decimal Places: 2
○ Scientific notation
○ Date
○ Dollar
○ Custom currency
○ String
○ Restricted Numeric (integer with leading zeros)

ⓘ The Numeric type honours the digit grouping setting, while the Restricted
   Numeric never uses digit grouping.

     Help                              Cancel      OK
```

## Decimals

If the data type is numeric, the variable 'Decimals' cell (see Figure 2.2) is where you can enter the number of decimal places you would like. This is similar to the equivalent function in Microsoft Excel. For example, if you enter 2 here, then any value would be stored with two decimal places, eg 6.05.

## Label

The variable 'Label' cell (see Figure 2.2) is where you can enter a textual description of the variable. This can be much longer than what you entered in the Variable Name field. In the case of an employee engagement survey, often the whole question is entered, eg 'When I get up in the morning, I feel like going to work'. This example is used in the 'engagement' case study (Chapter 5) as a measure of 'vigour', which is the variable name. It is part of a set of questions where the participant is asked to answer how much they agree or disagree with the statements on a scale of 1 to 5.

## Values

Generally in HR analytics statistical modelling we will use numeric values to represent categorical variable labels. See Chapter 3 for a more detailed explanation of categorical variables. What we mean by this is when, for example, a value of 0 may represent 'female' and a value of 1 may represent 'male'. We sometimes do this because representing the values as numeric in this way opens up a whole world of analysis that we would not otherwise be able to carry out were we to use the text (or 'string') value. Another example might be to enter performance rating meanings; for example: 1 = very poor performer; 2 = does not meet expectations; 3 = meets expectations; 4 = exceeds expectations; 5 = superhuman. If, while viewing the data in data view, you wish to view the categorical value to see the true identity of the value rather than the number, you can flip between the two using the button shown in Figure 2.4. You can also do this by using the menu items – View -> Value Labels.

**FIGURE 2.4**

## Missing

Depending on the source of the data we have entered or imported into SPSS, we may have some values in there that should actually be treated as missing data. For example, a convention exists where the value '99' or '999' may actually represent the 'null response' value from another system; 99 or 999 is sometimes used to represent missing values as they will be meaningless with certain variables (that only have one character). If we know what these missing data labels are, we can tell SPSS to treat these as missing data (ie they will be ignored), rather than treat them as the actual values in that place. You can set these in the variable 'Missing' cell (see Figure 2.2).

## Columns

In the variable 'Columns' cell (see Figure 2.2) you can use the up and down arrows to set the width of the column for when the data is being viewed in the data view mode.

## Align

In the variable 'Align' cell (see Figure 2.2), this is simply where you set the alignment of the cell in data view mode, ie left or right justified, or centred.

## Measure

In the variable 'Measure' cell (see Figure 2.2) you can describe the 'level' of the measurement, which we can set to be nominal, ordinal or scale. If the values describe different categories of something that has no particular order, for example eye colour (blue, green, brown, black, hazel, grey, etc), then we would say that the data is nominal. If the data values describe different categories of something that does have an order, for example, salary band (band a, band b, band c) or performance rating (1, 2, 3, 4, 5) where we can look at increases and decreases, we would call the data 'ordinal'. If, however, the value is a continuous number, and not necessarily whole numbers, such as that which we would measure on a scale, for example 23.5 degrees Celsius, 124.6 miles, 46 kilogrammes, this data would be called 'scale' data.

Once you have set up variables in the variable view, you can either enter data directly into the data view, or import data from another file.

## Preparing the data

Data may be typed into the SPSS data view, or it may be imported from an existing file such as an Excel spreadsheet. See the example below, which will walk you through the process of entering and importing data.

The annual performance review project manager, Remi, has forwarded you an e-mail he has just received from the marketing team manager containing some key information about performance results of her team. For each of the five employees on the marketing team, the e-mail contains the following information:

- employee ID;
- performance rating;
- salary adjustment (percentage).

Until you train Remi and the other managers to enter data into a spreadsheet (which you will soon see is much easier) rather than an e-mail, for each manager you will have to go through the exercise set out below. The first step, then, is to create a new file and enter the data manually into the data view. Remi has at least promised to be consistent and provide you with the same information from each manager.

### Setting up variables in the variable view and entering data manually into the data view

You will need to set up each variable first in the variable view before entering the data in the data view. Opening SPSS will present you with a data view and a variable view. Click on the variable view to begin setting up the variables.

The first variable is employee ID, so let's call it EmpId in the 'Name' column (see Figure 2.5).

In the 'Type' column, click on the button with the three dots (see Figure 2.6) to bring up the Variable Type selection box (see Figure 2.7), select String and hit OK. Employee ID has both numbers and letters, so we can treat it as a character string.

The 'Width' defaults to 8, which is fine; we have no decimal places in a string, so we can leave that also.

**FIGURE 2.5**

|   | Name  |
|---|-------|
| 1 | EmpId |

**FIGURE 2.6**

| Type   |     |
|--------|-----|
| String | ... |

## FIGURE 2.7

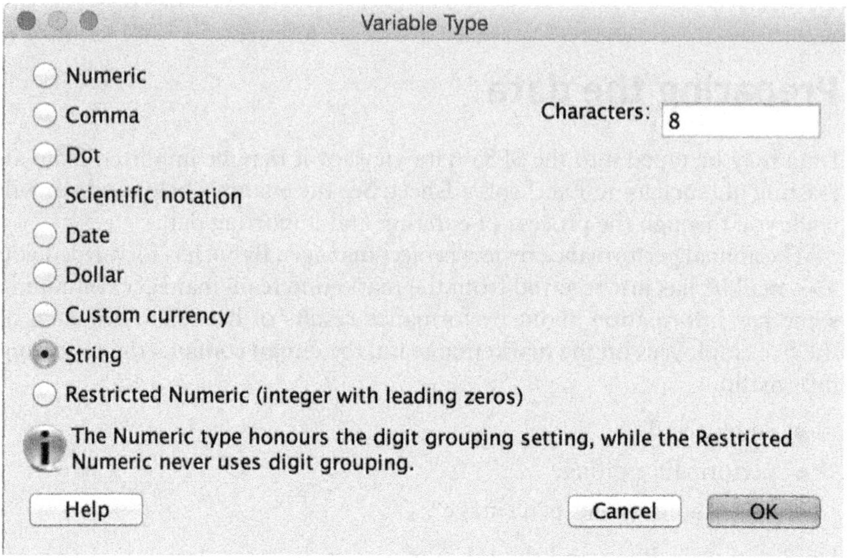

```
●  ●  ●                    Variable Type

   ○ Numeric
   ○ Comma                              Characters: 8
   ○ Dot
   ○ Scientific notation
   ○ Date
   ○ Dollar
   ○ Custom currency
   ● String
   ○ Restricted Numeric (integer with leading zeros)

   ⓘ  The Numeric type honours the digit grouping setting, while the Restricted
      Numeric never uses digit grouping.

   [ Help ]                                    [ Cancel ]    [ OK ]
```

For the 'Label', we need to put a description of the variable, which in this case is: 'Employee Unique Id' (see Figure 2.8); and the rest we can leave as the default.

## FIGURE 2.8

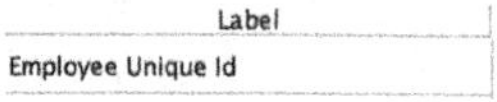

| Label |
|---|
| Employee Unique Id |

Now we can go to the data view by clicking on the tab at the bottom and entering in the data we have for employee ID. You will notice when you click on the Data View tab, the header is automatically updated (see Figure 2.9).

## FIGURE 2.9

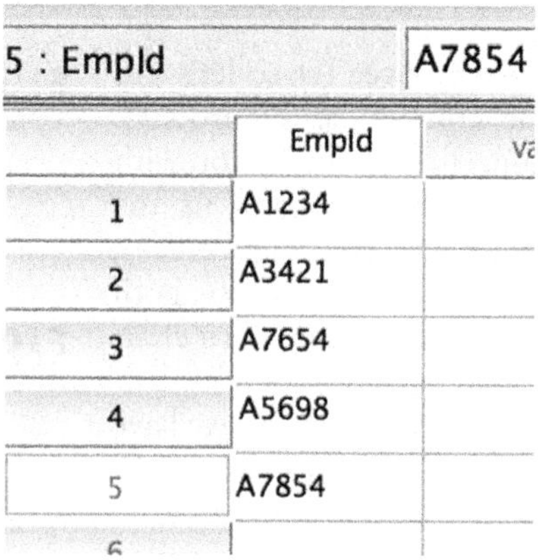

| 5 : EmpId |       | A7854 |
|---|---|---|
|   | EmpId | Va |
| 1 | A1234 |    |
| 2 | A3421 |    |
| 3 | A7654 |    |
| 4 | A5698 |    |
| 5 | A7854 |    |
| 6 |       |    |

We have now set up the employee ID variable and entered in the data. Now would be a good time to save the data file by going to the File menu (see Figure 2.10), selecting 'Save', and choosing the file name and location (see Figure 2.11).

**FIGURE 2.10**

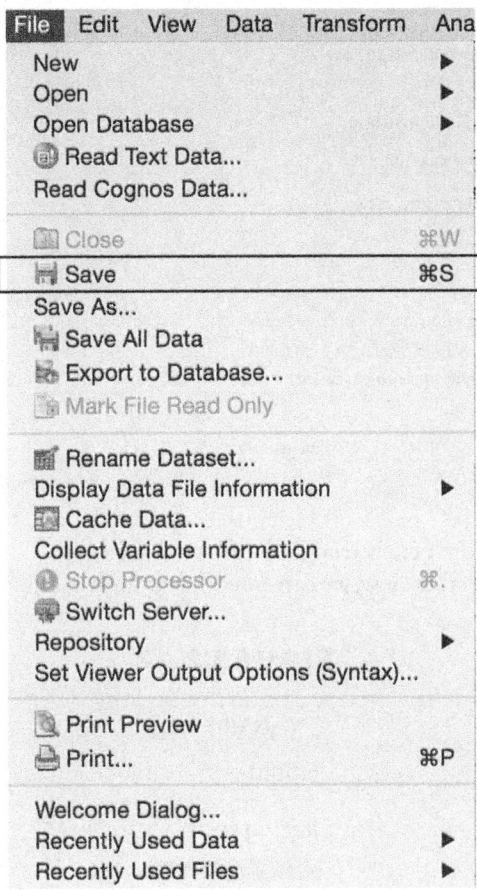

**FIGURE 2.11**

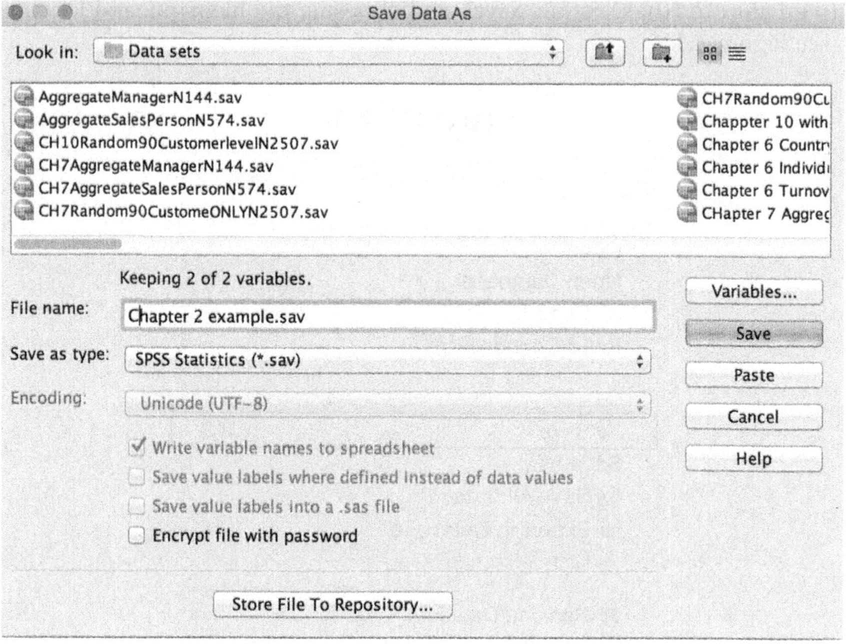
Save Data As
Look in:
Data sets
AggregateManagerN144.sav
AggregateSalesPersonN574.sav
CH10Random90CustomerlevelN2507.sav
CH7AggregateManagerN144.sav
CH7AggregateSalesPersonN574.sav
CH7Random90CustomeONLYN2507.sav
CH7Random90Cu
Chappter 10 with
Chapter 6 Countr
Chapter 6 Individ
Chapter 6 Turnov
CHapter 7 Aggreg
Keeping 2 of 2 variables.
File name:
Chapter 2 example.sav
Save as type:
SPSS Statistics (*.sav)
Encoding:
Unicode (UTF-8)
Write variable names to spreadsheet
Save value labels where defined instead of data values
Save value labels into a .sas file
Encrypt file with password
Store File To Repository...
Variables...
Save
Paste
Cancel
Help

Let's now go to the next variable: performance rating.

Back in the variable view, we can enter the name as 'Rating' (see Figure 2.12).

**FIGURE 2.12**

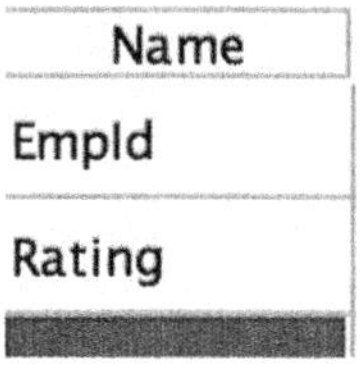
Name
EmpId
Rating

As we did above and then for the variable type we click on the button with the three dots again to bring up the variable type box and enter 'Numeric' (see Figure 2.13). We need to set the decimal points to 0 and click OK (see Figure 2.14).

**FIGURE 2.13**

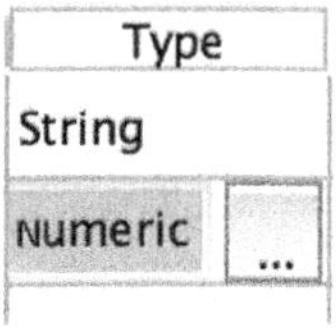
Type
String
Numeric
...

## HR Information Systems and Data

**FIGURE 2.14**

```
Variable Type

● Numeric
○ Comma                          Width: 8
○ Dot                            Decimal Places: 0
○ Scientific notation
○ Date
○ Dollar
○ Custom currency
○ String
○ Restricted Numeric (integer with leading zeros)

ⓘ  The Numeric type honours the digit grouping setting, while the Restricted
   Numeric never uses digit grouping.

   Help                          Cancel      OK
```

We can leave width and decimals as the default and then enter: 'Performance rating of employee' in the label (see Figure 2.15).

**FIGURE 2.15**

| Label |
|---|
| Employee Unique Id |
| Performance rating of employee |

Now we need to enter the value labels, which is where you will see just how useful this feature is; in the values column for the rating variable, click on the box with the three dots (see Figure 2.16).

**FIGURE 2.16**

| Values |
|---|
| None |
| None ... |

This will open the value labels dialogue box where you can start to enter the labels for performance ratings. One by one we can enter in our labels for each performance rating and hit 'Add' (see Figures 2.17, 2.18 and 2.19).

**FIGURE 2.17**

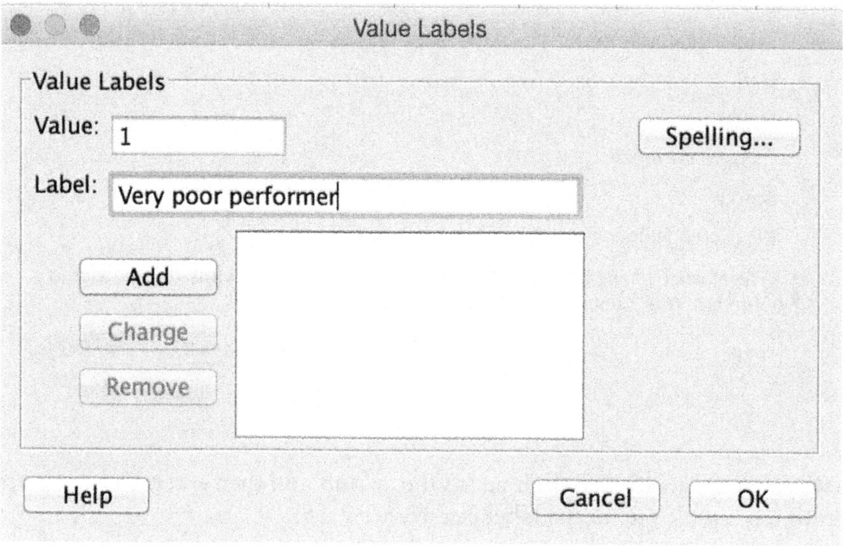

**FIGURE 2.18**

**FIGURE 2.19**

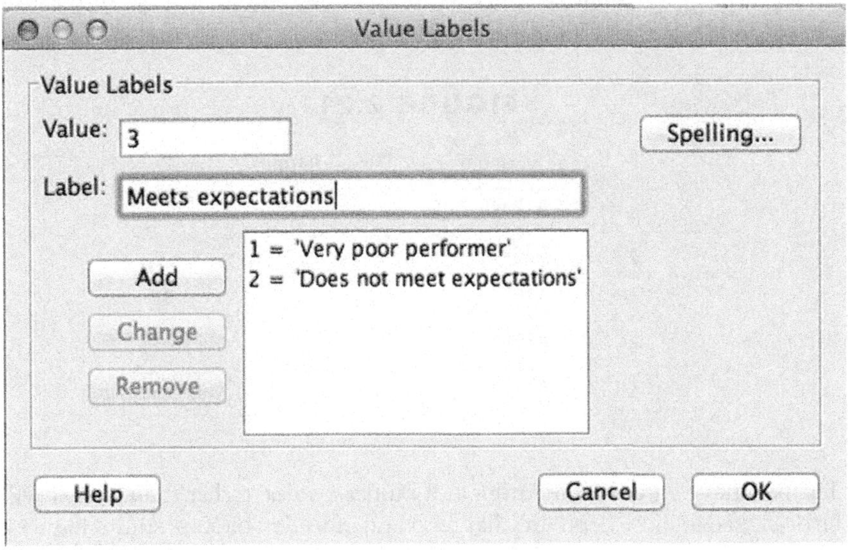

We can continue in this way until all the values have been entered (see Figure 2.20).

**FIGURE 2.20**

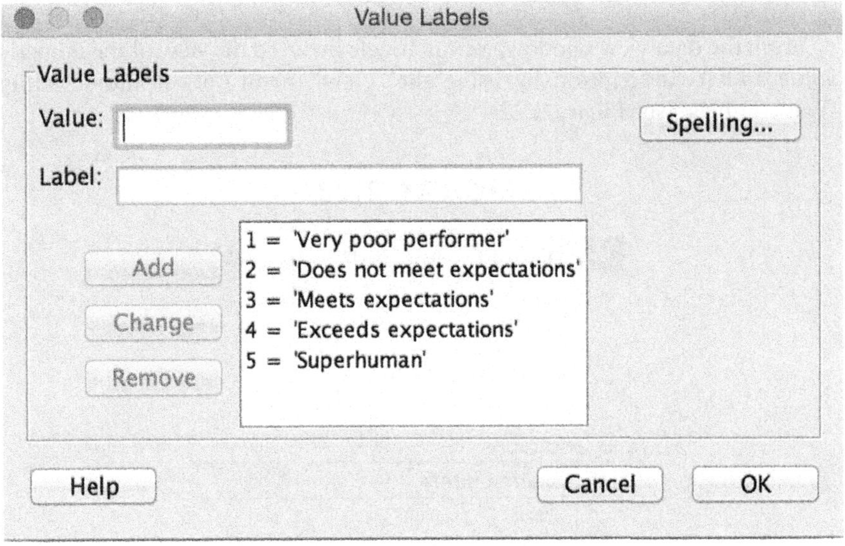

The rest of the columns in the variable view can be left as the default. Now when we go to the data view mode, we can enter in the data for ratings for each employee (see Figure 2.21).

**FIGURE 2.21**

|   | EmpId | Rating |
|---|-------|--------|
| 1 | A1234 | 3 |
| 2 | A3421 | 5 |
| 3 | A7654 | 3 |
| 4 | A5698 | 4 |
| 5 | A7854 | 3 |

The benefit of entering the rating as a numeric value rather than as text will be discussed in more depth in Chapter 3 and indeed in the case study chapters, but for now a simple explanation might be that storing the ratings as numbers allows us to perform arithmetic and calculate averages. It also allows us to talk about what causes an 'increase' or 'decrease' in performance – something we cannot test for if performance were stored as a text variable.

Finally, the 'Measure' column needs to be set up as 'ordinal'. This is because the numbers have an order – because the performance rating increases as the number goes up. Depending on the nature of the variable, you may also choose to change your variable to be a 'scale' measure type (more on this later).

From the data view window, we can toggle between the view of the numeric value and its description by using the 'View' menu option and selecting 'Value Labels' (see Figure 2.22).

**FIGURE 2.22**

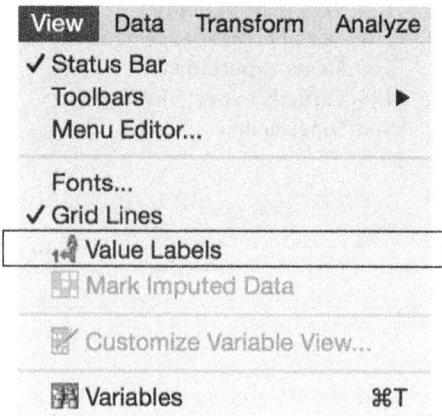

This will alter the view and show the value labels as follows (see Figure 2.23):

**FIGURE 2.23**

|   | EmpId | Rating |
|---|-------|--------|
| 1 | A1234 | Meets expectations |
| 2 | A3421 | Superhuman |
| 3 | A7654 | Meets expectations |
| 4 | A5698 | Exceeds expectations |
| 5 | A7854 | Meets expectations |

The final variable that Remi had asked the line managers to send through on the e-mail is to indicate the suggested salary adjustment as a percentage. As before, we go into the variable view and set up this variable. We can enter the name – here we have chosen 'SalaryAdj'. The type is numeric, and because some managers have entered in part percentages we need to set this up as having two decimal points. We can leave the columns 'Values', 'Missing' and 'Columns' as default and now focus on the 'Measure' column. Because the percentage salary increase is on a scale of 1 to 100, we select the type of measure as 'Scale'. The variable view now looks like this (see Figure 2.24):

**FIGURE 2.24**

|   | Name | Type | Width | Decimals | Label | Values | Missing | Columns | Align | Measure | Role |
|---|------|------|-------|----------|-------|--------|---------|---------|-------|---------|------|
| 1 | EmpId | String | 8 | 0 | Employee Unique Id | None | None | 8 | Left | Nominal | Input |
| 2 | Rating | Numeric | 8 | 0 | Performance Rating of employee | {1, Very po... | None | 19 | Right | Ordinal | Input |
| 3 | SalaryAdj | Numeric | 8 | 2 | Suggested percentage Salary Adjustment | None | None | 8 | Right | Scale | Input |

And, having entered the data into the data view, the entire data now looks like this (see Figure 2.25):

**FIGURE 2.25**

|   | EmpId | Rating | SalaryAdj |
|---|-------|--------|-----------|
| 1 | A1234 | 3 | 2.00 |
| 2 | A3421 | 5 | 25.00 |
| 3 | A7654 | 3 | 2.00 |
| 4 | A5698 | 4 | 10.00 |
| 5 | A7854 | 3 | 2.00 |

Now we have turned information included in an e-mail into a data file in SPSS on which we can perform some useful analysis.

In reality, and depending on the size of the organization, Remi (or Remi's equivalent in any organization) may send us 10 or 50 or 100 e-mails just like this one. This is when we can then highlight to Remi that SPSS actually has a wonderful data import facility and that it would save a lot of time if the data was received in one spreadsheet rather than many e-mails (but we can thank him for sending the first one in this way because it gave us a chance to test out how the manual set-up facility works in the data view and the variable view).

## Copying data from an Excel spreadsheet into the data view

Let's say that, the day after Remi sent the initial e-mail above, he has now seen the error of his ways and sent us the remainder of the information from the three remaining departments collated together in a spreadsheet that looks like this (see Figure 2.26):

**FIGURE 2.26**

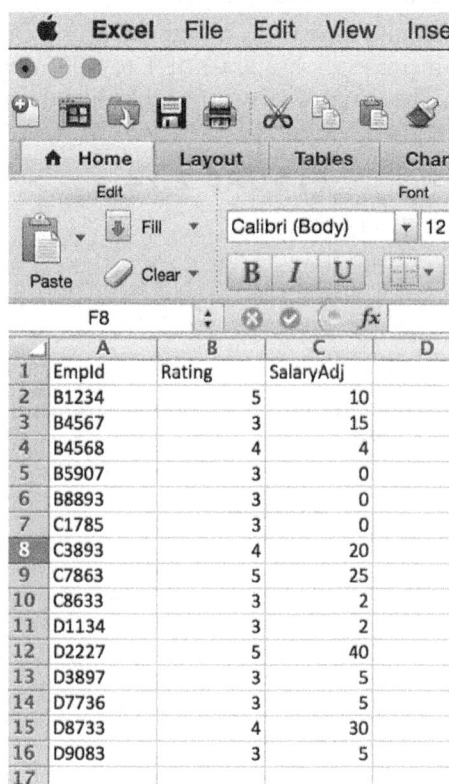

# HR Information Systems and Data

As a nifty trick, we can actually just copy and paste the data element into SPSS. We simply select the data we want (see Figure 2.27), like this:

**FIGURE 2.27**

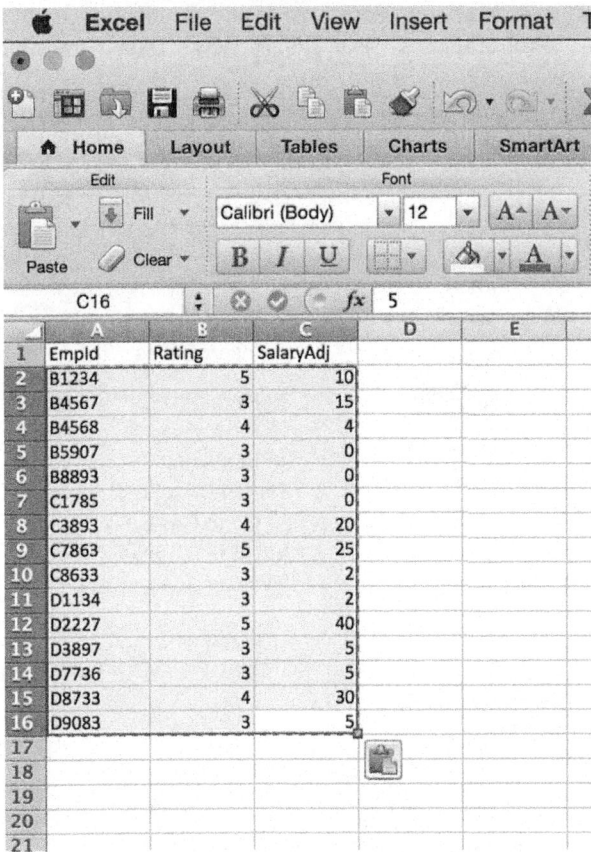

Copy this onto the clipboard in Excel by selecting Edit -> Copy or using the right mouse click, then flicking back to SPSS and paste this in under the data we already have by using Edit -> Paste (see Figure 2.28).

**FIGURE 2.28**

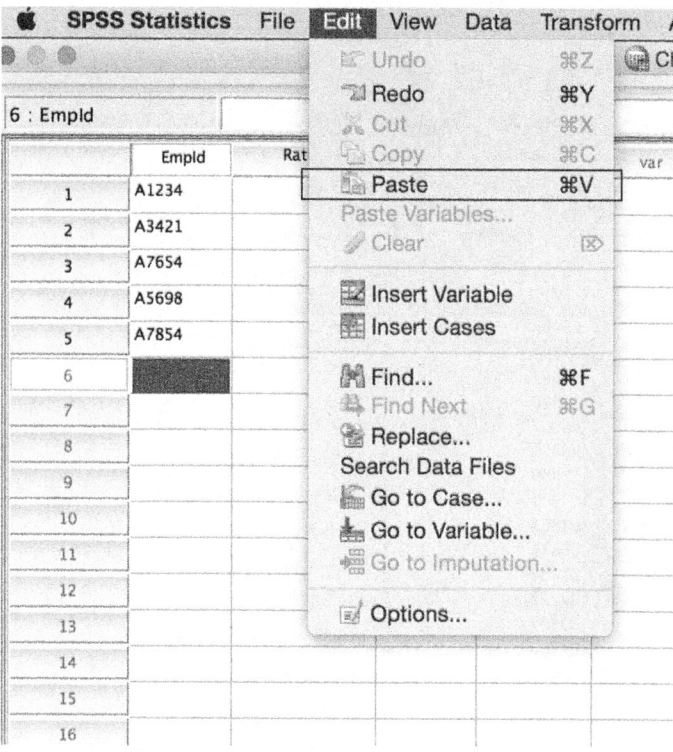

The data from the Excel spreadsheet will simply be copied into the data view. It should now look like this (see Figure 2.29):

**FIGURE 2.29**

|    | EmpId | Rating | SalaryAdj |
|----|-------|--------|-----------|
| 1  | A1234 | 3 | 2.00 |
| 2  | A3421 | 5 | 25.00 |
| 3  | A7654 | 3 | 2.00 |
| 4  | A5698 | 4 | 10.00 |
| 5  | A7854 | 3 | 2.00 |
| 6  | B1234 | 5 | 10.00 |
| 7  | B4567 | 3 | 15.00 |
| 8  | B4568 | 4 | 4.00 |
| 9  | B5907 | 3 | .00 |
| 10 | B8893 | 3 | .00 |
| 11 | C1785 | 3 | .00 |
| 12 | C3893 | 4 | 20.00 |
| 13 | C7863 | 5 | 25.00 |
| 14 | C8633 | 3 | 2.00 |
| 15 | D1134 | 3 | 2.00 |
| 16 | D2227 | 5 | 40.00 |
| 17 | D3897 | 3 | 5.00 |
| 18 | D7736 | 3 | 5.00 |
| 19 | D8733 | 4 | 30.00 |
| 20 | D9083 | 3 | 5.00 |
| 21 |       |   |      |

So now we have all the data from the performance review into SPSS and have worked through the examples of how to set up variables and enter data manually, as well as how to copy and paste from Microsoft Excel.

## Loading a complete data file from another source into SPSS

Another way to get data from a different source into SPSS is to use the menu commands to open and convert a data file. This is particularly useful if you have not already set up the variable view and are starting from scratch. Let's say we have another spreadsheet that contains HR profile data, including name, age, gender, start date and department. This information may have been exported from an HR information system such as Oracle or SAP. The spreadsheet may look like this (see Figure 2.30):

**FIGURE 2.30**

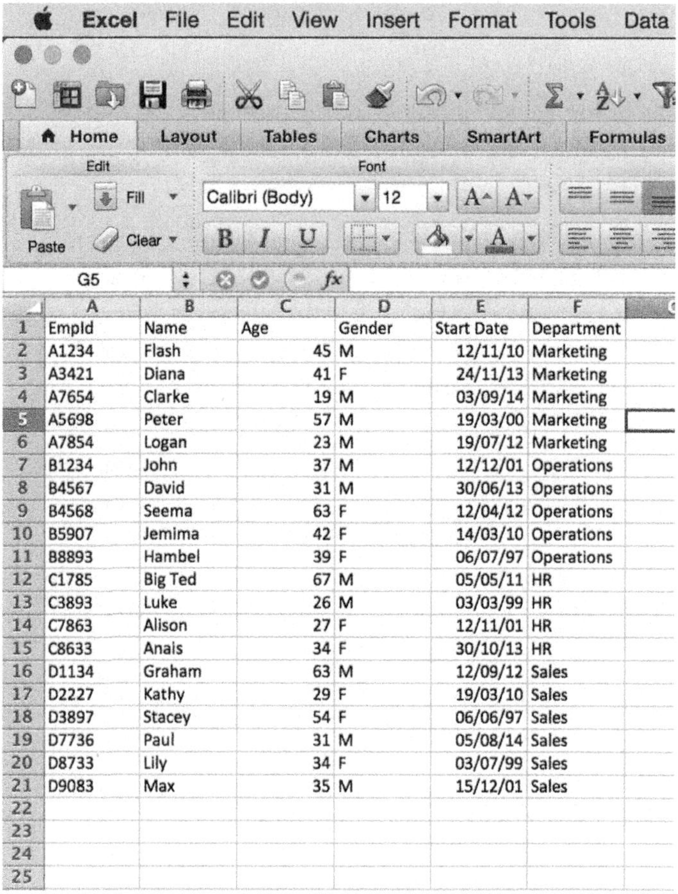

| | A | B | C | D | E | F |
|---|---|---|---|---|---|---|
| 1 | EmpId | Name | Age | Gender | Start Date | Department |
| 2 | A1234 | Flash | 45 | M | 12/11/10 | Marketing |
| 3 | A3421 | Diana | 41 | F | 24/11/13 | Marketing |
| 4 | A7654 | Clarke | 19 | M | 03/09/14 | Marketing |
| 5 | A5698 | Peter | 57 | M | 19/03/00 | Marketing |
| 6 | A7854 | Logan | 23 | M | 19/07/12 | Marketing |
| 7 | B1234 | John | 37 | M | 12/12/01 | Operations |
| 8 | B4567 | David | 31 | M | 30/06/13 | Operations |
| 9 | B4568 | Seema | 63 | F | 12/04/12 | Operations |
| 10 | B5907 | Jemima | 42 | F | 14/03/10 | Operations |
| 11 | B8893 | Hambel | 39 | F | 06/07/97 | Operations |
| 12 | C1785 | Big Ted | 67 | M | 05/05/11 | HR |
| 13 | C3893 | Luke | 26 | M | 03/03/99 | HR |
| 14 | C7863 | Alison | 27 | F | 12/11/01 | HR |
| 15 | C8633 | Anais | 34 | F | 30/10/13 | HR |
| 16 | D1134 | Graham | 63 | M | 12/09/12 | Sales |
| 17 | D2227 | Kathy | 29 | F | 19/03/10 | Sales |
| 18 | D3897 | Stacey | 54 | F | 06/06/97 | Sales |
| 19 | D7736 | Paul | 31 | M | 05/08/14 | Sales |
| 20 | D8733 | Lily | 34 | F | 03/07/99 | Sales |
| 21 | D9083 | Max | 35 | M | 15/12/01 | Sales |

HR Information Systems and Data | 35

To import this saved file into SPSS, we open SPSS, drop down the File menu and select File -> Open -> Data (see Figure 2.31).

**FIGURE 2.31**

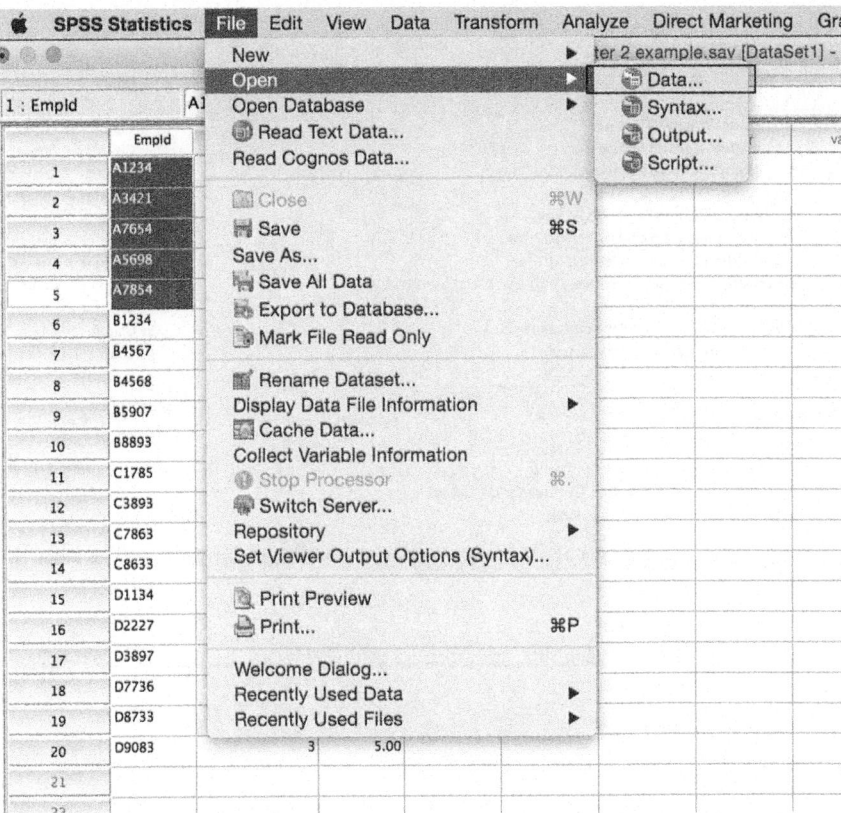

This will then open up the 'Open Data' dialogue box from where we can select an Excel file type in the 'Files of type' field (see Figure 2.32).

**FIGURE 2.32**

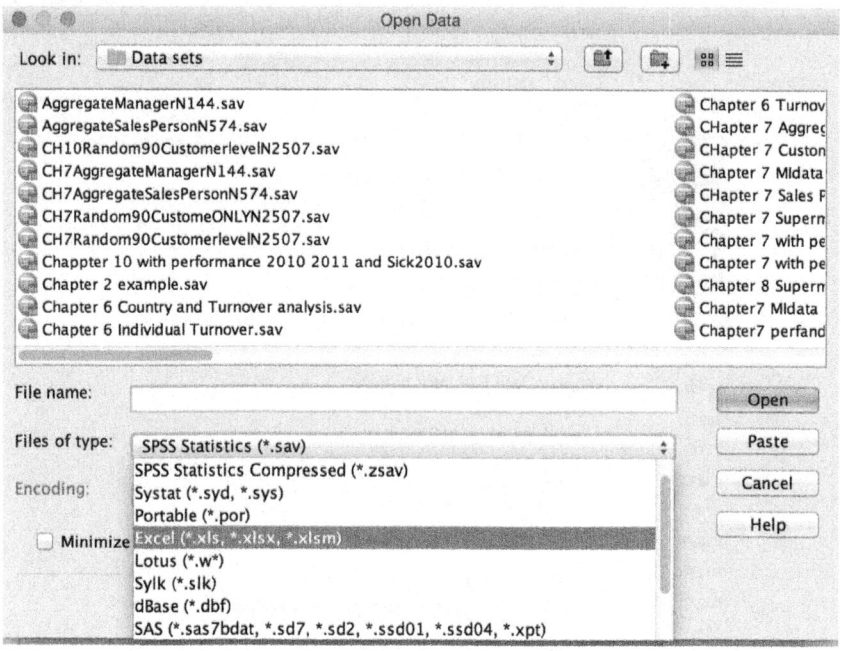

HR Information Systems and Data 37

This will filter the files to show only the Excel files, then you can select the one you want. In our example it is 'Ch 2 hr profile spreadsheet.xlsx' (see Figure 2.33). Note that SPSS recognizes files of many different types.

**FIGURE 2.33**

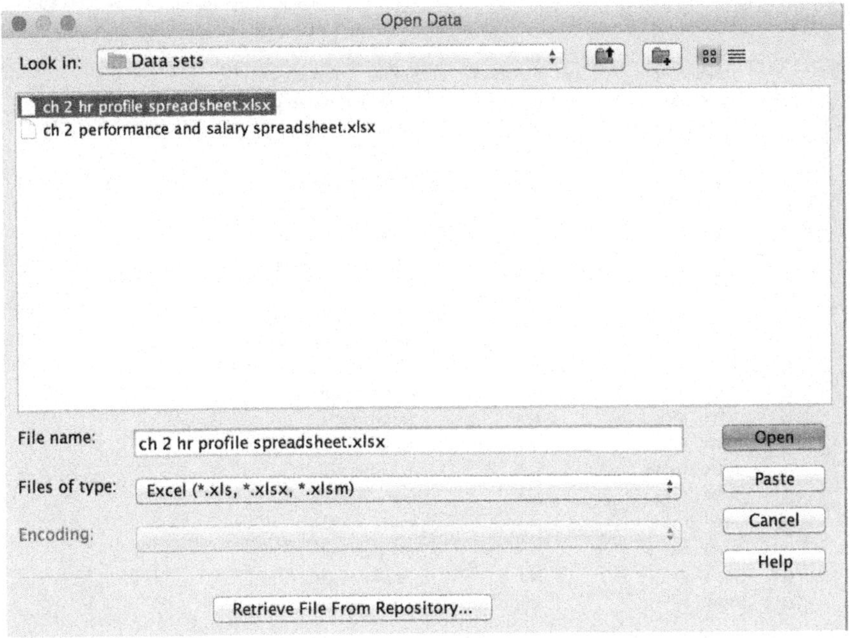

[Screenshot of 'Open Data' dialog showing Data sets folder with 'ch 2 hr profile spreadsheet.xlsx' selected and 'ch 2 performance and salary spreadsheet.xlsx' listed. File name: ch 2 hr profile spreadsheet.xlsx. Files of type: Excel (*.xls, *.xlsx, *.xlsm).]

And then click 'open'.

This will bring up another window. Here, you will need to select 'Read variable names from the first row of data' (Figure 2.34). This will populate the variable view (see Figure 2.35).

**FIGURE 2.34**

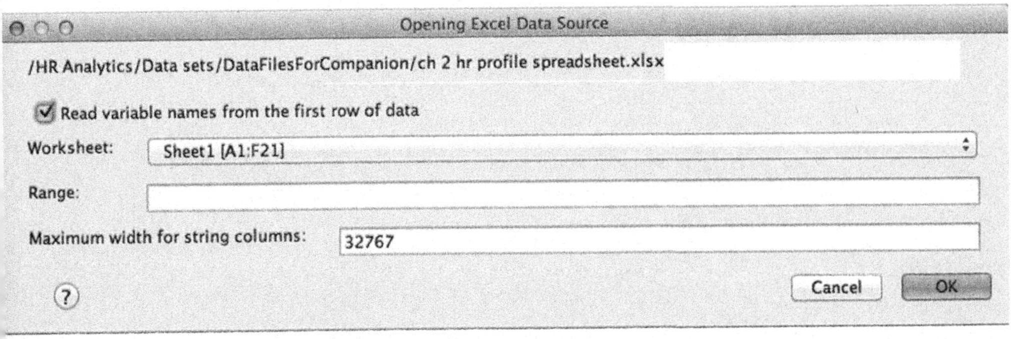

[Screenshot of 'Opening Excel Data Source' dialog. Path: /HR Analytics/Data sets/DataFilesForCompanion/ch 2 hr profile spreadsheet.xlsx. 'Read variable names from the first row of data' is checked. Worksheet: Sheet1 [A1:F21]. Maximum width for string columns: 32767.]

As you can see, SPSS has populated the information into the data view (see Figure 2.35).

## FIGURE 2.35

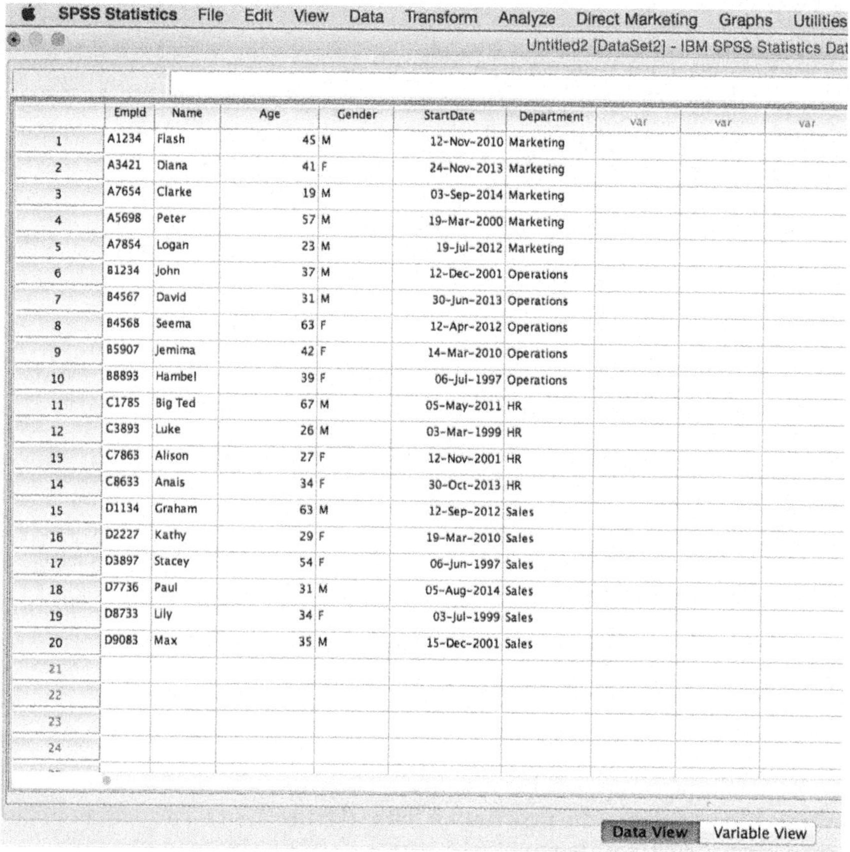

| | EmpId | Name | Age | Gender | StartDate | Department | var | var | var |
|---|---|---|---|---|---|---|---|---|---|
| 1 | A1234 | Flash | 45 | M | 12-Nov-2010 | Marketing | | | |
| 2 | A3421 | Diana | 41 | F | 24-Nov-2013 | Marketing | | | |
| 3 | A7654 | Clarke | 19 | M | 03-Sep-2014 | Marketing | | | |
| 4 | A5698 | Peter | 57 | M | 19-Mar-2000 | Marketing | | | |
| 5 | A7854 | Logan | 23 | M | 19-Jul-2012 | Marketing | | | |
| 6 | B1234 | John | 37 | M | 12-Dec-2001 | Operations | | | |
| 7 | B4567 | David | 31 | M | 30-Jun-2013 | Operations | | | |
| 8 | B4568 | Seema | 63 | F | 12-Apr-2012 | Operations | | | |
| 9 | B5907 | Jemima | 42 | F | 14-Mar-2010 | Operations | | | |
| 10 | B8893 | Hambel | 39 | F | 06-Jul-1997 | Operations | | | |
| 11 | C1785 | Big Ted | 67 | M | 05-May-2011 | HR | | | |
| 12 | C3893 | Luke | 26 | M | 03-Mar-1999 | HR | | | |
| 13 | C7863 | Alison | 27 | F | 12-Nov-2001 | HR | | | |
| 14 | C8633 | Anais | 34 | F | 30-Oct-2013 | HR | | | |
| 15 | D1134 | Graham | 63 | M | 12-Sep-2012 | Sales | | | |
| 16 | D2227 | Kathy | 29 | F | 19-Mar-2010 | Sales | | | |
| 17 | D3897 | Stacey | 54 | F | 06-Jun-1997 | Sales | | | |
| 18 | D7736 | Paul | 31 | M | 05-Aug-2014 | Sales | | | |
| 19 | D8733 | Lily | 34 | F | 03-Jul-1999 | Sales | | | |
| 20 | D9083 | Max | 35 | M | 15-Dec-2001 | Sales | | | |

And also populated details on the variable view (see Figure 2.36):

**FIGURE 2.36**

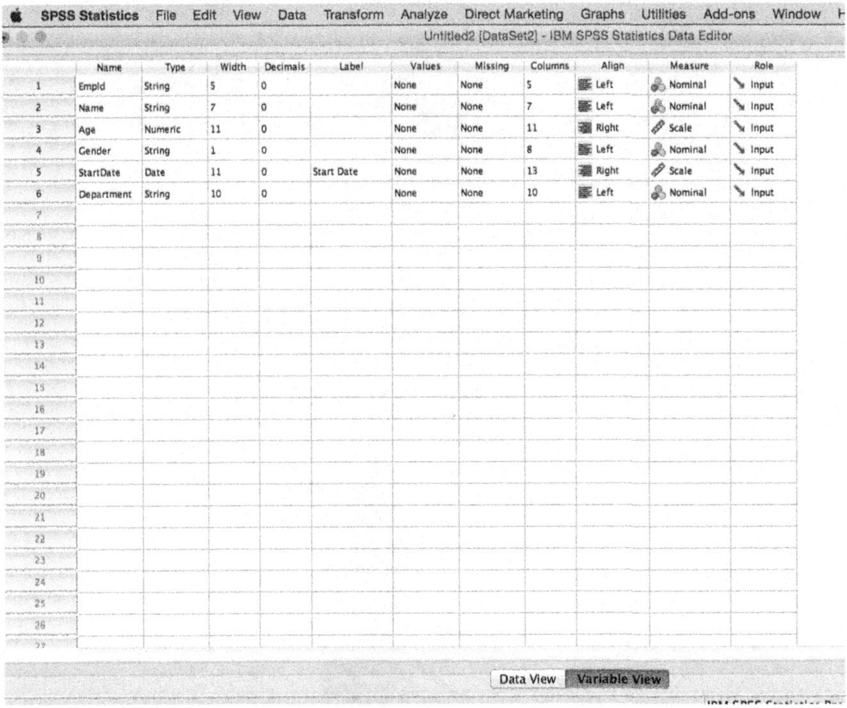

| | Name | Type | Width | Decimals | Label | Values | Missing | Columns | Align | Measure | Role |
|---|---|---|---|---|---|---|---|---|---|---|---|
| 1 | EmpId | String | 5 | 0 | | None | None | 5 | Left | Nominal | Input |
| 2 | Name | String | 7 | 0 | | None | None | 7 | Left | Nominal | Input |
| 3 | Age | Numeric | 11 | 0 | | None | None | 11 | Right | Scale | Input |
| 4 | Gender | String | 1 | 0 | | None | None | 8 | Left | Nominal | Input |
| 5 | StartDate | Date | 11 | 0 | Start Date | None | None | 13 | Right | Scale | Input |
| 6 | Department | String | 10 | 0 | | None | None | 10 | Left | Nominal | Input |

At this stage you will need to do the following in the variable view: 1) complete and tidy up the variable labels; 2) recode the text content of values for 'Department' and 'Gender'.

At this stage, we may want to edit the data for department and gender so that they are represented as numbers rather than strings. This is because, as mentioned earlier, we are able to perform more arithmetic and processes on numbers than we can on text or string values. To start, let's update the gender data as follows: 0 = F (female); 1 = M (male).

To do this we can use a simple search and replace. We select the gender column, then go to the Edit menu and select Edit -> Replace (see Figure 2.37). Then we replace 'F' with '0' when prompted on the following window and click 'Replace All' (see Figure 2.38).

**Predictive HR Analytics**

**FIGURE 2.37**

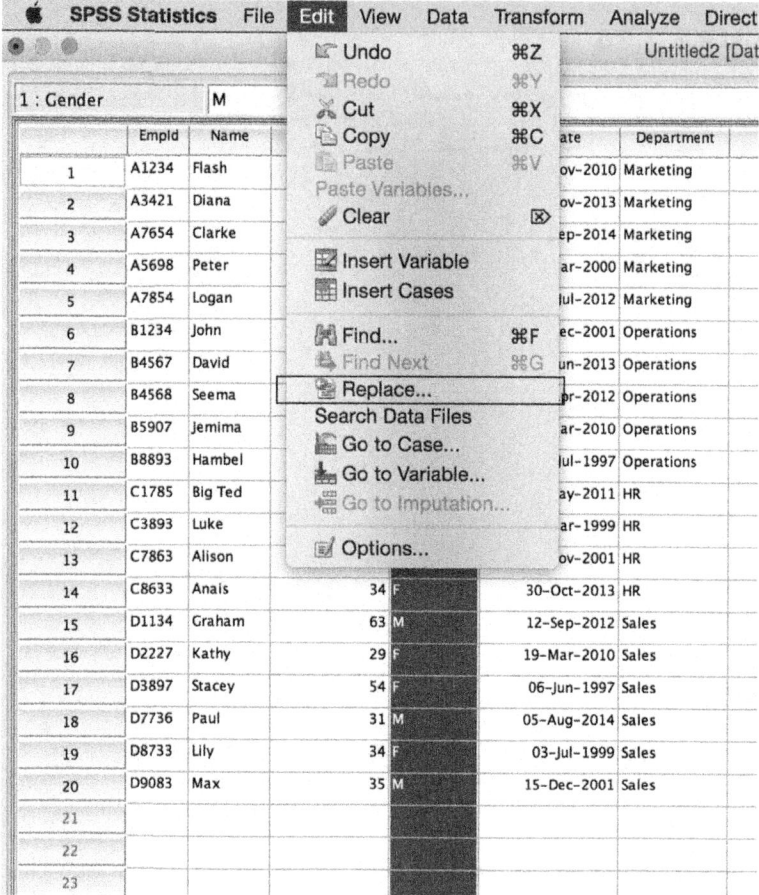

**FIGURE 2.38**

HR Information Systems and Data   41

You will then get a confirmation that this is complete (see Figure 2.39).

**FIGURE 2.39**

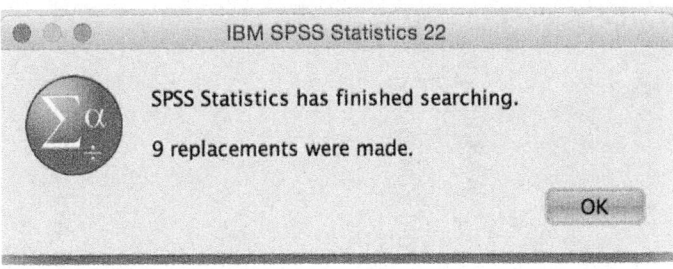

We then do exactly the same to replace 'M' with '1' and then our data view ends up looking like this (see Figure 2.40):

**FIGURE 2.40**

|    | EmpId | Name | Age | Gender | StartDate | Department |
|----|-------|------|-----|--------|-----------|------------|
| 1  | A1234 | Flash | 45 | 1 | 12-Nov-2010 | Marketing |
| 2  | A3421 | Diana | 41 | 0 | 24-Nov-2013 | Marketing |
| 3  | A7654 | Clarke | 19 | 1 | 03-Sep-2014 | Marketing |
| 4  | A5698 | Peter | 57 | 1 | 19-Mar-2000 | Marketing |
| 5  | A7854 | Logan | 23 | 1 | 19-Jul-2012 | Marketing |
| 6  | B1234 | John | 37 | 1 | 12-Dec-2001 | Operations |
| 7  | B4567 | David | 31 | 1 | 30-Jun-2013 | Operations |
| 8  | B4568 | Seema | 63 | 0 | 12-Apr-2012 | Operations |
| 9  | B5907 | Jemima | 42 | 0 | 14-Mar-2010 | Operations |
| 10 | B8893 | Hambel | 39 | 0 | 06-Jul-1997 | Operations |
| 11 | C1785 | Big Ted | 67 | 1 | 05-May-2011 | HR |
| 12 | C3893 | Luke | 26 | 1 | 03-Mar-1999 | HR |
| 13 | C7863 | Alison | 27 | 0 | 12-Nov-2001 | HR |
| 14 | C8633 | Anais | 34 | 0 | 30-Oct-2013 | HR |
| 15 | D1134 | Graham | 63 | 1 | 12-Sep-2012 | Sales |
| 16 | D2227 | Kathy | 29 | 0 | 19-Mar-2010 | Sales |
| 17 | D3897 | Stacey | 54 | 0 | 06-Jun-1997 | Sales |
| 18 | D7736 | Paul | 31 | 1 | 05-Aug-2014 | Sales |
| 19 | D8733 | Lily | 34 | 0 | 03-Jul-1999 | Sales |
| 20 | D9083 | Max | 35 | 1 | 15-Dec-2001 | Sales |

Now we need to set up gender as a 'Numeric' data type (see Figure 2.41).

**FIGURE 2.41**

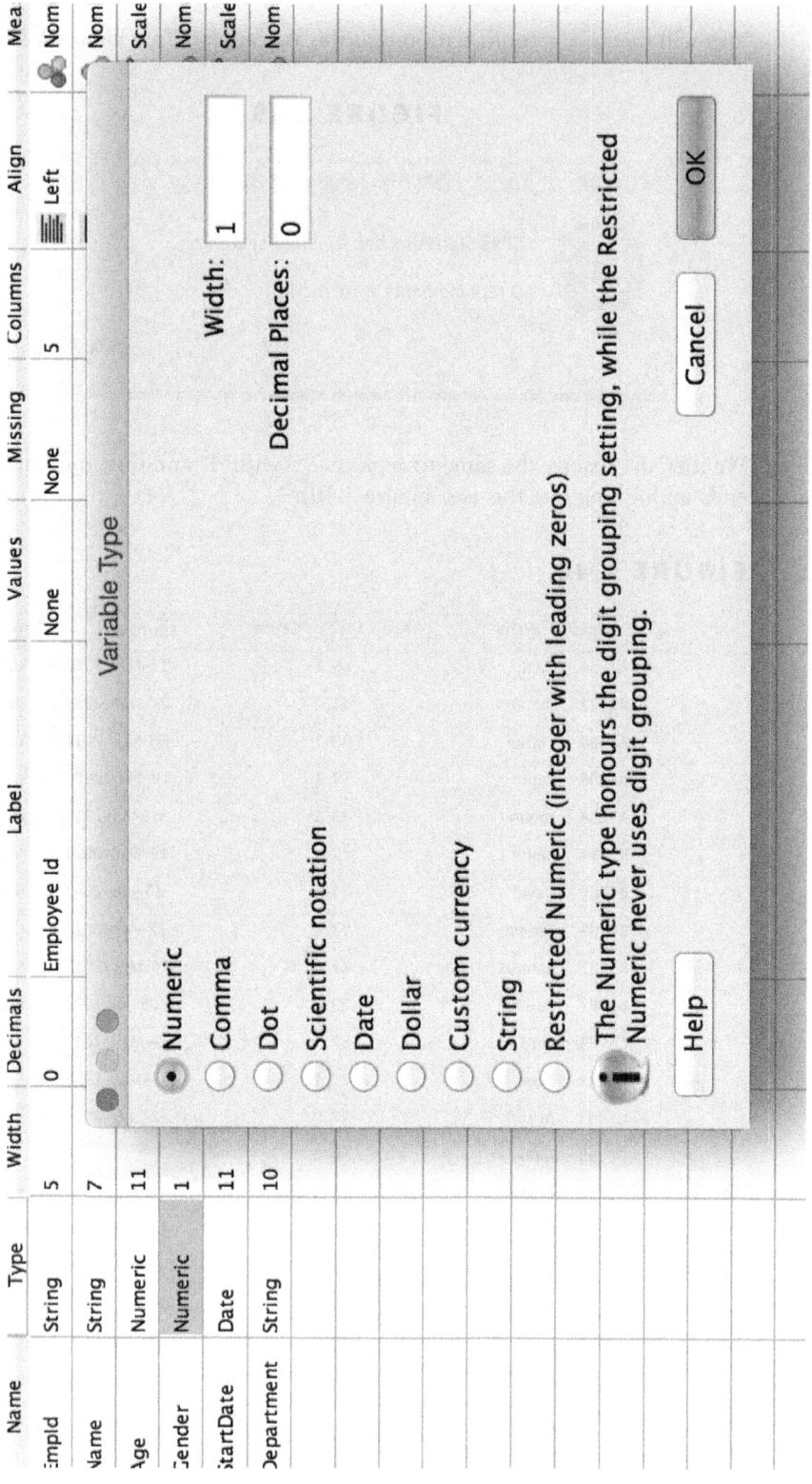

And finally, we update the value labels in a similar way to how we did this for the performance ratings earlier (see Figure 2.42).

**FIGURE 2.42**

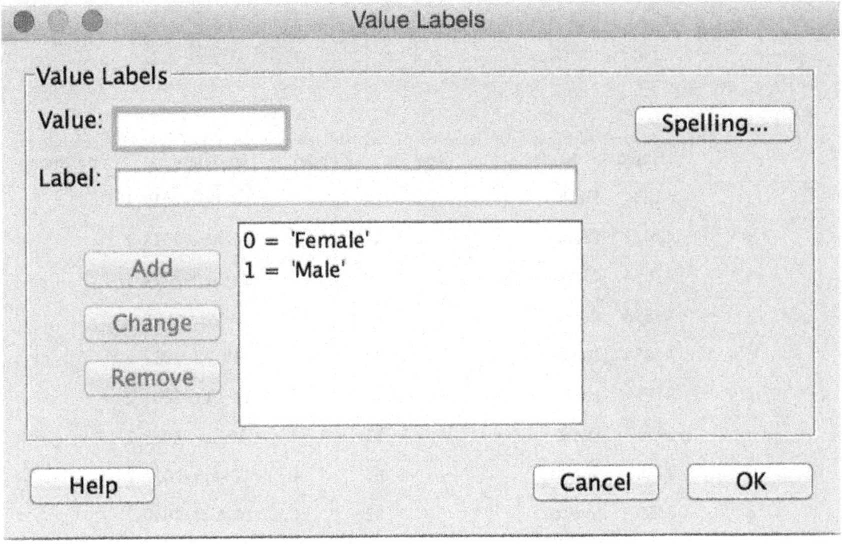

[Value Labels dialog box showing:
0 = 'Female'
1 = 'Male']

For the same reasons, we then go back to the data view and do exactly the same with the 'Department' variable, setting up the values as:

1 = 'Marketing'
2 = 'Operations'
3 = 'HR'
4 = 'Sales'

Predictive HR Analytics

We then use the Edit -> replace tool again to update the data in the data view to look like this (see Figure 2.43):

**FIGURE 2.43**

|    | EmpId | Name    | Age | Gender | StartDate   | Department |
|----|-------|---------|-----|--------|-------------|------------|
| 1  | A1234 | Flash   | 45  | 1      | 12-Nov-2010 | 1          |
| 2  | A3421 | Diana   | 41  | 0      | 24-Nov-2013 | 1          |
| 3  | A7654 | Clarke  | 19  | 1      | 03-Sep-2014 | 1          |
| 4  | A5698 | Peter   | 57  | 1      | 19-Mar-2000 | 1          |
| 5  | A7854 | Logan   | 23  | 1      | 19-Jul-2012 | 1          |
| 6  | B1234 | John    | 37  | 1      | 12-Dec-2001 | 2          |
| 7  | B4567 | David   | 31  | 1      | 30-Jun-2013 | 2          |
| 8  | B4568 | Seema   | 63  | 0      | 12-Apr-2012 | 2          |
| 9  | B5907 | Jemima  | 42  | 0      | 14-Mar-2010 | 2          |
| 10 | B8893 | Hambel  | 39  | 0      | 06-Jul-1997 | 2          |
| 11 | C1785 | Big Ted | 67  | 1      | 05-May-2011 | 3          |
| 12 | C3893 | Luke    | 26  | 1      | 03-Mar-1999 | 3          |
| 13 | C7863 | Alison  | 27  | 0      | 12-Nov-2001 | 3          |
| 14 | C8633 | Anais   | 34  | 0      | 30-Oct-2013 | 3          |
| 15 | D1134 | Graham  | 63  | 1      | 12-Sep-2012 | 4          |
| 16 | D2227 | Kathy   | 29  | 0      | 19-Mar-2010 | 4          |
| 17 | D3897 | Stacey  | 54  | 0      | 06-Jun-1997 | 4          |
| 18 | D7736 | Paul    | 31  | 1      | 05-Aug-2014 | 4          |
| 19 | D8733 | Lily    | 34  | 0      | 03-Jul-1999 | 4          |
| 20 | D9083 | Max     | 35  | 1      | 15-Dec-2001 | 4          |
| 21 |       |         |     |        |             |            |

# HR Information Systems and Data

We change the data type to 'Numeric', and update the value labels (Figure 2.44).

**FIGURE 2.44**

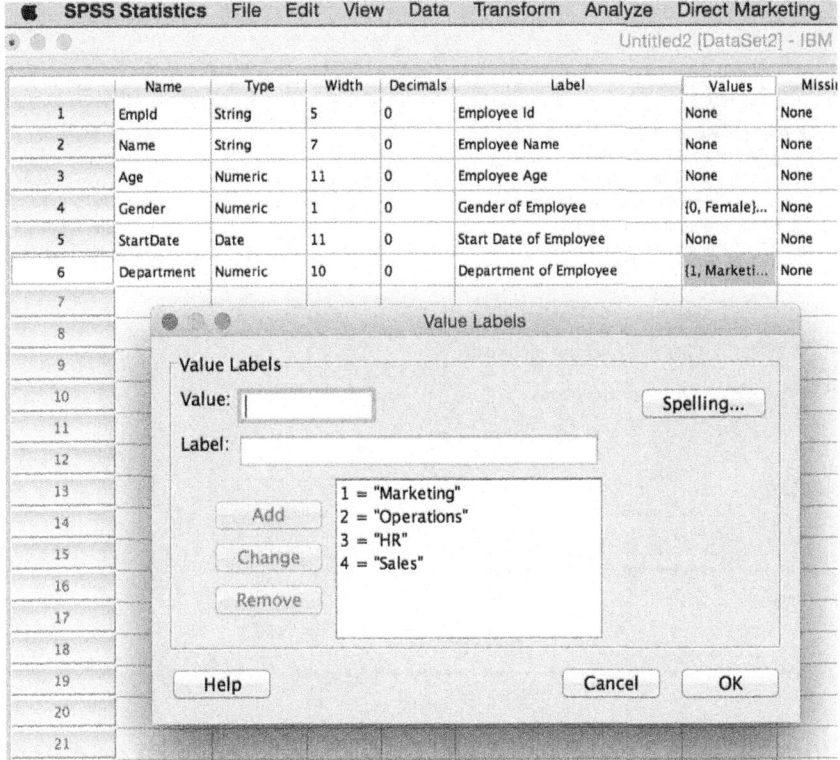

We then save this file using the File -> Save option on the menu. We will call this file 'Chapter 2 employee profile data.sav' (see Figure 2.45).

**FIGURE 2.45**

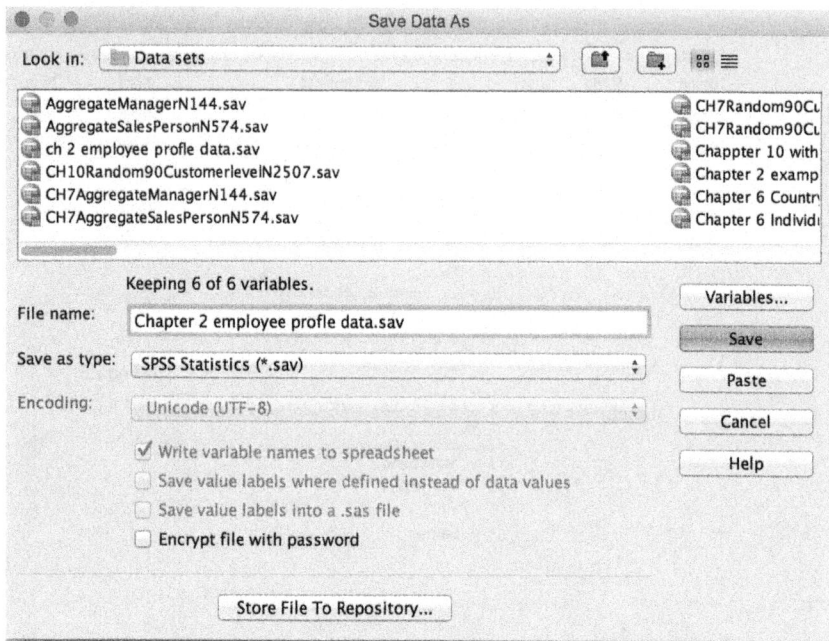

## *Joining two data sets in SPSS using employee ID as a key*

So now we have two data files in SPSS and we next want to join them together so we can perform some analysis.

Joining two files together in SPSS is very simple as long as you have one key field. The key field must be unique for each case (or each employee in this example) and it must be in both files. In our example here (and likely in many examples you will come across in HR analytics) that key is the employee ID. We will now take you through the steps to merge our two files in SPSS. As a reminder we have the following two files open: 1) Chapter 2 employee profile data.sav containing the employee ID, name, age, gender, start date and department; 2) Chapter 2 example.sav containing the employee ID, performance rating and salary adjustment.

# HR Information Systems and Data

## Step one: sort the data

First sort each file in ascending order by the key. This is done by selecting the Data menu and then Data -> Sort Cases (see Figure 2.46).

**FIGURE 2.46**

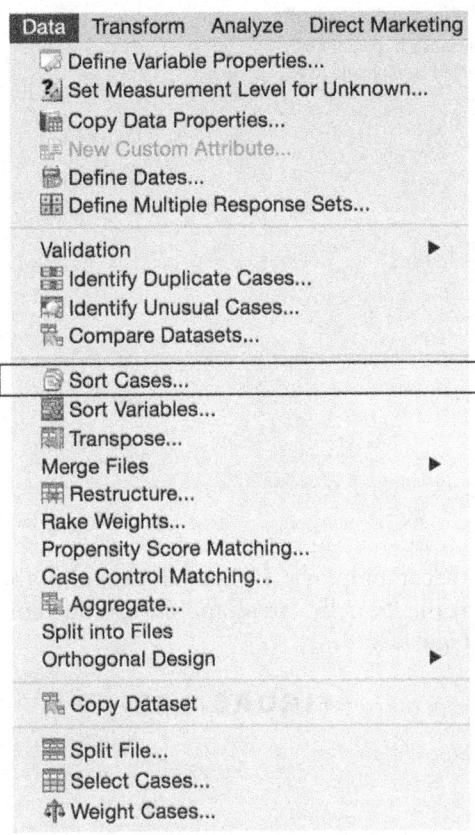

SPSS will then ask you which field you would like to sort by and in which order (see Figure 2.47).

**FIGURE 2.47**

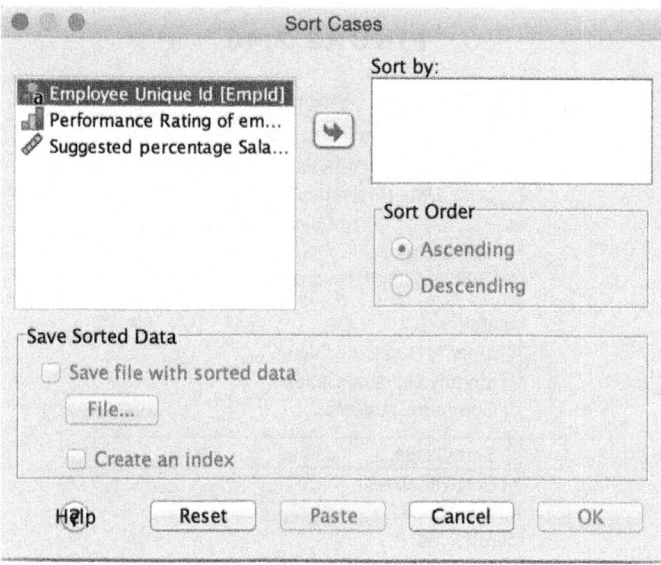

Here, we need to select 'Employee Unique Id' then click the arrow button to move this over to the 'Sort by' area; and ensure the 'Sort Order' is set to 'Ascending' (see Figure 2.48).

**FIGURE 2.48**

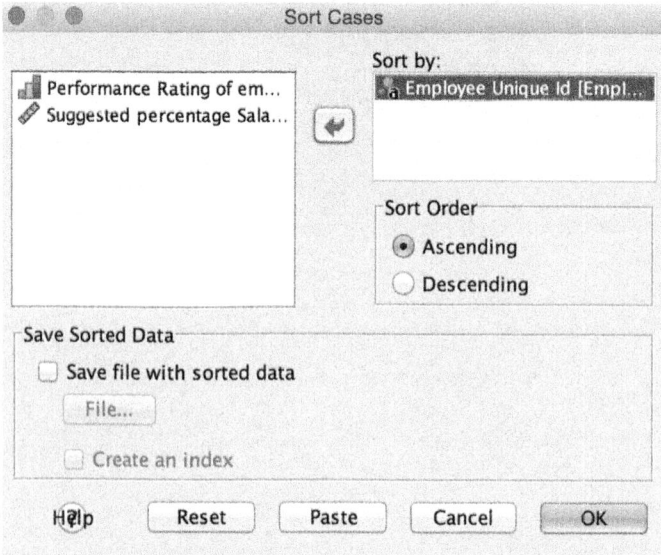

# HR Information Systems and Data

And click on 'OK'.

We then do the same with our other open file so that we end up with both files open and sorted (in ascending order) by employee ID.

## Step two: create a new file

In this example we want the merged file to be a completely new file, so the next step is to use the 'Save As' tool.

Next we open the employee profile data (Chapter 2 employee profile data.sav) and use File -> Save As to save it as a file name that we will use for our new merged file. In this example we will call it 'Chapter 2 employee profile and performance.sav' (see Figure 2.49).

**FIGURE 2.49**

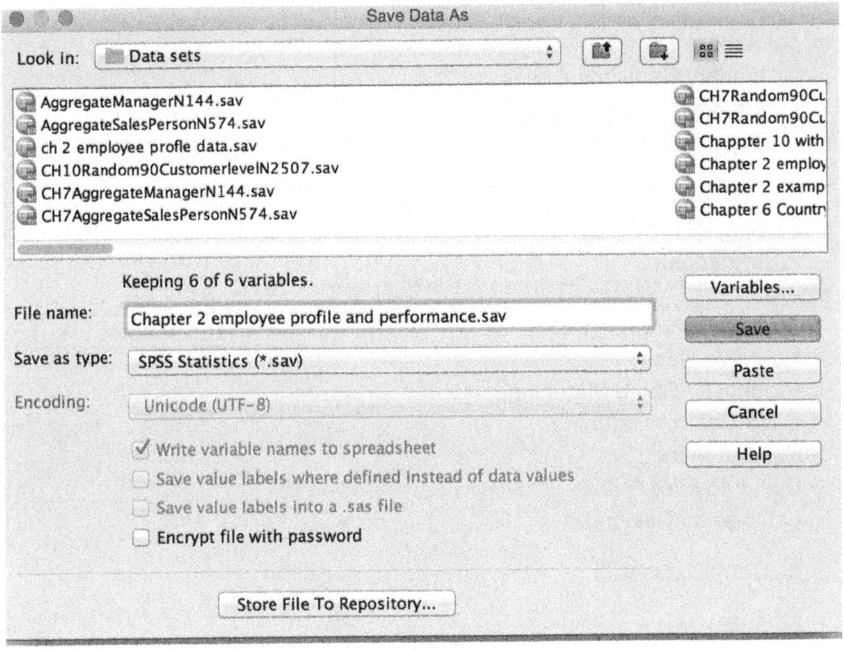

## Step three: merge the files

Next, from the new merge file (Chapter 2 employee profile and performance. sav) we go to the Data menu and select Data -> Merge Files -> Add Variables (see Figure 2.50).

**FIGURE 2.50**

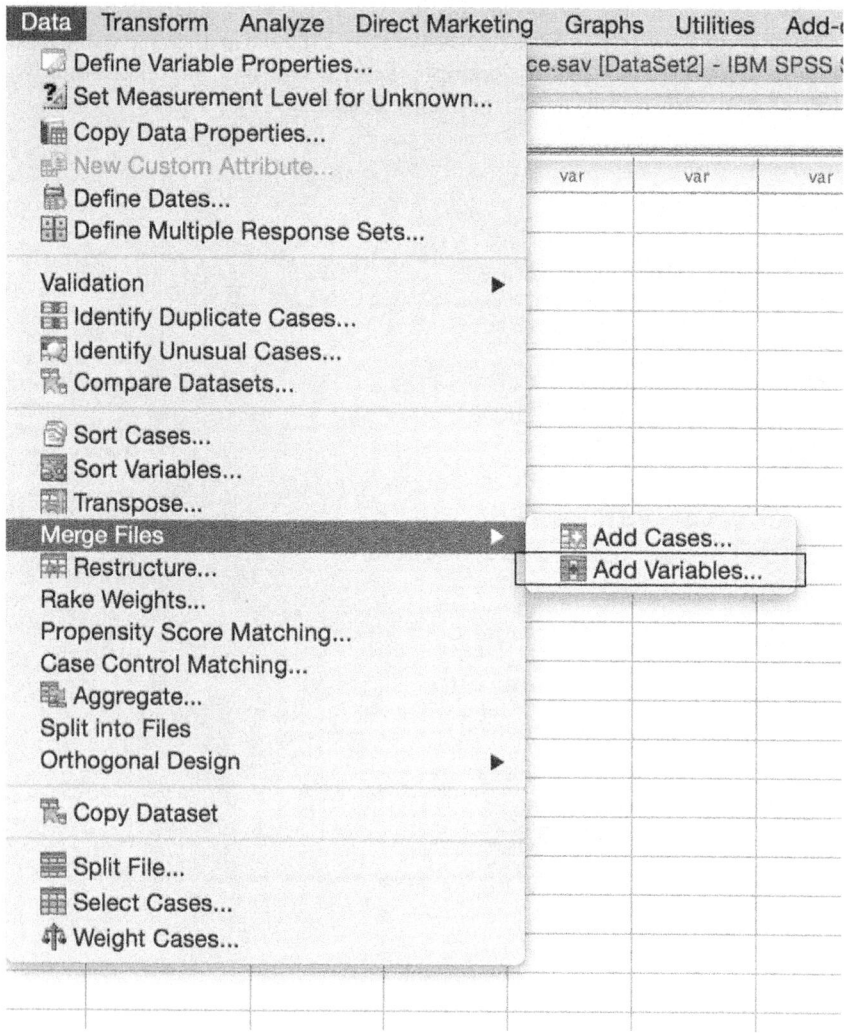

SPSS will then ask you to select a data set to merge with the active data set. Because we have the performance rating data open (Chapter 2 example.sav) this is in the open data set list. If it was not open, we would browse our file folders in order to find the file containing the data set. We select this and then 'Continue' (see Figure 2.51).

**FIGURE 2.51**

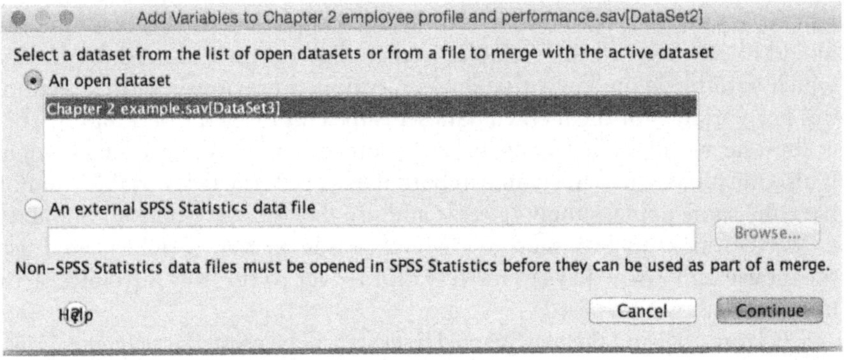

The next thing that SPSS will do is to ask you which variables you would like to see in the new data set. You do not have to include all of the variables in your newly merged file. You need to move the variables into either the 'Added Variables' area if you want them included, or to the 'Excluded Variables' area if you do not want them included (see Figure 2.52). As a default, SPSS will list all variables in the 'Added Variables' area and put any duplicates from the added data set into the 'Excluded Variables' area. SPSS will also help you to identify which variables are from the active data set (Chapter 2 employee profile and performance.sav) by putting a '(*)' after the variable name; and which variables are from the data set you are merging it

**FIGURE 2.52**

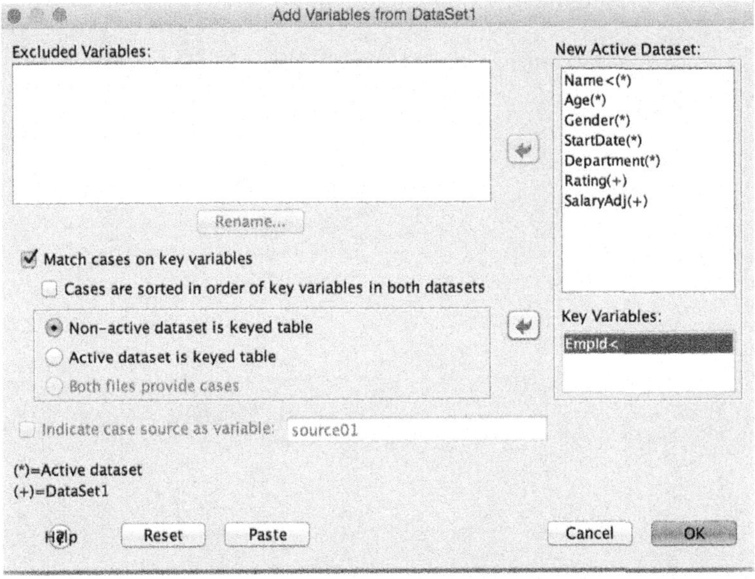

with (Chapter 2 example.sav) by putting a '(+)' after the variable name. You can select the variables using the mouse and can click the arrow keys to add or remove the variables from the final data set. In this example we would like to keep all the variables in there. Here, you also need to identify which variable is the key variable. As mentioned previously in this section, our key variable for the merged data set is the employee ID, or 'EmpId'. This is the one we identified as being common to both data sets and unique. It also must have the same name in both data sets. If the key variables do not have the same name, simply select it and use the 'Rename' button to update it. We then tick the box that says 'Match Cases on Key Variables', and use the mouse and arrow keys to move 'EmpId' over to the 'Key Variables' area (see Figure 2.52).

Click on 'OK' and the new merged data set will be created (see Figure 2.53).

**FIGURE 2.53**

| | EmpId | Name | Age | Gender | StartDate | Department | Rating | SalaryAdj | var |
|---|---|---|---|---|---|---|---|---|---|
| 1 | A1234 | Flash | 45 | 1 | 12-Nov-2010 | 1 | 3 | 2.00 | |
| 2 | A3421 | Diana | 41 | 0 | 24-Nov-2013 | 1 | 5 | 25.00 | |
| 3 | A5698 | Peter | 57 | 1 | 19-Mar-2000 | 1 | 4 | 10.00 | |
| 4 | A7654 | Clarke | 19 | 1 | 03-Sep-2014 | 1 | 3 | 2.00 | |
| 5 | A7854 | Logan | 23 | 1 | 19-Jul-2012 | 1 | 3 | 2.00 | |
| 6 | B1234 | John | 37 | 1 | 12-Dec-2001 | 2 | 5 | 10.00 | |
| 7 | B4567 | David | 31 | 1 | 30-Jun-2013 | 2 | 3 | 15.00 | |
| 8 | B4568 | Seema | 63 | 0 | 12-Apr-2012 | 2 | 4 | 4.00 | |
| 9 | B5907 | Jemima | 42 | 0 | 14-Mar-2010 | 2 | 3 | .00 | |
| 10 | B8893 | Hambel | 39 | 0 | 06-Jul-1997 | 2 | 3 | .00 | |
| 11 | C1785 | Big Ted | 67 | 1 | 05-May-2011 | 3 | 3 | .00 | |
| 12 | C3893 | Luke | 26 | 1 | 03-Mar-1999 | 3 | 4 | 20.00 | |
| 13 | C7863 | Alison | 27 | 0 | 12-Nov-2001 | 3 | 5 | 25.00 | |
| 14 | C8633 | Anais | 34 | 0 | 30-Oct-2013 | 3 | 3 | 2.00 | |
| 15 | D1134 | Graham | 63 | 1 | 12-Sep-2012 | 4 | 3 | 2.00 | |
| 16 | D2227 | Kathy | 29 | 0 | 19-Mar-2010 | 4 | 5 | 40.00 | |
| 17 | D3897 | Stacey | 54 | 0 | 06-Jun-1997 | 4 | 3 | 5.00 | |
| 18 | D7736 | Paul | 31 | 1 | 05-Aug-2014 | 4 | 3 | 5.00 | |
| 19 | D8733 | Lily | 34 | 0 | 03-Jul-1999 | 4 | 4 | 30.00 | |
| 20 | D9083 | Max | 35 | 1 | 15-Dec-2001 | 4 | 3 | 5.00 | |

And the variable view will be updated (see Figure 2.54):

**FIGURE 2.54**

| | Name | Type | Width | Decimals | Label | Values | Missing | Columns | Align | Measure | Role |
|---|---|---|---|---|---|---|---|---|---|---|---|
| 1 | EmpId | String | 5 | 0 | Employee Id | None | None | 5 | Left | Nominal | Input |
| 2 | Name | String | 7 | 0 | Employee Name | None | None | 7 | Left | Nominal | Input |
| 3 | Age | Numeric | 11 | 0 | Employee Age | None | None | 11 | Right | Scale | Input |
| 4 | Gender | Numeric | 1 | 0 | Gender of Emp... | {0, Female}... | None | 8 | Right | Nominal | Input |
| 5 | StartDate | Date | 11 | 0 | Start Date of E... | None | None | 13 | Right | Scale | Input |
| 6 | Department | Numeric | 10 | 0 | Department of... | {1, Marketi... | None | 10 | Right | Nominal | Input |
| 7 | Rating | Numeric | 8 | 0 | Performance R... | {1, Very po... | None | 12 | Right | Ordinal | Input |
| 8 | SalaryAdj | Numeric | 8 | 2 | Suggested per... | None | None | 8 | Right | Scale | Input |
| 9 | | | | | | | | | | | |
| 10 | | | | | | | | | | | |

You can see that the final data file contains all the variables from both files and we can now view one case (employee) and see the employee profile and the performance data all together in one place. Now we could go on and do all kinds of exciting analysis around performance ratings and gender or promotions by department or age, perhaps gender pay gaps, etc. Chapter 3 will take you through some very useful analysis tools that you could use on this data set.

The data in the above example is, of course, very small and in reality you may be running analysis on thousands or even hundreds of thousands of employees. Indeed the data now available to organizations is growing at an exponential rate, so we thought it would be important to talk about a term that you may hear around the world of HR analytics – big data.

# Big data

The term 'big data' is often used to describe big sets of data that are so large that traditional methods for storing, analysing and sharing data can be inadequate. Gartner (2012) defines big data as 'high volume, high velocity, and/or high variety information assets that require new forms of processing to enable enhanced decision making, insight discovery and process optimization'.

As an organization develops, databases grow in size because information is constantly being gathered. Sometimes hundreds, even thousands, of servers are required to store all of the information required by an organization. So bringing all this together for analysis is not a trivial matter. Because of the sheer size of the data, it is uncommon for predictive analysis to take place across the entire spectrum of big data; most predictive analysis uses data files that can be comfortably stored on a PC (and be files of 'PC-sized' data). Depending on the organization, the term 'big data' could be referring to hundreds of gigabytes or hundreds of terabytes.

This concept has grown in the last decade as organizations such as Google, Facebook and LinkedIn struggled to manage the vast amount of information they were collecting (Bersin and O'Leanard, 2013), and the relational databases such as Oracle and Sybase were not originally designed to manage that degree of volume, velocity (frequency of updates) and variety of data.

As already mentioned, however, this is not a book about information management – but a quick summary of the four types of databases you are likely to come across is as follows:

- Relational databases (eg SAP, Oracle or Sybase) store information in tables. These tables are linked together and information is queried using a structured query language (SQL). Most HR systems use relational databases.
- Multidimensional databases (eg Cognos, Business Objects), also called online analytic processing (OLAP) databases. These take data out of traditional relational systems and create a data warehouse. They store data by 'dimension' (ie such as a division, or a year of hire) and precalculate the information so that when you query the database it is quick to respond with answers to queries such as turnover by department or new hires per month.
- Object-oriented databases (eg Workday), which store data as 'objects'. So the 'employee object' would store data about employees such as name, address, start date, etc. It also stores 'rules' or 'methods' such as 'gender must be M or F' or 'start date must be after 1900'. With object-oriented databases, the analyst can change an object and the entire system changes along with it. So if you added a new field to the employee object, such as 'languages spoken', then the other parts of the system could use this field as well, immediately. Without getting into the details, suffice to say that object-oriented databases are far more flexible and easy to change than traditional relational databases.
- Big data databases or no SQL databases (eg Hadoop). These databases are designed specifically to handle enormous amounts of data, going up to hundreds of terabytes or even thousands of terabytes (called petabytes). It breaks down data into small pieces that can then be processed in parallel. Two key benefits of big data technologies are that they can run queries on vast amounts of data quickly, and that they work on both structured and unstructured data.

As mentioned earlier, most HR databases are relational databases, and some of the shortcomings of the big data databases (such as the inability to query one single employee) mean that the intention of big data databases is not to replace these, but to work together with them.

# HR Information Systems and Data

If you are an HR analytics expert or work closely with, or in, an HR MI team, you are likely to already be well aware of the concepts described in this section; indeed the major HR software vendors are investing heavily in analytics platforms, tools and solutions (Bersin and O'Leonard, 2013).

Indeed Oracle (including PeopleSoft), SAP and Workday, as well as many other HR solution providers, have introduced analytics products integrated with Hadoop big data technology. Additionally many data analysis tools, including Excel, have interfaces that work with big data technology.

According to a US McKinsey Report (2011) the introduction of big data is estimated to result in 140,000–150,000 more deep analytical talent positions in the United States. The same report estimates that the US healthcare industry could put a value of $300 billion each year on the increased efficiency and quality improvements that would take place by analysing big data effectively to drive efficiency. Benefits are also estimated in the retail sector to increase operating margin by as much as 60 per cent, and other levers highlighted in government include savings of more than US $100 billion in operational efficiency costs alone using big data. Additionally, the benefits of being able to use big data to reduce fraud, errors and tax gaps between potential and actual revenue have yet to be estimated.

McKinsey warns that organizations need to address many challenges ahead in trying to capture the full potential of big data, and the key, number-one pressing challenge is in having people with deep analytical skills, able to analyse the big data and help organizations to make decisions based on the findings. They identify five ways in which big data will create value in the future:

1 create transparency;
2 enable experimentation to discover needs, expose variability and improve performance;
3 segment populations to customize actions;
4 support human decision making with automated algorithms;
5 innovate new business models, products and services.

It is benefit number four where sophisticated analytics such as those outlined in this book can make considerable improvements in decision making and help organizations to minimize risk. Finally, creative use of analytics and big data can uncover valuable insights.

The analytics skills you will use in working through this book, together with a good understanding of the systems you are working with, will make you a valuable commodity in your organization in this information age. Chapter 3 will take you through analysis strategies. We will discuss, in detail, various commonly used statistical tests and strategies and take you through how and when to use them in order to understand what your data is telling you.

# References

Bersin and O'Leonard (2013) [accessed 20 November 2015] Analyst Blogs, *Bersin by Deloitte* [Online] http://www.bersin.com/Blog/
Gartner (2012) [accessed 30 November 2015] IT Glossary: Big Data, *Gartner* [Online] http://www.gartner.com/it-glossary/big-data
Kane, J (2012) [accessed 22 April 2015] A Review of the Top Five Statistical Software Systems, *Professional Statistical Services*, 24 November 2012, 02:03 [Online] http://www.prostatservices.com/statistical-consulting/articles-of-interest/a-review-of-the-top-five-statistical-software-systems
US McKinsey Report (2011) [accessed 20 November 2015] Big Data: The Next Frontier for Innovation, Competition and Productivity [Online] www.mckinsey.com/mgi

# Analysis strategies

03

In this chapter, we discuss everything you need to get started on predictive HR analytics. You could think of this chapter as your analytic compass. In Chapter 2 we discussed the types of information that you are likely to uncover around your organization, where you are likely to find it, and the type of database it may be stored in. Once you have the data, we now discuss moving from simply producing reports to showing the different analytic techniques that you can use as part of your predictive HR analytics toolkit. Understanding the different techniques will allow you to conduct more meaningful analysis, using statistics to uncover what is really going on and predict what is likely to occur in the future.

Below, we delve into different analytic tests; each of these does something different and can be applied to different data to answer different analytic questions. We discuss specifically which statistical tests to use on which type of variables and when. If you are like most people and do not have a photographic memory, you will find Table 3.4 (Statistical tests by data type, pages 69–71), and Table 3.5 (Case study examples, pages 72–74) to be very useful points of reference.

In Chapter 2 we discussed the five most commonly used statistical software packages, which may be useful if you are deciding which package to use at your organization or university. In this book we set out our examples using SPSS, so in this chapter we set out some screenshots of where the various analyses tests are in the SPSS menu system.

## From descriptive reports to predictive analytics

At present, most HR functions lack the capability to use the available HR data to its full potential, usually because they lack the knowledge or experience, or even the foresight to appreciate the enormous possibilities presented by HR analytic modelling. Indeed the ability to tap into the rich vein of human capital metrics that can be available to organizations will reveal new insights and knowledge about the organization that would have been very difficult to consider up to now.

Descriptive HR reports usually produced by MI teams refer to the illustration of a set of data, a 'snapshot' of what is occurring at that time, presenting the current state of play. Sets of data cut across various parts of an organization; for example: recruitment data such as time to hire, costs to hire per employee, recruiter productivity; workforce demographics such as age, gender, tenure; or headcount data such as percentage turnover and costs per head. For the vast majority of HR functions, this is the limit of the HR analytic capability. With these reports, the most sophisticated statistical techniques that tend to be used are usually calculating a percentage of the population that can be classified in a certain way (eg leaver or non-leaver) or an average figure that might represent an indication of how a particular group fares on a particular metric (eg average salary or average performance rating); these descriptive reports do not help us fully to understand what is going on in our organization. When running these reports the analysts do not generally interrogate the data fully for other possible explanatory factors (which can help clarify why something might be happening) nor do they tend to test or check the degree to which their data might be robust and valid and whether it might be reasonable to make claims on the basis of any data they may be presenting. In addition, presenting descriptive reports does not in any way help us to try and make predictions about what we might find in the future.

Bersin (2012) outlines the importance of using predictive analytics to help organizations predict or understand the performance of a person or group of people based on historical data. Once sufficient data has been collected over time, it is then possible to analyse patterns and trends based on this historical data. As already mentioned in Chapter 1, Huselid (2014) proposed that: 'Analytics present a tremendous opportunity to help organizations understand what they don't yet know... By identifying trends and patterns, HR professionals and management teams can make better strategic decisions about the workforce challenges that they may soon face.'

There are many examples of predictive analytics in this book. However, to get the ball rolling let's consider that, instead of just having a report showing turnover statistics per region, we are actually able to analyse the turnover percentage against the demographic data over a number of years. Predictive analytics would be able to understand what is likely (ie with statistical significance) to cause a low or a high turnover percentage, whether it be a particular region, a certain employee profile or a certain job role.

Once the organization has access to the available data, there really is no limit to the predictive models that could be analysed. Although this is incredibly powerful, it introduces its own challenges, one of the biggest being what, exactly, we should be analysing and what models we should run in the first place. This will be driven by a combination of business need and data availability and will likely evolve as time goes on. We will work through some examples of predictive models in the case study chapters in this book (Chapters 4–9). To give you a further idea, however, we can use predictive modelling to analyse what factors predict turnover of key talent;

to investigate the patterns of team diversity across the organization and what this may mean in terms of outcomes; or assessing what factors associated with recruitment, selection and induction predict the retention of new joiners.

## Statistical significance

Throughout this book, we discuss and perform various statistical tests. The key aim of the statistical testing is to determine whether the results point to a 'statistically significant' outcome.

The basic idea behind statistical significance is linked to hypotheses testing. This simply involves us developing a 'research hypothesis' and what is called a 'null hypothesis'. To test the research hypothesis we carry out particular statistical analysis on the associated data and obtain a test statistic. The test statistic then tells us whether a particular pattern of results (which may support the research hypothesis) can be relied upon and if it is robust enough for us to make various assumptions about what is going on in our population (eg in our organization if we are trying to explore data linked to employees); or whether it is more likely that we came by our particular set of findings by chance alone (in other words the results we find are not robust).

If there is strong evidence from our data that there is something really meaningful going on, and our test indicates that a finding is unlikely to have occurred by chance alone, we would say that we have grounds to: 'reject the null hypothesis' in favour of the 'research hypothesis' (or 'alternate' hypothesis as it is sometimes called). In very simple and loose terms, the 'null hypothesis' suggests that the results are not strong enough for us to draw any firm conclusions about the findings. So for us to be able to draw any conclusions from our data we want to be able to push this 'null hypothesis' to one side in favour of the 'research hypothesis'.

Like many terms in this book, this may be better explained by using an example. Let's say our hypotheses are as follows:

- *Research hypothesis:* attendance at a customer-service training course by sales employees will increase customer satisfaction survey scores.
- *Null hypothesis:* attendance at a customer-service training course by sales employees will have *no* impact on customer satisfaction survey scores.

So, in its simplest form, what we might do in researching this hypothesis (in a particular organization) is to collect and analyse data relating to who went on the customer-service training course and who did not. We could then collect data from the customer satisfaction survey (both before and after the training), making sure to record who the customer was served by. We would then run a statistical test (we will cover later in the book which statistical test we should run on what data) to understand whether there was a 'statistically significant' improvement in the customer satisfaction scores for those sales staff who attended the training course.

The statistical test would produce a test statistic, from which we could determine whether the result is statistically significant. If the test did indicate 'statistical significance', we would have grounds to reject the 'null hypothesis' that the customer-service training course has no impact on customer satisfaction survey scores.

The criterion used universally for testing significance is 95 per cent confidence. This 95 per cent cut-off for significance is a long-standing convention that has been recognized for almost 100 years (generally since 1925 when Fisher published his book *Statistical Methods for Research Workers*). Statistics is a moving field and the mathematical science underlying statistical analysis is continually being debated. The use of this 95 per cent certainty cut-off and the 'null hypothesis test for significance' is no exception. However, in this book we will follow the 100-year-old convention of using 95 per cent confidence to determine whether a result is significant, and we will use the 95 per cent level of certainty as our target cut-off.

So if we can be at least 95 per cent confident (from statistical tests) that the pattern of data found would be unlikely to occur by chance, we would say that the finding is 'statistically significant'. If we want to be 95 per cent certain about our findings then another way of putting this is that we want to be able to say that there is only a 5 per cent likelihood that our findings might be due to chance alone. The term used to indicate the level of significance in statistical tests is the probability level. A 5 per cent likelihood is presented as a 0.05 probability. This is called a p-value and this is what our statistical tests present: the probability that our findings could be due to chance alone. So with the statistical tests we want our p-values to be 0.05 or lower (commonly indicated as $p<0.05$). We want the likelihood that our findings are due to chance alone to be less than 5 per cent in order for us to be 95 per cent (or more) confident that our findings are meaningful. Thus we want $p<0.05$ (note: 5 per cent is the same as saying a p-value of 0.05, because it is $0.05 \times 100$).

It is important to remember this 0.05 p-value. We always want our statistical tests to indicate a significance level of 0.05 in order for us to say we have a 'statistically significant' finding.

$$p<0.05$$

$P<0.05$ will be the key to our decision making in interpreting the analysis results for most of the statistical analysis in this book.

Importantly, sometimes our statistical tests indicate that we can be more than 95 per cent confident that our findings are meaningful and not due to chance alone. For example, our statistical test may indicate that we can be 99 per cent confident that our results would not occur by chance and thus the p-value presented here will be $p=0.01$. If the p-value of the result is smaller than 0.01 then we indicate $p<0.01$.

Equally, our test results may indicate that we can be 99.9 per cent confident that our findings would not occur by chance; the associated p-value for this would be 0.001. This in effect would be saying that our findings are so strong that we can be *really* confident that the results are robust. If our p-value is smaller than 0.001 then we would generally present this as p<0.001. This, in effect, says the following: 'the likelihood that the results we find would occur by chance alone is less than 1 in 1,000'. Therefore, the smaller the p-value the more confident we can be with our results.

Importantly, if our p-value is more than 0.05 (p>0.05) we have not reached our desired 95 per cent level of confidence in our results. This means that our findings are not 'statistically significant' and, because our results might be due to chance, we cannot cast aside the null hypothesis.

It is important to remember the p<0.05, cut-off p-value. It will be the key to most of the statistical analysis in this book. As you go through the case study chapters in particular, and also when you carry out your own analysis, you will find yourself eagerly scanning the SPSS (or similar) statistical output tables looking for a p-value of 0.05 or less. Note that p values are usually labelled as 'sig.' in SPSS output.

We will go through the meaning of statistical significance with each test in more detail as we cover each test later in this chapter.

# Data integrity

It is important to note how critical it is that the data you are analysing is up to date and reliable. It is the practice of many organizations to put onto employees and line managers the ownership of keeping HR and people-management information up to date, and it is critical that the processes surrounding key people-management activities be sufficiently robust to ensure that the information in the database is comprehensive and regularly updated.

Linking data from different sources usually just requires a unique identifier such as an employee ID on which the other information relates. Data can be combined in data warehouses, databases such as Microsoft Access, spreadsheet packages such as Microsoft Excel, and loaded up into statistical software packages such as SPSS. Care is needed to ensure the integrity of the information. Indeed a key challenge with developed HR analytics is to understand the complexity of the data available, linking it up, and getting it to a format where it can be swiftly analysed. As mentioned earlier in this chapter, there are many different sources of data in the organization from which HR professionals can mine; however, it may take considerable data manipulation on these files and information sets to get predictive models to run. This can take a considerable amount of time, skill and experience in data handling and statistical analysis to ensure the models that are being run are suitable for the data they are analysing.

The type of data is critical in determining which type of analysis should be carried out. In the next three sections of this chapter, we go through the different types of data and how to recognize them, some common statistical analysis tests that can be carried out on organizational (and indeed other) data, and which statistical tests should be used on which types of data.

## Types of data

The data that we collect, or that is collected in an organization, can be grouped into certain types based on what it is measuring and how it behaves. Each data field, whether it is salary, name, gender, or anything else in the data set, is termed a variable. Variables can be classed as either categorical or continuous.

Put simply, variables are things that can vary, or change. It might be, for example, eye colour (which varies from person to person), temperature (which varies from day to day), or performance rating (which varies from employee to employee). This notion of variance is absolutely central in statistical analyses. If we think about any characteristic or data linked to employees (eg age, gender, salary, engagement levels, bonuses, competency rating, performance rating, whether they are a leaver or not, etc) in our organization, this characteristic will vary across individuals. Ultimately, it is this variation that we analyse with our statistical tests.

## Categorical variable types

A categorical variable is one that is made up of categories. For example, we talk about 'role' level in the diversity case study when analysing the prevalence of women in senior-level roles. The 'role levels' existing within the organization in question are: clerical, administrative, graduate consultant, consultant, senior consultant, principal consultant and partner. Each employee is only one or the other. They may be a graduate consultant, they may be a partner, but they cannot be both a graduate consultant and a partner. There is no overlap. When you think about what this data looks like, there is no immediate quantitative or numerical value. Indeed it is best thought of as a collection of labels or names representing some category within our organization or employee group. And clearly because these types of variables have no numerical value, it is not possible to add, subtract, multiply or divide them any more than you could add a graduate consultant to a senior consultant and hope to get a partner.

It is worth noting here that categorical variables can use numbers as labels. However, this does not mean they are meaningful numbers with which we can use arithmetic. An example would be if the base country code might be recorded in the HR PeopleSoft system as a number, for example:

01 – Australia
02 – United Kingdom

03 – United States
04 – Hong Kong
05 – Singapore
06 – Canada

So although the system stores country as a number, it is not a numeric value with which we could meaningfully add, subtract, multiply or divide. Clearly you cannot hope to multiply the UK by three and get Canada. Hence the numbers are just labels here too.

There are three different types of categorical variable: binary, nominal and ordinal, as set out below.

## *Binary variable*

Binary variables are categorical variables that are unique in that they name only two distinct entities or ideas. Certainly it is the simplest form of categorical variable. Binary variables are also referred to as binomial or dichotomous. Some examples are:

Gender: male/female

Attended customer service training: yes/no

## *Nominal variable*

Nominal variables are categorical variables that name three or more distinct entities. They are in no particular order and each value is mutually exclusive. Some examples are below:

Home office location: Australia, United Kingdom, Canada, United States, Singapore, Hong Kong, etc.

Division: Sales, Legal, HR, Finance, etc.

## *Ordinal variables*

Ordinal data takes things a step further. It is essentially categorical data for which there is a meaningful order. So it increases or decreases in order. Importantly, although there may be an order to the variable, and each case in the variable may have a number associated with it representing some kind of order (eg in the case of a rank), a characteristic of an ordinal variable is that the meaningful interval between each position or number in the order may not be equal. If you ranked all employees in an organization on the basis of their salary, the rank you give each person would represent an order; however, the actual amount of salary that each person (and thus ranked position) differs by will not necessarily be equal. The person who is paid the most, who is first in the variable, may get £200,000, the second person may get £190,000 and the third person may get £100,000. As such the meaningful intervals underlying the ordered numbers may not be equal. Aside from this salary ranking, some other examples are presented below:

> Role level: 1) graduate, 2) consultant, 3) senior consultant, 4) managing consultant, 5) vice principal
>
> Job satisfaction: 1) very dissatisfied, 2) dissatisfied, 3) neither satisfied nor dissatisfied, 4) satisfied, 5) very satisfied

So, in summary, the values within a categorical data variable are labels, or names. There are three types of categorical data: binary, nominal and ordinal. Binary is when there are only two possible values, nominal is when there are three or more possible values, and ordinal is when the values are in a meaningful order. Because they are names only, we cannot perform any arithmetic on them. For this reason, we cannot quantify the difference between different points on the scale.

## Continuous variable types

Continuous variables can take on any numerical value on a measurement scale. There are two key types of continuous variable: interval variables and ratio variables.

### *Interval variables*

Interval data is measured on a numeric scale. The numbers are continuous – so as well as knowing the order, interval data records the exact value. This means that, unlike ordinal data where there is a limited set of responses, with interval data the value could be anything on a scale:

> Daily temperature (Celsius): some examples might be 21.4, 37.8. 16.0, 8.5, etc. Although it is likely to be between –50 and +50, it could really take on any value on that temperature scale, including as many decimal points as you care to record.
>
> Start date: some examples might be 6/6/1994, 28/9/2013, 4/5/2015, etc. Whilst we can measure the difference between two dates, we cannot add or multiply this data.

So we have the ability to quantify the difference between each value. So, for example, if you wanted to know the difference in temperature from one day to the next, you could calculate the space in between, or *interval*, by simply subtracting.

Interval data lacks a zero starting point, which makes comparisons of magnitude not possible. Whilst we can say that the difference between 8 and 9 degrees is the same as the difference between 22 and 23 degrees, we cannot say, however, that 20 degrees is twice as hot as 10 degrees in the same way that we could say that 20 apples are twice as many as 10 apples. It is more complex than that because temperature does not start at zero and there is no such thing as having no temperature. There is such a thing as having no apples though.

So you cannot have 'no date' when measuring date or 'no temperature' when measuring temperature. Even a zero temperature is still a tangible temperature and even year zero on our calendar was still an actual year.

## *Ratio variables*

Ratio data is similar to interval data in that it is a continuous numerical value but, unlike interval data, there is a defined zero point. As in the earlier example, if we had a variable 'number of apples on table' it would start at zero and then go up to any number (depending on the size of your table). Some examples in an organizational context are below:

Annual salary (£): Some examples might be 16000, 120000, 564482, 34909, 86269, etc.

Height (cm): 170, 182, 163, 134.5, etc.

Weight (kg): 67, 48, 120.3, 98.4, etc.

Job tenure (years): 0.25, 0.5, 1, 23, 20, etc.

These values are meaningful numerically and can be added, subtracted, divided and multiplied. Ratio data enables you to say things like 'the average annual salary of men in this organization is 2.78 times greater than the average annual salary of women'. Tables 3.1 and 3.2 provide a summary of these five data types.

**TABLE 3.1** Categorical variable types – variables divided into distinct categories

| Data Type | Description | Examples |
| --- | --- | --- |
| Binary | Only two categories | Pregnant or not pregnant; male or female; someone who has left versus someone still employed |
| Nominal | Three or more categories | Division or function (eg HR, Risk, Finance, Sales, etc); country (eg Canada, Australia, India) |
| Ordinal | Categories have a meaningful order | Customer satisfaction scale (very dissatisfied, dissatisfied, neutral, satisfied, very satisfied); ranked sales position of employee or team (1st, 2nd, 3rd, etc) |

**TABLE 3.2** Continuous variable types – variables with a distinct numerical value

| Data Type | Description | Examples |
|---|---|---|
| Interval | Numerical value. No defined 'zero' starting point. | Temperature; year. |
| Ratio | Continuous numerical data with a defined zero starting point. Ratios of scores on a scale also make sense. | Height; weight; salary; age; job tenure; sales figures (€£$); % linked to an individual object such as individual, team, department (eg % of the team who indicated that they were 'engaged' or staff turnover % in each team or division). |

With continous data, the measure of difference between two points is quantifiable and equal intervals on the variable represent equal differences in the item being measured.

# Using group/team-level or individual-level data

Depending on the topic and what it is you are trying to achieve, it may be more appropriate to analyse the data at a team level, or at an individual level. Typically, more sensitive information such as employee engagement survey results will, for ethical reasons, only be available at a team level (organizations usually make promises of confidentiality and anonymity with engagement surveys; see Chapter 5). Equally, it may be more appropriate when assessing leadership effectiveness to assess the aggregated performance of the team they are leading. On the other hand, there are examples where it makes more sense to conduct the analysis at an individual level, particularly where we are looking at the attributes of an individual rather than the attributes of a team. Some examples are given in Table 3.3.

# Dependent variables and independent variables

As mentioned earlier in this chapter, the type of statistical test to use is reliant on the type of data being analysed. Before we get into this, it is

**TABLE 3.3** Data measurement levels with examples

| Level | Example Measures |
|---|---|
| Team | Employee opinion survey output (such as team engagement index, team leadership index, aggregate % confidence in leadership, composite team scores on work–life balance), store/branch customer feedback, store/branch customer loyalty, team staff turnover %, team size, team leader rating. |
| Individual | Performance appraisal rating, behavioural rating, sales performance figures, checkout scan rate, individual customer feedback, peer feedback, call rates, call loads, leaver status, length of service, gender. |

important to understand the difference between dependent variables and independent variables. Why? Because it is actually the data type of your dependent variable (rather than independent variables) or variables that will determine the type of statistical test you need to use. You can only determine this if you actually know the difference between the two! So what is the difference? The answer to the question really lies in what it is you are trying to model or what it is you are trying to explain or account for with your research question or analysis.

## Dependent variables

The dependent variable (or variables), also called the 'outcome variable' or the 'DV' for short, refers to what it is you are trying to model, predict or account for variation in. In our discussion about statistical significance earlier in this chapter, we outlined the research hypothesis as follows:

*'Attendance at the customer service training course by the sales team will increase customer satisfaction survey scores.'*

In this example, our outcome variable, the one we are trying to model, predict or account for variation in (and change if we can!) is the customer satisfaction survey score. This is our dependent variable. Customer satisfaction is expected to be affected by changes in the customer service training-course attendance, which is our independent variable. Thus we would expect that variation in customer satisfaction scores within our workforce might (to some degree) be dependent upon whether or not someone has been on a training course.

## Independent variables

The independent variable (or variables), also called 'predictor variable' or 'IV' for short, refers to the variable that we think has an effect, cause or influence on the outcome or dependent variable. So, in our example, we can now say the following:

*Dependent variable*: customer satisfaction survey scores.

*Independent variable*: customer service training-course attendance.

This is because we think (or we hypothesize) that there is a possibility that customer service training-course attendance has an impact on customer satisfaction survey scores.

One caution here is that, even when we do find a significant relationship or link between two variables (where we assume that one is an independent variable and the other a dependent variable), it does not necessarily mean that changes in the independent variable 'cause' changes in the dependent variable. It would just mean that there is a relationship between the two where change in one relates to or is associated with changes in another. A classic example of this is the sales of ice cream and the prevalence of skin cancer. It has been found that countries that have high ice-cream sales are also likely to have high rates of skin cancer. Does this mean that ice cream causes skin cancer? No. In reality the cause is something else: probably something to do with the sun. In countries where there are higher temperatures, there are higher sales of ice cream and there are also higher rates of skin cancer. So whilst the information is useful, we can only determine relationships (and not causality) in cross-sectional analysis. We will talk more about challenges with inferring causality from analysis later in the book (Chapter 12).

Importantly, dependent variables might be binary, nominal, ordinal, interval or ratio, and independent variables might be binary, nominal, ordinal, interval or ratio. The combination present in the data that we want to analyse will determine which analytic test we can use.

# Your toolkit: types of statistical tests

As mentioned earlier in this chapter, the type of statistical test used depends on two main things. First, the nature of the research question that you are hoping to answer, and second, the data types of your independent and dependent variables. Table 3.4 gives a brief summary of what to use (note that the list is confined to the subset of tools we use in the case studies in this book, which we believe would meet the need in 95 per cent of the analysis that HR analytics professionals will need to run).

### A note on parametric tests and parametric data

Most of the statistical procedures in Table 3.4 are 'parametric tests'.

**TABLE 3.4** Statistical tests by data type

| Dependent Variable (DV) | Independent Variables (IV) | Analysis Test | Nature of the Test; what type of research question is it trying to explore? |
|---|---|---|---|
| Categorical DV (Binary, Nominal, or *Ordinal) | Categorical and only one IV | **Chi-square** analysis – applied to a crosstabs of frequencies. | **Chi-square** analysis explores whether the frequencies and proportions found across particular categories (eg male versus female) might vary or be linked to another category (eg part-time versus full-time). |
| | Continuous or together continuous and categorical | **Logistic regression** analysis. | **Logistic regression** analysis attempts to predict the likelihood of something in particular occurring (eg whether someone leaves the organization versus whether they stay) on the basis of possible characteristics across a range of independent variables (eg performance criteria, gender, salary increases, promotion, etc). |
| Continuous DV (Interval or Ratio – and sometimes *Ordinal) | Categorical-Binary IV – Group A versus Group B | **Independent samples t-test** | **Independent samples t-test** explores whether two groups of data differ on some dimension. Eg are males more stressed than females? Are females more engaged than males? |
| | 2-Category-Time Based Binary IV – Group A at Time 1 versus Group A at Time 2 | **Paired samples t-test** | **Paired samples t-test** explores whether two separate times/instances of data collection of the same group differ or are the same across time – has there been a change in some data? Are the leadership team performing better than they were a year ago? |

**TABLE 3.4** continued

| Dependent Variable (DV) | Independent Variables (IV) | Analysis Test | Nature of the Test; what type of research question is it trying to explore? |
|---|---|---|---|
| Continuous DV (Interval or Ratio – and sometimes *Ordinal) | Categorical IV with three or more groups; Group A versus Group B versus Groups C etc... | **One-way independent ANOVA** | **One-way independent ANOVA** explores whether three or more groups of data differ on some continuous dimension, eg are the HR function's employees more engaged than those from finance or marketing? |
| | Category-Time Based IV with three or more time points (eg Group A at Time 1 versus Group A at Time 2 versus Group A at Time 3) | **One-way repeated measures ANOVA** | **One-way repeated measures ANOVA** explores whether three or more separate times/instances of data collection differ or are the same across time – has there been a change in some metric (eg team engagement scores) across time? |
| | Continuous (assumed) DV and only one other continuous IV | **Pearson's correlation,** or **Simple linear regression** | **Pearson's correlation,** or **Simple linear regression** – if you want to look at the degree to which two continuous variables are related in some way – with correlations you may just be interested in the 'co'-relation between two variables; with simple regression you might be making some assumptions about which variable could be 'caused' or 'predicted' by the other.[†] |
| | Time-based categorical IV with two or more time points – Time 1 versus Time 2 (etc) in combination with one or more categorical IVS (eg gender) | **Repeated measures ANOVA** (generalized linear model). The DV metric will have been collected on more than two occasions with the same objects (eg employees or teams) but the sample can be broken up into one or more other category (eg male versus female; received training versus not; HR versus marketing versus finance etc). | **Repeated measures ANOVA** (generalized linear model) explores whether two or more separate times/instances of data collection differ or are the same across time – has there been a change in some metric across time? This approach also enables you to explore whether particular comparator groups vary in the degree to which each differs across time (eg male versus female; received training versus not; HR versus marketing versus finance etc). |

**TABLE 3.4** continued

| Dependent Variable (DV) | Independent Variables (IV) | Analysis Test | Nature of the Test; what type of research question is it trying to explore? |
|---|---|---|---|
| Continuous DV (Interval or Ratio – and sometimes *Ordinal) | Two or more continuous IVs | **Multiple regression (linear)** | **Multiple regression** analysis – here we are trying to predict and account for variation in a continuous dependent variable (eg sales €£$ figures for each individual – importantly we do this by exploring the degree to which this variation can be 'accounted for' by the degree to which two or more other (possible) causal factors/IVS share variance with this DV. For example – might the variation in $ sales that an employee achieves in a week be linked to the number of hours worked in a week and the age of the employee? |
| | Both categorical and continuous IVs | **Multiple regression (linear)** | **Multiple regression** analysis: as immediately above – with the difference that some of the IVs included represent memberships of a particular category/group (eg male versus female). If the number of categories in a particular IV is above two then dummy variables have to be created. See discussion in Chapter 7. |

\* Although technically incorrect, in practice, sometimes ordinal data is treated as continuous data for the purpose of analysis. An example is answering multiple-item questions in a survey to give your line manager a score of 1 to 5 (where 1 means very poor and 5 means very good). Technically you cannot select anything other than 1, 2, 3, 4 or 5. Many analysts, though, will treat this data as continuous to perform arithmetic to get findings such as Manager A having a mean of 3.2 versus Manager B having a mean of 3.9.

† Again we caveat this statement by raising the issue that correlation does not imply causality (see Chapter 12).

**NOTE** – There are many different tests available not discussed here. We restrict our test choices to the most straightforward tests with regard to HR analytics.

Statisticians use the word 'parameter' when talking about characteristics of the population that the sample data (that they are analysing) comes from, and parametric tests are making various assumptions about the populations that the data being analysed is drawn from. One of the key assumptions of parametric tests (that enable us to draw conclusions about the wider population) is that distributions linked to the data form a normal distribution. This is when the data is distributed symmetrically around the centre (or mean) and is shaped like a bell curve, which you may have come across before. Characteristically most of the results will be nearest the mean, and then, as you move away from the mean in either direction, the numbers will get smaller.

Sometimes, however, the data that we analyse might not behave in this way. The distribution curve of the data may lean (be skewed) to the left (+) or the right (–), or it may be bunched up and 'pointy' (*lepto*kurtic: the data distribution *leapt* up in the middle) or more spread out and flat (*platy*kurtic: flat like a *plate*) than we would expect for a normal distribution. In this case we have to be careful when drawing assumptions from the tests; we may need to use other tests that are robust against violations of assumptions of normality.

As we have discussed, it is only continuous data on which we can do arithmetic and calculate means and standard deviations. Hence it is only when we are analysing continuous data that we need to test whether the data is parametric. Statistical analysis software packages will do this for you when the data is analysed and, where relevant, use the non-parametric statistical test. Further details on how this is done in SPSS are in the case study chapters (Chapters 4–9).

The best way to learn these methods is to use them in an organizational example in context. This is where the case studies in this book are very useful. Table 3.5 provides a summary of the case study examples for each statistical test mentioned.

**TABLE 3.5** Case study examples

| Test | Case Study Examples |
|---|---|
| Chi-square analysis | 1 Diversity case study (Chapter 4) example 1: gender and job grade analysis using frequency tables and chi-square. Page 111. |
| | 2 Employee turnover case study (Chapter 6) example 1b: exploring differences in individual staff turnover across a number of different countries using cross-tabulation and the chi-square test. Page 198. |
| | 3 Recruitment and selection case study (Chapter 8) examples 1 and 2: diversity analyses looking at potential bias in the recruitment and selection decisions. Pages 287 and 290. |

## TABLE 3.5  *continued*

| Test | Case Study Examples |
|---|---|
| Logistic regression analysis | 1  Employee turnover case study (Chapter 6) example 3: using logistic regression to set up a predictive model for individual turnover. Page 217.<br>2  Recruitment and selection case study (Chapter 8) example 2: predicting candidate rejection or shortlisting taking into account graduate gender and ethnicity. Page 290.<br>3  Recruitment and selection case sudy (Chapter 8) example 4: predicting graduate turnover. Page 310.<br>4  Predictive modelling case study (Chapter 10) example 3: predictive modeling and obtaining probabilities for the likelihood of employees leaving. Page 383.<br>5  Predictive modelling case study (Chapter 10) example 6: using historical patterns to predict the likelihood of new graduate candidates leaving. Page 406. |
| Independent samples t-test | 1  Diversity case study (Chapter 4) example 2b: comparing ethnicity and gender across two functions in an organization using the independent samples t-test. Page 128.<br>2  Engagement case study (Chapter 5) example 4: using the independent samples t-test to determine whether engagement levels are significantly different depending on functional grouping and location. Page 177. |
| Paired samples t-test | 1  Monitoring the impact of interventions case study (Chapter 9) example 1: assessing stress before and after an intervention using a paired samples t-test. Page 325. |
| One-way independent ANOVA | 1  Employee turnover case study (Chapter 6) example 2: exploring team-level turnover by country using the one-way ANOVA test. Page 203. |
| One-way repeated measures ANOVA | 1  Monitoring the impact of interventions case study (Chapter 9) example 3: value change. Exploring staff commitment levels at three different time points in a values change project. Page 336. |
| Within and between ANOVA: General Linear Model | 1  Monitoring the impact of interventions case study (Chapter 9) example 2: testing stress before and after intervention by gender using a repeated measures ANOVA. Page 330.<br>2  Monitoring the impact of interventions case study (Chapter 9) example 4: value change. Assessing the change in staff commitment over time by department. Page 344.<br>3  Monitoring the impact of interventions case study (Chapter 9) example 5: measuring the impact of a supermarket checkout training intervention on scan rates over time. Page 352. |

**TABLE 3.5** *continued*

| Test | Case Study Examples |
|---|---|
| **Multiple linear regression** | **1** Diversity case study (Chapter 4) example 3: using multiple linear regression to model and predict ethnic diversity variation across teams from base location, function, group size, team lead gender, and team gender breakdown. Page 135.<br>**2** Engagement case study (Chapter 5) example 5: using multiple linear regression to predict team level engagement. Page 183.<br>**3** Turnover case study (Chapter 6) example 4: using multiple linear regression to predict team level turnover. Page 226.<br>**4** Performance case study (Chapter 7) examples 1a and 1b: using multiple linear regression to predict customer loyalty and reinvestment in a financial services organization. Pages 241 and 246.<br>**5** Performance case study (Chapter 7) example 2: using multiple linear regression when combining customer survey data with 'pulse' survey to predict customer loyalty in a financial services organization. Page 249.<br>**6** Performance case study (Chapter 7) example 3: using multiple linear regression when combining performance appraisal data, sickness records and pulse survey data to predict individual performance in a manufacturing organization. Page 253.<br>**7** Performance case study (Chapter 7) example 4: using stepwise multiple linear regression to find the best model for predicting performance using combined performance appraisal data, sickness records and pulse survey data in a manufacturing organization. Page 258.<br>**8** Performance case study (Chapter 7) example 5: tracking performance over time using stepwise regression with combined performance appraisal data, sickness records and pulse survey data in a manufacturing organization. Page 264.<br>**9** Performance case study (Chapter 7) example 6: using multiple regression to predict sickness absence using employee attitude scores in a manufacturing organization. Page 268.<br>**10** Performance case study (Chapter 7) example 7: using multiple regression to explore patterns of performance with employee profile data in a manufacturing organization. Page 270.<br>**11** Performance case study (Chapter 7) example 8: using data interrogation techniques and multiple linear regression to predict checkout scan rates from employee profile data in a retail organization. Page 276.<br>**12** Performance case study (Chapter 7) example 9: using dummy variables in multiple linear regression to determine the presence of high-performing age groups in predicting scan rates in a retail organization. Page 279.<br>**13** Recruitment and selection case study (Chapter 8) example 3: assessment centre selection technique validation, predicting graduate performance from demographic, assessment centre and onboarding data. Page 307.<br>**14** Monitoring the impact of interventions case study (Chapter 9) example 6: conditional panel model predicting change in checkout scan rates with supermarket operators. Page 359.<br>**15** Predictive modelling case study (Chapter 10) example 1: predictive modelling of customer reinvestment intentions. Page 367.<br>**16** Predictive modelling case study (Chapter 10) example 2: predictive modelling the impact of training on checkout scan rates. Page 373.<br>**17** Predictive modelling case study (Chapter 10) example 4: predictive modelling the impact of induction day on graduate performance. Page 394.<br>**18** Predictive modelling case study (Chapter 10) example 5: predicting expected performance of graduate candidates. Page 398. |

Other analysis examples used in the book using simple descriptive statistics:

- Diversity case study (Chapter 4). Example 2a: exploring ethnic diversity across teams using descriptive statistics. Page 122.
- Turnover case study (Chapter 6). Example 1A: exploring differences in individual staff turnover across a number of different countries using frequencies tables. Page 194.
- Predictive modelling case study (Chapter 10): obtaining descriptive statistics to enable various predictive models. Page 382.

## Statistical tests for categorical data (binary, nominal, ordinal)

Here we outline each test in greater detail. Importantly, in each of the case study chapters we discuss further what the tests are doing in context. So in order to get to grips with each test the reader will also want to read each test in the context of each case study example in subsequent chapters.

### Cross-tabulation and the chi-square ($\chi^2$) test

Remembering from earlier in this chapter that the categorical data is all about categories and names on which we cannot do any arithmetic, we can be certain that if adding, subtracting, multiplying and dividing are not possible, then calculating means or standard deviations are out of the question! We can, then, only analyse the number of things that fall into each category, or the frequencies. This limitation determines which analytic test we can use. With categorical data, we can only analyse frequencies. The best way to start is by doing a cross-tabulation of the frequency of occurrence for each category of interest. This is similar to the results that you might get if you produced a pivot table in Excel. Then, we apply the chi-square (or $\chi^2$) test to the crosstabs frequencies; in this case we do this in order to analyse the significance of any link or relationships between two or more categorical variables.

A very simple example might be a cross-tabulation showing the results of frequencies of men and women in our organization (of 15,338 employees) and whether they were promoted or not in 2015. It would look something like the results shown in Table 3.6.

**TABLE 3.6** Observed gender and promotion values

| Gender | 2015 Promotions | | |
|---|---|---|---|
| | Promoted | Not Promoted | Total |
| Male | 127 | 6784 | 6911 |
| Female | 49 | 8378 | 8427 |
| Total | 176 | 15162 | 15338 |

By combining gender and promotions in this way, we end up with four discrete categories:

- male promoted;
- male not promoted;
- female promoted;
- female not promoted.

If we wanted to look at this descriptively we would want to calculate some percentages to get a feel for the data. For example, 54.94 per cent of the employees are female and 45.06 per cent are male. Only 1.147 per cent of employees were promoted in 2015. Of those promoted, just over 72 per cent were male; just under 2 per cent of men were promoted but the proportion of women who were promoted was just over 0.5 per cent. We can describe these findings and tell a story; however, we need to check whether there is a significant link between gender and promotion rates in 2015 before making any claims about statistically significant patterns.

If we want to see whether there is a statistically significant relationship between gender and 2015 promotions, we would do the chi-square test. The chi-square test compares the frequencies that you actually observed in particular conditions with the frequencies you would expect to get if there were absolutely no relationship between the two variables. If, in our organization, there is no relationship between gender and promotion rates, our chi-square tests could tell us that a set of frequencies could be gained by chance alone.

So in our example, the chi-squared statistic is obtained by calculating the overall difference between the observed frequency in each of the four categories and the 'expected' frequency in each of the four categories (that we would find if there were no real link between gender and promotions in our organization), and dividing it by the model total.

## Analysis Strategies

### Chi-square example (SPSS will do this for you!)

The equation (that SPSS calculates when you click your mouse) looks like this:

$X^2 = \sum ((\text{observed value} - \text{expected value})^2/\text{expected value})$

Or the sum of ((observed value − expected value)²/expected value) for each of the four categories.

Note that there is a slight variation on this equation when we have a 2 × 2 table, as in the example below, which is referred to as a Yates's continuity correction:

$X^2 = \sum ((|\text{observed value} - \text{expected value}| - 0.05)^2/\text{expected value})$

For simplicity we are going to ignore this version of the equation as it is only used with 2 × 2 tables.

Looking at our crosstabs of gender and 2015 promotion counts, we have the observed values for each category, but what are the 'expected' values that our equation refers to here? These are calculated by using the total values and the general proportions of males versus females found in the organization regardless of promotions.

Another way of putting this with our example is that the 'expected frequency' in each of the promotion versus not-promoted/male versus female condition is what you would expect if you simply translated the proportion of our organization that was promoted in 2015 into our populations of males and females in our organization. For example, if 1.1 per cent of our organization was promoted in 2015, then the 'expected frequency' of promoted versus non-promoted employees would amount to 1.1 per cent versus 98.9 per cent of both our male and female population (if there was no link between gender and promotion rates). But in reality, it may be the case that more than 1.1 per cent of males were promoted and less than 1.1 per cent of females were promoted... as in this case.

Let's work through the equation for each category:

1. Male promoted:

    Observed value = 127
    Expected value that we would probably have if there was no link between gender and promotions
    = (total # men) × (total # promoted) / total people
    = 6,911 × 176/15,338
    = 79.3

For simplicity, we will round this down to 79; so if gender was not linked to promotions we should have 79 males who were promoted in 2015 – the observed figure is obviously higher than this.

2   Male not promoted:

Observed value = 6,784
Expected value
= (total # men) x (total # not promoted) / total people
= 6,911 x 15,162 / 15,338
= 6,831.7

For simplicity, let's round this to 6,832 – so if gender was not linked to promotions we should have 6,832 males who were not promoted in 2015.

3   Female promoted:

Observed value = 49
Expected value
= (total # women) x (total # promoted) / total people
= 8,427 x 176 / 15,338
= 96.7

For simplicity, we will round this to 97 – so if gender was not linked to promotions we should have 97 females who were promoted in 2015 – the observed figure is obviously lower than this.

4   Female not promoted:

Observed value = 8,378
Expected value
= (total # women) x (total # not promoted) / total people
= 8,427 x 15,162 / 15,338
= 8,330.3

For simplicity, let's round this to 8,330 – so if gender was not linked to promotions we should have 8,330 females who were not promoted in 2015.

Looking at these figures, we can see that we would expect more women to be promoted and fewer men to be promoted than we actually observed in our organization if there was no link between gender and promotions. But could these numbers have come about by chance anyway, with no particular significant relationship between promotion and gender? Let's work out the chi-square statistic and test it!

So, going back to the formula:

$$\chi^2 = \chi((\text{observed value} - \text{expected value})^2 / \text{expected value})$$

= (observed male promoted − expected male promoted)²/expected male promoted + (observed male not promoted − expected male not promoted)²/expected male not promoted + (observed female promoted − expected female promoted)²/expected female promoted + (observed female not promoted − expected female not promoted)²/ expected female not promoted

= (127 − 79)²/79 + (6,784 − 6,832)²/6,832 + (49 − 97)²/97 + (8,378 − 8,330)²/8,330

= 2,304/79 + 2,304/6,832 + 2,304/97 + 2,304/8,330

= 29.16 + 0.34 + 23.75 + 0.28

= 53.53

This chi-squared ($\chi^2$) statistic is then checked against a $\chi^2$ distribution with known properties in a table (online or in a stats book) along with the degrees of freedom that, in this case, is calculated as (r−1)(c−1) where r is the number of rows and c is the number of columns. So (2−1)(2−1) = 1 x 1 = 1.

Any stats book will usually include statistical tables outlining critical values of the chi-square distribution. When you look up what the critical values of a chi-square test for a 2 x 2 table (1 degree of freedom), these amount to the following:

$p < 0.05$ = 3.84
$p < 0.01$ = 6.63
$p < 0.001$ = 10.83

These figures tell us how big the chi-square value needs to get to in order for us to be 95 per cent, 99 per cent or 99.9 per cent confident that our results are not due to chance alone.

Our value of 53.53 is far greater than the chi-square value required for us to be 99.9 per cent confident that our findings are not due to chance.

We can confidently say that *as a proportion of males and females in our organization*, males get promoted significantly more frequently than females.

Thus there is a link between gender and the likelihood of being promoted in our organization (and there is less than a 1 in 1,000 chance that this result would occur by chance alone).

You will be happy to know that SPSS does all of these calculations for you. All you need to do is have a data set with each employee entered – with an indication of whether they were promoted in 2015 and whether they are male or female (a simple cut-and-paste job from Excel). You merely open the file, select the gender variable and the promotion variable, and ask for a chi-square to be carried out. In total, carrying this out will involve clicking your mouse five times or so; SPSS will provide:

- a cross-tabs table as set out in Table 3.6;
- the degrees of freedom;
- the $\chi^2$ statistic;
- the p-value.

To run the chi-square test in SPSS, go to the 'Analyze' menu, select 'Descriptive Statistics' and then 'Crosstabs' (as shown in Figure 3.1).

**FIGURE 3.1** Running the chi-square in SPSS

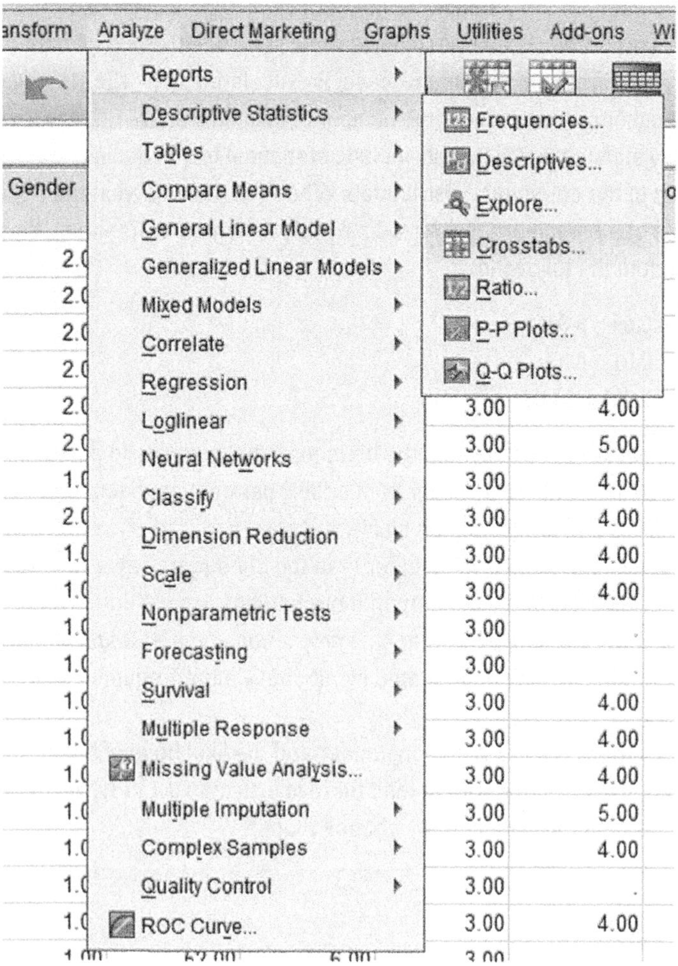

# Analysis Strategies

This will bring up another box where you can select the rows and columns of your cross-tabulation (or pivot) table. You will also need to select the chi-square statistic in the 'Statistics' button option and select how you would like the output table to look in the 'Cells' button option.

For worked-through examples of the chi-square ($\chi^2$) test using SPSS, including analysis of the SPSS output, see the following examples (these are also outlined in Table 3.5).

## Chi-square examples in the book's case studies

- Diversity case study (chapter 4). Example 1: gender and job grade analysis using frequency tables and chi-square. Page 111.
- Employee turnover case study (Chapter 6). Example 1b: exploring differences in individual staff turnover across a number of different countries using cross-tabulation and the chi-square test. Page 198.
- Recruitment and selection case study (Chapter 8). Examples 1 and 2. A diversity analysis looking at potential bias in the recruitment and selection decisions. Pages 287 and 290.

The chi-square analysis used here covered the situation where we were analysing the relationship between two categorical variables. If, however, there were three or more categorical variables, we could set up a chi-square analysis for particular combinations of categorical variables; yet we might prefer to use a technique called loglinear analysis. This is not a technique covered in this book (indeed you can also use logistic regression in this situation and we do cover that in a number of chapters); however, if you would like to learn more about loglinear analysis, see Field (2009).

## *Logistic regression analysis*

If the dependent variable is binary and the independent variables are either categorical or continuous, then you can use logistic regression analysis to model or predict the dependent variable. To extend the example given previously, we could try to model what factors can help predict whether someone was promoted in 2015: from a range of factors that include gender we could include contractual status, education level, training, job tenure, etc.

Another simple example of when we might use logistic regression in an organizational context might be when we are trying to predict factors that explain why someone might leave our organization. The data stored in our HR database in relation to this might be something like 'left/leaver' or 'active employee'. This example is a binary (2 level) categorical: yes or no variable. If we wanted to try to find predictors of whether someone is likely to be a leaver then we may wish to include a number of possible independent variables such as age (continuous), gender (categorical) and assessment centre scores (continuous), amongst others.

Analysis of historical data using logistical regression analysis will help us to find patterns in the data and create models with which to make some future predictions. In Chapter 10 we use this approach to predict the likelihood that graduate candidates might leave in the first year after they are hired. We use independent variables such as:

- Assessment-centre scores (are extroverts more likely to leave; are candidates with higher numerical reasoning scores more likely to stay?).
- Gender (are male or female candidates more likely to stay after a year?).
- Age (are younger candidates less likely to stay beyond a year?).

Here, with our analysis we are attempting to predict the likelihood of something happening; the likelihood of one particular occurrence of a set of possible occurrences (in this case the likelihood of someone being a 'leaver'). This is different from linear regression (to be discussed next), where the dependent variable is continuous. In linear regression we would be predicting the expected proportion (and direction) of change in a dependent variable that can be attributed to any particular independent variable; or, to put it another way, what makes the dependent variable increase or decrease (such as predicting the sales figures achieved by the new joiner – and what factors account for a particular proportion of change in these figures – what would make these sales higher or lower? Do young women bring in higher figures on average? Does a high assessment-centre score mean high sales figures?).

However, more on linear regression later... To return to logistic regression, we are trying to model or predict the likelihood of the occurrence of a binary categorical variable.

Just as in the chi-square test, there is an equation behind this. The equation will take the data as the input, calculate the estimated statistics/coefficients and 'parameters' (estimated characteristics of our organization) and produce an output of key information. With binary logistic regression this includes (but is not limited to) the following (which are all output in SPSS):

- *Model chi square*: to test how well the model fits the data using an observed versus expected comparison of the data you would expect if you used only the model logistic regression equation to calculate it versus the actual data.
- *Model chi-square p-value (Sig.)*: uses the model chi-square value to provide a p-value for the overall model (remembering that we need the p-value to be <0.05 for the model to be significant). This tells you whether your model significantly predicts your dependent variable.
- *The Nagelkerke R-square*: this is a 'pseudo R-square' figure that gives an estimate of the percentage variation that we account for in our dependent variable with our proposed model. For example, if this came out as 60 per cent in our example, we could say that 60 per cent

of the variance in our data set – that indicated whether someone left or not after the first year – is accounted for by the model we have created (eg using age, gender and assessment-centre scores).

- *P-value (Sig.) for each independent variable*: remembering again that any p-value <0.05 is significant. Having the p-value for each independent variable will tell us which independent variables potentially significantly 'impact' the dependent variable. In our example, it will tell us if age, gender or assessment-centre scores (or a combination of the three) have a significant impact (or significantly predict) the likelihood of a graduate leaving in the first year.

- *Odds ratios (Exp(B))*: indicates the changes in probability (or 'odds') of the occurrence in the dependent variable incurred by a change in one unit of the independent variable. In our example, it would be the increase (or decrease) in the chances of someone leaving in the first year with every increase (or decrease) in assessment-centre scores.

---

If you are using a statistical software package such as SPSS, you will not need to understand or work with the background equation for logistic regression. If you are curious, though, and would like to know what it looks like, here you go:

$$P(Y) = 1/(1+e^{-(b_0 + b_1X_{1i} + b_2X_{2i} + \ldots + b_nX_{ni})})$$

where 'e' is the base of natural logarithms, i is the instance of the variable, Y is the dependent variable, x(1 to n) are the n independent variables, and b is the degree to which that independent variable impacts the dependent variable in the equation.

Put another way:

$$Ln(p/(1-p)) = b_0 + b_1x_{1i} + b_2x_{2i} + b_nx_{ni}$$

where p is the probability that Y=1 and Ln denotes the natural logarithm.

---

That is quite enough talk of logarithms and equations in this chapter, and indeed the sum total of logarithmic talk. Let's get back to what you need to know to master HR analytics.

When the dependent variable (or outcome variable) has only two options, as it does in this example (yes or no), the analysis is referred to as 'binary logistic regression'. If the dependent variable has more than two options, for example if we were trying to predict the colour of somebody's eyes, the analysis we would carry out is called 'multinomial logistic regression'. Other terms you may hear are 'dichotomous logistic regression' and 'binomial logistic regression' (this is the same as binary logistic regression), or 'polychotomous logistic regression'.

To run a binary logistic regression analysis in SPSS, go to the Analyze menu, select 'Regression' and then 'Binary Logistic' if the dependent variable is binary (ie has only two possible outcomes such as 'yes' or 'no'), or 'multinomial logistic' if the dependent variable has more than two possible outcomes (such as red, white or blue) (see Figure 3.2).

**FIGURE 3.2**  Running a binary logistic regression analysis in SPSS

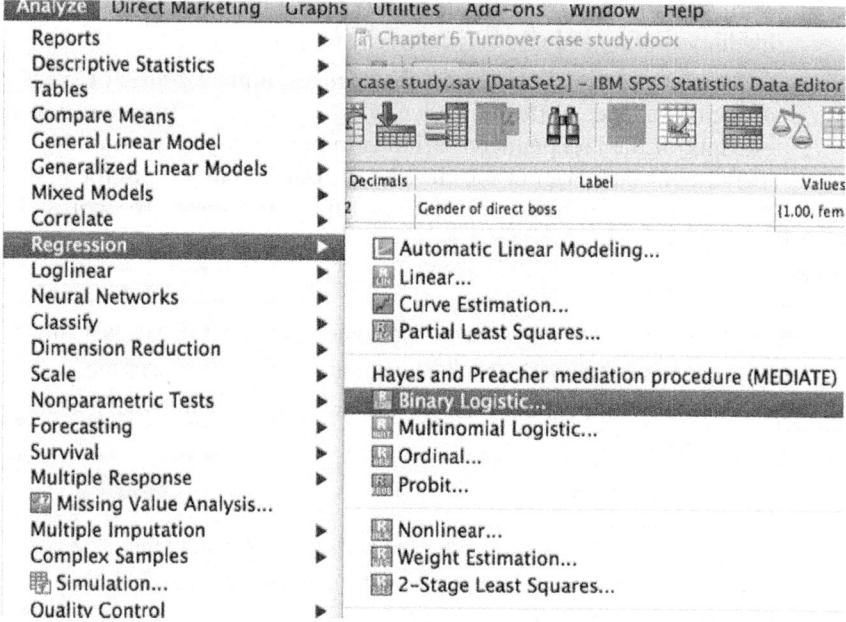

For worked-through examples of binary logistic regression analyses using SPSS, including a discussion of the SPSS output, see the following examples (these are also outlined in Table 3.5).

## Logistic regression analysis case study examples

- Employee turnover case study (Chapter 6). Example 3: using logistic regression to set up a predictive model for individual turnover (see page 217).

- Recruitment and selection case study (Chapter 8). Example 2: predicting candidate rejection or shortlisting taking into account graduate gender and ethnicity (see page 290).

- Recruitment and selection case study (Chapter 8). Example 4: predicting graduate turnover (see page 310).

- Predictive modelling case study (Chapter 10). Example 3: predictive modelling and obtaining probabilities for the likelihood of employees leaving (see page 383).

- Predictive modelling case study (Chapter 10). Example 6: using historical patterns to predict the likelihood of new graduate candidates leaving (see page 406).

# Statistical tests for continuous/interval-level data

## T-tests (two sample)

Two sample t-tests are used to identify whether there is a difference between two samples. The two samples can either be data taken from two completely different groups of objects (eg groups of employees or teams) or the two samples could be data taken on two separate occasions from the same group of objects (such as employees or teams). When the dependent variable is continuous (for example '€£$ sales') and there is only one independent variable, which is categorical and binary (for example, group 1 versus group 2 or Time 1 versus Time 2), then you should use a t-test.

There are two types of two sample t-tests:

- The independent samples t-test for use when the two samples have different people (or indeed teams... bears, pigeons, etc) – for example a group of men versus a group of women – and you are interested in testing for differences between these two groups on a particular continuous dependent variable (eg '€£$ sales'). For example: do women sell significantly more insurance products than men?

- Paired samples t-test can be used when you are interested in whether a sample of workers or a sample of teams (that have the same employees over time) changes significantly on some particular continuous dependent variable (eg '€£$ sales' or engagement scores) across two different occasions of data collection (thus two repeated samples). For example, you could compare customer satisfaction ratings of 100 employees in June 2014 with the customer satisfaction ratings of the same 100 people in September 2014 after they had all undergone training.

In both types of t-test, we have two samples of data collection and look for differences on a particular continuous dependent variable. We could use descriptive statistics and simply compare the means (either between the two groups that we are comparing at any one time or between the two sets of data collected with the same group across time). If the means are similar, then we might conclude that there is no difference between the two samples of data (or that 'the samples come from the same population'). Unless we test this for significance, however, we will not understand the degree of confidence that we should have in any difference in means (and thus the population that the samples of data represent) that we might find.

We discussed hypothesis testing earlier in this chapter in the section on statistical significance. Here, we might say the following:

- *Research hypothesis*: there is a difference between the samples in the data that we are comparing.
- *Null hypothesis*: there is no difference between the samples in the data that we are comparing.

Using a repeated measures t-test example:

- *Research hypothesis*: there is a significant difference in sales figures when you compare Time 1 (before attendance at a training course) with Time 2 (after attendance at a training course).
- *Null hypothesis*: there is no difference in employees' sales figures when you compare Time 1 (before attendance at a training course) with Time 2 (after attendance at a training course).

Intuitively, the larger the difference between the sample means, the more confident we would be that the research hypothesis was true or, in our example, that the training course did impact the sales figures and we could reject the null hypothesis (cast it aside like a chalice of bitter wine...).

## *Independent samples t-test*

Also known as the 'between-subjects' t-test or the 'independent measures' t-test, the independent samples t-test is for comparing the difference between two groups when we have different people in each group that we compare. An example of using this in an organizational context might be to compare the average engagement levels for staff who work part-time with those who work full-time. We could also have teams as our object of data collection and still use an independent t-test: for example, we could look at the difference in team level engagement scores for finance teams versus sales teams in our organization.

Conceptually, the way the independent t-test works is that it compares the difference between the sample means that we find to the difference between the sample means that we would expect to get if the null hypothesis were true (that there were no real differences between the two samples/populations):

t =
((observed difference between sample means) – (expected difference between sample means of the samples ie 0))/(estimate of the standard error of the difference between two sample means.

> The standard error is an estimate of the standard deviation of a sampling distribution where means from multiple samples of the same N have been plotted, so it is an estimated measure of the variability, or spread, of multiple sample means. So if the standard error is small, we would expect most samples to have very similar means.

Put simply, the independent t-test checks whether the difference in the means between groups is big enough for us to say that the likelihood that we would randomly find two groups that had such large differences in means is so slim that we have a meaningful, statistically significant difference.

Importantly, there are three things that will influence whether a difference between means of two groups of employees (or any object of study such as teams, etc) is likely to yield a significant (and thus meaningful) difference. The first of these is how big the observed differences are between the two groups; the second is how many cases (eg employees or teams) we have in each sample that we are comparing; and the third is how much variation we tend to have on our measures within each of our sample groups.

To conduct an independent t-test with SPSS we would select the 'Analyze' menu, then select 'Compare Means' and 'Independent Samples t-test' (see Figure 3.3).

**FIGURE 3.3** Selecting the independent samples t-test in SPSS

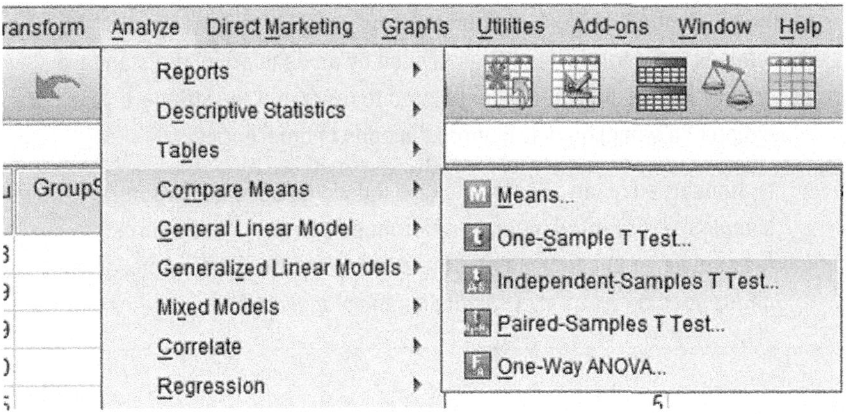

For worked-through examples of the independent samples t-test using SPSS, including a discussion of the SPSS output, see the following examples (these are also outlined in Table 3.5).

## Independent samples t-test case study examples

- Diversity case study (Chapter 4). Example 2b: comparing ethnicity and gender across two functions in an organization using the independent samples t-test (see page 128).
- Engagement case study (Chapter 5). Example 4: using the independent samples t-test to determine whether engagement levels are significantly different in two locations (see page 177).

## *Paired samples t-test*

Also known as the 'dependent t-test', the 'related t-test', the 'matched-pairs t-test' or the 'repeated t-test', the paired samples t-test compares the difference between two groups of data when we have the same people in each group. An example of using this is the one referred to previously where group 1 is the sales team before the training course and group 2 is the sales team after the training course. The dependent variable we are measuring in each group is the sales revenue data.

> Conceptually, the way that a paired samples t-test works is that it compares the means of differences found between the individual cases (eg employees) when comparing Time 1 with Time 2, with the mean of differences that we would expect if there were no change over time (thus 0) or the mean of differences over time that we would expect if the null hypothesis were true. Then this is divided by an estimate of the standard error of means of differences (estimated to represent the standard deviation of a sampling distribution of means of differences)
>
> t = ((observed mean of differences in individual cases between samples) – (expected mean of differences between cases across the sample, ie 0)) / (estimate of the standard error of the means of differences between two sample means of a given N).

Luckily, SPSS calculates this for us... In SPSS we would select the 'Analyze' menu, then select 'Compare Means' and 'Paired Samples t-test' (see Figure 3.4).

**FIGURE 3.4**  Selecting the paired samples t-test in SPSS

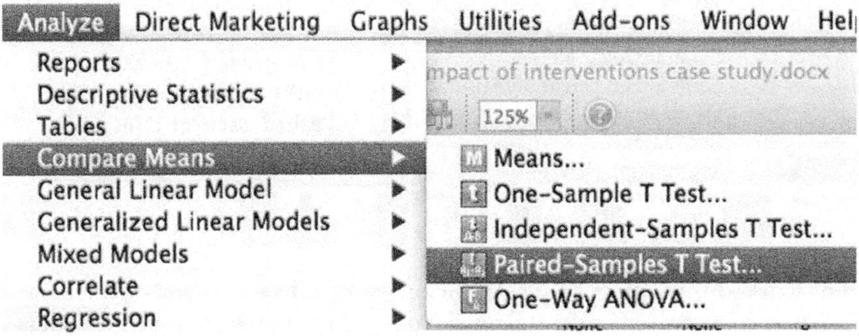

### Paired samples t-test case study examples

- Monitoring the impact of interventions case study (Chapter 9). Example 1: assessing stress before and after an intervention using a paired samples t-test (see page 325).

## *One-way independent analysis of variance (ANOVA) test*

Similar to the independent samples t-test, the one-way ANOVA test is used when the dependent variable is continuous, the independent variables are categorical, and when there are different participants (or entities) in each category. Again we are comparing the means of groups. The difference with the one-way ANOVA is that we have more than two groups to compare.

So the one-way ANOVA test is a powerful method for testing the significance of the difference between sample means where more than two conditions are used. It effectively tests the null hypothesis that all the samples are drawn from the same population and that there is no difference between them. Because there are more than two groups, if the test suggests there is a difference, then further testing (called 'post-hoc testing') is needed in order to determine specifically which samples are different and by how much (Coolican, 2009).

To run the one-way ANOVAs in SPSS, we would select the 'Analyze' menu and then select 'Compare Means' and 'One Way ANOVA' (see Figure 3.5).

**FIGURE 3.5**  Selecting a one-way ANOVA

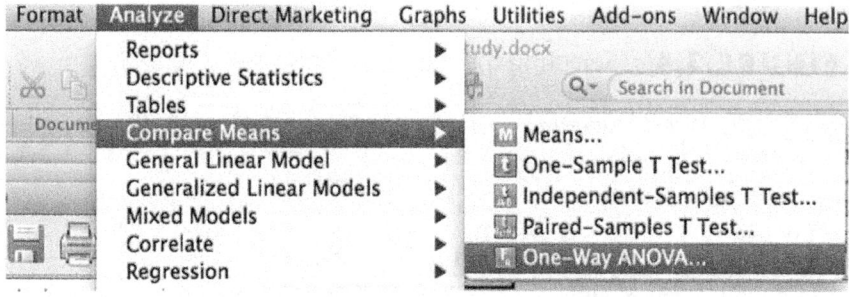

For worked-through examples of the one-way independent ANOVA, including post-hoc analysis and a full explanation of the output that SPSS produces, see the following examples.

### One-way ANOVA examples

- Employee turnover case study (Chapter 6). Example 2: exploring team-level turnover by country using the one-way ANOVA test (see page 203).

## *Post-hoc tests*

The ANOVA tests can only tell us whether the samples differ or not, but this is only half of the story. If the ANOVA test comes back indicating there is a significant difference (three or more) between the samples/groups of workers, surely the next question would be 'which groups are different from each other?' followed closely by 'and how different is it?'

The post-hoc tests will answer this for us. There are many different types of post-hoc tests available and it can be a bit confusing when deciding which one to use. If you are interested in further reading on these tests, we recommend reading Field (2009). Table 3.7, however, provides a high-level summary. Please be aware that this table is very simplified and only a subset of the information available on this topic. It should, however, get you through most situations that you are likely to come across in HR analytics.

**TABLE 3.7** Post-hoc tests

| Situation | Test | Benefit |
|---|---|---|
| If the group variances are not equal. | Games-Howell | A good idea to select this in all analysis alongside the other tests because we don't know until after the ANOVA has run whether the group variances are equal or not (until we look at Levene's test.) That way, it will be there if you need it without having to run the ANOVA again. If you don't need it, you can ignore it. |
| Equal sample sizes and population variances are similar. | REGWQ or Tukey | Good statistical sensitivity to correctly reject the null hypothesis (that there is no difference between the group means). |
| | Bonferroni | More conservative than REGWQ or Tukey (so less chance of getting a significant result) but good to use if you want guaranteed control that you will not make a Type I error (ie that you wil not incorrectly reject the null hypothesis that the group means are the same). |
| Sample sizes are slightly different. | Gabriel's procedure | Good statistical sensitivity to correctly reject the null hypothesis in this situation. |
| Sample sizes are very different. | Hochberg's GT2 | Offer's best performance in this situation. |

To then run the post-hoc testing, we would select the 'Post Hoc' button on the 'One-Way ANOVA' box that appears once you have selected to run an ANOVA (see Figure 3.6).

**FIGURE 3.6**

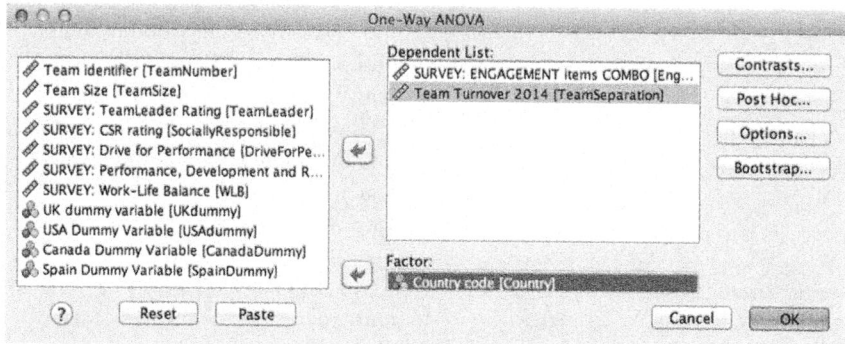

This will then bring up a second box (Figure 3.7), from which you can select the post-hoc tests that you would like to run.

**FIGURE 3.7**

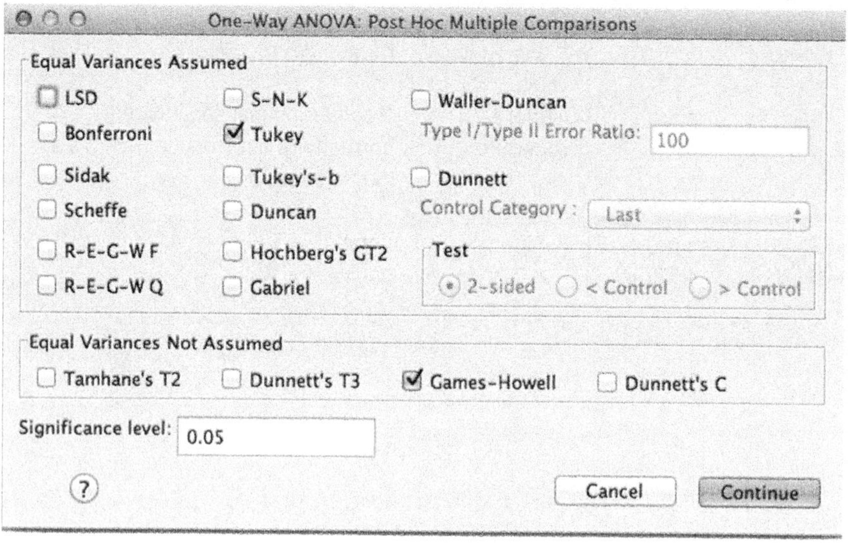

## One-way repeated measures analysis of variance (ANOVA)

Just as the one-way independent ANOVA can be compared to the independent samples t-test, the one-way repeated measures ANOVA can be compared to the paired samples t-test. In both cases, the dependent variable is continuous and we are comparing samples that have been collected at different time points and the same participants/cases (eg employees or teams) are found at each time point. The key difference is that we use the paired samples t-test for two different sets of samples collected (eg two time points of data), and the one-way repeated measures ANOVA for more than two groups.

So the one-way repeated measures ANOVA compares the means of differences with three or more groups where each group has the same participants/cases – eg employees or teams. In HR analytics, examples of this might be comparing the engagement levels of the same group of people at three or more time points in a corporate merger, or perhaps if the same function may have experienced a fundamentally changing work environment over an extended period of time and the HR director was keen to track stress levels every six months over a two-year period.

To run the one-way repeated measures ANOVA in SPSS, we would select the 'Analyze' menu and then select 'General Linear Model' and 'Repeated Measures' (see Figure 3.8).

### FIGURE 3.8

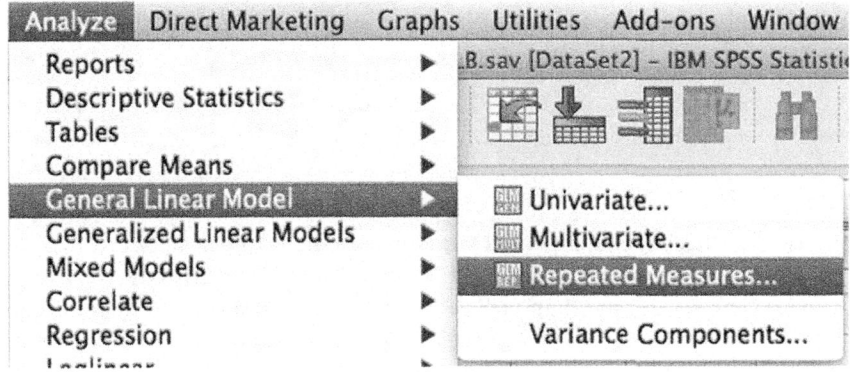

### Repeated measures ANOVA examples

- Monitoring the impact of interventions case study (Chapter 9). Example 3: value change. Exploring staff commitment levels at three different time points in a values change project (see page 336).

## Within and between ANOVA – general linear model

A further variation on the repeated measures ANOVA and the one-way ANOVA mentioned here is the 'within and between' ANOVA – general linear model variation. We will not go into too much detail about this type of analytic model here, as we walk through some examples (including the output) in Chapter 9 and the various combinations of this model can get very complicated. However, it is in effect an extension of our repeated measures one-way ANOVAs, but it can take into account any change or differences (across two or more time points); importantly between two or more different groups.

We will walk through some examples in Chapter 9. If we wanted to run such a test then we select the Analyze→General Linear Model→Repeated Measures option in SPSS (see Figure 3.9).

### FIGURE 3.9

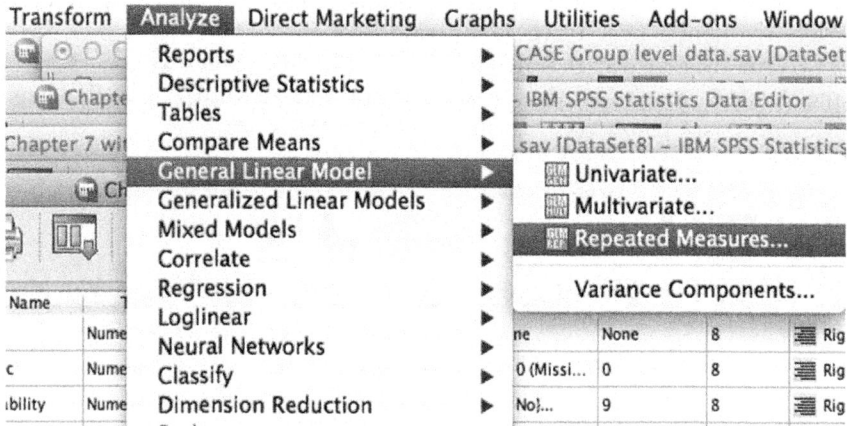

As this analysis has a repeated measures element and a between groups element to it, we have to set up these elements accordingly. One of the examples that we use in Chapter 9 involves testing for a change in employee stress levels across two time points (before and after a work–life balance intervention) and this change is compared with males versus females.

Once the General Linear Model→Repeated Measures option has been selected, the analyst needs to indicate how many 'levels' in the 'time' factor. Here we have stress at Time 1 and Time 2 so here we would select two levels in 'Within Subject Factor', 'Number of Levels' option box (see Figure 3.10) then click 'Define'.

**FIGURE 3.10**

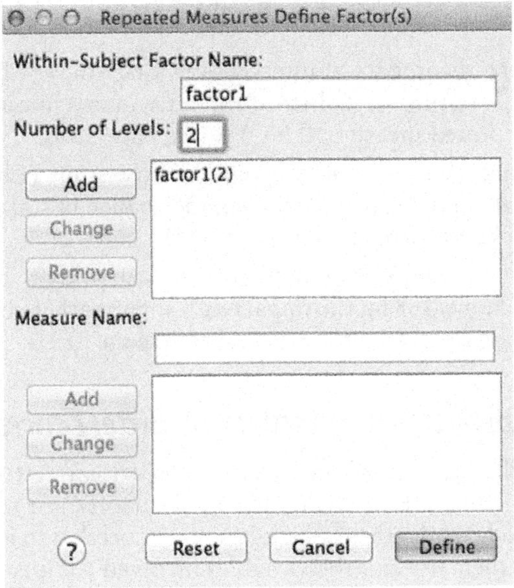

Then we have to select the two 'time' variables (in this case Stress at Time 1 and Stress at Time 2) and the grouping variable (in this case 'Gender' because we are comparing male and female), into the 'Within-Subjects Variables' (see Figure 3.11) and the 'Between-Subjects Factor(s)' selection boxes respectively.

**FIGURE 3.11**

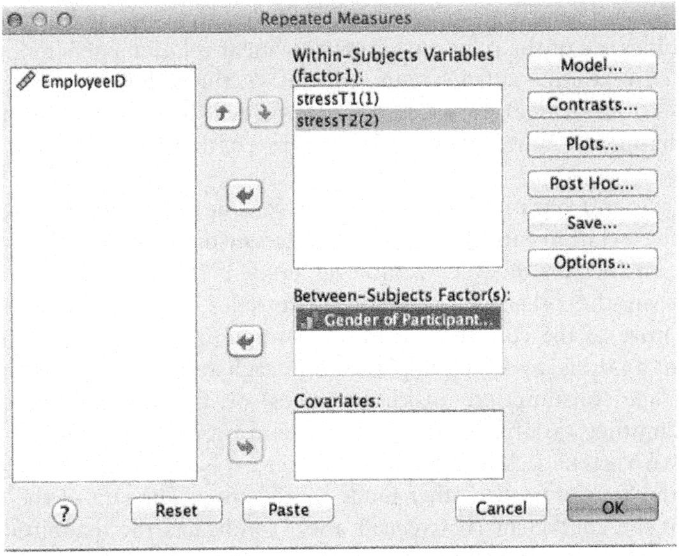

We discuss this form of analysis more in Chapter 9, which is the only chapter in which we carry out this form of analysis. The two examples we 'walk through' are:

1 Monitoring the impact of interventions case study (Chapter 9). Example 2: testing stress before and after intervention by gender using a repeated measures ANOVA (see page 330).
2 Monitoring the impact of interventions case study (Chapter 9). Example 4: value change; assessing the change in staff commitment over time by department (see page 344).
3 Monitoring the impact of interventions case study (Chapter 9). Example 5: measuring the impact of a supermarket checkout training intervention on scan rates over time (see page 352).

## *Pearson's (product-moment/zero-order) correlation*

Determining whether two continuous variables are correlated or not is a key activity in predictive HR analytics and the Pearson's test of correlations is the key tool used. Whilst the use of a Pearson's correlation is to some extent determined by the nature of the variables involved (eg it is not appropriate to use a categorical variable with a Pearson's correlation test), when one carries out certain types of predictive modelling SPSS will by default produce Pearson's correlation coefficients amongst all variables involved in the models. The Pearson's test of correlation gives the analyst an indication of the extent to which there is a significant linear relationship between two variables. When running the Pearson's test with SPSS a correlations coefficient ('r') is produced, which gives a considerable amount of information. It tells us the direction of any relationship (eg a positive or negative relationship between two variables) and the magnitude of the relationship (whether the relationship is strong, weak or non-existent). The Pearson's test will also indicate the significance of the relationship: is our linear relationship significant?

The correlation coefficient ranges from −1, through 0 to +1. Where two variables are not in any way correlated you will have an r=0.00 (this very rarely happens). Where two variables are completely correlated we will have an r=1 or −1.

The sign in front of the correlation coefficient indicates a positive versus a negative relationship. A positive (+) relationship indicates that you tend to find an increase in one variable in tandem (to some degree) with an increase in the other. Average ice-cream sales per person and average temperature of the country is a good example of this. The country is the object of analysis, average temperature in each country is one variable and the average consumption (in kilogrammes) of ice cream per person each year is another variable. You would expect a positive relationship between these two variables. A negative correlation (−) is obviously the reverse; as one variable goes up the other tends to go down. The size of the absolute value of the coefficient (between 0 and 1) indicates the magnitude of the relationship. A medium to strong correlation might have an 'r' of somewhere between 0.5 to 1.0 or −0.5 to −1.0. A medium correlation would be somewhere between 0.3 to 0.5 or –0.3 to –0.5. A weak or low correlation would be somewhere between 0.1 to 0.3 or –0.1 to –0.3. Importantly, the Pearson's correlation coefficient test will tell you how significant any relationship is, as well as the magnitude and direction of its linear relationship.

With SPSS you can obtain correlation coefficients by selecting the Analyze→Correlate→Bivariate menu option (see Figure 3.12).

**FIGURE 3.12** Selecting a correlation option in the SPSS menu

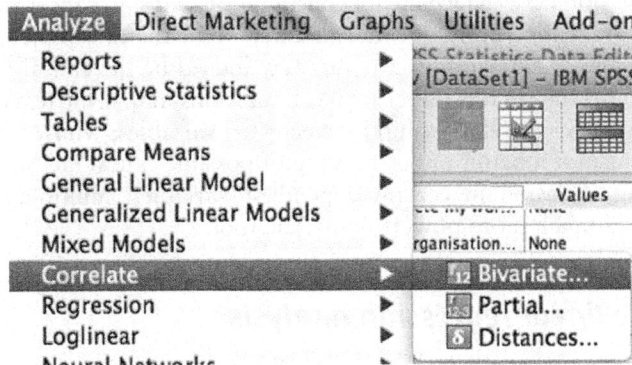

Then you would select the variables that you would want to correlate in the 'Variables:' selection box (see Figure 3.13).

**FIGURE 3.13** Selecting variables to correlate

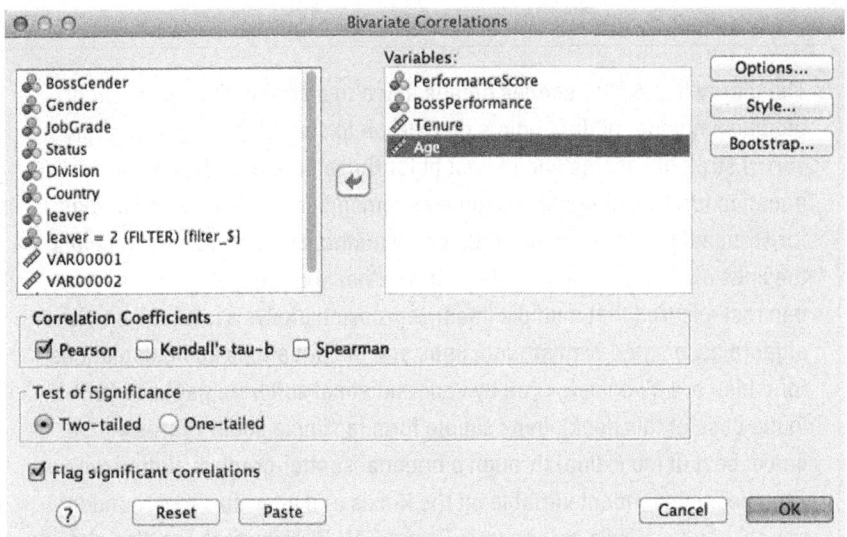

It is very important to recognize that, whilst sometimes an analyst might make some assumptions that a significant correlation may suggest evidence of causality between an X and a Y variable (eg engagement as an X and performance as a Y), a Pearson's correlation coefficient merely shows the extent to which two variables co-relate. A correlation does not imply causality; any inferences relating to causality that an analyst makes are based on analyst-imposed or inferred assumptions. Just looking at the ice-cream sales and skin cancer example mentioned previously can help demonstrate the danger of making assumptions of causality from correlations. There may be a correlation between ice-cream consumption and skin cancer rates across countries, but eating an ice cream is unlikely to be the causal factor here – a third variable of exposure to hot sun may indeed be the causal factor. The Pearson's correlation test therefore has limitations in that the test only looks at the shared linear relationship between two variables; whilst not without its problems, for a better understanding of possible causal factors at play in influencing variation in certain dependent variables, multiple regression analysis is a much more powerful analytic tool.

## *Multiple linear regression analysis*

Despite the long-winded name, multiple linear regression analysis is a straightforward procedure by which we collect data about our dependent variable (which must be continuous) and our independent variables (which can be either continuous or categorical). We then analyse the data in a software package such as SPSS in order to obtain evidence for which of the independent variables could be having a significant impact on the dependent variable, and what that impact is.

> The theory behind the scenes comes down to a straight line on a graph: plotting a number of data points on a graph to see if they form into some sort of straight line, the line of best fit for those data points, and the equation for that straight line. You may remember (or may not) equations for straight lines from secondary-school mathematics as something along the lines of $y = mx + c$. Regardless of whether you remember or not, you can rest assured that multiple linear regression analysis is based on clever algebra associated with straight lines and the equations and calculations for which are all done for you by your statistical software package (SPSS in the case of this book). In its simple form (a simple linear regression) a line of best fit (solid line) through a notional scatter graph is plotted with an assumed independent variable on the x-axis and an assumed dependent variable on the y-axis, as shown in Figure 3.14. On this graph we also plot an alternative possible 'line of best fit'.

**FIGURE 3.14**  Simple linear algebra

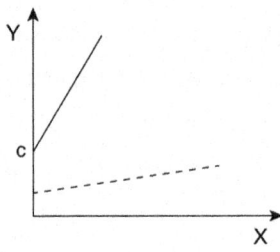

In the example shown in Figure 3.14, the value of c is simply the point where the line touches the y-axis, and the value of m is the gradient. So on the solid line, the gradient would be much higher (steeper) than the dotted line. This means that for every unit increase in x on the solid line, it will result in a much bigger change in the value of y than an increase in the value of x on the dotted line, because the gradient is much less steep. As it were, if the solid and the dotted lines were two different sides of a mountain and the y-axis represented the altitude and the x-axis represented the number of steps taken, one step forward on the solid line will get you to a much higher altitude than will one step forward on the dotted line. In this example, c would be the altitude of your starting point at the bottom of the mountain (which is rarely zero). So the greater the gradient, the greater a change in the value of x will have on the value of y.

Instead of y = mx + c, we expand this out to enable us to include many variables in our 'model'. Importantly, in regression analysis, we use an 'a' to represent the point at which the line intercepts the y-axis and a '*b*' (to represent a gradient coefficient) instead of c and m. So 'y=mx+c' becomes: 'y=a+*b*x'. When we have multiple independent variables in our model the equation becomes more complex and longer:

$$y = a + b_1x_1 + b_2x_2 + b_3x_3 \text{ (and so on)}$$

where y is the dependent variable, x is the independent variable(s), a is the constant value and *b* is the gradient for each of the independent variables.

So if we use our mountain analogy and add 'length of legs of climber' as another variable, our model might look something like:

$$\text{Altitude} = a + b_1(\text{number of steps}) + b_2(\text{leg length})$$

We would run a different model for each route (both the dotted and the solid).

If we plugged in the data for, say, 1,000 climbers over the two routes, SPSS would then generate for us something that looked like this:

Route 1 (solid):
Altitude = 300m + 3 (number of steps) + 5 (leg length)

Route 2 (dotted):
Altitude = 240m + 1 (number of steps) + 5 (leg length)

You can see from this that one step on route 1 will get you three times higher than one step on route 2.

Applying this to HR analytics and using the data available to us through many of the sources described early in this chapter, we might say, for example:

Job satisfaction score =
3 + 0.05 (size of bonus in $1,000) + 0.2 (managerial level) +
0.4 (performance rating)

In its simplest form of interpretation, we might say that if the average job satisfaction level (on a 1 to 7 scale) in our organization was 3 for non-managers, getting a thousand-dollar bonus should increase this by 0.05 (to 3.05) and then being at the first step of a managerial level should increase the expected level of satisfaction by 0.2 (to 3.25) and getting an increase in a notional performance rating of 1 should again increase this job satisfaction level by another 0.4 (to 3.65). Thus Bob (a non-manager with no bonus and an average performance rating of 3) should have a satisfaction level (perhaps) of 3; importantly 0.65 lower than Sally (a level one manager, who received a $1,000 bonus and a performance rating of 4).

When we run a multiple regression analysis, we are looking for a number of key things (in terms of the statistical output of interest):

1 Multiple $R^2$: the multiple $R^2$ is very important in our multiple regression analysis. It is an indicator of the total amount of variance in our dependent variable that can be accounted for by its shared relationship with all independent variables in the model (whilst taking into account the shared relationships amongst the independent variables and the dependent variables). This is a value between 0 and 1; 1 being 100 per cent of the variance in our dependent variable and 0 being 0 per cent. The closer the value of $R^2$ is to 1, the better our

model is at accounting for variation in our dependent variable of interest.

2 Model parameters: SPSS will calculate the model parameters, which are the F-statistic (the regression ANOVA statistic) and the model degrees of freedom. Simply put, in multiple linear regression, these two parameters are then used to calculate the statistical significance of the regression model. The degrees of freedom figures are directly related to the sample size and the number of variables that we have included in our model. The F-statistic is calculated on the basis of ratios of the variation in our dependent variable (sum of squares) that our model accounts for versus what remains unaccounted for (this statistic is therefore linked to the $R^2$). The F-test is the 'test-statistic' and we can refer to statistical tables to find out what value of f we need to reach before we can be 95 per cent, 99 per cent or 99.9 per cent confident that our model accounts for variation in our dependent variable. In the days before statistical software packages, statisticians would calculate these parameters by hand, and then reference a table to look up the level of significance resulting from the given parameters. Like other software packages, though, SPSS will calculate the statistical significance value at the same time (which, you may argue, removes the need to manually calculate the model parameters). It is good practice, though, to always report the model parameters along with the statistical significance.

3 Statistical significance: from the statistical significance section earlier in this chapter, we know that we are looking for a p-value of 0.05 or less in order for the result to be significant. In multiple linear regression, SPSS will give us a p-value for the model.

4 Finally, the coefficients for each assumed independent variable that we include in our model. These are our '$b$' values – or our line gradients for each independent variable in the model. For each independent variable, SPSS will provide the $b$ value for the equation as well as the significance of that independent variable in the model. As well as the $b$ value, SPSS will also provide the 'Beta' value, which is linked to the $b$ value but is unique and important in its own right. The Beta value is an indication of the importance of a particular independent variable (IV) in the prediction (accounting of variance) of the dependent variable (DV) and it also gives an indication of the direction of the unique linear relationship that exists between the IV and the DV, whilst taking into account the interrelationships between all IVs (and the DV) in the model. Importantly it gives information about the '*unique* contribution of each variable to the prediction of the y[DV]' (Howell, 2002).

To run multiple linear regression analysis in SPSS, you would go to the 'Analyze' menu and select 'Regression'→'Linear'.

## FIGURE 3.15  Selecting linear regressions in SPSS

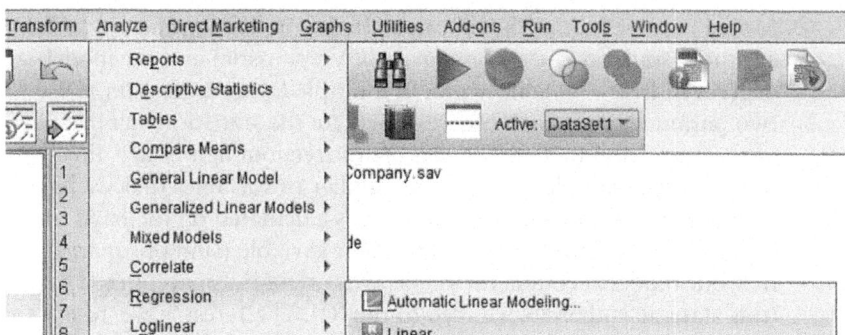

Because multiple regression analysis is such an important analytic tool for the predictive HR analyst, there are many worked-through examples of multiple linear regression, including discussions of the output, in the case study chapters (in almost every case Pearson's correlation coefficients are also provided). The examples that we work through are listed below.

## Multiple linear regression examples

- Diversity case study (Chapter 4). Example 3: using multiple linear regression to model and predict ethnic diversity variation across teams from base location, function, group size, team lead gender and team gender breakdown (see page 135).
- Engagement case study (Chapter 5). Example 5: using multiple linear regression to predict team-level engagement (see page 183).
- Turnover case study (Chapter 6). Example 4: using multiple linear regression to predict team-level turnover (see page 226).
- Performance case study (Chapter 7). Examples 1a and 1b: using multiple linear regression to predict customer loyalty and reinvestment in a financial services organization (see pages 241 and 246).
- Performance case study (Chapter 7). Example 2: using multiple linear regression when combining customer survey data with 'pulse' survey to predict customer loyalty in a financial services organization (see page 249).
- Performance case study (Chapter 7). Example 3: using multiple linear regression when combining performance appraisal data, sickness records and pulse survey data to predict individual performance in a manufacturing organization (see page 253).
- Performance case study (Chapter 7). Example 4: using stepwise multiple linear regression to find the best model for predicting performance using combined performance appraisal data, sickness

records and pulse survey data in a manufacturing organization (see page 258).
- Performance case study (Chapter 7). Example 5: tracking performance over time using stepwise regression with combined performance appraisal data, sickness records and pulse survey data in a manufacturing organization (see page 264).
- Performance case study (Chapter 7). Example 6: using multiple regression to predict sickness absence using employee attitude scores in a manufacturing organization (see page 268).
- Performance case study (Chapter 7). Example 7: using multiple regression to explore patterns of performance with employee profile data in a manufacturing organization (see page 270).
- Performance case study (Chapter 7). Example 8: using data interrogation techniques and multiple linear regression to predict checkout scan rates from employee profile data in a retail organization (see page 276).
- Performance case study (Chapter 7). Example 9: using dummy variables in multiple linear regression to determine the presence of high-performing age groups in predicting scan rates in a retail organization (see page 279).
- Recruitment and selection case study (Chapter 8). Example 3. assessment-centre selection technique validation, predicting graduate performance from demographic, assessment centre and onboarding data (see page 307).
- Monitoring the impact of interventions case study (Chapter 9). Example 6: conditional panel model predicting change in checkout scan rates with supermarket operators (see page 359).
- Predictive modelling case study (Chapter 10). Example 1: predictive modelling of customer reinvestment intentions (see page 367).
- Predictive modelling case study (Chapter 10). Example 2: predictive modelling the impact of training on checkout scan rates (see page 373).
- Predictive modelling case study (Chapter 10). Example 4: predictive modelling the impact of induction day on graduate performance (see page 394).
- Predictive modelling case study (Chapter 10) Example 5: predicting expected performance of graduate candidates (see page 398).

# Factor analysis and reliability analysis

In human resources, it is very common for us to try to measure something that cannot easily be measured such as 'engagement', 'leadership' or 'job satisfaction'. Unfortunately we cannot take out our ruler and set square, go up to an employee and measure their level of engagement – 'Ah, 4.2 this time, great news, Josephine.' Instead, we need to look at what we can measure directly, such as answers to a survey question, and then measure how closely we think those direct measures actually reflect what it is that we are trying to measure. The latter is sometimes termed the 'latent variable' or 'latent construct'.

## Factor analysis

What factor analysis will do for us is to take a number of different indices (such as a number of different survey questions) and analyse whether the responses appear to be measuring an expected variable (or variables). It helps tell us whether multiple indices are tapping the same variable of interest. In essence it can help tell us which indices we should and should not use to represent and tap any particular (latent) variable or measure (eg engagement or job satisfaction). This is very useful in survey design to identify which questions are most useful in measuring our particular variable and which are not; it can help us to simplify or reduce the size of the data set that we are analysing to a more manageable level (by helping us to remove the least useful measures). A more extensive discussion of factor analysis can be found in Chapter 5, linked to the measurement of engagement.

To run a factor analysis in SPSS, you need to select 'Dimension Reduction' from the 'Analyze' menu and then 'Factor' (see Figure 3.16).

**FIGURE 3.16** Selecting factor analysis in SPSS

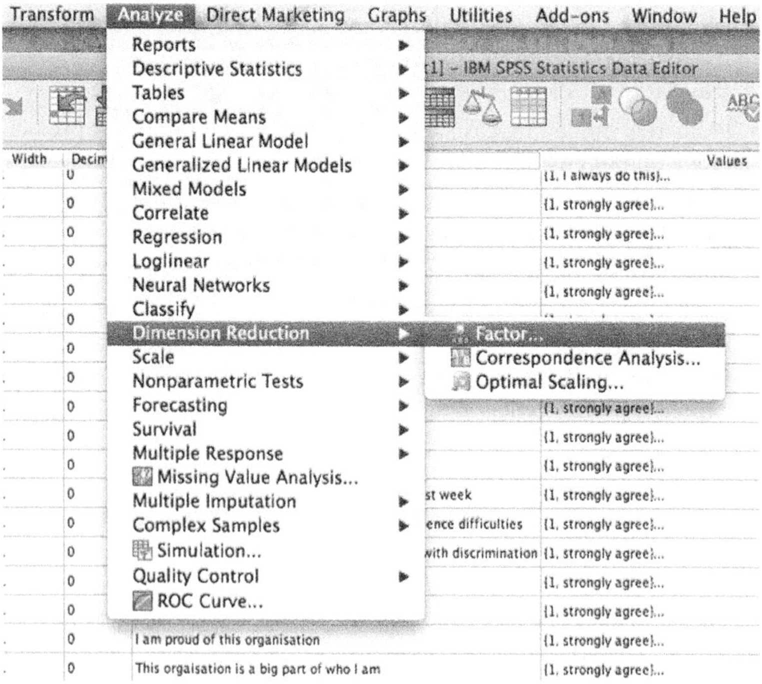

For worked-through examples of factor analysis, including interpretation of the output, see the following factor analysis examples:

- Engagement case study (Chapter 5). Example 1: two constructs: exploratory factor analysis (see page 158).
- Engagement case study (Chapter 5). Example 3: analysing group-level engagement data (see page 170).

## *Reliability analysis*

As outlined in the engagement case study (Chapter 5), even if you are using factor analysis to validate a survey questionnaire it is a good idea to use reliability analysis to check if the measures consistently reflect or tap the construct or latent variable that they are expected to measure. So if we asked the same person the same question again and again, we would expect to consistently get much the same answer, if it was a reliable measure. Put another way, we can test the degree to which results/responses to the different measures we are using (to measure a particular construct or latent variable) follow a similar pattern. As we discuss in more depth in Chapter 5, with specific examples, we would expect responses to follow a consistent pattern across items with a scale when it is measuring a single construct – because the idea, trait, attitude or perception in the person's head that we are trying to measure should end up causing them to respond in a similar way across all of the items designed to measure this idea (assuming the items measure this single idea). For example, if someone is very extroverted, then this level of extraversion should influence how they respond to a set of questionnaire items designed to measure extraversion; and highly extroverted people are likely to follow a certain pattern of responding across a multiple-item extraversion scale (and introverts are likely to follow a different but consistent pattern across a multiple-item extraversion scale). See Chapter 5 for a more in-depth discussion of reliability analysis.

SPSS will run a reliability analysis and output something called 'Cronbach's alpha' for each of the variables. The Cronbach's alpha statistic gives an indication of how much variation exists (and is shared) in the responses given. The Cronbach's alpha ranges from 0 to 1. If there is no internal consistency in the results, we would expect the value to be 0, while an accepted rule of thumb for the Cronbach's alpha to be considered to reflect a 'good' or 'acceptable' level of shared variance, indicating the measures are internally consistent, is 0.7.

To run a reliability analysis in SPSS, you need to go to the 'Analyze' menu and select 'Scale' and then 'Reliability analysis'.

For a worked-through example of reliability analysis, including analysis of the output, see the following example:

- Engagement case study (Chapter 5). Example 2: reliability analysis on a four-item engagement scale (see page 166).

**FIGURE 3.17** Selecting reliability analysis in SPSS

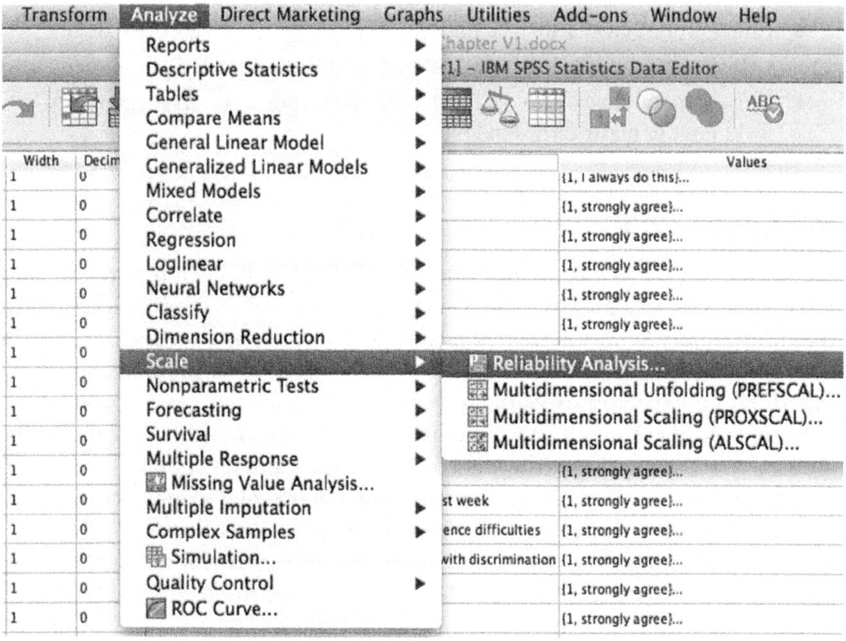

## What you will need

In order to run these analyses with relative ease (and a few clicks of your mouse) you can use SPSS. As discussed in Chapter 2, you do not have to use SPSS to run these statistical tests, as there are a number of packages on the market. The good news is that there is lots of overlap between the packages, and once you understand the main statistical analytic approaches, and have had a go at the analyses with a particular package, it is relatively straightforward to transfer those skills to another system (unless the system you move to requires knowledge of syntax to conduct the analysis, which will slow things up). Rest assured, although in this book we will only be using SPSS, the skills you learn and the methods we will take you through may be applied in most other systems.

## Summary

As mentioned previously, this chapter can be considered a reference section that you can return to when considering which type of analysis might be most appropriate for your modelling needs. This chapter should put you in a good position to start to work through the case studies in the following chapters. Once you do start to work through these and see the application in a real-world sense, the theory, analysis and tests described in this chapter should become clearer, as will the benefits of using statistical analysis in HR data.

# References

Bersin, J (2012) The HR Measurement Framework, Bersin and Associates Research Report, November

Coolican, H (2009) *Research Methods and Statistics in Psychology*, Hodder Education, Abingdon

Field, A (2009) *Discovering Statistics Using SPSS*, Sage, London

Fisher, R A (1925) *Statistical Methods for Research Workers*, Oliver and Boyd, Edinburgh

Howell, D C (2002) Statistical Methods for Psychology (5th Ed), Duxbury, Belmont CA

Huselid, M (2014) [accessed 30 November 2015] The Corporate Mirror, *D'Amore-McKim School of Business* [Online] http://www.damoremckimleadersatworkblog.com/corporate-mirror-looking-big-data-analytics-workforce-management/#sthash.4qx5y7F3.dpuf

# Case study 1
# Diversity analytics

04

No doubt you will have come across diversity and inclusion (D&I) at some point in your career or studies up to this point. Done well, D&I good practice should be integrated into every part of an employee's life cycle, including recruitment, onboarding, development, performance management, promotions and exiting. Managed poorly, perhaps some of the problems will be apparent through bias, unfairness, regretted resignations and a lack of innovation and customer empathy in corporate strategies.

In this chapter, we cover the following:

- Equality, diversity and inclusion (D&I).
- Common approaches to measuring and managing D&I.
- Example 1: gender and job grade analysis using frequency tables and chi square.
- Example 2a: exploring ethnic diversity across teams using descriptive statistics.
- Example 2b: comparing ethnicity and gender across two functions in an organization using the independent samples t-test.
- Defining multiple linear regression.
- Using multiple linear regression to model and predict ethnic diversity variation across teams from base location, function, group size, team lead gender, and team gender breakdown.
- Testing the impact of diversity: interacting diversity categories in predictive modelling.

## Equality, diversity and inclusion

Many countries, including Australia, Belgium, Bolivia, France, Germany, Hong Kong, Italy, the Netherlands and the UK, have equality legislation in place. The countries mentioned here have, at the time of writing, updated their legislative frameworks in the last five years. In many cases governments require regulated reporting of data from organizations to show that there is no unfair treatment on the basis of protected characteristics such as gender, ethnicity, age and disabilities. Inclusion and the management of diversity focus on the positive benefits to the organization of managing this well; predictive analytics are key to determining where problems and opportunities may exist in the organization, and where resources should be concentrated to improve the working environment.

According to the CEB Corporate Leadership Council (2013), diversity can be defined as: 'the collective mixture of differences and similarities that includes, for example, individual and organizational characteristics, values, beliefs, experiences, backgrounds, preferences and behaviours'; and inclusion as: 'the achievement of a work environment in which all individuals are treated fairly and respectfully, have equal access to opportunities and resources, and can contribute fully to the organization's success'.

## Why focus on diversity and inclusion?

Organizations are increasingly raising the priority of D&I through efforts such as inclusiveness and unconscious bias training; leadership programmes; sponsorship programmes for talented young female or ethnic minority staff; and through large-scale culture change programmes where all people processes in the firm are scrutinized and updated to ensure that no bias is occurring. Why? There are two key arguments for wanting to successfully manage diversity and inclusion. The first is the social case for diversity, whereby employers have a moral obligation to treat employees with fairness and dignity and should ensure that decisions are made without resorting to prejudice and stereotypes. The challenge here is that moral obligations and social justice are not the prime concern of organizations. By nature organizations are driven by profit and efficiency, and indeed a business plan guided by social justice would be detrimental to the bottom line (Noon, 2010).

The other key argument is the diversity business case. Some of the key benefits cited by researchers and academics include the ability to maximize people potential, better understand customers, draw from a wider candidate pool, develop a more positive company image, engender greater discretionary effort from employees, increase employee engagement and improve retention, innovation and team performance (Kandola and Fullerton, 1994). A particular challenge highlighted in the literature for the business case for diversity, however, is that it is difficult to quantify, and that it can take a long time to realize the benefits. The analytics presented in this chapter break down some of the data and demystify the link between a diverse organization and some of the benefits that can be realized.

# Approaches to measuring and managing D&I

## Diversity dashboards

As discussed in previous chapters, when analysing their workforce, current HR functions tend to stop at simply describing the characteristics of the workforce within their organization. In our diversity example this would be the equivalent of saying 'Did you know that 12 per cent of our senior managers are Black or Asian ethnicity and 20 per cent of our senior managers are women...?' To which a response might be: 'So what?' or 'I'll look at this later'. Why? Because there is no context. Is 12 per cent what we should expect, or should it be more like 30 per cent? What is the likelihood that we would get 20 per cent women completely by chance anyway? And does this proportion actually reflect a male-weighted gender ratio in our organization? How do we know if this is due to bias, discrimination or some identifiable factor inhibiting inclusion?

Descriptive reports, often produced at quarterly or monthly intervals, aside from being rather uninteresting reading can very quickly become 'checkbox' exercises, produced to fulfil a requirement, but rarely reviewed closely unless external pressures (either external to the organization or the HR function) are applied. Examples of these external pressures in D&I may be regulatory reports as required in the financial and public sectors, or particular requests for information if the organization is taking part in a benchmarking exercise.

## *Diversity benchmarking*

For organizations, knowing their diversity statistics engenders a key benefit in that it can enable them to conduct benchmarking activities with regard to D&I. A number of organizations such as Stonewall, The Business Disability Forum, *The Times* (Top 50 Places for Women to Work report), Saratoga Human Capital Measurement and Benchmarking, etc, collect and analyse information on organizational D&I data and advertise the best organizations on the basis of their D&I statistics. The reports produced can often produce gap analyses to help organizations understand where they may fall short on particular demographic membership linked to diversity (compared to industry averages). A note of caution with external benchmarking activities is that it is important to be careful interpreting any differences that might be found when comparing one's own organization with others in relation to diversity statistics. Even in the same industry, jobs and functions are usually structured differently, so the same role may be classified as a 'senior manager' in one firm and a 'middle manager' in another firm.

Just looking at the numbers and comparing them against others, however, is not particularly helpful unless you fully understand what it means for your organization. What we need to know is what the numbers are telling us and how we should use this information to make sound decisions about the future of the business. This is where predictive analysis using simple statistical tools bridges the gap.

Ultimately, descriptive D&I reports tend to be current 'state of play' descriptive snapshots of the organization. Examples of these types of reports may include female representation by seniority level, promotion data by age and gender, representation of ethnic minorities among employees who joined the firm in the past three years, performance ratings given to staff with/ without disabilities, etc.

### Moving towards predictive models

D&I reports are a great example of the kind of descriptive reports that the HR function (or sometimes a separate management information (MI) function working closely in collaboration with HR) often produces. To what extent, however, can we rely on descriptive reports to provide us insights into D&I issues within the organization? With a few simple steps the level of interrogation that can be applied to the data can fundamentally increase the rigour of the analysis presented and its importance in defining corporate strategy. The examples throughout the remainder of this chapter will demonstrate how the incorporation of predictive statistical methods can be used to enhance the analysis of diversity data.

# Example 1: gender and job grade analysis using frequency tables and chi square

In showing how HR functions can take a step forward and interrogate their descriptive data in more detail, we can use a simple diversity analysis that explores whether or not women tend to be under-represented in senior roles within the organization. From a commercial perspective, the organization may be interested in having a greater diversity of thought in senior, strategic discussions; and from a people perspective, the organization may want to understand the degree to which there is a gender balance of positive role models for younger employees. The analysis required here is to check for possible discrimination or (for example) unconscious bias within the organization. To check for this, what an HR analyst may do is simply to look at how many women versus men work in different job grades.

With our diversity case study example 1 (named Chapter4Diversity1.xls; Chapter4Diversity1.sav file), we have a management consulting firm, SlidesRUs, with 1,493 employees. Of these, 746 are female and 745 are male. On first look, this seems to represent an organization with an even gender balance of 50 per cent male and 50 per cent female. There are eight different job grades in the organization and these are listed with their numbers in Table 4.1.

If there was no evidence of any kind of glass ceiling or discrimination/ unconscious bias within this organization then we would expect there to be an equal proportion (approximately) of men and women in each of the eight grades shown in Table 4.1.

The actual gender ratios in this current organization, however, are far from an even split of gender in each of the grades. Figure 4.1 shows the proportions of male and female in each of the grades in graphical form.

**TABLE 4.1** SlidesRUs employee numbers breakdown by role

| Grade | Role | Number of People Currently in Role |
|---|---|---|
| 1 | Clerical/Officer | 39 |
| 2 | Administrator/Assistant | 343 |
| 3 | Graduate/Trainee Consultant | 263 |
| 4 | Consultant | 243 |
| 5 | Senior Consultant | 250 |
| 6 | Managing Consultant | 239 |
| 7 | Principal Consultant | 81 |
| 8 | Partner | 33 |

**FIGURE 4.1** Graphical representation (description) of % of the male/female groups across the eight grades within the organization

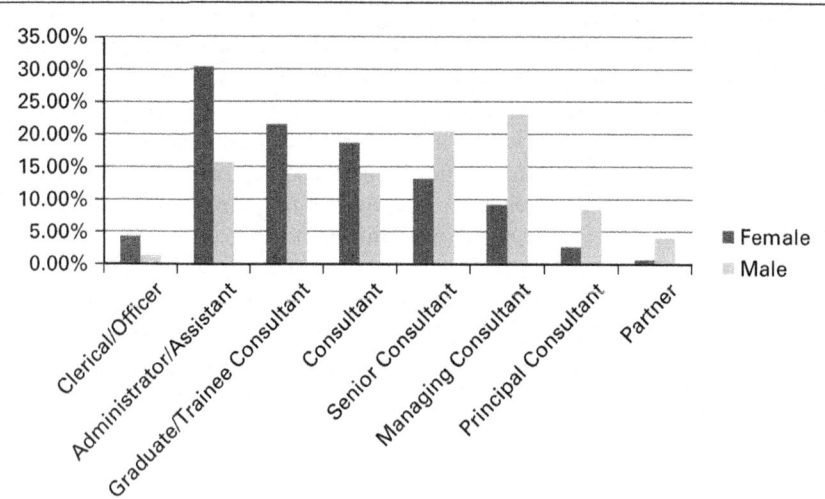

In the graph, we can see how men and women are spread across the organization. We can see that over one-third of women are in the Administrator/Assistant role, and then the number gradually decreases as the role becomes more senior. We can see that the most prevalent roles for men (where the male and female ratio leans more towards the male side) are the Managing Consultant and Senior Consultant roles.

At the moment, this is generally the kind of analysis that HR functions can and do provide in relation to HR diversity – such graphs can easily be produced with Excel. The bar graphs represent the proportion of the gender groups in each of the grades. Because the proportions of men and women in this organization are even, this bar chart is visually meaningful and is easy to interpret. One can see just from casting an eye over this graph that men dominate the more senior roles on the right-hand side and women dominate the more junior roles on the left-hand side. The data can also be presented in a different form, with the bars representing the proportion of each grade that is made up of women versus men (see Figure 4.2). The graph looks quite different but presents the same general message: that women are found more in the junior grades.

**FIGURE 4.2** Graphical representation (description) of the male/female % within each grade

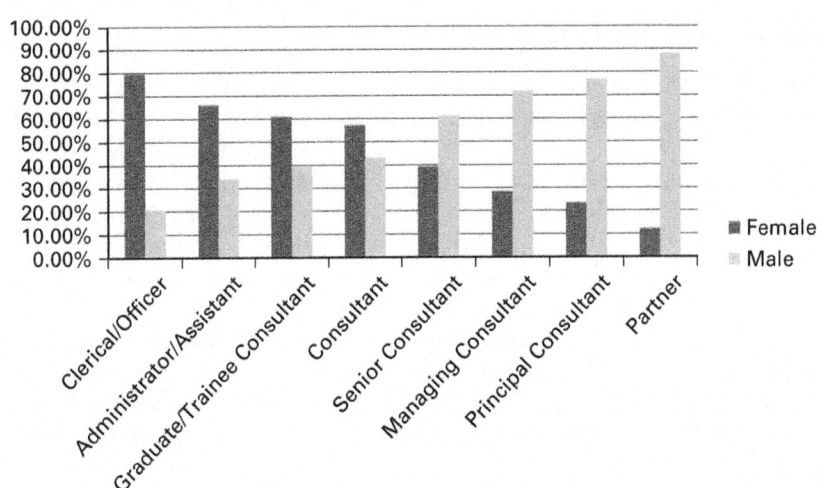

What the graph in Figure 4.2 tells us is that, looking at all of the Clerical/Officer roles, almost 80 per cent of them are held by women and just over 20 per cent are held by men; conversely, looking at all the partner roles, almost 90 per cent are held by men and just over 10 per cent are held by women.

## Interrogating the description

One of the main problems with this kind of analysis is that the data has generally not been subject to any kind of interrogation. To a degree, the data speaks for itself and seems to show a very strong pattern. However, even with such a pattern, it is not possible to say that there is a D&I problem with any degree of certainty. Were an HR professional to stand in front of a board of directors or an executive committee to argue for a case that there may be a glass ceiling or bias/ discrimination problem within the organization, the graphs in Figure 4.1 and Figure 4.2 do not hold up under scrutiny and could be passed off as coincidence or circumstance.

Imagine if you or your team spent a month putting this report together as part of a D&I proposition, only for it to be pulled apart with questions that the report cannot answer or suggestions that the data is just a coincidence. Or worse, if you embarked on an expensive programme based on the data when, in actual fact, there was no robust evidence to suggest there was a D&I problem at this organization – and the proportion of women in senior roles could indeed be explained by chance.

It is essential that an HR analyst has interrogated this data to ensure that there is a statistically significant pattern (See Chapter 3, page 59 for our discussion on significance).

## *The chi-square test*

The chi square is a simple test that we can use to interrogate the patterns presented in the graphs shown in Figure 4.1 and Figure 4.2. This test will immediately tell the analyst how certain they can be that the pattern is statistically meaningful. It will tell the HR analyst whether such a pattern could actually be a fluke or due to chance alone. Or, putting it another way, it will tell the HR analyst (and therefore any decision maker that they are trying to persuade) that it is *not* a fluke and is *not* due to chance alone, and is therefore something that should not be ignored.

The test follows a very simple idea. It checks whether the data pattern found (eg in Figure 4.2) is what we would expect to find if there was no link (or association) between gender and seniority in our organization. In other words, it tells the reader whether there is evidence that a gender bias might exist.

Looking at this from a purely statistical perspective (with all other factors being equal), if there were no gender bias or discrimination, we would expect the male:female ratio to be very close to 50:50 in any job grade because this is the gender ratio across our organization as a whole. So it would look something like Table 4.2.

For simplicity, where the number of people currently in role is an odd number, the extra person added is a woman for the first four grades and a man for the last four grades. For comparison, the *actual* number of men and women in the organization is illustrated in Table 4.3.

A chi-square test enables us to check the actual frequencies of males and females in each job grade within our organization against what we would expect to have if there were no bias (or link between gender and job level).

Simply put, the bigger the bias, the bigger the chi-square statistic will be. What does 'the bigger the bias' mean in this case? Well, as we have roughly 50:50 males and females in this particular organization, a 'no bias' scenario would be one where each job level is made up of about half males and half

**TABLE 4.2** SlidesRUs expected gender breakdown of employee numbers by role

| Grade | Role | Expected Number of Men in Role | Expected Number of Women in Role | Number of People Currently in Role |
|---|---|---|---|---|
| 1 | Clerical/Officer | 19 | 20 | 39 |
| 2 | Administrator/Assistant | 171 | 172 | 343 |
| 3 | Graduate/Trainee Consultant | 131 | 132 | 263 |
| 4 | Consultant | 121 | 122 | 243 |
| 5 | Senior Consultant | 125 | 125 | 250 |
| 6 | Managing Consultant | 120 | 119 | 239 |
| 7 | Principal Consultant | 41 | 40 | 81 |
| 8 | Partner | 17 | 16 | 33 |

females, as illustrated in Table 4.2. This pattern should be maintained as the roles get more senior.

However, the more we find that men dominate the senior roles, the greater 'evidence' that some kind of bias exists. The calculations going on behind the chi-square test calculation involve a check of what we actually have in terms of gender proportions compared to what we would have if there were no evidence of any bias. The greater the difference between the gender patterns in each grade (that we actually *observe* in our organization) and what we would *expect* (if no bias existed), the more our chi-square test will start to tell us that something is really going on that we cannot ignore (ie the chi-square statistic shows that statistical significance is found).

Our statistical software package (see Chapter 2 for our discussion of statistical software packages) then applies this information and calculates for us the statistical likelihood of finding our gender distribution by chance alone (if there was no link between gender and job grade). In other words, it tells us whether there is a meaningful and unexpected pattern of gender variation across the job grades.

**TABLE 4.3** SlidesRUs observed gender breakdown of employee numbers by role

| Grade | Role | Observed Number of Men in Role | Observed Number of Women in Role | Number of People Currently in Role |
|---|---|---|---|---|
| 1 | Clerical/Officer | 8 | 31 | 39 |
| 2 | Administrator/Assistant | 116 | 227 | 343 |
| 3 | Graduate/Trainee Consultant | 103 | 160 | 263 |
| 4 | Consultant | 104 | 139 | 243 |
| 5 | Senior Consultant | 152 | 98 | 250 |
| 6 | Managing Consultant | 171 | 68 | 239 |
| 7 | Principal Consultant | 62 | 19 | 81 |
| 8 | Partner | 29 | 4 | 33 |

Let's take a closer look at the data that our chi-square analysis produces.

When we run a chi-square analysis in SPSS (here we will use the SPSS data file: 'Chapter 4Diversity1.sav'), a number of useful things are produced at the click of a button. Figure 4.3 shows what SPSS produces with our data set when we ask it to interrogate our descriptions produced above in Table 4.2 and Table 4.3.

The output presented in Figure 4.3 gives us a considerable amount of information just by clicking a few buttons. Aside from the rich amount of information that is provided with regard to descriptive statistics (in the Gender * JobGrade cross-tabulation) on our organization (eg the proportions of male/female within each job grade, the proportion of the gender groups that each grade makes up), it also provides the expected count of males and females in each grade that should be found in the organization if there were no bias in any way. This is a useful target for HR to present as an internal gender ratio benchmark comparison that each job grade *should* have.

## FIGURE 4.3  SPSS output for our chi-square analysis of our data gender and grade description

**Case Processing Summary**

|  | Cases | | | | | |
| --- | --- | --- | --- | --- | --- | --- |
|  | Valid | | Missing | | Total | |
|  | N | Per cent | N | Per cent | N | Per cent |
| Gender * JobGrade | 1491 | 99.9% | 2 | 0.1% | 1493 | 100.0% |

**Gender * JobGrade Crosstabulation**

| | | | JobGrade | | | | | | | |
|---|---|---|---|---|---|---|---|---|---|---|
| | | | Clerical / Officer | Administrator / Assistant | Graduate / Trainee Consultant | Consultant | Senior Consultant | Managing Consultant | Principal Consultant | Partner | Total |
| Gender | Female | Count | 31 | 227 | 160 | 139 | 98 | 68 | 19 | 4 | 746 |
| | | Expected Count | 19.5 | 171.6 | 131.6 | 121.6 | 125.1 | 119.6 | 40.5 | 16.5 | 746.0 |
| | | % within Gender | 4.2% | 30.4% | 21.4% | 18.6% | 13.1% | 9.1% | 2.5% | 0.5% | 100.0% |
| | | % within JobGrade | 79.5% | 66.2% | 60.8% | 57.2% | 39.2% | 28.5% | 23.5% | 12.1% | 50.0% |
| | | % of Total | 2.1% | 15.2% | 10.7% | 9.3% | 6.6% | 4.6% | 1.3% | 0.3% | 50.0% |
| | Male | Count | 8 | 116 | 103 | 104 | 152 | 171 | 62 | 29 | 745 |
| | | Expected Count | 19.5 | 171.4 | 131.4 | 121.4 | 124.9 | 119.4 | 40.5 | 16.5 | 745.0 |
| | | % within Gender | 1.1% | 15.6% | 13.8% | 14.0% | 20.4% | 23.0% | 8.3% | 3.9% | 100.0% |
| | | % within JobGrade | 20.5% | 33.8% | 39.2% | 42.8% | 60.8% | 71.5% | 76.5% | 87.9% | 50.0% |
| | | % of Total | 0.5% | 7.8% | 6.9% | 7.0% | 10.2% | 11.5% | 4.2% | 1.9% | 50.0% |
| Total | | Count | 39 | 343 | 263 | 243 | 250 | 239 | 81 | 33 | 1491 |
| | | Expected Count | 39.0 | 343.0 | 263.0 | 243.0 | 250.0 | 239.0 | 81.0 | 33.0 | 1491.0 |
| | | % within Gender | 2.6% | 23.0% | 17.6% | 16.3% | 16.8% | 16.0% | 5.4% | 2.2% | 100.0% |
| | | % within JobGrade | 100.0% | 100.0% | 100.0% | 100.0% | 100.0% | 100.0% | 100.0% | 100.0% | 100.0% |
| | | % of Total | 2.6% | 23.0% | 17.6% | 16.3% | 16.8% | 16.0% | 5.4% | 2.2% | 100.0% |

**Chi-Square Tests**

|  | Value | df | Asymp. Sig. (2-sided) |
| --- | --- | --- | --- |
| Pearson Chi-Square | 164.699[a] | 7 | .000 |
| Likelihood Ratio | 171.620 | 7 | .000 |
| Linear-by-Linear Association | 157.403 | 1 | .000 |
| N of Valid Cases | 1491 | | |

a. 0 cells (0.0%) have expected count less than 5. The minimum expected count is 16.49.

The key statistics of interest here are the Pearson's chi-square statistic of 164.99 and the significance statistic of .000 in the 'Asymp. Sig. (2-sided)' column. This tells us that there is a pattern in our gender proportions that is meaningful. Indeed this tells us that we have a statistically significant link (or 'association' in this case) between gender and grade. As our descriptive statistics show that females are under-represented in the senior grades and over-represented in the junior grades, this significance figure is saying that we can be certain that this finding is meaningful to a 1 in 1,000 level of certainty (see Chapter 3 for our discussion of significance). Or, put differently, there is less than 1 in 1,000 chance that this gender proportion could happen by coincidence, hence we know that some other factor has influenced this proportion (this other factor could be some form of discrimination, but we will not know this without further exploration). Either way, we know that our gender pattern is not occurring by coincidence with this level of certainty. We reached a significance level of p<0.001 and, although we have the number to only three decimal places, we know that 0.000 is less than 0.001, and hence we can confidently say our result is 'less than 1 in 1,000 chance'.

> **Snapshot hidden gem**
>
> In this organization women are under-represented in senior roles (to a level of certainty that means it pretty much could never happen by chance alone) and no one could try to deny it due to the overwhelming evidence.

*Statistical interpretation caveat:* it is of course one thing to say that women are under-represented in senior roles in an organization and another thing to say that there is some form of discrimination or bias going on. A highly competent HR analytics expert would be very careful not to say that the analysis says more than it actually does. The statistical result needs to be carefully combined with a rational and considered set of arguments as to why the very strong pattern of female under-representation may be occurring. It would also be sensible to develop a plan for further research within the organization in order to try to explore why these patterns exist.

### Running the chi square

We are going to walk through the steps involved in running a chi-square analysis using the data set that produced the above statistics. This data is a representative random sample from an actual organization and the data set used includes information about the gender of the employee, the gender of their boss, their job grade, their age, tenure and a number of other demographic details. We will visit this data set again in subsequent chapters. For now, all we are using in this data set is the gender and job-grade information.

Producing the analysis set out in Figure 4.3 is very straightforward in SPSS. Once we open our SPSS data set that we earlier prepared (see page 21 in Chapter 2), all we do is left-click on our mouse a number of times (in the right places) to get our results. The first thing we do is select the 'Analyze' pull-down menu and select the 'Descriptive Statistics' option then the subsequent 'Crosstabs' option (see Figure 4.4).

**FIGURE 4.4** Running the chi square

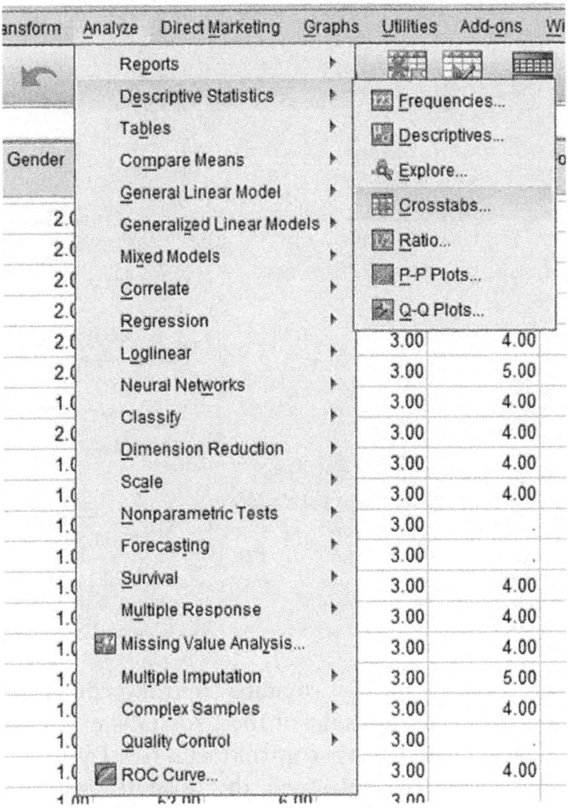

After selecting these options, the Crosstabs control menu will appear (see Figure 4.5). Here you select the Gender variable into the 'Row(s):' selection box (by clicking on the variable in the top left-hand box then clicking on the top arrow button) and the JobGrade variable into the 'Column(s)' box (by clicking on the variable in the top left-hand box then clicking on the middle arrow button). Then click on the 'Statistics' button positioned on the top right of the Crosstabs menu box and the 'Crosstabs: Statistics' control menu will appear (see Figure 4.5). In this, select the 'Chi-square' tick box then click on the 'Continue' box.

## Predictive HR Analytics

**FIGURE 4.5**  Getting SPSS to run a chi square

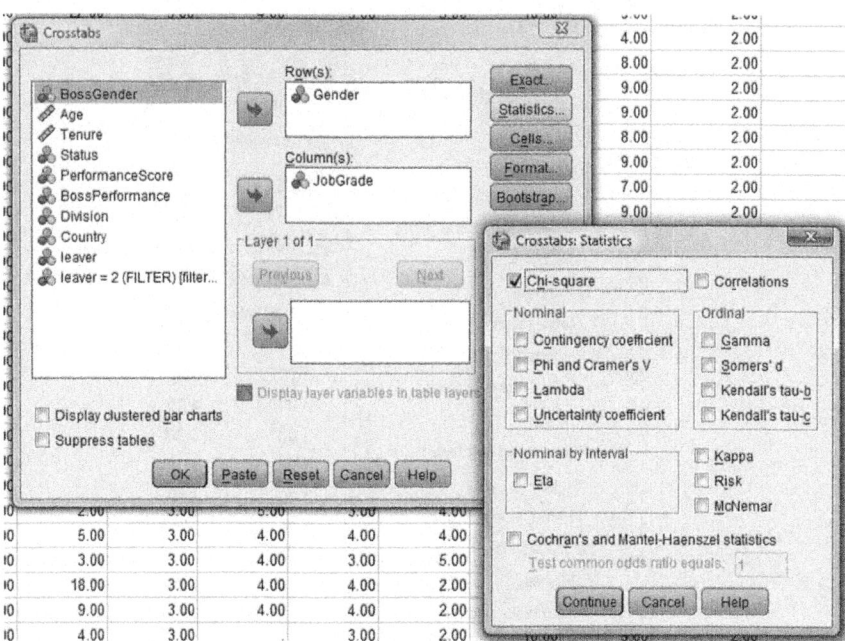

Then when you are back in the Crosstabs control menu click on the 'Cells' button positioned on the top right of the Crosstabs menu box and within the new 'Crosstabs: Cell Display' control menu (see Figure 4.6) tick on the 'Observed' and 'Expected' option in the 'Counts' box and the 'Row', 'Column' and 'Total' options in the 'Percentages' box. Then Click on 'Continue' and once back to the 'Crosstabs' control menu click on the 'OK' button (see Figure 4.6).

The analysis produced in Figure 4.3 (set out previously) will now appear in your SPSS output screen ready for the HR analytics master to use in persuasive arguments to get the senior management to take D&I seriously in the organization.

So, instead of the discussion around the executive committee table going like this:

*Scenario one – descriptive data only:*

> *ExCo member*: 'Well, the gender proportions across the grades vary quite a bit so that data could easily be a coincidence.'
>
> *HR analyst*: 'The pattern looks very strong and has done for a number of years...'
>
> *ExCo member*: 'Well, could you please produce this same report every month for six months so we can keep an eye on it.'
>
> *ExCo member (unspoken)*: 'I've seen this pattern over a number of years but we will never actually prioritize this because we don't believe this is a problem.'

**FIGURE 4.6** Selecting what to display in the Crosstabs output table

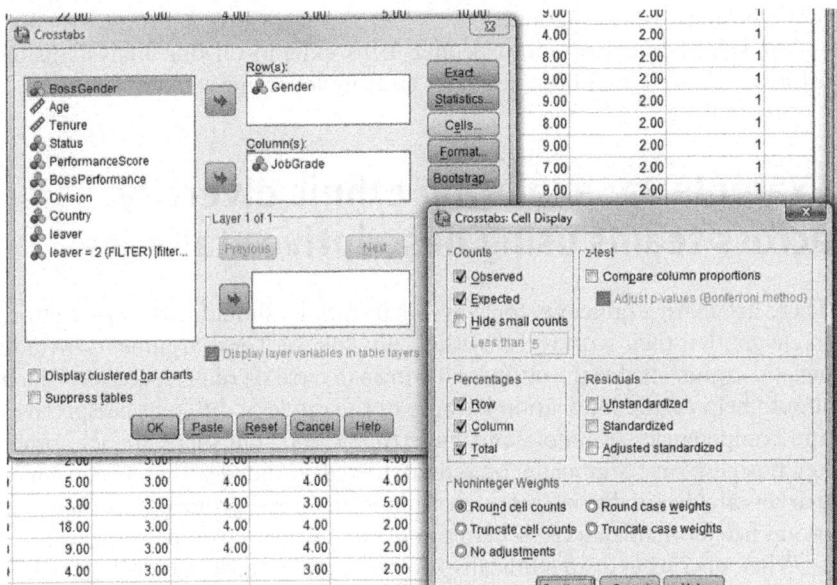

– with the chi-square analysis, it would go something like this:

*Scenario two – using some statistical analysis:*

>   *ExCo member*: 'Well, the gender proportions vary quite a bit so that data could easily be a coincidence.'
>
>   *HR analyst*: 'It is no coincidence. If you look at this chi-square test checking for statistical significance, you can see that the chance of this being a coincidence is less than 1 per cent, in fact the likelihood of this being a coincidence is less than 1 in 1,000. We have a real problem and, with some further analysis into what the contributing factors may be, my team has some suggestions for how to address it.'
>
>   *ExCo member*: 'I'm very impressed with your technical competency and I am grateful you have brought this to our attention. Thank you. Let's arrange a separate meeting to discuss possible causes and go through some of these suggestions.'

If you have ever seen the movie *Groundhog Day* whereby Bill Murray relives the same day again and again, you will understand what life will be like for the HR professional in scenario one. They will be producing the same descriptive report each month, having the same conversation with the executive committee (or probably someone lower down) again and again until they are reassigned to do analysis on something else and start a new cycle of conversations again.

Scenario two presents a far stronger argument and really helps the executive to see what is happening in the business. It also provides greater credibility to the data and has a good chance of really making a difference in the business where it counts.

But D&I is not just about gender. Let's expand on our analysis using information we have about ethnicity and employee engagement.

# Example 2a: exploring ethnic diversity across teams using descriptive statistics

There are many arguments for why organizations should make every effort to ensure that their workforce is ethnically diverse. These arguments include general arguments for the utility of having a diverse set of perspectives, which should help ensure innovation because of the range of different perspectives and competencies (Kandola and Fullerton, 1998). But there are also other key business-case arguments presented, linked to the idea that as consumer markets are diverse having representation from diverse groups as an employee group helps organizations to better understand their customers' needs.

When operating in an ethnically diverse country (such as the UK), the HR analytics expert needs to be very aware of the possible importance that ethnic origin might have for employees in the workplace. It is well documented that some industries tend to find it harder to demonstrate a good level of representation of Black, Asian or Minority Ethnic (BAME) (see 'Use of BAME' on p. 143) employees than others. This difficulty in ensuring a good level of representation may be for a number of reasons. The Race for Opportunity report 'Aspiration and Frustration' (Race for Opportunity, 2010) shows that ethnic minorities living and working in Britain consider certain professions – including banking, politics, law and journalism – as closed to them. Organizations need to understand why this is the case, look at what is happening in their own organization and develop a plan to address under-representation.

## *Exploring diversity in teams within a large organization*

In understanding patterns of ethnic diversity within our organization, one possible set of analysis that can be conducted would be to analyse patterns of team diversity in order to investigate whether specific ethnic groups are clustered together – and, also, if there are variations in the level of BAME representation in teams within our organization, might we be able to identify patterns that could help explain this?

Following on from the previous discussion about BAME candidates feeling as though some industries are not open to them, or that they feel excluded in certain industries, it would be useful to identify whether any bias is occurring at a more micro level in the organization. Are some teams more welcoming to BAME staff? Do some teams attract, develop and retain BAME individuals more effectively than others? If we found, for example, that a certain type of team had a low level of BAME representation, can we identify what factors might be influencing this? Might we be able to find some evidence within the organization that certain factors could be associated with low levels of BAME representation in teams? If we can find such evidence we can then identify possible levers with which to try to increase representation.

If we assume that the organization is interested in ensuring levels of diversity in teams, and there are a large number of teams that can be analysed meaningfully, then there are a number of interesting predictive models that can be run to identify patterns of team diversity (or lack of diversity).

Here, we will talk about 'predicting' diversity. By this, we mean identifying patterns that might exist, which show that more BAME individuals are found in some professions or job types but not others. We could say that we 'predict' levels of BAME representation by identifying the particular job type found in certain teams and exploring its relationship with BAME levels. If there were a high representation of BAME in certain job types this might mean that BAME individuals actually feel more welcome in such jobs (either at recruitment or once they have joined). Similarly, analysis of teams may show that more BAME individuals are found in a certain type of team (eg sales-based teams) but they are not found in other types of team (eg admin-based teams). Depending on the statistical significance, we could say that we 'predict' variation in team-level BAME on the basis of the job type that we tend to find in the team. This allows the organization to look at which teams might be better at attracting, developing and retaining BAME employees.

An assumption with predictive analysis is that factors can be identified that predict (and potentially influence or cause variation in) a dependent factor. So this can be easily applied here to see which team factors (department, team size, gender split, etc, influence or cause variation in the proportion of BAME staff).

In addition to this, there may be lots of information available at the team level that would be quite useful information in a D&I analysis that is not available at the individual employee level; in particular, scores from an employee attitude or employee engagement survey. As discussed in Chapter 5, many organizations are provided with engagement survey information at the team level but not at the individual level and we could fairly easily, therefore, link team-level BAME representation statistics with team-level scores produced by an engagement survey.

## *Team diversity case study example*

In this second diversity example we have branch/departmental/team-level data from two functions within a (very large) financial organization.

First a few important points on ethnicity data:

1 Ethnicity data is often collected on a diversity form completed by employees on joining the organization, and is sometimes updated in subsequent exercises whereby the analytics team may ask staff to review this.
2 Ethnicity data is rarely mandatory, so it is reasonable to expect some blank data in the report. SPSS will help to identify complete records and use the appropriate test.
3 The term 'BAME' – Black, Asian or Minority Ethnic – is primarily used in the UK. In other countries one might expect different definitions of 'Minority Ethnic'. For example, if your analysis was in China, perhaps 'Asian' would not be in the minority! It is important to look at the data closely before grouping 'ethnic minorities' together, particularly if you are in a multinational institution. In the United States, you might see terms such as 'visible minorities' and an emphasis on analysing Hispanic/Latino ethnicities. Indeed it is important to consider these differences in the data capture process as well.

Now, back to our financial institution.

There are 29,976 employees in these two functions across the UK and these employees are organized into 928 teams or employee units. These are sometimes branches, sometimes departments and sometimes teams within larger work settings. The data from the employee engagement survey is organized into these 928 units for analysis. It is also important to note that they have been organized with a 'work unit' key that was used by the engagement survey provider in order to supply engagement survey data in aggregate form (to protect identities in this anonymous survey, no unit here is identified if it has fewer than 10 employees). The data set that we are working with, therefore, is average/aggregate data at the work team level and there are 928 objects of analysis in the SPSS data set, entitled 'Chapter4Diversity Case Group Level Data.sav'.

The variables in the data set include the following information (Table 4.4):

**TABLE 4.4** Employee engagement survey variables for diversity analysis

| Variable Label | Description |
| --- | --- |
| DepartmentGroupNumber | Team/unit key identifier |
| GroupSize | Number of employees in the unit |
| PercentMale | Percentage of the unit made up of males |
| BAME | Percentage of the unit made up of Black, Asian or Minority Ethnic employees |

**TABLE 4.4** *continued*

| Variable Label | Description |
|---|---|
| NumberTeamLeads | Number of team leaders in the unit (in general this organization has a team leader for every seven or so employees |
| NumberFeMaleTeamLeads | Number of team leads in the unit who are female |
| Location | Geographical location: 1 = Central London, 2 = Greater London, 3 = Rest of UK |
| LondonorNot | Geographical location recoded to 1 = Central London or Greater London and 2 = Rest of UK |
| Function | Function 1 = Sales staff (customer-facing people) or 2 = Professional Service (non-customer-facing people) |
| EMPsurvEngage_1 – EMPsurvEngage_9 | Proportion of the unit who answered favourably (with either 'agree' or 'strongly agree' on a 1 to 5 'strongly disagree' to 'strongly agree' response scale) to each of nine employee engagement questions: <br><br> I work with full intensity in my job; I try my hardest to perform as well as I can in my work; I concentrate hard in my job; My mind is always focused on my job; I strive very hard to complete my work well; I would recommend this organization as a place to work; My job inspires me; Time flies at work; I am proud of the work I do |
| EMPsurvEngagement | Average unit/team score for the nine engagement questions |
| EMPorgIntegrity1 – EMPorgIntegrity5 | Proportion of the unit who answered favourably (with either 'agree' or 'strongly agree' on a 1 to 5 'strongly disagree' to 'strongly agree' response scale) to each of five employee 'organizational integrity' questions: <br><br> My organization listens to staff; My organization does the right thing; My organization treats external stakeholders with respect; My organization encourages staff to point out questionable practices; We all do the right thing in this organization |

**TABLE 4.4** *continued*

| Variable Label | Description |
|---|---|
| EmpSurvOrgIntegrity | Average unit/team score for the five organizational integrity questions |
| EMPsurvSUP1 – EMPsurvSUP4 | Proportion of the unit who answered favourably (with either 'agree' or 'strongly agree' on a 1 to 5 'strongly disagree' to 'strongly agree' response scale) to each of four 'supportive supervisor' questions: |
| | My supervisor listens to me; My supervisor cares about my well-being; My supervisor helps ensure we get things done; My supervisor is there when he/she is needed |
| EmpSurvSupervisor | Average unit/team score for the four 'supportive supervisor' questions |

There are a number of ways that we could analyse the data set provided, which would give us information about potential predictors of variation in BAME prevalence across the teams.

First – let's look at basic descriptive information linked to gender and BAME prevalence across the teams. We can easily produce averages and range information with SPSS. Going into SPSS, we analyse the descriptive statistics by selecting 'Analyze' from the toolbar, and then 'Descriptive Statistics' and 'Descriptives' (see Figure 4.7).

**FIGURE 4.7**

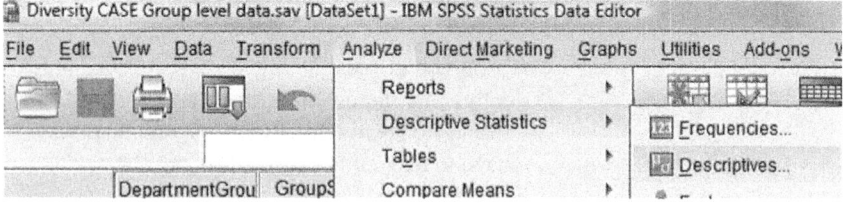

We can then choose which variables we would like to look at. In this example, 'PercentMale' and 'BAME' are selected, meaning we would like to look at the percentage of the unit made up of males and the percentage of the unit made up of BAME employees (see Figure 4.8).

## FIGURE 4.8

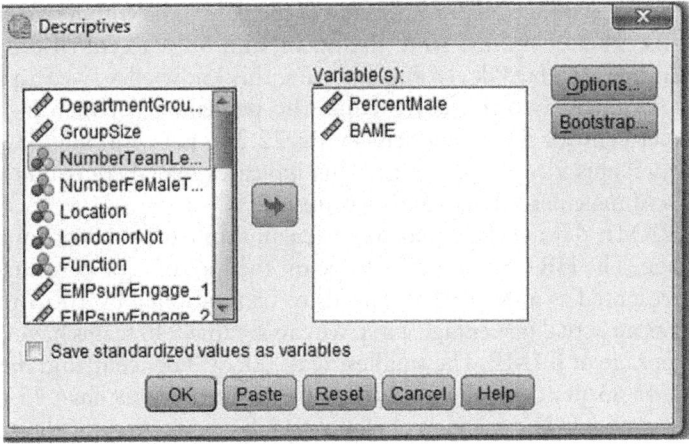

Giving the output shown in Figure 4.9:

## FIGURE 4.9

```
DESCRIPTIVES VARIABLES=PercentMale BAME
  /STATISTICS=MEAN STDDEV MIN MAX.
```

### Descriptives

**Descriptive Statistics**

|  | N | Minimum | Maximum | Mean | Std. Deviation |
|---|---|---|---|---|---|
| Percentage of the work unit that are male | 927 | 1 | 100 | 58.95 | 22.266 |
| Percentage Black Asian and Minority Ethnic | 746 | .00 | .45 | .1184 | .11331 |
| Valid N (listwise) | 746 |  |  |  |  |

Looking at Figure 4.9, we can see that 927 groups (or teams) reported the percentage of the team that are male, whilst only 746 teams reported the percentage of BAME individuals in the group. This reflects the discussion earlier about ethnicity data – because it is rarely mandatory, we should expect to find some gaps in the data. Breaking down the information in Figure 4.9, let's look at the figure showing the percentage of team members who are male.

We have 927 teams who were able to report the percentage male. The smallest/minimum male percentage was a team who had 1 per cent men, while the maximum shows that at least one team had 100 per cent men. The mean/average percentage of men in the teams was 58.95 per cent, and the standard deviation was 22.266 per cent, meaning that there was quite a wide variation in the percentage of males in the teams across our organization.

Remember that standard deviation is a measure to quantify the amount of dispersion or variation across the data and, in a normal distribution such as this one, we would expect 95 per cent of the data to be within two standard deviations (plus or minus) from the mean, and 68 per cent of the data to be within one standard deviation. So, using this knowledge, we can say that in approximately two-thirds of teams the percentage of men is between 36.684 per cent (or 58.95 per cent minus 22.266 per cent) and 81.216 per cent (58.95 plus 22.226 per cent). This indicates that there is quite a wide variation of male percentages across teams.

The BAME data represented has been multiplied by 100 to make it a percentage. The HR analyst needs to be on the lookout for percentage data that is presented as a decimal and needs to be multiplied by 100, or when it is stored as an actual percentage. First, we can see that 746 teams have reported the percentage of BAME. The smallest was .00, or 0 per cent, and the largest was .45, or 45 per cent, showing that one or more teams have 45 per cent BAME members. The mean is .1184, or 11.84 per cent, and the standard deviation is .11331, or 11.331 per cent. From what we know about normal distributions, we can deduce that approximately two-thirds of the teams have their percentage of BAME between one standard deviation below or above the mean; here 0.509 per cent (11.84 minus 11.331) and 23.171 per cent (11.84 plus 11.331).

Now we can look at these statistics across the two functions that we have in the data set to really investigate what is happening in this organization with regard to ethnicity.

The financial institution can be split at a very high level between those on the front line who are customer facing (called 'Sales' in our data set) and those who support the front-line staff in roles such as Product Development, Marketing, HR, Finance, etc (this group are called 'Professional Service' in our data set).

So what we want to do here is compare two functions in the organization (or two samples), namely customer facing (Sales) and non-customer facing (Professional Service), on BAME.

For this we will use a test that looks at differences between two independent (different) samples on a variable we are really interested in: this is the independent samples t-test.

# Example 2b: comparing ethnicity and gender across two functions in an organization using the independent samples t-test

The independent samples t-test is simple and practical. Used in certain situations, it will give you greater confidence in the group comparisons you are making. Essentially we should use the independent samples t-test when we have one grouping (independent) variable (eg two functions: Sales or Professional Service in our example, which determines which group people belong to) and one variable that we want to compare the two groups on – the dependent variable (team level BAME in our example).

We want to test whether there is a significant difference *between the means* of BAME prevalence in teams from the two functional groups. The rationale for this terminology is that, potentially, the BAME prevalence across the teams may to some extent be dependent upon the type of teams (ie the function).

Why are we doing this again? For both commercial reasons and for employee engagement and well-being reasons our organization would like to ensure there is a good representation of BAME individuals to enhance the diversity of our organization. Research has indicated that BAME individuals are often clustered into particular professions because they may feel that others are closed-off to them and potentially some professions may not make BAME individuals very welcome. Indeed Race for Opportunity (2014) suggested that banking is one of the professions that BAME individuals often felt was closed to them.

We want to test whether there may be instances of this in our organization by first testing whether there is a difference in the proportion of BAME individuals in 'Sales' (customer-facing banking roles, which are usually more highly paid) than in 'Professional Service' (non-customer-facing professions such as HR, finance, risk assessment, etc). This will help us to identify whether this problem exists in our organization and then carefully diagnose and recommend a D&I strategy that is specific to the needs of this organization.

So is there a difference in the prevalence of BAME in Sales versus Professional Service? Let's test it.

In fact, it seems like such a good idea, let's do the test for percentage of males too. Why hold back with our button clicking?

In SPSS we go to the 'Analyze' menu again, select 'Compare Means' (because we are comparing the means of the two samples), then we select 'Independent Samples T-Test' (see Figure 4.10).

**FIGURE 4.10**

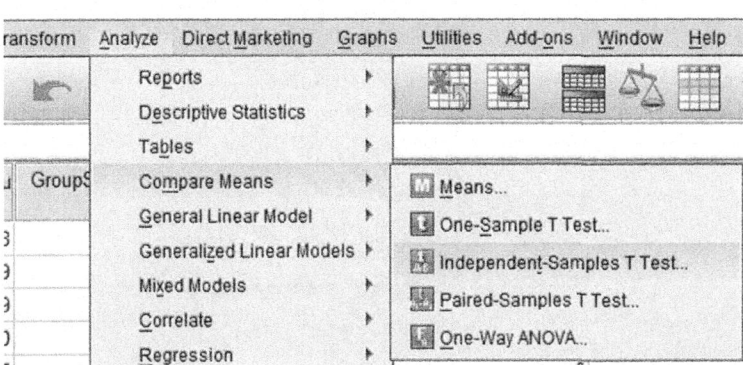

We need to put our independent variable (again, the one that determines which group a person belongs to (ie Sales or Professional Service) into the 'Grouping Variable' field, then we put the dependent variables (the ones we are testing, here PercentMale and BAME) into the 'Test Variable(s):' box (see Figure 4.11).

**FIGURE 4.11**

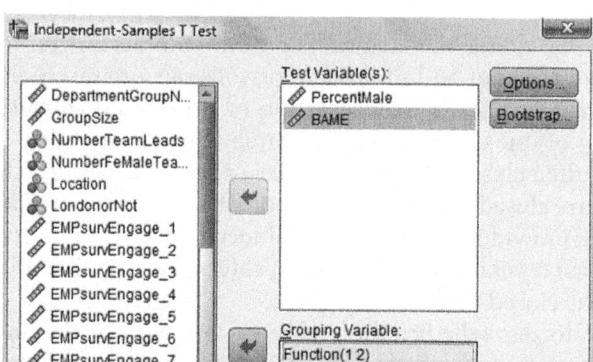

Then click on 'Define Groups' so that we can tell SPSS which group is which.

We have set up the data file for the 'Function' variable to be the following: 1 = Sales; 2 = Professional Service. So SPSS knows that a value of 1 means the person is in Group 1 (Sales); and that a value of 2 means the person is in Group 2 (Professional Service) – we just need to select the comparator groups in the t-test (Figure 4.12).

**FIGURE 4.12**

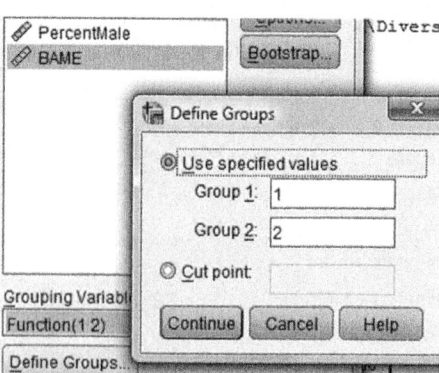

Then we hit 'Continue' and 'OK' and SPSS produces the output. Similar to unwrapping an ambiguously shaped Christmas present, we can now reveal what the test has produced (Figure 4.13).

## FIGURE 4.13

**Group Statistics**

| | Sales staff or Professional Services | N | Mean | Std. Deviation | Std. Error Mean |
|---|---|---|---|---|---|
| Percentage of the work unit that are male | Sales | 502 | 71.26 | 16.267 | .726 |
| | Professional Service | 425 | 44.40 | 19.455 | .944 |
| Percentage Black Asian and Minority Ethnic | Sales | 404 | .0968 | .09767 | .00486 |
| | Professional Service | 342 | .1439 | .12479 | .00675 |

**Independent Samples Test**

| | | Levene's Test for Equality of Variances | | t-test for Equality of Means | | | | | 95% Confidence Interval of the Difference | |
|---|---|---|---|---|---|---|---|---|---|---|
| | | F | Sig. | t | df | Sig. (2-tailed) | Mean Difference | Std. Error Difference | Lower | Upper |
| Percentage of the work unit that are male | Equal variances assumed | 30.992 | .000 | 22.892 | 925 | .000 | 26.859 | 1.173 | 24.556 | 29.161 |
| | Equal variances not assumed | | | 22.557 | 828.765 | .000 | 26.859 | 1.191 | 24.522 | 29.196 |
| Percentage Black Asian and Minority Ethnic | Equal variances assumed | 35.396 | .000 | -5.770 | 744 | .000 | -.04703 | .00815 | -.06303 | -.03103 |
| | Equal variances not assumed | | | -5.655 | 640.609 | .000 | -.04703 | .00832 | -.06336 | -.03070 |

## Analysis of the percentage of BAME in teams

So, remembering what we said earlier about completion rates for ethnicity data collection initiatives, we can see that we have 404 teams within the Sales function who have reported the percentage BAME, and we have 342 teams within the Professional Service function who have reported the percentage BAME. This shows that we are comparing two groups of different size, so behind the scenes SPSS will account for this in the calculations.

We can also see that the mean value for the percentage of BAME in the Sales function is .0968, or 9.6 per cent, compared to the mean value for the percentage of BAME in the Professional Service function, which is .1439, or 14.39 per cent. The standard deviation of the BAME in Sales and Professional Service functions is 9.767 per cent and 12.49 per cent respectively.

## Levene's test

One last thing we need to consider when comparing the two groups is whether they have a similar spread of values. For example, imagine if all the percentage BAME for the Sales function were clustered around the mean, ie all the teams in the Sales function actually reported a very similar prevalence of BAME (which would involve a small variation or spread in the data), yet within the Professional Service functions some teams had almost 100 per cent BAME, while others had only 1–2 per cent, or even zero (which would involve a large variation or spread in the data). We need to consider this difference in spread or variance patterns in the BAME prevalence in teams when comparing the two groups, because it will represent an important difference between the two.

Professor Howard Levene came up with a test that would clearly tell us if the two groups were similar enough that we could assume 'equal variance'. If Levene's F-test statistic produces a significance value of greater than 0.05, then we can assume that the functional groups have similar patterns of spread or variance in team BAME prevalence, or they have 'equal variance' (that they are not significantly different in their patterns of variance). However, if Levene's F-test statistic produces a significance value of less than 0.05 ($p<0.05$), then the functional groups that we are comparing can be considered to have very different variation in team BAME prevalence; the functional groups do not have 'equal variance'.

So, looking at our result, Levene's test shows a significance value of 0.000, so we cannot assume equal variance patterns in BAME across our two functional groupings as $p<0.05$. It follows that we should look at the values in the 'Equal variances not assumed' row (Figure 4.13) when we want to know whether the proportions (percentage) of BAME differ across the teams when comparing the two functional groupings. Just to be clear, Levene's test does not tell us whether the means of BAME prevalence are significantly different in their levels, but it does tell us that the spread or variation of BAME prevalence is different when we compare the two groups. The t-test tells us whether the proportions (levels) of BAME differ significantly when we compare Professional Service with front-line Sales functions.

We can see in Figure 4.13 that the t-value for BAME when equal variables are not assumed is –5.655; the degrees of freedom are 640.61, and the significance (known as the p-value) is .000 ($p<0.001$). The degrees of freedom is a statistical parameter that is used in SPSS to determine the significance p-value. It refers to the number of values in the calculation of a statitic that are free to vary.

If we were all students in Levene's class, before the days of statistical software we would have worked out this t-value and degrees of freedom with a pen and paper, and then looked up the corresponding p-value in a table to ascertain how significantly different the two groups are (if at all). However, SPSS gives this information to us and we just need to be able to interpret the output. So, to follow formal conventions for reporting these statistics, you would say something like: 'The t-test was significant: $t(640.61) = -5.655$, $p<0.001$. There is a significant difference in percentage BAME between the two functions. Sales (mean=.0968, SD=.09767) have a lower percentage BAME in their teams than Professional Service (mean=.1439, SD=.12479).'

The p-value means that the probability of this happening by chance alone is less than 1 in 1,000 – so there must be something else (other than random fluctuations) at play (we don't know what or why these functions differ – but we now know that this is an issue in our organization that needs to be addressed).

The format of the above write-up is recommended so that you can use it to compare with other, similar tests. When you are presenting this to senior executives, though, the best way to present this might be just to keep it simple and say something like:

> **Snapshot hidden gem**
>
> 'In comparing the Sales and the Professional Service functions, the proportion of BAME staff is significantly lower in Sales than in Professional Service. The average proportion of BAME staff in teams within the Sales is 9.7 per cent, and by comparison the average proportion of BAME staff in teams within the Professional Service function is 14.39 per cent. Deeper analysis shows that the likelihood of this difference occurring by chance alone is less than 1 in 1,000; suggesting we have an issue that needs attention within the Sales function.'

As HR professionals, the next step might be to recommend interviewing BAME individuals in the Sales teams about their experiences. Depending on the outcome and assuming that you find some evidence of a potential bias, you might recommend interventions such as reviewing approaches for recruitment, retention and development of BAME individuals in the Sales function, or diversity training such as unconscious bias and inclusive leadership.

A quick note on negative t-values as we had in this example: in all cases, the bigger the absolute t-value, the more there are differences *between* the two groups than *within* the two groups. Given that the important thing is the absolute value, or size of the t-value, rather than whether it is negative or not, feel free to ignore the negative sign here because it is only negative because we (fairly arbitrarily) coded our first group 'Sales' as 1 and our second group 'Professional Service' as 2, which has a higher mean than the first group. If we coded the groups the other way around we would not have a negative t-value. So a negative t-value is a function of which group you put into the analysis first (to compare with another group). Importantly, the value of the mean for each group tells us the important information and the t-test is just testing whether the groups are significantly different.

## *Analysis of the percentage of men in teams*

With our analysis above we also tested whether there was a difference between Sales and Professional Services functional groups with regard to the proportion of teams that are male. So, in interpreting our output for this we can see that again in Figure 4.13 our Levene's statistic has a p-value (shown in the Figure as 'Sig.') associated with it that is below 0.05. When we look at our corresponding t-value statistics where unequal variances are assumed, we can see that we have a significant difference in gender proportions across the two groups (Sales versus Professional Services). We would follow conventions and write up the statistics in the following way: 'The t-test was significant: $t(925)=22.892$, $p<0.001$. There is a significant difference in the percentage of men between the two functions. Sales have a higher percentage of men (mean=71.26, SD=16.267) in their teams than Professional Service (mean=44.4, SD=19.455).'

But of course this actually means:

> ### Snapshot hidden gem
>
> 'In comparing the Sales and the Professional Service functions, the proportion of male staff is significantly higher in Sales than in Professional Service groups within our organization. The average percentage of male staff in teams within Sales is 71.26 per cent, and by comparison the average proportion of male staff in teams within the Professional Service function is 44.4 per cent. Deeper analysis shows the chance of this difference occurring by chance alone is less than 1 in 1,000, suggesting that we have a clear issue of male dominance within our Sales function; this potentially needs attention if we want gender proportions to be similar across our organization.'

As with the BAME example, it suggests there is also a potential gender issue in the Sales team. The t-value is far higher in the second example, suggesting that the gender issue is greater than the ethnicity issue.

So the independent samples t-test has then helped us here to identify that the prevalence of women and of BAME employees is significantly lower in the Sales function compared to the Professional Service function. Because the dependent variables (percentage of the team who are ethnic minorities, and percentage of team who are men) are continuous variables (ie a meaningful number rather than a category) and because there are only two groups (Sales versus Professional Services), the independent samples t-test was the most appropriate choice here. For more information around which test to use in which situation, see Chapter 3, page 68). Another good example of when to use an independent samples t-test in diversity may be to test the difference between male and female average salary. Gender would be the independent variable and the dependent (continuous) variable would be salary.

So we now know that our organization faces some challenges in BAME, particularly in the Sales function. This opens things up for us now to delve deeper into what might be the possible reasons for this. Multiple regression will help us explore to a greater extent what factors might be at play or are associated with variations in diversity across our teams. Here we can use multiple regression to predict diversity statistics in teams; in particular we can try to predict the BAME proportions in teams using a number of possible internal factors that we have available.

First, let's recap on multiple regression and why we might use it.

# Example 3: using multiple linear regression to model and predict ethnic diversity variation across teams

## Multiple linear regression

To be clear, the term 'regression' here has nothing to do with age regression, past-life regression or some form of Freudian psychoanalytic regression therapy. Rather it refers to the attempt to model the relationship between two or more independent (or 'explanatory') variables and a dependent (or 'response') variable by analysing many observations. That model could then be used to predict and inform future behaviours with a degree of statistical confidence.

So as interesting as the exercise might have been, we will not be accessing any childhood or past life memories (not even once, let alone multiple times – unless of course you were a statistician in your past life, which may explain why you were drawn to this book). To simplify things, let's use an example and talk about factors that influence whether an individual might be satisfied in their job.

In a simple example, an employee pulse survey (see Chapter 5 for a discussion of pulse surveys) might ask people to report satisfaction in their job on a scale of 1 to 7, where 1 is 'very dissatisfied' (and 4 is 'neutral', etc); and another question might be to ask them whether they think the level of pay they receive is fair compared to the effort they put in, by putting the answer on a scale of 1 to 5, where 1 is 'very unfair' and 5 is 'very fair' (with 3 as neutral). Initial analysis may find a relationship between these two variables, and running the data through SPSS may tell us that the correlation between job satisfaction and pay fairness is r=0.4. Then an extremely rough regression formula might look like this:

Job satisfaction =
4 (neither satisfied nor dissatisfied) + 0.4 * (perceived fairness)

So if pay fairness was the main driver of job satisfaction and you did something at work that increased a sense of fairness (eg paid people a merit bonus), which increased a person's judgement of fairness by a response scale increase of 1 (for example representing a fairness increase from a 4 to a 5 on the response scale), then this should lead to a boost of their satisfaction levels by 0.40.

Now, if we take into account that having supportive co-workers (on a scale of 1 = 'very unsupportive' to 5 = 'very supportive'; with 3 as neutral) might be correlated with job satisfaction in a unique way and add that to the model in SPSS with pay fairness and job satisfaction, and the resultant correlation value is 0.3, we could add this to the equation as follows:

Job satisfaction =
4 (neither satisfied nor dissatisfied) + 0.4 * (perceived fairness) +
0.3 * (perceived co-worker support)

What this means is that the level of job satisfaction that someone feels increases by 0.4 for every one-point increase in perceived fairness, and increases by a further 0.3 for every one-point increase in perceived co-worker support.

So here we can start to build up a model that can help predict people's expected levels of job satisfaction, given the observed unique relationships that we find between perceived pay fairness, co-worker support and the general average levels of satisfaction in our organization. If we have the necessary data and we have identified predictive models from our analysis we can add other factors that are found to be important predictors of job satisfaction such as perceived organizational support, job autonomy and job variety. The same logic can be applied to a model that tries to predict the prevalence of BAME in our teams across our organization.

In our HR analytics example, we want to use multiple regression to determine what factors appear to predict a low prevalence of BAME individuals in teams. What is especially useful about multiple regression is that it can help you to establish the relationship between the dependent variable (BAME percentage in this case) and multiple possible predictor variables, in this case: base location, function, group size, team lead gender and team gender breakdown.

But that is not all. It will also help you to examine just how much each predictor variable has an impact on the dependent variable on its own (for example, after taking function and percentage 'male' into account, we may wish to know the extent to which team location, on its own, predicts the prevalence of BAME). And, finally, it will help show which of the predictor variables has the greatest impact on the dependant variable; this will give us the key information we need to identify where the problem areas are, and then to define a bespoke solution for the organization.

Next let's look at whether we can find predictors of BAME – using multiple regression.

Going into SPSS: again with our data file *'Chapter 4Diversity Case Group Level Data.Sav'*, go to the 'Analyze' menu option and select 'Regression' and then 'Linear' (see Figure 4.14).

### FIGURE 4.14

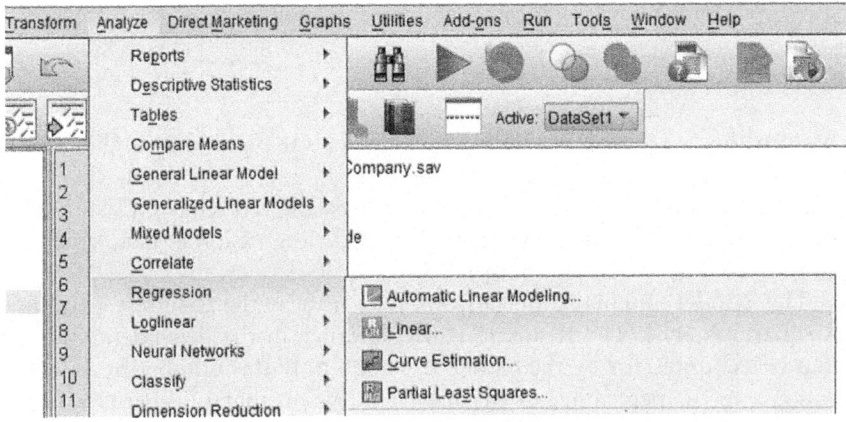

The variable we want to investigate predictors for is BAME, so we note that down as our dependent variable. In this example, variables we have in our data set that we want to test for as to whether they have an impact on BAME prevalence in teams are:

- LondonorNot (whether the team is located in London).
- Function (which function – Sales or Professional Service).
- GroupSize (the number of employees in the team).
- NumberFeMaleTeamLeads (number of team leads in the team who were female).
- PercentMale (percentage of the team made up of males).

So these are our independent variables.

We select the BAME variable from the list of variables in our data set (set out in the left-hand box in Figure 4.15); using the arrow button, insert it into our 'Dependent' option box. We then select the variables: LondonorNot, Function, GroupSize, NumberFeMaleTeamLead and PercentMale and click them into the 'Independent(s):' box (again, see Figure 4.15).

**FIGURE 4.15**

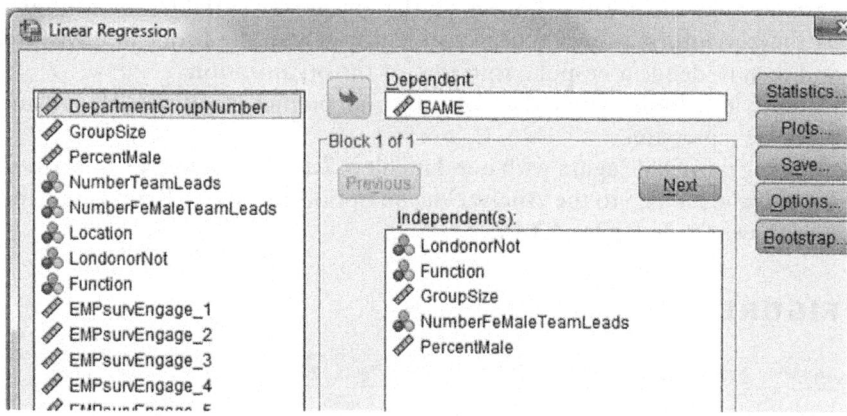

We run this regression model by clicking on 'OK' and we get the output shown in Figure 4.16.

The first table in Figure 4.16, 'Variables entered/removed', shows us which predictor variables were entered into the regression model, which are all the variables we entered into SPSS.

The 'Model Summary' output box tells us that the R-square (Multiple R-square) is .174. The R-square is the variance in the dependent variable that is accounted for by the model. If we multiply this number by 100 that will give us the percentage of variance. This means that 17.4 per cent of the variance in BAME prevalence across the teams (the 700+ that we have BAME data for) in our organization is accounted for by its shared relationship with the independent variables (ie whether they are in London or another location, whether they are sales staff or professional services staff, the number of employees in the work unit, the number of female team leads in the work unit, and the percentage of the overall work unit that are male) outlined above (whilst taking into account the degree to which the independent variables are amongst themselves related).

The regression ANOVA (analysis of variance) table tests whether the model that includes our five independent variables significantly predicts the prevalence of BAME. We say that the model 'accounts for variance in BAME' because, in theory, if the variables in the model change then the prevalence

## FIGURE 4.16

→ Regression

**Variables Entered/Removed[a]**

| Model | Variables Entered | Variables Removed | Method |
|---|---|---|---|
| 1 | Percentage of the work unit that are male, London or Other location, How many employees in the work unit, Number of female team leads in the work unit, Sales staff or Professional Services[b] | | Enter |

a. Dependent Variable: Percentage Black Asian and Minority Ethnic

b. All requested variables entered.

**Model Summary**

| Model | R | R-Square | Adjusted R-Square | Std. Error of the Estimate |
|---|---|---|---|---|
| 1 | .417[a] | .174 | .168 | .10331 |

a. Predictors: (Constant), Percentage of the work unit that are male, London or Other location, How many employees in the work unit, Number of female team leads in the work unit, Sales staff or Professional Services

**ANOVA[a]**

| Model | | Sum of Squares | df | Mean Square | F | Sig. |
|---|---|---|---|---|---|---|
| 1 | Regression | 1.627 | 5 | .325 | 30.492 | .000[b] |
| | Residual | 7.727 | 724 | .011 | | |
| | Total | 9.354 | 729 | | | |

a. Dependent Variable: Percentage Black Asian and Minority Ethnic

b. Predictors: (Constant), Percentage of the work unit that are male, London or Other location, How many employees in the work unit, Number of female team leads in the work unit, Sales staff or Professional Services

**Coefficients[a]**

| Model | | Unstandardized Coefficients | | Standardized Coefficients | t | Sig. |
|---|---|---|---|---|---|---|
| | | B | Std. Error | Beta | | |
| 1 | (Constant) | .199 | .028 | | 7.091 | .000 |
| | London or Other location | -.085 | .008 | -.361 | -10.674 | .000 |
| | Sales staff or Professional Services | .038 | .010 | .166 | 3.940 | .000 |
| | How many employees in the work unit | .000 | .000 | -.015 | -.427 | .669 |
| | Number of female team leads in the work unit | .000 | .004 | -.004 | -.118 | .906 |
| | Percentage of the work unit that are male | .000 | .000 | -.052 | -1.225 | .221 |

a. Dependent Variable: Percentage Black Asian and Minority Ethnic

of BAME will change; so variation in our independent variables can account for a significant degree of variance in our dependent variable.

The ANOVA table in Figure 4.16 shows the statistical significance of the regression (ANOVA) model. The F-value here is in effect a figure that is highly linked to the R-squared value, but it is the statistic that SPSS uses to obtain the level of significance that our model has, in terms of how good it is at predicting variation on BAME (greater than you might get if you were predicting variation in BAME prevalence across teams by random factors). SPSS gives us a significance value for our regression model with an F-value of 30.492, as being 0.000, or we would say $p<0.001$, which means there is less than 1 in 1,000 chance that we would get this result by chance alone, so the model is significant – we should use it!

But how do we know which variables had an impact on BAME? And, for that matter, which variables have the most impact? Let's look at the 'Coefficients' table in Figure 4.16.

There is a lot of information on this table, but to pull out the pieces that are of most use, and getting to grips with the fact that we are comfortable with SPSS calculating the significance level for us and that we trust it, let's look down the significance column (Sig.) in the coefficients table.

Here, we can see that the following two variables individually have a significant impact: 1) London or Other location; 2) Sales staff or Professional Services. The others are not contributing to the prediction of variation in BAME across teams in our organization in a meaningful way (these are factors that seem to be unrelated to BAME prevalence in our organization). So we can consider removing them from our model (though if our sample is big enough it is sometimes worthwhile leaving these factors in to make sure that any residual relationship they have with our other independent variables is factored out). Just looking at points 1) and 2) above, to what extent and in what way do they contribute?

Well, lucky for us, SPSS calculated standardized beta values, which give us this information. These are called standardized coefficients, or Beta values. The greater the beta value (positive or negative), the greater the potential impact that it has on the dependent variable.

So, looking at the Beta values for our two significant variables, we can see the following:

**1** Beta value for the 'London or Other location' variable is Beta=–0.361.

**2** Beta value for the 'Sales staff or Professional Services' variable is Beta=0.166.

This says that teams from the 'Sales' functions have a lower BAME prevalence compared to 'Professional Service' functions and London also has a higher BAME prevalence when taking the functional differences into account. Or, putting it another way:

> **Snapshot hidden gem**
>
> We have a significantly higher proportion of BAME in our teams within the 'Professional Service' functions as compared to 'Sales' teams even when we take into account that the diversity levels tend to be much higher in our London teams than our outside London teams. This is potentially very useful information given the fact that there tend to be rather large differences in the general population prevalence of BAME across different geographical locations.

The census chart shown in Figure 4.17, downloaded from the UK Race for Opportunity website, shows the percentage of BAME individuals in the workforce across different parts of the UK. These figures should be taken into account when assessing predictors of BAME in our organization across the teams.

In Figure 4.17, you can see that in London, for example, the percentage of BAME residents is over 40 per cent, whilst in the north-west it is only 9.8 per cent. So if all things were equal and our BAME representation in teams represented that of the local population then we might expect to find this pattern. Importantly, however, when we take the geographical differences into account across our organization we still find a big tendency for a lesser prevalence of BAME in our 'Sales' function compared to 'Professional 'Services'.

# Testing the impact of diversity: interacting diversity categories in predictive modelling

One of the key things that an HR analytics master will consider doing with regard to D&I is to see whether variation in important HR-related outcomes such as engagement, turnover, sickness absence and performance might be 'predicted' by particular categories/groups of interest to the D&I specialist. Also whether certain predictive models work in the same way for particular categories. Because in these analyses diversity is being used as a predictor of these important HR-related business outcomes, the predictive models for these will be outlined in other case study chapters within this book, and we discuss conducting analysis with interactions in Chapter 11. We also focus on additional diversity analyses in our case study in Chapter 8 (recruitment and selection).

**FIGURE 4.17** Percentage of BAME individuals in the UK workforce

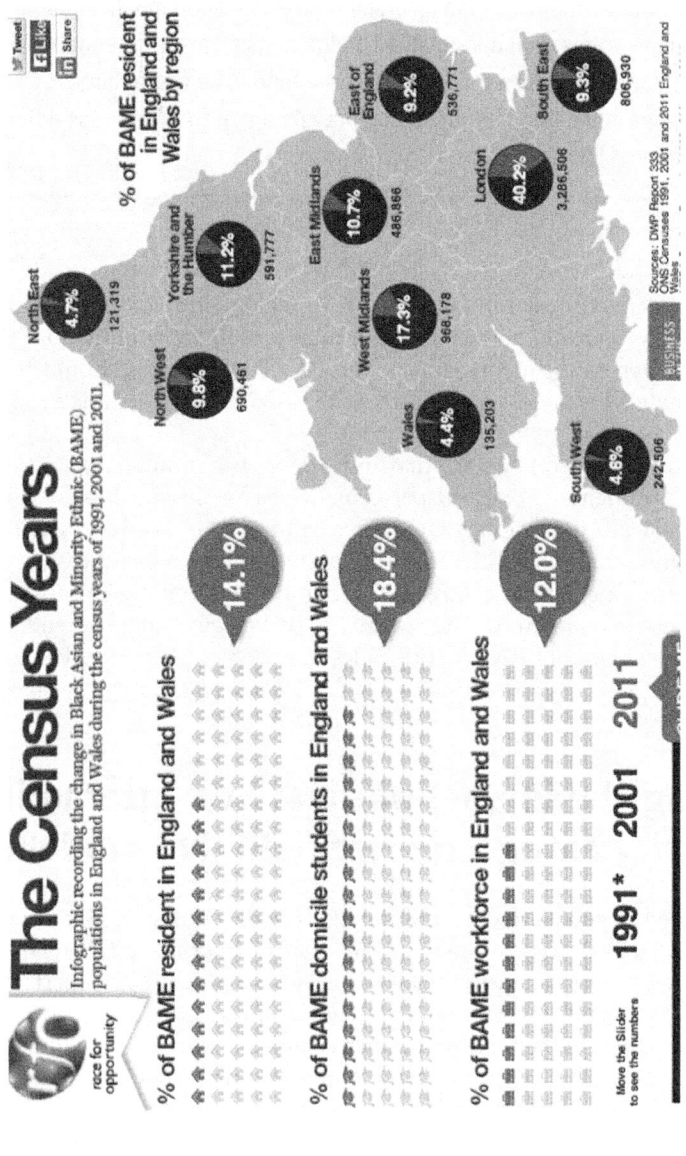

**SOURCE:** Business in the Community, Race for Opportunity:
http://raceforopportunity.bitc.org.uk/research_insight/ethnic_minority_fact_sheets

# A final note

Throughout this chapter we have discussed common approaches to measuring and managing D&I and worked through two examples covering ethnicity and gender. It is important to note here that this is just the tip of the iceberg when it comes to what can and should be measured as part of a comprehensive D&I programme. Many easily observed indices of diversity include gender and ethnicity as well as disabilities, age, marital status and sexual orientation. The management of diversity reaches far more broadly than exploring these primary characteristics; secondary characteristics include factors such as parental status, social status, nationality, language, accent, communication style, appearance, location, hobbies, educational background, religion – and even the department a person works in the organization itself can lead to bias.

As mentioned at the beginning of this chapter, the ability to quantify the benefits of having a diverse and inclusive organization is the number-one key challenge in the diversity business case. In this chapter, we have used frequency tables, chi-square analysis, independent samples t-tests and multiple linear regression to model, predict and investigate diversity data. These methods can be applied to any diversity characteristics for which there is data available and, as we discuss in Chapter 11, can be used in a business case.

# References

CEB Corporate Leadership Council [accessed May 2013] Creating Competitive Advantage Through Workforce Diversity [Online] https://clc.executiveboard.com/Public/Default.aspx

Kandola, B and Fullerton, J (1998) *Diversity in Action: Managing the mosaic*, Chartered Institute of Personnel and Development, London

Noon, M (2010) Managing equality and diversity, in *Human Resource Management: A contemporary approach*, ed J Beardwell and T Claydon, FT Prentice Hall, Edinburgh

Race for Opportunity (2010) [accessed November 2014] Aspiration and Frustration [Online] http://diversity.bitc.org.uk/research-insight/research-articles/aspiration-and-frustration

### *Use of BAME*

The term BAME, widely used in the UK to refer to members of the non-white community, may soon be outdated. In the absence of a widely agreed alternative at the time of writing however, we will continue to use it throughout this book.

# Case study 2
# Employee attitude surveys – engagement and workforce perceptions

05

Over the last decade or so, the idea of employee engagement has become one of the key people issues discussed at executive and senior manager level. Having engaged employees can be seen as one of the key objectives to which HR functions are expected to strive. With an enormous amount of literature written about it (including a UK government-sponsored research report (Macleod and Clarke, 2009) and vast amounts of money being spent on it, from an HR analytics point of view), employee engagement is something that HR professionals, people managers and students of HR or management need to be highly knowledgeable about.

In order to access levels of engagement within their organizations many large corporates will use external research companies such as Towers Watson, Gallup, Mercer and Hay Group, to name just a few, whilst others design and run their own employee engagement surveys. Regarding the former, this chapter will talk through how to get the most out of working with these external providers, understanding what they are doing for the organization, and asking the right questions to get meaningful results and outcomes. After reading this chapter you will understand their methods, which will make for a far more productive working relationship. Regarding the latter, this chapter will help you if you want to design your own in-house employee engagement survey; it will help you to ensure that the questions that you are measuring are tapping what you want them to measure using validity and reliability testing, and how to interpret the results when you run models to predict employee engagement. Ultimately, this chapter will help you to get the outcome you want for your organization.

You may choose to use a combination of the above. For example, your organization may use an external research company for the larger employee engagement survey and then you may use the methods below to structure ongoing 'pulse' surveys on a subset of the population such as one division that had particularly low engagement scores.

In this chapter, we cover the following:

- What is employee engagement?
- How is it measured?
- Interrogating the measures.
- Results, analysis and outcomes.
- Actions and business context.

## What is employee engagement?

There is, quite simply, no agreed definition of employee engagement. MacLeod and Clarke (2009) quote David Guest, professor of organizational psychology and human resource management at King's College London, as pointing out that 'much of the discussion of engagement tends to get muddled as to whether it is an attitude, a behaviour or an outcome or, indeed, all three' and that 'the concept of employee engagement needs to be more clearly defined... or it needs to be abandoned'. The research report then goes on to discuss that 'there is too much momentum and indeed excellent work being done under the banner of employee engagement to abandon the term'. Undeniably, academics and HR professionals (including professional survey companies that make a business out of employee engagement) have very different ideas about what engagement is.

Within the world of academic research, two main definitions of engagement are used. One of the first to be presented is a measure of 'behavioural work engagement' by Kahn (1990). Defined as: 'the simultaneous employment and expression of a person's "preferred self" in task behaviours that promote connections to work and to others, personal presence (physical, cognitive, and emotional) and active, full performances' (1990: 700). An example of a scale used to measure this (Rich, LePine and Crawford, 2010) includes survey questions based on physical, emotional, and cognitive engagement.

A second measure used in academia is a measure of 'work engagement' referred to as the Utrecht Work Engagement Scale (UWES) and defined as 'a positive, fulfilling work-related state of mind that is characterized by vigour, dedication and absorption' (Schaufeli and Bakker, 2003). The full questionnaire scale items used to measure this can be found in Schaufeli and Bakker (2010) and on the following web page: **http://www.wilmarschaufeli.nl/publications/Schaufeli/Tests/UWES_GB_17.pdf**.

In the world of HR professionals and consultancies a number of different definitions also exist, for example:

From consultancies:

- Mercer (2011) defines employee engagement as: 'A psychological state in which employees feel a vested interest in the company's success and are both willing and motivated to perform to levels that exceed the stated job requirements.'
- The Hay Group Insights Employee Effectiveness Framework defines employee engagement as a function of commitment and discretionary effort (Hay Group, 2012).
- Towers Watson (2012) defines employee engagement as 'the willingness and ability to go the extra mile'.

From businesses:

- 'Employee engagement is when the business values the employee and the employee values the business' (MacLeod and Clarke, 2009).

And even:

- 'You sort of smell it, don't you, that engagement of people as people. What goes on in meetings, how people talk to each other. You get the sense of energy, engagement, commitment, belief in what the organization stands for' (Lord Currie, cited in MacLeod and Clarke, 2009).

So, enough said. From the definitions, it seems that engagement is somewhere between being in the zone, feeling positive, enjoying work, feeling proud of it, having commitment to organizational success, going the extra mile, having a bit of energy around it all and feeling valued – or a combination of some or all of those things – depending on who you talk to.

In support of some of the extremely bold claims often found in the practitioner literature, a considerable amount of research has been carried out to explore the importance of engagement; this research seems to show a consistent pattern in that engagement tends to be positively correlated with both task and contextual performance, well-being measures and negatively related to intention to quit (see Table 5.1).

To recap on correlation, it shows the relationship between two variables. Because the p-value is <0.001 for all outcomes, we know that the relationship is significant. Looking at each variable in turn and remembering with correlations that the magnitude of correlation ranges from 0 to 1 with 1 the highest, we can see that task performance and contextual performance have a moderate positive relationship with engagement. So we might *infer* from this (remembering that correlation does not *imply* causality) that when engagement goes up, task performance (performance on work activities) and contextual performance (performance on social workplace behaviours) goes up a moderate amount. Health has a weaker, but significant positive relationship with engagement; so when engagement goes up, health and well-being go up by a small amount. Finally, voluntary turnover intention

**TABLE 5.1** Summary of research findings exploring the outcomes of engagement

| Outcomes | Corrected Correlations | Source |
| --- | --- | --- |
| Task performance | 0.43 | Study 1 (k = 14, N = 4562) |
| Contextual performance | 0.34 | Study 1 (k = 10, N = 3654) |
| Health | 0.20 | Study 2 (k = 17, N = 11593) |
| Turnover intention | −0.26 | Study 2 (k = 4, N = 1893) |

k = number of unique samples; N = total sample size. For all correlations p< 0.001
**SOURCE:** Peccei (2013)

(the measurement of whether employees plan to leave their position) has a weak, but significant, negative relationship with intention to leave; so when engagement goes down, intentions to leave the organization go up by a small degree.

# How do we measure employee engagement?

Employee engagement is not a tangible idea, so it cannot be measured as easily as, say, salary, sales performance figures or attendance at leadership training.

The only way to gather information about how engaged an individual might be is to ask them. Rather than just having a one-question survey with the question 'how engaged are you?', to which the answer would be as variable as each individual's own definition of employee engagement, thus rendering the survey useless, we can ask a range of questions that will indicate to us how engaged that person is, based on the definitions we choose. Asking someone 'how engaged are you?' could lead to a wide variety of responses depending upon what the respondent had in their head when thinking about engagement. Some people, for example, might answer the question in the context of how long they had been engaged to their future marriage partner. Asking a range of questions specifically designed to measure a range of aspects associated with what we mean by 'engagement' ensures that the researcher has some control over the measurement of engagement and can (to some extent) ensure that the idea of engagement in the employees' heads is as defined. This means that we can compare across the organization in a controlled and measured way and that we find out what we need to. We will discuss later in this chapter about how to choose questions in order to be sure we are measuring what we want to measure.

As an example of a range of questions that we could use, let's look at one of the academic definitions of employee engagement mentioned previously: behavioural work engagement and the associated Rich, LePine and Crawford (2010) set of questions. These questions are fully tested and validated measures of engagement. The full set of 17 questions can be found in Rich, LePine and Crawford (2010), but to give you a quick view, below is a sample:

Employees answer questions on a five-point response scale ranging from 1 'strongly disagree' to 5 'strongly agree', with the statements:

- 'I exert my full effort to my job' [measuring physical engagement].
- 'I am proud of my job' [measuring emotional engagement].
- 'At work, my mind is focused on my job' [measuring cognitive engagement].

The other academic engagement example presented above, the UWES (Schaufeli and Bakker, 2003), also uses 17 questions. The full set of questions can be found in Schaufeli and Bakker (2010), but to give you a quick view, below is a sample (again on a response scale from 'strongly disagree' to 'strongly agree'):

- 'When I get up in the morning, I feel like going to work' [vigour].
- 'My job inspires me' [dedication].
- 'Time flies when I'm working' [absorption].

Interestingly, professional measures of engagement used by consultancies and survey companies tend to be quite different from those used in academic research. Examples of some of the main measures used include the Q12 measure used by Gallup and an employee engagement measure used by Towers Watson.

The Q12 measure, although often mistaken for a measure of employee engagement, does not actually measure engagement; according to Gallup it measures: 'the actionable issues for management – those predictive of attitudinal outcomes such as satisfaction, loyalty, pride and so on'. Unfortunately the items cannot be presented here as a scale because Gallup has a copyright associated with their 12 questions (although, as mentioned, examples of similar individual items can be found in freely available measures presented by academic researchers over a number of decades), but the Gallup questions can be found relatively easily with a simple internet search of 'Gallup Q12 questions'. Also, interested readers should read the chapter by Schaufeli and Bakker (2010) where these researchers set out both the Q12 and the UWES scales, along with a discussion of the psychometric properties of these measures.

A brief examination of the Q12 items shows that the 12 true/false questions measure a wide scope of issues (eg having a good friend in the workplace; whether resources are made available; whether there are opportunities for development and growth, etc). Importantly, the Q12 is not an engagement measure as such but more of a measure that aims to tap a range of issues associated with employee engagement. Gallup presents some meta-analysis results that also, similar to the research conducted by academics, shows a consistently positive relationship with the Q12 measure and performance (Gallup, 2008).

One other example of professional survey companies' measures of employee engagement is a scale by Towers Watson, whose conceptualization of engagement includes employees having a belief in company goals and objectives, an emotional connection with the organization, and a willingness to give extra effort to support success. A definition such as this will have a number of links with traditional measures of organizational commitment, which has been heavily researched in the academic field for many decades.

Below is an example of some questions taken from one validated organizational commitment scale (Allen and Meyer, 1990), measured on a five-point scale ranging from 'strongly disagree' to 'strongly agree':

- 'I would not recommend a close friend to join this organization.'
- 'I am extremely glad that I chose this organization to work for, over others I was considering at the time I joined.'
- 'I really feel as if this organization's problems are my own.'

So whether you are designing your own survey questionnaire or partnering with a consultancy to run an employee survey (so as to benchmark measures), you need to be sure that the questions included in your employee survey are good indicators of what you are trying to measure (and that they are reliable). How can you be sure about this?

Before answering this we shall make the following assumptions:

- You want to survey your employee base to find out what people are thinking, feeling and doing.
- You want to measure the attitudes and perceptions that you think you are measuring.
- You presumably want to conduct a survey in order to take prescriptive action based on meaningful findings.
- You do not want to waste everyone's time with unreliable measures or meaningless results.
- You do not want to waste money on expensive interventions carried out based on recommendations from meaningless survey results.

In short, it is absolutely worth the time and effort to understand how to interrogate the measures.

# Interrogating the measures

## Interrogating measures of engagement and associated constructs used in surveys

Put simply, a good measure of a concept (such as engagement) is one that accurately and consistently taps the degree to which employees vary or differ on that concept. So a good measure of engagement will accurately and consistently identify when employees vary in engagement.

To fully understand what makes a good measure, we need to refer to a few central ideas linked to survey measurement theory. Yes, we are referring to 'theory'. When an academic starts talking about theory, practitioners often roll their eyes because there is a danger that it will not have any practical relevance. However, here the words of Kurt Lewin apply: 'there is nothing more practical than a good theory' (1952: 169). Measurement theory argues (amongst a range of things) that a measure has two key ideas linked to it: a 'construct' and an 'indicator'. The construct is the idea that the measure is trying to tap into. In the example above, the construct is 'engagement' and an example indicator could be the statement 'I am proud of my job', which leads to a 1–5 response. To ensure rigorous measurement, one indicator is not enough on its own. Just as you would look at many indicators when trying to assess whether a potential candidate is likely to be a good new hire (such as CV, online profile, performance at interview, assessment-centre results, references and recommendations, etc), it is necessary to look at many indicators when trying to ascertain the levels of engagement.

When presenting a measure of a construct a survey provider/consultancy should be able to clearly explain exactly what that construct entails: they should be able to present a clear definition of exactly what they are attempting to measure, and the indicators they are using to do so. If, as with engagement, this construct refers to a state or trait expected to be inside an employee, then a construct is referring to a state in someone's head (or maybe even somewhere else in their body... but let's not get drawn into some abstract Cartesian dualistic debate about whether 'my body is my mind' and 'my mind is my body'). Importantly, a measure of engagement should tap into how engaged someone is, or their state of engagement. Hence the construct is what we are trying to measure.

The measure will have an indicator; an indicator is what is used to gauge the construct in employees' heads. A question, or a range of questions, in a survey will be the 'indicator' or 'indicators'; importantly, the questions are used to *indicate* the level of the construct in the employees' heads (this is quite an important point in measurement theory).

So if, for example, we have a question in a questionnaire that requires employees to answer on a 1–5 'strongly disagree' to 'strongly agree' response scale with the statement 'I am fully engaged', then the idea is that the number an employee chooses – 1, 2, 3, 4 or 5 – will 'indicate' the degree of engagement that the employee feels (in their heads... or heart, depending upon how one conceptualizes engagement). So in our organization, employees will vary in their answers to this question: some will say 1, some 2, some 3, some 4 and some 5. A good measure of engagement, with precise indicators, will produce 'accurate' variation in the numbers recorded in the survey. If, for example, the wording of the question was complex or confusing, the results across employees may vary depending on how well the person understands the question. This would be an imprecise measure of engagement and hence the results will be quite inaccurate. So, by accurate here we mean that engagement levels vary in employees' heads, and the variation that our survey records indicate will correspond closely to the variation in employees' heads.

Of course, it is unlikely that any indicator will indicate or gauge engagement in employees' heads perfectly. This is where classical test theory comes in and has a very practical relevance to HR analytics.

## Classical test theory and construct measurement

Classical test theory can be used to further understand the mechanics of measurement testing. Before proceeding, it is worth adding that we should also consider things that might influence how someone will respond to survey questions that are outside the survey questions themselves. For example, did the person just have a particularly bad commute? Were they just involved in a meeting where they found out their project had been cancelled? Did they just receive news that they have been nominated for promotion? Or perhaps their partner just left them because they have been spending too much time at work? There is a strong possibility that provocations like this could influence their answer to the question.

Classical test theory considers all the types of influences discussed. It can be represented as follows:

$$X = t + e$$

Where each set of survey results contain a $\underline{t}$rue component and an $\underline{e}$rror component:

- X = set of survey results – the degree to which the numbers produced in our survey records vary (ie the engagement survey results).
- t = true component: an indication of $\underline{t}$rue variation in levels of engagement in employees' heads.
- e = error component: measurement $\underline{e}$rror.

So the numbers produced in the survey and the degree to which these numbers vary in our survey records will be made up of two things: 1) some indication of true variation in feelings (or states) of engagement in employees' heads; and 2) measurement error.

Or, put another way:

Variation in employee answers to survey questions =
variation in actual true engagement levels + some error.

If an indicator is a bad measure of a construct, then the error will be large. Variation will exist in the numbers recorded in our survey records that does not correspond with actual true variation in engagement amongst our employees. This variation can be considered 'measurement error'. So with $X=t+e$, variation from our indicator is made up of true variation in our construct plus error in our measure; a very simple notion really. Despite the theory, this is a very practical idea, as it raises the issue that a company's engagement survey may produce engagement results that have some degree of error in the measurement of engagement...

The main aim of measurement testing is to try to tease out, separate and identify $e$ from $t$ in order to establish whether $X$ is a good measure of our construct.

## *What is a good (valid) measure?*

A good measure is one that has indicators that accurately tap the construct under investigation. Importantly, the first thing that is needed to ensure a good measure is a clear definition of what the construct actually is. Only if we have this can we hope to understand whether an associated measure is good. By good, we mean valid. Validity refers to whether the measure accurately represents the construct intended, for example, whether the survey questions intended to ascertain whether an employee is engaged actually do measure whether an employee is engaged. In measurement model testing there are a number of different types of validity, as set out below.

### Face validity

Face validity is more an art than science. It is not measured in any sophisticated statistical way, rather it relies on an experienced professional who knows and understands the construct to cast their steely eye over the indicators, consider them carefully, and say something like 'Yes, on the face of it, these indicators seem to be good measures of the construct.' The notion of face validity revolves around the idea that the indicators actually look as if they should measure the construct at hand. When factor and reliability analyses are conducted, the results can often tell us whether any particular questions might be problematic (see below). When this happens, we can carefully read the items and make a sensible judgement about whether they might be tapping another construct instead of the one we are trying to measure.

### Construct validity

Construct validity is when the indicators do actually measure the construct at hand, and we know this because they behave analytically in a way that we would expect them to behave. We will cover below how to determine this and what it looks like. In our example, we would want our measure of engagement to show good factor analysis structure, good reliability statistics and tend to correlate with other measures (eg performance scores and supervisor ratings of motivation) in a way that we would expect. We will cover these later in this chapter.

### Discriminant validity

The notion of discriminant validity revolves around the idea that the measures actually demonstrate that they are *not* measuring some other construct. We could determine this by using factor analysis, or by analysing a correlation matrix of all measures in a data set, both of which will tell us the relationships that the measure has with other variables.

For example, if one of our measures of engagement is a question about having pride in the organization, we would expect it to correlate highly with other engagement measures, but not quite so high with non-engagement measures such as performance scores, 360-degree feedback ratings, or answers to other questions about leadership effectiveness.

### Criterion validity

After performing statistical tests, do the measures demonstrate the appropriate degree of statistical robustness that tells us they are measuring the construct?

## *Measure contamination*

Measure contamination is when the measures are actually sharing variance with other constructs due to imprecise measurement, measurement error and inaccurate indicators.

# Conceptual explanation of factor analysis

The basic idea behind factor analysis in relation to survey research is actually very simple. It is a form of analysis that helps check that questionnaire items in a survey are actually measuring the construct that they are supposed to be measuring, rather than other constructs. Well, that is the simple explanation, though in reality it is a little more complicated. The analysis examines the pattern of respondents' answers to a set of questionnaire items to see if responses follow a particular pattern. If responses to a certain set of questions (specifically designed to measure a particular construct) tend to group together then this provides some evidence that the items are measuring this construct. The example below should help to make this clearer as to why this is the case. Conceptually, you would expect all the questions about the same construct to yield a similar answer – a perhaps overly simple example might be:

Employee questionnaire:

1 Do you feel your line manager guides you in your career?
2 Do you feel your line manager cares about your development?
3 Do you feel your line manager does all he/she can to help you be successful?
4 Is your working environment hygienically clean?
5 Do you feel you need a shower after you leave the office?
6 Are there unexplained odours near your workstation?

Here, you would expect the responses to questions 1 to 3 to be similar because they seem to be all about measuring line manager support. Questions 4, 5 and 6, however, appear to be measuring something entirely different (office cleanliness?). So here you would expect items 1–3 to share variance (ie go up and down at the same time – probably depending on whether the line manager is supportive); and items 4–6 to share variance (ie go up and down at the same time probably based on what sort of office environment people have), but you would not expect 1–3 to share variance with 4–6 (although having said this, if the employees' line manager regularly spilled a Thai curry lunch over his or her subordinates, there might be some shared variance across the items; presumably this would be rare, so the amount of shared variance in the data set across these two sets of items would still be limited). It is clear here that the questions are not all tapping into the same construct.

The next example is more similar to what you would see in an employee engagement survey. Note that this is *not* a recognized engagement scale and the authors have created items loosely based on questions used by various researchers to present as an example here.

So let's say that a survey provider has a questionnaire with the following nine questions that are supposed to measure employees' 'engagement'. The response scale ranges from 1 to 5 where 1 = strongly disagree and 5 = strongly disagree:

1 I work with full intensity in my job [intensity].
2 I try my hardest to perform as well as I can in my work [performance].
3 I concentrate really hard in my job [concentration].
4 My mind is always totally focused on my job [focus].
5 I strive very hard to complete my work as well as I can [quality].
6 Time flies at work [absorption].
7 I would recommend this organization as a place to work [recommend].
8 I feel a sense of belonging with my organization [belonging].
9 I am proud of the work I do [pride].

If this is a good and valid multi-item measure of engagement then we would expect respondents to answer all questions in a similar way (ie to give a similar point on the 1 to 5 scale for all nine items).

If people had very low levels of engagement, we might expect them to answer 1 or 2 on most of these items, and people who are highly engaged to answer 4 or 5 on most of these. The important point is that if the items truly gauge the state of engagement in the employee's head, their individual responses should not vary too much across all these items. We would expect some variation, but the pattern of responses should be reasonably consistent across the items for each person if it is tapping into a single construct of engagement.

See Figure 5.1, which is a diagrammatic representation of a construct of engagement where employees' responses to the nine items above are generally consistent across the nine items because they neatly tap the state of engagement in their heads.

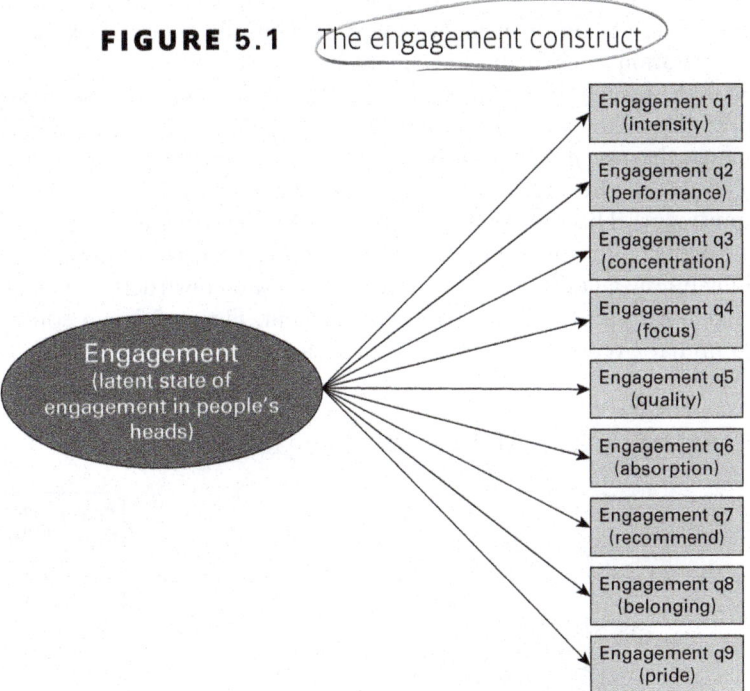

**FIGURE 5.1** The engagement construct

Factor analysis will enable us to examine the extent to which people respond in a consistent pattern across the nine questions. It will then confirm one of four outcomes:

1  The question responses show a consistent pattern (and indeed form a good measure of engagement).
2  The question responses do not show a consistent pattern (and hence the questions are not a good measure of engagement).
3  The question responses show a consistent pattern across some of the items but not all (this could suggest that some of the items form a good measure of engagement but some do not).

**4** The question responses show a consistent pattern across two or more sets of items (this might suggest that our measure actually taps more than one construct).

If the items used here actually measure more than one construct then the factor analysis will tell you this. It might be the case that some of the questions were badly designed and these badly designed items actually measured something other than engagement. This would be evident in analysing the pattern of responses, as you will see in the example below.

The analysis may indicate that there were two sets of responses found, suggesting that the scale was measuring two separate constructs rather than one single construct of engagement. If a two-construct pattern was found then it may also be the case that the designer of the survey actually defined engagement with two separate notions, ie with some items designed to measure one notion or element of engagement and other items measuring another notion or element of engagement.

So if we defined 'engagement' as a combination of 'organizational engagement' and 'psychological job engagement', we might actually design some items to gauge the psychological job engagement (eg mental focus) and design others to tap the organizational engagement aspect (eg organizational commitment). This may then lead to a two-factor structure being identified in the pattern of responses rather than a single factor. The analysis would be picking up the fact that we are measuring two sub-constructs of engagement or two slightly different forms of engagement. Figure 5.2 is a conceptual/diagrammatic representation of such a scenario.

**FIGURE 5.2**  Two-'sub-factor' engagement structure

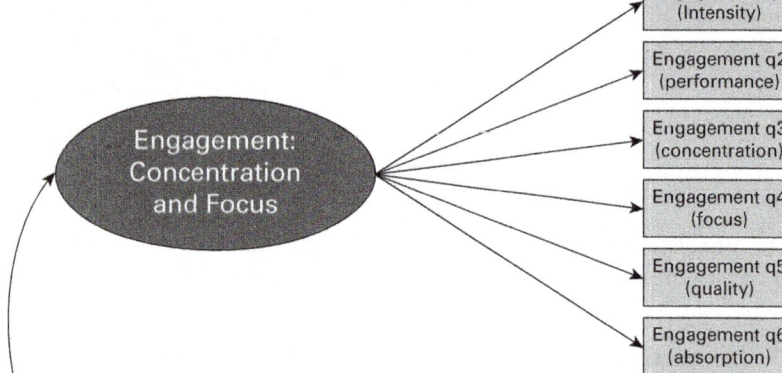

The state of engagement that the survey provider is working with in the case of Figure 5.2 (see questionnaire items listed previously) is made up of two slightly different ideas: mental concentration in people's heads when they engage in their job, and the degree to which these employees feel a sense of engagement with their organization or 'organizational commitment'. If the engagement scale has three items that ask questions more around organizational engagement and six items that focus on mental engagement linked to concentration, people's answers on these two subsets are likely to be slightly different – factor analysis can pick this up and identify that there are two sub-factors to our engagement scale.

So if a multi-item measure is actually measuring more than one construct, factor analysis will identify this. Factor analysis can also be used to check that different measures, designed to gauge different constructs, actually do seem to be measuring different constructs. For example, we could have nine items designed to measure engagement in a questionnaire (above) and four items designed to measure whether employees feel that their line manager is supportive, by asking the following four questions on the same scale:

- My line manager supports me (support).
- My line manager helps me out when I am faced with difficulties (help).
- My line manager gives me good guidance when I really need it (guidance).
- My line manager knows how to get the best out of me (best).

We could use factor analysis to ensure that the 13 items measure two separate constructs. We would expect that there may be some differences in how people tend to respond to the four 'manager' items as compared to the nine engagement items. If our items are measuring these two constructs then this should happen. See Figure 5.3.

One of the things that an HR analytics expert needs to be able to assess, with regard to either their own in-house engagement survey or with engagement surveys provided by external providers, is the degree to which items grouped together to form a single combined composite measure are actually measuring the unified construct (ie the degree to which these questions are actually measuring engagement of a range of different mental states). The composite measure that a survey provider presents is likely to be an aggregate average score for engagement derived from responses to the range of questions intended to measure engagement, perhaps called an 'engagement index'.

Putting our above definitions of validity into practice, the items should have *face validity*, in that they look like the kind of questions that would measure 'engagement' in accordance with the definition used. However, the construct also needs to demonstrate *criterion validity* in that the factor analysis statistics (calculated using SPSS in the two-construct example below) demonstrate that the items do indeed 'load' together to measure a single factor. Also, the *criterion validity* should demonstrate that the engagement scale separates from other measures used and, finally, when combined as a composite should demonstrate different magnitudes of correlations with other constructs compared to any other scale, showing that the scale demonstrates *discriminant validity*.

**FIGURE 5.3** Two-factor structure: engagement and manager support

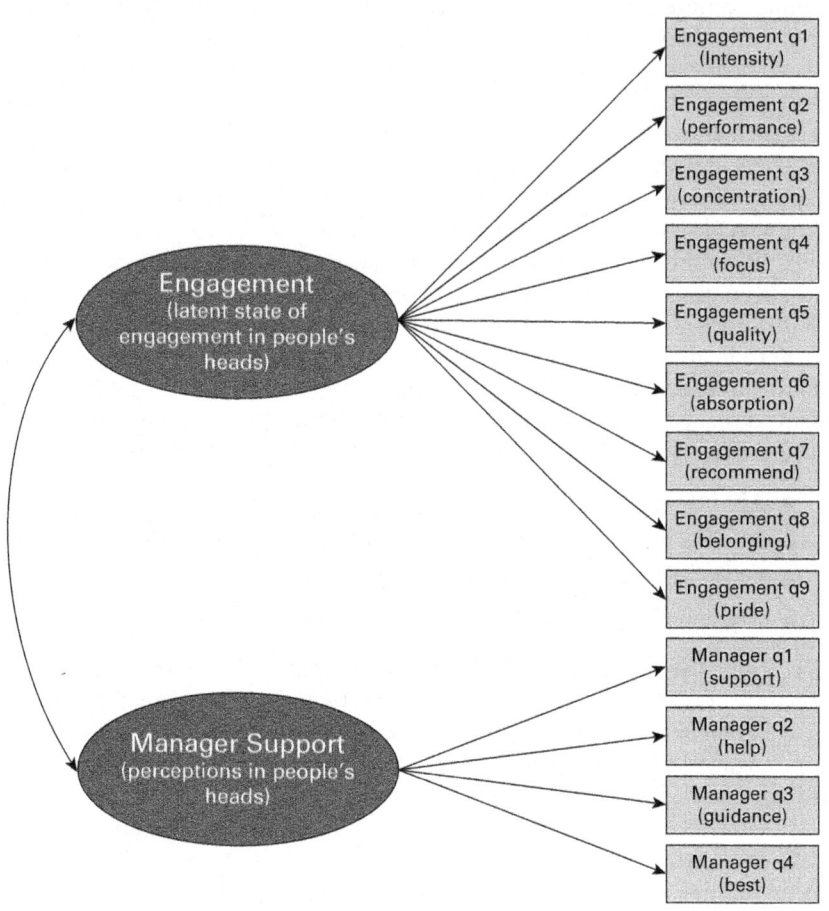

# Example 1: two constructs – exploratory factor analysis

In this section we will be using the SPSS data file named 'Chapter 5 RAW Survey Results.sav'. In this file you will see 34 different variables that hold individual survey responses of 832 employees. The first five variables hold data linked to employees' demographic profiles and the remaining variables (6–34) are employee responses on a 1 'strongly disagree' to 5 'strongly agree' response scale for a range of specific questions (these are indicated). The variables are as follows:

1 Sex (gender).
2 jbstatus (job status).

Case Study 2

3 age (age category).
4 tenure (years in job).
5 ethnicity (ethnicity category).
6 ManMot1 – My manager motivates me.
7 ManMot2 – My manager knows how to get the most out of me.
8 ManMot3 – My manager encourages me to do my best.
9 ManMot4 – My manager is great.
10 ocb1 – I work harder than my job requires.
11 ocb2 – I put a huge amount of effort into my job.
12 ocb3 – I help out my teammates.
13 ocb4 – I go the extra mile.
14 aut1 – I have the freedom to choose how I work.
15 aut2 – I can decide how to work during the day.
16 aut3 – I am given enough leeway to get the job done.
17 Justice1 – Procedures are fair here.
18 Justice2 – Procedures are applied fairly.
19 Justice3 – Procedures are the same for all.
20 JobSat1 – I am satisfied in my job.
21 JobSat2 – My job is good.
22 Quit1 – I am thinking of leaving.
23 Quit2 – I am ready to look for other work.
24 Quit3 – I have looked for employment elsewhere in the last week.
25 Man1 – Management help workers out when they experience difficulties.
26 Man2 – Management supports employees who are faced with discrimination.
27 Man3 – Management acts decisively.
28 Eng1 – I share the values of this organization.
29 Eng2 – I am proud of this organization.
30 Eng3 – This organization is a big part of who I am.
31 Eng4 – I would recommend this organization as a place to work.
32 pos1 – This organization cares about my well-being.
33 pos2 – This organization is interested in my contribution.
34 pos3 – This organization is there for me when I need help.

In this analytic example, we use exploratory factor analysis to assess construct structure and criterion validity in a survey that has seven questions.

The survey includes the following seven questions, in which respondents are asked to answer on a scale of 1 to 5 where 1 = strongly agree and 5 =

strongly disagree (a word summary is given in brackets afterwards for reference purposes later):

1. I share the values of this organization (values).
2. I am proud of this organization (pride).
3. This organization is a big part of who I am (who I am).
4. I would recommend this organization as a place to work (recommend).
5. This organization cares about my well-being (cares).
6. This organization is interested in my contribution (interested).
7. This organization is there for me when I need help (helps).

Before we proceed, it is useful at this point to review the questions and reflect, based on your knowledge of this topic, whether you believe the questions look as though they might fall into two categories. We will come back to this point later.

So let's go into SPSS and perform factor analysis on the results. Go to the 'Analyze' menu and select 'Dimension Reduction', then the 'Factor' option (see Figure 5.4).

### FIGURE 5.4

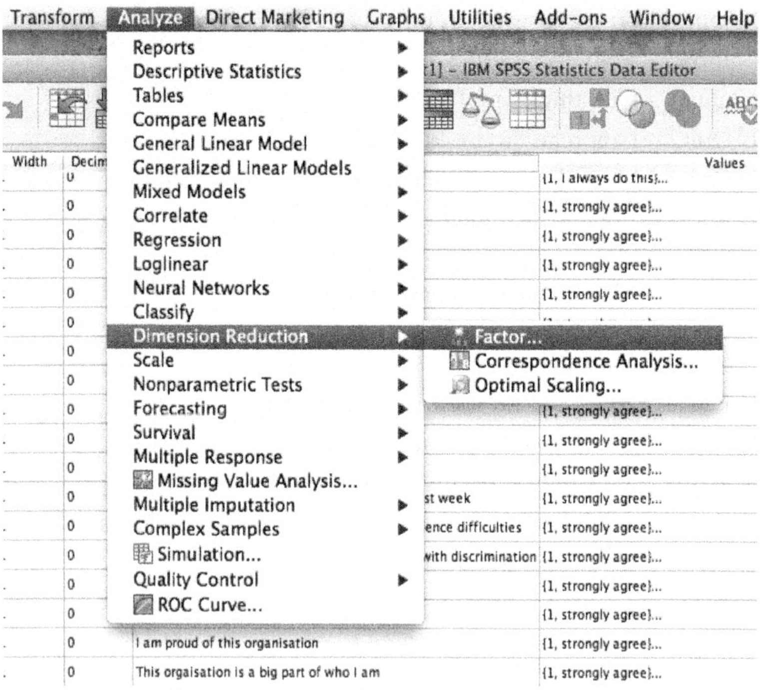

Next, select the seven relevant questions and move them over to the right-hand side 'Variables:' selection box using the arrow button. Then click on 'Rotation' (Figure 5.5).

**FIGURE 5.5** Selecting the variables

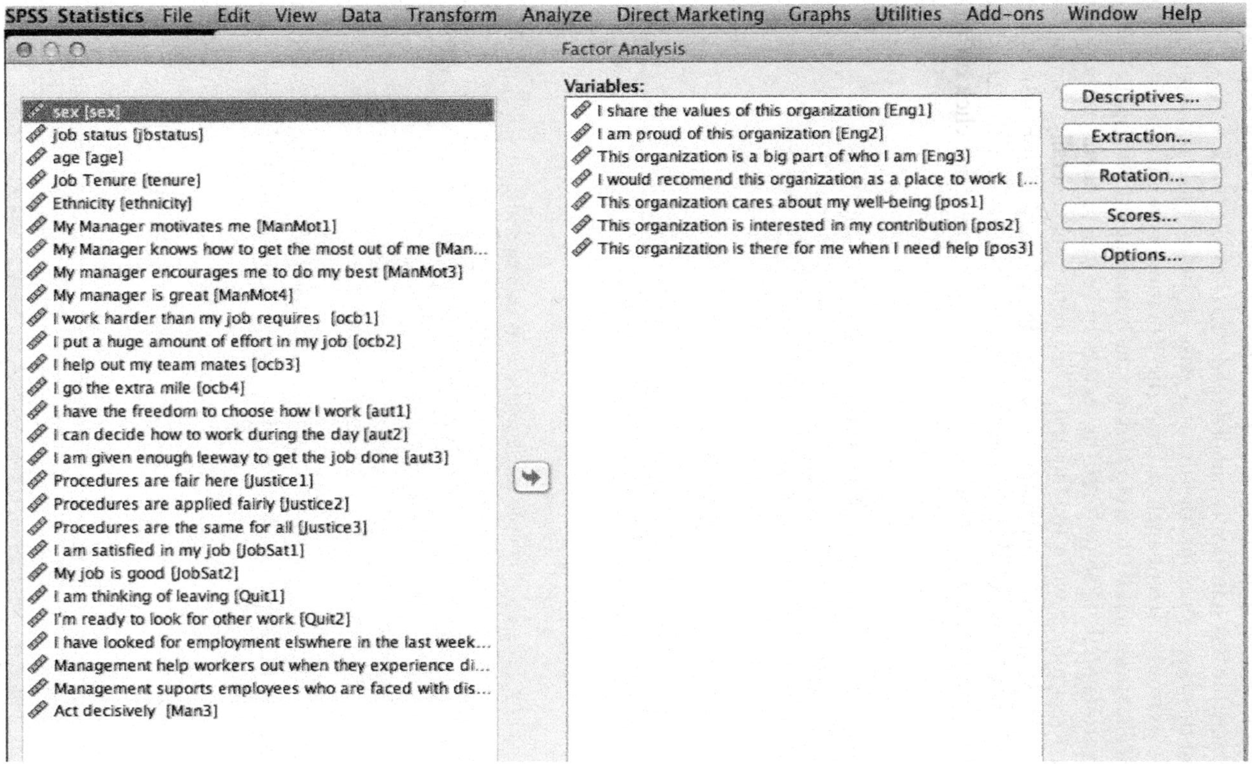

What we are doing here is selecting the items on which to perform factor analysis. By selecting 'Rotation', we will be preparing to tell SPSS to place (and rotate) the factors into the best possible position (this idea of rotation is a little complex to explain and there is a danger that the explanation may cause the less statistically minded reader to close the book; so let's just imagine, in this case, someone looking at a glass jar full of pink and white marshmallows from different angles). Once the 'Rotation' box is clicked, a dialogue box will appear, and we need to click on the button next to 'Varimax' (Figure 5.6). Varimax tells SPSS to force the factors to be independent (rather than allow correlation between the factors). This method is generally recommended as the most versatile and helps us to identify different factors where they exist. It would be useful, then, to see the 'Rotated solution' and the 'Loading plots', so select these in the display area as shown below. Then click on 'Continue' and then 'OK'.

**FIGURE 5.6** Rotation

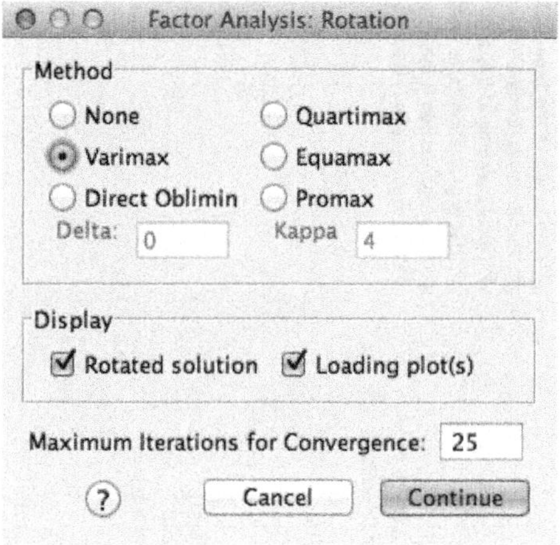


The output produced will include the 'Total Variance Explained' and the 'Rotated Component Matrix'. Let's take a look at 'Total Variance Explained' first (Figure 5.7):

**FIGURE 5.7** Factor analysis total variance explained

Eigenvalues

**Total Variance Explained**

| Component | Initial Eigenvalues | | | Extraction Sums of Squared Loadings | | | Rotation Sums of Squared Loadings | | |
|---|---|---|---|---|---|---|---|---|---|
| | Total | % of Variance | Cumulative % | Total | % of Variance | Cumulative % | Total | % of Variance | Cumulative % |
| 1 | 3.458 | 49.406 | 49.406 | 3.458 | 49.406 | 49.406 | 3.120 | 44.569 | 44.569 |
| 2 | 1.767 | 25.244 | 74.651 | 1.767 | 25.244 | 74.651 | 2.106 | 30.082 | 74.651 |
| 3 | .637 | 9.104 | 83.754 | | | | | | |
| 4 | .424 | 6.058 | 89.812 | | | | | | |
| 5 | .272 | 3.888 | 93.700 | | | | | | |
| 6 | .231 | 3.297 | 96.997 | | | | | | |
| 7 | .210 | 3.003 | 100.000 | | | | | | |

Extraction Method: Principal Component Analysis.

>1, groupings correspond to meaningful construct, so there is a factor we can use

SPSS has gone away and produced seven factors (which are different from the seven question items). These are called 'Components' in the table and basically group the question items together in various combinations to try to find if any of them seem to be measuring the same underlying construct. How does it know? Well, each time two variables behave similarly, we know they have a high correlation with each other. When SPSS produces a new component (grouping measure – such as engagement) then it will calculate the correlation that each item has with that component. These are called 'factor loadings'.

In order to determine which components should be included, SPSS calculates the square of the factor loadings and then adds them together to give what is called an eigenvalue. As a rule of thumb, if the eigenvalue is greater than one, you have a factor that you can use. If it is less than one, then this grouping of items does not correspond to a meaningful construct.

Looking at Figure 5.7, you can see that SPSS has calculated the eigenvalues for each of the seven factors. Only the first two factors have eigenvalues greater than one, so it has ignored the rest. Looking at component 1 (or factor 1), it has a total eigenvalue of 3.458 and accounts for 49.406 per cent of variance in the items. Component 2 (or factor 2) has a total eigenvalue of 1.767 and accounts for 25.244 per cent of the variance in the items.

Looking at the two together, the cumulative percentage value tells us that they both account for 74.651 of the variance in all of the items.

The next step is to identify which items (questions) load together into which factors. This is where the subsequent rotated component matrix (Figure 5.8) comes in. Figure 5.8 shows the loadings of each item on each component (factor) after they have been rotated. It is possible to see that the first four questions have high (above 0.6) factor loadings on component 1, and the bottom three questions have high factor loadings (above 0.6) on component 2.

**FIGURE 5.8**
Rotated component matrix

Rotated Component Matrix[a]

|  | Component 1 | Component 2 |
|---|---|---|
| I share the values of this organization | .844 | .105 |
| I am proud of this organization | .893 | .064 |
| This organization is a big part of who I am | .871 | .148 |
| I would recomend this organization as a place to work | .897 | .164 |
| This organization cares about my well-being | .188 | .689 |
| This organization is interested in my contribution | .050 | .876 |
| This organization is there for me when I need help | .092 | .895 |

Extraction Method: Principal Component Analysis.
Rotation Method: Varimax with Kaiser Normalization.

a. Rotation converged in 3 iterations.

Reviewing our questions, is this what you thought might happen? Looking at the first four questions, they do appear to be asking something a little bit similar to each other, but a little bit different to the bottom three questions.

In actual fact, the first four questions appear to be asking questions that could be about organizational engagement, whilst the final three questions appear to be asking questions about perceived organizational support (see Eisenberger *et al* (1986) for their full perceived organizational support (POS) measure).

In diagrammatic form, it would look like this:

**FIGURE 5.9**  Two-factor structure: engagement and perceived organizational support

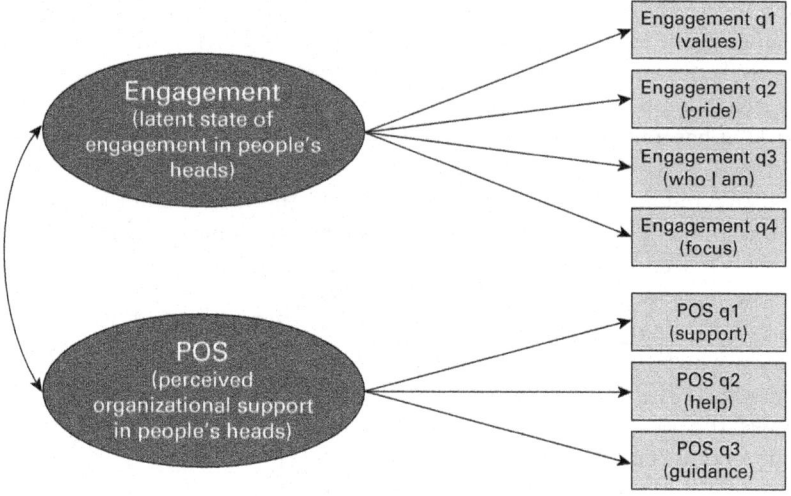

### Snapshot hidden gem

Our questions are measuring two latent variables: engagement and perceived organizational support.

The results of the survey can give the overall picture on these constructs as well as point towards areas/teams/regions that are doing well or not so well on these measures. And, although both constructs are related, and indeed low POS may contribute to low engagement, this information will be critical to decision making for taking action on specific areas to improve the overall level of engagement in the organization.

# Reliability analysis

Reliability analysis (internal consistency reliability in particular) shares a number of common ideas with factor analysis as a questionnaire testing technique in that it enables us to establish the degree to which respondents' answers to a specific set of survey items (eg the nine items from the engagement scale presented at the start of this chapter) tend to follow a similar pattern.

We would expect employee responses to follow a similar pattern across items with a scale when it is measuring a single construct – because the level of an idea, trait, attitude or perception in the person's head that we are trying to measure should end up causing them to respond in a similar way across all of the items designed to measure this idea (assuming the items measure this single idea).

If, as we suggested above, a person's engagement level or the degree of engagement that they 'have' is actually something in their heads, then this degree of engagement will compel them to answer a set of engagement items in a similar way. Therefore, although there will be some variation in how any individual responds to the set of nine items (above), there should be a good deal of internal consistency in responses if the scale measures the same construct. Another way of putting this is that the variance in the items will be 'shared' if they tap the same construct.

Reliability analysis assesses this internal consistency or this 'shared variation'. It actually gives us an indication of how much a scale has internal consistency or shared variation by providing us with a figure of *how much variation* in the scale items is shared (the extent of average covariance between multiple items). This particular statistic is called *Cronbach's alpha* and ranges from 0.0 to 1.0.

If there is no internal consistency in respondents' answers across a particular set of items, then our Cronbach's alpha figure could be 0. If every individual in our survey sample gave the same answer for every item (eg a disengaged employee answered 1,1,1,1,1,1,1,1,1 to all nine questions and a highly engaged employee gave 5,5,5,5,5,5,5,5,5 to all nine questions) – then we would have perfect-shared variance, perfect internal consistency and our alpha would be equal to 1. In reality, scales will tend to fall between 0 and 1. The level of shared variance within our set of items that is considered a 'good' or 'acceptable' level of variance in a scale that is supposed to be measuring the same construct is 0.70. So any scale that has an alpha figure greater than 0.70 is considered to be a decent measure with decent levels of internal consistency. Note that a scale that has a Cronbach's alpha value of 0.70 still has some variation in how people responded across the multiple items that is not shared across the items. In the case of our nine-item scale, as soon as individuals do not give the same response to all nine items we will have some 'unshared' variance in responses. Note that we are suggesting that if people give exactly the same response to a set of questionnaire items, this indicates a reliable measure. However, the analytics expert needs to

be aware of insufficient effort responding patterns (IER) (see Meade and Craig, 2012) that can plague workplace engagement surveys – this is where people tick the same response without attending to the content of the question.

## Reliability testing

So, in summary, a measure is reliable when the scale measures a construct with a limited amount of measurement error, ie a minimal amount of variation in how people tend to respond across a set of items.

Reliability can only be tested with multiple items, and reliability analysis checks whether the items seem to produce variance that is consistent with scales across respondents. Importantly, the testing compares the item responses with other item responses in order to check whether the items/indicators might be measuring the same construct.

An example of an unreliable measure is a questionnaire scale that has items that could be interpreted differently by different people. With low reliability, more variance will occur in responses that do not represent variance in the actual construct in the heads of respondents. Measurement error is therefore occurring.

## Necessity of multiple item indicators

Many professional survey providers use single-item measures to measure a construct, ie just one question to determine whether someone is engaged. Whilst this is a very efficient method of measuring constructs in a survey (as you only need to ask a limited number of questions to measure a variety of constructs), single-item measures suffer from a key problem in terms of measurement testing in that they cannot be tested for reliability.

With a single-item question we cannot be sure that variation in responses is not due to some problem with the question: for example, is there measurement error due to ambiguous wording of the question, or are there meaningful variations in respondents' heads? When we measure constructs with multiple indicators, we can and should consider how they operate together and hence we need multiple indicators to model validity and reliability of a measure.

# Example 2: reliability analysis on a four-item engagement scale

Scale reliability can be determined in a fairly straightforward manner using SPSS.

## Case Study 2

In this example, we test a four-item scale that is testing discretionary effort – or organizational citizenship behaviour (OCB) – using the following questions:

- I work harder than my job requires.
- I put a huge amount of effort into my job.
- I help out my teammates.
- I go the extra mile.

These questions are associated with a response scale of 1 to 5 where: 1 = I always do this; 2 = I frequently do this; 3 = I sometimes do this; 4 = I occasionally do this; 5 = I never do this.

Employee responses to a survey that included this set of questions can be found in the data file we used before: 'Chapter 5 RAW Survey Results.sav'; remember that in total 832 employees completed this survey. Open this file with SPSS, go into the 'Analyze' menu and select 'Scale' and 'Reliability Analysis' (see Figure 5.10).

**FIGURE 5.10** Reliability analysis in SPSS

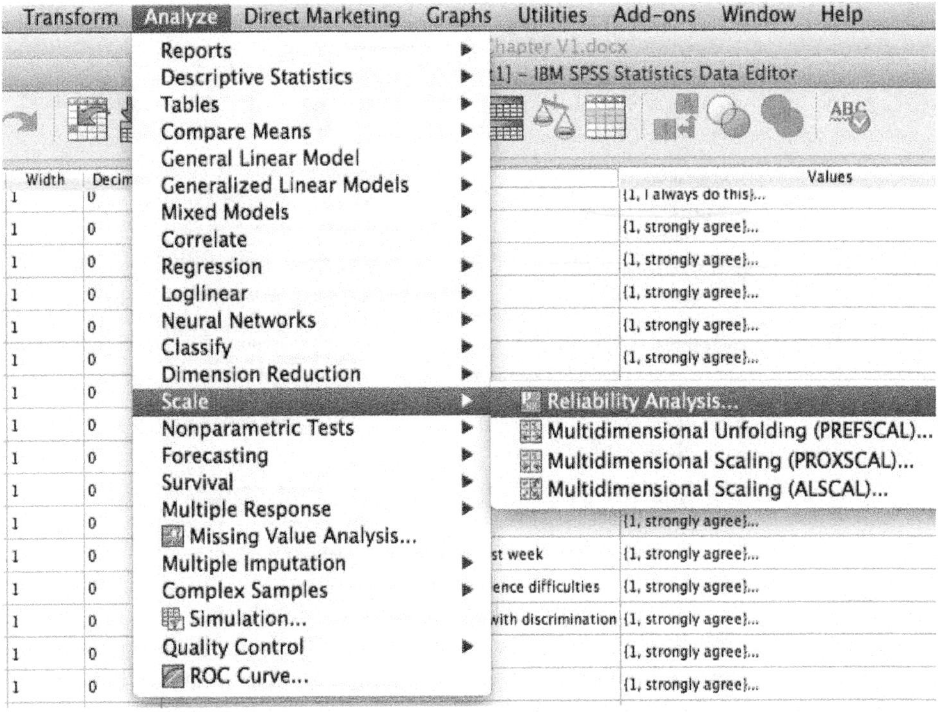

Then select the relevant items on the left-hand side and move them to the items box on the right-hand side using the arrow button (Figure 5.11).

**FIGURE 5.11**

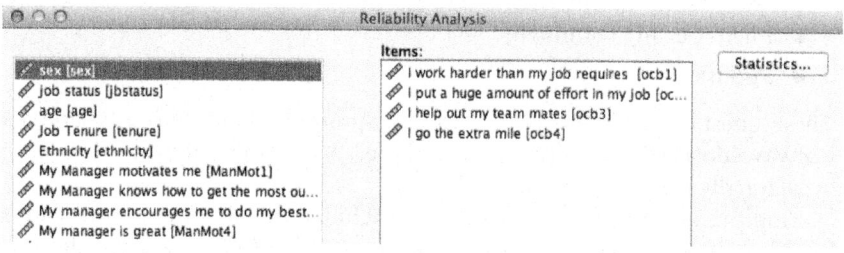

Click on 'Statistics' and a dialogue box will appear. In the 'Descriptives for' area, tick: 'Item', 'Scale' and 'Scale if item deleted' (Figure 5.12).

**FIGURE 5.12**  Reliability analysis statistics

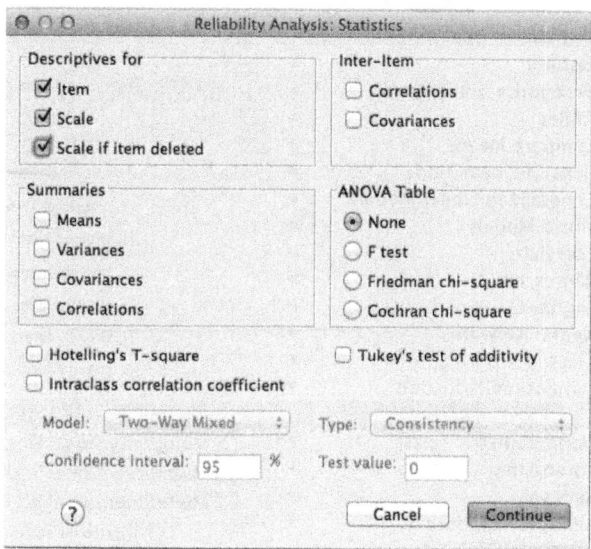

What this selection does is tell SPSS to produce descriptive statistics for individual items and the complete scale. It also tells SPSS to display scale summary statistics including Cronbach's alpha; it also shows what the Cronbach alpha would be if each item were to be deleted from the scale (ie it would tell us if that one question has more unshared 'unique' variation than the rest in the group).

Then click 'Continue' and 'OK'.

The output here tells us that the reliability of this set of questions in measuring discretionary effort is 0.681. This is below 0.70, which could be better (see Figure 5.13).

**FIGURE 5.13** Reliability analysis output

**Reliability Statistics**

| Cronbach's Alpha | N of Items |
|---|---|
| .681 | 4 |

**Item–Total Statistics**

| | Scale Mean if Item Deleted | Scale Variance if Item Deleted | Corrected Item-Total Correlation | Cronbach's Alpha if Item Deleted |
|---|---|---|---|---|
| I work harder than my job requires | 7.56 | 6.491 | .523 | .599 |
| I put a huge amount of effort in my job | 7.15 | 5.947 | .578 | .557 |
| I help out my team mates | 6.96 | 5.421 | .593 | .531 |
| I go the extra mile | 6.31 | 5.359 | .297 | .787 |

In the 'Item–Total Statistics' box in Figure 5.13 the last column on the right-hand side gives the Cronbach's alpha value if that item was dropped from the scale. Looking through these values, it shows that the Cronbach's alpha would be much higher (0.787) if the last question, 'I go the extra mile', was deleted from the responses. Hence this item has a lot of measurement error and is causing a lack of reliability, possibly because it is slightly ambiguous and may be interpreted differently by different people. Although from a face validity point of view 'I go the extra mile' might be a reasonable question to ask if one wants to measure 'going the extra mile', and this might be valid to a degree, because it could have a number of interpretations it could lead to low reliability and high measurement error. Without this item the remaining three items show a good Cronbach's alpha of 0.787. Thus:

> **Snapshot hidden gem**
>
> The three items of 'I work harder than my job requires', 'I put a huge amount of effort into my job', and 'I help out my teammates' form a coherent scale and can be interpreted as being a reliable measure of organizational citizenship behaviour.

# Example 3: reliability and factor testing with group-level engagement data

Whilst factor analysis and reliability analysis should really be conducted on individual-level responses, this information is generally not available where the services of an external survey provider have been paid for; survey companies tend to hold the data due to confidentiality issues (see Chapter 12). Therefore, if the survey data is not available, the above discussion gives some idea of what questions to ask the survey provider.

Below are some other questions you might want to ask your survey provider:

- Why are we only using one-item scales? (if that is the case).
- How have you assessed whether the single item is valid and reliable?
- Do any multi-item indicators separate into sub-factors?
- Do items measuring different constructs separate into different factors?
- What levels of reliability are you getting with your multi-item scales?
- What are the Cronbach alpha coefficients of the multi-item composite measures?
- Has the survey provider tested for a problem of insufficient effortful responding (IER)?
- What sort of discriminant validity tests have you conducted with your measures?

When the survey providers produce reports, they do not (for good reasons) present individual survey responses. What they often provide, however, are group-level statistics, for example the proportion of each team that has a positive response (eg 'Agree' or 'Strongly Agree' to an engagement item). If the organization is large enough and if there are enough teams, we can actually conduct reliability analysis at a team level with this data. Whilst this analysis might not be as sensitive as with data at individual level, it provides some data with which to test the measurement integrity of scales used by survey providers.

The data set 'Chapter 5 SURVEY PROVIDER ENGAGEMENT DATA TEAM LEVEL.sav' measures the percentage of team members who answered positively on nine engagement measures in 212 teams. The nine engagement measures represent an engagement measure used by Engagement Survey Inc. The nine question items are as follows:

- I feel a sense of pride with my organization.
- I would recommend this employer to a friend.
- I am really engaged.
- I can manage my workload.

- My work does not interfere with my home life.
- I have good work–life balance.
- My organization is socially responsible.
- My organization makes sure that no one gets hurt in the workplace.
- My organization is ethical.

These items are answered on a scale of 1 to 5 where 1= strongly disagree and 5 = strongly agree. The data that the survey provider supplied was originally in the form of an Excel spreadsheet and then transferred to an SPSS file.

As we did with the individual examples, let's first perform factor analysis to determine whether the items load onto separate constructs. So, going into SPSS, from the 'Analyze' menu, select 'Dimension Reduction' and 'Factor'. Then select the nine engagement variables from the left-hand side and move them over to the 'Variables:' selection box on the right-hand side and click on the 'Rotation' button.

As before, a dialogue box will appear, on which you need to select the 'Varimax' method, 'Rotated Solution' and 'Loading Plots' (Figure 5.14). Then 'Continue' and 'OK'.

**FIGURE 5.14** Selecting variables for factor analysis in SPSS

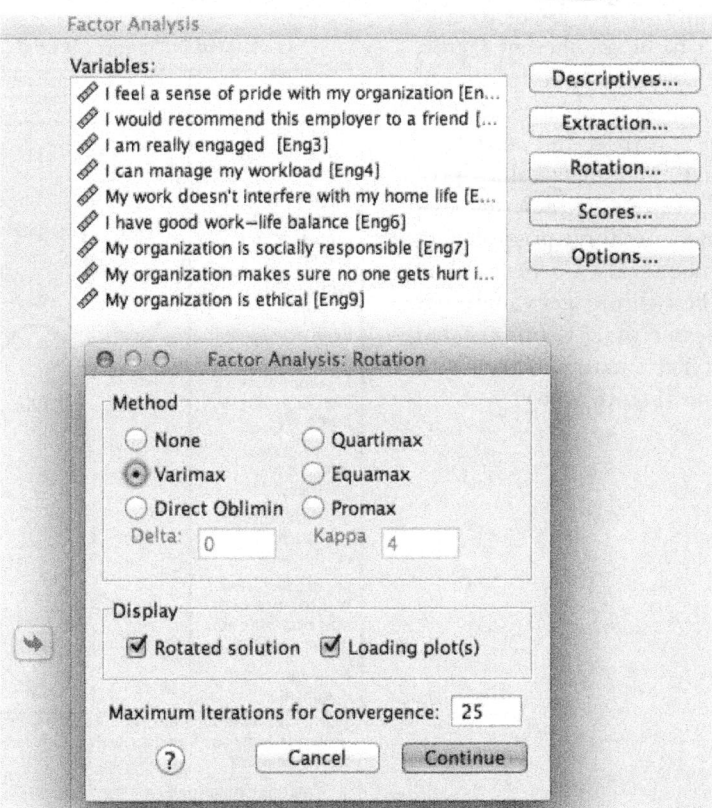

As the output shows, even with this team-level data (rather than individual responses) using percentage of team responses that are positive, this engagement scale shows evidence of being made up of three separate constructs. There are three factors with eigenvalues above 1, as can be seen in 'Total Variance Explained' in Figure 5.15.

**FIGURE 5.15** Total variance explained in team-level engagement data

Total Variance Explained

| Component | Initial Eigenvalues | | | Extraction Sums of Squared Loadings | | | Rotation Sums of Squared Loadings | | |
|---|---|---|---|---|---|---|---|---|---|
| | Total | % of Variance | Cumulative % | Total | % of Variance | Cumulative % | Total | % of Variance | Cumulative % |
| 1 | 4.507 | 50.074 | 50.074 | 4.507 | 50.074 | 50.074 | 2.666 | 29.621 | 29.621 |
| 2 | 1.617 | 17.964 | 68.038 | 1.617 | 17.964 | 68.038 | 2.423 | 26.921 | 56.543 |
| 3 | 1.370 | 15.224 | 83.262 | 1.370 | 15.224 | 83.262 | 2.405 | 26.720 | 83.262 |
| 4 | .620 | 6.888 | 90.150 | | | | | | |
| 5 | .425 | 4.719 | 94.870 | | | | | | |
| 6 | .209 | 2.322 | 97.192 | | | | | | |
| 7 | .168 | 1.868 | 99.060 | | | | | | |
| 8 | .084 | .936 | 99.995 | | | | | | |
| 9 | .000 | .005 | 100.000 | | | | | | |

Extraction Method: Principal Component Analysis.

As discussed in the section on factor analysis previously in this chapter, an eigenvalue needs to be greater than 1 for us to consider it to be a coherent factor; or to consider a collection of items to measure a particular unique construct. In Figure 5.15 we have three eigenvalues produced above 1, which suggests that there are three possible factors in our scale. Corresponding with these three eigenvalues that are greater than 1, our rotated component matrix has three columns (Figure 5.16).

**FIGURE 5.16** Rotated component matrix in team-level engagement data

Rotated Component Matrix[a]

| | Component | | |
|---|---|---|---|
| | 1 | 2 | 3 |
| I feel a sense of pride with my organization | .883 | .134 | .230 |
| I would recommend this employer to a friend | .907 | .147 | .147 |
| I am really engaged | .878 | .207 | .264 |
| I can manage my workload | .263 | .839 | .049 |
| My work doesn't interfere with my home life | -.029 | .859 | .211 |
| I have good work–life balance | .279 | .911 | .189 |
| My organization is socially responsible | .275 | .082 | .805 |
| My organization makes sure no one gets hurt in the workplace | .101 | .194 | .786 |
| My organization is ethical | .240 | .155 | .955 |

Extraction Method: Principal Component Analysis.
Rotation Method: Varimax with Kaiser Normalization.

a. Rotation converged in 4 iterations.

This tells us that the responses to the nine-item scale seem to be clustering into three possible separate factors/constructs. In considering the factor loadings in Figure 5.16, we can see that each of the columns tends to have three items that load together onto each of the components with loadings that are greater than 0.70. This provides us with information about what items tend to load together into particular factors.

> **Snapshot hidden gem**
>
> Our data suggests that if the survey provider created a composite measure comprised of all nine survey questions and used it as an indicator of team-level engagement, they would be misrepresenting the survey data and ignoring the fact that the nine questions (as shown in Figure 5.16) seem to be clustering into three separate constructs. Looking at the face validity of the questions, the first three appear to be about engagement, questions 4–6 are similar and appear to be about work–life balance, whilst the last three are more about perception of the organization's ethics.

Figure 5.17 presents a very stylish three-dimensional graph that shows how these items plot in 3D rotated space (Figure 5.16 is really the one that we look at to get proper indication of loadings and cross loadings – but this 3D graph is rather interesting... let's face it, who wouldn't want this on their report?).

**FIGURE 5.17** A very stylish 3D graph

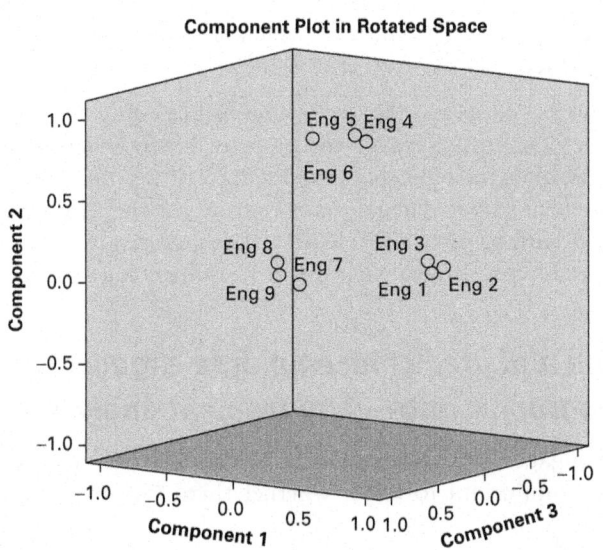

So separating these three constructs would result in a more in-depth picture of what is going on in the hearts and minds of the people in this organization. It would enable us to look at variances in all three constructs separately and take prescriptive action around engagement, well-being and ethics that would be far more useful than if we had bundled all the information together into one 'engagement' measure. Indeed the separated engagement questions (1–3) might show quite a different result on their own than the three merged together.

# Analysis and outcomes

## What organizations tend to do with surveys at the moment

There are pros and cons of using survey consultancies/research companies to run employee surveys and some of these have already been explored in this chapter. A summary of what survey companies usually provide is given below:

- A ready-made measure of engagement used by hundreds of organizations.
- Benchmark norms of 'employee engagement' scores that the organization can compare itself to. For example across peers in the same industry, and to compare against 'high performing' or 'top quartile' organizations'.
- Interactive reports where the organization can obtain bespoke scores cut across organizational functions, teams and demographic groups.
- A team and subordinate group average 'engagement score' (that is often used as a performance indicator for supervisor/leader).
- A breakdown of data to show which teams, regions, etc are more engaged/feel they have a better leader.

Whether you are designing the survey yourself or using the skills gleaned in this chapter to interrogate your survey provider to ensure you are getting meaningful results, the next step is an analysis of what else you can do with your engagement survey data. Perhaps some of the survey output data could be combined with some of the HR MI data that already exists about teams in order to really probe into what might be influencing engagement.

## Analysing and predicting employee engagement with MI/demographic data – engagement analysis example

Given that engagement is such a key behaviour for organizations to want to develop, it is important to know whether there are any team-level factors that might 'predict' engagement. The following data set includes a combination of team-level HR metrics, employee demographic data and engagement survey data. There are 29,976 employees in these functions across the UK and these employees are organized into 928 teams or employee units. These are sometimes branches, sometimes departments and sometimes teams within larger work nestings. They have, however, been organized with a 'work unit' key that was used by the engagement survey provider in order to supply engagement survey data in aggregate form (to ethically protect identities in this anonymous survey, no unit here is identified if it has fewer than 10 employees). The data set that we are working with, therefore, is average/aggregate data at the work-team level and there are 928 objects or units of analysis in the data set; this data is stored in 30 variables (note our discussion on team analyses, pp 421–23 and 443). The data set can be found in the SPSS file 'CHAPTER 5 Engagement CASE Group level data.sav'.

The variables in the data set include the following (Table 5.2):

**TABLE 5.2** Employee engagement survey variables

| Variable Label | Description |
| --- | --- |
| DepartmentGroupNumber | Team/unit key identifier |
| GroupSize | Number of employees in the unit |
| PercentMale | Percentage of the unit made up of males |
| BAME | Percentage of the unit made up of Black, Asian or Minority Ethnic employees |
| NumberTeamLeads | Number of team leaders in the unit (in general this organization has a team leader for every seven or so employees |
| NumberFeMaleTeamLeads | Number of team leads in the unit who are female |
| Location | Geographical location: 1 = Central London, 2 = Greater London, 3 = Rest of UK |
| LondonorNot | Geographical location recoded to 1 = Central London or Greater London and 2 = Rest of UK |
| Function | Function drawn from: 1 = Sales staff (customer-facing people) or 2 = Professional Service (non-customer-facing people) |

**TABLE 5.2** *continued*

| Variable Label | Description |
|---|---|
| EMPsurvEngage_1 – EMPsurvEngage_9 | Proportion of the unit who answered favourably (with either 'agree' or 'strongly agree' on a 1 to 5 'strongly disagree' to 'strongly agree' response scale) to each of nine employee engagement questions: I work with full intensity in my job; I try my hardest to perform as well as I can in my work; I concentrate hard in my job; My mind is always focused on my job; I strive very hard to complete my work well; Time flies at work; I would recommend this organization as a place to work; I feel a sense of belonging with my organization; I am proud of the work I do |
| EMPsurvEngagement | Average unit/team score for the nine engagement questions |
| EMPorgIntegrity1 – EMPorgIntegrity5 | Proportion of the unit who answered favourably (with either 'agree' or 'strongly agree' on a 1 to 5 'strongly disagree' to 'strongly agree' response scale) to each of five employee 'organizational integrity' questions: My organization listens to staff; My organization does the right thing; My organization treats external stakeholders with respect; My organization encourages staff to point out questionable practices; We all do the right thing in this organization |
| EmpSurvOrgIntegrity | Average unit/team score for the five organizational integrity questions |
| EMPsurvSUP1 – EMPsurvSUP4 | Proportion of the unit who answered favourably (with either 'agree' or 'strongly agree' on a 1 to 5 'strongly disagree' to 'strongly agree' response scale) to each of four 'supportive supervisor' questions: My supervisor listens to me; My supervisor cares about my well-being; My supervisor helps ensure we get things done; My supervisor is there when he/she is needed |
| EmpSurvSupervisor | Average unit/team score for the four 'supportive supervisor' questions |

This data set will be used in examples 4 and 5 below.

# Example 4: using the independent samples t-test to determine differences in engagement levels

## The independent samples t-test

The first thing we can do is to run a t-test with the team-level engagement results as the dependent variable.

So what we want to do here is to compare two regional and geographical groupings in the organization (or two samples) namely 'London' or 'Not London', on their engagement survey results. This is testing the strongly held belief (held by senior management at the organization) that people in regional offices are less engaged than those based in the 'dynamic' London branches. The independent samples t-test is used when we have one independent variable with two groups (the location in our example), which determines which group people belong to, and one dependent variable (team engagement in our example). We want to test whether there is a significant difference between the team means of the two groups on the dependant variable.

In SPSS we go to the 'Analyze' menu again, select 'Compare Means' (because we are comparing the means of the two samples), then we select, 'Independent Samples T-Test' (Figure 5.18).

**FIGURE 5.18** Independent samples t-test

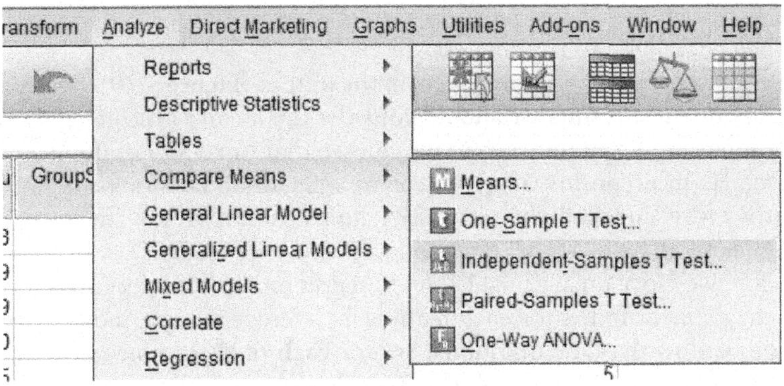

We need to put our independent variable ('London' or 'Not London') into the 'Grouping Variable' field, then we put the dependent variable ('Engagement') into the 'Test Variable' box. Then click on 'Define Groups' so that we can tell SPSS which group is which.

We have set up the data file lookup in SPSS as follows:

1 = London

2 = Other Location

As we have set up the data file with these value labels SPSS knows that a value of 1 means that the person is in Group 1 (London); and that a value of 2, means the person is in Group 2 (Other Location). We insert these numbers as in Figure 5.19 and click 'Continue'.

**FIGURE 5.19**   Setting up our independent t-tests

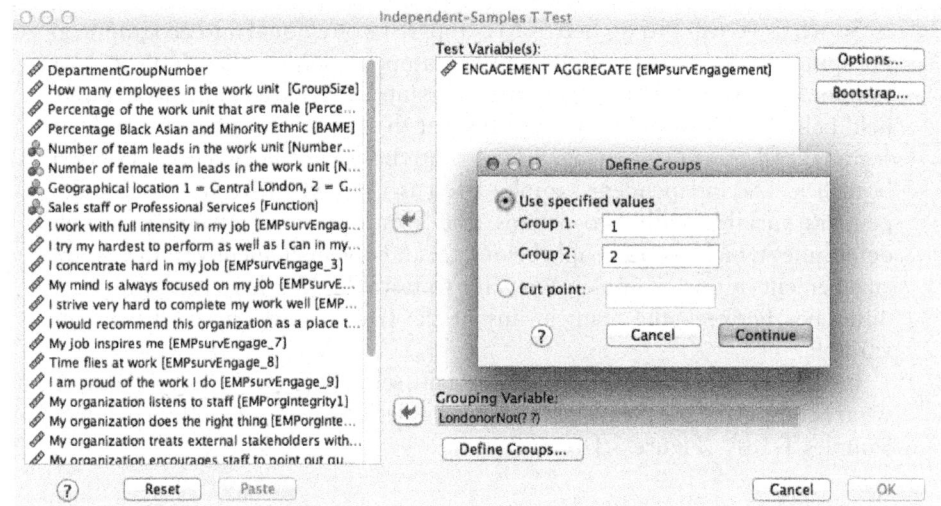

We then click 'OK' to run the test.

We can see a number of things from the output (Figure 5.20). Before interpreting our t-test results we should consider the mean of the groups that we are comparing. From our output we can see that our 533 London teams are on average (mean positive engagement answers for all London teams = 81.55) slightly more engaged than our 394 non-London teams (mean positive engagement answers for all non-London teams = 80.67).

Before we move on, we might want to reflect on what these means represent. The engagement index for each team is an average of nine indices for each team linked to the nine questions. So, for each of these nine questions, the team members will have ticked a 1-to-5 scale and the indicator for the team associated with each question is the proportion of the team who ticked either 4 or 5 for each question. The engagement index is therefore a team average of proportions of positive responses for each of the nine questions. The 81.55 mean figure (London teams), represents the average of 533 team averages of the nine indices (which are the percentage of the teams who

**FIGURE 5.20** First t-test result: engagement comparing inner London versus non-London teams

## T-Test

**Group Statistics**

| | London or Other location | N | Mean | Std. Deviation | Std. Error Mean |
|---|---|---|---|---|---|
| ENGAGEMENT AGGREGATE | London | 533 | 81.5478 | 10.10528 | .43771 |
| | Other Location | 394 | 80.6726 | 9.88519 | .49801 |

① London has higher avg. engagement

**Independent Samples Test**

| | | Levene's Test for Equality of Variances | | t-test for Equality of Means | | | | | 95% Confidence Interval of the Difference | |
|---|---|---|---|---|---|---|---|---|---|---|
| | | F | Sig. | t | df | Sig. (2-tailed) | Mean Difference | Std. Error Difference | Lower | Upper |
| ENGAGEMENT AGGREGATE | Equal variances assumed | .014 | .904 | 1.316 | 925 | .189 | .87525 | .66522 | -.43026 | 2.18077 |
| | Equal variances not assumed | | | 1.320 | 856.938 | .187 | .87525 | .66302 | -.42609 | 2.17659 |

② No sig diff in the patterns of variation, so we look @ top row results

③ No sig diff in engagement scores

answered 4 or 5 on each of the nine engagement questions). The 80.67 mean figure (non-London teams) represents the average of 394 team averages of the nine indices (which are the percentage of the teams who answered 4 or 5 on each of the nine engagement questions).

Here, the non-London averages are slightly lower than the London averages. This kind of finding is a good example of a situation where a statistical test such as the t-test is very useful. We could make an assumption that our non-London and London teams differ and that London employees are more engaged. However, could this difference be due to random fluctuation of engagement levels across teams in our organization? Teams vary in levels of engagement and some of this variation will be random variation (teams will never, for purely random reasons, all have exactly the same engagement scores) and we should not take some degree of variation seriously.

To see if these geographical locations differ significantly in a meaningful way we need to carry out the t-test. You will also recall from our earlier discussion of t-tests (Chapter 4) that a pre-test checking for assumption violations should be carried out. This is the Levene's test and our output shows that the Levene's here has a very low F-value (0.014) and this is not significant (p>0.05), suggesting that the patterns of variation in team engagement means across the two locations are similar – the pattern of variance is not significantly different. This means we can assume equal variance (patterns) and interpret the t-test results from the top row of our output. So 'equal variances are assumed' and the t-test result (a t-value of 1.316) has a significance value associated with it of 0.189. So here our t-test is p>0.05, which means we do not have a significant difference in engagement scores when we compare London teams with non-London teams.

> ### Snapshot hidden gem
>
> The difference in engagement means of 81.55 for London compared to 80.67 for other locations should not be taken seriously as it could easily have occurred by random chance fluctuations in team engagement levels.

Without doing this test, if an engagement provider tells us that there is a difference in engagement scores when you compare London with non-London, all you could do is nod and say: 'okay'. You might even take action on the back of this, when actually it may not be the best option for your organization.

In a formal write-up convention, we would write: 'The t-test was not significant: t(925)= 1.316, p>0.1. There is no significant difference in engagement between teams based in London and those that are based in non-London locations; London (mean=81.5478, SD=10.10528) is not significantly different to Other Locations (mean=80.6726, SD=9.88519).'

So on this example, we would not want to recommend any specific action or any adjustment to the organization's engagement strategy with regards to the importance of location. Next, let's do the exact same test, but with function as the independent variable (and keeping the dependent variable as engagement).

Again, we need to put our independent variable (function) into the 'Grouping Variable' field, then we put the dependent variable (engagement) into the 'Test Variable' box. Then click on 'Define Groups' so that we can tell SPSS which group is which. We set up the group comparison as follows: 1 = Sales: 2 = Professional Service – and click 'OK' to run the test.

Immediately we can see from Figure 5.21 that the average engagement scores for our Sales team functions (with a mean of 79.15) are a bit lower than teams from the Professional Service function (mean of 83.57). Whilst there is a difference here, it is not that big; our t-test will, however, inform us whether we should interpret this difference as meaningful or whether it could again be due to random fluctuation that we tend to find in team engagement levels across the organization.

We can see from the results that our Levene's pre-test checking for assumption violations shows that the variation in team engagement scores when comparing the two functions has a significant F-value (5.442) ($p=0.020$, so $p<0.05$): suggesting that the patterns of variation in team engagement means across the two functions do vary – the *pattern* of variance is significantly different. This means that we cannot assume equal variance (patterns) and we need to interpret the t-test results from the bottom row of our output (which puts the numbers through a tougher test and is robust against such violations). The p-value or significance level for our *t*-test (with a value of –6.943 and a degrees of freedom of 923), is 0.000, which means that the chance of finding such a pattern of team engagement differences by chance alone is less than 1 in 1,000 ($p<0.001$).

> **Snapshot hidden gem**
>
> Team engagement scores are significantly different across the functions. We can actually say with 99.9 per cent confidence that there is a significant difference in engagement results between people who work in the Sales Function (customer facing) and people who work in the Professional Services function (non-customer facing). Professional Services teams are significantly more engaged than those in the Sales function. Given that it is people in the sales function who deal directly with customers, this highlights a key challenge to be addressed in any engagement strategy.

In formal write-up convention, we would say: 'The t-test was significant: $t(923.209)= -6.943$, $p<0.001$. There is a significant difference in engagement scores of teams where employees work in the Sales function compared to teams from Professional Services. Sales teams (mean=79.1454, SD=10.30226) are significantly less engaged than teams from Professional Services (mean=83.5741, SD=9.11327).'

Ho: No sig diff
Ha: Sig diff

**FIGURE 5.21** Second t-test result: engagement comparing Sales versus Professional Service teams

## T–Test

**Group Statistics**

| | Sales staff or Professional Services | N | Mean | Std. Deviation | Std. Error Mean |
|---|---|---|---|---|---|
| ENGAGEMENT AGGREGATE | Sales | 502 | 79.1454 | 10.30226 | .45981 |
| | Professional Service | 425 | 83.5741 | 9.11327 | .44206 |

**Independent Samples Test**

| | | Levene's Test for Equality of Variances | | t-test for Equality of Means | | | | | |
|---|---|---|---|---|---|---|---|---|---|
| | | F | Sig. | t | df | Sig. (2-tailed) | Mean Difference | Std. Error Difference | 95% Confidence Interval of the Difference |   |
| | | | | | | | | | Lower | Upper |
| ENGAGEMENT AGGREGATE | Equal variances assumed | 5.442 | .020 | -6.873 | 925 | .000 | -4.42870 | .64435 | -5.69325 | -3.16415 |
| | Equal variances not assumed | | | -6.943 | 923.209 | .000 | -4.42870 | .63784 | -5.68049 | -3.17691 |

# Example 5: using multiple regression to predict team-level engagement

In the following example, we run an ordinary least squares (OLS) multiple linear regression model to predict team-level engagement scores with a number of other team-level survey measures provided by our external survey company; we also use some team demographic information (obtained from MI data) as possible predictors of team-level engagement. Some of this information includes diversity-based information such as team gender proportions and the proportion of team members who are made up of BAME – Black, Asian or Minority Ethnic – employees (a more detailed discussion on diversity demographics can be found in Chapter 4). So we are still using the same data set ('Chapter 5 Engagement CASE Group level data.sav') as with the t-tests but we are going to utilize more of this data set – integrating more varied metrics from different data sets. So here we are going to predict team-level engagement (EMPsurvEngagement) from unit demographics and other survey composites.

As discussed in Chapter 3, multiple regression can be used to predict variation in a dependent variable by using two or more independent variables, using a model in the form of:

$$Y_i = (b_0 + b_1 X_{i1} + b_2 X_{i2} + \ldots + b_n X_n) + \varepsilon_i$$

where $Y_i$ is the value of the dependent variable for the i'th participant (where 'i' could be 1, 2, 3, etc and refers to the specific case/employee in the sample), $b_0$ is the constant, $b_1$ is the coefficient of the first independent variable ($X_1$), $b_2$ is the coefficient of the second independent variable ($X_2$), and $b_n$ is the coefficient of the n'th independent variable ($X_n$) (where 'n' is the number of independent variables), and $\varepsilon_i$ is the error in prediction. Field (2009).

In this example, y is equal to team-level engagement, and the values of X are the other variables.

So in this model team-level engagement index (EMPsurvEngagement) is the dependent variable and the following variables are independent variables:

- Team survey composite – supervisor aggregate score.
- Team survey composite – integrity aggregate score.
- How many employees in the team.
- Percentage of males in the team.
- Percentage of BAME in the team.
- London versus Other location.
- Sales versus Professional Services function.

So, replacing the y and x's with the values in our example, our model will look something like:

Team Engagement =
a + $b_1$ (supervisor score) + $b_2$ (integrity score) + $b_3$ (work unit size) + $b_4$ (% male) + $b_5$ (% BAME) + $b_6$ (London or other) + $b_7$ (Sales or Prof Svcs)

Basically, we are suggesting (and testing) that team-level engagement might be (to a significant extent) a function of the type of work that people do in the teams, where the teams are based, the ethnic diversity in the team, the gender mix in the team, how big the team is, their general judgements of the organization's moral integrity and how good the supervisor is. Just from looking at this list, it is possible that any of these factors might actually influence a team's engagement score. As such it is important to take into account as many possible meaningful factors as we can in trying to predict engagement levels.

So, going into SPSS, we select 'Analyze', then 'Regression', and 'Linear' (Figure 5.22).

**FIGURE 5.22** Conducting a multiple regression analysis predicting team-level engagement

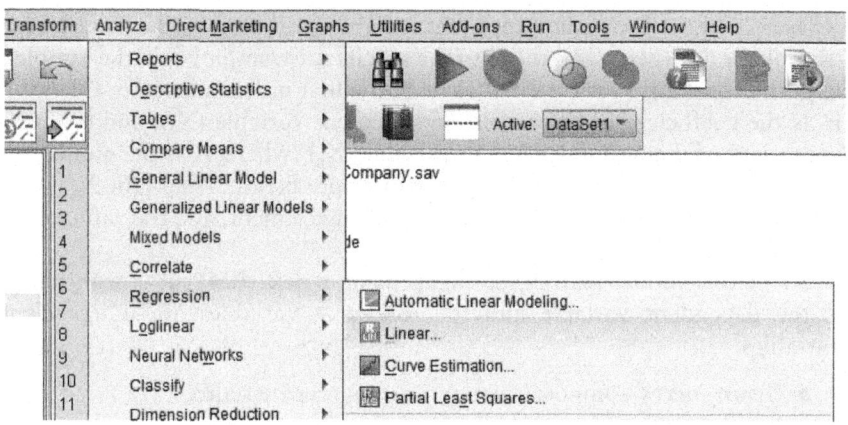

Then select the Engagement Aggregate [EMPSURVEngagement] as the dependent variable using the arrow button and move the seven independent variables over to the 'Independents' box (Figure 5.23). Then click 'OK'.

**FIGURE 5.23** Setting up the model predicting team engagement

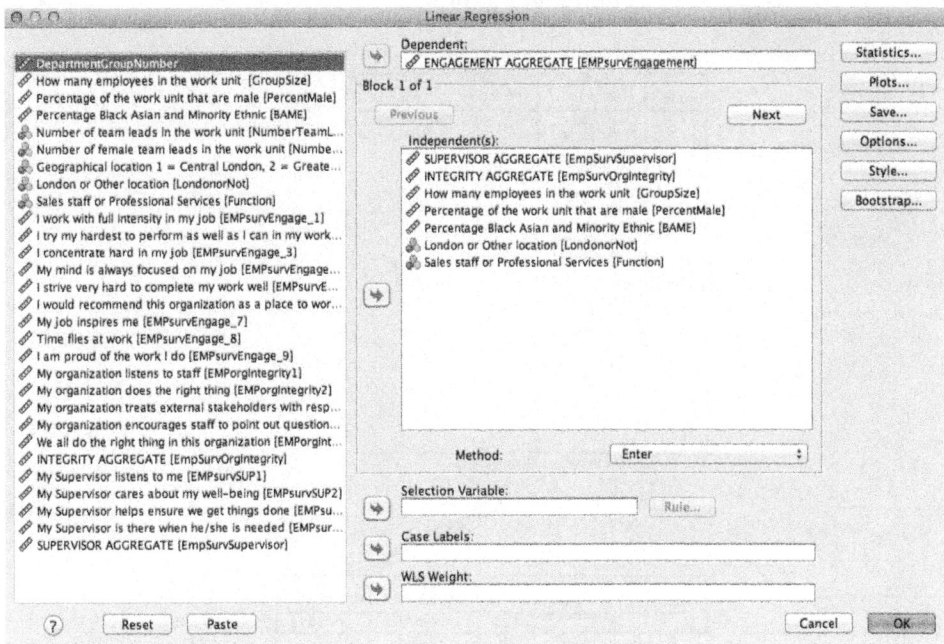

SPSS then produces the following regression output (Figure 5.24).

From the first table in Figure 5.24, we can see that 'Variables entered/removed' shows up; this presents the predictor variables that were entered into the regression model, which are all the variables we entered into SPSS.

The model summary table in Figure 5.24 tells us that the R-square is 0.378. Multiplying this by 100 gives the percentage of variance in the dependent variable that is accounted for by the model. This means that 37.8 per cent of the variance in the average team engagement index (the average of proportions of the team who answered 4 or 5 to the nine engagement survey items) can be accounted for when modelling the variance found in the independent variables (or predictor variables). Importantly, this is the variance of engagement that can be accounted for when modelling and identifying its variance shared with all of the independent variables at the same time (whilst considering the interrelationships amongst the independent variables).

The regression ANOVA table (analysis of variance) in Figure 5.24 tests the significance of how well the model predicts variations in the team-engagement index and is linked to the $R^2$ figure. Here the regression ANOVA F-value is 64.150, with associated degrees of freedom of 7 (for the regression) plus 738 (for the residual), giving a total of 745. The results show the

**FIGURE 5.24** Analysis output for our model predicting team engagement

**Variables Entered/Removed**[a]

| Model | Variables Entered | Variables Removed | Method |
|---|---|---|---|
| 1 | Sales staff or Professional Services, London or Other location, How many employees in the work unit, INTEGRITY AGGREGATE, SUPERVISOR AGGREGATE, Percentage Black Asian and Minority Ethnic, Percentage of the work unit that are male[b] | . | Enter |

a. Dependent Variable: ENGAGEMENT AGGREGATE
b. All requested variables entered.

① Model explains 37.8% of variance

**Model Summary**

| Model | R | R-Square | Adjusted R-Square | Std. Error of the Estimate |
|---|---|---|---|---|
| 1 | .615[a] | .378 | .372 | 8.00652 |

a. Predictors: (Constant), Sales staff or Professional Services, London or Other location, How many employees in the work unit, INTEGRITY AGGREGATE, SUPERVISOR AGGREGATE, Percentage Black Asian and Minority Ethnic, Percentage of the work unit that are male

② The model is sig.

**ANOVA**[a]

| Model | | Sum of Squares | df | Mean Square | F | Sig. |
|---|---|---|---|---|---|---|
| 1 | Regression | 28786.027 | 7 | 4112.290 | 64.150 | .000[b] |
| | Residual | 47309.074 | 738 | 64.104 | | |
| | Total | 76095.101 | 745 | | | |

a. Dependent Variable: ENGAGEMENT AGGREGATE

**Coefficients**[a]

| Model | | Unstandardized Coefficients | | Standardized Coefficients | t | Sig. |
|---|---|---|---|---|---|---|
| | | B | Std. Error | Beta | | |
| 1 | (Constant) | 53.537 | 3.405 | | 15.724 | .000 |
| | SUPERVISOR AGGREGATE | .487 | .030 | .492 | 16.303 | .000 |
| | INTEGRITY AGGREGATE | -.002 | .005 | -.012 | -.396 | .692 |
| | How many employees in the work unit | -.033 | .018 | -.052 | -1.798 | .073 |
| | Percentage of the work unit that are male | -.139 | .017 | -.303 | -8.211 | .000 |
| | Percentage Black Asian and Minority Ethnic | .880 | 2.853 | .010 | .309 | .758 |
| | London or Other location | -.729 | .657 | -.035 | -1.109 | .268 |
| | Sales staff or Professional Services | -1.246 | .747 | -.061 | -1.667 | .096 |

a. Dependent Variable: ENGAGEMENT AGGREGATE

③ Sig

④ As male % increases, engagement decreases

statistical significance of the regression ANOVA as being .000, or we would say p<0.001, which means there is less than 1 in 1,000 chance that we would find this pattern of shared variance (between our team engagement index scores and our seven independent variables) randomly by chance alone, so the model is significant.

Now we need to look at the coefficients table to assess which of our independent variables potentially have an impact on engagement and the degree to which they uniquely contribute to the prediction of variation in team engagement (and in what way or what direction they seem to be related to variation in team engagement).

The coefficients table in Figure 5.24 tells us that of the seven possible drivers of engagement only two seem to come out as significantly predicting variation in levels of team engagement. These significant predictors can be identified as the following:

1 Supervisor aggregate (with a significant standardized Beta= +0.492, p<0.001).

2 Percentage of the work unit who are male (with a significant standardized Beta=−0.303, p<0.001).

### Snapshot hidden gem

Team perceptions of how supportive their supervisors are is the most important driver of team engagement. The better the team tends to rate their supervisor then the higher the team's level of engagement. Importantly, gender diversity is also found to be a key potential driver of engagement. The higher the proportion of males that are found in the teams then the less engaged the teams tend to be. Team size is nearly a significant factor – clearly Sales staff versus Professional Services (which showed a significant t-test) loses its importance when we take into account the range of other factors.

A potential interpretation of why the functional groups no longer come out as being significant may be because of variations in gender mix and levels of supervisory support across the two functional groups; these factors may be possible causes of the earlier differences that we found in team engagement across Sales versus Professional Services. These interesting results show us the greater diagnostic possibilities of using more complex predictive statistics in our analysis than we would have if we just had descriptive means to work with. If we had not run this regression analysis, we might have mistakenly diagnosed the type of job as the possible cause of variations in fluctuations in engagement, when in fact the potential causal factor may well be something that is associated with the different jobs, such as gender-mix differences across the jobs and potential differences in supervisory style that we tend to find across the two functional groups.

## Actions and business context

The analysis outlined in the previous section provides a wealth of information that will help the organization determine where to focus engagement activities. Recommendations may now be focused on supervisor training as well as the diversity training across the organization as a whole. Analysis of diversity data has also been addressed in Chapter 4.

This analysis highlights the importance of thoroughly understanding and diagnosing the current organizational behaviours before rolling out any engagement interventions. Depending on the outcome of a set of analyses (such as those discussed in this chapter), interventions, which are typically found on the engagement agenda in organizations, may include increased communication, town halls, more access to senior leaders, career development, recognition schemes, better onboarding for new staff, mentoring, and informal social events.

A final note on employee engagement surveys: individuals give up their time and often put a lot of thought into their answers to employee opinion surveys (as you would want them to do!). This care and thought needs to be repaid by timely publishing of the survey results across the organization along with a plan of what changes will take place as a result of the answers in an attempt to address the survey results, and what that means for each individual. Attitudes and behaviours change with the environment and if you take too long over the results, analysis and action from the survey then there is an increased likelihood that the survey will lose credibility; even worse, the prescriptive action will not be as relevant, particularly if you are working in a dynamic environment where outside influences such as business restructures, press attention or competitor success may impact people's engagement levels.

We talk about ethics and data sensitivity in Chapter 12; however, it should go without saying that employee opinion surveys are a key area where these must be considered. If people are completing a survey with the understanding that it is anonymous, under no circumstances should that individual-level data be shared.

# References

Allen, N J and Meyer, J P (1990) The measurement and antecedents of affective, continuance, and normative commitment to the organization, *Journal of Occupational Psychology*, 63, pp 1–18

Eisenberger, R, Huntington, R, Hutchison, S and Sowa, D (1986) Perceived organizational support, *Journal of Applied Psychology*, 71, pp 500–07

Gallup (2008) [accessed 25 November 2015] Meta Analysis Research [Online] http://strengths.gallup.com/private/resources/q12meta-analysis_flyer_gen_08%2008_bp.pdf

Hay Group (2012) [accessed 30 November 2015] [Online] http://www.haygroup.com/downloads/ww/misc/insight_external_brochure_singles.pdf

Kahn, W (1990) Psychological conditions of personal engagement and disengagement at work, *Academy of Management Journal*, December 1990, p 33

Lewin, K (1952) *Field Theory in Social Science: Selected theoretical papers by Kurt Lewin*, Tavistock, London

MacLeod, D and Clarke, N (2009) [accessed 20 November 2015] Engaging for Success [Online] http://www.engageforsuccess.org/wp-content/uploads/2012/09/file52215.pdf

Meade, A W and Craig, S B (2012) Identifying careless responses in survey data, *Psychological Methods*, 17 (3), pp 437–55

Mercer (2011) [accessed 30 November 2015] Engaging Employees to Drive Global Business Success [Online] https://www.dgfp.de/wissen/personalwissen-direkt/dokument/86227/herunterladen

Peccei, R (2013) Employee engagement: an evidence-based review, in *Managing Human Resources: Human resource management in transition*, 5th edn, ed S Bach and M R Edwards, John Wiley, New York

Rich, B L, LePine, J A and Crawford, E R (2010) Job engagement: antecedents and effects on job performance, *Academy of Management Journal*, 53, pp 617–35

Schaufeli, W B and Bakker, A B (2003) *Utrecht Work Engagement Scale: Preliminary manual*, Department of Psychology, Utrecht University, Netherlands

Schaufeli, W B and Bakker, A B (2010) Defining and measuring work engagement: bringing clarity to the concept, in *Work Engagement: A handbook of essential theory and research*, ed A B Bakker and M P Leiter, Psychology Press, New York

Towers Watson (2012) [accessed 20 November 2015] Global Workforce Study, *Towers Watson* [Online] http://www.towerswatson.com/assets/pdf/2012-Towers-Watson-Global-Workforce-Study.pdf

# Case study 3
# Predicting employee turnover

## 06

## Employee turnover and why it is such an important part of HR management information

Employee turnover usually refers to all leavers of an organization, including those who resign, are made redundant, take retirement, or exit the organization for any other reason. In this chapter, however, we are only concerned with voluntary turnover and its possible causes.

In this chapter, we cover:

- Descriptive turnover analysis as a day-to-day activity.
- How to measure turnover at individual and team levels.
- Exploring differences in turnover between different countries at both individual and team levels using two practical examples from a multinational organization.
- Predicting turnover at both individual and team levels using survey and profile data using two practical examples from a multinational organization.
- Modelling the costs of turnover and the business case for action.

The cost of employee turnover can be substantial and has been projected at 93–200 per cent of each single leaver's salary depending on his or her skill, level of responsibility and how difficult it is to replace them (Griffeth and Hom, 2001). When this is accumulated across all leavers in an organization, the cost is substantial and it is hence a key area where sound analysis into causes and problem diagnosis can make an enormously valuable contribution to the organization's bottom line. Putting a figure on the cost of employee turnover is valuable because it can help the business case to justify programmes and interventions to address the problem. Costs of voluntary turnover will vary depending on the organization and type of role. Griffeth

**TABLE 6.1** Costs of employee turnover

| Separation Costs | Replacement Costs | Training Costs |
| --- | --- | --- |
| • Exit interviews | • Job advertisements | • Formal orientation |
| • Administrative costs | • Recruitment | • Formal job training |
| • Separation benefits such as unused vacation time paid out | • Administrative processing | • Offsite training |
| | • Entrance interviews | • On-the-job training |
| | • Applicant selection | • Productivity inefficiency |
| • Lost revenues due to vacancy | • Assessment centres/testing | |
| • Productivity declines | • Travelling and relocation expenses | |
| • Overtime costs for extra labour during job vacancy | • Pre-employment screening | |
| • Hiring temporary personnel during job vacancy | • Medical examination (if applicable) | |
| • Client reassignment costs (if a customer-facing role) | | |

and Hom (2001) break down some of these costs as separation costs, replacement costs and training costs. Table 6.1 provides further detail.

In some roles it can take up to 12 months for the new joiner to be brought up to speed, build internal networks, gain client trust, etc to the level of competence and productivity experienced by the predecessor, and organizations are looking at efficient onboarding methods in order to reduce this time to productivity (Watkins, 2013).

As this book is about predictive HR modelling and analytics, we will not cover how to calculate the costs of employee turnover; however, if you are interested in exploring this further then Griffeth and Hom (2001) cover this in detail.

As mentioned, we are only looking at voluntary turnover. It is worth noting here that, whilst we would like to reduce the costs involved in voluntary turnover, and, as an organization it is invaluable to understand why people leave, it can be argued that some voluntary turnover is potentially desirable and the goal is not necessarily to have 0 per cent voluntary turnover. Some voluntary turnover is potentially functional, for example a poor performer who is deeply unhappy with their career choice and realizes that the job is not for them; it may be best for such a person to seek employment elsewhere, and/or resign voluntarily in favour of a different career. However, as a general rule, one can consider low voluntary turnover to indicate that the organization is doing something right in terms of how it manages the people-management environment.

One of the most common activities that an HR information or management information (MI) function will conduct is the regular reporting of turnover statistics. This is partly because of the potentially massive costs associated with replacing people who leave, including recruiting and then getting new joiners up to the same level of productivity (as well as the importance of having people in the right place at the right time doing the right things).

## Descriptive turnover analysis as a day-to-day activity

Most organizations will view turnover reports in a spreadsheet showing the percentage of people in a team, function or division who have left over a given period, but very little analysis will be conducted to explore why this might be. There may be some graphs on a spreadsheet showing which countries or teams have the highest turnover rates, but little modelling or controlling for other explanatory factors will be carried out. The result is often unfounded speculation about possible causes, such as 'the culture is different in Asia and people are more likely to move jobs' or 'the nature of sales is to chase the money so turnover will naturally be higher in that team', etc. This potentially leads to overgeneralized assumptions and a likely misdiagnosis of organizational problems, masking the real issues, which may run far deeper. The real causes of the problem, or predictors, can potentially be found with inferential statistical testing across a number of data sources taking into account a variety of possible causes of turnover simultaneously.

Without proper analysis, causes may be misdiagnosed and interventions may be misdirected. An example might be if the MI report shows that the 'Sales' team in Australia seems to have particularly high turnover compared to other countries, so the leadership team decide to introduce a 'retention bonus' in Australia whereby anyone who resigns to go to a competitor is offered a bonus to stay. Whilst this might decrease the turnover numbers to a degree, it does not address the root cause; further analysis using inferential statistics in this particular case may have revealed a much more specific root issue that needed to be addressed (such as poor leadership, a gender bias that favours men over women for promotion, or even a lack of training to enable staff to do the job they need to do on a particular technical skill). Having this kind of knowledge would have enabled the organization to direct their resources towards more specific, impactful interventions.

## Measuring turnover at individual or team level

Organizational turnover is often presented as a percentage of all employees on a monthly or yearly basis. For example, the UK's Chartered Institute of

Personnel and Development (CIPD) 2014, recommends the following formula:

$$\frac{\text{Total number of leavers over the period}}{\text{average total number of employees over the period}} \times 100$$

The measures of employee flows, as set out below, have all been seen in organizations. Note that item number 1 is the same as the CIPD recommendation and the one that we will be using in our example.

## Measures of employee flows

Note, these are usually presented as a percentage (× 100):

1. Separation rate = $\dfrac{\text{Number of members who left during period}}{\text{Average number of members during period}}$

2. Accession rate = $\dfrac{\text{Number of new members added during the period}}{\text{Average number of members during period}}$

3. Stability rate = $\dfrac{\text{Number of new joiners who stayed during a period}}{\text{Number of members at the beginning of a period}}$

4. Instability rate = $\dfrac{\text{Number of new joiners who leave during a period}}{\text{Number of members at the beginning of a period}}$

5. Survival rate = $\dfrac{\text{Number of new joiners who remain during period}}{\text{Number of new joiners during period}}$

6. Wastage rate = $\dfrac{\text{Number of new joiners who leave during a period}}{\text{Number of new joiners during period}}$

According to the UK CIPD, separation rate is a common measure of employee turnover at organizational or unit level, and hence is the measure that we will use in this chapter. Individual turnover is more simple to measure – either a person has left or they have not – however, it is not quite so simple to model and predict.

# Exploring differences in both individual and team-level turnover

As mentioned, an activity that to some extent is the 'bread and butter' of MI and HR information professionals is regular reporting on staff turnover. Indeed a very common report that HR people have to produce is staff turnover levels across difference 'cuts' or sub-samples of the organization. However, it is not always the case (as explained in Chapter 3) that much of the analysis that HR functions carry out is tested for any kind of significance. Thus the analysis most often presented is an analysis that has been produced without the analyst checking whether any pattern found could easily have been due to random fluctuations (one needs to recognize that some voluntary turnover might have absolutely nothing to do with the organization – it may just be that some random factor led certain employees to leave their jobs). As individual turnover is a dichotomous event (leaver versus non-leaver) this restricts (or determines) the type of analysis that we can do to check for significance. For example, it would not necessarily make sense to explore linear relationships with a dichotomous variable, mainly because such data is not numerically meaningful (you cannot, for example, have 'more' gender, or have 'more' stayer/leaver). We deal with this issue in greater depth later in this chapter (though see Chapter 3 for a discussion of this issue).

One aspect of the analysis that we do here ('crosstabs') is the kind of analysis that the HR function might naturally do; however, we add a level of statistical interrogation to the data. We explore and interrogate differences in individual staff turnover patterns across a number of different countries. For this we use a crosstab analysis (cross-tabulation, similar to the diversity analysis we conduct in Chapter 4, example 1) and we apply a chi-square test to the results to check for significance.

# Example 1a: using frequency tables to explore regional differences in staff turnover

The data set we use for this analysis is called: 'Chapter 6 Individual Turnover.sav' and includes data on 1,653 employees within a financial services organization across 10 countries.

The following variables are in this data set:

1. BossGender (gender of line manager/direct boss: 0 = female, 1 = male).
2. Gender (gender of individual: 0 = female, 1 = male).
3. Age (actual number).
4. LengthOfService (number of completed years).
5. AppraisalRating (performance appraisal rating on a scale of 1 to 5, with 5 being the highest).
6. Country (1 = Belgium; 2 = Sweden; 3 = Italy; 4 = France; 5 = Poland; 6 = Mexico; 7 = Spain; 8 = UK; 9 = United States; 10 = Australia).
7. LeaverStatus (whether or not the individual has left the organization: 0 = stayer; 1 = leaver).

First let's explore the data set in terms of how many people left over the last year and how many people are based in the different countries, by using a frequencies table.

Go into SPSS and select 'Descriptive Statistics' from the 'Analyze' menu and then 'Frequencies' (Figure 6.1).

**FIGURE 6.1**

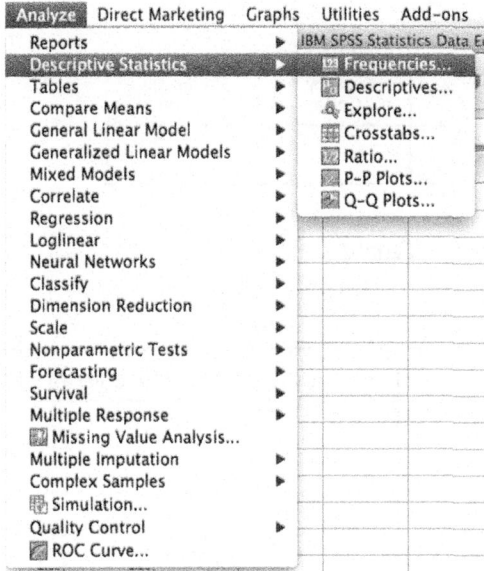

First select frequencies of the 'Country Code' and the 'Stayer or Leaver' variables into the 'Variable(s):' box (see Figure 6.2).

**FIGURE 6.2**

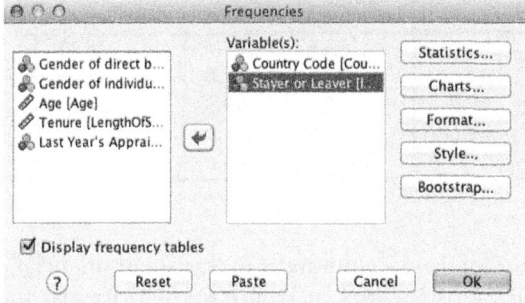

Then Click 'OK' and this will produce the following output (Figure 6.3):

## FIGURE 6.3

### ➜ Frequencies

**Statistics**

|   |         | Country Code | Stayer or Leaver |
|---|---------|--------------|------------------|
| N | Valid   | 1653         | 1652             |
|   | Missing | 0            | 1                |

## Frequency Table

**Country Code**

|       |           | Frequency | Per cent | Valid Per cent | Cumulative Per cent |
|-------|-----------|-----------|----------|----------------|---------------------|
| Valid | Belgium   | 40        | 2.4      | 2.4            | 2.4                 |
|       | Sweden    | 36        | 2.2      | 2.2            | 4.6                 |
|       | Italy     | 70        | 4.2      | 4.2            | 8.8                 |
|       | France    | 37        | 2.2      | 2.2            | 11.1                |
|       | Poland    | 40        | 2.4      | 2.4            | 13.5                |
|       | Mexico    | 46        | 2.8      | 2.8            | 16.3                |
|       | Spain     | 76        | 4.6      | 4.6            | 20.9                |
|       | UK        | 196       | 11.9     | 11.9           | 32.7                |
|       | USA       | 1065      | 64.4     | 64.4           | 97.2                |
|       | Australia | 47        | 2.8      | 2.8            | 100.0               |
|       | Total     | 1653      | 100.0    | 100.0          |                     |

**Stayer or Leaver**

|         |        | Frequency | Per cent | Valid Per cent | Cumulative Per cent |
|---------|--------|-----------|----------|----------------|---------------------|
| Valid   | Stayer | 1441      | 87.2     | 87.2           | 87.2                |
|         | Leaver | 211       | 12.8     | 12.8           | 100.0               |
|         | Total  | 1652      | 99.9     | 100.0          |                     |
| Missing | System | 1         | .1       |                |                     |
| Total   |        | 1653      | 100.0    |                |                     |

So we have data for 1,653 employees in this small financial services organization and the 'Statistics' box in Figure 6.3 tells us that there is only one employee for whom we do not know whether they are a stayer or a leaver, because the data is missing for that person.

Looking at the 'Country Code' table, we can see that the United States is (by far) the country with the most employees, while some other countries have very small populations (and we know from our research into the organization that they are start-up offices). If we were doing any analysis that might be sensitive in terms of dealing with confidential private information for employees (eg analysing survey responses) we would need to carefully consider whether or not to include some of those countries because it might expose the individuals (see our discussion on this in Chapter 12 – ethical considerations).

However, as we are just analysing fairly generic 'HR produced' data here we can consider these small populations not to be at any risk from the analysis. Ideally, chi square requires subgroups to have more than five cases in each cell (ie data for five people in each country), and if any fall below this we might want to consider removing some of the countries from analysis.

Looking at the 'Stayer or Leaver' table, we can see that there were 211 voluntary leavers over the past year. We can see that the crude snapshot (just calculated from the data we have here) separation rate is 12.8 per cent = 211/1,653 = 12.8 per cent. This is the figure calculated in the 'Per cent' column.

We can assume that this indicates a separation rate of 12.8 per cent. To provide a reference for this, Table 6.2 gives an account of the 2013 average voluntary turnover rates by industry as provided by Compensation Force (2014). From this we can see that the average for banking and finance is actually 12.8 per cent (we didn't plan this – honest!). So it appears that this financial services organization has the industry average turnover figure.

**TABLE 6.2**   Average turnover rates by industry 2013

| 2013 Voluntary Turnover | |
| --- | --- |
| All industries | 10.4% |
| Banking and Finance | 12.8% |
| Healthcare | 12.5% |
| Hospitality | 18.2% |
| Insurance | 6.8% |
| Manufacturing and Distribution | 8.4% |
| Not for Profit | 11.0% |
| Services | 11.0% |
| Utilities | 5.2% |

**SOURCE:** Compensation Force (2014)

A quick note on benchmarks, though – just because it is better than or the same as the industry average does not mean it is good.

It would be interesting at this point to investigate how the turnover patterns compare across the 10 different country locations. We can do this by a simple cross-tabulation. Additionally, we can also run a chi-square test to ascertain whether there is a significant difference between what we would expect the separation rate to be in each country and what we observe it to be.

# Example 1b: using chi-square analysis to explore regional differences in individual staff turnover

## Cross-tabulation and chi square

Go into SPSS and select 'Analyze' and then 'Descriptive Statistics' and 'Crosstabs' (Figure 6.4).

**FIGURE 6.4**

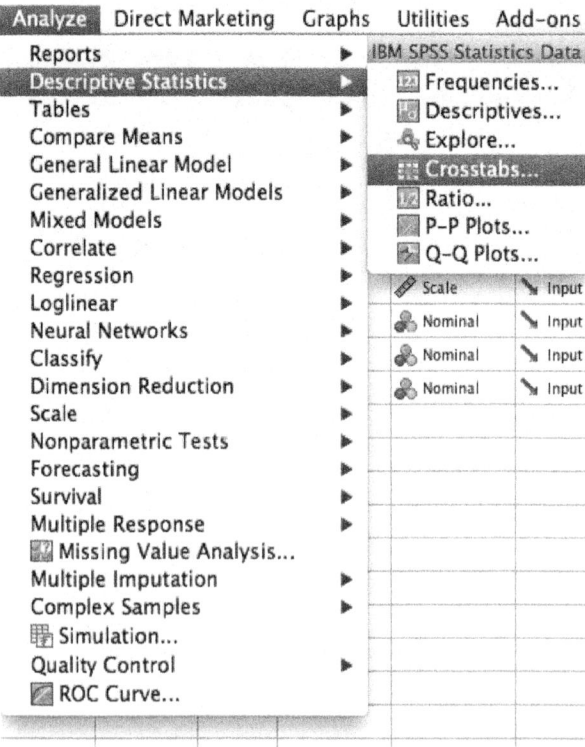

Then select 'LeaverStatus' and 'Country' into the Crosstabs 'Row(s):' and 'Column(s):' boxes and click on the statistics button (Figure 6.5a), which will open up a new dialogue box (Figure 6.6).

**FIGURE 6.5a**

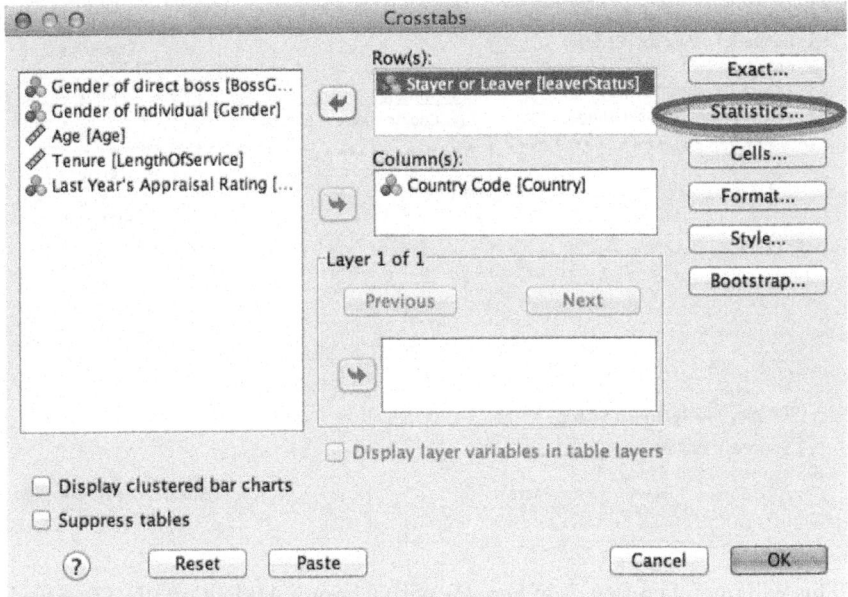

**FIGURE 6.6**

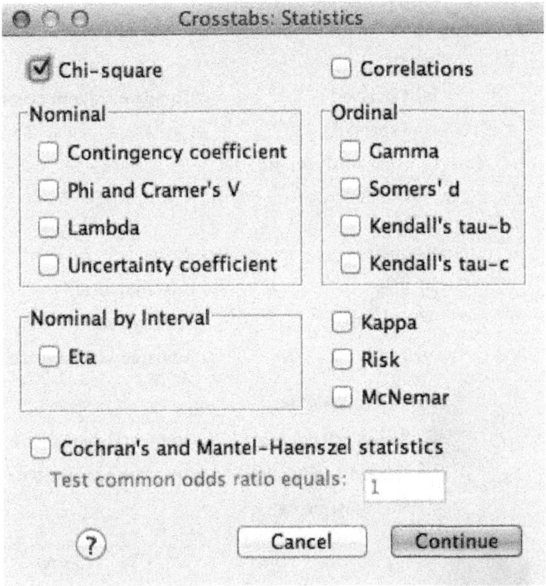

Then select the chi-square option and then 'Continue'. Then, back in the main Crosstabs menu (Figure 6.5b), select 'Cells'.

**FIGURE 6.5b**

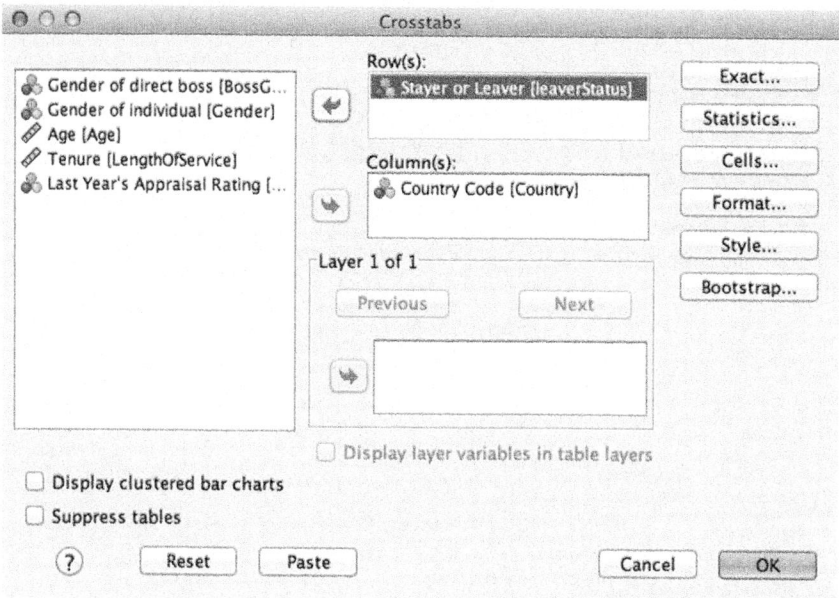

This will open Figure 6.7; in here (as with Chapter 4) click on the 'Observed' option in the 'Counts' selection box and the 'Row Column' and 'Total' option in the 'Percentages' selection box, then click 'Continue'.

**FIGURE 6.7**

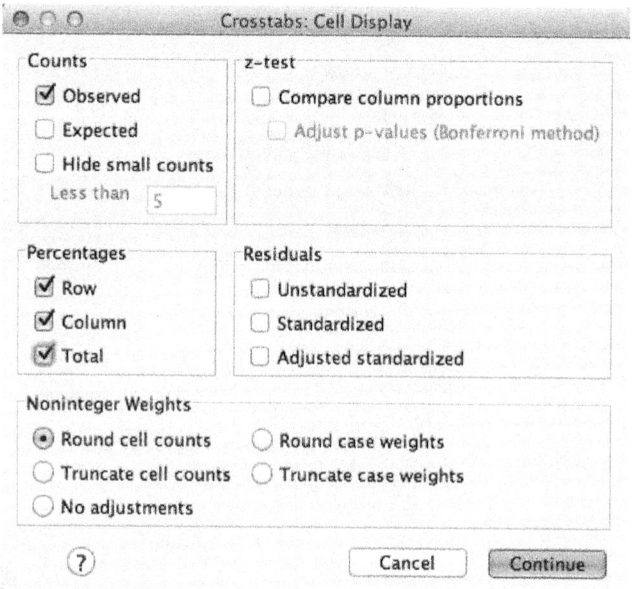

Your 'crosstabs' and chi-square results will be produced in the output box (Figure 6.8).

## FIGURE 6.8

### Crosstabs

**Case Processing Summary**

| | Cases | | | | | |
|---|---|---|---|---|---|---|
| | Valid | | Missing | | Total | |
| | N | Per cent | N | Per cent | N | Per cent |
| Stayer or Leaver * Country Code | 1652 | 99.9% | 1 | 0.1% | 1653 | 100.0% |

**Stayer or Leaver * Country Code Crosstabulation**

| | | | Country Code | | | | | | | | Total |
|---|---|---|---|---|---|---|---|---|---|---|---|
| | | | Belgium | Sweden | Italy | France | Poland | Mexico | Spain | UK | USA | Australia | |
| Stayer or Leaver | Stayer | Count | 33 | 28 | 55 | 31 | 35 | 39 | 64 | 168 | 949 | 39 | 1441 |
| | | % within Stayer or Leaver | 2.3% | 1.9% | 3.8% | 2.2% | 2.4% | 2.7% | 4.4% | 11.7% | 65.9% | 2.7% | 100.0% |
| | | % within Country Code | 82.5% | 77.8% | 78.6% | 83.8% | 87.5% | 84.8% | 84.2% | 85.7% | 89.2% | 83.0% | 87.2% |
| | | % of Total | 2.0% | 1.7% | 3.3% | 1.9% | 2.1% | 2.4% | 3.9% | 10.2% | 57.4% | 2.4% | 87.2% |
| | Leaver | Count | 7 | 8 | 15 | 6 | 5 | 7 | 12 | 28 | (115) | 8 | 211 |
| | | % within Stayer or Leaver | 3.3% | 3.8% | 7.1% | 2.8% | 2.4% | 3.3% | 5.7% | 13.3% | 54.5% | 3.8% | 100.0% |
| | | % within Country Code | 17.5% | 22.2% | 21.4% | 16.2% | 12.5% | 15.2% | 15.8% | 14.3% | (10.8%) | 17.0% | 12.8% |
| | | % of Total | 0.4% | 0.5% | 0.9% | 0.4% | 0.3% | 0.4% | 0.7% | 1.7% | 7.0% | 0.5% | 12.8% |
| Total | | Count | 40 | 36 | 70 | 37 | 40 | 46 | 76 | 196 | 1064 | 47 | 1652 |
| | | % within Stayer or Leaver | 2.4% | 2.2% | 4.2% | 2.2% | 2.4% | 2.8% | 4.6% | 11.9% | 64.4% | 2.8% | 100.0% |
| | | % within Country Code | 100.0% | 100.0% | 100.0% | 100.0% | 100.0% | 100.0% | 100.0% | 100.0% | 100.0% | 100.0% | 100.0% |
| | | % of Total | 2.4% | 2.2% | 4.2% | 2.2% | 2.4% | 2.8% | 4.6% | 11.9% | 64.4% | 2.8% | 100.0% |

### Chi-Square Tests

| | Value | df | Asymp. Sig. (2-sided) |
|---|---|---|---|
| Pearson Chi-Square | 14.509[a] | 9 | .105 |
| Likelihood Ratio | 13.335 | 9 | .148 |
| Linear-by-Linear Association | 9.774 | 1 | .002 |
| N of Valid Cases | 1652 | | |

*No sig diff b/w countries*

As we can see from the main crosstabs table in Figure 6.8 (which is the kind of data that MI functions produce all of the time using Excel and pivot tables), the pattern clearly shows some differences in terms of percentages of staff turnover across the different countries. In Australia, 17 per cent of staff (eight employees) left in 2014, whereas 22.2 per cent of staff left in Sweden in 2014 (eight employees). The country with the most amount of leavers was the United States with 115 leavers, though this was only 10.8 per cent of the country population; only five people left in Poland, but this was 12.5 per cent of the 40 employees employed there. The variations in these leaver percentages are the sort of variations that may cause some concern when presented in a report. It would be easy to think that a country with a 22.2 per cent turnover rate is a real problem, especially when you compare it with the turnover rate of 10.8 per cent in another country.

However, random factors across the globe may influence whether someone has left their job, so you would expect some variation across countries; we can only tell if these variations might be statistically meaningful (in that there might be something about the countries that 'causes' or 'explains' variation in turnover rates in our company) by conducting an inferential test.

The chi-square inferential test in Figure 6.8 shows a Pearson chi-square test parameter value of 14.509 with 9 degrees of freedom, giving a p-value (significance value) of 0.105. Using our rule of thumb that $p<0.05$ is the point at which we determine significance, we would say that there is no significant difference between what we would expect the country turnover figures to be, and what we observe the country turnover figures to be, suggesting that, although the variations in country turnover rates look like a big problem, these are more likely to be due to chance alone.

> **Snapshot hidden gem**
>
> Even though the descriptive report suggested quite large differences between countries in terms of turnover rates, the chi-square analysis confirmed there was no significant difference between what you would expect to see in each country (given its size) and what was observed.

Note that in the data set used here, the leaver status is categorical, ie 1 = stayer, 2 = leaver; and the country variable is also categorical (ie 1 = Belgium, 2 = Sweden, 3 = Italy, etc). Because both the independent variable and the dependent variable are categorical, and because we are looking simply at the association or link between the two variables, the best test for us to use, looking at Table 3.4 (showing which test to use) in Chapter 3 and following the reasoning through, we can see that the chi square is the best test in this situation.

In the next example, we look at a different type of data – team data. In this data set, the dependent variable is a continuous number, showing the team separation rate (ie the number of team members left during the period/average number of members during the period). So here, while we are still looking at the association between two variables, the difference is that the dependent variable is continuous. As the country variable is still a categorical variable, the best test for us to use is the one-way ANOVA test (see Table 3.4 in Chapter 3).

# Example 2: using one-way ANOVA to analyse team-level turnover by country

As a reminder, the one-way ANOVA test is a powerful method for testing the significance of the difference between sample means (ie between the means of country samples) where more than two categorical conditions/groups are compared. It effectively tests the null hypothesis that all the samples are drawn from the same population and that there is no difference between them. If the test suggests there is a difference, then further testing (called 'post-hoc testing') is needed to determine which samples are different and by how much (Coolican, 2009).

The data set used is 'Chapter 6 Turnover team DATA.sav' and the data variables look like this:

1 Team identifier (unique team number).
2 Team size (number of people in the team).
3 Team turnover 2014 (separation rate between 0 and 1).
4 Country (1 = UK; 2 = United States; 3 = CANADA; 4 = SPAIN).
5 SURVEY: ENGAGEMENT items COMBO (composite engagement percentage across the team).
6 SURVEY: TeamLeader Rating (composite team leader percentage across the team).
7 SURVEY: CSR rating (composite corporate social responsibility percentage across the team).
8 SURVEY: Drive for Performance (composite percentage team score on perceived 'Drive for performance' percentage).
9 SURVEY: Performance, Development and Reward (composite percentage team score on perceived fairness of performance, development and reward across the team).
10 SURVEY: Work-Life Balance (composite percentage team score on perceived work–life balance across the team).

**11** UK dummy variable (0 = not UK; 1 = UK).

**12** USA dummy variable (0 = not United States; 1 = United States).

**13** Canada dummy variable (0 = not Canada; 1 = Canada).

**14** Spain dummy variable (0 = not Spain; 1 = Spain).

Here we are going to explore the turnover differences between the four countries in the data set (the UK, United States, Canada and Spain). Here we have 2,910 employees employed across four countries organized in 212 teams. We have team-level engagement survey data provided by our external survey company; for each team we have an average positive response score from a 2013 engagement survey that measured scales of engagement, team leader rating, organizational corporate social responsibility (CSR) rating, perceived culture of 'drive for performance' (the organization's motto), fairness of performance development and reward, and perceived work–life balance (WLB). We also have an indicator of which country the team is based in along with the 2013–14 staff turnover percentage for each team.

First, let's do a frequencies table in SPSS to take a closer look at the data.

Going into the 'Analyze' menu, we select 'Descriptive Statistics' and then 'Frequencies' (Figure 6.9).

### FIGURE 6.9

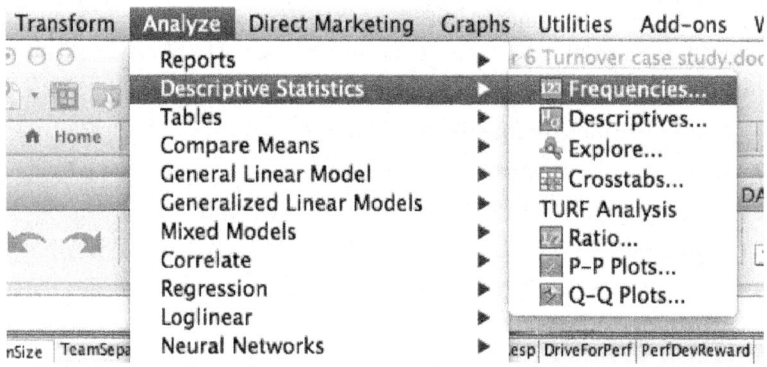

Then select 'Country Code' and move it over to the right panel under the 'Variable(s):' selection box and click 'OK' (Figure 6.10).

## Case Study 3

**FIGURE 6.10**

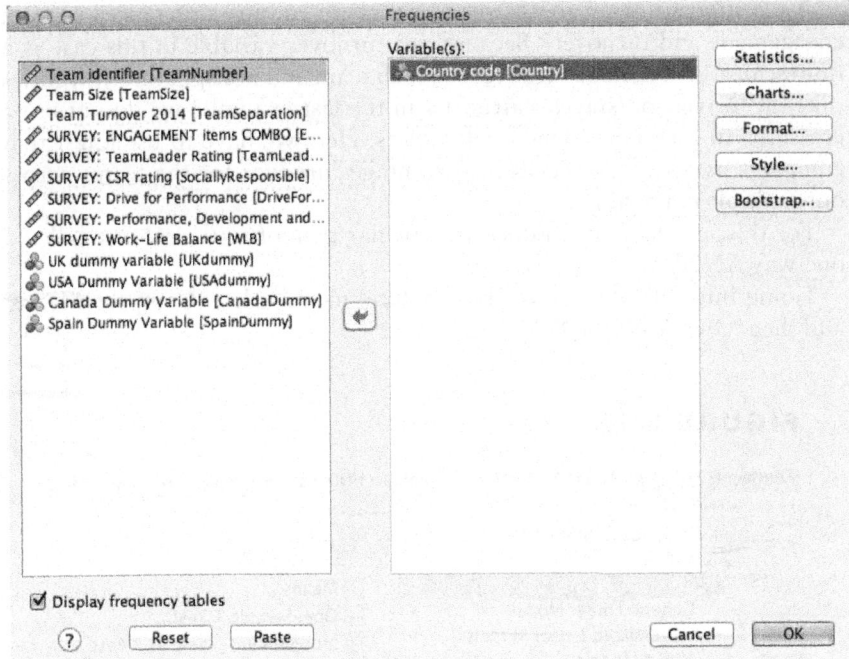

The following output is produced (Figure 6.11).

**FIGURE 6.11**

→ **Frequencies**

**Statistics**

Country code

|   |         |     |
|---|---------|-----|
| N | Valid   | 212 |
|   | Missing | 0   |

**Country code**

|       |        | Frequency | Per cent | Valid Per cent | Cumulative Per cent |
|-------|--------|-----------|----------|----------------|---------------------|
| Valid | UK     | 52        | 24.5     | 24.5           | 24.5                |
|       | USA    | 73        | 34.4     | 34.4           | 59.0                |
|       | Canada | 32        | 15.1     | 15.1           | 74.1                |
|       | Spain  | 55        | 25.9     | 25.9           | 100.0               |
|       | Total  | 212       | 100.0    | 100.0          |                     |

We have data for 212 teams and the 'Country code' box in Figure 6.11 shows us that the teams are not evenly distributed across the countries.

A question we want to answer is: are there country differences in team engagement and turnover? Because our turnover variable in this case is a ratio scale of percentage turnover for each team and not split into categories (like the 'leaver' or 'stayer' categories in the last example) we do not use a crosstabs to ascertain country differences. Here we have to use a test that compares average differences in percentage turnover for the teams across our multiple countries.

For this, we need to conduct a particular type of statistical test called a one-way ANOVA.

Going into SPSS, we go to the 'Analyze' menu, select 'Compare Means' and then 'One-Way ANOVA' (Figure 6.12).

**FIGURE 6.12**

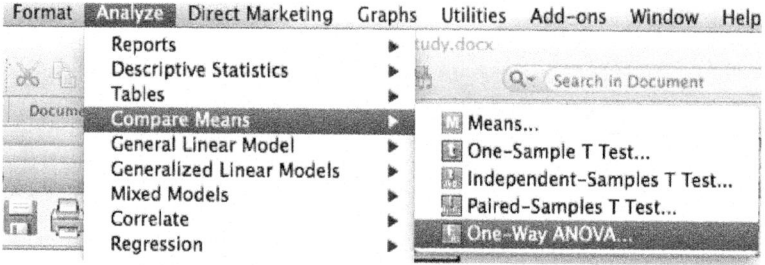

Then we select the following variables from the list on the left-hand side and move them to the right-hand-side box labelled 'Dependent List:'. These variables are 'SURVEY: ENGAGEMENT Items COMBO' and 'Team Turnover 2014'. Then select the 'Country Code' variable and move it to the 'Factor' list on the right-hand side (Figure 6.13).

**FIGURE 6.13**

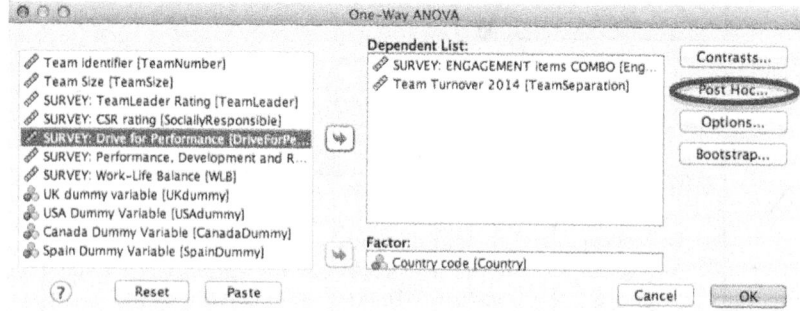

Then click on the 'Post Hoc' button, which opens up a new dialogue box as follows (Figure 6.14):

**FIGURE 6.14**

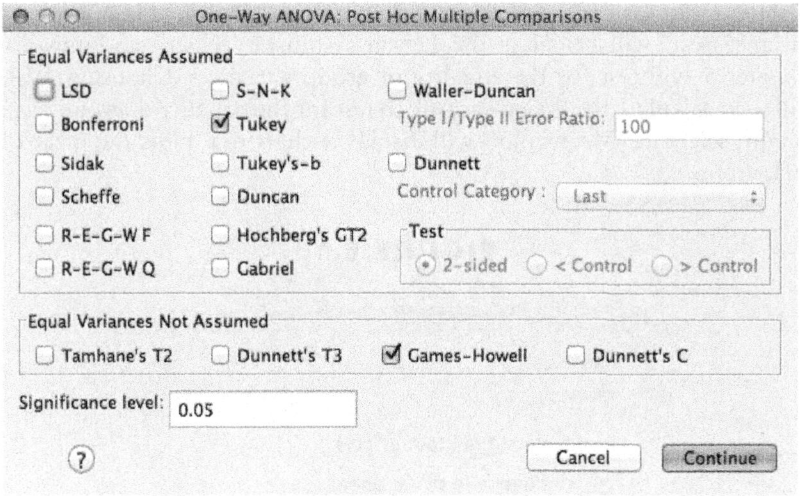

The post-hoc test simply helps to determine *which* means differ once the ANOVA has determined that differences exist. On the post-hoc dialogue box (Figure 6.14), we select 'Tukey' and 'Games-Howell'. We will talk about these selections later in the section on post-hoc testing. Finally, we select a significance level of 0.05, which is our generally agreed rule of thumb value for this book. Click 'Continue'.

Back at the one-way ANOVA dialogue box again, click on 'Options' Figure 6.15.

**FIGURE 6.15**

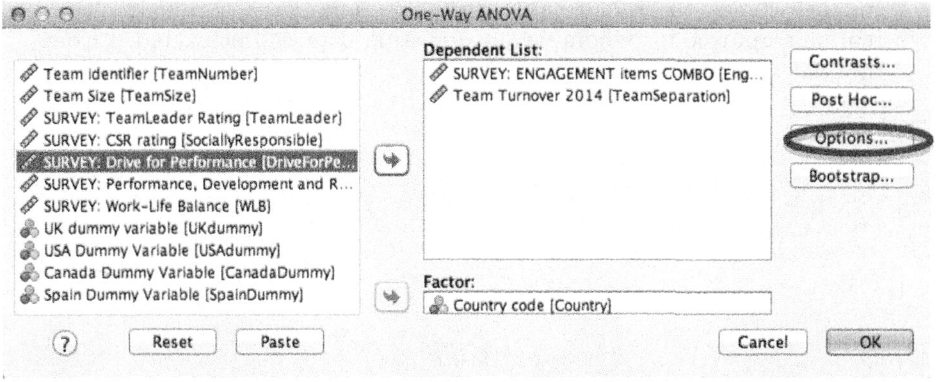

In the subsequent window (Figure 6.16) in the 'Statistics' section select: 'Descriptive', 'Homogeneity of variance test', and 'Welch'. Select 'Means plot'. In the 'Missing Values' section, select: 'Excludes cases analysis by analysis'.

Choosing 'Descriptive' will show the number of employees, mean, standard deviation, etc for each dependent variable. Choosing the 'Homogeneity of variance test' will calculate the Levene's statistic, which we know from Chapter 5 will test for the equality of group variances. Choosing 'Welch' will then calculate the Welch statistic to test for the equality of group means. Finally, selecting 'Means plot' will display a chart that plots the means for each group.

**FIGURE 6.16**

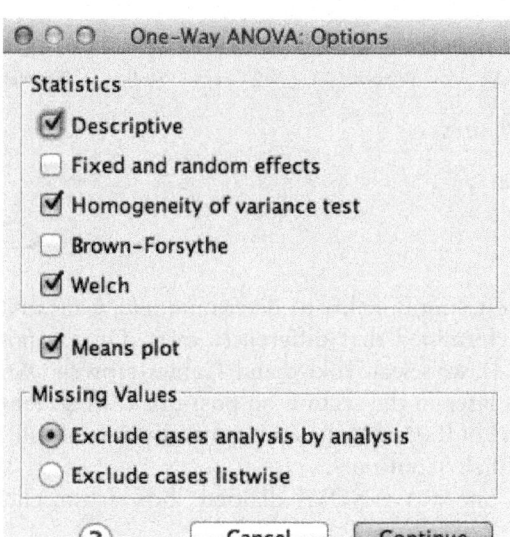

We then choose to exclude cases analysis by analysis. This simply means that an employee for whom we have missing data will be excluded from the analysis.

Case Study 3

Click 'Continue'. This will produce the following output (Figure 6.17):

## FIGURE 6.17

→ Oneway

### Descriptives

| | | N | Mean | Std. Deviation | Std. Error | 95% Confidence Interval for Mean | | Minimum | Maximum |
|---|---|---|---|---|---|---|---|---|---|
| | | | | | | Lower Bound | Upper Bound | | |
| SURVEY: ENGAGEMENT items COMBO | UK | 52 | 82.6923 | 8.43787 | 1.17012 | 80.3432 | 85.0414 | 44.00 | 99.00 |
| | USA | 73 | 86.6164 | 10.56807 | 1.23690 | 84.1507 | 89.0822 | 44.00 | 99.00 |
| | Canada | 32 | 81.6875 | 17.74085 | 3.13617 | 75.2912 | 88.0838 | 34.00 | 99.00 |
| | Spain | 55 | 69.4909 | 10.45957 | 1.41037 | 66.6633 | 72.3185 | 34.00 | 79.00 |
| | Total | 212 | 80.4670 | 13.24733 | .90983 | 78.6735 | 82.2605 | 34.00 | 99.00 |
| Team Turnover 2014 | UK | 52 | .1587 | .20358 | .02823 | .1020 | .2153 | .00 | .70 |
| | USA | 73 | .1601 | .13597 | .01591 | .1284 | .1919 | .00 | .70 |
| | Canada | 32 | .1891 | .12837 | .02269 | .1428 | .2353 | .00 | .60 |
| | Spain | 55 | .2665 | .22422 | .03023 | .2059 | .3272 | .00 | .70 |
| | Total | 212 | .1917 | .18354 | .01261 | .1669 | .2166 | .00 | .70 |

### Test of Homogeneity of Variances

| | Levene Statistic | df1 | df2 | Sig. |
|---|---|---|---|---|
| SURVEY: ENGAGEMENT items COMBO | 13.789 | 3 | 208 | .000 |
| Team Turnover 2014 | 10.273 | 3 | 208 | .000 |

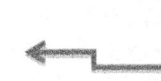

Levene's test is significant, therefore the variances between country with both SURVEY ENGAGEMENT items COMBO and Team Turnover 2014 are significantly different. This means we violate one of the assumptions of ANOVA: that the variances are equal or homogeneous.

### ANOVA

| | | Sum of Squares | df | Mean Square | F | Sig. |
|---|---|---|---|---|---|---|
| SURVEY: ENGAGEMENT items COMBO | Between Groups | 9691.811 | 3 | 3230.604 | 24.581 | .000 |
| | Within Groups | 27336.958 | 208 | 131.428 | | |
| | Total | 37028.769 | 211 | | | |
| Team Turnover 2014 | Between Groups | .438 | 3 | .146 | 4.551 | .004 |
| | Within Groups | 6.670 | 208 | .032 | | |
| | Total | 7.108 | 211 | | | |

### Robust Tests of Equality of Means

| | | Statistic[a] | df1 | df2 | Sig. |
|---|---|---|---|---|---|
| SURVEY: ENGAGEMENT items COMBO | Welch | 29.256 | 3 | 93.477 | .000 |
| Team Turnover 2014 | Welch | 3.446 | 3 | 98.758 | .020 |

a. Asymptotically F distributed.

← country sig. effects engagement
← country sig effects turnover

## Descriptives

So, what is the data in Figure 6.17 telling us? First, let's look at the 'Descriptives' table at the top. For the 'survey engagement items combo' we have:

- **N**: the number of employees measured in each country. We can see that the United States has the largest number of employees measured (73 employees) and Canada has the smallest (32 employees).
- **Mean**: the average calculated engagement combo score for each country in the top section, and the average team turnover in the bottom section. We can see here that the United States has the highest engagement score and Spain the lowest, while Spain has the highest

team turnover measured in 2014 (26.65 per cent) and the UK the lowest (15.87 per cent).

- **Standard deviation**: showing the standard deviation of the engagement combo score for each country. We can see that Canadian teams show a far greater degree of variation in engagement responses than other countries, and the UK much less variation. However, Spain shows greater variation in team turnover across teams and the United States the smallest.

- **Standard error**: showing the standard error of the mean. It takes into account both the standard deviation and the sample size to make estimates of characteristics of likely means of multiple samples from our population. It can be used to help calculate confidence intervals and make estimates of the likely mean of our population of teams. However, given that we are working with all of our possible teams in each country we can comfortably consider the means and standard deviations to represent characteristics of the teams in our countries. This shows us that the United States has the smallest standard error; this is to be expected because theirs is the largest sample and also it has the smallest standard deviation.

- **95 per cent confidence interval**: linked to the standard error statistic, the confidence interval shows the estimated range of your statistic where we can be 95 per cent certain that the mean of the relevant wider population should be contained. For example, with the 'survey engagement combo', the upper and lower bound intervals represent the range where you can be 95 per cent certain that the population of each country should be contained within this range. This is particularly important if your data represents a sample from the country populations rather than data of all employees within these countries. Specifically, we can be 95 per cent certain that the mean team engagement items combo for our employee population in Spain falls between 66.6633 and 72.3185; and 95 per cent certain that the average 2014 team turnover statistic in the United States (within our organization) falls between 12.84 per cent and 19.19 per cent. However, given that we are working with all of our possible teams in each country we can comfortably consider the means and standard deviations to represent characteristics of the teams in our countries.

- **Maximum and minimum**: showing the highest and lowest team value for each country on the survey engagement combo score. So for example, the minimum average team engagement combo score for the UK is 44, while the maximum average team engagement combo score for the UK is 99. The minimum team turnover figure for Canada is 0, whilst the maximum is 60 per cent.

Spending some time reviewing the 'Descriptives' table gives us a good feel for the data and what it might be trying to tell us.

## Test of homogeneity of variances

The next table in Figure 6.17, the 'Test of Homogeneity of Variances', uses the Levene's test that we used in the independent samples t-test example in Chapter 4 (diversity example 2). As a reminder, Levene's test will test whether the variance patterns of the particular statistic analysed (average team scores and team percentage turnover) across the groups (countries in this case) are the same. Put another way, it tests the null hypothesis that the variance patterns of the groups are the same. If the test comes out as significant (ie with p<0.05) then we could say that the variance patterns across the groups are significantly different (See Chapter 3 'Significance').

The reason this is important is that one of the assumptions of ANOVA is that the variance patterns of data in groups should be the same. In our example, the table shows a significance level of the Levene's test of 0.000 for both 'survey engagement items combo' and 'team turnover' in relation to country. In practice, what this means is that we need to use Welch's F-statistic rather than the F-statistic given in the ANOVA table.

If Levene's test had come out as not significant (ie with a p-value >=0.05) then we would report the F-statistic given in the ANOVA table when considering whether the countries are significantly different in terms of team turnover and engagement.

Next, then, let's go straight to the bottom table in Figure 6.17.

## Robust test of equality of means

First let's look at the 'SURVEY: ENGAGEMENT items COMBO' dependent variable, remembering that we are testing whether there is any significant difference in the team means of the 'engagement items combo' mean values across the countries. Looking at the table, we can see that we have a Welch's F-statistic of 29.256 with 3 degrees of freedom, giving a significance value of 0.000 (p<0.001). Hence we can say that there is a significant effect of 'country' on the team survey engagement combo values. We cannot say at this stage exactly what that country effect was (just that the team engagement levels differ across the countries somewhere) but we can look into that next.

Looking also at the tests for 'Team Turnover 2014', we can see that with the calculated parameters of Welch's F-statistic of 3.446 and degrees of freedom of 3, a significance value of 0.020 is calculated, so p<0.05 again. Hence we can say that there is a significant effect of country on the team turnover 2014 value.

To identify which countries differ, we need to look at the post-hoc tests.

## Post-hoc tests

After any ANOVA, you need to undertake further analysis to determine which groups differ. In our situation, we know from the Welch's F-statistic that 'country' has a significant impact on both 'SURVEY ENGAGEMENT items COMBO' and 'Team Turnover 2014'.

Note that there are many different types of post-hoc tests, which can be confusing when deciding which one to use. If you are interested in further reading on these tests, we recommend reading Field (2009). For the purposes of this book, though, Table 6.3 may help.

Please be aware that Table 6.3 is very simplified and only a subset of what is available. It should, though, get you through most situations that you come across in HR analytics.

**TABLE 6.3** Post-hoc tests

| Situation | Test | Benefit |
| --- | --- | --- |
| If the group variances are not equal. | Games-Howell | A good idea to select this in all analysis alongside the other tests because we don't know until after the ANOVA whether the group variances are equal or not (until we look at Levene's test). That way, it will be there if you need it without having to run the ANOVA again. If you don't need it, you can ignore it. |
| Equal sample sizes and population variances are similar. | REGWQ or Tukey | Good statistical sensitivity to correctly reject the null hypothesis or otherwise (the null hypothesis that there is no difference between the group means). |
|  | Bonferroni | More conservative than REGWQ or Tukey (so less chance of getting a significant result) but good to use if you want guaranteed control that you will not make a Type I error (ie that you will not incorrectly reject the null hypothesis that the group means are the same). |
| Sample sizes are slightly different. | Gabriel's procedure | Good statistical sensitivity to correctly reject the null hypothesis in this situation. |
| Sample sizes are very different. | Hochberg's GT2 | Offers best performance in this situation. |

In this example, we selected the Games-Howell test – because, as it turns out, Levene's test told us that the group variances are not equal. So, ignoring Tukey test in this instance (which we would have used if Levene's was not significant), we look at the Games-Howell test.

Because we have no specific hypothesis about the effect that 'country' may have on either 'Team Turnover 2014' or 'SURVEY: ENGAGEMENT items COMBO', then we carry out this post-hoc test to compare all countries with each other.

In Figure 6.18 we present the post-hoc testing for team engagement; Figure 6.19 shows team turnover post-hoc results.

So, for each country, the difference between country means is shown in the 'Mean Difference (I-J)' column. For example, looking at the Games-Howell result first line in Figure 6.18, we see that mean difference in team engagement between the UK and the United States is (–3.9241). If we were to calculate this manually, we would look back to the descriptives table and calculate it as follows:

$$\begin{aligned} &\text{UK mean} - \text{US mean} \\ &= 82.6923 - 86.6164 \\ &= -3.9241 \end{aligned}$$

Then it compares the UK mean to the Canada mean and the Spain mean in the same way.

Moving to the right, we can see the standard error of that difference, the significance level (this is what we should focus on here) and the 95 per cent confidence interval.

After this, it compares the United States to the other three countries, Canada to the other three countries, and finally Spain to the other three countries in the same way.

Looking down the significance column for the Games-Howell (bottom half) of the table in Figure 6.18 we can see that there is a significant difference ($p<0.05$) between:

- Differences in SURVEY: ENGAGEMENT items COMBO values for UK and Spain ($p = 0.000$, $p<0.001$).
- Differences in SURVEY: ENGAGEMENT items COMBO values for USA and Spain ($p = 0.000$, $p<0.001$).
- Differences in SURVEY: ENGAGEMENT items COMBO values for Canada and Spain ($p = 0.005$, $p<0.01$).
- Differences in SURVEY: ENGAGEMENT items COMBO values for Canada and USA ($p = 0.469$, $p>0.05$).
- Differences in SURVEY: ENGAGEMENT items COMBO values for Canada and UK ($p = 0.990$, $p>0.05$).
- Differences in SURVEY: ENGAGEMENT items COMBO values for USA and UK ($p = 0.103$, $p>0.05$).

**FIGURE 6.18** Post-hoc testing for team engagement

## Post Hoc Tests

**Multiple Comparisons**

| Dependent Variable | | (I) Country code | (J) Country code | Mean Difference (I-J) | Std. Error | Sig. | 95% Confidence Interval | |
|---|---|---|---|---|---|---|---|---|
| | | | | | | | Lower Bound | Upper Bound |
| SURVEY: ENGAGEMENT items COMBO | Tukey HSD | UK | USA | -3.92413 | 2.08034 | .237 | -9.3121 | 1.4638 |
| | | | Canada | 1.00481 | 2.57577 | .980 | -5.6662 | 7.6758 |
| | | | Spain | 13.20140* | 2.21744 | .000 | 7.4584 | 18.9444 |
| | | USA | UK | 3.92413 | 2.08034 | .237 | -1.4638 | 9.3121 |
| | | | Canada | 4.92894 | 2.43053 | .181 | -1.3660 | 11.2238 |
| | | | Spain | 17.12553* | 2.04694 | .000 | 11.8241 | 22.4269 |
| | | Canada | UK | -1.00481 | 2.57577 | .980 | -7.6758 | 5.6662 |
| | | | USA | -4.92894 | 2.43053 | .181 | -11.2238 | 1.3660 |
| | | | Spain | 12.19659* | 2.54886 | .000 | 5.5952 | 18.7979 |
| | | Spain | UK | -13.20140* | 2.21744 | .000 | -18.9444 | -7.4584 |
| | | | USA | -17.12553* | 2.04694 | .000 | -22.4269 | -11.8241 |
| | | | Canada | -12.19659* | 2.54886 | .000 | -18.7979 | -5.5952 |
| | Games-Howell | UK | USA | -3.92413 | 1.70268 | .103 | -8.3596 | .5113 |
| | | | Canada | 1.00481 | 3.34735 | .990 | -7.9698 | 9.9794 |
| | | | Spain | 13.20140* | 1.83257 | .000 | 8.4153 | 17.9875 |
| | | USA | UK | 3.92413 | 1.70268 | .103 | -.5113 | 8.3596 |
| | | | Canada | 4.92894 | 3.37127 | .469 | -4.0983 | 13.9562 |
| | | | Spain | 17.12553* | 1.87592 | .000 | 12.2363 | 22.0148 |
| | | Canada | UK | -1.00481 | 3.34735 | .990 | -9.9794 | 7.9698 |
| | | | USA | -4.92894 | 3.37127 | .469 | -13.9562 | 4.0983 |
| | | | Spain | 12.19659* | 3.43871 | .005 | 3.0134 | 21.3798 |
| | | Spain | UK | -13.20140* | 1.83257 | .000 | -17.9875 | -8.4153 |
| | | | USA | -17.12553* | 1.87592 | .000 | -22.0148 | -12.2363 |
| | | | Canada | -12.19659* | 3.43871 | .005 | -21.3798 | -3.0134 |

**FIGURE 6.19** Post-hoc testing for team turnover

| Team Turnover 2014 | | | | Mean Diff | Std Error | Sig. | Lower | Upper |
|---|---|---|---|---|---|---|---|---|
| Tukey HSD | UK | USA | | -.00148 | .03250 | 1.000 | -.0856 | .0827 |
| | | Canada | | -.03041 | .04024 | .874 | -.1346 | .0738 |
| | | Spain | | -.10789* | .03464 | .011 | -.1976 | -.0182 |
| | USA | UK | | .00148 | .03250 | 1.000 | -.0827 | .0856 |
| | | Canada | | -.02893 | .03797 | .871 | -.1273 | .0694 |
| | | Spain | | -.10641* | .03197 | .006 | -.1892 | -.0236 |
| | Canada | UK | | .03041 | .04024 | .874 | -.0738 | .1346 |
| | | USA | | .02893 | .03797 | .871 | -.0694 | .1273 |
| | | Spain | | -.07748 | .03982 | .212 | -.1806 | .0256 |
| | Spain | UK | | .10789* | .03464 | .011 | .0182 | .1976 |
| | | USA | | .10641* | .03197 | .006 | .0236 | .1892 |
| | | Canada | | .07748 | .03982 | .212 | -.0256 | .1806 |
| Games–Howell | UK | USA | | -.00148 | .03241 | 1.000 | -.0865 | .0835 |
| | | Canada | | -.03041 | .03622 | .835 | -.1254 | .0646 |
| | | Spain | | -.10789* | .04137 | .050 | -.2159 | .0001 |
| | USA | UK | | .00148 | .03241 | 1.000 | -.0835 | .0865 |
| | | Canada | | -.02893 | .02772 | .725 | -.1021 | .0442 |
| | | Spain | | -.10641* | .03417 | .013 | -.1960 | -.0168 |
| | Canada | UK | | .03041 | .03622 | .835 | -.0646 | .1254 |
| | | USA | | .02893 | .02772 | .725 | -.0442 | .1021 |
| | | Spain | | -.07748 | .03780 | .178 | -.1765 | .0216 |
| | Spain | UK | | .10789* | .04137 | .050 | -.0001 | .2159 |
| | | USA | | .10641* | .03417 | .013 | .0168 | .1960 |
| | | Canada | | .07748 | .03780 | .178 | -.0216 | .1765 |

*. The mean difference is significant at the 0.05 level.

And:

- Differences in Team Turnover 2014 values for UK and Spain (p = 0.050, p>0.05).
- Differences in Team Turnover 2014 values for USA and Spain (p = 0.013, p<0.05).
- Differences in Team Turnover 2014 values for Canada and Spain (p = 0.178, p>0.05).
- Differences in Team Turnover 2014 values for Canada and USA (p = 0.715, p>0.05).
- Differences in Team Turnover 2014 values for Canada and UK (p = 0.835, p>0.05).
- Differences in Team Turnover 2014 values for USA and UK (p = 1.00, p>0.05; this is no surprise as the mean of team turnover for both of these countries is much the same at 16 per cent).

> **Snapshot hidden gem**
>
> We can now deduce that the impact that 'country' has on both 'SURVEY: ENGAGEMENT items COMBO' values and 'Team Turnover' within our ANOVA (and Welch) is mainly due to how different Spain is compared to the other countries in our data set. We can say that Spain has significantly lower engagement than all other countries based on the survey engagement items combo values, and significantly higher turnover than both the UK and the United States. However, the remaining countries do not show any significant differences from each other.

Recommendations that may come from the above would be to investigate possible causes of the low engagement in Spain (see Chapter 5, engagement case study, for more details about analysis linked to engagement). Now that we can be certain that Spain has a significantly higher turnover than both the UK and the United States, a recommendation can be made to direct resources into investigating why this is – using predictive models such as the regression analysis later in this chapter. It may be a combination of things, including market conditions (such as local competition for talented employees), employee engagement and desire to leave (as the results here seem to hint), or other factors such as length of service or appraisal rating. Regardless, we can be confident in recommending that resources be directed towards Spain to more closely diagnose the turnover situation and prescribe action. Figure 6.20 shows the mean levels of 'Team Turnover 2014' for each country.

**FIGURE 6.20**  Mean levels of 'Team Turnover 2014'

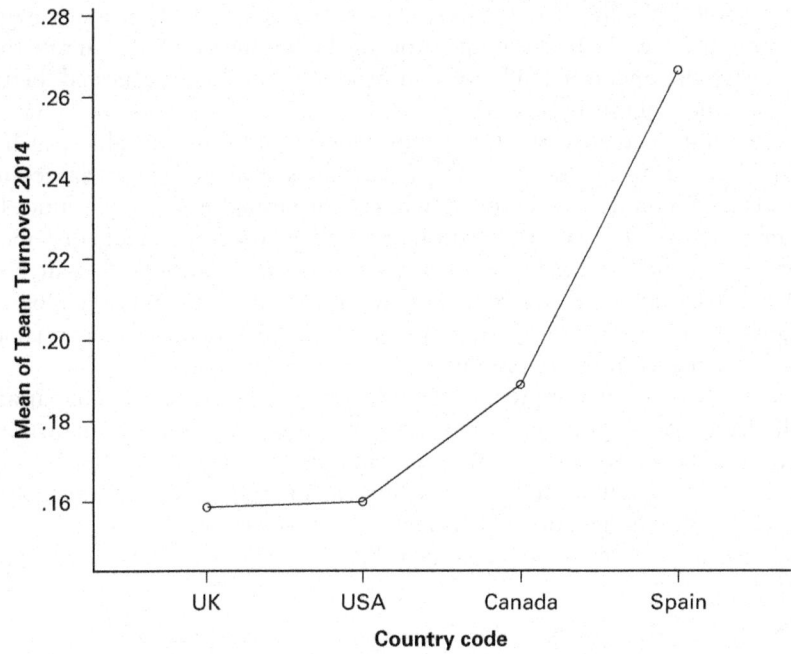

In the two examples below, we use regression modelling to predict turnover. In the first example, we look at individual turnover. Now, because individual turnover is a binary event – ie there are only two outcomes – we will use logistic regression; and because team turnover is a continuous variable – a percentage that could take on any value between 1 and 100 on a linear scale – we use multiple linear regression to predict it.

# Example 3: predicting individual turnover

The data set that we used in this example is 'Chapter 6 Individual Turnover.sav'; the predictive models use binary/dichotomous data as the logistic regression.

## *Logistic regression*

We discuss logistic regression in more detail in Chapter 3 and Chapter 4; here is a quick recap. We see in Chapter 5 (engagement case study) – and in other chapters to follow – that we can use ordinary least squares (OLS) multiple linear regression to model and predict performance based on recorded/ historical data. Some dependent variable measures are ideal for this type of regression because they are often continuous variables. What is a continuous variable? It is one that could be measured along a continuum and has a numerical value: for example, the average scan rate (how many items) per minute for each checkout operator; the higher the average scan rate then the faster the operator tends to scan products (thus this suggested 'better' performance on this indicator).

Not all dependent variables are continuous, and some variables, such as individual turnover, are categorical variables. Categorical variables are discrete, or nominal. They do not have a meaningful numeric value: for example, the office country location or whether someone is male or female. For this type of variable (if we want to account for variation in this categorical variable), the regression modelling we need to undertake is called logistic regression. In logistic regression, the predictor variables (independent variables) may be categorical or continuous.

So, as discussed in Chapter 3, the nature of the data included in our variable will dictate which type of statistical analysis we use. And while team turnover in the example above is a continuous number (ie the percentage of people who left in a specific time period within each team), individual turnover is a binary event: either someone has left or they have not.

As a reminder, the data in this file is linked to 1,653 employees and looks like this:

1 BossGender (gender of line manager: 0 = female, 1 = male).
2 Gender (gender of individual: 0 = female, 1 = male).
3 Age (actual number).
4 LengthofService (number of completed years).
5 AppraisalRating (performance appraisal rating on a scale of 1 to 5, with 5 being the highest).
6 Country (1 = Belgium; 2 = Sweden; 3 = Italy; 4 = France; 5 = Poland; 6 = Mexico; 7 = Spain; 8 = UK; 9 = United States; 10 = Australia).
7 LeaverStatus (whether or not the individual has left the organization: 0 = stayer; 1 = leaver).

We are going to predict leaver status with the other variables in the data set. Going into SPSS, this involves selecting 'Analyze→Regression' and the 'Binary Logistic' regression option (see Figure 6.21).

**FIGURE 6.21** Binary logistic regression in SPSS

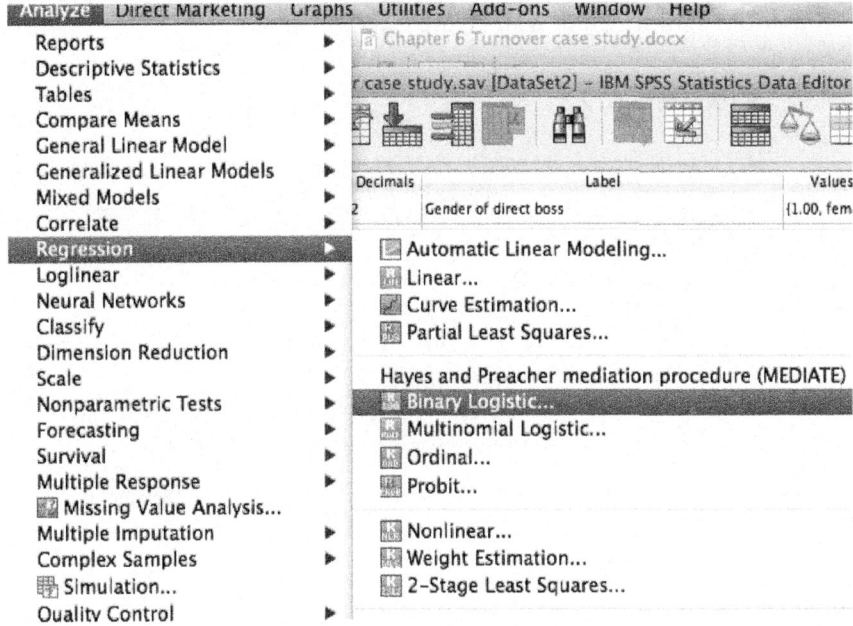

Then select 'Leaver Status' into the 'Dependent:' selection box and all remaining variables into the 'Covariates:' selection box (see Figure 6.22).

**FIGURE 6.22** Logistic regression for individual leavers

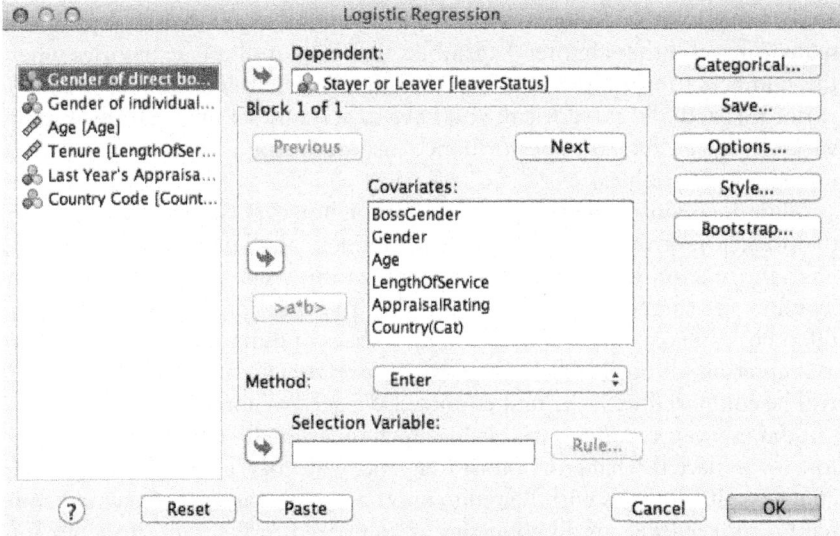

Before running the analysis, tell SPSS that the 'Country Code' variable is a categorical variable. Click on the 'Categorical' button (see Figure 6.22 for this button) and the window in Figure 6.23 will appear.

**FIGURE 6.23**

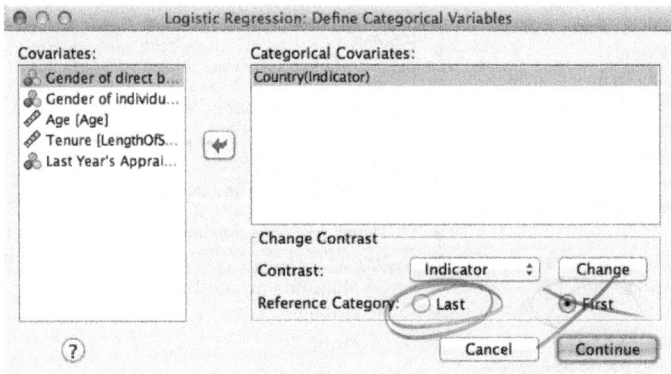

In this 'Categorical' menu box, you need to select the 'Country' variable and pull it across into the 'Categorical Covariates:' box (see Figure 6.23). And then tick the 'Reference Category:' 'Last' option (if it is not selected already). Then click on the 'Change' button and press 'Continue'.

This is an important process because SPSS would otherwise treat the 1–10 country coding as a numerical variable and the analysis would assume that this was a single numerical scale – it would check to see if 'the *more* country a person works in, are they *more* likely to be a leaver'. This of course makes no sense. You cannot have *more country*. In other types of analysis (eg with OLS linear regression – as outlined in Chapter 3 and used many times in other chapters) variables that have multiple categories where the numbers are in effect labels, we cannot just tell SPSS that a predictor variable is actually categorical; you have to actually set up separate 'dummy variables' (see Chapter 7, performance case study, for a discussion on setting up 'dummy' variables).

With the binary logistic regression option, however, SPSS expects some of the predictor variables to have multiple numerically labelled categories and has a process for dealing with these. Importantly, when you tell SPSS to treat 'country' as categorical and indicate that the first category should be the reference category this is like setting up a series of dummies for each country and entering all but the first category as a reference category (all countries will be compared with the first country). We need to consider the fact that in our data set our country variable has Belgium as the first category and therefore if we selected 'Change Contrast Reference Category' to 'First' here, it would compare all countries with Belgium; in other words the analysis would compare turnover levels of all countries as compared to Belgium (if we wanted to change this we could simply recode whatever country is preferred as a reference category to 1 and recode the Belgium group as another number). However, remember that we selected 'Last' as our selected 'Change Contrast Reference Category' – this means that all countries will be compared with the last category in the variable, which in this case is Australia (category 10).

Clicking 'Continue' and 'OK' will give the following output (Figure 6.24).

## FIGURE 6.24

**Omnibus Tests of Model Coefficients**

|        |       | Chi-square | df | Sig. |
|--------|-------|------------|----|------|
| Step 1 | Step  | 49.799     | 14 | .000 |
|        | Block | 49.799     | 14 | .000 |
|        | Model | 49.799     | 14 | .000 |

① Model is Sig.

**Model Summary**

| Step | -2 Log likelihood | Cox and Snell R-Square | Nagelkerke R-Square |
|------|-------------------|------------------------|---------------------|
| 1    | 1204.203ᵃ         | .030                   | .056                |

a. Estimation terminated at iteration number 5 because parameter estimates changed by less than .001.

② can account for 5.6% turnover

and

**Classification Tableᵃ**

|        |                  |        | Predicted |        |                     |
|--------|------------------|--------|-----------|--------|---------------------|
|        |                  |        | Stayer or Leaver | | Percentage Correct |
|        | Observed         |        | Stayer    | Leaver |                     |
| Step 1 | Stayer or Leaver | Stayer | 1441      | 0      | 100.0               |
|        |                  | Leaver | 209       | 0      | .0                  |
|        | Overall Percentage |      |           |        | 87.3                |

a. The cut value is .500

**Variables in the Equation**

|        |                | B     | S.E. | Wald   | df | Sig.  | Exp(B) |
|--------|----------------|-------|------|--------|----|-------|--------|
| Step 1ᵃ | BossGender    | -.184 | .163 | 1.268  | 1  | .260  | .832   |
|        | Gender         | -.608 | .162 | 14.151 | 1  | .000  | .544   |
|        | Age            | -.001 | .009 | .021   | 1  | .886  | .999   |
|        | LengthOfService| -.017 | .011 | 2.488  | 1  | .115  | .983   |
|        | AppraisalRating| -.248 | .097 | 6.499  | 1  | .011  | .780   |
|        | Country        |       |      | 9.188  | 9  | .420  |        |
|        | Country(1)     | -.249 | .604 | .170   | 1  | .680  | .779   |
|        | Country(2)     | .002  | .594 | .000   | 1  | .998  | 1.002  |
|        | Country(3)     | -.059 | .516 | .013   | 1  | .909  | .943   |
|        | Country(4)     | -.455 | .624 | .532   | 1  | .466  | .634   |
|        | Country(5)     | -.734 | .649 | 1.281  | 1  | .258  | .480   |
|        | Country(6)     | -.415 | .597 | .485   | 1  | .486  | .660   |
|        | Country(7)     | -.572 | .535 | 1.141  | 1  | .285  | .565   |
|        | Country(8)     | -.506 | .471 | 1.154  | 1  | .283  | .603   |
|        | Country(9)     | -.698 | .434 | 2.592  | 1  | .107  | .497   |
|        | Constant       | .168  | .657 | .066   | 1  | .798  | 1.183  |

a. Variable(s) entered on step 1: BossGender, Gender, Age, LengthOfService, AppraisalRating, Country.

The tables in Figure 6.24 give us a huge amount of information, SPSS also produces other results, which we do not need to consider at this point. So to simplify things, here we focus on the information given in Figure 6.24.

## Omnibus tests of model coefficients

In the top table shown in Figure 6.24 we have an index of how good our model is at accounting for turnover across our organization. Here we see that our model chi square is 49.799 and this is deemed to be significant ($p<0.001$). Thus, importantly in this case, our five independent variables plus our nine country categories (with a reference category of Australia) significantly account for variation in the leaver versus stayer variable in our data set. In other words, we can identify features that may well account for whether or not people have left.

## Model summary

The second table in Figure 6.24 has two key estimations of R-square statistics. As we have discussed in previous sections, our R-square figure is an indication of the degree of variation in our dependent variable that is accounted for by the variation in our predictor variables. The Nagelkerke R-square is a figure that most closely equates with the multiple R-square figure in multiple linear regression (that we have used in previous chapters). Here the Nagelkerke R is referred to as a pseudo R-square in that it gives an estimated indication of the percentage variation (whether people leave or not) that we account for in our dependent variable with our proposed model. So on the assumption that this works the same as an R-square statistic produced with linear multiple regression, here this indicates that just from looking at these six variables in our data set, we can account for 5.6 per cent of turnover across our organization. Whilst this may seem like a small percentage, we need to consider all of the possible causes of people leaving an organization and be impressed that these few predictors actually account for a not-insubstantial amount of variation.

## Variables in the equation

The bottom table in Figure 6.24, the busiest table, gives us lots of information about the particular unique patterns of prediction of turnover from our model.

See Chapter 3 for our more detailed explanation of logistic regression; however, it is clear from the analysis that gender and appraisal ratings are the two factors (that we have looked at here) that significantly account for individual staff turnover. Looking down the significance column, these two factors have p-values below 0.05 ($p<0.05$). Gender has a significance level of $p<0.001$ and appraisal rating is 0.011, $p<0.05$. To interpret what this means we need to look further at something called odds ratios.

## Odds ratios

At this point it might be useful to take a step back and explain odds ratios.

The most well-known use of odds in everyday life is betting on horses or sports. At the time of writing this chapter (spring 2015), the odds of Australia winning the 2015 Rugby World Cup were 10/1, or '10 to 1'. In this way, the bookmaker believes that the odds of Australia winning are 10/1. These are relatively good odds, and anyone who follows rugby will know that Australia is a strong rugby nation and, in the seven Rugby World Cup events that have taken place since inception, Australia have won it twice.

By comparison, countries that do not have such a strong record for rugby such as Romania and Canada will have higher odds because there is less chance of them winning. At the time of writing these are 5,000/1 and 2,000/1 respectively. Indeed the table of the odds at one of the UK's leading bookmakers looked like this:

New Zealand 11/8
Canada 2,000/1
Scotland 200/1
South Africa 11/2
United States 3,000/1
Italy 1,000/1
Australia 10/1
Romania 5,000/1
Fiji 1,000/1
France 22/1

Argentina 75/1
England 9/2
Tonga 2,000/1
Samoa 300/1
Ireland 7/1
Uruguay 5,000/1
Japan 1,000/1
Wales 16/1
Namibia 5,000/1
Georgia 2,000/1

Talking about money for a moment, if you put £10 down on Australia to win, you would win £100 if Australia did indeed win. If, however you put £10 down for Romania to win and they surprised everyone and came through to win the cup, you would win £50,000. You would be taking a bigger risk, but the payout would be higher. The bookmakers calculate these odds to ensure that the big payouts are unlikely. How do they know who is more likely to win? Bookmakers are known to use logistic regression to determine this by modelling independent variables such as past performance, stadium size and the distance that the team has to travel. Indeed Paddy Power, a UK bookmaker, famously employed Professor Stephen Hawking to determine the optimum conditions of England to succeed in the football world cup, as well as how the team could triumph in a penalty shootout.

Which method did Stephen Hawking use? Logistic regression, of course! He used it to find what they could do to maximize the odds of winning. This was referenced in many newspaper articles and blogs; however, Moore-Bridger and Lynch (2014) in the *London Evening Standard* described that Hawking, using logistic regression, found that the four conditions (independent variables) that account for the probability of winning a penalty shootout (dependent variable) are:

- Have a run-up of more than three steps.
- Use the side foot rather than laces.

- Put the ball in the top left or right corners.
- Choose a fair-haired player, because statistically they are more likely to score.

Odds ratios are calculated and interpreted in a similar way.

So while OLS multiple linear regression uses ordinary least squares to find a best-fitting line and comes up with coefficients that predict the change in the dependent variable for one unit change in the independent variable, logistic regression estimates the probability of an event occurring. So what we want to predict is not a precise numerical value of a dependent variable (because it is a binary variable, not a continuous variable), but rather the probability (p) that the value of it is (1) 'leaver' rather than (0) not-leaver – or 'stayer' (much as we were predicting the probability of a team winning the World Cup (1) versus not winning the World Cup (0).

In our example, logistic regression estimates the probability of an individual leaving the organization. Logistic regression allows us to calculate odds ratios, which are the ratio of the odds of the event occurring to it not occurring.

Say Australia progresses to the final and the probability of winning the World Cup has now increased to 0.8. Therefore p=0.8. Then the probability of not winning would be 0.2. (calculated as 1–p). It may be helpful to think of it as an 80 per cent chance of winning and 20 per cent chance of not winning.

The odds of winning are then defined as p/(1–p), or 0.8/0.2. We would say that the odds of winning are 4 to 1 on. The odds of not winning would be 0.2/0.8, or 1 to 4, or '1 to 4' against.

In our turnover example, the odds ratio is the likelihood or odds of Y=1 (rather than 0) if the value of x is increased by one unit. In our example using leaver status and the continuous variable tenure it would be:

Odds Ratio = ratio of the probability that Leaver Status (Y) = Leaver (1)/Leaver Status (Y) = 0 (stayer) if the value of Tenure (x) is increased by one unit.

So if the odds ratio for tenure was 2.00, we could say that odds of an individual being a 'leaver' compared to being a 'stayer' doubles for every additional year of service. Another way of looking at this is that you are twice as likely to be a leaver as a stayer for every one year you stay with the organization.

If we include a categorical variable such as country, SPSS will automatically create the 'dummy' variables for you (though you have to indicate whether the first or last category is the reference category). To demonstrate, we have the following 10 country categories: 1 = Belgium; 2 = Sweden; 3 = Italy; 4 = France; 5 = Poland; 6 = Mexico; 7 = Spain; 8 = UK; 9 = United States; 10 = Australia.

When you indicate that the last country category is the reference category (which we did in setting up this analysis), SPSS will form nine comparators (dummy variables) for each country with which to compare Australia.

Country (1)         (1 = Belgium; 0 = not Belgium)
Country (2)         (1 = Sweden; 0 = not Sweden)
Country (3)         (1 = Italy; 0 = not Italy)
Country (4)         (1 = France; 0 = not France)
Country (5)         (1 = Poland; 0 = not Poland)
Country (6)         (1 = Mexico; 0 = not Mexico)
Country (7)         (1 = Spain; 0 = not Spain)
Country (8)         (1 = UK; 0 = not UK)
Country (9)         (1 = United States; 0 = not United States)
Reference country   (1 = Australia; 0 = not Australia)

So an odds ratio for country (9) of .497 would mean that after controlling for all other factors, if an individual was based in the United States, they are nearly half as likely to be a leaver than if they were based in Australia (our reference country category in this case).

The logistic regression model equation does look very similar to the linear regression equation, except that it looks at the probability of y instead of the value y. In the equation below, p refers to the probability that y=1, and Ln is the natural logarithm (that makes it all work). For more information on natural logarithms see Field (2009).

### Multiple logistic regression

$$Ln(p/(1-p)) = b_0 + b_1x_{1i} + b_2x_{2i} + b_nx_{ni}$$

where p is the probability that Y=1, i is the instance of the variable and n is the number of independent variables. This is not a million miles away from the OLS linear regression equation:

$$y = a + b_1x_1 + b_2x_2 + \ldots + b_nx_n$$

Exp(B) is the odds ratio for each independent variable. So remember that 1 is a leaver and 0 is a stayer. With 'Gender' in Figure 6.24, we have Exp(B) of 0.544. This means that the probability of leaving/probability of staying = 0.544 if the gender = 1 (rather than 0) ie men, rather than women.

Because the odds ratio here is less than 1, we know that the probability of staying is greater than the probability of leaving if the individual is male. So women are more likely to leave. We could present this in a number of ways:

1 The odds of men leaving the organization are 0.544 to 1 on; or we could flip it and say:
2 The odds of men leaving the organization are (1/0.544=) 1.8382 to 1 against.
3 The odds of men staying are 1.8382 to 1, or:
4 Women are 1.8382 times more likely to leave than men.

As a reminder, an odds ratio of 1.0 would mean that men are no more likely to stay or leave than women.

If we look at our other significant finding, which is the previous year's performance appraisal rating, we can see that the odds ratio (Exp(B)) is 0.780. So the probability of staying/probability of leaving ratio is 0.78 if the performance rating goes up one point.

This means that the lower the appraisal rating the year before then the more likely the individual is to have left. Again it might be easier to convert the odds ratio here and do the sum 1 / 0.780 = 1.282. This means that a person who got a particular rating (eg 3 in a 1–5 scale) in their appraisal would be 28.2 per cent more likely to stay the following year than a person who got a lower appraisal rating of 2. Lower rating = more likely to leave.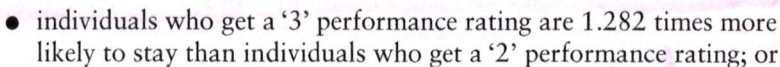
For example:

- individuals who get a '3' performance rating are 1.282 times more likely to stay than individuals who get a '2' performance rating; or:
- individuals who get a '4' performance rating are 28.2 per cent more likely to stay the following year than individuals who get a '3' performance rating.

As we can see from the results, country differences do not come out as significant in accounting for turnover.

> **Snapshot hidden gem**
>
>
> Country differences do not come out as significant in accounting for turnover. However, women are more than twice as likely to leave as men and a higher appraisal rating will increase the chances of employees staying (thus women who get a low performance rating are a 'higher risk of leaving' category than other employees).

# Example 4: predicting team turnover

Here, we predict team-level turnover using a linear regression model that includes six employee attitude/engagement (composite) survey measures, controlling for team size and including country as a measure.

We use the same team-level data set as above: 'Chapter 6 Turnover team DATA.sav'.

The data looks like this:

1. Team identifier (unique team number).
2. Team size (number of people in the team).
3. Team turnover 2014 (separation rate between 0 and 1).
4. Country (1 = UK; 2 = United States; 3 = Canada; 4 = Spain).
5. SURVEY: ENGAGEMENT items COMBO (composite engagement percentage across the team).
6. SURVEY: TeamLeader Rating (composite team leader percentage across the team).
7. SURVEY: CSR rating (composite corporate social responsibility percentage across the team).
8. SURVEY: Drive for Performance (composite percentage team score on perceived 'Drive for performance' percentage).
9. SURVEY: Performance, Development and Reward (composite percentage team score on perceived fairness of performance, development and reward across the team).
10. SURVEY: Work–Life Balance (composite percentage team score on perceived work–life balance across the team).
11. UK dummy variable (0 = not UK; 1 = UK).
12. USA dummy variable (0 = not United States; 1 = United States).
13. Canada dummy variable (0 = not Canada; 1 = Canada).
14. Spain dummy variable (0 = not Spain; 1 = Spain).

Because the team turnover variable is a continuous variable, we will use OLS multiple linear regression. It is important to remember that, at any point, if you are unsure which method to use, refer back to Table 3.4 in Chapter 3.

As the country variable is a categorical variable and because we are using linear regression we need to include the pre-prepared dummy variables in the analysis. You will see above that the last four variables indicate whether the countries are UK, United States, Canada or Spain; in each of these country columns a 1 indicates that the teams are from that country and a 0 indicates that the team is from another country. Remember that logistic regression sets up dummy variables automatically in SPSS, but linear regression does not. In our regression model, we therefore include three country dummy variables but exclude a reference category. Thus when a country dummy coefficient is presented in the output it is comparing that country with whatever reference country category we chose (by excluding it from the analysis). In the following model we will enter United States, Canada and Spain dummy variables – remember that the exclusion of the UK dummy variable makes this location the 'reference' category that the other countries are compared to.

Our model then looks like this:

Team Turnover =
$b_0 + b_1(\text{engagement}) + b_2(\text{teamleader}) + b_3(\text{CSR}) + b_4(\text{Drive for performance}) + b_5(\text{PDR}) + b_6(\text{WLB}) + b_7(\text{USA}) + b_8(\text{Canada}) + b_9(\text{Spain})$

To reiterate, we are using OLS multiple linear regression rather than binary logistic regression because our team-level turnover dependent variable is not a leaver versus stayer dichotomous variable, it is an interval-level measure that involves a percentage of team members who have left in the last year. Thus we can meaningfully explore linear relationships with this variable and use a multiple linear regression.

To do this we go into SPSS, select 'Analyze', then 'Regression' and 'Linear' (see Figure 6.25).

### FIGURE 6.25

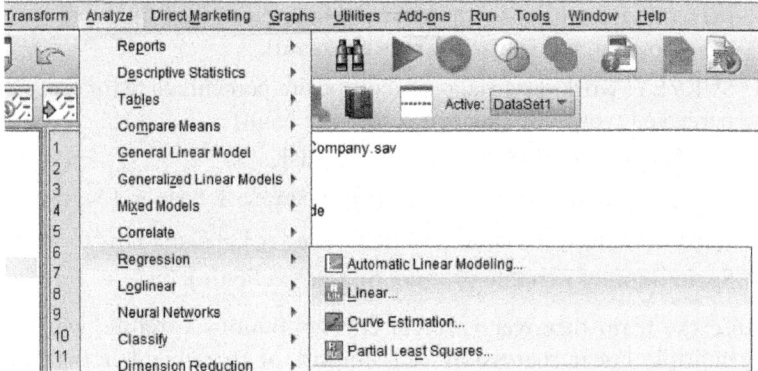

Then in the 'Linear' regression set-up menu we select 'Team Turnover 2014' as the 'Dependent:' variable and the other variables as per the model equation into the 'Independent():' variables selection box (Figure 6.26).

# Case Study 3

**FIGURE 6.26**

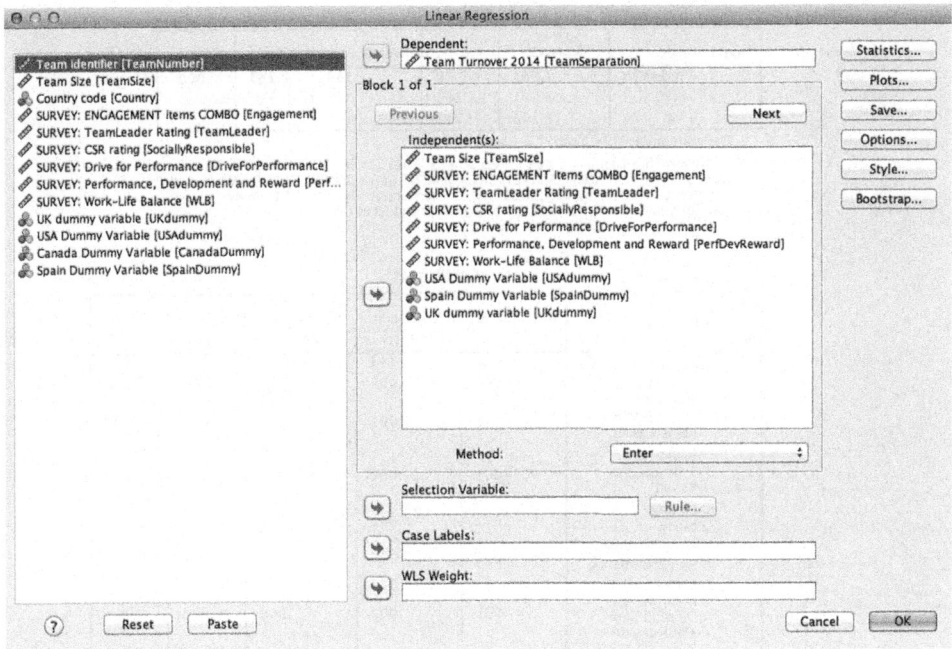

After clicking 'OK', the following results are produced (Figure 6.27 and Figure 6.28).

**FIGURE 6.27**

**Model Summary**

| Model | R | R-Square | Adjusted R-Square | Std. Error of the Estimate |
|---|---|---|---|---|
| 1 | .515[a] | .265 | .229 | .16118 |

a. Predictors: (Constant), UK dummy variable, SURVEY: Drive for Performance, Team Size, SURVEY: CSR rating, SURVEY: ENGAGEMENT items COMBO, SURVEY: Work-Life Balance, Spain Dummy Variable, SURVEY: TeamLeader Rating, USA Dummy Variable, SURVEY: Performance, Development and Reward

Looking at the model summary (Figure 6.27) we can see that the (Multiple) $R^2$ is 0.265, meaning that 26.5 per cent of the variance in team turnover is accounted for by its shared relationship with all of the independent variables in the model.

## FIGURE 6.28

ANOVA[a]

| Model | | Sum of Squares | df | Mean Square | F | Sig. |
|---|---|---|---|---|---|---|
| 1 | Regression | 1.887 | 10 | .189 | 7.263 | .000[b] *Model is sig.* |
| | Residual | 5.221 | 201 | .026 | | |
| | Total | 7.108 | 211 | | | |

a. Dependent Variable: Team Turnover 2014
b. Predictors: (Constant), UK dummy variable, SURVEY: Drive for Performance, Team Size, SURVEY: CSR rating, SURVEY: ENGAGEMENT items COMBO, SURVEY: Work–Life Balance, Spain Dummy Variable, SURVEY: TeamLeader Rating, USA Dummy Variable, SURVEY: Performance, Development and Reward

Coefficients[a]

| Model | | Unstandardized Coefficients | | Standardized Coefficients | t | Sig. |
|---|---|---|---|---|---|---|
| | | B | Std. Error | Beta | | |
| 1 | (Constant) | .402 | .153 | | 2.631 | .009 |
| | Team Size | -.001 | .005 | -.010 | -.165 | .870 |
| | SURVEY: ENGAGEMENT items COMBO | -.006 | .001 | -.449 | -5.422 | .000 |
| | SURVEY: TeamLeader Rating | -.001 | .001 | -.048 | -.496 | .620 |
| | SURVEY: CSR rating | .001 | .002 | .081 | .877 | .382 |
| | SURVEY: Drive for Performance | .002 | .001 | .192 | 2.588 | .010 |
| | SURVEY: Performance, Development and Reward | .001 | .002 | .090 | .824 | .411 |
| | SURVEY: Work–Life Balance | .000 | .001 | -.008 | -.095 | .924 |
| | USA Dummy Variable | -.045 | .040 | -.116 | -1.105 | .270 |
| | Spain Dummy Variable | -.025 | .046 | -.060 | -.545 | .586 |
| | UK dummy variable | -.053 | .042 | -.125 | -1.273 | .204 |

a. Dependent Variable: Team Turnover 2014

Looking at the regression ANOVA table (Figure 6.28), which tests the significance of how well the model predicts variation in team turnover, we can see that the regression ANOVA F-value is 7.263, with an associated degrees of freedom of 10 and 201. These parameters give a significance level of 0.000 (p<0.001). So we would say it is less than 0.001, which means there is less than 1 in 1,000 chance that we would find this pattern of shared variance (between the team turnover and the other variables) by chance alone. Hence the model is significant.

Now, looking at the significance value of the coefficients, we can see that the 'SURVEY: ENGAGEMENT Items COMBO' is significant at p<0.001; and that 'SURVEY: Drive Performance' is significant at p<0.05.

Further investigation would be needed here to explore whether having too high an emphasis on a 'drive for performance' culture could foster team norms and behaviours that could end up making people want to leave.

> **Snapshot hidden gem**
>
> When you take into account the various country effects in the model, alongside the survey measures, it seems that the country differences no longer come out as being as important in predicting team turnover as much as levels of engagement (Beta = –0.449, p<0.001) and, interestingly, perceptions of the team experiences of the company's 'drive for performance' culture (Beta = +0.192, p<0.05). This is interesting because engagement does seem to predict turnover, in that the more engaged the teams seem to be, the lower the turnover rate. However, where team members indicate that they experience a high level of a 'drive for performance' cultural focus (presumably team norms differ in the degree to which they focus on trying to be high performers) then these teams seem to have a higher turnover.

## Modelling the costs of turnover and the business case for action

In our logistic regression example presented above, we realized that gender plays a role in accounting for turnover across our global organization. In that model, when we included lots of our controls, (in the form of additional independent variables) we managed to account for 5.6 per cent of turnover across our organization. You will recall that the turnover rate in the organization is 12.8 per cent. If we wanted to translate this into some numbers that executives may pay attention to, we could work out what is the average cost of replacing individuals who leave, work out the total cost of turnover in our organization and then make a rough estimate in £ or $ of how much we are accounting for with 12.8 per cent. Then, we could go further and isolate the monetary cost of any particular factor that we find to be important. For example, if we find that gender accounts for 2.4 per cent of variation in our turnover statistics, we can work out in monetary terms what the gender effect on turnover equates to in staff replacement costs.

We carry out more complex modelling activities in Chapter 10; however, in a simple analysis, we can look at variables in isolation (that have been found to be significant in our model, such as gender) and run a simple logistic regression to get a general idea of the *potential* percentage of variance in turnover that each might loosely account for. For example, we could use 'gender' as the only independent variable and 'stayer or leaver' as the dependent variable; this will give us a rough idea of the total amount of variance in individual turnover that this particular factor could potentially account for.

**FIGURE 6.29**

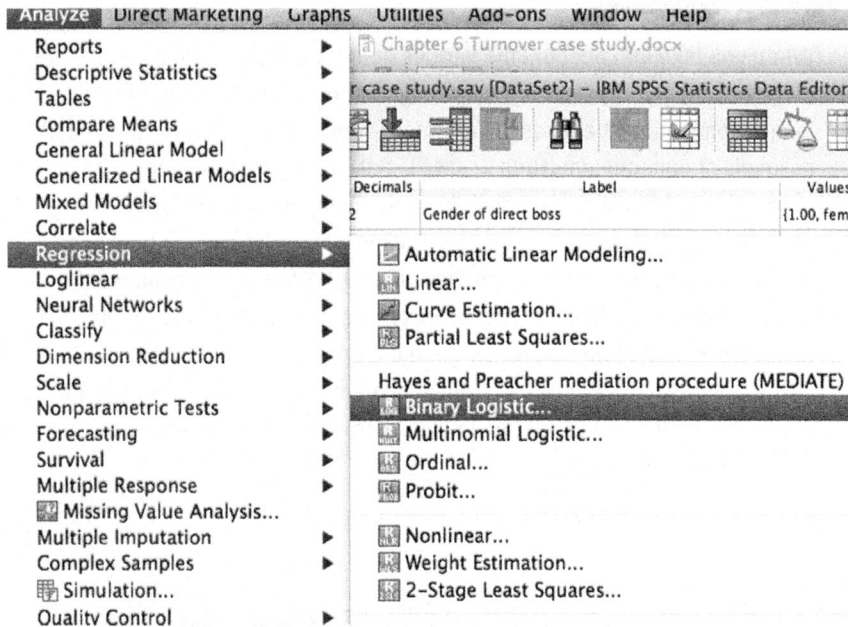

Going into SPSS, we would select 'Analyze', then 'Regression' and 'Binary Logistic' (Figure 6.29).

We would then select 'Stayer or Leaver' as the dependent variable and 'Gender' as the independent variable, as per Figure 6.30.

**FIGURE 6.30**

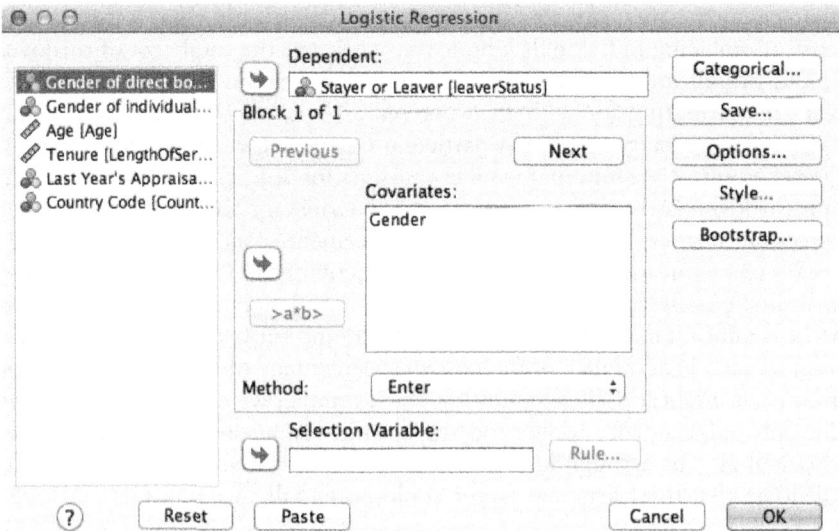

The following model will run and here we get indices of how much variation in turnover 'gender' may have in isolation (Figure 6.31).

## FIGURE 6.31

### Block 1: Method = Enter

**Omnibus Tests of Model Coefficients**

|        |       | Chi-square | df | Sig. |
|--------|-------|------------|----|----|
| Step 1 | Step  | 20.837     | 1  | .000 |
|        | Block | 20.837     | 1  | .000 |
|        | Model | 20.837     | 1  | .000 |

*Model is sig*

**Model Summary**

| Step | -2 Log likelihood | Cox and Snell R-Square | Nagelkerke R-Square |
|------|-------------------|------------------------|---------------------|
| 1    | 1233.166[a]       | .013                   | .024                |

*2.4% of variation*

a. Estimation terminated at iteration number 5 because parameter estimates changed by less than .001.

**Classification Table[a]**

|        |                  |        | Predicted |        |                     |
|--------|------------------|--------|-----------|--------|---------------------|
|        |                  |        | Stayer or Leaver |  | Percentage Correct |
|        | Observed         |        | Stayer    | Leaver |                     |
| Step 1 | Stayer or Leaver | Stayer | 1441      | 0      | 100.0               |
|        |                  | Leaver | 209       | 0      | .0                  |
|        | Overall Percentage |      |           |        | 87.3                |

a. The cut value is .500

**Variables in the Equation**

|           |          | B      | S.E. | Wald    | df | Sig. | Exp(B) |
|-----------|----------|--------|------|---------|----|------|--------|
| Step 1[a] | Gender   | -.690  | .154 | 19.992  | 1  | .000 | .501   |
|           | Constant | -1.633 | .094 | 303.274 | 1  | .000 | .195   |

a. Variable(s) entered on step 1: Gender.

## Omnibus tests of model coefficients

Again, in Figure 6.31 we have an index of how good our model is at accounting for turnover across our organization. Here we see that our model chi square is 20.837 and this is deemed to be significant ($p<0.001$). This shows us that the logistic regression model fits the data well enough to be considered significant.

## Model summary

The 'Model Summary' table in Figure 6.31 shows two key R-square statistics. As we have discussed in previous sections, our R-square figure is an indication of the degree of variation in our dependent variable that is accounted for by the variation in our predictor variables. The Nagelkerke R-square (referred to as a pseudo R-square) is a figure that most closely equates with the R-square figure in linear regression and this shows that, by just looking at gender, we can account for 2.4 per cent of turnover across our organization.

## Variables in the equation

This table shown in Figure 6.31 tells us that gender has a significant impact ($p<0.001$) on turnover and the Exp(b) gives the odds ratio on the probability that the individual is a leaver versus a stayer, which is 0.501.

The important item to pull out of this analysis, though (and probably the one that everyone will understand), is that gender may well have as much as a 2.4 per cent impact on individual turnover – and if someone (someone like you?) were to recommend an intervention that would remove the gender portion of turnover and retain women at least as well as the organization can retain men, then the organization could potentially reduce turnover by 2.4 per cent.

Just looking at this statistic, let's say that our total cost of turnover is something like £4 million including all of the separation, replacement and training costs (as outlined at the beginning of this chapter). If we could reduce this by 2.4 per cent then this would save £96,000. With this knowledge, we could potentially use this information to build a business case for making some investment into trying to understand and deal with the factors that may be leading women across the globe to be more likely to leave than men. As a caveat to this, from the above analysis, in exploring these factors it is likely that we will need to consider whether there are gender differences in performance ratings that tend to be given to men versus women. The reason this would be important is that performance appraisal ratings are also found to be an important predictor of individual turnover (see above) and therefore there may be some key link between gender, performance ratings and voluntary turnover.

## More robust modelling

Strictly speaking, if we wanted to be much more robust in modelling the potential cost savings from our turnover driver analysis, we should explore the percentage of variance in turnover that each factor might account for: eg how much variance in turnover does gender account for after controlling for performance appraisal ratings? To do this we would just find the Nagelkerke R-square figure when performance appraisal rating is set as a predictor of individual turnover (coincidently also 0.024) and then we see how much this figure increases when we include gender as a predictor. When we do this the Nagelkerke R-square figure increases to 0.039, thus gender uniquely accounts for 1.3 per cent of individual turnover (0.039–0.024= 0.013). Using these techniques we can identify and attempt to partition the potential variance (and cost) in turnover that can be isolated with each factor when taking into account other possible causes of turnover. With this information we can then potentially translate this information into £ (or $, €, etc) potential cost savings that dealing with these factors could bring.

One further caveat here. In Chapter 11 we discuss more complex forms of analysis and address the importance of testing for interactions in our models. As well as running a turnover model that includes both gender and performance in predicting turnover, we might want to see whether there is an interaction between performance ratings and gender in predicting turnover. For example, is a 1 grade differential in a performance appraisal rating more or less important in accounting for leaver status with women compared to men? We discuss interactions further in Chapter 11.

## Summary

You can see that, by using the methods outlined in this chapter, it is possible to determine predictors of both individual and team turnover. Importantly, from our analysis we can then use this information to help identify factors that could help reduce turnover costs; at the same time our analysis could also eliminate factors (such as country differences in our example) that on the surface could otherwise be considered as being important. When we have information about or potential drivers of turnover we can isolate the unique variance that each factor might play in accounting for turnover and translate this into a potential cost saving (assuming we have an estimate of our current staff turnover costs) that focusing on these 'levers' could result in. This information can be used to build a business case for a turnover intervention programme that could make a real difference to the organization's bottom line. For further examples of possible ways to carry out modelling with regression analysis, especially in predicting actual and potential turnover probabilities, see Chapter 10 on business applications.

## References

CIPD Factsheet (2014) [accessed 20 November 2015] Employee Turnover and Retention [Online] http://www.cipd.co.uk/hr-resources/factsheets/employee-turnover-retention.aspx

Compensation Force (2014) [accessed 30 November 2015] Turnover Rates by Industry [Online] http://www.compensationforce.com/2014/02/2013-turnover-rates-by-industry.html

Coolican, H (2009) *Research Methods and Statistics in Psychology*, Hodder Education, Abingdon
Field, A (2009) *Discovering Statistics using SPSS*, Sage, London
Griffeth, R W and Hom, P W (2001) *Retaining Valued Employees*, Sage, London
Moore-Bridger and Lynch (2014) [accessed 19 June 2015] *London Evening Standard* [Online] http://www.standard.co.uk/news/uk/stephen-hawking-suarez-england-world-cup-win-9444698.html
Watkins, M (2013) *The First 90 Days: Strategies for getting up to speed faster and smarter*, Harvard Business Review Press, Boston

# Case study 4
# Predicting employee performance

07

In response to volatile markets and heightened economic uncertainty, organizations have placed increased emphasis on individual, team and organizational performance (Bach, 2012). Indeed, one could consider the HR analytic ability to predict future performance as the holy grail of HR analytics. The ability to identify, predict, understand and potentially influence high levels of employee or team performance can be considered critical to improving organizational performance and driving people strategy.

Performance management in organizations has evolved over the last 20 years from a stand-alone performance appraisal process to a more integrated system of measures and processes, including customer feedback, sales figures, team productivity and 360-degree feedback, to name just a few. The trend has also been to move responsibility for performance management away from the HR function towards line managers. Although this move has given line managers the opportunity to take more responsibility for the development and performance of their team members, it has introduced greater variation in the employee experience, thus placing greater emphasis on the strength of the performance management system and the competence and attitude of line managers to take their people-management responsibilities seriously (Brown and Hirsh, 2011; Armstrong and Baron, 2005).

The downside of this decentralized process is that it is often difficult to get one single view of the performance of all teams and individuals across the organization and across all of the indicators of performance. Indeed how do senior leaders know who is doing well across all of these, what they are doing right, and where should they invest their, often limited, learning and development funds to ensure the greatest return? How do we use this information to make the biggest difference to the bottom line?

In this chapter, we cover:

- What can we measure to indicate performance?
- What methods might we use?
- Practical examples from issues in real organizations.
- Ethical considerations in performance data.

# What can we measure to indicate performance?

One of the key challenges with conducting analyses of performance with HR data is deciding what sort of performance to try to predict. One might assume that the annual or biannual performance appraisal rating should be something we focus on trying to predict. However, while there might be good reasons why this is something we could try to do, there are other types of performance indices that can also provide some extremely useful information. What is important here is to remember that we need to not only measure performance, but to think about what measure we might have that may be a predictor of performance. Table 7.1 gives some indication of the types of measures we could be considering.

**TABLE 7.1** Team and Individual performance measures

| Level | Example Measures of Performance | Example Measures of what might influence Performance |
|---|---|---|
| Team | Employee opinion survey output (team engagement index, team leadership index), store/branch customer feedback, customer loyalty, customer reinvestment/ repeat business, staff turnover. | Team function, team leader competence; composite measures of individual team member attitude/engagement survey measures. |
| Individual | Performance appraisal rating, behavioural rating, sales performance figures, checkout scan rate, individual customer feedback, peer feedback, call rates, call loads. | Gender, age, tenure, job strain, sickness absence, pulse survey data (see Chapter 9 for a discussion of pulse surveys), hours worked, job satisfaction, person–organization fit, perceived organization support, perceptions of justice, salary, base country. |

With the move away from manufacturing industries to the service sector, customer satisfaction has become a major measure that we could focus on as a performance measure. In the service sector customer satisfaction, customer loyalty and the likelihood that customers reinvest could be considered very strong indicators of performance, because these factors ultimately impact the bottom line. Many organizations routinely collect customer satisfaction data; however, it is rare that these organizations have the HR analytic capability to be able to fully understand and explore what factors might predict these key performance outcomes.

Whilst measures such as sickness absence, staff turnover and engagement scores may not obviously be performance indices in a traditional sense, these indices are all performance measures of a kind. High sickness-absence rates, high staff turnover and low engagement will all be associated with a detrimental change in the organization's bottom line and are all things that a successful HR function will want to avoid. Therefore they can all be considered to be performance indices that we might want to try to analytically predict. We touch on sickness absence below, and we dealt with engagement in Chapter 5 and turnover in Chapter 6.

As we have discussed in previous chapters, sometimes information that we would want to include in our analytic model is not available at the individual level. As we discuss in Chapter 5 on engagement, individual engagement scores may not always be available due to the confidential nature of most employee opinion surveys. Also, with performance, it may not always be appropriate to judge performance at an individual level, especially when there may be teams involved in the work process. As such we might want to focus on team-level performance of some kind. The actual type of analysis and models that we can run will be dependent upon the availability of the data that we have, and organizations will differ fundamentally in this. For example, an organization that involves some form of selling could focus on getting new customers and the amount of revenue generated directly from sales. A call centre, for example, would focus on call rates, call loads and call duration.

## What methods might we use?

In analysing performance, the key thing we are looking for is relationships and predictors. We might want to answer questions along the lines of:

- What are the characteristics of a high-performing individual or team?
- Where can we invest money that is likely to show an increase in customer loyalty?
- What are the key employee characteristics, capabilities and attributes that make a high performer?

The methods we will use in this chapter are as follows:

- **Multiple linear regression:** this allows us to analyse a number of independent variables (for example, gender, age, team leader, country location) to see what, if any, impact they have on allowing us to predict a dependent variable (for example, performance rating) by forming a 'best fit' model. The multiple linear regression will tell us the proportion of variance in the dependent variable that is accounted for by all the independent variables collectively, which independent variables have a significant impact on the dependent variable, and the relative 'weighting' of each dependent variable.
- **Stepwise multiple linear regression:** this will allow us to undertake a number of iterative steps to try to find the most economical (and parsimonious) model that best fits the data we have, by successively adding and removing important independent variables.
- **Tracking over time using multiple linear regression:** tracking the values of a dependent variable over time allows us to better establish patterns of behaviour in the data. For example: rather than predicting high or low performance ratings, we can predict what causes an *increase* or a *decrease* in performance ratings over time. This can be far more powerful when determining which interventions may be more effective in improving organizational performance.
- **Using dummy variables in multiple linear regression:** using dummy variables is a way of manipulating the data to enable us to indicate either the absence or presence of a particular characteristic or trait. For example, in the nominal level variable 'contractual status', which might have four categories, instead of having 1 = 'full-time permanent', 2 = 'full-time fixed-term contract', 3 = 'part-time permanent' and 4 = 'part-time temporary' as the values, we might have 'full-time permanent' as one dichotomous variable (ie one that has only two categories or values) and record the value as either a 0 or 1 (where full-time permanent is 1). This is a dummy variable. We might set up another 'full-time fixed-term contract' variable and record the value as either a 0 or 1, another for 'part-time permanent' and record the value as either a 0 or 1 and the fourth as 'part-time temporary' and record the value as either a 0 or 1. Importantly, these four dummy variables should cover the whole data set. Having these dummy variables greatly increases our options for data analysis.

# Practical examples using multiple linear regression to predict performance

The nine examples below are all laid out in a similar manner. They are using data sets based on real data from organizations in the financial services, manufacturing and retail sectors:

- Example 1: uses multiple linear regression to predict customer loyalty and reinvestment in a financial services organization.
- Example 2: uses multiple linear regression and combines customer survey data and pulse survey data to predict customer loyalty in a financial services organization.
- Example 3: uses multiple linear regression and combines performance appraisal data, sickness records and pulse survey data to predict individual performance in a manufacturing organization.
- Example 4: uses stepwise multiple linear regression to find the best model for predicting performance using combined performance appraisal data, sickness records and pulse survey data in a manufacturing organization.
- Example 5: tracks performance over time using stepwise regression and combined performance appraisal data, sickness records and pulse survey data in a manufacturing organization.
- Example 6: uses multiple linear regression to predict sickness absence using employee attitude scores in a manufacturing organization.
- Example 7: uses multiple regression to explore patterns of performance with employee profile data in a manufacturing organization.
- Example 8: uses data interrogation techniques and multiple linear regression to predict checkout scan rates from employee profile data in a retail organization.
- Example 9: uses dummy variables in multiple linear regression to determine the presence of high-performing age groups in predicting scan rates in a retail organization.

The examples listed focus on using multiple linear regression. This is because this is the best method for this type of analysis, where we are trying to predict a particular outcome – in our case, high performance. Because of this, some of the examples and methods may seem repetitive; however, we hope they provide a broad scope of what is possible with all the data available in the organization, and that they may provide inspiration for what you may do with the data in your organization.

## Example 1a: using multiple linear regression to predict customer loyalty in a financial services organization

As we have seen in previous chapters, multiple regression can be used to model an independent variable and predict patterns of behaviour. In the example below, we will analyse customer input to try to understand what factors are most important in influencing customer satisfaction and customer loyalty. In this example, we have a data set based on the results of a customer satisfaction survey, which was sent out to customers who have been in contact with a sales person in a financial services organization.

Each customer was sent a survey that included seven questions, four of which specifically related to key sales-person competency elements:

**1** The sales person understanding your needs (Sat1). 1-5
**2** The sales person seems confident (Sat2). 1-5
**3** The sales person has a recommendation (Sat3). 1-5
**4** The sales person is knowledgeable (Sat4). 1-5

Here, customers were asked to grade the sales person on a scale of 1 to 5, where 1 was 'very dissatisfied' and 5 was 'very satisfied'.

The next two questions relate to loyalty and asked customers to put themselves on a scale of 1 to 5 where:

**5** Likelihood of reinvesting (Custloyalty):
  – 1 = Definitely going to go elsewhere with my investments.
  – 2 = Thinking about going elsewhere with my money.
  – 3 = Not sure about where I will place my future investments.
  – 4 = Thinking about investing here again.
  – 5 = Definitely will invest here again.
**6** How much they may or may not reinvest (InvestMore):
  – 1 = Definitely will not invest more than now here.
  – 2 = Unlikely to invest more than now here.
  – 3 = Planning to invest 0–50 per cent more than now in this organization.
  – 4 = Planning to invest 50–100 per cent more in this organization.
  – 5 = Going to double my investment or more in this organization.

The final question was about the gender of the sales person:

**7** Sex of sales person: 1 = female; 2 = male.

The data set used includes responses from 2,507 customer surveys: 'Chapter 7 Customer satisfaction ONLY N2507.sav'.

So here we have two dependent variables, or desired outcomes, and we would like to understand whether there is anything we can do as an organization to improve those. The two dependant variables are: customer loyalty and reinvestment.

Using the same approach as in the engagement case study (Chapter 5), we would expect the model to look something like:

Customer Loyalty =
 $a + b_1$ (understanding customer needs) + $b_2$ (sales confidence) + $b_3$ (giving a recommendation) + $b_4$ (product knowledge) + $b_5$ (gender)

So we want to test whether customer loyalty is a function of any or a combination of the above five factors. Our model will also tell us which factors are the most important. Intuitively, it makes sense that if a customer felt as though a sales person understood their needs, was very confident, was able to provide a recommendation, and had a high level of knowledge about their products that they would be more likely to feel a sense of loyalty. But which elements are most important? Which aspects should the organization invest in to maximize customer loyalty? And what part does gender play?

Our model should help us to answer these questions and help us to predict customer loyalty.

Going into SPSS, We select 'Analyze', then 'Regression' and 'Linear' (Figure 7.1).

**FIGURE 7.1** Conducting a multiple regression analysis predicting customer loyalty

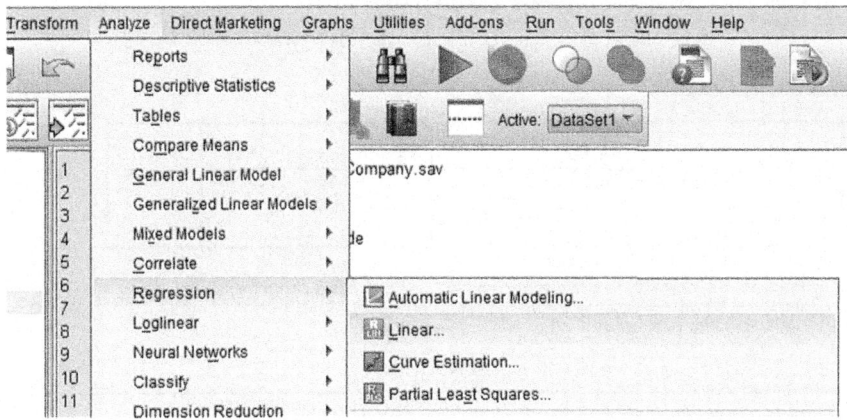

Then select the 'Customer Loyalty' variable as the 'Dependent:' variable using the arrow button and move the five independent variables (sales person understanding your needs, sales person seems confident, sales person has a recommendation, sales person is knowledgeable, sex of sales person) into the 'Independent(s):' selection box (Figure 7.2).

**FIGURE 7.2**

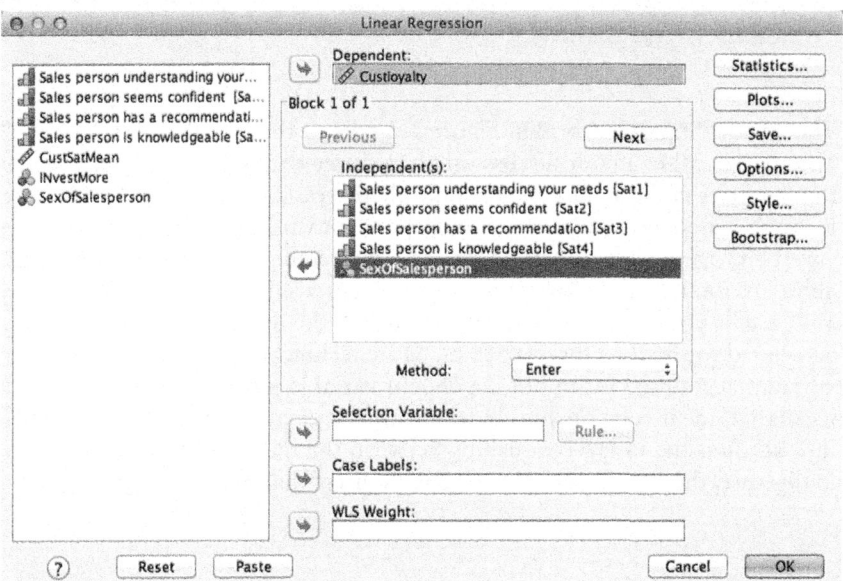

Then click 'OK'. This will produce the following output (Figure 7.3):

**FIGURE 7.3**

Model Summary

| Model | R | R-Square | Adjusted R-Square | Std. Error of the Estimate |
|---|---|---|---|---|
| 1 | .571[a] | .326 | .324 | .88886 |

a. Predictors: (Constant), SexOfSalesperson, Sales person has a recommendation, Sales person is knowledgeable, Sales person seems confident, Sales person understanding your needs

ANOVA[a]

| Model | | Sum of Squares | df | Mean Square | F | Sig. |
|---|---|---|---|---|---|---|
| 1 | Regression | 698.217 | 5 | 139.643 | 176.749 | .000[b] |
| | Residual | 1445.822 | 1830 | .790 | | |
| | Total | 2144.039 | 1835 | | | |

*Model is Sig.*

a. Dependent Variable: Custloyalty
b. Predictors: (Constant), SexOfSalesperson, Sales person has a recommendation, Sales person is knowledgeable, Sales person seems confident, Sales person understanding your needs

Coefficients[a]

| Model | | Unstandardized Coefficients | | Standardized Coefficients | t | Sig. |
|---|---|---|---|---|---|---|
| | | B | Std. Error | Beta | | |
| 1 | (Constant) | 1.853 | .130 | | 14.233 | .000 |
| | Sales person understanding your needs | .324 | .036 | .307 | 9.067 | .000 |
| | Sales person seems confident | -.034 | .033 | -.030 | -1.018 | .309 |
| | Sales person has a recommendation | .288 | .030 | .290 | 9.716 | .000 |
| | Sales person is knowledgeable | .053 | .032 | .048 | 1.664 | .096 |
| | SexOfSalesperson | -.114 | .051 | -.043 | -2.240 | .025 |

a. Dependent Variable: Custloyalty

The 'Model Summary' box in Figure 7.3 tells us that the R-square is 0.326. You may recall from our discussion on multiple regression in Chapter 3 that the R-square is the square of the multiple regression coefficient. Simply put, R shows the coefficient between the dependant variable and all the predictor variables together. So, the greater the R-square, the more the predictor variables are jointly predictive of the dependent variable. If you multiply it by 100, it tells you the percentage of variance in the dependant variable that is accounted for by the other variables. More technically, it is the percentage of variance accounted for in our dependent variable when taking into account its shared linear relationship with our independent variables (whilst taking into account the interrelationships between the independent variables). So, in this case, the R-square is 0.326, so we can say that 32.6 per cent, or almost one-third, of the variance in expressions of customer loyalty is accounted for by the particular combination of predictor variables used here.

Looking at the regression ANOVA in Figure 7.3, ie the regression ANOVA table, which tests the significance of how well the model predicts variation in customer loyalty, there are some important results to pull out. First, the regression ANOVA F-value is 176.749, with associated degrees of freedom of 5 and 1830. As mentioned in other chapters, these figures provide the parameters for us to determine the statistical significance in a statistical table such as those found in most stats textbooks. However, SPSS has calculated the statistical significance for us to be 0.000 (p<0.001). So we would say that our significance level reached has a p-value of 0.001, which means there is less than 1 in 1,000 chance that we would find this pattern of shared variance (between the customer loyalty scores and the other survey questions) by chance alone. Hence the model is significant.

Now we are aware that the model is significant, we need to review the coefficients table to ascertain which of our independent variables have an impact on customer loyalty, to what extent and also in what direction (ie some may potentially improve customer loyalty while others may decrease customer loyalty).

Using our knowledge of levels of significance and looking down the right-hand column of the table, it appears that three of the five predictor variables significantly predict customer loyalty; most important are 'sales person understanding your needs' and 'sales person has a recommendation'. Sales person knowledge and sales person confidence have no significant impact.

From this example, it would be reasonable to make the recommendation to invest in helping salespeople to better understand customer needs by, for example, listening and making the customer feel as though they have been listened to, asking questions and keeping appropriate records. Also training salespeople in how to be confident in making the right recommendations would likely result in a positive return on investment. Because the data shows the salesperson ID, it is possible to go back to the raw data to identify who is skilled at making recommendations and making the customer feel as though they have been understood, and share those skills with others in the team.

Although the results for 'sex of sales person' was less significant with a Beta = –0.043, p<0.05, or p is less than 5 in 100, we can say that there is more than a 95 out of 100 chance that the variance in customer loyalty is linked to the gender of the sales person. Because the Beta coefficient is negative, and because we used the following in the data set:

1 = female; 2 = male.

Then we can say that the higher this number, the lower the customer loyalty, or that customers with a female sales person are more likely to be loyal than customers of male salespeople.

We can also rewrite our model raw regression formula with the $b$ values:

Customer loyalty =
1.853 + 0.324 (understanding customer needs) −
0.034 (sales confidence) + 0.288 (giving a recommendation) +
0.053 (product knowledge) − 0.114 (gender)

> **Snapshot hidden gem**
>
> Understanding customer needs and having a recommendation are the two key drivers of customer loyalty indices – interestingly, women sales advisors keep their customers more than men do.

## Example 1b: using multiple linear regression to predict customer reinvestment in a financial services organization

Using the same data set, let's see if there is anything we can glean to try to understand what might help to increase the level of reinvestment for our customers:

Customer reinvestment =
$a + b_1$ (understanding customer needs) + $b_2$ (sales confidence) +
$b_3$ (giving a recommendation) + $b_4$ (product knowledge) + $b_5$ (gender)

Going into SPSS, we select 'Analyze', then 'Regression' and 'Linear' (Figure 7.4).

**FIGURE 7.4** Conducting a multiple regression analysis predicting customer reinvestment

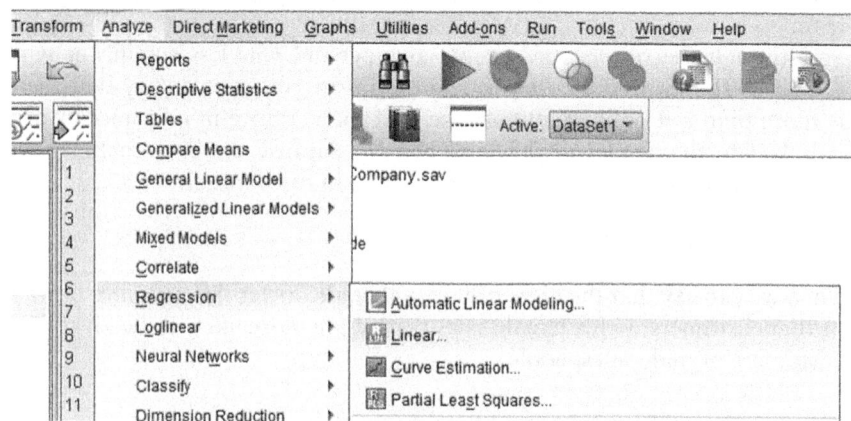

Then select the '(INvestMore)' variable as the 'Dependent:' variable using the arrow button and move the five independent variables (sales person understanding your needs, sales person seems confident, sales person has a recommendation, sales person is knowledgeable, sex of sales person) into the 'Independent(s):' selection box (Figure 7.5).

**FIGURE 7.5**

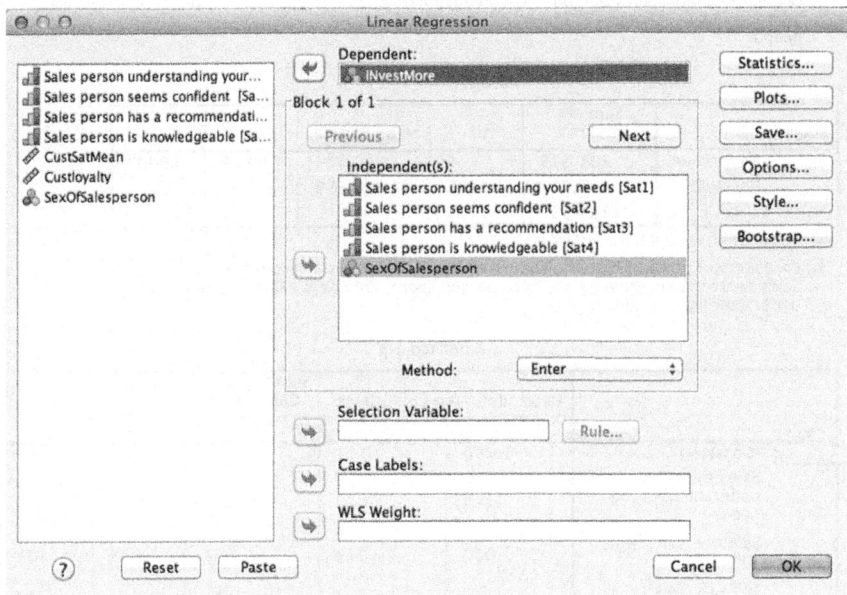

Then click 'OK'. This will produce the following output (Figure 7.6):

## FIGURE 7.6

**Model Summary**

| Model | R | R-Square | Adjusted R-Square | Std. Error of the Estimate |
|---|---|---|---|---|
| 1 | .413[a] | .170 | .168 | .74597 |

a. Predictors: (Constant), SexOfSalesperson, Sales person has a recommendation, Sales person is knowledgeable, Sales person seems confident, Sales person understanding your needs

**ANOVA[a]**

| Model | | Sum of Squares | df | Mean Square | F | Sig. |
|---|---|---|---|---|---|---|
| 1 | Regression | 201.815 | 5 | 40.363 | 72.534 | .000[b] |
| | Residual | 982.724 | 1766 | .556 | | |
| | Total | 1184.539 | 1771 | | | |

*Model is Sig.*

a. Dependent Variable: INvestMore
b. Predictors: (Constant), SexOfSalesperson, Sales person has a recommendation, Sales person is knowledgeable, Sales person seems confident, Sales person understanding your needs

**Coefficients[a]**

| Model | | Unstandardized Coefficients | | Standardized Coefficients | t | Sig. |
|---|---|---|---|---|---|---|
| | | B | Std. Error | Beta | | |
| 1 | (Constant) | 1.740 | .111 | | 15.685 | .000 |
| | Sales person understanding your needs | .176 | .030 | .219 | 5.789 | .000 |
| | Sales person seems confident | .030 | .029 | .034 | 1.035 | .301 |
| | Sales person has a recommendation | .140 | .025 | .186 | 5.540 | .000 |
| | Sales person is knowledgeable | .012 | .027 | .014 | .429 | .668 |
| | SexOfSalesperson | -.020 | .043 | -.010 | -.453 | .651 |

a. Dependent Variable: INvestMore

Using the same analysis method as in the above example, we can see that the R-square = 0.17, or that 17 per cent, approximately one-sixth, of the variance in customer reinvestment is accounted for by the predictor variables used here.

Looking at the ANOVA in Figure 7.6, ie the regression ANOVA table, which tests the significance of how well the model predicts variation in customer loyalty, there are again some important results to pull out. First, the regression ANOVA F-value is 72.534, with associated degrees of freedom of 5 and 1766 and the significance level of 0.000. So we would say that p<0.001, which means there is less than 1 in 1,000 chance that we would find this pattern of shared variance (between the customer reinvestment scores and the other survey questions) by chance alone. Hence the model is significant.

So, while the model only accounts for one-sixth of the output (customer reinvestment), it is significant and hence we can be confident that recommendations we make on the basis of this model should impact the customer reinvestment intentions (but it is important to set the expectations in such a way that that the impact will be conservative; see Chapter 10, page 367).

The model then looks like this:

Customer reinvestment =
1.740 + 0.176 (understanding customer needs) +
0.030 (sales confidence) + 0.140 (giving a recommendation) +
0.012 (product knowledge) – 0.020 (gender)

Knowing that the model is significant, as in the customer loyalty example, we can now look at the coefficients to ascertain which predictor variables have the most potential impact. Looking down the right-hand side again, we can see that the same two satisfaction variables seem to have an impact, ie the sales person understanding your needs and the sales person having a recommendation.

Interestingly, gender does not have a significant impact here, so although customers of female salespeople are more likely to express loyalty and indicate an intention to stay with the financial organization (thus continue investment), it does not necessarily mean that they will invest more money on top of what they already have there.

So the key findings here can be updated as follows:

> **Snapshot hidden gem**
>
> Understanding customer needs and having a recommendation are the two key drivers of customer reinvestment indices.

## Example 2: using multiple linear regression to predict customer loyalty

In this example we use the same multiple regression analysis technique, but we link data from three sources: the customer survey data used in the above example, including details of which sales person was linked to which respondent; HR employee data found in the employee database; and results of a small employee engagement 'pulse' survey, which did actually track employees in their responses. This enables us to explore whether engaged employees might have greater sales success and also whether any employee profile details have any impact.

It is important to note in the example here that the organization is using a limited engagement survey because it represents data included in a company 'health check'. In this case it actually identifies employees when asking survey questions (though this is not a comprehensive engagement survey) and only limited engagement information is available; however, being able to identify individuals in engagement questions provides particularly useful opportunities to link data sets. Here we have aggregated customer loyalty data at the individual sales-person level – meaning that we have averaged any customer loyalty responses for each sales person (where more than one customer answered a survey for each sales advisor, multiple responses were answered). Often when we combine data sets and choose to analyse data at a particular level, we may have to aggregate data linked to this particular level if there are multiple data points associated with one single variable. Here the employee is the 'level' that we are interested in and we can have multiple customer survey responses from multiple customers for each employee; thus we need to aggregate these multiple customer responses to get one customer score per employee (this actually has the potential to be a 'multi-level' data set-up, which we discuss further in Chapter 11).

The data set used in this example, is 'Chapter 7 Sales Person and aggregated customer loyalty N574.sav'.

## Predicting aggregated customer loyalty scores for each sales advisor

We use the following three survey questions, for which employees were asked to answer on a scale of 1 to 5 (where 1 = strongly agree and 5 = strongly disagree):

**1** My manager gives me useful feedback (qMan1).
**2** I would recommend this organization as a place to work (qEng1).
**3** I am really engaged in my work (qEng2).

We also have HR data linked to each employee included in the model as follows:

**4** Sex (1 = female, 2 = male).
**5** Manager status (0 = non-manager, 1 = manager).
**6** Age (actual number).
**7** Talent 2014 (0 = not key talent, 1 = key talent).

So, in this multiple regression example, the dependent variable is aggregate customer loyalty scores and the multiple regression model would look something like this:

Customer Loyalty Mean =
$a + b_1$ (Key Talent) + $b_2$ (Sex) + $b_3$ (Engaged in my work) +
$b_4$ (Age) + $b_5$ (Manager {or not}) + $b_6$ (Manager gives useful feedback) +
$b_7$ (recommend this organization)

Going into SPSS, we select 'Analyze', then 'Regression' and 'Linear' (Figure 7.7).

**FIGURE 7.7** Conducting a multiple regression analysis predicting customer loyalty

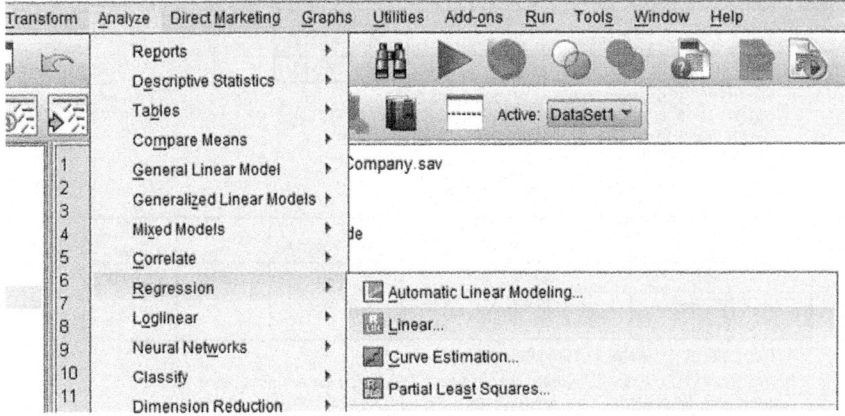

Select the aforementioned variables as before with 'Custloyalty_mean' as the 'Dependent: variable' and Talent2014, Sex, qEng2, Age, Manager, qMan1 and qENg1 into the 'Independent(s):' selection box (Figure 7.8).

**FIGURE 7.8**

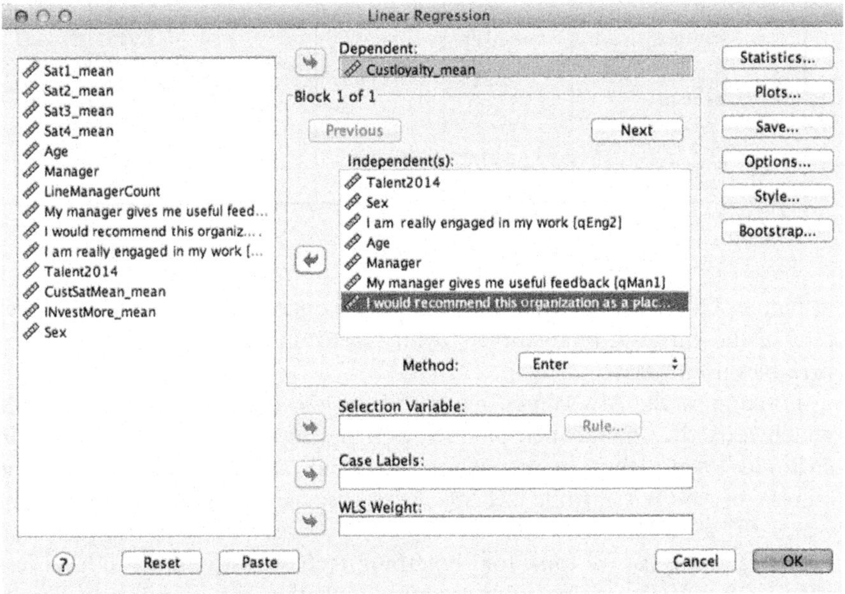

Click 'OK' and we get the following multiple regression results (Figure 7.9):

## FIGURE 7.9

**Model Summary**

| Model | R | R-Square | Adjusted R-Square | Std. Error of the Estimate |
|---|---|---|---|---|
| 1 | .207a | .043 | .020 | .72911 |

a. Predictors: (Constant), I would recommend this organization as a place to work, Age, Sex, KeyTalent2014, My manager gives me useful feedback, Manager, I am really engaged in my work

**ANOVA**a

| Model | | Sum of Squares | df | Mean Square | F | Sig. |
|---|---|---|---|---|---|---|
| 1 | Regression | 7.050 | 7 | 1.007 | 1.894 | .070b |
|   | Residual | 157.885 | 297 | .532 | | |
|   | Total | 164.934 | 304 | | | |

a. Dependent Variable: Custloyalty_mean
b. Predictors: (Constant), I would recommend this organization as a place to work, Age, Sex, KeyTalent2014, My manager gives me useful feedback, Manager, I am really engaged in my work

*Model NOT sig.*

**Coefficients**a

| Model | | Unstandardized Coefficients | | Standardized Coefficients | t | Sig. |
|---|---|---|---|---|---|---|
| | | B | Std. Error | Beta | | |
| 1 | (Constant) | 3.794 | .370 | | 10.262 | .000 |
|   | KeyTalent2014 | .007 | .136 | .003 | .052 | .959 |
|   | Sex | -.047 | .112 | -.024 | -.417 | .677 |
|   | I am really engaged in my work | .141 | .051 | .196 | 2.782 | .006 |
|   | Age | -.004 | .006 | -.037 | -.628 | .530 |
|   | Manager | .195 | .129 | .090 | 1.515 | .131 |
|   | My manager gives me useful feedback | -.048 | .044 | -.065 | -1.103 | .271 |
|   | I would recommend this organization as a place to work | -.011 | .051 | -.015 | -.213 | .832 |

a. Dependent Variable: Custloyalty_mean

*Only 1 sig. variables*

In Figure 7.9 we can see that the multiple R-square = 0.043, or that 4.3 per cent of the variance in customer loyalty is accounted for by the predictor variables used here.

Looking at the ANOVA in Figure 7.9, ie the regression ANOVA table, which tests the significance of how well the model predicts variation in customer loyalty, there are some important indicators to pull out. First, the regression ANOVA F-value is 1.894, with associated degrees of freedom of 7 and 297 and the significance level of 0.070. As discussed in Chapter 3, in statistical analysis, we look for something to have a significance level less than 0.05 (p<0.05) in order to determine whether it is significant. This is not the case here and hence it is <u>not recommended to use this model to make recommendations.</u>

It is important to be aware that models will not always be significant. A possible reason for this result not to be significant is that the number of cases is much smaller than in other examples. This is because we could only analyse rows or cases for which we had information on all three areas, ie customer survey, employee pulse survey and complete HR system data. As the pulse surveys (see page 321) are often only sent to a small random sample of employees, this is the most likely cause for the greatly reduced number of rows (or cases) that are included in the analysis.

Another reason may be that there is simply no relationship here, which can be disappointing at the end of an analysis. However, this is still a result and it still means something. It tells us that this is not the right model to use to predict customer loyalty.

Looking at the coefficients on their own, <u>the variable 'I am really engaged in my work' appears to correlate with customer loyalty because the significance value is 0.006, so that is something worth exploring further in other models.</u>

> **Snapshot hidden gem**
>
> Not all results are significant. Even when they are not, the data is still telling us something. In some cases it will suggest what we might want to investigate further.

## *Example 3: using multiple linear regression to predict individual performance*

In this example, we use a data set of 626 employees containing their performance appraisal ratings, sickness absence records and scores from the annual employee attitude survey from a manufacturing organization. The data, taken over the past two years, includes the following:

- Employee attitude survey data collected in November 2014.
- Performance appraisal data collected in January 2014.
- Performance appraisal data collected in January 2015.
- Number of days' sickness absence taken per employee during 2014.

Here, the HR analyst has linked data from the two sources and constructed composite survey measurements (average measures derived form multiple questionnaire items) using the unique employee ID.

We introduce some new terms here and a brief description for each is given below (for more information on engagement survey questions and their validity, see Chapter 5):

- *Perceived organizational support (POS)*: this is the degree to which employees believe that their organization values their contributions, cares about their well-being and fulfils socio-emotional needs (Eisenberger *et al*, 1986).
- *Distributive justice perceptions*: this is fostered where rewards and outcomes are perceived to be consistent with implicit norms for allocation, such as equity or equality (Colquitt, 2001).
- *Procedural justice perceptions*: this is fostered through voice during a decision-making process or influence over the outcome or by adherence to fair process criteria such as consistency, lack of bias, correctability, representation, accuracy and ethicality (Colquitt, 2001).
- *Job satisfaction*: this is defined as 'a pleasurable or positive emotional state resulting from the appraisal of one's job or job experiences' (Locke, 1976). It is said to have emotional, cognitive and behavioural components where the emotional component refers to feelings regarding the job such as boredom, anxiety or excitement; the cognitive component of job satisfaction refers to beliefs regarding one's job such as feeling that one's job is mentally demanding and challenging; and finally the behavioural component includes people's actions in relation to their work, which may include being tardy, staying late, or pretending to be ill in order to avoid work (Bernstein and Nash, 2008).
- *Person–organization fit*: this refers to the compatibility between an employee and their organization. It can lead to increased levels of trust and a shared sense of corporate community (Boon and Hartog, 2011).
- *Job strain*: this refers to a psychological response to a demanding work context and can be a consequence of having the perception of having little control over one's work, while facing high job demands (House and Rizzo, 1972).

The data set that we use in this example is another that we have not used before: 'Chapter 7 with performance 2014 2015 and Sick2014.sav'. The data looks like this:

**1** ID (employee ID).

**2** Gender (1 = female, 2 = male).

**3** JobTenure2014 (years with the organization as at November 2014).

**4** POS2014 (composite of perceived organizational support questions on a scale of 1 to 5 as at November 2014).

**5** DistJust2014 (composite of distributive justice questions on a scale of 1 to 5 as at November 2014).

**6** ProcJust2014 (composite of procedural justice questions on a scale of 1 to 5 as at November 2014).

**7** JOBSAT2014 (composite of job satisfaction questions on a scale of 1 to 5 as at November 2014).

**8** ValueFit2014 (composite of person organization fit questions on a scale of 1 to 5 as at November 2014).

9 JobStrain2014 (composite of job strain questions on a scale of 1 to 5 as at November 2014).
10 PerformanceRating2014 (performance rating given in January 2014 on a scale of 1 to 5, with 5 being the highest).
11 PerformanceRating2015 (performance rating given in January 2015 on a scale of 1 to 5, with 5 being the highest).
12 SickDays2014 (total number of sick days taken in 2014).

## Predicting 2015 performance from survey measures and sickness absence

In selecting which model to test here, we can make many choices (a situation that the HR analyst will often find themselves in). The first choice to make is which measure of performance we should use. We have two measures – January 2014 and January 2015 (giving the ratings from the previous year's performance).

> The temporal sequence of data included in the data set is of vital importance when considering which analytic model to run.

Our regression models make an implicit assumption that A causes B, or in this case that our independent variables may cause variation in performance. As such, if the independent variables available are collected in 2014, we probably want to make sure that the performance measure that we are to predict with these factors is the 2015 performance measure. If we try to predict the January 2014 performance measure with November 2014 staff attitudes then we are doing things backwards. So, we should choose the 2015 performance measure as a dependent variable here.

Let's first run a multiple regression model in SPSS (as in the above examples) looking at the link between employee attitudes, sickness absence and performance. Hence we are testing the following model:

Performance Rating 2015 (January) =
 $a + b_1$ (POS2014) + $b_2$ (DistJust2014) + $b_3$ (ProcJust2014) + $b_4$ (JOBSAT2014) + $b_5$ (ValueFit2014) + $b_6$ (JobStrain2014) + $b_7$ (sickdays2014)

Using exactly the same linear regression method we have used elsewhere and above, we can test this model by selecting 'Analyze→Regression→Linear and transferring the PerformanceRating2015 variable into the 'Dependent:' selection box and choosing the following variables as 'Independent Variables' and transferring them into the 'Independent(s):' selection box: POS2014, DistJust2014, ProcJust2014, JOBSAT2014, ValueFit2014, JobStrain2014 and sickdays2014. When we click 'OK' we get the following output (Figure 7.10):

## FIGURE 7.10

**Model Summary**

| Model | R | R-Square | Adjusted R-Square | Std. Error of the Estimate |
|---|---|---|---|---|
| 1 | .312[a] | .097 | .068 | .89916 |

a. Predictors: (Constant), Number of Days taken sick during 2014, Composite of Perceived Organizational Support, Composite of Person Organization Fit, Composite of Job Strain, Composite of Distributive Justice, Composite of Procedural Justice, Composite of Job Satisfaction

*Model is Sig.*

**ANOVA[a]**

| Model | | Sum of Squares | df | Mean Square | F | Sig. |
|---|---|---|---|---|---|---|
| 1 | Regression | 18.553 | 7 | 2.650 | 3.278 | .002[b] |
| | Residual | 172.207 | 213 | .808 | | |
| | Total | 190.760 | 220 | | | |

a. Dependent Variable: Performance ratings given January 2015 1–5 where 5 is highest

b. Predictors: (Constant), Number of Days taken sick during 2014, Composite of Perceived Organizational Support, Composite of Person Organization Fit, Composite of Job Strain, Composite of Distributive Justice, Composite of Procedural Justice, Composite of Job Satisfaction

**Coefficients[a]**

| Model | | Unstandardized Coefficients | | Standardized Coefficients | t | Sig. |
|---|---|---|---|---|---|---|
| | | B | Std. Error | Beta | | |
| 1 | (Constant) | .959 | .584 | | 1.641 | .102 |
| | Composite of Perceived Organizational Support | .196 | .130 | .168 | 1.500 | .135 |
| | Composite of Distributive Justice | -.126 | .102 | -.116 | -1.235 | .218 |
| | Composite of Procedural Justice | .163 | .140 | .121 | 1.163 | .246 |
| | Composite of Job Satisfaction | .033 | .100 | .037 | .331 | .741 |
| | Composite of Person Organization Fit | .062 | .114 | .041 | .544 | .587 |
| | Composite of Job Strain | .247 | .072 | .267 | 3.415 | .001 |
| | Number of Days taken sick during 2014 | -.018 | .008 | -.144 | -2.145 | .033 |

a. Dependent Variable: Performance ratings given January 2015 1–5 where 5 is highest

In the above example, we can see that the R-square = 0.097, or that 9.7 per cent (approximately one-tenth) of the variance in the performance rating given in January 2015 can be accounted for by the predictor variables used here.

Looking at the analysis of variance in Figure 7.10, ie the regression ANOVA table, which tests the significance of how well the model predicts variation in the 2015 performance rating, we can see that the regression ANOVA F-value is 3.278, with an associated total degrees of freedom of 220 and the significance level of 0.002 ($p<0.01$). So we could say it is less than 0.005, which means there is less than a 5 in 1,000 chance that we would randomly find this pattern of shared variance (between the 2015 performance ratings and the independent variables in the model). Hence the model is significant.

So, while the model only accounts for one-tenth of the output (2015 performance rating), it is significant and hence we can be confident in recommendations that we make on the basis of the significant results produced with this model (in that we may have found factors that may impact the performance outcome). It is important to set the expectations in such a way that the impact will be conservative (and always caveat our claims on the basis that our regression findings do not definitively 'prove' causality).

This is a regression method where you put all factors in as predictors and see what come out as significant predictors. This helps control for multiple factors and takes into account noise and inter-correlations between the factors measured. Looking at the Beta coefficients, you can see that the number of sick days taken in 2014 has a negative relationship with the 2015 performance rating, and the amount of job strain has a significant and positive relationship with the 2015 performance rating (we discuss this finding further in Chapter 11 where we present additional analytic strategies; this finding could be an example of where we might want to explore interactions between our predictors).

> **Snapshot hidden gem**
>
> The perceived level of job strain and the number of sick days taken in 2014 are the key potential drivers of performance on ratings given in 2015. Interestingly, the more an individual feels they have job strain, the more likely they are to receive a higher performance rating.

You can, however, use a slightly different method called stepwise regression. This method, in effect, just selects the most important factors contributing to the prediction of your dependent variable. It looks at the independent variables, it finds the strongest relationship, and then it enters this as a regression model. Then it looks to see if the variable with the next strongest relationship adds to the regression model if it is included. This process continues until the prediction of the dependent variable is not improved any more. Thus you get your most efficient regression model.

This process is called stepwise regression.

## Example 4: using stepwise multiple linear regression to model performance

If we enter the above independent variables into a stepwise regression model predicting performance then we get a cleaner, simpler, more parsimonious model. The notion of parsimony here refers to not having unnecessary factors included in our model with the argument 'simple is better'. Bear in mind, however, that when we do this our model is not 'controlling' for the possible effect of other (excluded) variables, so the analyst needs to think carefully about what approach to take.

Here, we again use the data file: 'Chapter 7 with performance 2014 2015 and Sick2014.sav'. To run stepwise regression with this example, we go into SPSS and select 'Regression' and 'Linear' from the 'Analyze' menu (as before) (see Figure 7.11).

**FIGURE 7.11**

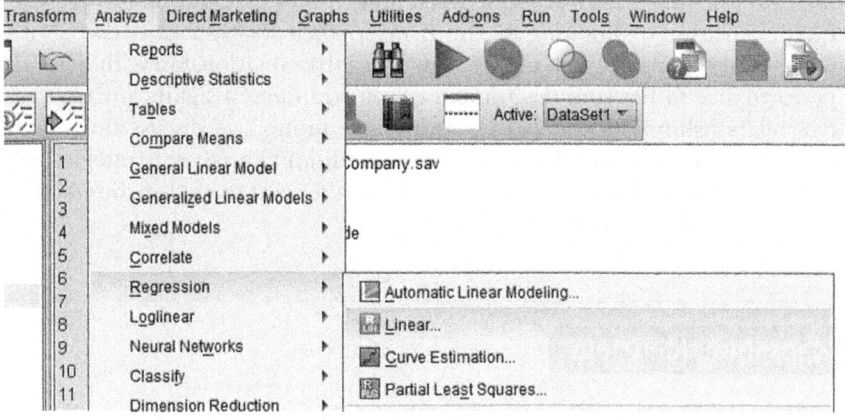

On the next screen, we then select the variables as normal. The key difference in stepwise regression is that we select 'Stepwise' in the 'Method' field (see Figure 7.12).

**FIGURE 7.12**

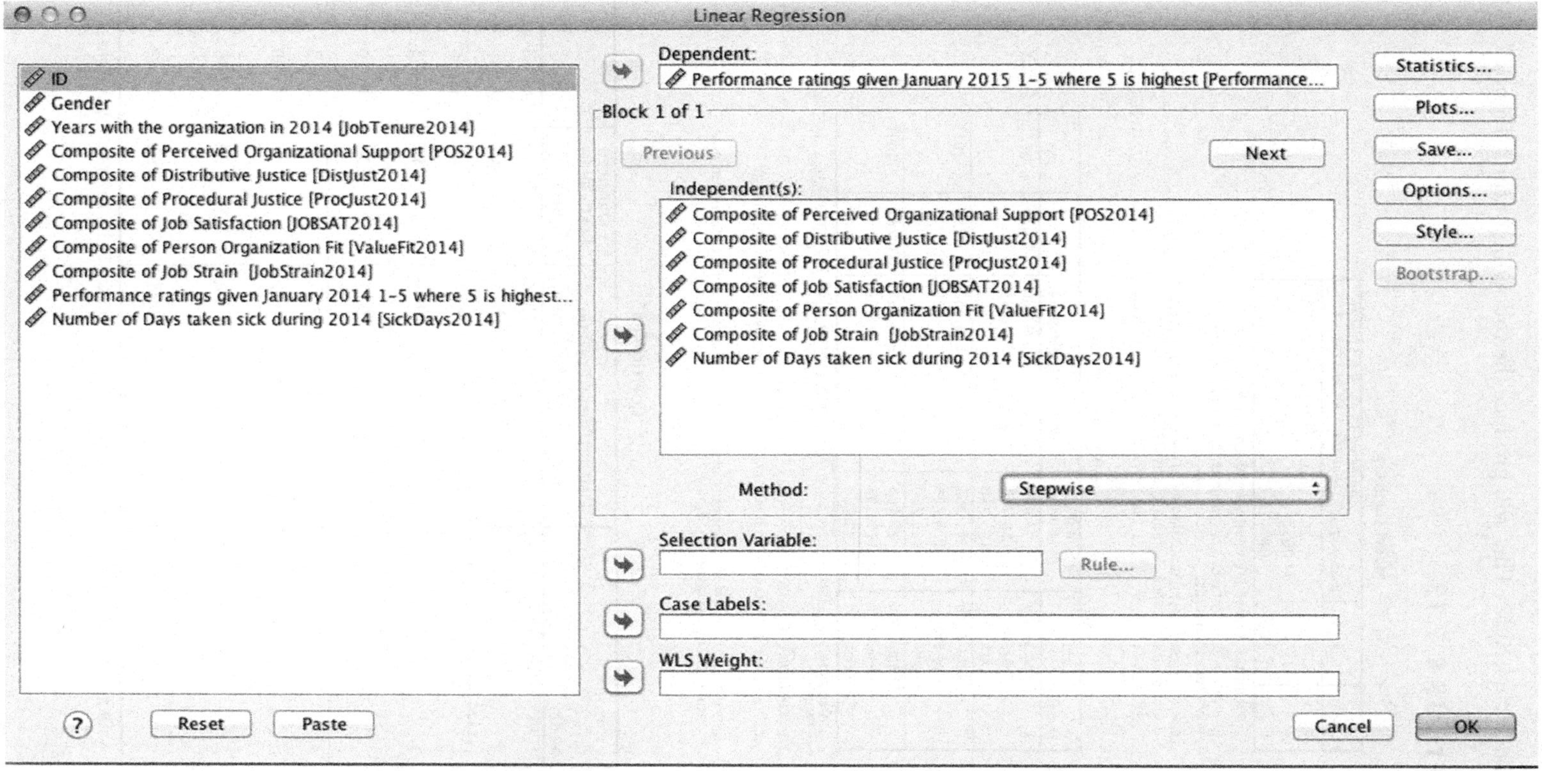

Then click 'OK'. This will produce the following output (Figure 7.13):

**FIGURE 7.13**

Model Summary

| Model | R | R-Square | Adjusted R-Square | Std. Error of the Estimate |
|---|---|---|---|---|
| 1 | .153[a] | .024 | .019 | .92226 |
| 2 | .250[b] | .063 | .054 | .90563 |
| 3 | .282[c] | .080 | .067 | .89955 |

a. Predictors: (Constant), Composite of Job Strain
b. Predictors: (Constant), Composite of Job Strain, Composite of Procedural Justice
c. Predictors: (Constant), Composite of Job Strain, Composite of Procedural Justice, Number of Days taken sick during 2014

ANOVA[a]

| Model | | Sum of Squares | df | Mean Square | F | Sig. |
|---|---|---|---|---|---|---|
| 1 | Regression | 4.486 | 1 | 4.486 | 5.274 | .023[b] |
|   | Residual | 186.274 | 219 | .851 | | |
|   | Total | 190.760 | 220 | | | |
| 2 | Regression | 11.965 | 2 | 5.982 | 7.294 | .001[c] |
|   | Residual | 178.796 | 218 | .820 | | |
|   | Total | 190.760 | 220 | | | |
| 3 | Regression | 15.166 | 3 | 5.055 | 6.247 | .000[d] |
|   | Residual | 175.595 | 217 | .809 | | |
|   | Total | 190.760 | 220 | | | |

a. Dependent Variable: Performance ratings given January 2015 1–5 where 5 is highest
b. Predictors: (Constant), Composite of Job Strain
c. Predictors: (Constant), Composite of Job Strain, Composite of Procedural Justice
d. Predictors: (Constant), Composite of Job Strain, Composite of Procedural Justice, Number of Days taken sick during 2014

Coefficients[a]

| Model | | Unstandardized Coefficients | | Standardized Coefficients | t | Sig. |
|---|---|---|---|---|---|---|
| | | B | Std. Error | Beta | | |
| 1 | (Constant) | 2.404 | .191 | | 12.568 | .000 |
|   | Composite of Job Strain | .142 | .062 | .153 | 2.297 | .023 |
| 2 | (Constant) | 1.311 | .408 | | 3.216 | .001 |
|   | Composite of Job Strain | .194 | .063 | .210 | 3.083 | .002 |
|   | Composite of Procedural Justice | .278 | .092 | .206 | 3.020 | .003 |
| 3 | (Constant) | 1.351 | .405 | | 3.333 | .001 |
|   | Composite of Job Strain | .208 | .063 | .225 | 3.299 | .001 |
|   | Composite of Procedural Justice | .269 | .092 | .199 | 2.936 | .004 |
|   | Number of Days taken sick during 2014 | −.016 | .008 | −.131 | −1.989 | .048 |

a. Dependent Variable: Performance ratings given January 2015 1–5 where 5 is highest

**FIGURE 7.13** *continued*

Excluded Variables[a]

| Model | | Beta In | t | Sig. | Partial Correlation | Collinearity Statistics Tolerance |
|---|---|---|---|---|---|---|
| 1 | Composite of Perceived Organizational Support | .215[b] | 2.886 | .004 | .192 | .780 |
| | Composite of Distributive Justice | .071[b] | .985 | .326 | .067 | .848 |
| | Composite of Procedural Justice | .206[b] | 3.020 | .003 | .200 | .923 |
| | Composite of Job Satisfaction | .185[b] | 2.491 | .013 | .166 | .791 |
| | Composite of Person Organization Fit | .117[b] | 1.687 | .093 | .114 | .916 |
| | Number of Days taken sick during 2014 | -.140[b] | -2.103 | .037 | -.141 | .984 |
| 2 | Composite of Perceived Organizational Support | .119[c] | 1.212 | .227 | .082 | .446 |
| | Composite of Distributive Justice | -.069[c] | -.805 | .421 | -.055 | .588 |
| | Composite of Job Satisfaction | .070[c] | .723 | .471 | .049 | .459 |
| | Composite of Person Organization Fit | .042[c] | .557 | .578 | .038 | .772 |
| | Number of Days taken sick during 2014 | -.131[c] | -1.989 | .048 | -.134 | .982 |
| 3 | Composite of Perceived Organizational Support | .143[d] | 1.462 | .145 | .099 | .440 |
| | Composite of Distributive Justice | -.063[d] | -.742 | .459 | -.050 | .587 |
| | Composite of Job Satisfaction | .061[d] | .632 | .528 | .043 | .458 |
| | Composite of Person Organization Fit | .059[d] | .786 | .433 | .053 | .763 |

a. Dependent Variable: Performance ratings given January 2015 1–5 where 5 is highest
b. Predictors in the Model: (Constant), Composite of Job Strain
c. Predictors in the Model: (Constant), Composite of Job Strain , Composite of Procedural Justice
d. Predictors in the Model: (Constant), Composite of Job Strain , Composite of Procedural Justice, Number of Days taken sick during 2014

The difference here, in stepwise regression, is that we now are able to compare a few models with a view to finding the model that best fits in the most parsimonious way. It is important to consider that whilst stepwise regression has some advantages in that the models presented at the end *only* include significant predictors, therefore they are more simple and parsimonious models, there are some potential downsides to this approach. The main disadvantage is that you are not 'controlling' for the effects of other possible influencers of your dependent variable. It might actually be important to do this and demonstrate that you have control of the possible effects of other factors. If, for example, someone interrogating your findings felt that some other factors (that the stepwise regression analysis failed to include as a model) could be important, it may give you (and them) greater confidence if you actually include these other factors in your model, even though they do not come out as significant predictors.

You will see by looking at the model summary, the ANOVA table and the coefficients table in Figure 7.13 that the analysis identifies the three best models, as follows:

- Model 1
  Model 1 shows that the key driver in determining the performance rating given in January 2015 is actually the amount of job strain reported two months before in November 2014 (Beta=0.153, p<0.05). The raw regression model looks like this:

  Performance Rating 2015 (January) = 2.404 + 0.142(JobStrain2014)

- Model 2
  Model 2 illustrates the key drivers of the performance rating given in January 2015 as a combination of job strain (Beta=0.210,p<0.05) reported in November 2014 and the procedural justice (Beta=0.206,p<0.05) felt by the individual in November 2014. The raw regression model looks like this:

  Performance Rating 2015 (January) =
  1.311 + 0.194(JobStrain2014) + 0.278(ProcJust2014)

- Model 3
  Model 3 is broader and illustrates the predictors of the performance rating given in January 2015 as a combination of job strain (Beta=0.225,p<0.05) felt in November 2014, procedural justice (Beta=0.199,p<0.05) felt in November 2014, and the total number of days taken sick in 2014 (Beta=–0.131,p<0.05). The raw regression model looks like this:

  Performance Rating 2015 (January) =
  1.351 + 0.208(JobStrain2014) + 0.269(ProcJust2014) – 0.016(sickdays2014)

The remainder of the variables (as shown in the 'Excluded Variables' table in Figure 7.13) do not help us to predict performance and thus are not included in these models.

What does the data show us? Well, interestingly, it appears that the people who felt more under strain (who lost sleep worrying about work) in November 2014 seem to have higher performance appraisal ratings in January 2015. This is potentially problematic from a health and well-being perspective. More strain and worry tend to lead to higher performance? One would not want to consider trying to increase the strain and worry on individuals as an organizational performance improvement strategy. But it might be a reflection of the fact that people who work hard and are under pressure, and indeed who might lose sleep worrying about their work, are subsequently rewarded with a higher performance rating (regardless of whether they are actually performing at a higher level).

The story does not stop there, however. The second model indicates that the people who feel that their employer acts in a just and fair way also have higher performance ratings. Why might this be? Well, one could interpret this as the employees who feel their employer is not fair or just may have lower levels of motivation or they may have a more disgruntled attitude than those who experience (or perceive) greater levels of procedural justice, thus this may play out in how their supervisor then rates them. It is worth considering for a moment how important it is to have the performance measure subsequent to the attitude survey rating in this model. If, for example, we inserted our 2014 performance measure here as a dependent variable instead of our 2015 performance measure, and we found a positive relationship between November 2014 justice perceptions and January 2014 performance ratings, it might be that a lower performance rating produced negative perceptions of justice, thus the causality would be reversed. Therefore it is essential that the performance rating that we use in our model (as a dependent variable) is given after the attitude/perceptual measure. We will get back to this issue below.

If we look at the third model that the analysis produces we also see that number of days' sick in 2014 is a significant predictor of 2015 performance. This means that the frequency of days for which people were absent due to illness seems to be reflected in their performance appraisal. So, in summary, the employees who receive the highest performance ratings are those who have the least amount of days off sick, who experience and perceive that their employer acts in a procedurally just manner, and who feel a sense of strain and worry about their work.

Strategically, how could we use this information to make recommendations to the organization's people strategy? First, it is worth highlighting to senior leaders that the data suggests we may be rewarding people for being under strain. This could be damaging, because it is the high performers who are seen as role models in the organization – and if they are losing sleep and are under pressure, then it may be a signal to others that if they want to be rewarded also then they need to be putting more strain and pressure on themselves, which is not healthy for them or for the organization.

A high level of job strain is likely to cause the individual to become ill, which would, in time, cause more days taken in sickness absence and eventually (according to this model) lead to a lower performance rating. So this approach would not lead to sustained, long-term, consistent high performance.

Let's look at the other key drivers: sickness absence and procedural justice. First, sickness absence. Many organizations invest in employee well-being programmes to help employees remain mentally and physically healthy, and there are many specialists in the field who can advise on employee well-being programmes. Even small, simple, low-cost suggestions such as providing fresh fruit, encouraging exercise through lunchtime or after-work clubs, or obtaining discounted gym membership for staff can go a long way to help employees to stay healthy. Other suggestions include teaching healthy habits to employees through external speakers, employee assistance programmes to help employees who are experiencing stress, offering on-site flu vaccinations or even an on-site doctor's office.

Finally, procedural justice. The more employees perceive their employer to be just and fair, the higher they are likely to perform. To improve this, it would almost certainly require further investigations into which procedures are deemed fair and just (and which are not) so that prescriptive action may be taken. This could be done through a review of processes combined with input from survey respondents.

> **Snapshot hidden gem**
>
> The perceived level of job strain, the perceived level of procedural justice felt and the number of sick days taken in 2014 are the key drivers of performance ratings given in 2015. Interestingly, the more an individual feels they have job strain, and the more they feel their employer is just and fair, the more likely they are to receive a higher performance rating. The lower the number of sick days taken, the higher the performance rating that they tend to be given.

## Example 5: using stepwise multiple linear regression to model change in performance over time

In this example, we are repeating the same model used in Example 4; however, here we are controlling for earlier levels of performance. In the example above we have predicted 2015 performance levels by exploring 2014 predictors. Our data set also has 2014 data that would be useful to use in our analysis. If we take earlier levels of performance into account we would, in effect, be able to filter out any role that earlier performance ratings may have in influencing our 2014 variables (which you would expect to be substantial as employees often get consistent performance ratings over the years). This is important because even though in our model above we are showing that 2015 performance may be influenced by 2014 experiences and perceptions, it is possible that these perceptions could have been influenced by 2014 performance ratings rather than the other way around. When we predict 2015 performance, if we have not controlled for earlier levels of performance we will not know for certain whether we are just showing relationships between 2014 performance and subsequent 2014 attitudes. If we include a 2014 performance measure in our regression model as an independent variable then we are in effect filtering out the impact that the January 2014 performance may have had on our November 2014 attitudes when accounting for variation in January 2015 performance. Importantly, when we include a 2014 performance measure as a control in our model, we are looking at the relationship between 2014 experiences (and sickness) on a *change* in performance rating between 2014 and 2015. This is actually a stronger predictive test and we are able to be more confident in any causal inferences that such analysis might identify.

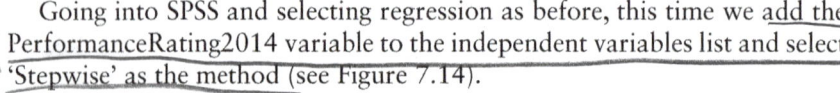
Going into SPSS and selecting regression as before, this time we add the PerformanceRating2014 variable to the independent variables list and select 'Stepwise' as the method (see Figure 7.14).

## FIGURE 7.14

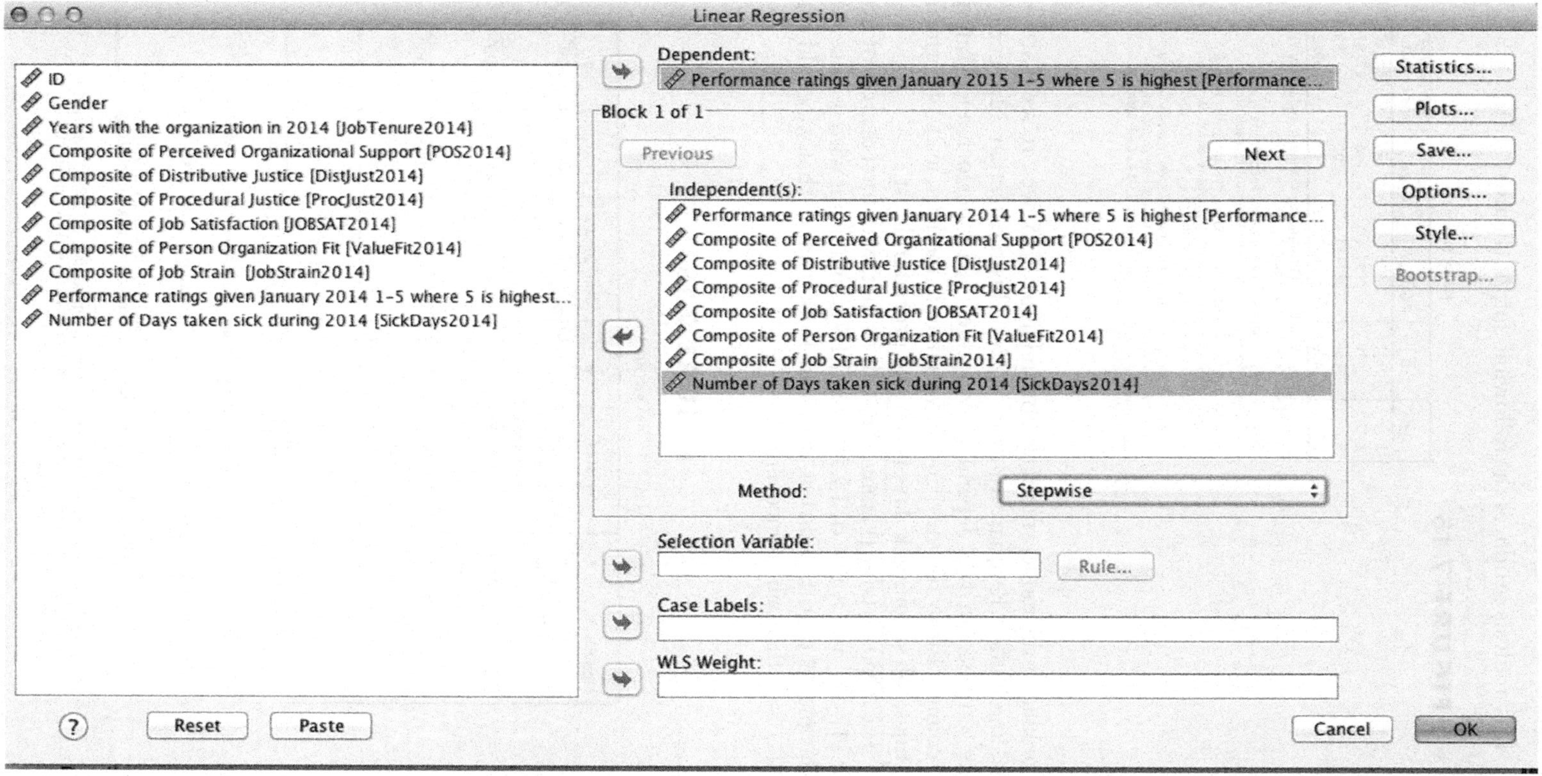

**Linear Regression**

- ID
- Gender
- Years with the organization in 2014 [JobTenure2014]
- Composite of Perceived Organizational Support [POS2014]
- Composite of Distributive Justice [DistJust2014]
- Composite of Procedural Justice [ProcJust2014]
- Composite of Job Satisfaction [JOBSAT2014]
- Composite of Person Organization Fit [ValueFit2014]
- Composite of Job Strain [JobStrain2014]
- Performance ratings given January 2014 1–5 where 5 is highest...
- Number of Days taken sick during 2014 [SickDays2014]

**Dependent:**
Performance ratings given January 2015 1–5 where 5 is highest [Performance...

Block 1 of 1
[Previous] [Next]

**Independent(s):**
- Performance ratings given January 2014 1–5 where 5 is highest [Performance...
- Composite of Perceived Organizational Support [POS2014]
- Composite of Distributive Justice [DistJust2014]
- Composite of Procedural Justice [ProcJust2014]
- Composite of Job Satisfaction [JOBSAT2014]
- Composite of Person Organization Fit [ValueFit2014]
- Composite of Job Strain [JobStrain2014]
- Number of Days taken sick during 2014 [SickDays2014]

**Method:** Stepwise

**Selection Variable:** [Rule...]

**Case Labels:**

**WLS Weight:**

[Reset] [Paste] [Cancel] [OK]

[Statistics...] [Plots...] [Save...] [Options...] [Style...] [Bootstrap...]

This analysis produces the following output (Figure 7.15):

**FIGURE 7.15**

Model Summary

| Model | R | R-Square | Adjusted R-Square | Std. Error of the Estimate |
|---|---|---|---|---|
| 1 | .417[a] | .173 | .170 | .83110 |
| 2 | .440[b] | .193 | .186 | .82297 |
| 3 | .459[c] | .211 | .200 | .81590 |
| 4 | .476[d] | .226 | .212 | .80982 |

a. Predictors: (Constant), Performance ratings given January 2014 1-5 where 5 is highest

b. Predictors: (Constant), Performance ratings given January 2014 1-5 where 5 is highest, Composite of Job Strain

c. Predictors: (Constant), Performance ratings given January 2014 1-5 where 5 is highest, Composite of Job Strain, Number of Days taken sick during 2014

d. Predictors: (Constant), Performance ratings given January 2014 1-5 where 5 is highest, Composite of Job Strain, Number of Days taken sick during 2014, Composite of Procedural Justice

Looking at the model summary box in Figure 7.15, we can see that model 4 has the highest R-square value of 0.226. This means that 22.6 per cent of the variance in the dependant variable (2015 performance ratings) is accounted for by the independent variables in model 4, ie 2014 performance ratings, job strain, sick days taken and procedural justice.

The ANOVA table (Figure 7.16) tells us that, with total degrees of freedom of 217 and an F-value of 15.565, model 4 is significant with p-value <0.001. This means that there is less than 1 in 1,000 chance that we could come to this result through chance alone.

**FIGURE 7.16**

ANOVA[a]

| Model | | Sum of Squares | df | Mean Square | F | Sig. |
|---|---|---|---|---|---|---|
| 1 | Regression | 31.320 | 1 | 31.320 | 45.342 | .000[b] |
| | Residual | 149.199 | 216 | .691 | | |
| | Total | 180.518 | 217 | | | |
| 2 | Regression | 34.904 | 2 | 17.452 | 25.768 | .000[c] |
| | Residual | 145.614 | 215 | .677 | | |
| | Total | 180.518 | 217 | | | |
| 3 | Regression | 38.060 | 3 | 12.687 | 19.058 | .000[d] |
| | Residual | 142.458 | 214 | .666 | | |
| | Total | 180.518 | 217 | | | |
| 4 | Regression | 40.831 | 4 | 10.208 | 15.565 | .000[e] |
| | Residual | 139.688 | 213 | .656 | | |
| | Total | 180.518 | 217 | | | |

Model is Sig.

a. Dependent Variable: Performance ratings given January 2015 1-5 where 5 is highest

b. Predictors: (Constant), Performance ratings given January 2014 1-5 where 5 is highest

c. Predictors: (Constant), Performance ratings given January 2014 1-5 where 5 is highest, Composite of Job Strain

d. Predictors: (Constant), Performance ratings given January 2014 1-5 where 5 is highest, Composite of Job Strain, Number of Days taken sick during 2014

e. Predictors: (Constant), Performance ratings given January 2014 1-5 where 5 is highest, Composite of Job Strain, Number of Days taken sick during 2014, Composite of Procedural Justice

Looking at the coefficients for Model 4 (Figure 7.17), we can see that our raw regression model 4 looks like this:

2015 performance ratings =
 0.467 + 0.377 (2014 performance ratings) + 0.175 (job strain) −
 0.016 (sick days taken) + 0.173 (procedural justice)

The above actually predicts an increase (or decrease) in performance between 2014 and 2015 and is thus much more interesting to us.

**FIGURE 7.17**

Coefficients[a]

| Model | | Unstandardized Coefficients B | Unstandardized Coefficients Std. Error | Standardized Coefficients Beta | t | Sig. |
|---|---|---|---|---|---|---|
| 1 | (Constant) | 1.447 | .209 | | 6.922 | .000 |
| | Performance ratings given January 2014 1–5 where 5 is highest | .397 | .059 | .417 | 6.734 | .000 |
| 2 | (Constant) | 1.091 | .258 | | 4.223 | .000 |
| | Performance ratings given January 2014 1–5 where 5 is highest | .392 | .058 | .411 | 6.709 | .000 |
| | Composite of Job Strain | .127 | .055 | .141 | 2.301 | .022 |
| 3 | (Constant) | 1.103 | .256 | | 4.303 | .000 |
| | Performance ratings given January 2014 1–5 where 5 is highest | .390 | .058 | .409 | 6.732 | .000 |
| | Composite of Job Strain | .142 | .055 | .158 | 2.572 | .011 |
| | Number of Days taken sick during 2014 | −.016 | .007 | −.133 | −2.177 | .031 |
| 4 | (Constant) | .467 | .400 | | 1.166 | .245 |
| | Performance ratings given January 2014 1–5 where 5 is highest | .377 | .058 | .396 | 6.519 | .000 |
| | Composite of Job Strain | .175 | .057 | .194 | 3.064 | .002 |
| | Number of Days taken sick during 2014 | −.016 | .007 | −.127 | −2.092 | .038 |
| | Composite of Procedural Justice | .173 | .084 | .130 | 2.056 | .041 |

a. Dependent Variable: Performance ratings given January 2015 1–5 where 5 is highest

*All sig.*

> **Snapshot hidden gem**
>
> The biggest predictor of 2015 performance is 2014 performance; however, change in performance between 2014 and 2015 is largely driven by job strain, number of sick days taken and the employees' perceptions of procedural justice.

Interestingly, one of the things that often happens when one carries out some analysis is that some results often lead us to explore further. If it is the case that sickness absence predicts performance, what is it that predicts sickness absence?

## Example 6: using multiple regression to predict sickness absence

Using the same data set, we can switch the dependent variable to the number of sick days taken, and include scores from the employee attitude survey as the independent variables. To do this we go into the SPSS 'Analyze' menu again, select 'Regression' and 'Linear' and then enter 'Number of days taken sick during 2014' as the dependent variable. We then enter the following as the independent variables, which are taken directly from the employee opinion survey results: composite of job satisfaction, composite of person organization fit, composite of job strain, composite of distributive justice, composite of procedural justice and composite of perceived organizational support. This will give the results illustrated in Figure 7.18.

Using the same analysis method as in the above example, we can see that in running a model that predicts number of days sick in 2014, the R-square = 0.044, or that 4.4 per cent of the variance in number of sick days taken is accounted for by the predictor variables used here.

Looking at the analysis of variance, ie the regression ANOVA table in Figure 7.18, which tests the significance of how well the model predicts variation in number of sick days taken, there are some important indicators to pull out. First, the regression ANOVA F-value is 2.047, with associated total degrees of freedom of 271, giving the significance level of 0.060. So the model does not quite meet the $p<0.05$ threshold for significance. If we had more data perhaps this would become significant, but as it is we cannot confirm this.

## FIGURE 7.18

**Model Summary**

| Model | R | R-Square | Adjusted R-Square | Std. Error of the Estimate |
|---|---|---|---|---|
| 1 | .210[a] | .044 | .023 | 6.71348 |

a. Predictors: (Constant), Composite of Job Satisfaction, Composite of Person Organization Fit, Composite of Job Strain, Composite of Distributive Justice, Composite of Procedural Justice, Composite of Perceived Organizational Support

**ANOVA[a]**

*Cannot confirm model is sig.*

| Model | | Sum of Squares | df | Mean Square | F | Sig. |
|---|---|---|---|---|---|---|
| 1 | Regression | 553.549 | 6 | 92.258 | 2.047 | .060[b] |
| | Residual | 11943.771 | 265 | 45.071 | | |
| | Total | 12497.320 | 271 | | | |

a. Dependent Variable: Number of Days taken sick during 2014
b. Predictors: (Constant), Composite of Job Satisfaction, Composite of Person Organization Fit, Composite of Job Strain, Composite of Distributive Justice, Composite of Procedural Justice, Composite of Perceived Organizational Support

**Coefficients[a]**

| Model | | Unstandardized Coefficients B | Std. Error | Standardized Coefficients Beta | t | Sig. |
|---|---|---|---|---|---|---|
| 1 | (Constant) | -.897 | 3.863 | | -.232 | .817 |
| | Composite of Perceived Organizational Support | 1.811 | .860 | .215 | 2.107 | .036 |
| | Composite of Person Organization Fit | 1.045 | .760 | .096 | 1.376 | .170 |
| | Composite of Job Strain | .928 | .470 | .140 | 1.974 | .049 |
| | Composite of Distributive Justice | .150 | .661 | .019 | .227 | .820 |
| | Composite of Procedural Justice | -1.180 | .921 | -.120 | -1.280 | .202 |
| | Composite of Job Satisfaction | -1.110 | .673 | -.166 | -1.649 | .100 |

a. Dependent Variable: Number of Days taken sick during 2014

As it is so close to significance, let's take a look at what the results are hinting at.

The raw regression model looks like this:

Number of days sickness absence =
  −0.897 + 1.811 (perceived organizational support) +
  1.045 (person organization fit) + 0.928 (job strain) +
  0.150 (distributive justice) − 1.180 (procedural justice) −
  1.110 (job satisfaction)

Although we saw a positive relationship between job strain and performance in the last example, we can see from this analysis that job strain also predicts sickness absence. This suggests that people who feel under pressure may end up getting higher ratings only if this does not make them sick. This is a well-known idea – that a bit of pressure can increase performance but too much may have a negative affect (it can make people sick). So our analysis here shows some evidence of this. Importantly, however, we also see that the more employees experience support from their employer then the more days off sick they tend to take. This can help us to understand some of the processes involved in ensuring high sustainable performance: having demanding and challenging jobs, making sure procedures are in place at the organization that are fair and just, and ensuring a supportive culture. From this set of analysis, we seem to have identified some conditions for a sustainable high-performance workplace. The research literature exploring possible stress reactions (see Cooper, Dewe and O'Driscoll, 2001 for a review) identifies a number of factors that may intervene in experiences of workplace pressure – and 'support' is one of these possible 'buffers' that may mitigate the negative effects of workplace pressure. Such a process (ie a factor to potentially buffer a negative experience) is referred to as a moderating process (testing for moderation will be discussed in Chapter 11).

## Growth trajectories and analytic demands

One of the things we may be interested in is identifying predictors of certain patterns of performance over time. For example, we might want to look at the changes in individual performance ratings or levels of engagement over three or four years of employment, and what factors may influence that over time; the more waves of data that we have, the more interesting and powerful our analysis can get. This type of analysis can be extremely useful in the long term, especially in terms of predictive utility, but it comes with its challenges and will be discussed further in Chapter 11.

## Example 7: exploring patterns in performance linked to employee profile data

The data file we are using with this example is: 'Chapter 7 MIdata perf9450.sav'. The data here is from a large multinational manufacturing organization and contains details of 9,450 employees across four countries, looking at age, tenure, gender and benchmark position salary.

The data looks like this:

**1** Perf (performance appraisal: 1 = low; 2 = medium; 3 = high).
**2** Joiner (recent joiner: 1 = old timer, 2 = new hire).

3 SalaryBenchmark (benchmark salary: 1 = <80 per cent; 2 = 80–89.99 per cent; 3 = 90–109.99 per cent; 4 = 110–120 per cent; 5 = >120 per cent of benchmark).
4 CountryCode (country where employee is based: (1 = United States; 2 = UK; 3 = Netherlands; 4 = Russia).
5 Gender (1 = male; 2 = female).
6 AgeCat (age group: 1 = 20–29; 2 = 30–39; 3 = 40–49; 4 = 50–59; 5 = 60–64; 6 = 65+).
7 TenureCat (years with the organization: 1 = less than 1 year; 2 = 1–2 years; 3 = 3–5 years; 4 = 6–10 years; 5 = 11–15 years; 6 = more than 16 years).
8 Leaver (whether or not the employee left the organization: 1 = stayer; 2 = leaver).

Notice in the listed variables where there is more than one value such as 'Perf' and 'AgeCat' that the numbers assigned to the values have a numerical meaning, ie the higher the number in 'Perf', the higher the performance rating, so the number is meaningful numerically. In the 'TenureCat' variable, although not interval-level data, the higher the number, the longer the person has been with the organization. This helps with our analysis in highlighting whether the dependent variable increases or decreases (and to what extent) with an increase or a decrease in the independent variable. In the 'CountryCode' variable, however, the number assigned to the country has no numerical meaning, so a model like the one we have been using for the above examples does not work for a variable like country (ie an increment in the numeric value would *not* mean the employee moves closer to Russia – just as a mean value of 3.5 for a team would *not* suggest they are based somewhere between the Netherlands and Russia, say in Poland?); clearly in this variable, the numbers are just labels.

In this situation, in order to include these country categories in our analysis we need to set up new variables that we refer to as *dummy* variables.

We set up the new variables so that there are two choices in each, as follows:

9 USAdummy (shows if the employee is based in the United States or not: 1 = yes; 0 = no).
10 UKdummy (shows if the employee is based in the UK or not: 1 = yes; 0 = no).
11 Netherlandsdummy (shows if the employee is based in the Netherlands or not: 1 = yes; 0 = no).
12 Russiadummy (shows if the employee is based in Russia or not: 1 = yes; 0 = no).

After constructing dummy variables in this way, we now want to include them in the analysis; importantly, with dummy variables we choose one of them to act as a baseline or reference category (country in this case). To break down this idea further, say the United States is the head office of this particular organization. We might want to know whether performance ratings might be influenced by whether they work in a country *other* than the United States; does it make a difference if someone works in the UK, in the Netherlands or in Russia compared to the United States? So we would select United States as our reference. How do we reflect this in our analysis? As mentioned previously, we simply leave the reference category dummy variable out of the model but include all of the other country dummy variables. Although it is not intuitive to leave out the most strategically important country (or the country with the most employees), think of it as analysing the difference it makes if someone is not based in this country. This will become clearer as we discuss the results.

So, again, we run the multiple regression in SPSS in exactly the same manner as the examples above (Analyze→Regression→Linear) (see Figure 7.19). We put performance appraisal as the 'Dependent:' variable and the Salary-Benchmark, Gender, AgeCat, TenureCat, UKDummy, NetherlandsDummy and Russia Dummy into the 'Independent(s):' selection box.

**FIGURE 7.19**

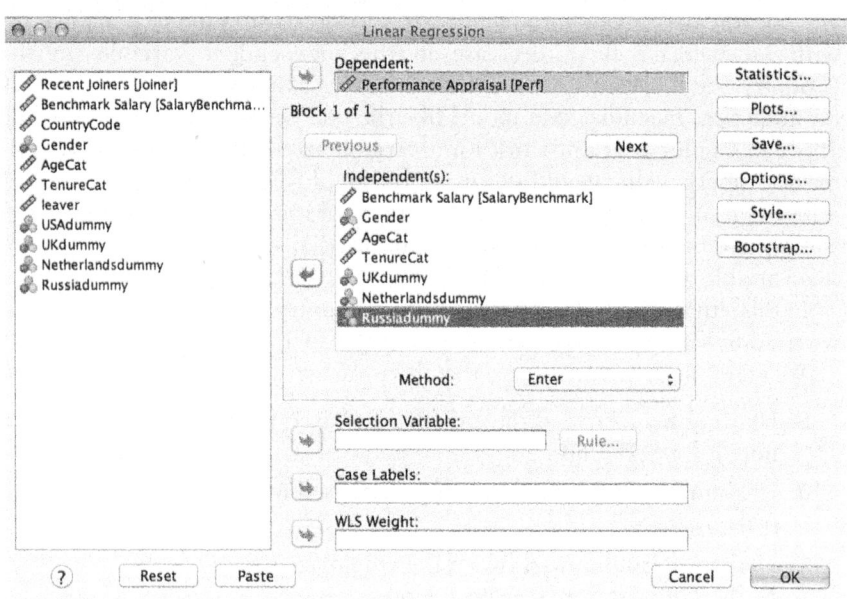

The following output is produced (Figure 7.20):

## FIGURE 7.20

**Model Summary**

| Model | R | R-Square | Adjusted R-Square | Std. Error of the Estimate |
|---|---|---|---|---|
| 1 | .374a | .140 | .139 | .48723 |

a. Predictors: (Constant), Russiadummy, Benchmark Salary, Netherlandsdummy, TenureCat, UKdummy, AgeCat, Gender

*Model is sig.*

**ANOVAa**

| Model | | Sum of Squares | df | Mean Square | F | Sig. |
|---|---|---|---|---|---|---|
| 1 | Regression | 341.129 | 7 | 48.733 | 205.281 | .000b |
| | Residual | 2097.629 | 8836 | .237 | | |
| | Total | 2438.758 | 8843 | | | |

a. Dependent Variable: Performance Appraisal
b. Predictors: (Constant), Russiadummy, Benchmark Salary, Netherlandsdummy, TenureCat, UKdummy, AgeCat, Gender

*M=1, so males get higher ratings*
*All variables sig.*

**Coefficientsa**

| Model | | Unstandardized Coefficients | | Standardized Coefficients | t | Sig. |
|---|---|---|---|---|---|---|
| | | B | Std. Error | Beta | | |
| 1 | (Constant) | 2.645 | .031 | | 84.633 | .000 |
| | Benchmark Salary | .130 | .008 | .180 | 17.052 | .000 |
| | Gender | -.732 | .021 | -.654 | -34.758 | .000 |
| | AgeCat | -.071 | .006 | -.127 | -11.153 | .000 |
| | TenureCat | .026 | .005 | .063 | 5.600 | .000 |
| | UKdummy | .068 | .013 | .057 | 5.067 | .000 |
| | Netherlandsdummy | .538 | .030 | .208 | 17.713 | .000 |
| | Russiadummy | .661 | .023 | .563 | 28.469 | .000 |

a. Dependent Variable: Performance Appraisal

*Higher ratings than U.S.*

Analysing the data we can see from the R-square that 14 per cent of the variance in the dependent variable (performance appraisal rating) is accounted for by variance in the independent variables. The model is significant, with an F-value of 205.28, a regression degrees of freedom of 7, and a residual degrees of freedom of 8,843.

The raw regression model looks like this:

Performance appraisal rating =
2.645 + 0.130 (benchmark salary) − 0.071 (age) + 0.026 (tenure) − 0.732 (gender) + 0.068 (UK) + 0.538 (Netherlands) + 0.661 (Russia)

With very large data sets the significance column here can often be rather unhelpful. This is one of the challenges with running inferential statistical models with 'big data'. The Beta column, however, does give us some important information as to what are the most important factors that could be influencing performance across the organization and in what direction (and by how much). It is clear, for example, that gender seems to be very important in predicting performance rating. As males are coded as 1 and females as 2 in this data set, it seems that males get higher ratings, as this is a negative relationship (Beta=-0.654, p<0.001).

The data also suggests that employees in the Netherlands (Beta=0.208, p<0.001) and Russia (Beta=0.563, p<0.001) tend to receive higher performance ratings than their US counterparts. It would definitely be worth conducting further analysis to look at how the organization's performance appraisal ratings schemes are applied across different countries.

> **Snapshot hidden gem**
>
> The biggest predictor of performance ratings in this organization is gender, showing that men receive significantly higher performance ratings than women. Employees from Russia and the Netherlands also receive significantly higher performance ratings.

The hidden gem above potentially points to procedural inconsistencies in the performance ratings process, so the recommendation on the back of this analysis would be to more strictly monitor the calibration process and the assessment process to ensure that line managers are not favouring male employees over female employees, and that employees in the Netherlands and Russia are being assessed against equivalent criteria (compared to the headquarters in the United States) to ensure a fair process.

## *Exploring the use of supermarket checkout scan rates as a measure of employee performance*

Many supermarkets in the UK impose a scan-rate target on their employees who work on the checkout. An article in the *Daily Mail* newspaper on 8 July 2012 reported on a leading supermarket imposing a target on staff whereby they must scan each item in three seconds or less, or face being moved to another department.

The example given below explores patterns of checkout scan rates across various demographic employee characteristics of a 'fictitious' supermarket chain. The variables in the data sample are outlined below. The dependent variable measured in this example is the average number of items scanned per minute (per employee), and the target in this particular supermarket was 22 items per minute. Obviously, as we are exploring predictors of performance in this chapter, employee variation in this scan rate

(Scanspminute) is the key performance indicator that we try to predict here (we use this data set again in Chapter 9). The data file we use here is 'Chapter 7 Supermarket Checkout.sav':

1. id (unique ID for each employee).
2. educ (number of years of education of the employee).
3. jobtime (number of weeks working with the supermarket).
4. disability (whether or not the employee has stated they have a disability: 0 = no; 1 = yes).
5. Gender (1= male; 2 = female).
6. Scanspminute (average number of items scanned per minute this week).
7. Store (which store: 1 = Portsmouth North; 2 = Portsea Island).
8. weeksinjob (number of weeks working on the checkout).
9. AgeCat (age category: 1 = 16–19; 2 = 20–24; 3 = 25–29; 4 = 30–34; 5 = 35–39; 6 = 40–44; 7 = 45–49; 8 = 50–54; 9 = 55–59; 10 = 60+).
10. Age 1 (16–19).
11. Age 2 (20–24).
12. Age 3 (25–29).
13. Age 4 (30–34).
14. Age 5 (35–39).
15. Age 6 (40–44).
16. Age 7 (45–49).
17. Age 8 (50–54).
18. Age 9 (55–59).
19. Age 10 (60+).

Let's look a bit more closely at the scan-rate data by age group.

Go into SPSS in the 'Analyze' menu and select 'Compare Means' and 'Means' (see Figure 7.21)

**FIGURE 7.21**

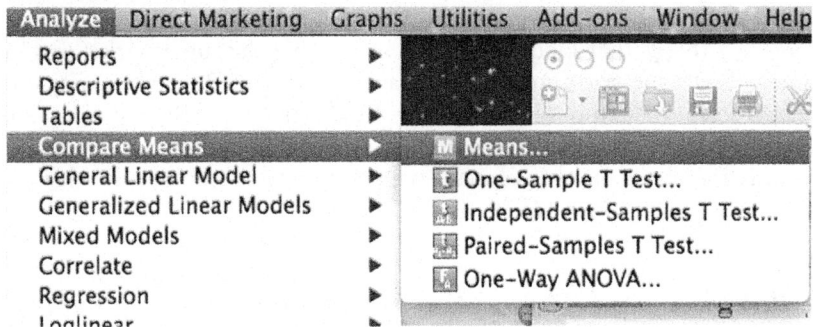

In the 'Means Dependent List:' selection box, transfer the average number of items scanned per minute this week as the dependent variable, and the 'AgeCATegory' as the independent variable (Figure 7.22).

## FIGURE 7.22

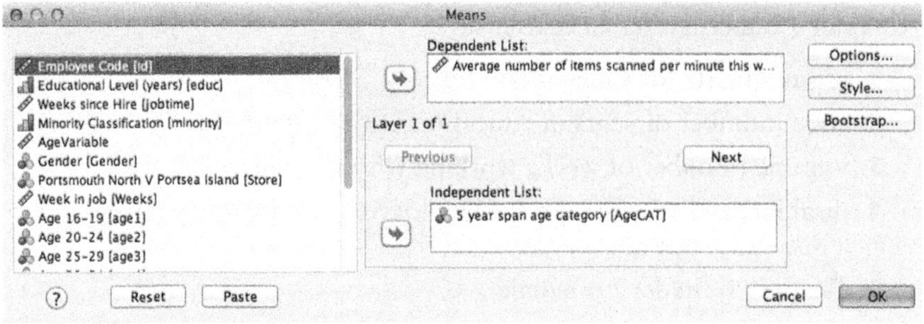

[SPSS Means dialog box screenshot]

Figure 7.23 shows the mean average number of items scanned per minute, the number of employees in each age group and the standard deviation, or spread of the values for each age group.

## FIGURE 7.23

Report

Average number of items scanned per minute this week

| 5-year span age category | Mean | N | Std. Deviation |
|---|---|---|---|
| 16–19 | 15.6842 | 19 | 4.65239 |
| 20–24 | 20.1297 | 111 | 3.26019 |
| 25–29 | 18.8191 | 141 | 2.99115 |
| 30–34 | 20.4611 | 36 | 3.98427 |
| 35–39 | 18.7667 | 33 | 4.30753 |
| 40–44 | 22.1743 | 35 | 4.89660 |
| 45–49 | 21.3129 | 31 | 3.30280 |
| 50–54 | 20.9862 | 29 | 2.26033 |
| 55–59 | 19.8571 | 35 | 3.65331 |
| 60+ | 12.3750 | 4 | 4.95606 |
| Total | 19.6871 | 474 | 3.79660 |

Some key things that Figure 7.23 tells us are that the supermarket employs almost three times the number of staff aged 20–24 and 25–29 than any other age category; that employees in the 40–44 age group are the only age group that meets the (22 items per minute) target on average, and that there is a lot of variation in the number of items scanned by those employees (this is also the case for age groups 16–19, 35–39, and 60+).

## Example 8: exploring patterns in supermarket checkout scan rates linked to employee demographic data

If we run a multiple regression analysis, we will be able to identify which of the demographic variables, if any, impact the number of items scanned per week.

As before, with multiple regression, we go into SPSS and select 'Analyze'→ 'Regression'→'Linear'. We transfer 'Average number of items scanned per minute this week' as the 'Dependent:' variable (Figure 7.24), and for the

**FIGURE 7.24**

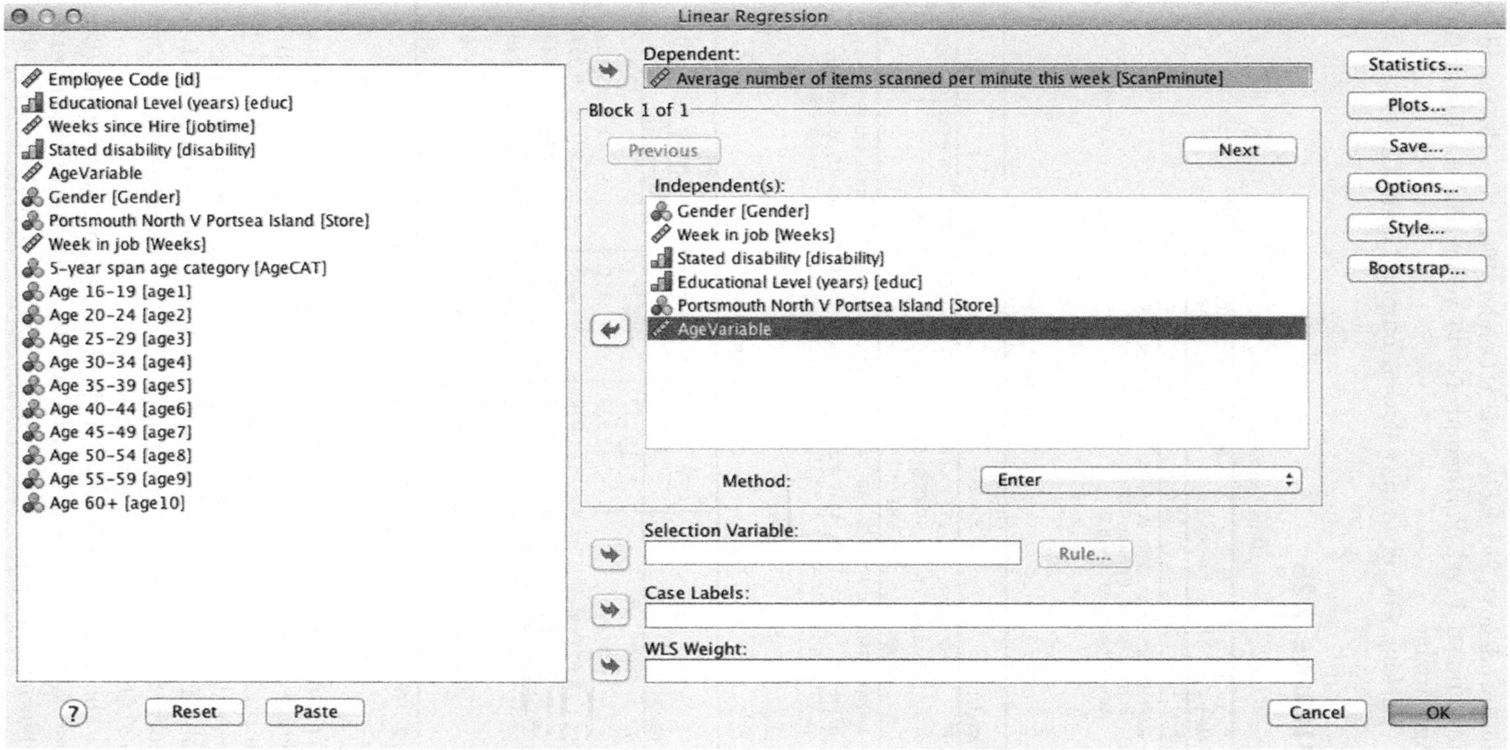
Linear Regression
Employee Code [id]
Educational Level (years) [educ]
Weeks since Hire [jobtime]
Stated disability [disability]
AgeVariable
Gender [Gender]
Portsmouth North V Portsea Island [Store]
Week in job [Weeks]
5-year span age category [AgeCAT]
Age 16-19 [age1]
Age 20-24 [age2]
Age 25-29 [age3]
Age 30-34 [age4]
Age 35-39 [age5]
Age 40-44 [age6]
Age 45-49 [age7]
Age 50-54 [age8]
Age 55-59 [age9]
Age 60+ [age10]
Dependent:
Average number of items scanned per minute this week [ScanPminute]
Block 1 of 1
Previous
Next
Independent(s):
Gender [Gender]
Week in job [Weeks]
Stated disability [disability]
Educational Level (years) [educ]
Portsmouth North V Portsea Island [Store]
AgeVariable
Method:
Enter
Selection Variable:
Rule...
Case Labels:
WLS Weight:
Statistics...
Plots...
Save...
Options...
Style...
Bootstrap...
Reset
Paste
Cancel
OK

'Independent(s):' variables select Gender, Week in job, Stated disability, Educational Level, Portsmouth North versus Portsea Island (store), and AgeVariable.

Clicking 'OK' gives the following output (Figure 7.25)

## FIGURE 7.25

**Model Summary**

| Model | R | R-Square | Adjusted R-Square | Std. Error of the Estimate |
|---|---|---|---|---|
| 1 | .507[a] | .257 | .248 | 3.29332 |

a. Predictors: (Constant), AgeVariable, Portsmouth North V Portsea Island, Gender, Stated disability, Week in job, Educational Level (years)

*Model is Sig.*

**ANOVA[a]**

| Model | | Sum of Squares | df | Mean Square | F | Sig. |
|---|---|---|---|---|---|---|
| 1 | Regression | 1752.846 | 6 | 292.141 | 26.935 | .000[b] |
|   | Residual | 5065.065 | 467 | 10.846 | | |
|   | Total | 6817.911 | 473 | | | |

a. Dependent Variable: Average number of items scanned per minute this week
b. Predictors: (Constant), AgeVariable, Portsmouth North V Portsea Island, Gender, Stated disability, Week in job, Educational Level (years)

*Females have better scan rates*

**Coefficients[a]**

| Model | | Unstandardized Coefficients | | Standardized Coefficients | t | Sig. |
|---|---|---|---|---|---|---|
| | | B | Std. Error | Beta | | |
| 1 | (Constant) | 17.212 | 1.384 | | 12.432 | .000 |
|   | Gender | 1.899 | .350 | .249 | 5.432 | .000 |
|   | Week in job | .039 | .006 | .301 | 6.967 | .000 |
|   | Stated disability | .232 | .375 | .025 | .620 | .536 |
|   | Educational Level (years) | -.138 | .059 | -.105 | -2.328 | .020 |
|   | Portsmouth North V Portsea Island | -.296 | .305 | -.039 | -.969 | .333 |
|   | AgeVariable | .016 | .013 | .050 | 1.188 | .235 |

a. Dependent Variable: Average number of items scanned per minute this week

We can see from the model summary in Figure 7.25 that the R-square is 0.257, which means that 25.6 per cent, or more than one-quarter, of the variation in the average number of items scanned per minute in this given week is shared with the independent variables in the model. The regression ANOVA table in Figure 7.25 shows us that, with the parameters given (F-statistic of 26.935 and degrees of freedom of 473), the model has a significance level of $p<0.001$ (our model is very significant).

Looking at the correlation coefficients, we can see that gender (Beta=0.249, $p<0.001$) and weeks in job (Beta=0.301, $p<0.001$) are the most significant influencers with p-values less than 0.001 ($p<0.001$) shown in the far-right column. The gender value is positive, showing that females have a significantly faster scan rate than males. Education level is also significant (Beta= –0.105, p<0.05), whereas more time in education does not seem to improve scan rates.

> **Snapshot hidden gem**
>
> The biggest predictors of the average number of items scanned this week are gender and weeks in the job. Women have a significantly higher scan rate than men, and also the longer employees are working on the checkout, the faster their scan rate. Interestingly, the educational level of employees had a negative impact (meaning the more time that employees spent in education, the lower their scan rate).

## Example 9: determining the presence or otherwise of high-performing age groups

If we want to develop a profile of the employee who has the highest scan rate, we would need to break down key categories in our workforce data set, in particular the age category. At the moment when we just include this in the regression there is no evidence of a linear relationship between age category and scan rate (Beta=0.050, p>0.05). Given the variation in mean scan rates across the age groups (see Figure 7.23), however, we may obtain more diagnostic sensitivity by coding the age groups into separate dummy variables, in a similar way to what we did with the countries in Example 7 above. As there are 10 age categories to our AgeCat variable, we create 10 new variables representing each of the age categories by themselves; we code the separate variables 1 and 0 depending on whether the employees' age falls into each of these categories. Let's run the multiple regression using the dummy age variables instead of the 'AgeCat' variable. Remember, with the country categories in Example 7 we selected the United States as the baseline (because it was the headquarters?). In this example, let's simply select the largest age group as the baseline/reference category. This is age 25–29, hence we leave this category out of the regression analysis and include all other age category dummies. So we run the scan-rate regression analysis again as before but instead of including the AgeCat variable we now include nine age-category dummies (apart from the 25–29 age group). Thus, use your mouse and select Analyze→Regression→Linear and set up the regression as before, but this time insert the nine age categories into the 'Independent(s):' selection box below the other demographic variables (Figure 7.26).

# FIGURE 7.26

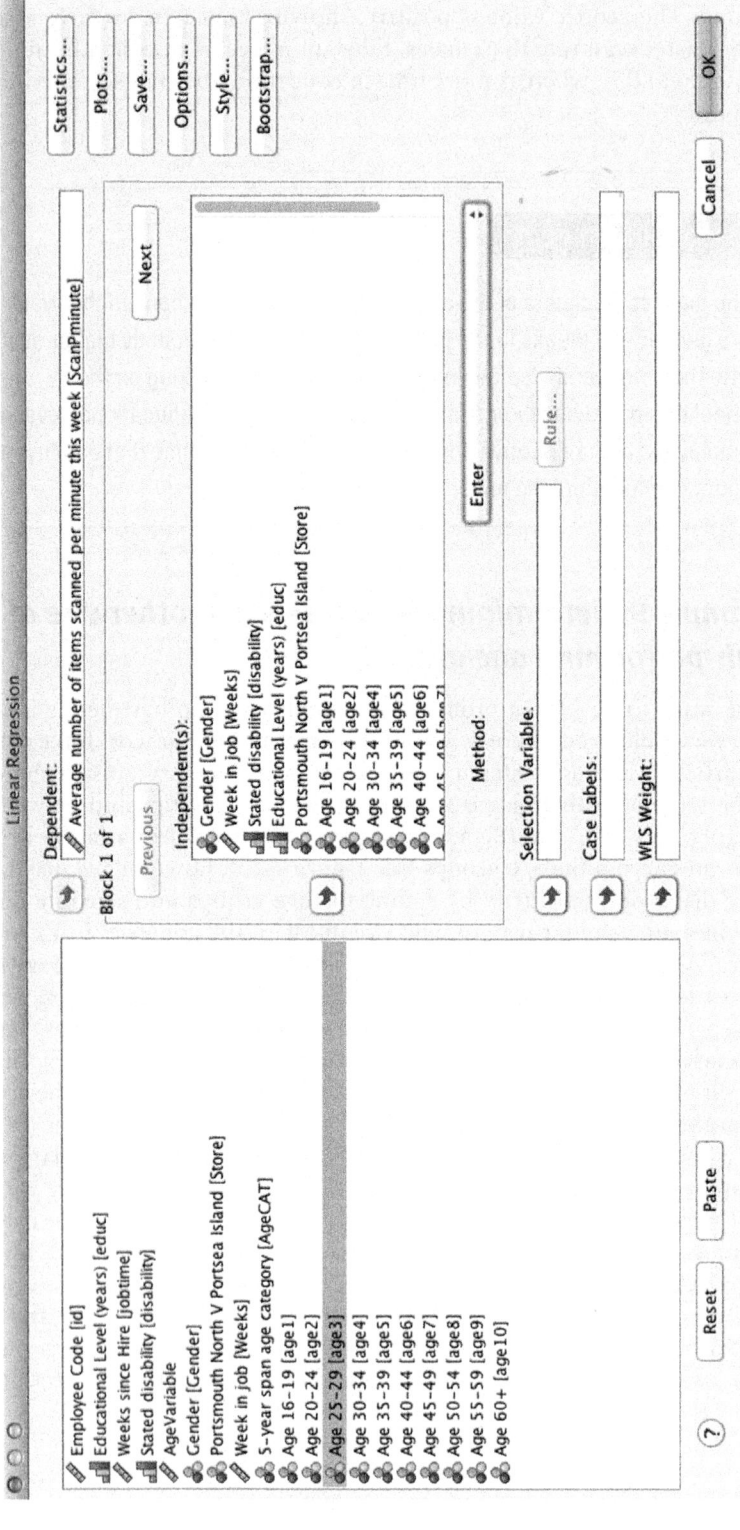

This produces the following output (Figure 7.27):

## FIGURE 7.27

**Model Summary**

| Model | R | R-Square | Adjusted R-Square | Std. Error of the Estimate |
|---|---|---|---|---|
| 1 | .633[a] | .401 | .383 | 2.98252 |

a. Predictors: (Constant), Age 60+, Portsmouth North V Portsea Island, Gender, Age 40-44, Age 50-54, Age 55-59, Stated disability, Age 35-39, Age 45-49, Age 16-19, Age 30-34, Week in job, Educational Level (years), Age 20-24

**ANOVA[a]**

*(Model is sig.)*

| Model | | Sum of Squares | df | Mean Square | F | Sig. |
|---|---|---|---|---|---|---|
| 1 | Regression | 2734.903 | 14 | 195.350 | 21.961 | .000[b] |
| | Residual | 4083.008 | 459 | 8.895 | | |
| | Total | 6817.911 | 473 | | | |

a. Dependent Variable: Average number of items scanned per minute this week
b. Predictors: (Constant), Age 60+, Portsmouth North V Portsea Island, Gender, Age 40-44, Age 50-54, Age 55-59, Stated disability, Age 35-39, Age 45-49, Age 16-19, Age 30-34, Week in job, Educational Level (years), Age 20-24

**Coefficients[a]**

| Model | | Unstandardized Coefficients | | Standardized Coefficients | t | Sig. |
|---|---|---|---|---|---|---|
| | | B | Std. Error | Beta | | |
| 1 | (Constant) | 19.472 | 1.166 | | 16.697 | .000 |
| | Gender | 2.734 | .346 | .359 | 7.898 | .000 |
| | Week in job | .028 | .005 | .212 | 5.200 | .000 |
| | Stated disability | -.299 | .351 | -.033 | -.851 | .395 |
| | Educational Level (years) | -.288 | .058 | -.219 | -4.972 | .000 |
| | Portsmouth North V Portsea Island | -.314 | .277 | -.041 | -1.134 | .257 |
| | Age 16-19 | -6.034 | .787 | -.312 | -7.666 | .000 |
| | Age 20-24 | -.692 | .413 | -.077 | -1.676 | .095 |
| | Age 30-34 | 2.012 | .562 | .141 | 3.578 | .000 |
| | Age 35-39 | -.160 | .585 | -.011 | -.274 | .784 |
| | Age 40-44 | 1.399 | .592 | .096 | 2.365 | .018 |
| | Age 45-49 | -.439 | .633 | -.029 | -.693 | .488 |
| | Age 50-54 | -.213 | .637 | -.013 | -.335 | .738 |
| | Age 55-59 | -1.350 | .621 | -.093 | -2.172 | .030 |
| | Age 60+ | -8.022 | 1.544 | -.193 | -5.194 | .000 |

a. Dependent Variable: Average number of items scanned per minute this week

In Figure 7.27 we can immediately see that the R-square is now 0.401 rather than 0.257 as before, so we can be confident that 40 per cent of the variance in the 'average number of items scanned per minute this week' measure can be accounted for by this more elaborate model that divided the age category variable into separate dummy variables. The regression ANOVA table tells us that with the parameters given (F-statistic of 21.961 and degrees of freedom of 473), the model is significant with a p-value<0.001. As you can see, by breaking the age category variable into separate age groups we have managed to account for 14.4 per cent more of the variation in our scan-rate performance measure. Clearly, the age category measure was not diagnostically sensitive enough as a basic ordinal variable (in linear relationship testing) and it needed to be broken up into smaller categories in order to be useful in our analysis.

The coefficients table in Figure 7.27 tells us that the key predictors are gender (Beta=0.359, p<0.001), weeks in the job (Beta=0.212, p<0.001), education (Beta=–0.219, p<0.001), age 16–19 (Beta=–0.312, p<0.001), age 30–34 (Beta=0.141 p<0.001), age 40–44 (Beta=–0.096 p<0.05), age 55–59 (Beta=–0.093, p<0.05) and age 60+(Beta=–0.193, p<0.001). Looking at the Beta values to get the direction, we can see that the criteria more likely to achieve a high number of scans per minute in this week are as follows:

> **Snapshot hidden gem**
>
> The biggest predictors of higher average number of items scanned this week are gender, weeks in the job, education and age categories. Interestingly, those who have achieved the highest number of scans this week are women, those aged 30–34, those with a high number of weeks in the job and those who have spent less time in education.

## Ethical considerations caveat in performance data analysis

But what do we recommend that the supermarket does with this information? Not hire employee school leavers or people over 60? This would be unfair and expose the organization to age discrimination claims. How about the financial services organization? Should we recommend that they only employ women in an effort to increase customer loyalty, because customers of female salespeople have higher customer loyalty? This would obviously not be a fair, ethical or sensible recommendation. Indeed we also need to be careful with the sensitive nature of pulse survey data, just as we do with employee engagement data (as mentioned in Chapter 5). It is important here, as in all of our analysis, to review the results in context and consider the wider impact of what the results suggest. More information about the ethics of analysis and findings can be found in Chapter 12.

# Considering the possible range of performance analytic models

You may have noticed that this case study chapter is the longest in the book; this reflects the emphasis that HR analytics as a discipline places on being able to predict performance and the need for us to present a number of different examples of models predicting performance. The types of analysis presented here only represent a small proportion of possible analytic models that can be run to predict performance. We touch on some other methods in Chapter 11 where we discuss more advanced analytic approaches, but ultimately there is no end to the forms of analysis that can be carried out.

The type of analysis carried out will always need to be carefully considered and, generally speaking, the analyst will choose a particular model set-up that has the potential to answer *specific business questions relevant to the context* of the organization. As discussed above (and demonstrated in our examples) there are many types of metrics that can be considered to be an important performance measure (none are likely to be a perfect gauge of employee performance); the performance indices that the analyst chooses will always depend on the business question that they are trying to answer. However, it is important for the analyst to question and interrogate the legitimacy of any performance indicator that they explore (especially due to the danger that the reliance of one particular metric can end up institutionalizing metric-oriented behaviour, or IMOB for short; see Chapter 12). Where possible, the analyst should try to predict a *range* of performance measures so that when diagnosing factors that might predict performance they apply the principles of a 'balanced scorecard' where possible.

Importantly, when analysts run specific models in predicting performance they will always need to ask themselves what the results actually mean in practice; they will need to question whether the results are producing findings that might lead to actionable interventions. They will also need to consider whether there are factors that might be influencing their results that have not been taken into account in their analytic models (this will be discussed further in Chapter 12). Having said this, when the analytic models produce some interesting significant results as predictors of performance, this information might be used to predict future performance (see Chapter 10); these factors can also (where appropriate) inform managerial practice and identify levers than can be focused on to help foster higher levels of organizational performance.

# References

Armstrong, M and Baron, A (2005) *Managing Performance: Performance management in action*, Chartered Institute of Personnel and Development, London

Bach, S (2012) Performance management, in *Managing Human Resources: HRM in transition*, 5th edn, ed S Bach and M R Edwards, John Wiley and Sons, New York

Bernstein, D A and Nash, P W (2008) [accessed November 2015] *Essentials of Psychology*, 4th edn, Cengage Learning, Boston [Online] http://books.google.com/books?id=4Do-bFrt9tUC.

Boon, C and Den Hartog, D N (2011) Human resource management, person–environment fit, and trust, *Trust and Human Resource Management*, pp 109–21

Brown, D and Hirsh, W (2011) Performance management: fine intentions, *People Management*, September, pp 34–37

Colquitt, J A (2001) On the dimensionality of organizational justice: a construct validation of a measure, *Journal of Applied Psychology*, **86** (3), pp 386–400

Cooper, C L, Dewe, P J and O'Driscoll, M P (2001) *Organizational Stress: A review and critique of theory, research and applications*, Sage, California

Daily Mail [accessed 25 November 2015] One Checkout Item Every Three Seconds, *Daily Mail* [Online] http://www.dailymail.co.uk/femail/article-2170377/Morrisons-imposes-new-second-targets-cut-till-queues.html

Eisenberger, R, Huntington, R, Hutchison, S and Sowa, D (1986) Perceived organizational support, *Journal of Applied Psychology*, **71**, pp 500–07

House, R J and Rizzo, J R (1972) Role conflict and ambiguity as critical variables in a model of organizational behavior, *Organizational Behavior and Human Performance*, 7, pp 467–505

Locke, E A (1976) The nature and causes of job satisfaction, in *Handbook of Industrial and Organizational Psychology*, pp 1297–349, ed M D Dunnette, Rand McNally, Chicago

# Case study 5
# Recruitment and selection analytics

08

In the process of recruiting and selecting new employees, organizations can often collect and record a considerable amount of information that can be utilized in many ways by an HR analytics expert. Much of the recruitment and selection-related analysis that an HR analytics team might wish to conduct could be considered a subset of other analysis forms that we present in other case study chapters. For example, an HR analyst may wish to explore factors and data collected in the recruitment and selection process in order to determine whether certain metrics, data or onboarding activities predict future performance. Thus, a case study of recruitment and selection analytics can include predictive models intended to account for employee performance after they join the firm (and the analyst should carefully study the predicting performance case study in Chapter 7). What makes such a model a recruitment and selection case study is the choice of independent variables, which will involve variables linked to data collected in the recruitment and selection phase.

Another type of predictive analysis that an HR analyst may wish to test is a model that explores recruitment and selection-related predictors of employee turnover. As well as looking at predictors of new joiner performance, the analyst would want to predict factors related to the recruitment and selection process that help predict whether these joiners actually stay (or leave). Thus the analyst should read the predicting turnover case study in Chapter 6, in particular Example 3 (page 217), where individual turnover is the phenomenon that we are trying to predict.

One of the key preoccupations that should be at the forefront of an HR analyst's priorities when conducting analysis in the recruitment and selection area is the degree to which recruitment and selection processes appear to be free from bias. Thus, diversity-related analysis of recruitment and selection activities (and data) should be a key subset of activities to focus on (and the analyst should carefully study the diversity case study in Chapter 4). For example, what are the gender male–female ratios of people who apply for jobs in the organization compared to the male–female ratios of people who are shortlisted, interviewed and ultimately offered a job? Also, the analyst may wish to conduct a similar analysis linked to ethnicity and other important demographic categorizations other than gender. The fact that recruitment and selection analysis can be considered a subset of other predictive analysis questions, therefore, means that this chapter will only present a few examples of particular analyses that could be conducted with recruitment and selection-related data.

# Reliability and validity of selection methods

One of the key areas of debate within the area of recruitment and selection revolves around the issue of what selection method can be considered to be the 'best' way of selecting new candidates. What do we mean by 'best' here? Such a question is of key importance when we want to apply analytic techniques to the area of recruitment and selection. Both reliability and validity are important in this regard (see the discussion of reliability and validity in relation to engagement set out in Chapter 5); in the area of recruitment and selection analysis these relate specifically to the method or range of methods used to form a judgement on a candidate that will influence whether they are offered a job or not. Importantly, these judgements will lead to a metric (eg aptitude test score, competency rating, personality test score) and the metric will often be the determinant of a hiring decision. As these metrics will generally be driving hiring decisions, the reliability and validity of these metric creation methods are therefore of key concern.

What do we mean by reliability and validity of selection methods? By reliability of selection methods, we mean the degree to which a particular method will consistently lead to the same judgement about an individual on a particular feature or characteristic, often across different settings. Importantly, human beings are fallible and judgements that we make about each other are fundamentally prone to bias; we are victims to the inevitability of human subjectivity. Thus, any selection method/selection metric creation tool that increases the consistency and reliability in making judgements about potential recruits will be a 'better' selection method. Of course, it is well known (Schmidt and Hunter, 1998) that unstructured interviews (that amount to a bit of a chat really) are one of the most unreliable methods of forming a judgement about potential recruits.

The validity of a selection method relates to the degree to which the particular method will accurately identify the people that the selectors intended to identify as being the right person for any particular job. In ensuring that the right person is identified, the methods will need to: 1) successfully discriminate between people who will perform well versus those who will struggle to perform well; and, 2) successfully discriminate between people who will want to stay versus people who will want to leave shortly after they join. Of course 1) and 2) are inextricably linked as someone who does not perform well is likely to not want to hang around for ever (though of course this statement makes certain assumptions about the nature of human motivation in the workplace...). Thus, we have two clear metrics that we can use to judge the validity of a metric, performance ratings and staff turnover data. From a predictive HR analytics point of view, given the considerable costs often incurred in the process of selecting the right candidate for a job (see Chapter 6 for a brief discussion of this), ensuring that the methods used are successfully predicting performance in the organization is an important analytic activity to carry out.

## Human bias in recruitment selection

There is so much potential for human bias to come into play in the recruitment and selection process that an entire chapter could be devoted to discussing this (and how an analyst might try to expose its occurrence). Examples of such general everyday judgement biases include 'halo' effects (where one characteristic stands out and influences judgements of other characteristics), leniency tendencies and harshness tendencies, as well as first or last impression effects. However, one of the key biases that the predictive HR analytics expert will want to explore is that associated with stereotyping, prejudice and discrimination. Thus, one of the case study examples we present here revolves around an exploration into patterns of demographics that might be found associated with recruitment and selection stages; specifically, whether the patterns of gender or ethnic minority proportions in the applicant pool remain consistent through various stages of the recruitment and selection period. As with the other analyses that we are presenting for this chapter, analysis exploring bias and recruitment activities is in essence a subset of diversity analysis; thus the following example could equally be found within our diversity case study in Chapter 4.

## Example 1: consistency of gender and BAME proportions in the applicant pool

The following example involves a data set that has been compiled in order to specifically conduct inferential testing linked to gender and BAME profiles of the pool of applications received, versus the applications shortlisted/interviewed and ultimately those who are offered a job. The following data set has information linked to 280 applications for graduate jobs in a large consultancy firm.

The data set that we use here is 'Chapter 8 RECRUITMENT_APPLICANTS.sav'. The applicant data set includes the following information within nine variables:

1 ApplicantCode (applicant code).
2 Gender (1 = male or 2 = female).
3 BAMEyn (Black, Asian or Minority Ethnic: 1 = yes or 2 = no).

**4** ShortlistedNY (0 = rejected or 1 = shortlisted).
**5** Interviewed (0 = not interviewed or 1 = interviewed).
**6** FemaleONpanel (1 = male only panel or 2 = female member on panel).
**7** OfferNY (1= made an offer or 0 = not offered).
**8** AcceptNY (1 = Accepted or 0 = declined).
**9** JoinYN (1 = joined or 0 = not joined).

As the variable and value labels indicate, the data set indicates the gender ('Gender' – variable 2) of each person that sent in an application for the graduate job as well as whether or not they were Black, Asian or Minority Ethnic ('BAMEyn' – variable 3). Importantly the 'ShortlistedNY' variable indicates whether, after an initial review of their application, they were considered to be an appropriate candidate for interview (in other words, considered potentially employable). The 'Interviewed' variable indicates whether they were interviewed or not, the 'FemaleONPanel' variable indicates whether there was a female interviewer included on the interview panel. Then a key variable here is whether the applicant was offered a job or not ('OfferNY') and the 'AcceptNY' variable indicates whether they accepted the offer. Finally the 'JoinYN' variable indicates whether the applicant joined the organization.

## Patterns of gender and BAME in the applicant pool

The first thing we will want to do is look at the patterns of gender and BAME in the applicant pool in general. To do this we can just run a frequency analysis with the data set. Thus we select Analyze→Descriptive Statistics→Frequencies and select the variables that we are interested in looking at, then click 'OK' (see Figure 8.1).

**FIGURE 8.1**

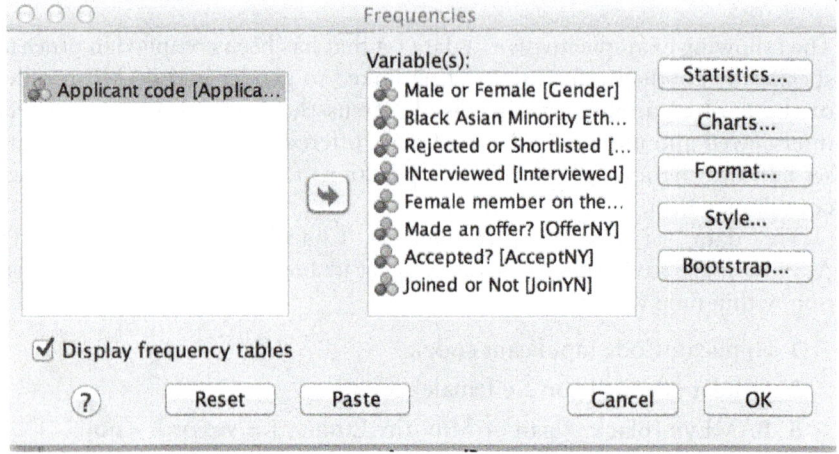

# Case Study 5

When we look at the following output tables (Figure 8.2) that SPSS produces we can see that of the 280 applicants for these jobs, the majority are female (72.1 per cent) and just under half (43.2 per cent) are categorized as Black, Asian or Minority Ethnic (BAME). Subsequently, 88 were shortlisted and 55 were interviewed, leading to 28 offers and 18 joining.

## FIGURE 8.2

**Male or Female**

| | | Frequency | Per cent | Valid Per cent | Cumulative Per cent |
|---|---|---|---|---|---|
| Valid | Male | 78 | 27.9 | 27.9 | 27.9 |
| | Female | 202 | 72.1 | 72.1 | 100.0 |
| | Total | 280 | 100.0 | 100.0 | |

**Black Asian Minority Ethnic Yes or No**

| | | Frequency | Per cent | Valid Per cent | Cumulative Per cent |
|---|---|---|---|---|---|
| Valid | BAME Yes | 121 | 43.2 | 43.2 | 43.2 |
| | BAME No | 159 | 56.8 | 56.8 | 100.0 |
| | Total | 280 | 100.0 | 100.0 | |

**Rejected or Shortlisted**

| | | Frequency | Per cent | Valid Per cent | Cumulative Per cent |
|---|---|---|---|---|---|
| Valid | Not Shortlisted | 192 | 68.6 | 68.6 | 68.6 |
| | Shortlisted | 88 | 31.4 | 31.4 | 100.0 |
| | Total | 280 | 100.0 | 100.0 | |

**Interviewed**

| | | Frequency | Per cent | Valid Per cent | Cumulative Per cent |
|---|---|---|---|---|---|
| Valid | Not Interviewed | 225 | 80.4 | 80.4 | 80.4 |
| | Interviewed | 55 | 19.6 | 19.6 | 100.0 |
| | Total | 280 | 100.0 | 100.0 | |

**Female member on the interview panel**

| | | Frequency | Per cent | Valid Per cent | Cumulative Per cent |
|---|---|---|---|---|---|
| Valid | Male only | 33 | 11.8 | 60.0 | 60.0 |
| | Female panel member | 22 | 7.9 | 40.0 | 100.0 |
| | Total | 55 | 19.6 | 100.0 | |
| Missing | System | 225 | 80.4 | | |
| Total | | 280 | 100.0 | | |

**FIGURE 8.2** *continued*

**Made an offer?**

| | | Frequency | Per cent | Valid Per cent | Cumulative Per cent |
|---|---|---|---|---|---|
| Valid | Offer not made | 27 | 9.6 | 49.1 | 49.1 |
| | Offer Made | 28 | 10.0 | 50.9 | 100.0 |
| | Total | 55 | 19.6 | 100.0 | |
| Missing | System | 225 | 80.4 | | |
| Total | | 280 | 100.0 | | |

**Accepted?**

| | | Frequency | Per cent | Valid Per cent | Cumulative Per cent |
|---|---|---|---|---|---|
| Valid | Declined | 10 | 3.6 | 35.7 | 35.7 |
| | Accepted | 18 | 6.4 | 64.3 | 100.0 |
| | Total | 28 | 10.0 | 100.0 | |
| Missing | System | 252 | 90.0 | | |
| Total | | 280 | 100.0 | | |

**Joined or Not**

| | | Frequency | Per cent | Valid Per cent | Cumulative Per cent |
|---|---|---|---|---|---|
| Valid | Not Joined | 10 | 3.6 | 35.7 | 35.7 |
| | Joined | 18 | 6.4 | 64.3 | 100.0 |
| | Total | 28 | 10.0 | 100.0 | |
| Missing | System | 252 | 90.0 | | |
| Total | | 280 | 100.0 | | |

# Example 2: investigating the influence of gender and BAME on shortlisting and offers made

A key question that we want to explore here is whether the proportion of those shortlisted for interview who are female or Black, Asian or Minority Ethnic (BAME) are representative of these groups from the applicant pool.

If it is the case that the proportion of female applicants is the same as the proportion of those shortlisted, then this immediately suggests that there is no evidence of any particular gender bias. Just from looking at the gender frequencies presented above, which indicate that 72 per cent of the applicant pool are female, we should expect a similar proportion of females to be present in the group of applicants that have been shortlisted, if the initial screening procedures have no particular bias.

Importantly, as we discussed in the diversity case study in Chapter 4, the analysis required to test whether there is evidence for any meaningful bias would require a crosstabs analysis and, in particular, a chi-square test to check whether there is statistically significant evidence of any gender preferences in the process of shortlisting. Thus in order to carry out this analysis, the analyst should select Analyze->Descriptive Statistics->Crosstabs. In the window that is then presented (see Figure 8.3) select 'Gender' in the 'Row(s):' box and 'ShortlistedNY' in the 'Column(s):' box.

**FIGURE 8.3**

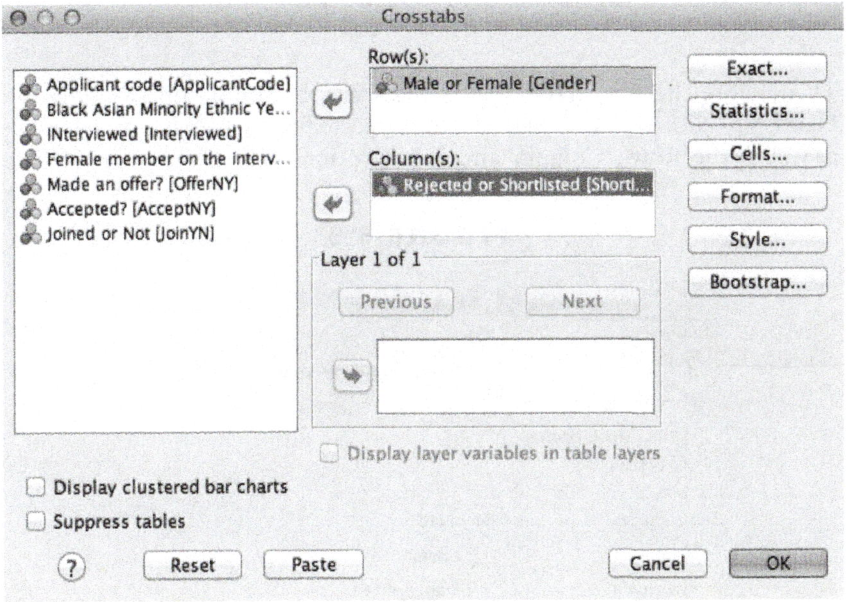

Before clicking 'OK', the analyst should click on the 'Statistics' button and select the chi-square tick box and click 'Continue' (See Figure 8.4).

**FIGURE 8.4**

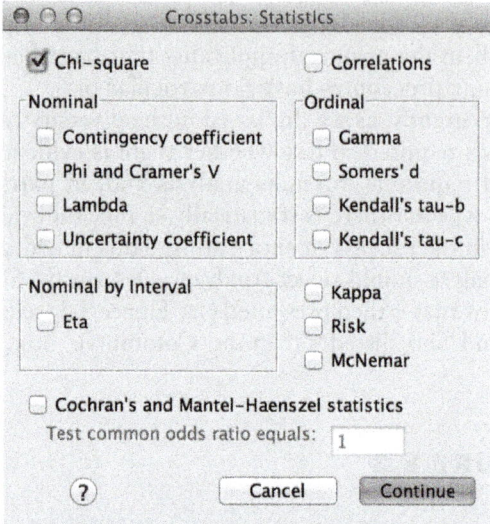

Then before clicking on 'OK' select the 'Cells' button. In this window (see Figure 8.5) click on the 'Observed' and 'Expected' options in the counts frame as well as the 'Row', 'Column' and 'Total' options in the 'Percentages' frame.

**FIGURE 8.5**

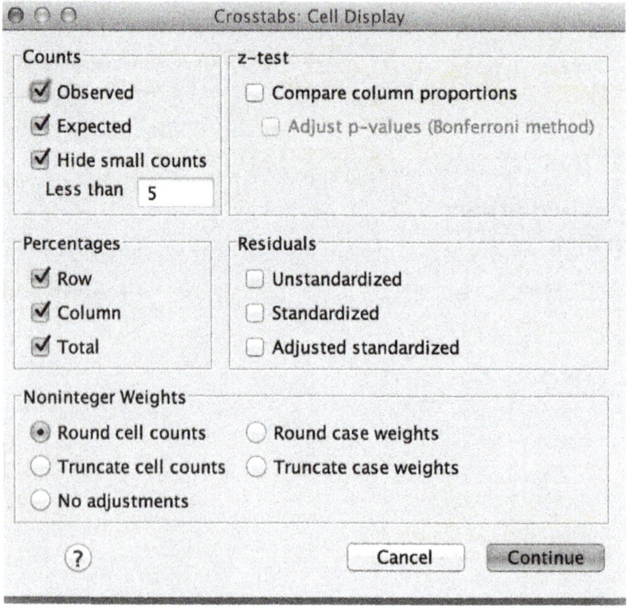

**FIGURE 8.6** Male or female rejected or shortlisted cross-tabulation

|  |  |  | Rejected or Shortlisted | | Total |
|---|---|---|---|---|---|
|  |  |  | Not Shortlisted | Shortlisted |  |
| Male or Female | Male | Count | 40 | 38 | 78 |
|  |  | Expected Count | 53.5 | 24.5 | 78.0 |
|  |  | % within Male or Female | 51.3% | 48.7% | 100.0% |
|  |  | % within Rejected or Shortlisted | 20.8% | 43.2% | 27.9% |
|  |  | % of Total | 14.3% | 13.6% | 27.9% |
|  | Female | Count | 152 | 50 | 202 |
|  |  | Expected Count | 138.5 | 63.5 | 202.0 |
|  |  | % within Male or Female | 75.2% | 24.8% | 100.0% |
|  |  | % within Rejected or Shortlisted | 79.2% | 56.8% | 72.1% |
|  |  | % of Total | 54.3% | 17.9% | 72.1% |
| Total |  | Count | 192 | 88 | 280 |
|  |  | Expected Count | 192.0 | 88.0 | 280.0 |
|  |  | % within Male or Female | 68.6% | 31.4% | 100.0% |
|  |  | % within Rejected or Shortlisted | 100.0% | 100.0% | 100.0% |
|  |  | % of Total | 68.6% | 31.4% | 100.0% |

Once these have been selected click 'Continue', then click 'OK'. The crosstabs will now be presented (see Figure 8.6). As we can see from the output, 38 out of the 78 males in the applicant pool were shortlisted and 50 from the 202 females were shortlisted. Also, although 72.2 per cent of the applicant pool are female, the proportion of those shortlisted who are female drops to 56.7 per cent. Thus the crosstabs provides some evidence that there may be a male-leaning preference in the shortlisting process (which could be due to the fact that the male candidates are stronger applicants; however, all things being equal we would not expect this pattern).

Although the frequency statistics above suggest that there may be some gender male preference in the shortlisting process, we do not at this stage know whether this could occur by chance alone. Therefore the chi-square results are required in order for us to understand how strong this tendency is and whether this is a statistically significant pattern. As Figure 8.7 shows, the Pearson's chi-square value of 14.77 is highly significant (with $p<0.001$) as is the 13.905 ($p<0.001$) chi square with the continuity correction (we use this with a 2 × 2 table). Therefore we can be completely confident that there is definitely a pro-male preference in the shortlisting process somewhere (which would probably require further investigation); there is less than a 1 in a 1,000 chance that we would find this pattern of gender proportions with the shortlisted versus not shortlisted populations by chance alone.

### FIGURE 8.7   Chi-square tests

|  | Value | df | Asymp. Sig. (2-sided) | Exact Sig. (2-sided) | Exact Sig. (1-sided) |
|---|---|---|---|---|---|
| Pearson Chi-Square | 14.997[a] | 1 | .000 | | |
| Continuity Correction[b] | 13.905 | 1 | .000 | | |
| Likelihood Ratio | 14.435 | 1 | .000 | | |
| Fisher's Exact Test | | | | .000 | .000 |
| Linear-by-Linear Association | 14.943 | 1 | .000 | | |
| N of Valid Cases | 280 | | | | |

a. 0 cells (0.0%) have expected count less than 5. The minimum expected count is 24.51.
b. Computed only for a 2x2 table

We would also need to carry out the same analysis on the shortlisted (versus non-shortlisted) applicant pool but this time comparing BAME classification. To run this we follow the same procedure as above (see Figure 8.3 above) but we select 'BAMEyn' into the row box rather than 'Gender Variable' (and we again select the 'ShortlistedYN' into the column box). After we have set up the analysis in the same way as above (by again selecting the chi-square option in the 'Statistics' menu option and the same details in the 'Cells' menu option), we run the analysis and our new output is produced (see Figure 8.8).

### FIGURE 8.8   BAME 'yes' or 'no' rejected or shortlisted cross-tabulation

|  |  |  | Rejected or Shortlisted | | Total |
|---|---|---|---|---|---|
|  |  |  | Not Shortlisted | Shortlisted |  |
| Black Asian Minority Ethnic Yes or No | BAME Yes | Count | 102 | 19 | 121 |
|  |  | Expected Count | 83.0 | 38.0 | 121.0 |
|  |  | % within Black Asian Minority Ethnic Yes or No | 84.3% | 15.7% | 100.0% |
|  |  | % within Rejected or Shortlisted | 53.1% | 21.6% | 43.2% |
|  |  | % of Total | 36.4% | 6.8% | 43.2% |
|  | BAME No | Count | 90 | 69 | 159 |
|  |  | Expected Count | 109.0 | 50.0 | 159.0 |
|  |  | % within Black Asian Minority Ethnic Yes or No | 56.6% | 43.4% | 100.0% |
|  |  | % within Rejected or Shortlisted | 46.9% | 78.4% | 56.8% |
|  |  | % of Total | 32.1% | 24.6% | 56.8% |
| Total |  | Count | 192 | 88 | 280 |
|  |  | Expected Count | 192.0 | 88.0 | 280.0 |
|  |  | % within Black Asian Minority Ethnic Yes or No | 68.6% | 31.4% | 100.0% |
|  |  | % within Rejected or Shortlisted | 100.0% | 100.0% | 100.0% |
|  |  | % of Total | 68.6% | 31.4% | 100.0% |

## FIGURE 8.9    Chi-square tests

|  | Value | df | Asymp. Sig. (2-sided) | Exact Sig. (2-sided) | Exact Sig. (1-sided) |
|---|---|---|---|---|---|
| Pearson Chi-Square | 24.452[a] | 1 | .000 | | |
| Continuity Correction[b] | 23.184 | 1 | .000 | | |
| Likelihood Ratio | 25.755 | 1 | .000 | | |
| Fisher's Exact Test | | | | .000 | .000 |
| Linear-by-Linear Association | 24.365 | 1 | .000 | | |
| N of Valid Cases | 280 | | | | |

a. 0 cells (0.0%) have expected count less than 5. The minimum expected count is 38.03.
b. Computed only for a 2x2 table

As the crosstabs table in Figure 8.8 shows, of the 280 applicants, 121 (43.2 per cent) are BAME and of these only 19 were shortlisted. This amounts to 15 per cent of the BAME part of the applicant pool. When you compare this to the fact that 43.4 per cent (69 applicants) of the non-BAME applicant pool (159) were shortlisted, this seems to show a real preference for non-BAME applicants in the shortlisting process. Importantly, as we did previously with gender, we need to test this pattern for significance using the chi-square test; our output for this is in Figure 8.9.

Importantly, what we see here is that the likelihood of finding this pro-non-BAME shortlisting preference by chance alone (given the proportions of BAME we find in our applicant pool) is less than a 1 in 1,000 chance (continuity correction chi square = 23.184, $p<0.001$). Thus, although lots of the applicant pool are BAME, relatively few of them are shortlisted. Such a finding would need to be investigated further to make sure that these shortlisting preferences were not being driven by some systematic discrimination or prejudice.

## Combining gender and BAME in predicting shortlisting

In the above analysis we have explored the patterns of shortlisting across two variables of gender and BAME; however, our analysis explores the patterns of shortlisting across these two variables separately. Importantly, when we conduct analysis of factors that might predict shortlisting, we should ideally take these two demographic variables into account at the same time. One of the reasons to do this is that there may be a relationship between BAME and gender in our applicant pool. If it were the case for example that most of the BAME applicant group were female, the two different sets of findings above might actually be due to BAME *or* gender preferences rather than both. Therefore it would be important to incorporate both into an analysis at the same time. One way of doing this is using logistic regression (as we did in the turnover case study in Chapter 6). We would use logistic rather than linear regression here because the outcome (shortlisted or not) is binary.

To conduct the logistic regression, we would select the Analyze→Regression→Binary Logistic menu option. In the window presented in Figure 8.10 the analyst would need to select the 'ShortlistedNY' variable into the 'Dependent:' box as well as select the 'Gender' and 'BAMEyn' variables into the covariates box. Then click 'OK'.

## FIGURE 8.10

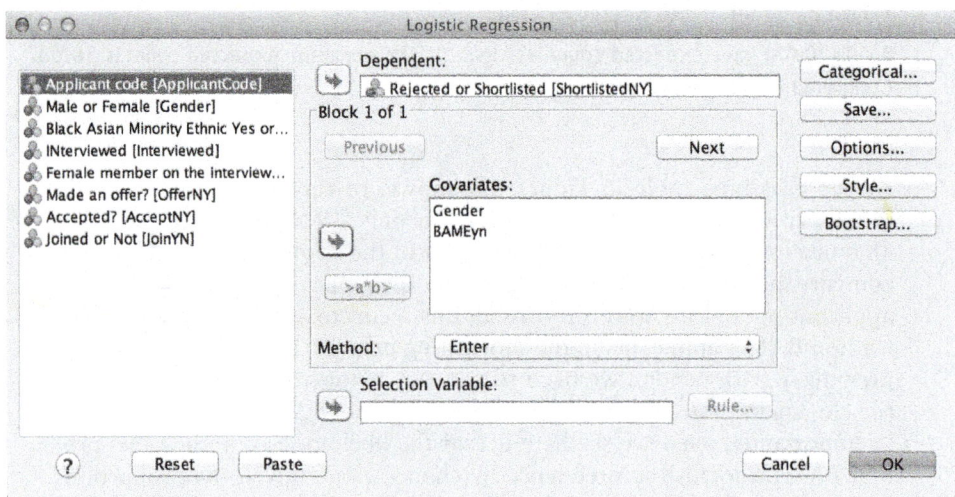

The following set of analysis results will be produced (see Figure 8.11 and Figure 8.12).

## FIGURE 8.11

**Variables in the Equation**

|  |  | B | S.E. | Wald | df | Sig. | Exp(B) |
|---|---|---|---|---|---|---|---|
| Step 0 | Constant | -.780 | .129 | 36.728 | 1 | .000 | .458 |

**Variables not in the Equation**

|  |  |  | Score | df | Sig. |
|---|---|---|---|---|---|
| Step 0 | Variables | Gender | 14.997 | 1 | .000 |
|  |  | BAMEyn | 24.452 | 1 | .000 |
|  | Overall Statistics |  | 39.630 | 2 | .000 |

Case Study 5

**FIGURE 8.11** *continued*

### Block 1: Method = Enter

**Omnibus Tests of Model Coefficients**

|        |       | Chi-square | df | Sig. |
|--------|-------|------------|----|------|
| Step 1 | Step  | 41.980     | 2  | .000 |
|        | Block | 41.980     | 2  | .000 |
|        | Model | 41.980     | 2  | .000 |

**Model Summary**

| Step | -2 Log likelihood | Cox and Snell R-Square | Nagelkerke R-Square |
|------|-------------------|------------------------|---------------------|
| 1    | 306.613[a]        | .139                   | .196                |

a. Estimation terminated at iteration number 5 because parameter estimates changed by less than .001.

The tables shown in Figure 8.11 tell us that gender and BAME seem to account for just under 20 per cent of the variation in shortlisting (Nagelkerke pseudo R-square = 0.1936, thus 19.36 per cent) and this model (chi square = 41.98) is highly significant (p<0.001). Importantly we need to look at the set of results shown in Figure 8.12 in order to identify whether gender and BAME *both* account for whether the applicants are shortlisted.

**FIGURE 8.12**

**Classification Table[a]**

|        |                        |                | Predicted |  |  |
|--------|------------------------|----------------|-----------|---|---|
|        |                        |                | Rejected or Shortlisted | | Percentage Correct |
|        | Observed               |                | Not Shortlisted | Shortlisted | |
| Step 1 | Rejected or Shortlisted | Not Shortlisted | 177 | 15 | 92.2 |
|        |                        | Shortlisted    | 59  | 29 | 33.0 |
|        | Overall Percentage     |                |     |    | 73.6 |

a. The cut value is .500

**Variables in the Equation**

|         |          | B      | S.E. | Wald   | df | Sig. | Exp(B) |
|---------|----------|--------|------|--------|----|------|--------|
| Step 1[a] | Gender   | -1.196 | .301 | 15.826 | 1  | .000 | .303   |
|         | BAMEyn   | 1.516  | .310 | 23.962 | 1  | .000 | 4.553  |
|         | Constant | -1.243 | .678 | 3.365  | 1  | .067 | .288   |

a. Variable(s) entered on step 1: Gender, BAMEyn.

The set of results shown in Figure 8.12 tells us three very important bits of information. First, when modelled together in accounting for shortlisting likelihood, gender and BAME demographic characteristics *both* independently (significantly) account for the likelihood of whether the applicant will be shortlisted. This information can be ascertained from the fact that the 'Sig.' column in the 'Variables in the equation' box shows p<0.001 for both the gender and the BAME row. Second, the Exp(B) gives us information about the odds of males versus females and BAME versus non-BAME getting shortlisted. To understand these odds ratios we need to bear in mind how the data set is coded.

1. Gender (1 = male or 2 = female).
2. BAMEyn (Black Asian or Minority Ethnic: 1 = Yes or 2 = No).
3. ShortlistedNY (0 = rejected or 1 = shortlisted).

The shortlisted dependent variable coding implies that as this variable increases to 1 from 0 then the applicant has been shortlisted. The gender coding implies that as the number gets higher from 1 to 2 then the applicant will be female rather than male. The BAMEyn coding implies that as the number gets higher from 1 to 2 then the applicant is non-BAME rather than BAME. As the Exp(B) figure is less than 1 (remember an Exp(B) of 1 equates to 50:50 even odds) and is 0.303, this tells us that as the gender variable goes up from 1 to 2 then the shortlisting is less likely; thus females (2) are less likely to be shortlisted than male (1). It is not straightforward to conceptualize what an odds ratio of less than 1 means; therefore it is often easier to transform the odds ratio to represent the odds of being the lower coded category of the predictor (in this case gender). When we do this, we see that male applicants are 3.3 times more likely than females to be shortlisted (calculated by dividing 1 by 0.303=3.3). The Exp(B) figure of 4.553 on the BAMEyn row of the results table tells us that as the BAME goes up from BAME to non-BAME, then the likelihood of the applicant getting shortlisted is greater (as the Exp(B) is above 1). Specifically, non-BAME applicants are 4.553 times more likely to get shortlisted than BAME applicants.

> **Snapshot hidden gem**
>
> Male applicants are 3.3 times more likely to be shortlisted for jobs in our organization than women applicants and non-BAME applicants are 4.5 times more likely to be shortlisted than BAME applicants. Analytics indicate that further investigation is required as to why this is the case.

### Comment and thoughts for additional analysis

The results here clearly suggest that there may be some bias in the shortlisting of the applicants in favour of male non-BAME. It would be important to add additional data to the logistic regression that would help us to get a better picture of whether there is something about the female and BAME applicants that might explain these preferences that is not linked to any kind of discrimination; for example it may be that the education or work experience patterns associated with these two groups could explain why they are not being shortlisted. Often, an interesting finding that an analysis uncovers will lead to the requirement of additional analysis to be conducted before the real picture of what is going on in the organization is obtained.

## Offers made – gender and BAME

One final analysis before we go on to explore predictive models with our selection data is to see whether the non-BAME and male preferences found in the shortlisting continues on into the selection phase after the interviews have been conducted. We can repeat the crosstabs and chi-square analysis that we conducted above, but look at who was made an offer after an interview compared to who were not made an offer. It is possible to run two sets of crosstabs in parallel.

If you look at Figure 8.13, you will see that we have selected the 'OfferNY' variable into the 'Column(s):' box and the 'Gender' and 'BAMEny' variables into the 'Row(s):' box. When we run this it produces two sets of crosstabs output (we have already selected the chi square and cell percentage etc; see Figure 8.4 and Figure 8.5 above).

**FIGURE 8.13**

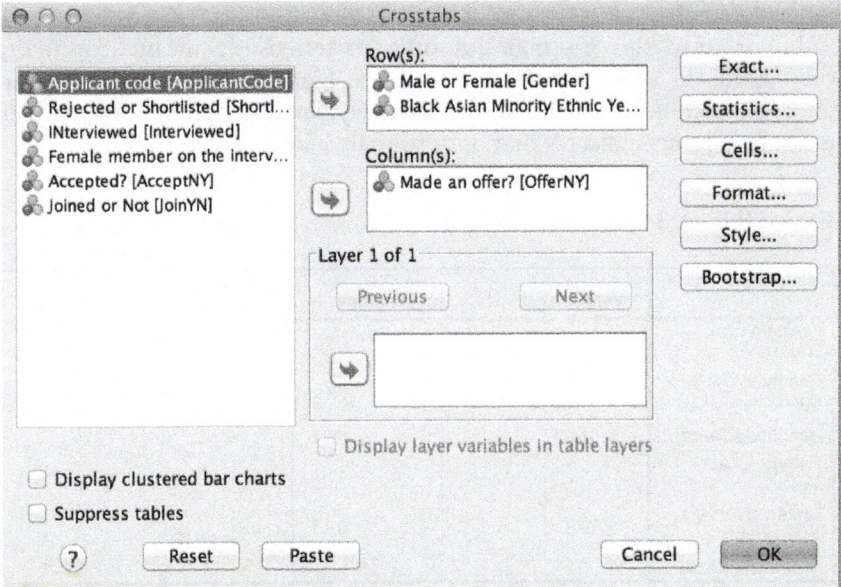

**FIGURE 8.14** Crosstab

|  |  |  | Made an Offer? | | Total |
|---|---|---|---|---|---|
|  |  |  | Offer Not Made | Offer Made |  |
| Male or Female | Male | Count | 9 | 18 | 27 |
|  |  | Expected Count | 13.3 | 13.7 | 27.0 |
|  |  | % within Male or Female | 33.3% | 66.7% | 100.0% |
|  |  | % within Made an offer? | 33.3% | 64.3% | 49.1% |
|  |  | % of Total | 16.4% | 32.7% | 49.1% |
|  | Female | Count | 18 | 10 | 28 |
|  |  | Expected Count | 13.7 | 14.3 | 28.0 |
|  |  | % within Male or Female | 64.3% | 35.7% | 100.0% |
|  |  | % within Made an offer? | 66.7% | 35.7% | 50.9% |
|  |  | % of Total | 32.7% | 18.2% | 50.9% |
| Total |  | Count | 27 | 28 | 55 |
|  |  | Expected Count | 27.0 | 28.0 | 55.0 |
|  |  | % within Male or Female | 49.1% | 50.9% | 100.0% |
|  |  | % within Made an offer? | 100.0% | 100.0% | 100.0% |
|  |  | % of Total | 49.1% | 50.9% | 100.0% |

With our first set of analysis output here (Figure 8.14), we can see that although approximately half of those interviewed are female (28 of 55), only about one-third (35.7 per cent) of the interviewees who are offered jobs are female.

Importantly, this pro-male job-offer pattern is significant (continuity correction chi square=4.104, p<0.05; see Figure 8.15). Given that this finding is significant even with the relatively small sample size here (which is not huge), this indicates that our pro-male bias is rather severe.

**FIGURE 8.15** Chi-square tests

|  | Value | df | Asymp. Sig. (2-sided) | Exact Sig. (2-sided) | Exact Sig. (1-sided) |
|---|---|---|---|---|---|
| Pearson Chi-Square | 5.269[a] | 1 | .022 |  |  |
| Continuity Correction[b] | 4.104 | 1 | .043 |  |  |
| Likelihood Ratio | 5.358 | 1 | .021 |  |  |
| Fisher's Exact Test |  |  |  | .031 | .021 |
| Linear-by-Linear Association | 5.173 | 1 | .023 |  |  |
| N of Valid Cases | 55 |  |  |  |  |

a. 0 cells (0.0%) have expected count less than 5. The minimum expected count is 13.25.
b. Computed only for a 2x2 table

When we look at the BAME analysis with the interview offer, we see that BAME applicants who get to interview (8 from 13) are as likely to get a job offer as the non-BAME who get to interview (20 from 42) (see Figure 8.16).

**FIGURE 8.16** Crosstab

*BAME w/ Offer   NonBAME w/ Offer*
*61.5% > 47.6%*

| | | | Made an Offer? | | |
|---|---|---|---|---|---|
| | | | Offer Not Made | Offer Made | Total |
| Black Asian Minority Ethnic Yes or No | BAME Yes | Count | 5 | 8 | 13 |
| | | Expected Count | 6.4 | 6.6 | 13.0 |
| | | % within Black Asian Minority Ethnic Yes or No | 38.5% | 61.5% | 100.0% |
| | | % within Made an offer? | 18.5% | 28.6% | 23.6% |
| | | % of Total | 9.1% | 14.5% | 23.6% |
| | BAME No | Count | 22 | 20 | 42 |
| | | Expected Count | 20.6 | 21.4 | 42.0 |
| | | % within Black Asian Minority Ethnic Yes or No | 52.4% | 47.6% | 100.0% |
| | | % within Made an offer? | 81.5% | 71.4% | 76.4% |
| | | % of Total | 40.0% | 36.4% | 76.4% |
| Total | | Count | 27 | 28 | 55 |
| | | Expected Count | 27.0 | 28.0 | 55.0 |
| | | % within Black Asian Minority Ethnic Yes or No | 49.1% | 50.9% | 100.0% |
| | | % within Made an offer? | 100.0% | 100.0% | 100.0% |
| | | % of Total | 49.1% | 50.9% | 100.0% |

This is supported by the non-significant chi-square result (continuity correction chi square =0.313. p>0.05) (see Figure 8.17).

**FIGURE 8.17** Chi-square tests

| | Value | df | Asymp. Sig. (2-sided) | Exact Sig. (2-sided) | Exact Sig. (1-sided) |
|---|---|---|---|---|---|
| Pearson Chi-Square | .770[a] | 1 | .380 | | |
| Continuity Correction[b] | .313 | 1 | .576 | | |
| Likelihood Ratio | .776 | 1 | .378 | | |
| Fisher's Exact Test | | | | .528 | .289 |
| Linear-by-Linear Association | .756 | 1 | .385 | | |
| N of Valid Cases | 55 | | | | |

a. 0 cells (0.0%) have expected count less than 5. The minimum expected count is 6.38.
b. Computed only for a 2x2 table

> **Snapshot hidden gem**
>
> The bias in the recruitment within our organization that favours male applicants at the early stages of the process (shortlisting) continues into the selection phase of hiring, as males are more likely to be offered a job after an interview than women. Although BAME applicants are less likely to be shortlisted and asked along for an interview (compared to non-BAME applicants), if they get to interview, they do not tend to experience the same level of bias at this stage (they are as likely to get a job offer as non-BAME).

Obviously, further analysis can be carried out that explores various combinations of other decisions made in the recruitment and selection process (eg such as whether a female member on the panel might be linked to offer/acceptance frequencies, etc). By now the analyst should be able to apply the above analytic techniques to explore these questions.

# Validating selection techniques as predictors of performance

As discussed above, a key activity that an HR analytics expert would wish to conduct is explore what selection factors (from data collected or associated with the selection process) predict post-hire employee performance. One reason to do this is to test how valid the selection processes are; a second reason is to identify selection factors that will predict who is likely to turn out to be a high performer. In the next example we have compiled a data set that merges HR information collected at the selection stage, specifically scores and ratings taken at graduate assessment centres; this particular organization is a large financial consultancy firm and hires a large cohort of graduates each year. The data file used for this analysis is called 'Chapter 8 Selection.sav' and contains data linked to 360 graduates within 30 different variables.

The data file we use here is 'Chapter 8 Selection.sav'. The variables are:

1. GradID — Employee Identifier
2. Gender — Male (1) or Female (2)
3. EducationHighest — Education Category: BSc (1) MSc (2) PhD (3)
4. BAMEYN — Black, Asian or Minority Ethnic: Yes (1) or No (2)
5. WorkExperience — Worked Before: Yes (1) No (2)

| | | |
|---|---|---|
| 6 | GradJOBfunction | Function Joined:<br>– (1) HR; (2) Finance; (3) Marketing;<br>– (4) Sales; (5) Risk; (6) Legal;<br>(7) Operations |
| 7 | ACPersonalityO | Assessment C Personality Openness (percentage) |
| 8 | ACPersonalityC | Assessment C Personality Conscientious (percentage) |
| 9 | ACPersonalityE | Assessment C Personality Extraversion (percentage) |
| 10 | ACPersonalityA | Assessment C Personality Agreeable (percentage) |
| 11 | ACPersonalityN | Assessment C Personality Neuroticism (percentage) |
| 12 | ACRatingINTCOMPA | Assessment C Competency Technical (1–5) |
| 13 | ACRatingINTCOMPB | Assessment C Competency Team Player |
| 14 | ACRatingINTCOMPC | Assessment C Competency Critical Thought |
| 15 | ACRatingINTCOMPD | Assessment C Competency Business Aware |
| 16 | ACRatingINTCOMPE | Assessment C Competency Drive Innovation |
| 17 | ACRatingAPTnumerical | Numerical Aptitude Test Score |
| 18 | ACRatingAPTverbal | Verbal Reasoning Aptitude Test Score |
| 19 | InductionDay | Attend Induction Day:<br>No (0) Yes (1) |
| 20 | InductionWeek | Attend Induction Week:<br>No (0) Yes (1) |
| 21 | OnBoardingBuddy | Given Joining Buddy:<br>No (0) Yes (1) |
| 22 | Year1performanceRating | Year 1 Performance Rating:<br>– (1) Fails to Meet Expectations<br>– (2) Just Meets Expectations<br>– (3) Meets Expectations Comfortably<br>– (4) Exceeds Expectations<br>– (5) A Star Performer |
| 23 | LeaverYr2 | Leaver in First 24 Months (0) No (1) Leaver |

| | | |
|---|---|---|
| 24 | HRDummyV | HR Dummy Variable |
| 25 | FinanceDummyV | Finance Dummy Variable |
| 26 | MarketingDummyV | Marketing Dummy Variable |
| 27 | SalesDummyV | Sales Dummy Variable |
| 28 | RiskDummyV | Risk Management Dummy Variable |
| 29 | LegalDummyV | Legal Dummy Variable |
| 30 | OperationsDummyV | Operations Dummy Variable |

The 30 variables in this data set contain some demographic and CV-related information associated with the graduates (Gender, EducationHighest, BAME, WorkExperience) and indicate which function the graduate joined (GradJOBfunction) and a set of variables that represent dummy variables for each function (see Chapter 7 for a discussion of dummy variables); these are the last seven variables in the data set (24–30 above). Variables 7–11 above indicate the score that each applicant was given with a personality test; these represent scores on personality dimensions of openness, conscientiousness, extraversion, agreeableness and neuroticism. Each graduate gets a percentage score for each of these personality dimensions.

The next five variables (12–16 above) represent a competency rating score given (agreed by an interview panel) on the organization's core competencies: A = Technical Capabilities, B = Team Player, C = Critical Thinking, D = Business Awareness and E = Drive and Innovation. Note that the competency rating scales range from 1 to 5, but we only have scores of 4 and 5 here because the applicants were not hired unless they were given 4 or 5 on all ratings. Then variables 17 and 18 are aptitude test scores conducted at the assessment centre: ACRatingAPTnumerical, which rates the graduate on numerical reasoning; and ACRatingAPTverbal, which rates them on verbal reasoning. Then there are three variables (19–21) that indicate whether the graduate attended the induction day (variable 19 above), an induction week (variable 20) and whether the graduate was assigned an 'onboarding buddy' (variable 21) after they joined. All of these 21 variables represent data that was collected at the selection stage/joining stage.

The next two variables include data drawn from the HR information system some time after the graduate joined; this includes the graduate performance appraisal rating at the end of year 1 (Year1performanceRating rated on a scale of 1 = fails to meet expectations to 5 = star performer) and whether they left the company in the first two years of their job (LeaverYr2). Importantly, some of the graduates left in the first year and as such will not have any performance rating on the Year1performanceRating variable.

First, we can produce some descriptive frequency statistics with our data set of 340 graduates (see Figure 8.18).

Note here that although 106 of the graduates left before the two-year anniversary, the fact that 42 graduates did not get a performance rating may well indicate that these 42 had left before their year-one performance rating was given, thus they left in the first 12 months of their tenure (this needs further investigation).

**FIGURE 8.18**

### Male or Female

| | | Frequency | Per cent | Valid Per cent | Cumulative Per cent |
|---|---|---|---|---|---|
| Valid | Male | 210 | 58.3 | 58.3 | 58.3 |
| | Female | 150 | 41.7 | 41.7 | 100.0 |
| | Total | 360 | 100.0 | 100.0 | |

### Education Category

| | | Frequency | Per cent | Valid Per cent | Cumulative Per cent |
|---|---|---|---|---|---|
| Valid | BSc | 144 | 40.0 | 40.0 | 40.0 |
| | MSc | 206 | 57.2 | 57.2 | 97.2 |
| | Phd | 10 | 2.8 | 2.8 | 100.0 |
| | Total | 360 | 100.0 | 100.0 | |

### Black Asian Minority Ethnic Yes or No

| | | Frequency | Per cent | Valid Per cent | Cumulative Per cent |
|---|---|---|---|---|---|
| Valid | BAME Yes | 80 | 22.2 | 22.2 | 22.2 |
| | BAME No | 280 | 77.8 | 77.8 | 100.0 |
| | Total | 360 | 100.0 | 100.0 | |

### Worked Before

| | | Frequency | Per cent | Valid Per cent | Cumulative Per cent |
|---|---|---|---|---|---|
| Valid | Yes Worked Before | 120 | 33.3 | 33.3 | 33.3 |
| | Just Studied | 240 | 66.7 | 66.7 | 100.0 |
| | Total | 360 | 100.0 | 100.0 | |

### Function Joined

| | | Frequency | Per cent | Valid Per cent | Cumulative Per cent |
|---|---|---|---|---|---|
| Valid | HR | 62 | 17.2 | 17.2 | 17.2 |
| | Finance | 66 | 18.3 | 18.3 | 35.6 |
| | Marketing | 70 | 19.4 | 19.4 | 55.0 |
| | Front Line Sales | 28 | 7.8 | 7.8 | 62.8 |
| | Risk Management | 30 | 8.3 | 8.3 | 71.1 |
| | Legal | 60 | 16.7 | 16.7 | 87.8 |
| | Operations | 44 | 12.2 | 12.2 | 100.0 |
| | Total | 360 | 100.0 | 100.0 | |

**FIGURE 8.18** *continued*

**Did they attend the Induction Day**

| | | Frequency | Per cent | Valid Per cent | Cumulative Per cent |
|---|---|---|---|---|---|
| Valid | No | 46 | 12.8 | 12.8 | 12.8 |
| | Yes | 314 | 87.2 | 87.2 | 100.0 |
| | Total | 360 | 100.0 | 100.0 | |

**Did they attend the Induction Week**

| | | Frequency | Per cent | Valid Per cent | Cumulative Per cent |
|---|---|---|---|---|---|
| Valid | No | 81 | 22.5 | 22.5 | 22.5 |
| | Yes | 279 | 77.5 | 77.5 | 100.0 |
| | Total | 360 | 100.0 | 100.0 | |

**Did they get an on-boarding Buddy**

| | | Frequency | Per cent | Valid Per cent | Cumulative Per cent |
|---|---|---|---|---|---|
| Valid | No | 32 | 8.9 | 8.9 | 8.9 |
| | Yes | 328 | 91.1 | 91.1 | 100.0 |
| | Total | 360 | 100.0 | 100.0 | |

**Performance rating 1 year in (1 fails to meet expectations– 5 A star performer)**

| | | Frequency | Per cent | Valid Per cent | Cumulative Per cent |
|---|---|---|---|---|---|
| Valid | Fails to Meet Expectations By some Margin | 27 | 7.5 | 8.5 | 8.5 |
| | Just meets expectations | 29 | 8.1 | 9.1 | 17.6 |
| | Meets Expectations comfortably | 114 | 31.7 | 35.8 | 53.5 |
| | Exceeds Expectations | 84 | 23.3 | 26.4 | 79.9 |
| | A Star Performer | 64 | 17.8 | 20.1 | 100.0 |
| | Total | 318 | 88.3 | 100.0 | |
| Missing | System | 42 | 11.7 | | |
| Total | | 360 | 100.0 | | |

**Left by Year 2**

| | | Frequency | Per cent | Valid Per cent | Cumulative Per cent |
|---|---|---|---|---|---|
| Valid | STAYER | 254 | 70.6 | 70.6 | 70.6 |
| | LEAVER | 106 | 29.4 | 29.4 | 100.0 |
| | Total | 360 | 100.0 | 100.0 | |

# Example 3: predicting performance from selection data using multiple linear regression

The first analysis that we present here involves predicting year-one performance appraisal ratings from demographic and CV information, assessment-centre ratings (that include personality, competency and aptitude scores), attendance at induction days and weeks, whether they were given an onboarding buddy as well as the function joined information. Thus, as our dependent variable is a 1-to-5 scale variable we will select the Analyze→Regression→Linear option to set up our regression model. Once our regression window appears (see Figure 8.19) we put the 'Year1performanceRating' (performance rating) variable into the 'Dependent:' box and transfer all but four of the variables (excluding the GradID, GradJOBfunction, LeaverYr2 and HRDummyV variables) into the 'Independent(s):' selection box. Then click 'OK'.

**FIGURE 8.19**

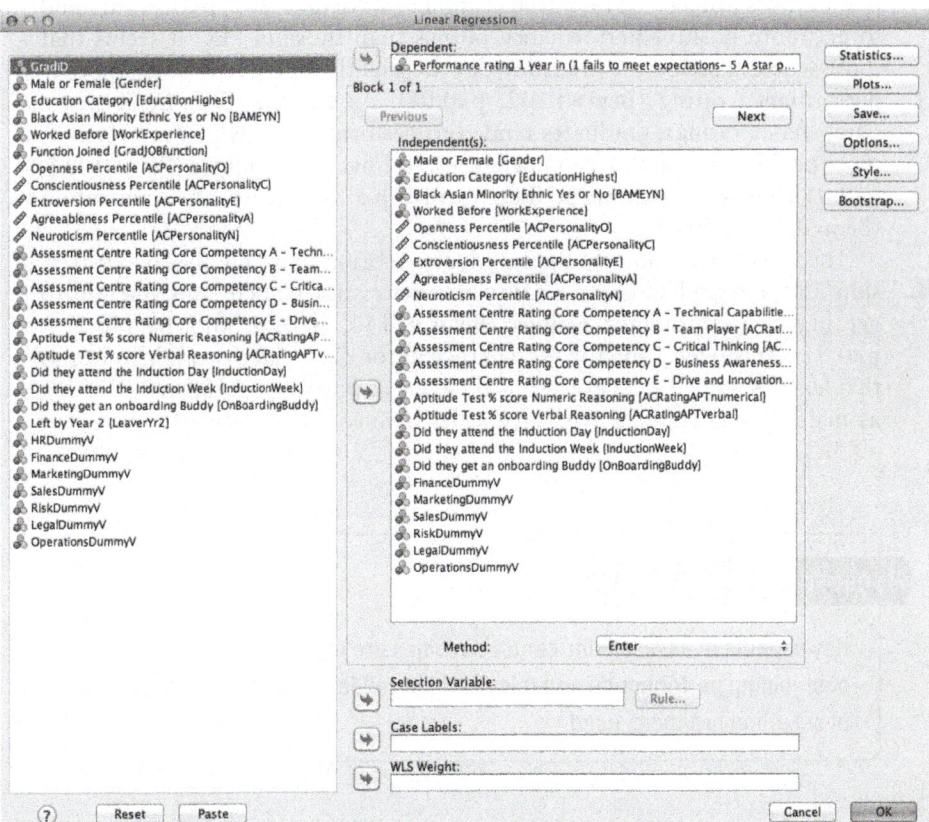

Note that we are including the function dummy variables rather than the 'GradJOBfunction' variable because it makes no sense including a multiple category descriptive variable in a linear regression as an independent variable – because an increase in the numerical values does not represent an increase in the function, the numbers are just labels. Furthermore, we include six rather than all of the seven function dummy variables because we need to set a function reference category that each of the six functions can be compared against when predicting performance (see Chapter 7, page 271, for a discussion of dummy variables). See Figure 8.20 for the regression output with this model.

The regression model shown in Figure 8.20 tells us a number of interesting things. First, our demographic, assessment centre, function and induction data accounts for a good deal of the variation (R-square=0.664) in performance ratings (some 66.4 per cent of this variation) and this model is highly significant, $f(25,292)=23.074$, $p<0.001$. If one looks at the individual Beta coefficients and their corresponding significance levels, we see that there are 10 key variables that can be identified as significant 'drivers' of subsequent performance ratings.

Three of the functional dummies are shown to be significant and all Betas are positive. As our 'HRDummyV' variable was omitted and thus HR is the excluded function, these indicate that graduates from Marketing (Beta=0.224, $p<0.01$), Risk (Beta=0.219, $p<0.01$) and Legal (Beta=0.357, $p<0.01$) all tend to get more positive performance ratings than those in HR. It seems that those who did attend the induction day are slightly more likely to get a better performance rating (Beta=0.102, $p<0.05$). As for the assessment-centre competency ratings, graduates tended to perform better who were rated as more positive on the three competencies: technical capabilities (Beta=0.155, $p<0.01$), business awareness (Beta=0.150, $p<0.01$), drive and innovation (Beta=0.123, $p<0.05$).

The results also indicate that graduates scoring more highly on extraversion and agreeableness personality characteristics tended subsequently to get higher performance ratings (Betas=0.144, $p<0.01$ and Beta=0.179, $p<0.01$ respectively). Finally the, coefficient for the gender variable indicates that females (coded as 2) are less likely to get as positive a performance rating as males (coded as 1) as we have a negative coefficient for gender (Beta= –0.362, $p<0.001$).

### Snapshot hidden gem

Key aspects of assessment-centre activities are found to predict post-joining performance and this provides validating evidence for a range of selection practices used.

## FIGURE 8.20

**Model Summary**

| Model | R | R-Square | Adjusted R-Square | Std. Error of the Estimate |
|---|---|---|---|---|
| 1 | .815[a] | .664 | .635 | .69911 |

a. Predictors: (Constant), OperationsDummyV, Black Asian Minority Ethnic Yes or No, Openness Percentile, RiskDummyV, Assessment Centre Rating Core Competency C – Critical Thinking, Neuroticism Percentile, Worked Before, Did they attend the Induction Day, Aptitude Test % score Verbal Reasoning, SalesDummyV, Did they get an onboarding Buddy, Education Category, Aptitude Test % score Numeric Reasoning, Assessment Centre Rating Core Competency B – Team Player, Assessment Centre Rating Core Competency D – Business Awareness, Did they attend the Induction Week, Extroversion Percentile, Agreeableness Percentile, Conscientiousness Percentile, Male or Female, Assessment Centre Rating Core Competency E – Drive and Innovation, Assessment Centre Rating Core Competency A – Technical Capabilities, FinanceDummyV, MarketingDummyV, LegalDummyV

**ANOVA[a]**

| Model | | Sum of Squares | df | Mean Square | F | Sig. |
|---|---|---|---|---|---|---|
| 1 | Regression | 281.954 | 25 | 11.278 | 23.075 | .000[b] |
| | Residual | 142.716 | 292 | .489 | | |
| | Total | 424.670 | 317 | | | |

a. Dependent Variable: Performance rating 1 year in (1 fails to meet expectations – 5 A star performer)

b. Predictors: (Constant), OperationsDummyV, Black Asian Minority Ethnic Yes or No, Openness Percentile, RiskDummyV, Assessment Centre Rating Core Competency C – Critical Thinking, Neuroticism Percentile, Worked Before, Did they attend the Induction Day, Aptitude Test % score Verbal Reasoning, SalesDummyV, Did they get an onboarding Buddy, Education Category, Aptitude Test % score Numeric Reasoning, Assessment Centre Rating Core Competency B – Team Player, Assessment Centre Rating Core Competency D – Business Awareness, Did they attend the Induction Week, Extroversion Percentile, Agreeableness Percentile, Conscientiousness Percentile, Male or Female, Assessment Centre Rating Core Competency E – Drive and Innovation, Assessment Centre Rating Core Competency A – Technical Capabilities, FinanceDummyV, MarketingDummyV, LegalDummyV

*[Handwritten note: As Gender increases from male=1 to female=2, likelihood for positive performance decreases]*

**Coefficients[a]**

| Model | | Unstandardized Coefficients B | Std. Error | Standardized Coefficients Beta | t | Sig. |
|---|---|---|---|---|---|---|
| 1 | (Constant) | -4.823 | 1.202 | | -4.014 | .000 |
| | Male or Female | -.858 | .131 | -.362 | -6.567 | .000 |
| | Education Category | .138 | .083 | .064 | 1.677 | .095 |
| | Black Asian Minority Ethnic Yes or No | -.019 | .104 | -.007 | -.186 | .853 |
| | Worked Before | .061 | .089 | .024 | .679 | .497 |
| | Openness Percentile | -.003 | .004 | -.045 | -.930 | .353 |
| | Conscientiousness Percentile | .008 | .003 | .144 | 2.978 | .003 |
| | Extroversion Percentile | .010 | .004 | .179 | 2.785 | .006 |
| | Agreeableness Percentile | .001 | .003 | .018 | .317 | .751 |
| | Neuroticism Percentile | -.001 | .002 | -.016 | -.419 | .676 |
| | Assessment Centre Rating Core Competency A – Technical Capabilities | .364 | .138 | .155 | 2.633 | .009 |
| | Assessment Centre Rating Core Competency B – Team Player | .131 | .120 | .046 | 1.091 | .276 |
| | Assessment Centre Rating Core Competency C – Critical Thinking | .090 | .140 | .032 | .644 | .520 |
| | Assessment Centre Rating Core Competency D – Business Awareness | .359 | .113 | .150 | 3.193 | .002 |
| | Assessment Centre Rating Core Competency E – Drive and Innovation | .346 | .165 | .123 | 2.088 | .038 |
| | Aptitude Test % score Numeric Reasoning | .010 | .007 | .070 | 1.407 | .161 |
| | Aptitude Test % score Verbal Reasoning | .008 | .010 | .039 | .770 | .442 |
| | Did they attend the Induction Day | .357 | .141 | .102 | 2.526 | .012 |
| | Did they attend the Induction Week | .023 | .129 | .007 | .182 | .856 |
| | Did they get an onboarding Buddy | .232 | .252 | .035 | .919 | .359 |
| | FinanceDummyV | .154 | .254 | .051 | .607 | .544 |
| | MarketingDummyV | .624 | .219 | .224 | 2.842 | .005 |
| | SalesDummyV | -.064 | .296 | -.016 | -.215 | .830 |
| | RiskDummyV | .923 | .245 | .219 | 3.773 | .000 |
| | LegalDummyV | 1.151 | .255 | .357 | 4.517 | .000 |
| | OperationsDummyV | .402 | .233 | .115 | 1.722 | .086 |

a. Dependent Variable: Performance rating 1 year in (1 fails to meet expectations – 5 A star performer)

*[Handwritten note: Grads in these depts have more positive reviews than HR]*

The fact that personality factors predict performance provides evidence that the use of personality tests in the assessment centre is a valid selection technique. The same can be argued for the use of competency-based interviews, the ratings from which are significant predictors of performance. The results also indicate that investing in an induction day has benefit too (as attendance on this predicts performance, we discuss this further in Chapter 10).

Before we move on to using this selection data to predict subsequent graduate turnover, we would want to reflect on some of the findings above. We can see that the function that the graduate is in tends to account for a fair bit of the variance in the performance appraisal ratings. This would probably need some investigating in order to understand whether there are some systematic differences in the performance scores given in different departments; such a difference may or may not be a problem, depending upon company policy regarding performance appraisal-rating calibration. Also, we can see that the aptitude test scores do not predict performance. If we assume that aptitude tests should predict performance in jobs, it may be the case that the verbal and numerical reasoning might have an influence on jobs in a varied fashion across different functions (eg numerical reasoning may be an important predictor of performance only in certain jobs, such as highly technical roles within the finance or risk division). The analysis here has not tested this and it might be something that the analytics expert should explore further (by looking at the correlations between these scores and performance with the separate functional groups).

Also, in reflecting on the results of the above analysis, it seems to show that female graduates do not perform as well as male graduates. Before drawing any conclusions from this, the analyst would need to consider (and explore analytically) whether there are functional variations in how performance appraisal ratings are applied in practice (managers across functions may vary in their generosity when giving ratings). Related to this, the analyst would need to consider whether the functions vary in male and female ratios. This apparent gender effect could also be demonstrating a gender bias in performance appraisal practices and the finding definitely needs to be investigated further. We will return to this analysis in Chapter 10 where we use the results of these regression models to predict expected levels of performance of candidates in an assessment centre (to potentially aid selection decisions).

# Example 4: predicting turnover from selection data – validating selection techniques by predicting turnover

For our last recruitment and selection example we continue to use the same graduate selection data set that we introduced in the previous example (in predicting performance): 'Chapter 8 Selection.sav'. Although this is the same data set, we set out details of the variables and coding again for ease of reference:

1. GradID — Employee Identifier
2. Gender — Male (1) or Female (2)
3. EducationHighest — Education Category: BSc (1) MSc (2) PhD (3)
4. BAMEYN — Black, Asian or Minority Ethnic: Yes (1) or No (2)
5. WorkExperience — Worked Before: Yes (1) No (2)
6. GradJOBfunction — Function Joined: (1) HR; (2) Finance; (3) Marketing; (4) Sales; (5) Risk; (6) Legal; (7) Operations
7. ACPersonalityO — Assessment C Personality Openness (percentage)
8. ACPersonalityC — Assessment C Personality Conscientious (percentage)
9. ACPersonalityE — Assessment C Personality Extraversion (percentage)
10. ACPersonalityA — Assessment C Personality Agreeable (percentage)
11. ACPersonalityN — Assessment C Personality Neuroticism (percentage)
12. ACRatingINTCOMPA — Assessment C Competency Technical (1–5)
13. ACRatingINTCOMPB — Assessment C Competency Team Player
14. ACRatingINTCOMPC — Assessment C Competency Critical Thought
15. ACRatingINTCOMPD — Assessment C Competency Business Aware
16. ACRatingINTCOMPE — Assessment C Competency Drive Innovation
17. ACRatingAPTnumerical — Numerical Aptitude Test Score
18. ACRatingAPTverbal — Verbal Reasoning Aptitude Test Score
19. InductionDay — Attend Induction Day: No (0) Yes (1)
20. InductionWeek — Attend Induction Week: No (0) Yes (1)
21. OnBoardingBuddy — Given Joining Buddy: No (0) Yes (1)
22. Year1performanceRating — Year 1 Performance Rating: (1) Fails to Meet Expectations (2) Just Meets Expectations (3) Meets Expectations Comfortably (4) Exceeds Expectations (5) A Star Performer

| 23 | LeaverYr2 | Leaver in First 24 Months (0) No (1) Leaver |
| --- | --- | --- |
| 24 | HRDummyV | HR Dummy Variable |
| 25 | FinanceDummyV | Finance Dummy Variable |
| 26 | MarketingDummyV | Marketing Dummy Variable |
| 27 | SalesDummyV | Sales Dummy Variable |
| 28 | RiskDummyV | Risk Management Dummy Variable |
| 29 | LegalDummyV | Legal Dummy Variable |
| 30 | OperationsDummyV | Operations Dummy Variable |

Here, we are going to predict whether our demographic or our selection-centre data predicts graduate turnover. Thus, as our dependent variable here is the 'LeaverYr2' binary variable (variable 23 set out in our list), we will select Analyze→Regression→Binary Logistic to set up our regression model.

Once our regression window appears (see Figure 8.21) we put the 'LeaverYr2' variable (0 = stayer; 1 = leaver) into the 'Dependent:' box and transfer all but the seven dummy function variables (variables 24–30 above) and the 'GradID' variable into the 'Independent(s):' selection box.

Whereas with the graduate performance linear regression model tested above we included the functional dummy variables, here, as we are using binary logistic regression we can simply enter the 'GradJobfunction' variable into our analysis. This is because with logistic regression analysis, SPSS has a feature to handle (and identify) categorical variables.

Once we have set up our logistic regression predicting graduate turnover (Figure 8.20) and before we click 'OK', we need to indicate that the 'GradJOBfunction' variable is categorical rather than numeric. As with previous chapters (eg Chapter 6), we indicate this by clicking on the `Categorical...` button (see Figure 8.21, in the top-right-hand corner of our screenshot) and in the following window (Figure 8.22) transfer the 'GradJOBfunction' variable into the 'Categorical Covariates:' selection box (using the arrow button).

The default set-up for the categorical variable reference category is that all the categories within the variable will be compared with the last category stored in the variable. As the HR function is the first category in this GradJOBfunction variable and we used the HRDummyV as a reference category with the above analysis, we should change the reference category in this analysis so that the first rather than the last category is the reference category. To do this you select the 'First' option in the 'Reference Category' part of the window (see the bottom of Figure 8.22) and click on the 'Change' button to apply this change; click 'Continue' then click 'OK'.

Before we go on to discuss the model results here, we should consider the first table produced in our results (see the 'Case Processing Summary' table in Figure 8.23). As we can see, there are 42 missing cases in this analysis, which may have some implications for the analysis. We know that 42 of the graduates have no performance rating; this means that these graduates are not being included in the analysis as we have 'Yr1Performance' as an independent variable in our model.

# FIGURE 8.21

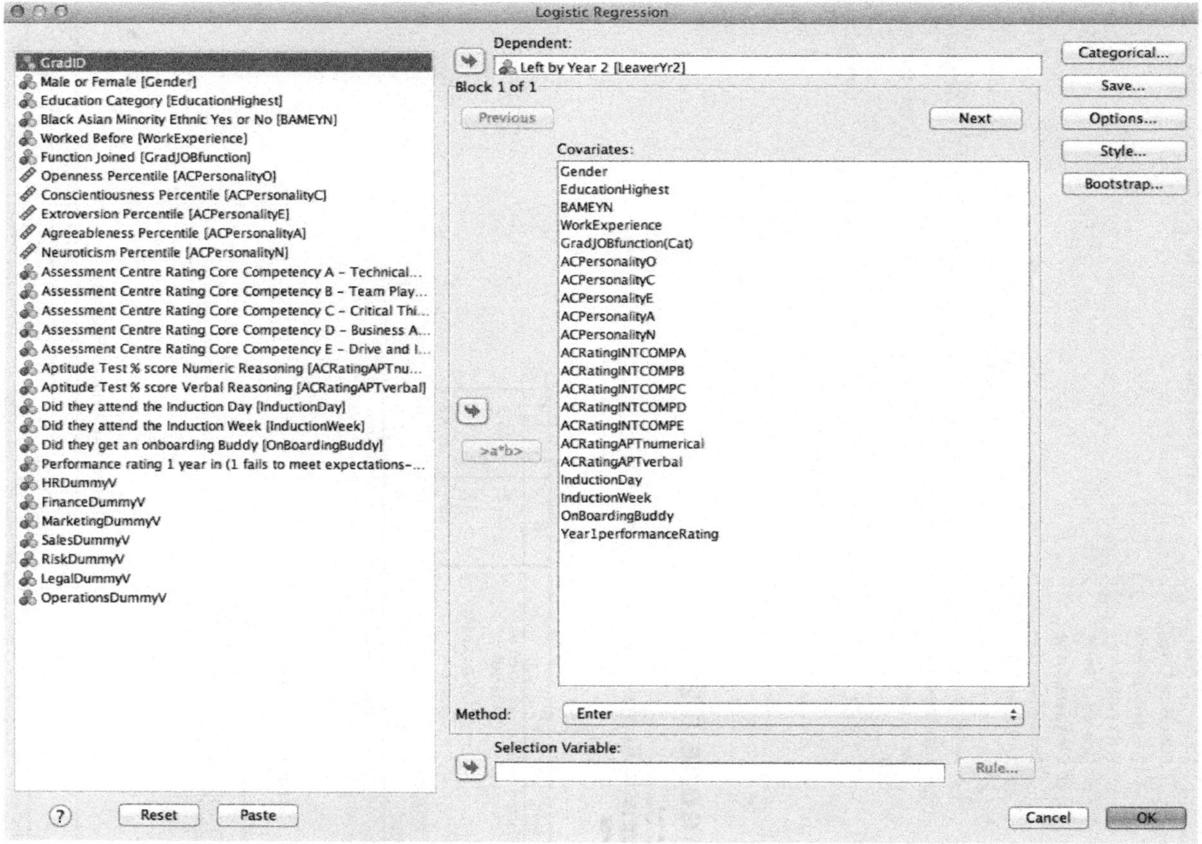

## FIGURE 8.22

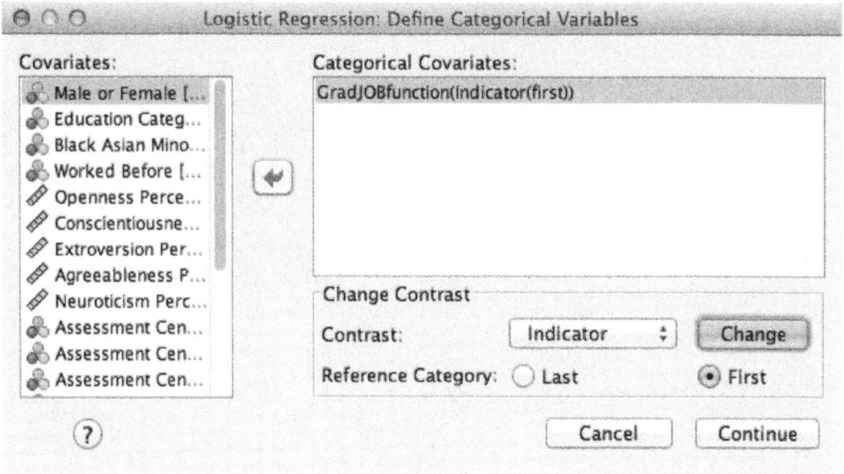

[Screenshot: Logistic Regression: Define Categorical Variables dialog box. Covariates list includes Male or Female, Education Categ..., Black Asian Mino..., Worked Before, Openness Perce..., Conscientiousne..., Extroversion Per..., Agreeableness P..., Neuroticism Perc..., Assessment Cen... (×3). Categorical Covariates: GradJOBfunction(Indicator(first)). Change Contrast: Contrast: Indicator; Reference Category: First selected.]

## FIGURE 8.23

Logistic Regression

**Case Processing Summary**

| Unweighted Cases[a] | | N | Per cent |
|---|---|---|---|
| Selected Cases | Included in Analysis | 318 | 88.3 |
| | Missing Cases | 42 | 11.7 |
| | Total | 360 | 100.0 |
| Unselected Cases | | 0 | .0 |
| Total | | 360 | 100.0 |

a. If weight is in effect, see classification table for the total number of cases.

**Dependent Variable Encoding**

| Original Value | Internal Value |
|---|---|
| STAYER | 0 |
| LEAVER | 1 |

**Categorical Variables Codings**

| | | Frequency | Parameter coding | | | | | |
|---|---|---|---|---|---|---|---|---|
| | | | (1) | (2) | (3) | (4) | (5) | (6) |
| Function Joined | HR | 50 | .000 | .000 | .000 | .000 | .000 | .000 |
| | Finance | 56 | 1.000 | .000 | .000 | .000 | .000 | .000 |
| | Marketing | 70 | .000 | 1.000 | .000 | .000 | .000 | .000 |
| | Front-Line Sales | 28 | .000 | .000 | 1.000 | .000 | .000 | .000 |
| | Risk Management | 26 | .000 | .000 | .000 | 1.000 | .000 | .000 |
| | Legal | 48 | .000 | .000 | .000 | .000 | 1.000 | .000 |
| | Operations | 40 | .000 | .000 | .000 | .000 | .000 | 1.000 |

As we can see from the 'Categorical Variables Codings' table in Figure 8.23, all of the functions have a 1.000 somewhere in their row apart from HR (in the top row), which confirms that the HR function will be the reference category that the other functions will be compared with (in terms of turnover). The following output (Figure 8.24) gives us key information here about our model.

**FIGURE 8.24**

### Block 1: Method = Enter

**Omnibus Tests of Model Coefficients**

|        |       | Chi-square | df | Sig. |
|--------|-------|------------|----|------|
| Step 1 | Step  | 117.146    | 26 | .000 |
|        | Block | 117.146    | 26 | .000 |
|        | Model | 117.146    | 26 | .000 |

**Model Summary**

| Step | -2 Log likelihood | Cox and Snell R-Square | Nagelkerke R-Square |
|------|-------------------|------------------------|---------------------|
| 1    | 263.615[a]        | .308                   | .441                |

a. Estimation terminated at iteration number 6 because parameter estimates changed by less than .001.

**Classification Table[a]**

|        |              |        | Predicted |        |            |
|--------|--------------|--------|-----------|--------|------------|
|        |              |        | Left by Year 2 |   | Percentage |
|        | Observed     |        | STAYER    | LEAVER | Correct    |
| Step 1 | Left by Year 2 | STAYER | 211     | 16     | 93.0       |
|        |              | LEAVER | 37        | 54     | 59.3       |
|        | Overall Percentage |    |           |        | 83.3       |

The chi-square figure (see the 'Omnibus Tests of Model Coefficients' box in Figure 8.24) is significant (chi square=117.146, $p<0.001$) and the Nagelkerke pseudo R-square in the 'Model Summary' box is .441, thus the model accounts for a good amount of the turnover (approximately 44.1 per cent) that we have in our model. The output table in Figure 8.25 gives us information about how important each of the variables is in predicting graduate turnover, and indeed the odds of the graduate being a leaver linked to what value they may have in each of the variables.

From Figure 8.25, we can see that there are eight significant predictors of graduate turnover here. The first is gender, which has a B of 1.476 ($p<0.05$) and an Exp(B) figure of 4.374. Given how gender is coded

**FIGURE 8.25**

Variables in the Equation

| | | B | S.E. | Wald | df | Sig. | Exp(B) |
|---|---|---|---|---|---|---|---|
| Step 1ª | Gender | 1.476 | .592 | 6.215 | 1 | .013 | 4.374 |
| | EducationHighest | -.061 | .356 | .030 | 1 | .863 | .941 |
| | BAMEYN | .118 | .436 | .073 | 1 | .787 | 1.125 |
| | WorkExperience | -.076 | .357 | .046 | 1 | .831 | .926 |
| | GradJOBfunction | | | 11.645 | 6 | .070 | |
| | GradJOBfunction(1) | 3.270 | 1.249 | 6.853 | 1 | .009 | 26.307 |
| | GradJOBfunction(2) | 2.895 | .997 | 8.441 | 1 | .004 | 18.088 |
| | GradJOBfunction(3) | 2.634 | 1.353 | 3.788 | 1 | .052 | 13.932 |
| | GradJOBfunction(4) | 2.863 | 1.133 | 6.386 | 1 | .012 | 17.509 |
| | GradJOBfunction(5) | 1.696 | 1.197 | 2.005 | 1 | .157 | 5.450 |
| | GradJOBfunction(6) | 2.766 | 1.081 | 6.545 | 1 | .011 | 15.900 |
| | ACPersonalityO | -.023 | .016 | 1.930 | 1 | .165 | .978 |
| | ACPersonalityC | -.009 | .011 | .620 | 1 | .431 | .991 |
| | ACPersonalityE | .017 | .015 | 1.330 | 1 | .249 | 1.017 |
| | ACPersonalityA | .001 | .014 | .009 | 1 | .924 | 1.001 |
| | ACPersonalityN | .021 | .010 | 4.536 | 1 | .033 | 1.021 |
| | ACRatingINTCOMPA | -.500 | .564 | .787 | 1 | .375 | .606 |
| | ACRatingINTCOMPB | .129 | .480 | .073 | 1 | .788 | 1.138 |
| | ACRatingINTCOMPC | -.326 | .559 | .340 | 1 | .560 | .722 |
| | ACRatingINTCOMPD | -.497 | .457 | 1.179 | 1 | .278 | .609 |
| | ACRatingINTCOMPE | .438 | .693 | .399 | 1 | .528 | 1.549 |
| | ACRatingAPTnumerical | -.061 | .036 | 2.789 | 1 | .095 | .941 |
| | ACRatingAPTverbal | .040 | .043 | .855 | 1 | .355 | 1.041 |
| | InductionDay | -1.969 | .569 | 11.997 | 1 | .001 | .140 |
| | InductionWeek | .054 | .511 | .011 | 1 | .916 | 1.055 |
| | OnBoardingBuddy | -.532 | 1.087 | .240 | 1 | .625 | .587 |
| | Year1performanceRating | .086 | .242 | .128 | 1 | .721 | 1.090 |
| | Constant | .951 | 5.341 | .032 | 1 | .859 | 2.587 |

a. Variable(s) entered on step 1: Gender, EducationHighest, BAMEYN, WorkExperience, GradJOBfunction, ACPersonalityO, ACPersonalityC, ACPersonalityE, ACPersonalityA, ACPersonalityN, ACRatingINTCOMPA, ACRatingINTCOMPB, ACRatingINTCOMPC, ACRatingINTCOMPD, ACRatingINTCOMPE, ACRatingAPTnumerical, ACRatingAPTverbal, InductionDay, InductionWeek, OnBoardingBuddy, Year1performanceRating.

neg = less likely to leave

(1 = male; 2 = female), this tells us that female graduates are 4.374 times more likely to leave than males in the first two years.

Four of the function dummy variables are also significant (in all cases the betas are positive and odds ratios are all above 1, which suggests that the graduates are more likely to leave in these functions than graduates in the HR function, which is the reference category of 0 here); thus Finance (1) graduates are 26.3 (Exp(B)) times more likely to leave than HR graduates. Marketing graduates are 18.09 (Exp(B)) times more likely to leave than HR graduates, Risk graduates are 17.51 (Exp(B)) times more likely to leave than HR graduates, and Operations graduates are 15.90 (Exp(B)) times more likely to leave than HR graduates. Those graduates who show higher levels of neuroticism are more likely to leave within the first two years (Exp(B)=1.021, B=0.021, p<0.05). Finally, if the graduate went on the induction day (0 = absent; 1 = attend) they are less likely to leave (Exp(B)=0.14, B=-1.969, p<0.05) in the first two years. Again, it is not straightforward to conceptualize as we have an odds ratio lower than 1 (0.14); therefore it is often easier to transform the odds ratio to represent the odds of being the lower coded category of the predictor (in this case induction-day absentee). When we do this, we see that absent graduates are 7.14 times more likely to be a leaver within two years than those who attended (1/0.14=7.14).

> **Snapshot hidden gem**
>
> Key aspects of assessment-centre activities are found to predict graduate turnover. It is clear that the HR function has higher retention than Finance, Marketing, Risk and Operations. Female graduates are much more likely to leave than male graduates; this needs further investigation. Also, non-attendance of induction day should be a key warning flag for possible future turnover (as attendance is significant it does, however, validate induction days as a useful onboarding activity).

# Further considerations

As mentioned elsewhere, it is often the case that when one begins to analyse and diagnose predictors of various important outcomes (such as turnover or low performance), the analysis uncovers diagnostic clues pointing towards what is going on within the organization and further analysis is often required. The fact that turnover varies considerably across the functions here, and women are more likely to leave means that it might be worth exploring whether the gender ratio of leavers varies considerably over the different functions. It might be the case that female turnover is extremely high in some of the functions with high turnover; this would be worth exploring. This is in effect an interaction analysis (we explain this in Chapter 11). Ultimately, as the HR analytics expert becomes more experienced, they will begin to see clues in the data that help them to really understand (and predict) what is going on in their organization.

## *Other considerations for analytic applications*

Here, as with all our chapters, we have only presented some examples of the kind of models that an analytics team could begin to explore with each topic or area. There are obviously many different types of analysis that focus on the area of recruitment and selection analytics that we do not cover here.

One thing that analysts linked to recruitment and selection teams may want to consider is the cost of recruitment and selection activities (and the cost per successful hire). This kind of information would be useful to feed into analysis where the HR analytics team want to validate particular selection techniques/activities. Cost information can be linked to analysis that we have carried out above.

Once the HR analytics team increase in their level of experience, the potential and opportunities of integrating different data (eg cost information) into models, interpretations and recommendations linked to analysis examples we present here will begin to expand.

# References

Schmidt, F and Hunter, J (1998) The validity and utility of selection methods in personnel psychology: practical and theoretical implications of 85 years of research findings, *Psychological Bulletin*, **124** (2), pp 262–74

# Case study 6
# Monitoring the impact of interventions

## Tracking the impact of interventions

One of the key tasks that an HR analytics practitioner will be involved in is helping evaluate the impact of an HR intervention. Often these interventions can involve a considerable financial investment and there may be an expectation that the intervention will have an impact. The obvious example is something like the introduction of a training programme; training programmes cost money and the evaluation of the effectiveness of training can be considered to be an activity that any good HR function should do automatically (there are literally hundreds of books out there explaining how to do this). The cost of any HR intervention, and its potential return, is something that HR practitioners have to consider in the planning and inception stage. It is often the case that before the intervention gets a sign-off HR will have to explicitly anticipate and present expected outcomes as part of a business case to justify the investment. Thus, having expertise in helping to track and monitor the potential impact of HR interventions is an essential capability that an HR analytic expert would be required to have.

Ultimately, to properly assess the impact or efficacy of any intervention programme, some assessment of *change* will be required. This may be, for example, a change in employee attitudes, perceptions or behaviour. For an intervention to have had an impact, some change must occur following its introduction. In the majority of cases, the only reason to introduce an HR intervention is to create change of some sort. Having said this, there may of course be a situation where the HR function wants to introduce an intervention to stop change (eg to make sure that positive attitudes or behaviours do not decline). In general the HR function wants to impact something, and something is expected to change after the intervention. Importantly, the HR analytics expert will be completely aware of this fact, as often the only way to track the impact of an intervention is to demonstrate and interrogate change in one or more appropriate metric.

## *What intervention; what measure?*

When contemplating how to track the impact of an intervention, the HR analytics expert will need to carefully consider what metric should be used. It is possible that some simple metrics may exist already that can be monitored over time and can give information that indicates impact. For example, if you were to implement an HR initiative (such as training) to improve performance, there may be performance indicators that are regularly collected (such as customer feedback results) that you could just track and watch for any change subsequent to implementation. Another example where a relevant direct metric may already exist (that can just be monitored) is where an HR intervention has been introduced to have a positive impact on well-being; sickness absence rates (assuming that these are recorded) and changes in these could simply be tracked. Thus some metrics will exist that can be accessed to track the impact of an intervention.

Importantly, great care must be taken to ensure that the metric used to track the impact is actually a valid indicator of something that the HR function hopes to influence with the intervention. The metric must fit the intended impact of an intervention in order to track the impact properly. As mentioned, in some cases this is simple and a metric exists; however, in other cases this is not possible. Although in Chapter 7 we gave an example of sickness absence rates as a possible measure of well-being, and this may be a reasonable indicator of well-being, it may not be the only or best measure. There may be a case for identifying other indicators as well: for example, employee levels of engagement, job satisfaction and/or levels of stress or psychological strain.

So the HR analytics expert needs to address each intervention and ask three key questions:

**1** What exactly would we expect this intervention to impact/what do we expect/hope to see a change in if it is successful?

**2** What possible measures or metrics exist at the moment that might help test for this change?

**3** Do we need to create a measure/index/metric that we can track to assess the impact of the intervention?

It may be that the analytics expert recommends that the organization create new methods to measure and track particular perceptions, attitudes, behaviours or performance indicators in order to monitor the effectiveness of an HR intervention. Importantly (ideally) this needs to be done before the intervention is implemented; a key way to be able to identify the impact of an intervention is to track the impact from before, after and beyond. Ultimately, from an analytics point of view, this requires a solid understanding of the analysis of 'change'.

A simple example might be if we are trying to improve the mathematics skills of cashier staff. We might give them a simple test at time zero, then another test just after some basic mathematics training, and then another test six months later to track progress and see if the knowledge has been retained. The test is a measure that we have had to introduce in order to track the impact of the intervention.

## Simple change testing

Importantly, when we introduce an intervention, what sort of change are we looking for? Depending on the metric and what we are hoping to affect, we would generally want an improvement of some sort. If, for example, we were trying to improve well-being, then we might want to track sickness absence rates and the change we would be looking for following an intervention would be a reduction in sickness absence rates. So the change would be downward change in sickness absence. An improvement in performance would imply a change in performance; depending upon the performance metric being considered this could involve an increase (eg increase in scan rate of checkout staff) or decrease (eg average length of calls in a call-centre environment). Regardless of the nature of the required change for an intervention to be considered, an ideal platform to assess change is where a *before-and-after* metric can be monitored; before-and-after monitoring of key metrics is often the only way to obtain a clear picture of the efficacy of any intervention. Aside from tracking established metrics or newly introduced metrics, conducting surveys to provide rich information before and after an intervention might often be the most sensible option. In this situation, the HR function may need to consider introducing either a panel or a pulse survey.

## Panels and pulses

The word 'panel' in research and analytics is a term that is used a lot. It is important to understand what it means and why is it a useful research tool that opens up analytic and diagnostic options. A panel is where a collection or sample of people is tracked over time, often multiple times.

In market research, panels are regularly used to monitor and understand consumer behaviour. Often, a sample of shoppers are paid to monitor and keep track of where they shop or what they buy over a period of time; market research companies are able to judge trends and patterns of change in purchasing behaviour. These panels can be monitored and employee purchasing behaviour, and change in this (eg following an advertising campaign on certain products) can be monitored and tracked. In addition to this, these people can also be interviewed and surveyed at various points to ask them about their reasons for buying certain products and reactions to certain products. Such a panel of consumers can provide invaluable information that would otherwise not be obtainable. Ultimately, though, from an HR point of view, an ideal 'panel' would be a sample of employees whose perceptions, attitudes and behaviour are tracked over multiple time points.

Due to the inevitable power dynamic between employees and the employer, there will be confidentiality issues and sensitivities in asking employees their attitudes and perceptions about their employment experiences. In the very nature of a panel, employees are identified in some way so that their perceptions, behaviour and attitudes can be tracked over time (thus enabling change to be observed). Therefore an organization has to be very careful as to how these confidentiality issues are handled if part of the data (metric) collection exercise includes surveys. However, with regard to monitoring the impact of intervention, tracking employees over time and monitoring change in a particular metric allows considerable opportunities to evaluate the impact of an intervention.

Distinct from a 'panel', a 'pulse' survey is something that HR functions often carry out; this often involves a short survey sent to a sample of staff carried out over regular intervals; thus multiple waves of data are often collected. Pulse surveys are used to provide a regular picture of staff perceptions and attitudes that can also potentially provide a picture of change occurring within the organization. The difference between a pulse and a panel is that a pulse does not necessitate the same people being monitored over time to observe their change; the ideal pulse does however need to involve the collection of a random sample from the organization in each wave of data collection to help ensure that the sample observed on each occasion is representative of the organization's population. In some ways, when tracking change, both the panel and the pulse as methods should theoretically provide information about change over time. For example, if we surveyed a random selection of 850 employees (from an organization that employed 10,000 people) a month before the introduction of an HR intervention (eg a work–life balance programme) and then another random selection of 850 employees again six months afterwards, we could potentially obtain a picture of how 'the organization' may have changed over time because each pulse should theoretically represent the organization (assuming the employee samples were a random sample). We could also survey a random selection of 100 employees one month before the HR intervention, track their responses and survey them again six months afterwards; with this panel we should be able to see whether this sample has changed over the time period. Importantly, with panels, our sample size does not need to be as big as with a pulse as we do not have to make absolutely sure that the two data collection samples 'represent' the organization.

## *Sampling issues and representativeness*

One of the reasons we have to use random samples in our analysis is that we want our data set to reflect characteristics of our organization, but we might not want to have to collect metrics or measures for an entire organization. Although we might want to understand the impact of an intervention on an entire organization and were considering setting up a survey to assess its impact (involving either a pulse or a panel), due to our understanding of sampling theory and something called the 'central limit theorem' we do not actually need to survey our entire organization.

The central limit theorem tells us that assuming we carefully sample from our organizational population, only a relatively small sample of employees need to be surveyed if we wish to begin to understand general characteristics of the organization (this is discussed again in Chapter 12). Therefore, even if we are conducting analysis with an extremely large organization with many thousands of employees globally, and we need to conduct surveys to track employee responses to enable an understanding of the possible impact of the intervention, only a sub-sample is required. As statisticians like to say: 'you don't need to eat the whole bowl of soup to get an idea of what the soup tastes like' (as long as you are careful how you select your spoonful). Thus conducting a mini research project to track employee responses to an intervention may not be prohibitively expensive or as time-consuming as one might assume.

## *The use of control conditions*

In scientific research, experiments are considered to be the only sufficient way of testing for some kind of causal impact. Even with sophisticated modelling of change and variance patterns using regression models, the problem of isolating causality in data will always still be present. As such, if one needs to try to assess the impact of interventions, it is always worth considering whether there may be a possible group of employees who could be compared to our target group as some kind of control condition. For example, if an organization wanted to introduce a new training initiative to increase staff performance, the analyst tracking the impact might want to compare a group of workers who have received the training with a group who have not. Even if training is provided for most of the organization, this is often staggered; thus conditions may be set up to enable the existence of a quasi control group.

## *Testing for embedded and sustainable impact of initiatives*

A famous finding from a ground-breaking series of workplace performance studies carried out in the early 1900s is that change can occur in employees purely when they are being observed. Elton Mayo and colleagues entered the Hawthorne plant of an electric component manufacturing company and carried out numerous experiments on workers to try to understand what factors helped lead to high performance and worker productivity. The so-called 'Hawthorne effect' refers to the situation where employees' performance and productivity seemed to change (and improve) in the workplace studies regardless of the actual experimental conditions that were introduced. Thus, the so-called 'Hawthorne effect' describes the phenomenon whereby, in the act of trying to assess the impact of an intervention, purely by paying attention to employees, a short-term boost in performance and productivity is often witnessed. A key implication that this has for the HR analytics expert who needs to track the impact of an intervention is that any observations of a change that follows the intervention need to be repeated over the long term. This has implications for the time period that is required to assess any sustainable impact of an intervention. Ideally any analysis of change should incorporate an assessment of change before the intervention and immediately after, as well as at a reasonable period after this.

## *Time versus intervention effects: isolating the effects of an intervention*

Temporal causes of change will often naturally occur in the workplace and, when testing for the possible causal effects of the introduction of an HR initiative or programme, the HR analyst needs to be able to isolate and separate natural temporal effects from the possible 'causal' effects of a new initiative. For example, if a doctor prescribes an intervention of antibiotics for tonsillitis, and then the patient gets better after one month, how do we know that the patient might not have got better after one month due to the passing of time (and the workings of the body's immune system) rather than due to the antibiotics? To be able to isolate the efficacy of the intervention we require some of the population to have experienced the intervention differently (as in some did not get the intervention) and ideally it requires the ability to isolate natural temporal fluctuations. Importantly in the analysis that is carried out, every effort needs to be made to isolate possible causes of any change that may be observed. This often requires the use of temporal analysis that incorporates the assessment of change in different groups who may have different experiences through the change period.

Thus rigorous statistical analysis will need to be conducted that tests change in different groups who may have been exposed to different experiences at the same time, as well as testing for general change in employees over time. One of the best ways to understand the impact of an event is to see change over time before and after an intervention. However, if a 'before' scenario has not been enabled then the analyst needs to do their utmost to be able to isolate groups of employees who have experienced different conditions, so as to strengthen the 'post-intervention' impact conclusions that they can draw. As you will see in one of the examples we give in this chapter, we introduce a training programme to try to improve (increase) checkout scan rate. One way to assess the impact of this is to compare the scan rate of employees who have been on a training course with a group of employees who have not been on a training course. This would, of course, only be possible if not all staff received training. However, an assessment of the true impact of the training intervention would not really be possible if some 'before' data was not obtained; because as the analysis shows here, the before-and-after change in scan rate varies considerably across the group who received training versus the group who did not. Thus, at the very least, an analyst should always try to get two simple measures of a before-and-after metric from a group of employees who have had direct experience of the intervention at hand. Below we go through various examples of different analytic techniques to apply to different types of change-related data; we start with the simplest.

### Using a related/repeated/paired sample t-test

If you are interested in exploring change over time linked to the same object or entity (eg team) or the same group of individual employees then the simplest form of statistical analysis that you can conduct is the paired sample t-test, also known as the repeated sample t-test or the related sample t-test. With this test, you obtain two sets of data from the same individual or object (eg team) and conduct a simple analysis to find out whether there are any statistical differences between each individual's scores over the two occasions; thus whether there has been a significant change in the metrics or measurements over time.

## Example 1: stress before and after intervention

In this example, a market research firm has identified a problem with stress in the workplace; an engagement survey identified work pressure and work hours as being positively associated with well-being indices of anxiety, depression and reported sleeping problems. Following a series of focus groups the HR function has identified that a work–life balance intervention is needed to alleviate the problem. Data that the analyst explored can be found in the data set 'Chapter 9 intervention WLB.sav'. This file is a relatively simple data set with four variables; these are:

1. EmployeeID.
2. Gender (1 = male; 2 = female).
3. stressT1 (1–5 where 1 = very low stress; 5 = very high stress).
4. stressT2 (1–5 where 1 = very low stress; 5 = very high stress).

The organization introduced a work–life balance (WLB) programme that included working from home and flexible hours. The survey measured stress levels as part of a simple survey before the change (stressT1); it introduced the new programme and then three months later distributed questionnaires again to measure the same stress measure (stressT2) a second time. Importantly, there is an employee ID column that the analyst used to match the two waves of data.

As the analyst needs to track employee stress levels over time, some way of linking findings from the two questionnaires was required. To do this the employees were asked to enter their e-mail address on the questionnaires; when circulating the questionnaire the analyst made a commitment that identifying information would never be stored in the same data set as the responses to the other attitude questions. The analyst allocated separate employee identification codes to e-mail addresses in a separate Excel spreadsheet and linked the two sets of e-mail addresses and ID codes separately in order to link the data for analysis. Importantly, this data set remains anonymous even though the stress measures have been linked to individuals across time.

The SPSS file here includes basic data collected from 534 employees; the stress measure used is a very basic single-item 'in the past week, what levels of stress would you say you have experienced' with a scale of 1 = 'very low stress' to 5 = 'very high stress'.

Before we conduct a paired samples t-test the analyst could simply check the mean stress levels at Time 1 compared to Time 2.

To do this the analyst should select the following option: Analyze→ Compare Means→ Means (Figure 9.1).

Question: Are there differences in stress levels at Time 1 + Time 2?

**FIGURE 9.1**

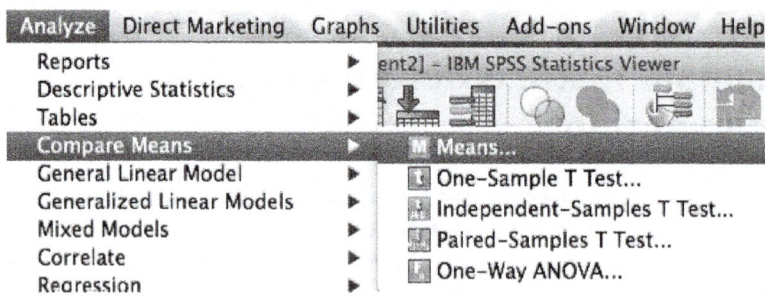

Transfer 'StressT1' and 'StressT2' into the 'Dependent List:' (Figure 9.2).

**FIGURE 9.2**

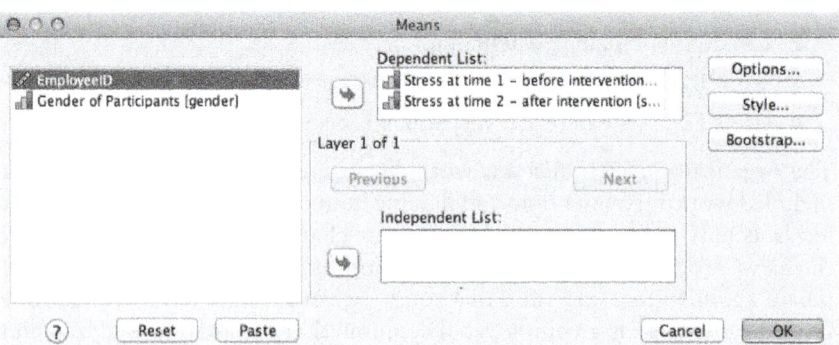

The SPSS output from this analysis (Figure 9.3) simply shows the descriptive information about the two stress level variables in the data set. The average of stress at Time 1 is 3.27 (on the 1-to-5 scale) and this is higher than at Time 2 where the average stress level is 2.90. Other information is presented, for example the N associated with the Stress 1 measure is 525. This means that of the 534 respondents in the data set, there were nine cases of missing data for this measure. At Time 2, however, the N was 300 employees, which means that a considerable number of employees who filled out the first questionnaire did not do so the second time.

**FIGURE 9.3**

**Means**

*Responded to 1st*

*534 were sent emails both times*

**Case Processing Summary**

| | Cases | | | | | |
|---|---|---|---|---|---|---|
| | Included | | Excluded | | Total | |
| | N | Per cent | N | Per cent | N | Per cent |
| Stress at time 1 – before intervention | 525 | 98.3% | 9 | 1.7% | 534 | 100.0% |
| Stress at time 2 – after intervention | 300 | 56.2% | 234 | 43.8% | 534 | 100.0% |

*Responded to 2nd*

**Report**

| | Stress at time 1 – before intervention | Stress at time 2 – after intervention |
|---|---|---|
| Mean | 3.27 | 2.90 |
| N | 525 | 300 |
| Std. Deviation | 1.051 | 1.083 |

Because of the uneven Ns across the two waves of stress data, we would have to be very careful drawing any conclusions about change in stress between Time 1 and Time 2 as these are in effect two very different groups of employees. One is made up of over 500 employees, whereas the sample of the latter time period has more than 200 fewer employees. Therefore, if we just looked at the stress level mean of the full Time 1 data and compared this to the lower stress mean at Time 2, we could not be sure as to whether the difference in the average stress levels indicates a reduction in stress or whether it indicates that the people who did not respond across both times had higher stress than those who did respond (which might actually make a lot of sense). Because of this we should really compare the two stress levels when there are 'pairs' of data at Time 1 and Time 2; when we do this we can check for the significance of the paired differences/changes that may have occurred. Simply checking for changes on one particular metric for a group of individuals over time requires a particular statistical test – here you would use a repeated/paired samples t-test. To conduct this test you click on Analyze→Compare Means→Paired-Samples T Test (Figure 9.4).

*Question: Are there significant differences in stress levels at Time 1 & Time 2?*

**FIGURE 9.4**

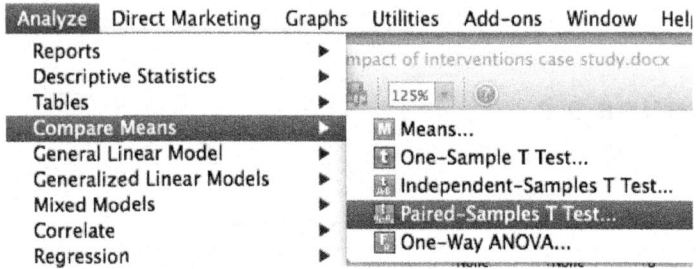

Select the 'Stress at Time 1' and 'Stress at Time 2' in the variable list and click these over as Variable 1 and Variable 2 into the 'Paired Variables:' box. Then click 'OK' (Figure 9.5).

**FIGURE 9.5**

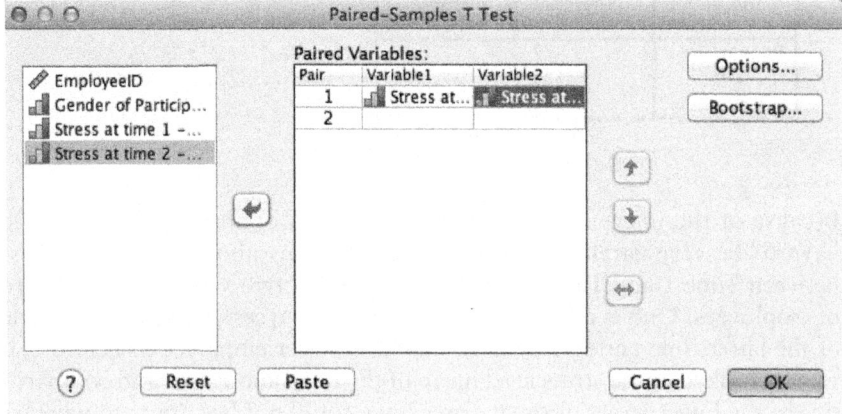

Case Study 6

The following output is produced (Figure 9.6):

**FIGURE 9.6**

*[handwritten note: 294 people did both surveys]*

**Paired Samples Statistics**

| | | Mean | N | Std. Deviation | Std. Error Mean |
|---|---|---|---|---|---|
| Pair 1 | Stress at time 1 – before intervention | 3.20 | 294 | 1.041 | .061 |
| | Stress at time 2 – after intervention | 2.90 | 294 | 1.085 | .063 |

**Paired Samples Correlations**

| | | N | Correlation | Sig. |
|---|---|---|---|---|
| Pair 1 | Stress at time 1 – before intervention and Stress at time 2 – after intervention | 294 | .209 | .000 |

**Paired Samples Test**

| | | Paired Differences | | | | | t | df | Sig. (2-tailed) |
|---|---|---|---|---|---|---|---|---|---|
| | | Mean | Std. Deviation | Std. Error Mean | 95% Confidence Interval of the Difference | | | | |
| | | | | | Lower | Upper | | | |
| Pair 1 | Stress at time 1 – before intervention – Stress at time 2 – after intervention | .306 | 1.338 | .078 | .153 | .460 | 3.923 | 293 | .000 |

The results in Figure 9.6 provide us with some key information. The 'Paired Samples Statistics' box gives the mean levels of stress at Time 1 and Time 2, the N of the 'paired data' as well as information about how the stress levels tend to vary. Interestingly we can see that the N here is 294 rather than 534 – clearly, although we have some data on 534 individuals we only managed to collect stress data at both time points from 294 employees. This means that 240 employees who responded to the survey did not complete the survey at Time 1 *and* Time 2. This is very important information that the analyst needs to bear in mind when analysing the responses; who are these 240 employees? Why did they not complete the surveys at both time points? Might there be characteristics that we could identify with this group that could have a bearing on the results? Putting these questions aside, from the 'paired' results it looks like the Time 2 mean stress level (mean = 2.90) is lower than it was at Time 1 (mean = 3.20). As these are matched pairs of stress variables, these employees seem to have shown a reduction in stress levels after the WLB programme was introduced.

Importantly, however, we need to check whether these changes are significant or not. To check for significance we look at the 'paired samples test' output. The key statistic here is the t-value of 3.923; this is the result of the t-test with 293 (df) (degrees of freedom). The test is significant at the p<0.001 level. Thus, in summary, stress levels are lower at Time 2 than Time 1, the mean stress levels reduced from 3.2 to 2.9 and this change is significant, t(293)=3.923, p<0.001. Thus, there is evidence here to suggest that the WLB intervention has had a positive impact on stress levels across the market research firm.

# Example 2: stress before and after intervention by gender

In the above analysis we conduct a straightforward t-test comparing the entire data set across the two time points. If, however, we want to check whether these differences occur with two different groups (eg males versus females) then we will need to use a more complicated analysis. The statistical test we will be using here consists of a particular subset of an analysis referred to as general linear model (GLM).

### General linear model (GLM): within and between – repeated measures

Here we are using the same data set again: 'Chapter 8 intervention WLB.sav'. You will recall that this simple data set has four variables:

1 EmployeeID.
2 Gender (1 = male; 2 = female).
3 stressT1 (1–5, where 1 = very low stress; 5 = very high stress).
4 stressT2 (1–5, where 1 = very low stress; 5 = very high stress).

Here we are going to ask SPSS to test for: a) the significance of a general change in stress levels across Time 1 and Time 2; b) any general gender differences in stress levels; and c) differences in the change in stress when comparing men with women. Thus this analysis performs a number of different statistical checks. To run the analysis, select: Analyze→General Linear Model→Repeated Measures (see Figure 9.7).

**FIGURE 9.7**

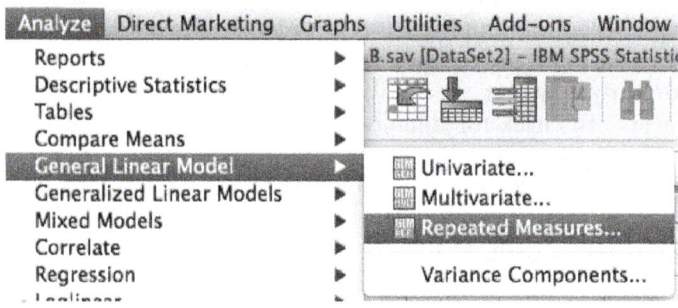

Once the following window appears (Figure 9.8), type the number 2 in the 'Number of levels:' box (signifying two time points), click the 'Add' button so that 'factor1(2)' appears in the box and then click the 'Define' button.

**FIGURE 9.8**

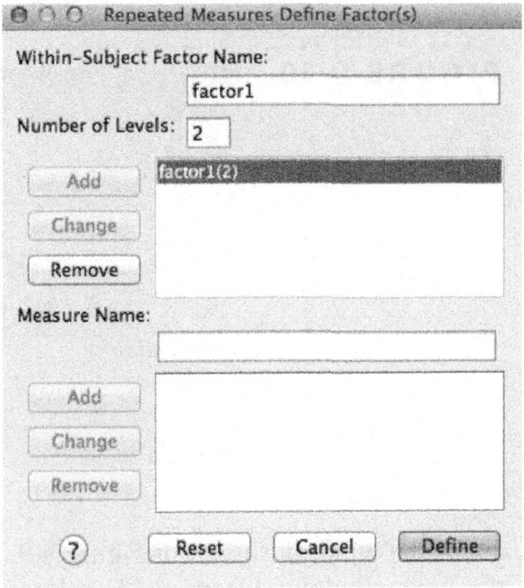

Once the following window (Figure 9.9) appears you need to select the two repeated measure variables (StressT1 and StressT2) into the 'Within-Subjects Variables (factor 1):' box and select 'Gender' into the 'Between-Subjects Factor(s):' box.

**FIGURE 9.9**

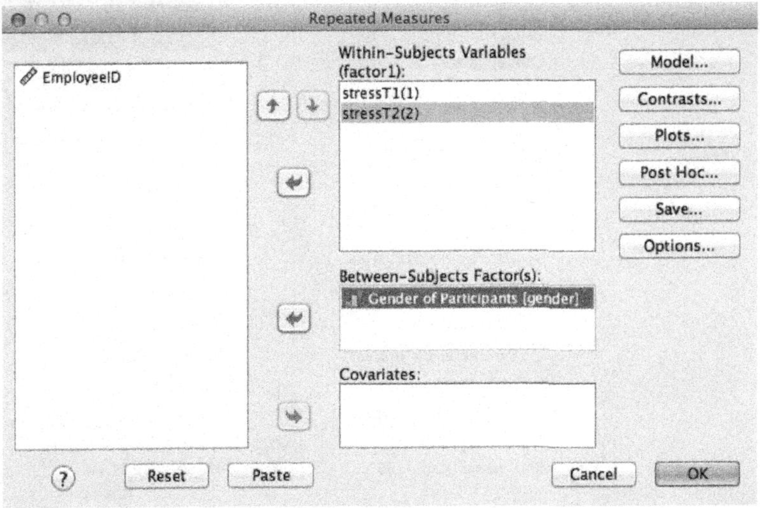

Before clicking 'OK' you need to click on the 'Plots...' button to get SPSS to provide some graphical information. In this plots window (Figure 9.10) select 'factor1' into the 'Horizontal Axis:' selection box and 'gender' into the 'Separate Lines:' selection box then click the 'Plots: Add' button so that the entry 'factor1*gender' appears in the box (see Figure 9.10) then click 'Continue'.

**FIGURE 9.10**

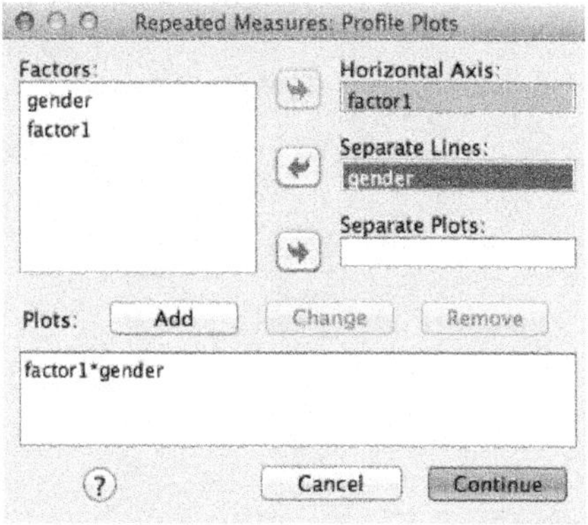

Once back in the window shown in Figure 9.9, select the 'Options' button ['EM Means'] and in the next window (Figure 9.11) select the 'gender', 'factor1', and 'gender*factor1' options into the 'Display Means for:' box. Then click 'Continue'. The 'gender*factor1' simply means showing the means of each combination of gender and factor, as you will see in the output table.

**FIGURE 9.11**

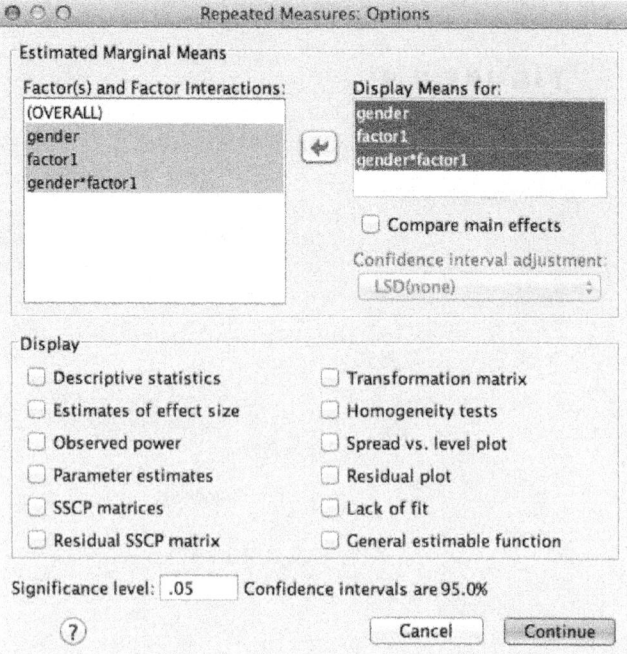

Then click 'OK' and lots of output will be produced (Figure 9.12).

**FIGURE 9.12** Estimated marginal means

1. Gender of Participants [Main effect = combining both times, females more stressed]

Measure: MEASURE_1

| Gender of Participants | Mean | Std. Error | 95% Confidence Interval | |
|---|---|---|---|---|
| | | | Lower Bound | Upper Bound |
| male | 2.902 | .074 | 2.757 | 3.048 |
| female | 3.158 | .063 | 3.035 | 3.281 |

[Stress @ time 1+2 regardless of gender]

2. factor1

Measure: MEASURE_1

| factor1 | Mean | Std. Error | 95% Confidence Interval | |
|---|---|---|---|---|
| | | | Lower Bound | Upper Bound |
| 1 | 3.169 | .060 | 3.050 | 3.287 |
| 2 | 2.892 | .064 | 2.765 | 3.018 |

[This shows decrease over time]

3. Gender of Participants * factor1

Measure: MEASURE_1

| Gender of Participants | factor1 | Mean | Std. Error | 95% Confidence Interval | |
|---|---|---|---|---|---|
| | | | | Lower Bound | Upper Bound |
| male | 1 | 2.951 | .092 | 2.770 | 3.132 |
| | 2 | 2.854 | .098 | 2.661 | 3.046 |
| female | 1 | 3.386 | .078 | 3.232 | 3.540 |
| | 2 | 2.930 | .083 | 2.766 | 3.093 |

[Females seem to decrease over time more, now test sig.]

The 'Estimated Marginal Means' output in Figure 9.12 tells you a number of important things. First, that the average stress levels of males is 2.902 and 3.158 for females when you combine the two sets of temporal stress data together. This is called a main effect of gender and the means indicate that females in general seem to express higher stress levels than males. The second box presents the mean stress levels at the first and second levels of the 'time' 'factor1' – in other words stress levels at Time 1 compared to Time 2 regardless of gender; the means indicate that the stress levels in general have gone down between Time 1 and Time 2. The third set of means separates the males and the females and presents their mean levels of stress at the two temporal factor levels (Time 1 and Time 2). As you can see, the average stress levels of males goes down slightly from 2.953 at Time 1 to 2.854 at Time 2, and for females the stress levels go down from 3.386 at Time 1 to 2.930 at Time 2. These means are also presented in the mean plots (see Figure 9.13).

**FIGURE 9.13** Profile plots

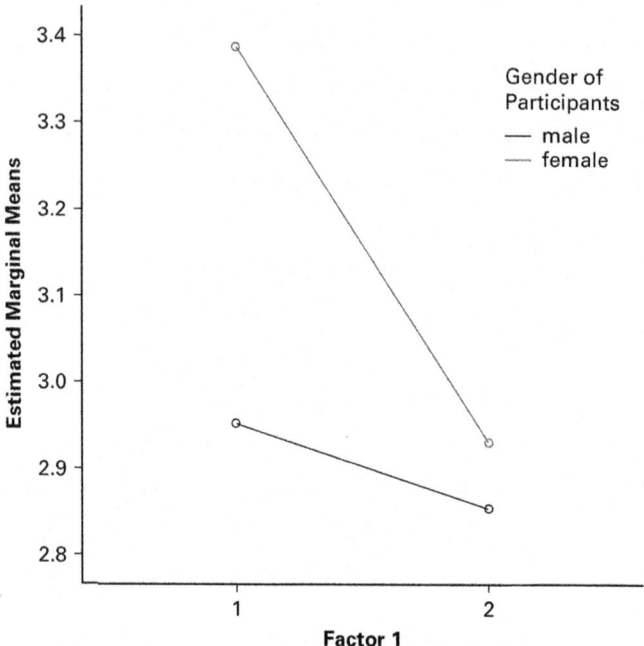

The plot visually represents what has happened with stress in our organization across time and between genders. Importantly we need to check various aspects of these findings (gender differences in stress in general, temporal changes in stress in general across time, and temporal changes in stress across time when comparing men with women). To assess this we need to look at the remaining results (Figure 9.14), in particular the 'Tests of Within-Subjects Effects', the 'Tests of Within-Subjects Contrasts' (these two sets of results give the same results here because we only have two time periods – to be discussed later) and the 'Tests of Between-Subjects Effects'.

To interpret these results let us first look at the 'Tests of Within-Subjects Contrasts'. The: 'factor1 Linear' row reports an F of 12.430 with a significance of $p<0.001$. This is very similar to the paired samples t-test conducted above and it tells us that the general change (drop in this case) in stress over time is significant. The 'Tests of Between-Subjects Effects' results show that the 'gender' row has an F of 6.971, which is significant to the level of $p<0.01$. This indicates that in general (when combining Time 1 and Time 2 results), men report significantly less stress than women. Finally, the 'factor1*gender Linear' row of the 'Tests of Within-Subjects Contrasts' has an F of 5.213

## FIGURE 9.14

*change in stress is sig.*

**Tests of Within-Subjects Effects**

Measure: MEASURE_1

| Source | | Type III Sum of Squares | df | Mean Square | F | Sig. |
|---|---|---|---|---|---|---|
| factor1 | Sphericity Assumed | 10.967 | 1 | 10.967 | 12.430 | .000 |
| | Greenhouse-Geisser | 10.967 | 1.000 | 10.967 | 12.430 | .000 |
| | Huynh-Feldt | 10.967 | 1.000 | 10.967 | 12.430 | .000 |
| | Lower-bound | 10.967 | 1.000 | 10.967 | 12.430 | .000 |
| factor1 * gender | Sphericity Assumed | 4.599 | 1 | 4.599 | 5.213 | .023 |
| | Greenhouse-Geisser | 4.599 | 1.000 | 4.599 | 5.213 | .023 |
| | Huynh-Feldt | 4.599 | 1.000 | 4.599 | 5.213 | .023 |
| | Lower-bound | 4.599 | 1.000 | 4.599 | 5.213 | .023 |
| Error(factor1) | Sphericity Assumed | 257.625 | 292 | .882 | | |
| | Greenhouse-Geisser | 257.625 | 292.000 | .882 | | |
| | Huynh-Feldt | 257.625 | 292.000 | .882 | | |
| | Lower-bound | 257.625 | 292.000 | .882 | | |

*The change over time by gender is sig.*

**Tests of Within-Subjects Contrasts**

Measure: MEASURE_1

| Source | factor1 | Type III Sum of Squares | df | Mean Square | F | Sig. |
|---|---|---|---|---|---|---|
| factor1 | Linear | 10.967 | 1 | 10.967 | 12.430 | .000 |
| factor1 * gender | Linear | 4.599 | 1 | 4.599 | 5.213 | .023 |
| Error(factor1) | Linear | 257.625 | 292 | .882 | | |

**Tests of Between-Subjects Effects**

Measure: MEASURE_1
Transformed Variable: Average

| Source | Type III Sum of Squares | df | Mean Square | F | Sig. |
|---|---|---|---|---|---|
| Intercept | 5255.051 | 1 | 5255.051 | 3923.162 | .000 |
| gender | 9.337 | 1 | 9.337 | 6.971 | .009 |
| Error | 391.132 | 292 | 1.339 | | |

?

and this is significant at the p<0.05 level. This information is key here, as combined with the plot presented in Figure 9.13 it tells us that females show a significant reduction in stress between Time 1 and Time 2 at a significantly greater level of change than the reduction that men seemed to show between Time 1 and Time 2; this suggests that there is a significant 'interaction' between gender and change in stress across Time 1 and Time 2.

> **Snapshot hidden gem**
>
> Whilst employees in our market research firm show a marked reduction in stress levels when you compare stress before the WLB programme is introduced with stress after, the positive impact on stress levels that this HR intervention has on workforce stress levels seems to be much greater with female rather than male employees. Analytics indicate that the HR intervention has had a positive impact on well-being.

## Example 3: value-change initiative

The following example takes us through a scenario where a financial advisory company wants to introduce a new set of socially responsible corporate values and is investing in a 'Values Festival' event, which involves a full day of activities (that all employees participate in) where the new values, and how they translate into everyday behaviour, are introduced:

*'Our Values'*
*RESPECT for Key Stakeholders:*
*Communities, Customers, Shareholders and Employees*

Because the organization is investing a considerable sum of money into this activity, the management want to make sure that the values take hold. Therefore they ask their engagement survey (six-monthly panel) provider to include some questions that can give an indication of the level of employee commitment to these new values. Just before the values event, the managers (who wanted to check for the impact of the values festival) were able to include a set of questions in this externally organized survey sent to a random sample of the organization (800 employees from four key strategically important functions within the organization). The employees were sent the online questionnaires six months later and then another six months after this. The following items were included (note that the name of the organization has been replaced with 'ORG'):

1. In my actions I am always respectful of the local communities associated with ORG
2. In my actions I am always respectful of ORG's customers
3. In my actions I am always respectful of ORG's shareholders
4. In my actions I am always respectful of ORG's employees.

An anonymized data set has been provided to the HR analytics team. This data includes three waves of data collection with 438 employees from the panel; the data can be found in the following SPSS data set: 'Chapter 9 value change.sav'.

Here there are 16 variables, the first of which (FUNCTION) outlines which of four functions the employee works for (HQ Admin, Sales, HR, Marketing). Twelve of the variables include employee responses to the four individual value questions for each of the three waves. The final three variables are average composite measures of the four items for each of the waves:

1. FUNCTION (department the employee works in 1: HQ Admin; 2: Sales; 3: HR; 4: Marketing).
2. Vals1t1 (value commitment community Time 1).
3. Vals2t1 (value commitment customers Time 1).
4. Vals3t1 (value commitment shareholders Time 1).
5. Vals4t1 (value commitment employees Time 1).
6. Vals1t2 (value commitment community Time 2).
7. Vals2t2 (value commitment customers Time 2).
8. Vals3t2 (value commitment shareholders Time 2).
9. Vals4t2 (value commitment employees Time 2).
10. Vals1t3 (value commitment community Time 3).
11. Vals2t3 (value commitment customers Time 3).
12. Vals3t3 (value commitment shareholders Time 3).
13. Vals4t3 (value commitment employees Time 3).
14. ValsCompositeT1 (composite of the four value commitment items at Time 1).
15. ValsCompositeT2 (composite of the four value commitment items at Time 2).
16. ValsCompositeT3 (composite of the four value commitment items at Time 3).

*Vals1 = community*
*Vals2 = customers*
*Vals3 = shareholders*
*Vals4 = employees*

## General linear model (GLM): repeated measures

The first analysis that we do here is to see whether the staff commitment to the values changes over time; if the value-change programme is to have an impact on staff then we would hope to see an increase in the commitment over the three waves of data collection. Here, we need to test for a significant change over time in the three sets of values, and we use the three composite measures of value commitment six months apart. The statistical analysis that we use for this is GLM repeated measures. To conduct this analysis click on: Analyze→General Linear Model→Repeated Measures (Figure 9.15).

① *Question: Change in values over time?*

**FIGURE 9.15**

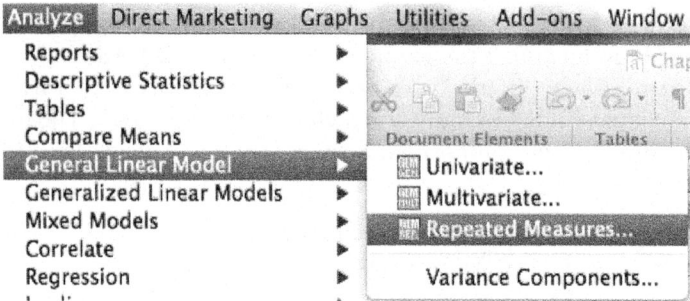

When the following window appears (Figure 9.16) type 'Values' in the 'Within-Subject Factor Name:' box and enter '3' in the 'Number of Levels:' box, then click the 'Add' button so that 'Values(3)' appears in the selection box. Then click 'Define'.

**FIGURE 9.16**

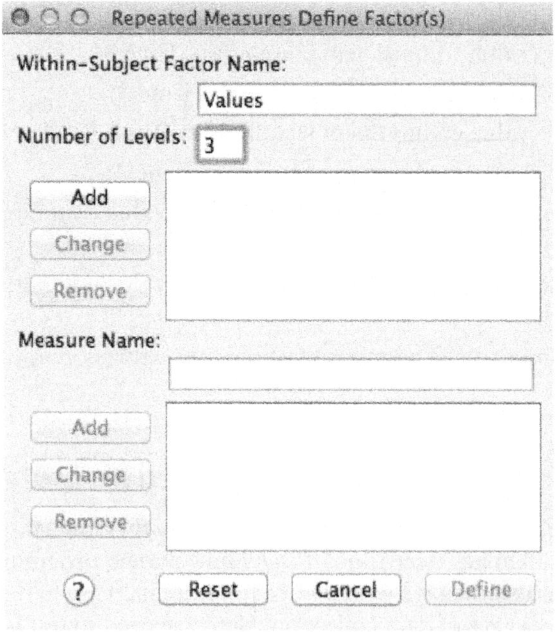

Once you have clicked 'Define', the following window will appear (Figure 9.17); in this you should select the variables 'ValsCompositeT1', 'ValsCompositeT2' and 'ValsCompositeT3' into the 'Within-Subjects Variables (Values):' selection box. The (1), (2) and (3) following the variables once selected represent the three levels of this values variables; they represent the three waves of data collection for values. Once these have been selected click the 'Plots...' button.

**FIGURE 9.17**

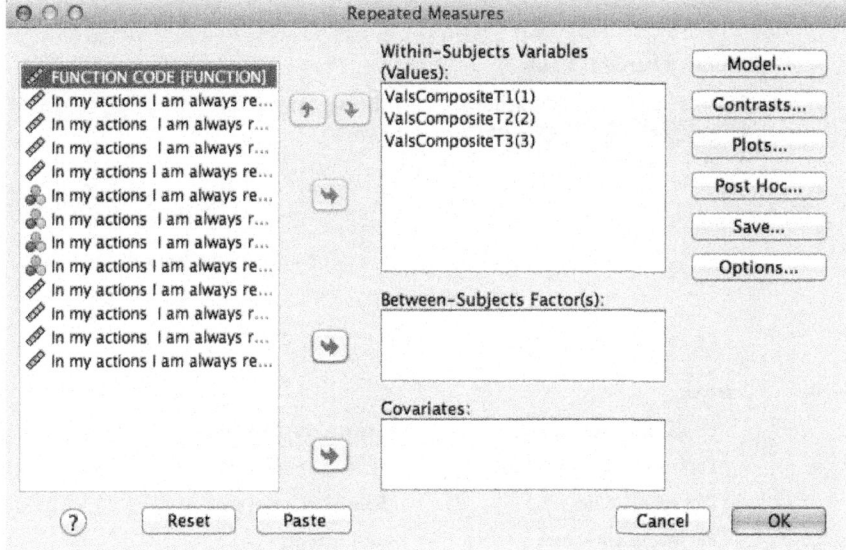

The window in Figure 9.18 will appear; here you should select the 'Values' factor and insert it into the 'Horizontal Axis:' selection box. Then click 'Add', then click 'Continue'.

**FIGURE 9.18**

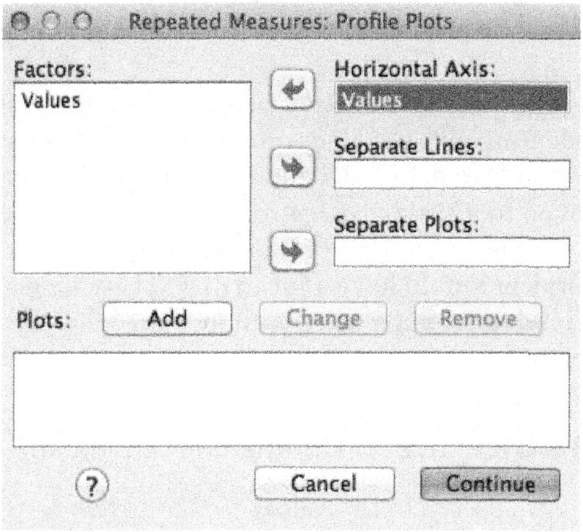

Once Figure 9.17 appears again select the 'Options' button ['EM Means'] and the following window appears (Figure 9.19); here select 'Values' factor into the 'Display Means for:' selection box then click 'Continue'.

**FIGURE 9.19**

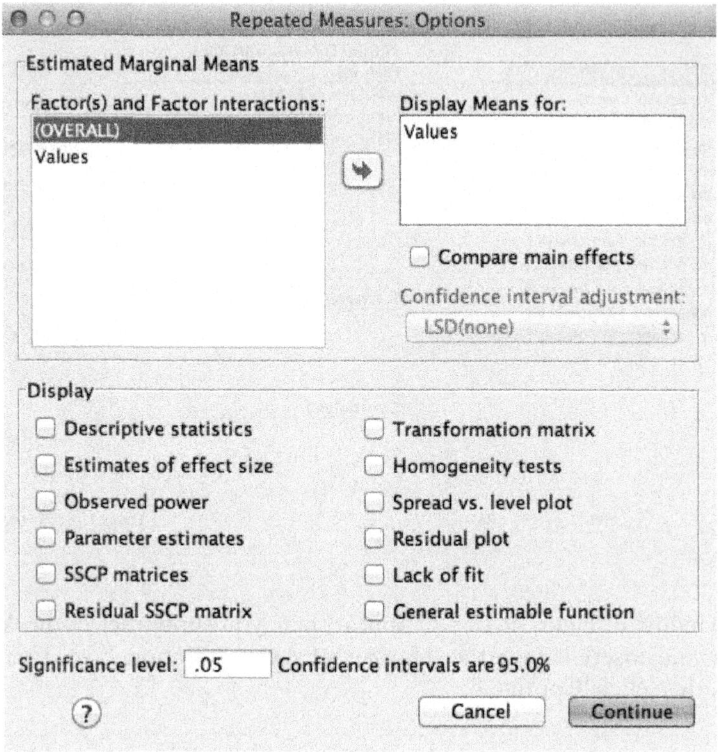

*[Screenshot of SPSS "Repeated Measures: Options" dialog box. Estimated Marginal Means section shows Factor(s) and Factor Interactions: (OVERALL), Values; Display Means for: Values. Checkbox options include Compare main effects, Confidence interval adjustment: LSD(none). Display section has checkboxes for: Descriptive statistics, Estimates of effect size, Observed power, Parameter estimates, SSCP matrices, Residual SSCP matrix, Transformation matrix, Homogeneity tests, Spread vs. level plot, Residual plot, Lack of fit, General estimable function. Significance level: .05. Confidence intervals are 95.0%. Buttons: Cancel, Continue.]*

Once Figure 9.17 appears again click 'OK' to run the analysis. Now a whole series of output will be produced. We will look at important elements of this one at a time.

<u>First let's look at the average level of value commitment over the three time points.</u> The mean level of value commitment (see Figure 9.20) increases from 4.112 at Time 1, to 4.122 at Time 2 and finally 4.188 at Time 3. These averages are linked to a scale of 1 = strongly disagree to 5 = strongly agree; so, in general, people are fairly committed to each of the values; neutral levels of commitment would have a mean of 3. <u>These increases do not seem too large in themselves, though there is an increase (that we will need to test for significance).</u>

**FIGURE 9.20** Estimated marginal means

Values

Measure: MEASURE_1

| Values | Mean | Std. Error | 95% Confidence Interval | |
|---|---|---|---|---|
| | | | Lower Bound | Upper Bound |
| 1 | 4.112 | .022 | 4.069 | 4.154 |
| 2 | 4.122 | .024 | 4.076 | 4.169 |
| 3 | 4.188 | .022 | 4.145 | 4.230 |

*Increasing over time*

In the mean plots (see Figure 9.21) we can see the increase visually; there seems to be a steeper increase in commitment in the later six-month period compared to the slight increase in the first six-month period.

**FIGURE 9.21**   Profile plots

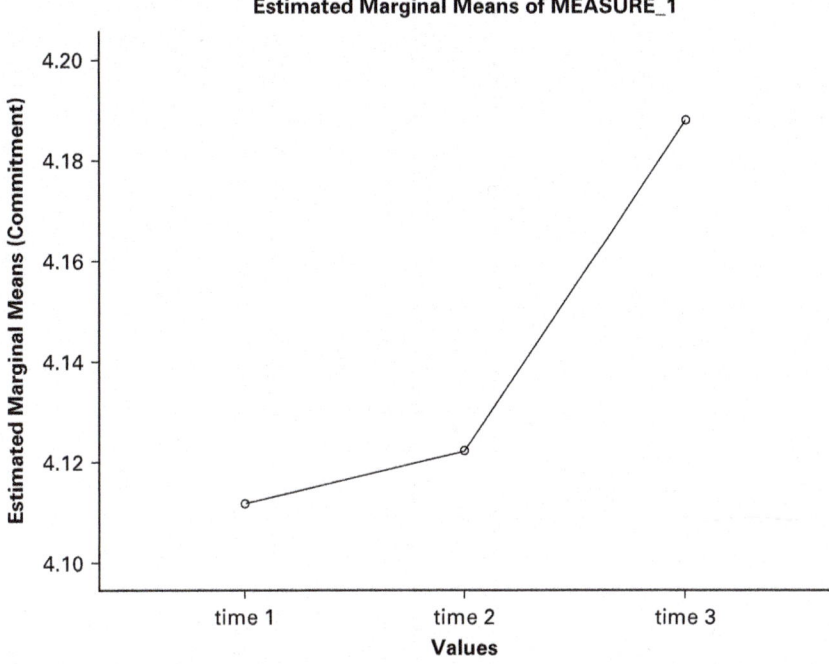

The first statistical result we should look at is the Mauchly's 'Test of Sphericity' (see Figure 9.22).

The repeated measures ANOVA test makes the assumption of something called sphericity. Sphericity is the assumption that the variance of the differences between each pair of scores is equal. So in our example, the test of sphericity is testing for whether the variance of the difference between scores at Time 1 and at Time 2 is the same as the variance of the difference between scores at Time 1 and at Time 3, and the same as the variance of the difference between scores at Time 2 and at Time 3. This test applies when there are more than two points of data from the same participant (just as we have here with data from the same people at more than two time points). The Mauchly test, then, explores whether the variance patterns of the differences between the sets of time-point data look different (when looking at particular combinations of time-point data). If the test is violated, SPSS will run similar (robust) statistical tests alongside the within-subjects ANOVA part of the test, namely the Greenhouse-Guisser and the Huynh-Feldt tests, which should be used (if the Mauchly test for sphericity is significant, which ideally we do not want it to be).

## FIGURE 9.22

Measure: MEASURE_1

**Mauchly's Test of Sphericity**[a]

| Within Subjects Effect | Mauchly's W | Approx. Chi-Square | df | Sig. | Epsilon[b] | | |
|---|---|---|---|---|---|---|---|
| | | | | | Greenhouse-Geisser | Huynh-Feldt | Lower-bound |
| Values | .979 | 9.310 | 2 | .010 | .979 | .984 | .500 |

Tests the null hypothesis that the error covariance matrix of the orthonormalized transformed dependent variables is proportional to an identity matrix.

a. Design: Intercept
   Within Subjects Design: Values

b. May be used to adjust the degrees of freedom for the averaged tests of significance. Corrected tests are displayed in the Tests of Within-Subjects Effects table.

So, once again, the test for sphericity examines whether the pattern of differences across the different sets of repeated measures violates the assumption of sphericity. Ideally we do not want this test to be significant, as it would be saying that the variance of differences in our data looks unusual when you compare across the particular time phases. In our case, Mauchly's test is significant (Figure 9.22, p<0.05). Because of this, when considering whether the repeated measures of value commitment change significantly over time we need to consider the Huynh-Feldt row of results in the top box of our 'Tests of Within-Subjects Effects' (Figure 9.23) – the set of results we need to look at has 'Values' in the 'Source' box. If our Mauchly test was not significant we would refer to the row of results 'Sphericity Assumed'; however, as Mauchly's test was significant we check the Huynh-Feldt row, which has an F of 6.159 that is significant at p<0.01, so repeated measures ANOVA (the Huynh-Feldt) is significant.

Thus we can say that our results change over the three time points. We see a significant increase in value commitment across the 12-month period here. The second set of results here test for a linear versus quadratic (curvilinear)

**FIGURE 9.23**

Tests of Within-Subjects Effects

Measure: MEASURE_1

| Source | | Type III Sum of Squares | df | Mean Square | F | Sig. |
|---|---|---|---|---|---|---|
| Values | Sphericity Assumed | 1.476 | 2 | .738 | 6.159 | .002 |
| | Greenhouse-Geisser | 1.476 | 1.958 | .754 | 6.159 | .002 |
| | Huynh-Feldt | 1.476 | 1.967 | .750 | 6.159 | .002 |
| | Lower-bound | 1.476 | 1.000 | 1.476 | 6.159 | .013 |
| Error(Values) | Sphericity Assumed | 103.756 | 866 | .120 | | |
| | Greenhouse-Geisser | 103.756 | 847.921 | .122 | | |
| | Huynh-Feldt | 103.756 | 851.732 | .122 | | |
| | Lower-bound | 103.756 | 433.000 | .240 | | |

Tests of Within-Subjects Contrasts

Measure: MEASURE_1

| Source | Values | Type III Sum of Squares | df | Mean Square | F | Sig. |
|---|---|---|---|---|---|---|
| Values | Linear | 1.255 | 1 | 1.255 | 11.231 | .001 |
| | Quadratic | .221 | 1 | .221 | 1.729 | .189 |
| Error(Values) | Linear | 48.370 | 433 | .112 | | |
| | Quadratic | 55.385 | 433 | .128 | | |

Tests of Between-Subjects Effects

Measure: MEASURE_1
Transformed Variable: Average

| Source | Type III Sum of Squares | df | Mean Square | F | Sig. |
|---|---|---|---|---|---|
| Intercept | 22321.721 | 1 | 22321.721 | 54395.360 | .000 |
| Error | 177.686 | 433 | .410 | | |

change over time. The results from the 'Tests of Within-Subjects Contrasts' show that there is a linear increase over time (F=11.231, p<0.001) but not a quadratic increase (F=1.728, p>0.05). A significant quadratic effect would suggest that the nature of the change across the sets of time comparisons was significantly different (this might happen if value commitment went up between Time 1 and Time 2 but down between Time 2 and Time 3); something like this this did not happen here as the changes were consistently upward.

The finding here is that, across the three waves of data collection, commitment to the company's new values appears to increase steadily. This provides evidence that the values are potentially being embedded within the workforce.

Something that is important to check for, however, is whether this value 'embedding' is found across all parts of the workforce (such as the different functions).

## Example 4: value-change initiative by department

In Example 2, we tested for a change in stress across different groups (male/female) within our workforce. Here, we can conduct an analysis that examines whether the value commitment change we witness over time occurs within different groups of workers. For this we use a GLM repeated measures – within and between test (where the value commitment measures are the repeated 'within' element and the functions are the 'between' group comparison element).

### General linear model (GLM): within and between repeated measures

The statistical analysis that we use for this is GLM repeated measures. To conduct this analysis click on: Analyze→General Linear Model→Repeated Measures (see Figure 9.15 above). As with example 3, the 'Repeated Measures Define Factor(s)' window appears (as with Figure 9.16) and you need to type 'Values' in the 'Within-Subject Factor Name:' box and enter '3' in the 'Number of Levels:' box, then click ' Add' so that 'Values(3)' appears in the selection box. Then click 'Define'. Figure 9.24 appears; in this you should select the variables 'ValsCompositeT1', 'ValsCompositeT2' and 'ValsCompositeT3' into the 'Within-Subjects Variables (Values):' selection box (as above). Then you should select the 'FUNCTION' variable into the 'Between-Subjects Factor(s)' selection box. Once these have been selected click the 'Plots...' button.

## Case Study 6

**FIGURE 9.24**

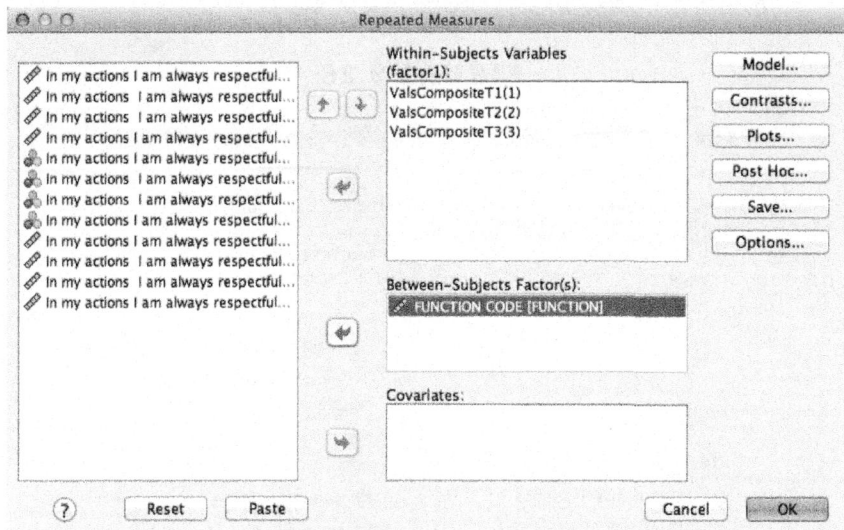

In the 'Repeated Measures: Profile Plots' window (see Figure 9.25) select the 'Values' factor into the 'Horizontal Axis:' selection box and the 'FUNCTION' factor into the 'Separate Lines:' selection box. Then click 'Add'. Once 'Values*FUNCTION' appears in the selection box click 'Continue'.

**FIGURE 9.25**

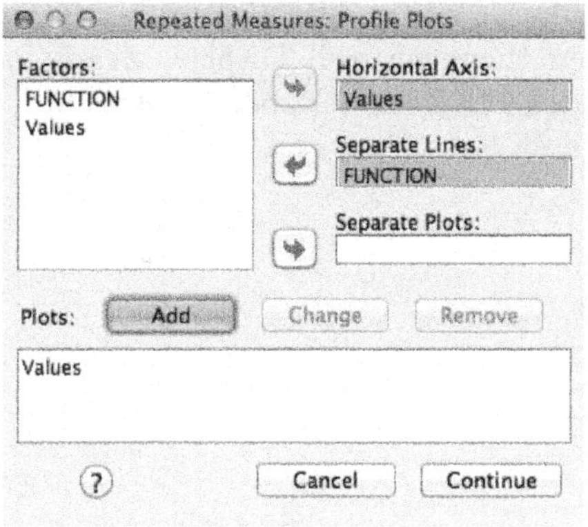

Once back in the main 'Repeated Measures' window (Figure 9.24 above) select the 'Options' button and Figure 9.26 will appear.

[handwritten annotation: 'EM Means']

**FIGURE 9.26**

[Screenshot of Repeated Measures: Options dialog box showing Estimated Marginal Means section with Factor(s) and Factor Interactions list containing (OVERALL), FUNCTION, Values, FUNCTION*Values, and Display Means for box containing Values, FUNCTION, FUNCTION*Values. Compare main effects checkbox with Confidence interval adjustment: LSD(none). Display section with checkboxes for Descriptive statistics, Estimates of effect size, Observed power, Parameter estimates, SSCP matrices, Residual SSCP matrix, Transformation matrix, Homogeneity tests, Spread vs. level plot, Residual plot, Lack of fit, General estimable function. Significance level: .05, Confidence intervals are 95.0%. Cancel and Continue buttons.]

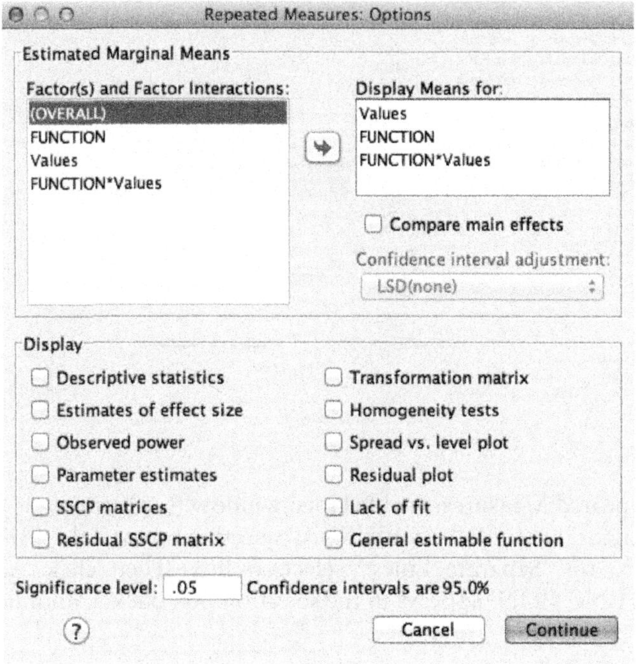

Here select the 'Values', 'FUNCTION' and 'FUNCTION*Values' factor selections and insert them into the 'Display Means for:' box. Then click 'Continue'. Once back in the main 'Repeated Measures' window click 'OK'. Your analysis will now run.

**FIGURE 9.27** Estimated marginal means

**1. Values**  *General mean for 3 times*

Measure: MEASURE_1

| Values | Mean | Std. Error | 95% Confidence Interval | |
|---|---|---|---|---|
| | | | Lower Bound | Upper Bound |
| 1 | 4.081 | .030 | 4.021 | 4.141 |
| 2 | 4.092 | .033 | 4.027 | 4.157 |
| 3 | 4.209 | .031 | 4.149 | 4.269 |

**2. FUNCTION CODE**

Measure: MEASURE_1

| FUNCTION CODE | Mean | Std. Error | 95% Confidence Interval | |
|---|---|---|---|---|
| | | | Lower Bound | Upper Bound |
| HQ | 4.072 | .026 | 4.022 | 4.123 |
| SALES | 4.156 | .054 | 4.051 | 4.261 |
| HR | 4.233 | .028 | 4.177 | 4.288 |
| MARKETING | 4.049 | .074 | 3.903 | 4.194 |

*General diff. in means across functions*

**3. FUNCTION CODE * Values**

Measure: MEASURE_1

| FUNCTION CODE | Values | Mean | Std. Error | 95% Confidence Interval | |
|---|---|---|---|---|---|
| | | | | Lower Bound | Upper Bound |
| HQ | 1 | 4.050 | .032 | 3.988 | 4.112 |
| | 2 | 4.035 | .034 | 3.968 | 4.102 |
| | 3 | 4.132 | .032 | 4.070 | 4.195 |
| SALES | 1 | 4.054 | .066 | 3.925 | 4.183 |
| | 2 | 4.098 | .071 | 3.958 | 4.238 |
| | 3 | 4.315 | .066 | 4.185 | 4.445 |
| HR | 1 | 4.220 | .035 | 4.151 | 4.288 |
| | 2 | 4.256 | .038 | 4.182 | 4.330 |
| | 3 | 4.223 | .035 | 4.154 | 4.291 |
| MARKETING | 1 | 4.000 | .091 | 3.821 | 4.179 |
| | 2 | 3.979 | .099 | 3.786 | 4.173 |
| | 3 | 4.167 | .091 | 3.987 | 4.346 |

The first set of information that we would probably want to look at here (Figure 9.27) is the means for the three sets of value commitment measures across the three occasions and the value commitment means associated with the four functions. The top set of means presented in Figure 9.27 sets out the average value commitment levels across the three separate occasions. As with before there is some increase between Time 1 and Time 2 but a greater increase occurs between the second and third phases of data collection. It is worth noting here that the means are slightly different to the results presented in the previous analysis; this is because we were not previously including information on function, which may have some missing data. Whenever variables are combined with another variable in GLM analysis there is always the possibility that statistics from the samples might vary, as missing data alters the actual sample being used each time. It is important that you are sensitive to these issues. The second set of results in Figure 9.27

shows that there are some differences in the means across the functions (in general; disregarding the temporal differences) with the mean level of value commitment being highest in the HR function and the lowest in the Marketing function. However, when we look at the third set of results we see that the means of the value commitment differ quite a bit across the three waves depending upon what function we are considering. For example, the HQ row shows a very slight dip between waves 1 and 2 and an increase between waves 2 and 3; the Sales function shows a general increase across all three waves. To further understand the apparent patterns of change we can look at the plot (Figure 9.28) below.

**FIGURE 9.28**  Estimated marginal means of MEASURE_1

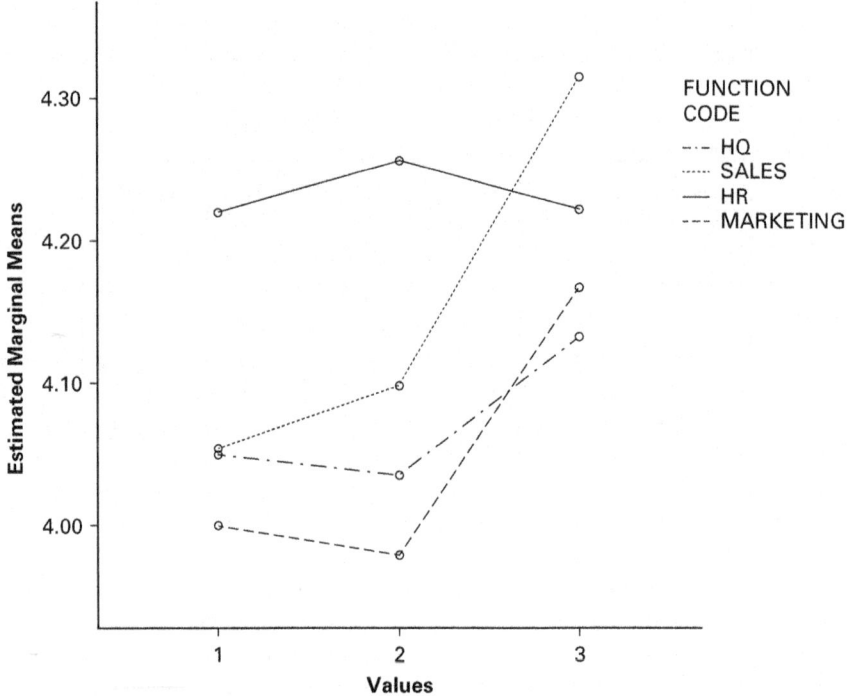

From the looks of this graph the four functions have slightly different trajectories of change across the three time periods, which may hold some important information if we want to understand the impact of the value-change event (which occurred between waves 1 and 2). However, we need to test for significant differences across the waves, taking into account the differences across the functions. Before we interpret the analysis we need to consider the fact that the Mauchly test for sphericity (Figure 9.29) is again significant ($p<0.05$) and we need to take this into account when selecting which results to interpret (Figure 9.30).

④ Question: Is there sig diff across job function?

## FIGURE 9.29

**Mauchly's Test of Sphericity[a]**

Measure: MEASURE_1

| Within Subjects Effect | Mauchly's W | Approx. Chi-Square | df | Sig. | Epsilon[b] Greenhouse-Geisser | Huynh-Feldt | Lower-bound |
|---|---|---|---|---|---|---|---|
| Values | .981 | 8.196 | 2 | .017 | .981 | .993 | .500 |

Tests the null hypothesis that the error covariance matrix of the orthonormalized transformed dependent variables is proportional to an identity matrix.

a. Design: Intercept + FUNCTION
   Within Subjects Design: Values

b. May be used to adjust the degrees of freedom for the averaged tests of significance. Corrected tests are displayed in the Tests of Within-Subjects Effects table.

## FIGURE 9.30

**Tests of Within-Subjects Effects**

Measure: MEASURE_1

| Source | | Type III Sum of Squares | df | Mean Square | F | Sig. |
|---|---|---|---|---|---|---|
| Values | Sphericity Assumed | 2.170 | 2 | 1.085 | 9.176 | .000 |
| | Greenhouse-Geisser | 2.170 | 1.963 | 1.106 | 9.176 | .000 |
| | Huynh-Feldt | 2.170 | 1.986 | 1.093 | 9.176 | .000 |
| | Lower-bound | 2.170 | 1.000 | 2.170 | 9.176 | .003 |
| Values * FUNCTION | Sphericity Assumed | 2.066 | 6 | .344 | 2.912 | .008 |
| | Greenhouse-Geisser | 2.066 | 5.889 | .351 | 2.912 | .009 |
| | Huynh-Feldt | 2.066 | 5.957 | .347 | 2.912 | .008 |
| | Lower-bound | 2.066 | 3.000 | .689 | 2.912 | .034 |
| Error(Values) | Sphericity Assumed | 101.690 | 860 | .118 | | |
| | Greenhouse-Geisser | 101.690 | 844.028 | .120 | | |
| | Huynh-Feldt | 101.690 | 853.777 | .119 | | |
| | Lower-bound | 101.690 | 430.000 | .236 | | |

*[handwritten: There are sig diffs in values across functions]*

**Tests of Within-Subjects Contrasts**

Measure: MEASURE_1

| Source | Values | Type III Sum of Squares | df | Mean Square | F | Sig. |
|---|---|---|---|---|---|---|
| Values | Linear | 1.767 | 1 | 1.767 | 16.148 | .000 |
| | Quadratic | .403 | 1 | .403 | 3.174 | .076 |
| Values * FUNCTION | Linear | 1.325 | 3 | .442 | 4.038 | .008 |
| | Quadratic | .741 | 3 | .247 | 1.943 | .122 |
| Error(Values) | Linear | 47.045 | 430 | .109 | | |
| | Quadratic | 54.645 | 430 | .127 | | |

*[handwritten: Linear sig diff; No quadratic sig diff; sig interaction]*

**Tests of Between-Subjects Effects** — *[handwritten: similar to one-way ANOVA]*

Measure: MEASURE_1
Transformed Variable: Average

| Source | Type III Sum of Squares | df | Mean Square | F | Sig. |
|---|---|---|---|---|---|
| Intercept | 10975.396 | 1 | 10975.396 | 27747.090 | .000 |
| FUNCTION | 7.599 | 3 | 2.533 | 6.404 | .000 |
| Error | 170.087 | 430 | .396 | | |

*[handwritten: sig diffs between the 4 functions]*

When considering whether the repeated measures of value commitment change significantly over time we again need to consider the Huynh-Feldt row of results in the top box of our 'Tests of Within-Subjects Effects' (Figure 9.30) – the set of results we need to look at has 'Values' in the 'Source' box. If our Mauchly test was not significant we would refer to the row of results 'Sphericity Assumed'; however, Huynh-Feldt row has an F of 9.176, which is significant at $p<0.001$. Thus we can say that our results change over the three time points. So we see a significant increase in value commitment across the 12-month period here (we would expect this from the above findings).

Before we move on to see whether there are differences in changes across time in value commitment when comparing our functions, we should look at whether there are significant differences between the value commitment of the four functions in general. For this, we look at the between-subjects set of results. The 'Tests of Between-Subjects Effects' in Figure 9.30 shows that the general differences across the functions are significant ($F=6.404$, $p<0.001$); this part of the test is similar to a one-way ANOVA result that we looked at in Chapter 6 (page 203).

As we know that there are significant general changes across time in the value commitment measures, we now will want to test for the pattern of the change in general. The second set of results in the output test for a linear versus quadratic (curvilinear) change over time. The results from the 'Tests of Within-Subjects Contrasts' show that there is a linear increase over time ($F=16.148$, $p<0.001$) but not a quadratic increase ($F=3.17$, $p>0.05$).

The next thing we need to consider is how our patterns of change over time vary across the different functions. The second row in our first set of results in Figure 9.30, 'Tests of Within-Subjects Effects', which has 'Values* FUNCTION' in the output shows us that there is a significant interaction between function and value change (Huynh-Feldt – $F = 2.912$, $p<0.01$). This indicates that we can confidently say that there are significant differences in the changes in value commitment when we compare our four functions; our plot graph above (Figure 9.28) helps explain the pattern that we find. The second piece of analysis (the second row block) presented in the 'Tests of Within-Subjects Contrasts' set indicate that there is a significant interaction between the linear change effects and the function (Values*Function Linear $F=4.038$, $p<0.01$); this makes sense as there is clearly less of a linear increase in the value commitment with the HR function (that does not really increase much over the three periods) compared to say the Sales function (that shows a greater increase). However, there is no significant interaction between quadratic effects and function (Values*Function Quadratic $F=1.943$, $p>0.05$); this suggests that the nature of any change in commitment to the values does not change dramatically across the four functions.

The brief summary given in the 'hidden gem' actually requires some context to be able to understand fully what is going on. To some extent the HR function might be a little disappointed that there was not an immediate increase in value commitment between the first and the second wave of data collection; however, the circumstances of the organizational context were such that a new performance appraisal system that included judging employees

> **Snapshot hidden gem**
>
> We find that in our organization the introduction of new socially responsible corporate values is followed by an increase in staff commitment to these values; however, we find that the increase varies across the functions – HR generally shows a steady high level of commitment but all other functions show an increase. The sales team in particular started with the lowest level of commitment but increased considerably over the 12-month period.

on whether they showed commitment to the values of the organization was introduced between the second and third waves. Thus it makes sense that the value commitment was found in the long term once this performance-appraisal value benchmark was introduced. When examining changes over time it is always important to consider what events were going on during the time of data collection; contextual information is often important to consider when interpreting change over time.

Before we move on from this example, one thing we need to consider is the nature of the sample that we are effectively analysing. In the frequency output in Figure 9.31, it is clear that the sample sizes in our four functions vary considerably. The Marketing group has only 24 employees, the financial Sales group has only 46 employees, the HR function has 164 and HQ has 200. Whilst we can be confident that the panel results do show significant changes over time, an analyst will need to consider the degree to which there may be something meaningful in the pattern of responses that have been provided for analysis. The analyst will need to check a number of things. The first thing to check is the relative size of the four functions in the organization itself. Second, the degree to which these differences in employee numbers across the functions in the data set represent the variation in relative size of the functions in both the organization itself and target population that the survey company sampled from. If these proportions are not in line with what is expected then further investigation needs to be carried out to understand why these samples vary as they do.

**FIGURE 9.31**

Between-Subjects Factors

|  |  | Value Label | N |
|---|---|---|---|
| FUNCTION CODE | 1.00 | HQ | 200 |
|  | 2.00 | SALES | 46 |
|  | 3.00 | HR | 164 |
|  | 4.00 | MARKETING | 24 |

# Example 5: supermarket checkout training intervention

In Chapter 7 we presented supermarket checkout performance data with the explanation that many supermarkets have a scan-rate target with their employees who work on the checkout. The management of this supermarket introduced a special training programme (for staff who wanted to attend; participation was voluntary) to share good scan-rate techniques. One of the features of the course included training on how to manage overly talkative customers who interfere with the scan rate, without coming across as rude. Given that such a training programme is quite specific and it has a clear aim of improving scan rates of checkout staff, deciding on a metric to track its efficacy is fairly straightforward (and we do not have to collect any more data than the HR systems routinely collect in this organization). We simply identify who went on the (voluntary) training course and track their scan rate in the week following the training course. We have inserted data on this into the previous data set that we used in Chapter 7. The new data set is called 'Chapter 9 Supermarket Checkout Training.sav' and it has the following variables:

1. id (unique ID for each employee).
2. educ (number of years of education of the employee).
3. disability (whether or not the employee has stated they have a disability: 0 = no; 1 = yes).
4. Gender (1 = male; 2 = female).
5. Scanspminute (average number of items scanned per minute this week).
6. Store (which store: 1 = Portsmouth North; 2 = Portsea Island).
7. weeks (number of weeks working on the checkout).
8. AgeCat (age category: 1 = 16–19; 2 = 20–24; 3 = 25–29; 4 = 30–34; 5 = 35–39; 6 = 40–44; 7 = 45–49; 8 = 50–54; 9 = 55–59; 10 = 60+).
9. Age 1 (16–19).
10. Age 2 (20–24).
11. Age 3 (25–29).
12. Age 4 (30–34).
13. Age 5 (35–39).
14. Age 6 (40–44).
15. Age 7 (45–49).
16. Age 8 (50–54).
17. Age 9 (55–59).
18. Age 10 (60+).

**19** Training (whether or not the employee participated in the training course: 0 = no; 1 = yes).

**20** ScanPminuteTime2 (average number of items scanned per minute in the week after training).

You will see that two variables have been added to the data set, which represent a new variable that indicates whether the checkout operator went on the training course and the new average scan rate in the week after the training course was delivered.

Here we initially analyse this data using the same GLM analysis utilized with the values change example (as it takes into account change over time and compares between groups at the same time). Here, we have two groups now, those who participated in the training and those who did not. We also have two waves of scan-rate data for all (regardless of whether the checkout operator attended the training course).

As with the analysis examples presented above click on Analyze→General Linear Model→Repeated Measures. In the 'Repeated Measures Define Factor(s)' window (Figure 9.32) type '2' into the 'Number of Levels' box and then click 'Add', followed by 'Define'.

**FIGURE 9.32**

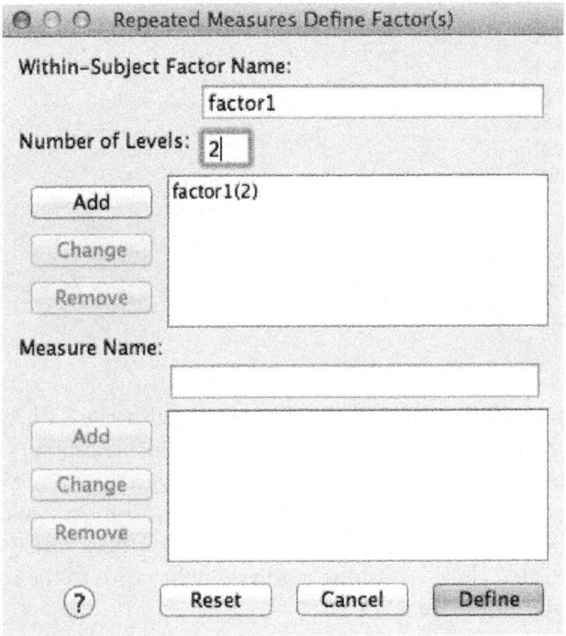

Once you have clicked 'Define' you will be presented with Figure 9.33. Here select the 'ScanPminute' and 'ScanPminuteTime2' variables from the variable list and enter them into the 'Within-Subjects Variables (factor 1):' selection box. Also transfer the 'Training' (Participated in the new training) variable into the 'Between-Subjects Factor(s):' box. Before you click 'OK' you need to set up a few other options. First click on the 'Plots' button.

**FIGURE 9.33**

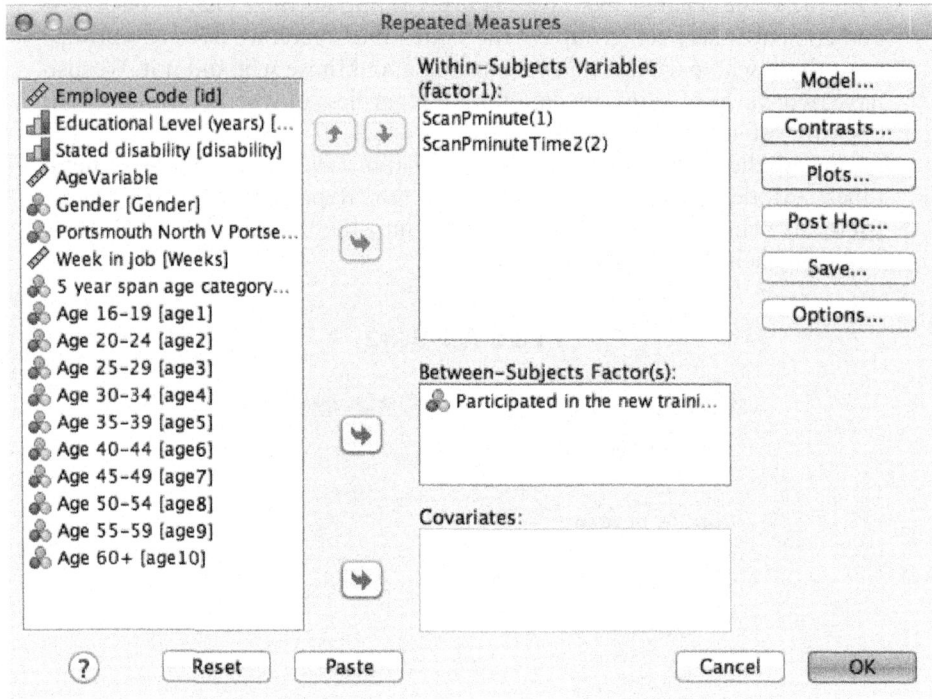

After selecting 'Plots' you will be presented with the following dialogue box (Figure 9.34). In here you need to select the 'Training' variable in the 'Separate Lines:' box and insert the 'factor1' variable into the 'Horizontal Axis:' selection box. Then click the 'Add' button to make sure that 'factor1*Training' appears in the 'Plots:' selection box. Once these options have been selected click 'Continue' and you will return to the repeated measures set-up box in Figure 9.33.

**FIGURE 9.34**

*[Repeated Measures: Profile Plots dialogue box. Factors: Training, factor1. Horizontal Axis: factor1. Separate Lines: Training. Plots: factor1*Training.]*

Then click on the 'Options' button. ['EM Means'] In this dialogue box (Figure 9.35) you need to select 'Training', 'factor1' and 'Training*factor 1' over into the 'Display Means for:' box, and then click 'Continue'.

**FIGURE 9.35**

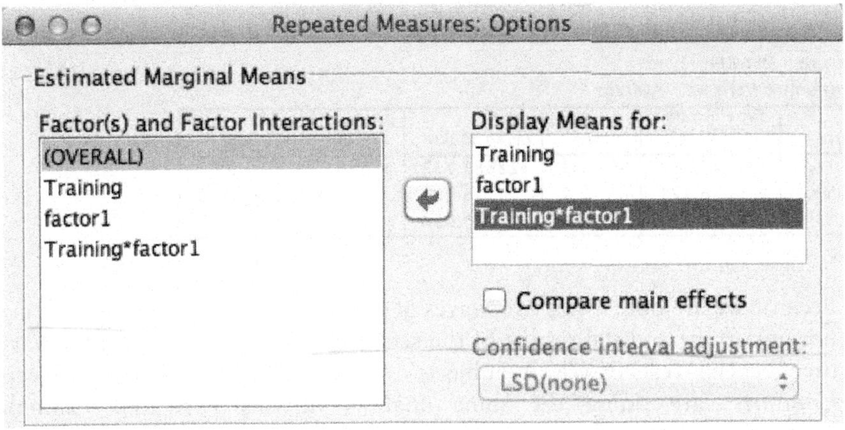

*[Repeated Measures: Options dialogue box. Estimated Marginal Means — Factor(s) and Factor Interactions: (OVERALL), Training, factor1, Training*factor1. Display Means for: Training, factor1, Training*factor1. Compare main effects unchecked. Confidence interval adjustment: LSD(none).]*

Once you return to the repeated measures set-up box click 'OK' and your analysis will run (see Figure 9.36).

## FIGURE 9.36

**Tests of Within-Subjects Effects**

Measure: MEASURE_1

| Source | | Type III Sum of Squares | df | Mean Square | F | Sig. |
|---|---|---|---|---|---|---|
| factor1 | Sphericity Assumed | 570.136 | 1 | 570.136 | 151.284 | .000 |
| | Greenhouse-Geisser | 570.136 | 1.000 | 570.136 | 151.284 | .000 |
| | Huynh-Feldt | 570.136 | 1.000 | 570.136 | 151.284 | .000 |
| | Lower-bound | 570.136 | 1.000 | 570.136 | 151.284 | .000 |
| factor1 * Training | Sphericity Assumed | 234.431 | 1 | 234.431 | 62.205 | .000 |
| | Greenhouse-Geisser | 234.431 | 1.000 | 234.431 | 62.205 | .000 |
| | Huynh-Feldt | 234.431 | 1.000 | 234.431 | 62.205 | .000 |
| | Lower-bound | 234.431 | 1.000 | 234.431 | 62.205 | .000 |
| Error(factor1) | Sphericity Assumed | 1695.892 | 450 | 3.769 | | |
| | Greenhouse-Geisser | 1695.892 | 450.000 | 3.769 | | |
| | Huynh-Feldt | 1695.892 | 450.000 | 3.769 | | |
| | Lower-bound | 1695.892 | 450.000 | 3.769 | | |

**Tests of Within-Subjects Contrasts**

Measure: MEASURE_1

| Source | factor1 | Type III Sum of Squares | df | Mean Square | F | Sig. |
|---|---|---|---|---|---|---|
| factor1 | Linear | 570.136 | 1 | 570.136 | 151.284 | .000 |
| factor1 * Training | Linear | 234.431 | 1 | 234.431 | 62.205 | .000 |
| Error(factor1) | Linear | 1695.892 | 450 | 3.769 | | |

**Tests of Between-Subjects Effects**

Measure: MEASURE_1
Transformed Variable: Average

| Source | Type III Sum of Squares | df | Mean Square | F | Sig. |
|---|---|---|---|---|---|
| Intercept | 312681.732 | 1 | 312681.732 | 13586.703 | .000 |
| Training | 56.121 | 1 | 56.121 | 2.439 | .119 |
| Error | 10356.212 | 450 | 23.014 | | |

Because we are only using two waves of data the sphericity assumptions are not important and the results of the sets of analysis presented do not vary (in effect the 'Tests of Within-Subjects *Effects*' and 'Tests of Within-Subjects *Contrasts*' are doing the same analysis in this particular example as we only have two waves of temporal data). Here the main results of the across-time (within-subjects factor) related analysis are significant; the 'factor1' row is significant (F=151.284, p<0.001) as is the 'factor1*Training' (F=62.205, p<0.001). This suggests that there is a change over time in the scan-rate performance data and that there is an interaction between scan-rate change and whether people have been on a training course or not.

The above results also show in the 'Tests of Between-Subjects Effects' output that the general effect of training is not significant (when disregarding change over time). This is an interesting null finding; however, the significant interaction of 'factor1*Training' suggests that the story is going to be more complicated. To interpret what is going on we need to look at the marginal means (Figure 9.37) and the mean plot (Figure 9.38), which we selected in our analysis set-up.

**FIGURE 9.37** Estimated marginal means

**1. Participated in the new training course**

*Difference, but we already know between-subjects diffs are not sig*

Measure: MEASURE_1

| Participated in the new training course | Mean | Std. Error | 95% Confidence Interval | |
|---|---|---|---|---|
| | | | Lower Bound | Upper Bound |
| Not participated | 20.116 | .194 | 19.735 | 20.498 |
| Participated | 19.584 | .280 | 19.035 | 20.134 |

**2. factor1**

*Sig, temporal effect*

Measure: MEASURE_1

| factor1 | Mean | Std. Error | 95% Confidence Interval | |
|---|---|---|---|---|
| | | | Lower Bound | Upper Bound |
| 1 | 19.003 | .185 | 18.639 | 19.366 |
| 2 | 20.698 | .182 | 20.339 | 21.056 |

**3. Participated in the new training course * factor1**

Measure: MEASURE_1

| Participated in the new training course | factor1 | Mean | Std. Error | 95% Confidence Interval | |
|---|---|---|---|---|---|
| | | | | Lower Bound | Upper Bound |
| Not participated | 1 | 19.812 | .211 | 19.397 | 20.227 |
| | 2 | 20.420 | .208 | 20.012 | 20.829 |
| Participated | 1 | 18.193 | .304 | 17.596 | 18.791 |
| | 2 | 20.976 | .300 | 20.387 | 21.564 |

Here are the descriptive statistics for the different 'marginal means'. The mean scan rate in general (combining Time 1 and Time 2 data) for the people who did not participate (mean=20.116) is higher than for those who did participate in training (19.584). Our analysis above suggests that these between-subjects differences are not significant, however. Our 'factor1' marginal means show that regardless of training participation the overall scan-rate mean has increased from 19.003 before the training to 20.698 after the training. As mentioned above, this is a significant 'factor1' temporal effect.

The key set of statistics, however, is the scan-rate means at Time 1 versus Time 2 (factor1) for employees who participate in training versus those who did not; especially as the analysis results indicate that there is a significant 'factor1*Training' interaction. Clearly those who chose to go on the training course tended to have a lower scan-rate mean before the training course (mean=18.193) compared to those who did not participate (mean=19.812). This may be explained by the fact that those with lower scan rates are under pressure from management to increase this and they are probably more likely to volunteer for the training course than those with higher scan rates. The results also show that whilst there seems to be some increase in scan rate for the training non-participators from Time 1 to Time 2 (mean=20.420) this rate of increase was not as much as for those who did participate (Time 2 mean = 20.976) and this interaction was significant (p<0.001). The mean plot figure clearly demonstrates that the training course seems to have had an effect on scan rate. One of the strengths of this particular analysis compared to the change analysis conducted previously is that we actually include a 'treatment' versus 'control' condition in our analysis. By treatment, we mean that we have a subset of our organization that has been 'treated' differently to a 'control' group; in this case the treatment is attendance on a training course. In effect we are setting up a quasi experiment, and when we show that change occurs with those receiving the treatment, but others who have not received this treatment do not show as much of a change, then this gives us strong confidence that the training course has had an impact (we need to consider whether we have a Hawthorne effect, of course… yet regardless of this possibility the training course seems to have had an impact).

**FIGURE 9.38**   Profile plots

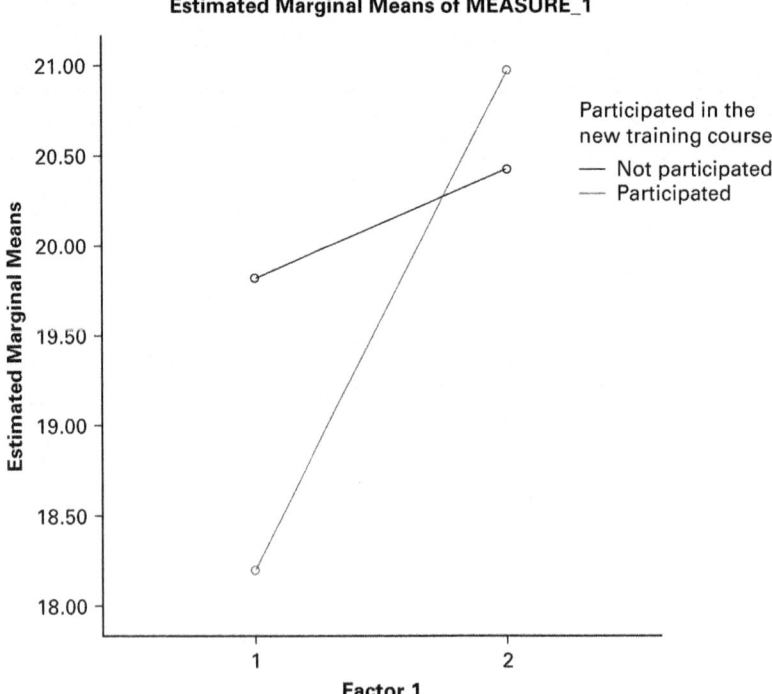

## Case Study 6

> **Snapshot hidden gem**
>
> We find that checkout staff tended to increase their scan rate over time; however, attendance at a scan-rate training course significantly boosts the improvement in scan rate (those who attend show the potential to be faster scanners than those who do not attend).

# Example 6: supermarket checkout training course – Redux

## *Conditional panel regression models assessing change in metrics whilst controlling for other factors*

So far the change analysis that we have carried out above tends to involve fairly straightforward mean testing and the data sets have also tended to be fairly straightforward; we have not tended to try to test for change effects whilst controlling for other factors that could be influencing change in the possible dependent variable. When we have two groups in the organization where one has experienced an intervention and another has not, a powerful way of testing for the impact of such an intervention whilst controlling for other factors is an analytic approach called conditional panel regression (Finkel, 1995). Here, we use multiple regression analysis to predict our Time 2 scan rate whilst controlling for our baseline Time 1 scan rate (as we did in Chapter 7 when modelling performance ratings whilst controlling for the previous year's ratings); in doing this we are in effect predicting 'change' in scan rate.

The logic of this analysis might not immediately seem obvious, so we will discuss this a little more here. When you conduct a regression analysis you are in effect trying to predict variation in a particular dependent variable. In Chapter 7 we predicted checkout scan rate as a dependent variable; in doing this we were trying to see whether variation in certain independent variables predicts the variation in checkout scan rate. Importantly, when you have two phases, or waves, of scan-rate data per individual taken at different time points (Time 1 scan rate versus Time 2 scan rate) you can set the latter scan-rate data as a dependent variable and insert the earlier scan rate as an independent variable.

Assuming that individual differences are an important factor accounting for scan rate (if someone is fast at Time 1 then they are likely to be fast at Time 2), operators' Time 1 scan rate is likely to predict the Time 2 scan rate; thus accounting for variation in the Time 2 scan rate to a considerable degree. It is *very* unlikely that the Time 2 scan rate will be exactly the same as the

Time 1 scan rate for each checkout operator; as such there will be some error in prediction of Time 2 scan rate when using Time 1 scan rate as an independent variable. The more there is a difference in employee scan rates when comparing Time 1 with Time 2 then the greater the 'error' in prediction; where Time 1 scan rate differs from Time 2 scan rate then the predicted value that we would get for Time 2 scan rate if we just used Time 1 scan rate as a guide would not always be correct – it would have some error (in prediction of Time 2 scan rate). Importantly, if we set up a model where scan rate at Time 2 is regressed onto a number of independent variables and we tried to account for variation in this scan rate but we included Time 1 scan rate as a control, the relationship that Time 1 scan rate shares with these independent variables and Time 2 scan rate is filtered out of the regression model. In effect we are no longer predicting variation in Time 2 scan rate; we are in effect predicting the difference in scan rate between Time 1 and Time 2 (Time 2 scan rate – Time 1 scan rate). Thus, we are predicting a change in scan rate between Time 1 and Time 2.

Using a multiple regression analysis as a change model enables us to include an independent variable that signifies whether someone has been on a training course; thus we can test whether training-course attendance seems to have an impact on change in scan rate. In addition to this we can also control for a whole range of other factors that we know might be important in accounting for individual scan rate (see Chapter 7, page 281) at the same time. Hopefully this will become clearer when we look at the conditional change panel regression analysis output. Again we are using the same supermarket data set as above: data file 'Chapter 9 Supermarket Checkout Training.sav.'.

To conduct this analysis we select Analyze→Regression→Linear and we see our familiar linear regression window that we have interacted with before (in Chapters 4, 5, 6 and 7). In this window (Figure 9.39), select the 'ScanPminuteTime2' measure as the regression's 'Dependent:' variable. Then select the following 16 variables as independent variables (file: Chapter 9 Supermarket Checkout Training.sav) (note that the 'Age 3 (25–29)' category is excluded from the analysis as we want this to be our reference age category (see Example 9 in Chapter 7):

1. educ (number of years of education of the employee).
2. disability (whether or not the employee has stated they have a disability: 0 = no; 1 = yes).
3. Gender (1 = male; 2 = female).
4. Store (which Store: 1 = Portsmouth North; 2 = Portsea Island).
5. Weeks (number of weeks working on the checkout).
6. Age 1 (16–19).
7. Age 2 (20–24).
8. Age 4 (30–34).
9. Age 5 (35–39).

**10** Age 6 (40–44).

**11** Age 7 (45–49).

**12** Age 8 (50–54).

**13** Age 9 (55–59).

**14** Age 10 (60+).

**15** Training (whether or not the employee participated in the training course: 0 = no; 1 = yes).

**16** ScanPminute (average number of items scanned per minute this week, our Time 1 scan-rate measure).

## FIGURE 9.39

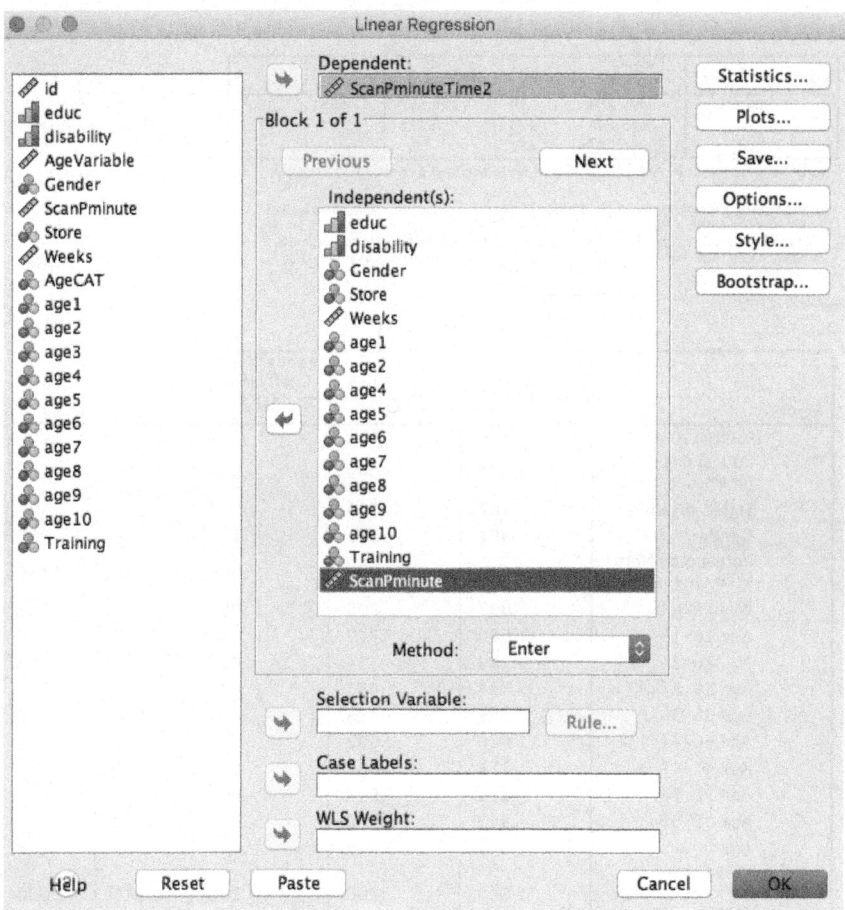

Notice that in Figure 9.39 the 'ScanPminute' variable inserted as an independent variable is in effect a control variable that means we are actually predicting change in scan rate; also note that the training variable included as an independent variable is the key intervention variable, as it will tell us whether going on a training course accounts for Time 1 to Time 2 change in scan rate. Once you click 'OK' the following output should be produced (Figure 9.40):

**FIGURE 9.40**

**Model Summary**

| Model | R | R-Square | Adjusted R-Square | Std. Error of the Estimate |
|---|---|---|---|---|
| 1 | .744[d] | .553 | .537 | 2.47558 |

a. Predictors: (Constant), Average number of items scanned per minute this week, Portsmouth North V Portsea Island, Age 55-59, Stated disability, Age 50-54, Age 35-39, Age 60+, Age 45-49, Participated in the new training course, Age 30-34, Age 16-19, Age 40-44, Week in job, Age 20-24, Educational Level (years), Gender

**ANOVA[a]**

| Model | | Sum of Squares | df | Mean Square | F | Sig. |
|---|---|---|---|---|---|---|
| 1 | Regression | 3304.106 | 16 | 206.507 | 33.696 | .000[b] |
| | Residual | 2665.894 | 435 | 6.128 | | |
| | Total | 5970.000 | 451 | | | |

*Model is significant*

a. Dependent Variable: Average number of items scanned per minute in the week after training

b. Predictors: (Constant), Average number of items scanned per minute this week, Portsmouth North V Portsea Island, Age 55-59, Stated disability, Age 50-54, Age 35-39, Age 60+, Age 45-49, Participated in the new training course, Age 30-34, Age 16-19, Age 40-44, Week in job, Age 20-24, Educational Level (years), Gender

**Coefficients[a]**

| Model | | Unstandardized Coefficients | | Standardized Coefficients | t | Sig. |
|---|---|---|---|---|---|---|
| | | B | Std. Error | Beta | | |
| 1 | (Constant) | 7.586 | 1.201 | | 6.318 | .000 |
| | Educational Level (years) | -.077 | .049 | -.061 | -1.553 | .121 |
| | Stated disability | -.162 | .300 | -.018 | -.539 | .590 |
| | Gender | .991 | .312 | .136 | 3.176 | .002 |
| | Portsmouth North V Portsea Island | .033 | .237 | .005 | .140 | .889 |
| | Week in job | .007 | .005 | .054 | 1.471 | .142 |
| | Age 16-19 | -1.580 | .719 | -.083 | -2.196 | .029 |
| | Age 20-24 | -.109 | .354 | -.013 | -.309 | .758 |
| | Age 30-34 | .434 | .481 | .032 | .902 | .367 |
| | Age 35-39 | .786 | .495 | .055 | 1.590 | .113 |
| | Age 40-44 | 1.010 | .502 | .073 | 2.012 | .045 |
| | Age 45-49 | .123 | .561 | .008 | .220 | .826 |
| | Age 50-54 | -.116 | .548 | -.008 | -.213 | .832 |
| | Age 55-59 | -.353 | .520 | -.026 | -.679 | .497 |
| | Age 60+ | .675 | 1.315 | .017 | .513 | .608 |
| | Participated in the new training course | 1.600 | .260 | .206 | 6.146 | .000 |
| | Average number of items scanned per minute this week | .610 | .038 | .630 | 15.932 | .000 |

*Women increase over time because β is positive*

a. Dependent Variable: Average number of items scanned per minute in the week after training

*More increase than 25-29 control*

The first thing to notice here is that the regression model accounts for 55.3 per cent of variance in our dependent variable and our model is highly significant ($F(16,435)=33.696$, $p<0.001$). Thus we can account for 55.3 per cent of variation on our Time 2 scan rate with this model (which, as models go, is quite good).

Out of all 16 independent variables in the model, five are significant. As we would expect with a panel model like this, the Time 1 scan rate is the biggest predictor of Time 2 scan rate with a Beta of 0.630 ($p<0.001$); the more the checkout person scans at Time 1 then the more they tend to scan at Time 2 – this is a fairly strong positive coefficient. Of vital importance, however, is that the training course variable is also significant (Beta=0.206, $p<0.001$), providing strong evidence that the training programme has a significantly positive impact on change (an increase) in scan rates of check-out operatives; thus training potentially increases scan rates. Also, gender is also a significant predictor of change with a Beta of 0.136, $p<0.01$), suggesting that women tended to show an increase over time; also 40–44-year-olds (Beta=0.073, $p<0.05$) seemed to show more of an increase in scan rates across time than our reference age category of 25–29-year-olds; 16–19-year-olds showed a greater decrease over time compared to the same reference category (Beta=–0.083). Obviously, of these results, the key finding is that attendance at the scan-rate training leads to a greater increase in scan rate than you see with people who did not attend.

> **Snapshot hidden gem**
>
> We find that attendance at a scan-rate training course significantly boosts the improvement in checkout operative's scan rate (those who attend show the potential to be faster scanners than those who do not attend); importantly, however, females show a greater increase in scan rate over time whilst controlling for training attendance.

# Evidence-based practice and responsible investment

The above examples are generally examples of where organizations have either deliberately set up conditions where important predicted outcomes of an intervention are created or metrics are made available to monitor whether an intervention has the desired impact. This is obviously very sensible management practice and indeed something that an effective HR function will want to do; both to help set up conditions where the expected returns from an investment can be identified but also to be able to ensure that the intervention has positive returns. It is as important to identify when an intervention has a negative outcome as it is to identify when it has a positive outcome; something can be done about an intervention that is not working when the impact of the intervention is monitored. Without tracking the impact of an intervention it may be the case that management will never know whether the investment has paid off or whether it is having negative consequences.

### See no evil, hear no evil, speak no evil

Whilst many organizations make investment decisions based on what the management think is the best thing to do, it might often be the case that a decision has been made by management to introduce a change or HR intervention on grounds that do not necessarily make rational sense. Sometimes management can make decisions to implement a change on ideological grounds, on grounds that competitors are doing it or for irrational reasons even; these decisions can sometimes be made even when the case for interventions might not be that strong. Indeed, often investments into a new intervention can be so huge or so difficult to undo that the last thing management would want is a set of metrics that could risk the exposure of this. Ultimately, in the spirit of accountable and sustainable treatment of employees, the HR analytics expert should always try to present a case for tracking the impact of an intervention wherever possible; the HR analytics function should always be on the lookout for situations where the impact of any management change can be monitored and tracked on its workforce.

# References

Finkel, S E (1995) *Causal Analysis With Panel Data: Quantitative applications in the social sciences*, Sage, California

# Business applications
## Scenario modelling and business cases

10

So far in this book we have set out and discussed a variety of different analytic techniques and walked through the analysis of various models. Whilst we have in general used predictive analytic techniques, these have tended to be used to diagnose key drivers of important HR outcomes (such as employee turnover and performance) or to help us evaluate the effectiveness of an initiative or intervention. Once a budding HR analytics expert has gone through the case study chapters and run various analyses for themselves with his or her organization's own HR data, perhaps the following might happen.

The analyst goes into the boardroom/executive committee/senior management group/HR director's office and she/he presents the sophisticated predictive analysis and the models, pointing out the significant findings that included drivers of HR outcomes and a proposed course of action. Four of the five people in the room nod in affable agreement, impressed at the analyst's skills and clearly enlightened at what the analysis shows. Then the analyst looks at David in the corner. David is not smiling; instead he is frowning. He looks up and the long pause causes others to look at David also. There is an air of anticipation in the room. He takes one last observable glance at the meeting papers outlining the analysis before raising his head, taking off his reading glasses and uttering the words 'So what?'

It feels like a slap in the face and a bit rude actually. Where are his manners? Maybe he didn't understand? But then the words that follow suggest he understood completely.

'Should I now go and change my departmental plan, my day-to-day tasks, the management of my team leaders?' he asks. 'What is to stop us from all agreeing that this statistically significant model,' he says (doing finger quotation marks around the words 'statistically significant'), 'is great to have, but then leaving this meeting, going back to our jobs, and never giving it another thought?'

The others in the room start to look uncomfortable and a little embarrassed. At this point the analyst realizes that David is actually on his/her side. Despite his spikey exterior, David is impressed with the model and actually wants to use it. So do the others; the problem is they just don't know how. In other words, nice model, but 'So what?'

The important question now is how you can translate these analyses and results into tangible predictive business applications. Aside from the obvious business implications of being able to diagnose drivers of HR outcomes, we might now want to ask the 'So what?' question. From the types of analyses that we have carried out so far, there are a number of things that the HR analytics expert can do with the knowledge gained that can help us to answer this 'So what?' question.

Here lies the real value in statistical models. The models have been created and analyses run. In this chapter we can present a few examples of how the statistical models that we outline can be applied further; some of these examples demonstrate how the analyst can make real and tangible predictions from the analysis conducted. In this chapter we discuss the following:

**Predictive modelling scenarios**
Using the regression models we built in the 'turnover and performance' case studies (Chapters 6 and 7) to model future scenarios, we will work out who is more likely to leave and how their performance might be impacted when environmental factors change. We will also use financial models to build a business case for particular HR initiatives.

**Evidence-based decision making**
We will use the models that we built in the recruitment and selection case studies (Chapter 8) as a basis for making important people-related decisions, thus helping to reduce the likelihood for bias by adding additional evidence-based information to our decision-making process.

## Predictive modelling scenarios

Here we use an example model that we ran in Chapter 7 to explore predictors of customer satisfaction with financial sales representatives. We will briefly revise the analysis and show how you can take the findings in order to model the potential impact of focusing on particular drivers with a view to understanding how this could lead to an increase in our factor of interest; with the modelling we can potentially draw some conclusions about how our particular HR outcome (in this case customer reinvestment intentions) could be influenced.

# Example 1: customer reinvestment

In Chapter 7 we explored predictors of customer reinvestment intentions in a financial sales environment. This was example 1b in Chapter 7 (performance case study, see page 246) (using the data file: Chapter 7 Customer satisfaction ONLY N2507.sav).

You may recall that we looked at the results of a customer satisfaction survey in a financial services organization in order to determine the drivers of customer reinvestment intentions (expressed in a customer satisfaction survey). To recap, the survey asked investing customers to grade their sales person on a scale of 1 to 5, where 1 was 'dissatisfied' and 5 was 'extremely satisfied' on the following measures:

**1** Sales person understanding your needs (Sat1).
**2** Sales person seems confident (Sat2).
**3** Sales person has a recommendation (Sat3).
**4** Sales person is knowledgeable (Sat4).

Then the survey asked customers to rate themselves on two measures that indicate a degree of customer loyalty (a 1-to-5 scale was used in each case). The first loyalty measure related to intentions to reinvest and the second measure indicated how much they intended to reinvest. The response items for these two measures used the following 1-to-5 response scales:

**5** Likelihood of reinvesting (CustLoyalty):
  – 1 = Definitely going to go elsewhere with my investments.
  – 2 = Thinking about going elsewhere with my money.
  – 3 = Not sure about where I will place my future investments.
  – 4 = Thinking about investing here again.
  – 5 = Definitely will invest here again.
**6** How much they may or may not reinvest (INvestMore):
  – 1 = Definitely will not invest more than now here.
  – 2 = Unlikely to invest more than now here.
  – 3 = Planning to invest 0–50 per cent more than now in this organization.
  – 4 = Planning to invest 50–100 per cent more in this organization.
  – 5 = Going to double my investment or more in this organization.

The final question was about the gender of the sales person:

**7** Sex of sales person: 1 = female; 2 = male.

If we present the predictive model that we analysed in Chapter 7 (see Figure 7.6, page 248) as a diagram, when we run the multiple regression equation, the model would look like Figure 10.1:

**FIGURE 10.1** Diagram of the regression model predicting customer reinvestment intentions from customer satisfaction data (analysis presented in Figure 7.5 of Chapter 7)

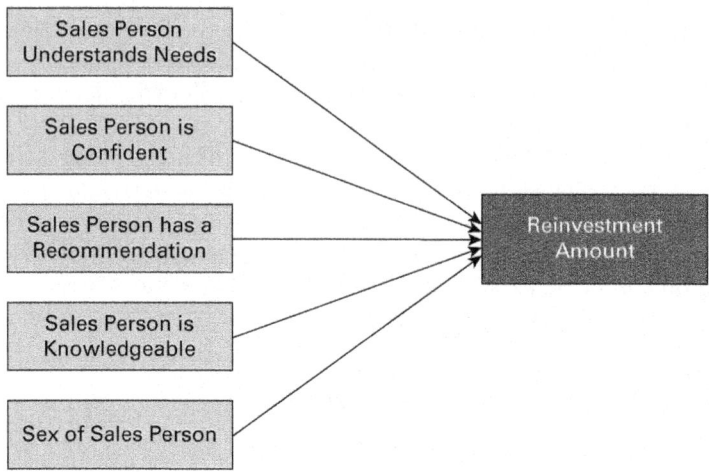

And the resulting output from the analysis can be found in Figure 10.2.

When we translate the model results to a raw regression equation we have the following:

Customer reinvestment =
1.740 + 0.176 (understanding customer needs) +
0.030 (sales confidence) + 0.140 (giving a recommendation) +
0.012 (product knowledge) – 0.020 (gender)

And the significant drivers (independent variables) came out to be:

- understanding customer needs ($p<0.001$); and
- giving a recommendation ($p<0.001$).

With this information, we realized the snapshot hidden gem:

*Understanding customer needs and having a recommendation are the two key drivers of customer reinvestment indices.*

In considering what we can do with this information, we can now take this further and look at the potential impact that bespoke changes would have on customer reinvestment.

Remembering that the independent variables are on a scale of 1 to 5 it looks like this:

1 – very dissatisfied;
2 – somewhat dissatisfied;
3 – neither satisfied nor dissatisfied;
4 – somewhat satisfied;
5 – extremely satisfied.

## FIGURE 10.2

**Model Summary**

| Model | R | R-Square | Adjusted R-Square | Std. Error of the Estimate |
|---|---|---|---|---|
| 1 | .413[a] | .170 | .168 | .74597 |

a. Predictors: (Constant), SexOfSalesperson, Sales person has a recommendation, Sales person is knowledgeable, Sales person seems confident, Sales person understanding your needs

**ANOVA[a]**

| Model | | Sum of Squares | df | Mean Square | F | Sig. |
|---|---|---|---|---|---|---|
| 1 | Regression | 201.815 | 5 | 40.363 | 72.534 | .000[b] |
|   | Residual | 982.724 | 1766 | .556 | | |
|   | Total | 1184.539 | 1771 | | | |

a. Dependent Variable: INvestMore

b. Predictors: (Constant), SexOfSalesperson, Sales person has a recommendation, Sales person is knowledgeable, Sales person seems confident, Sales person understanding your needs

**Coefficients[a]**

| Model | | Unstandardized Coefficients | | Standardized Coefficients | t | Sig. |
|---|---|---|---|---|---|---|
| | | B | Std. Error | Beta | | |
| 1 | (Constant) | 1.740 | .111 | | 15.685 | .000 |
|   | Sales person understanding your needs | .176 | .030 | .219 | 5.789 | .000 |
|   | Sales person seems confident | .030 | .029 | .034 | 1.035 | .301 |
|   | Sales person has a recommendation | .140 | .025 | .186 | 5.540 | .000 |
|   | Sales person is knowledgeable | .012 | .027 | .014 | .429 | .668 |
|   | SexOfSalesperson | -.020 | .043 | -.010 | -.453 | .651 |

a. Dependent Variable: INvestMore

Currently, the average scores for the independent variables on these scales (in our data set) are:

- Understanding customer needs is 3.47.
- Sales confidence is 3.79.
- Giving a recommendation is 3.43.
- Product knowledge is 3.59.

And knowing that we have set the value of 1 as female and 2 as male for the gender variable, then the average gender score is 1.78.

If we plug those average values into the model equation, we should get a value for the dependent reinvestment variable that is close to the average figure for this variable (INvestMore) in our data set, which is 2.92:

Customer reinvestment
= 1.740 + 0.176 (3.47) + 0.030 (3.79) + 0.140 (3.43) +
  0.012 (3.59) − 0.020 (1.78)
= 2.95

The value of 2.95 is the predicted/expected level of customer reinvestment based on our model when inputting average values for each independent variable. In conducting some modelling with our equation, we can translate this predicted value to be the average of the customer reinvestment scores with the salespeople that our model included (not all people were included as there was some missing data with particular individuals on certain variables). We established in our case study that the model was significant with a p-value of 0.001, so there is less than a 1 in 1,000 chance that we would find this pattern of shared variance (between the customer reinvestment scores and the other survey questions) by chance alone. Hence the model is significant.

So, back to David's big 'So what?' question. Knowing from the R-square value of 0.326 and the p-value of 0.000 in the case study, we can be 99.9 per cent confident that the model 'accounts for' almost 33 per cent, or approximately one-third, of the variance in the dependent variable. Let's try a couple of scenarios.

Something we can do with these results is model the impact of a hypothetical increase with particular drivers of probable reinvestment amounts; we can see how our predicted level of reinvestment changes when we adjust significant drivers of dependent variable. We could, for example, ask: 'What if we managed to increase our level of understanding customer needs to a point where the average customer rating was 4.00 (somewhat satisfied) rather than the current average of 3.47 (somewhere between neither satisfied nor dissatisfied and somewhat satisfied)?'

To recap, the survey response values for our outcome customer reinvestment variable are:

*How much they may or may not reinvest:*

1 = Definitely will not invest more than now here.
2 = Unlikely to invest more than now here.
3 = Planning to invest 0–50 per cent more than now in this organization.
4 = Planning to invest 50–100 per cent more in this organization.
5 = Going to double my investment or more in this organization.

And we are working with an average value for this in our data set of 2.95.

We then plug our new value for understanding customer needs into the model regression equation (in much the same way as we did in the previous calculation) and we can work out the expected level of customer reinvestment; all other things remaining the same, we get the following result:

= 1.740 + 0.176 (4.00) + 0.030 (3.79) + 0.140 (3.43) + 0.012 (3.59)
− 0.020 (1.78)
= 3.04

We can see that changing our understanding customer needs value from 3.47 (somewhere between neither satisfied nor dissatisfied and somewhat satisfied) to 4.00 (somewhat satisfied) increases the average expected level of customer reinvestment and pushes the average further into level 3 (planning to invest 0–50 per cent more than now). This is a substantial move in the right direction for organizational revenue.

But what if we also trained our salespeople so that they had an increased understanding of customer needs, and who were 'always' able to give a recommendation that met each customer's needs? What if the average score was 4.5 for both of the two key drivers of our customer reinvestment outcome?

Plugging those two new values into the model:

= 1.740 + 0.176 (4.5) + 0.030 (3.79) + 0.140 (4.5) + 0.012 (3.59)
− 0.020 (1.78)
= 3.24.

This is a much higher value and shows how much a change in the two variables we know to have the most impact ('understanding customer needs' and 'giving a recommendation') will impact the outcome we are interested in, ie the amount of customer reinvestment. This is very powerful modelling.

Moving the average from 2.95 to 3.24 in monetary terms means there are more customers who plan to invest 0–50 per cent more than they do now, and for the average now to be quite a bit over 3, it also means we have a much greater prevalence of customers who would indicate a '4' value on the survey, which means they intend to invest 50–100 per cent more than they do now. So, let's extrapolate and say that an increase of .29 on a scale of 1 to 5 is an average increase in likelihood to reinvest of .29/5 = 0.058, or let's round it to 6 per cent.

We could here use this information to build an estimate of the possible increase in reinvestment to enable a business case for investing in training. If you were writing a business case for a new training programme to increase the ability of salespeople to understand customer needs and make a recommendation, you might show a potential business case for investing in training on the basis that this training will help increase customers' satisfaction. You could suggest that the return on that investment might be a 6 per cent increase in the amount your customers invest if you were able to increase average customer satisfaction ratings on these two driver variables by 0.5 (on the 1-to-5 scales). Whilst we recognize here that we are working with a 1-to-5 scale that is not exactly discrete in terms of the amount of customer reinvestment that a customer is saying that they may invest, it would be reasonable to translate an increase in the scale to a rough estimate of the potential increase in investment potential (our analyst would have to explain this assumption and caveat that this is a rough estimate; but an estimate based in rigorous modelling nonetheless).

> **Snapshot hidden gem**
>
> If the annual customer investment figures totalled US $1.2 billion last year, and our model suggests that an increase in understanding customer needs and giving a recommendation should influence an increase in customer investment by 6 per cent, then we predict a possible increase of approximately $72 million of additional customer investment by getting more customer satisfaction in those two factors.

Obviously this would be a very big and specific claim to make and there is no guarantee that your training will definitely lead to a 0.5 increase in satisfaction on the two driver dimensions. It would be sensible for the analyst to model a range of possible increases and translate these to some kind of discrete sensitivity analysis of potential financial returns that various scenarios of different increases in the two satisfaction drivers could lead to. Importantly when we are talking about such large sums of money, even a relatively small increase in customer satisfaction could lead to a decent return, thus covering costs of new training initiatives.

Remembering that this is a linear regression model, it is important to keep in mind that it does not prove causality, and our results give us information about relationships between variables and the probabilities that these relationships are not products of random factors. So while the levels of significance that our results presented above are considerable, and we can be 99.9 per cent confident that the independent variables in our model 'account for' or 'share' variation in our customers' reports of intended investment increases, the results do not offer 'proof' for causality. We should be careful to caveat our claims on the basis that our regression findings show statistical relationships between variables but do not prove that one thing causes another; ie while increasing an understanding of customer needs and the ability to make a recommendation will result in an increase in customer reinvestment, we cannot be sure that this is the direct *cause* – there may be other factors at play.

It would also be sensible to caveat our business-case predictions with the reminder that these are customers' self-report predictions of their reinvestment intentions and that self-report intentions do not always lead to action (their intentions might not lead to actual investments – for many reasons).

The analyst needs to be aware that there are a number of different ways of modelling the possible impact of increases in predictors and this is just one possible way.

However, despite these caveats, the analytical evidence-based rigour used in the modelling here can be presented and defended, and assumptions can be set out. Here, the analyst will have:

1 conducted rigorous statistical analysis exploring the drivers of customer reinvestment intentions;
2 identified how much the key drivers predict variations in reinvestment intentions;
3 demonstrated how focusing on the key drivers could influence customer reinvestment;
4 developed a model that can help get a sense of potential financial return that might be possible with a training initiative that could increase the drivers by a range of possible values.

At this point, it would be worth pointing out an additional analysis linked to the above that the analytics team could undertake to follow this up. Given that the analysts must know who the sales representatives are and who the customers are in this scenario (otherwise they would not have been able to link the customer surveys with the analysts), the analyst could also track how much the customers did invest the following year and conduct this analysis with actual increases (or decreases) in investment rather than self-report customer intentions. With actual monetary figures to play with as a dependent outcome variable, the power of this kind of analysis (and the accuracy of the claims made) increases considerably; the analyst could actually model the monetary value of potential increases in our drivers rather than an estimate based on a less accurate 1-to-5 Likert scale (that requires assumptions to be made).

# Example 2: modelling the potential impact of a training programme

In scenario one we explored and modelled the drivers of potential customer reinvestment on the basis of sales representative-linked customer satisfaction survey data. Here we turn to an example predictive modelling scenario where we model the potential tangible impact (on individual employee performance) of a training programme; we conduct some scenario modelling using an example used in both Chapter 7 and Chapter 9, where we explored factors predicting supermarket scan rate with checkout operators.

As a recap, in Chapter 7 we presented supermarket checkout performance data with the explanation that many supermarkets have a scan-rate target with their employees who work on the checkout. The management of this supermarket introduced a special training programme (for staff who wanted to attend; ie participation was voluntary) to share good scan-rate techniques. We then introduced a new data set in Chapter 9 where we included additional data into the data set that showed who participated in the training course and we included new scan-rate (post-training period) data.

The new data set was called 'Chapter 9 Supermarket Checkout Training. sav' and it has the following variables:

1. id (unique ID for each employee).
2. Educ (number of years of education of the employee).
3. Disability (whether or not the employee has stated they have a disability: 0 = no; 1 = yes).
4. Gender (1 = male; 2 = female).
5. Scanspminute (average number of items scanned per minute this week).
6. Store (which store: 1 = Portsmouth North; 2 = Portsea Island).
7. Weeks (number of weeks working on the checkout).
8. AgeCat (age category: 1 = 16–19; 2 = 2–24; 3 = 25–29; 4 = 30–34; 5 = 35–39; 6 = 40–44; 7 = 45–49; 8 = 50–54; 9 = 55–59; 10 = 60+).
9. Age 1 (16–19).
10. Age 2 (20–24).
11. Age 3 (25–29).
12. Age 4 (30–34).
13. Age 5 (35–39).
14. Age 6 (40–44).
15. Age 7 (45–49).
16. Age 8 (50–54).
17. Age 9 (55–59).
18. Age 10 (60+).
19. Training (whether or not the employee participated in the training course: 0 = no; 1 = yes).
20. ScanPminuteTime2 (average number of items scanned per minute in the week after training).

With the 'Redux' model (example 6) that we ran in Chapter 9 (page 362) we predicted Time 2 (post-training) scan rate with demographic factors, pre-training scan rate and whether the operator participated in a training session. This model therefore predicted 'change' in scan rate (see Figure 10.3 for a visual presentation of the model tested).

Figure 10.4 shows how we set up this model in the linear regression set-up box.

Business Applications: Scenario Modelling and Business Cases    375

**FIGURE 10.3** Diagram of the regression model predicting post-training scan rate when controlling for pre-training scan rate and training participation (example 6 in Chapter 9)

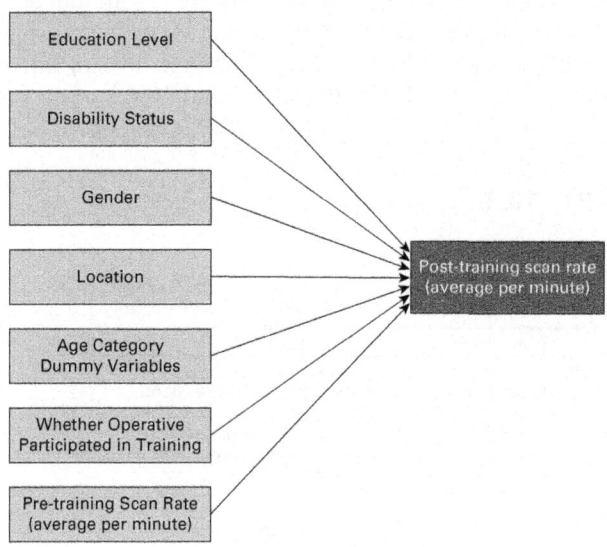

**FIGURE 10.4**

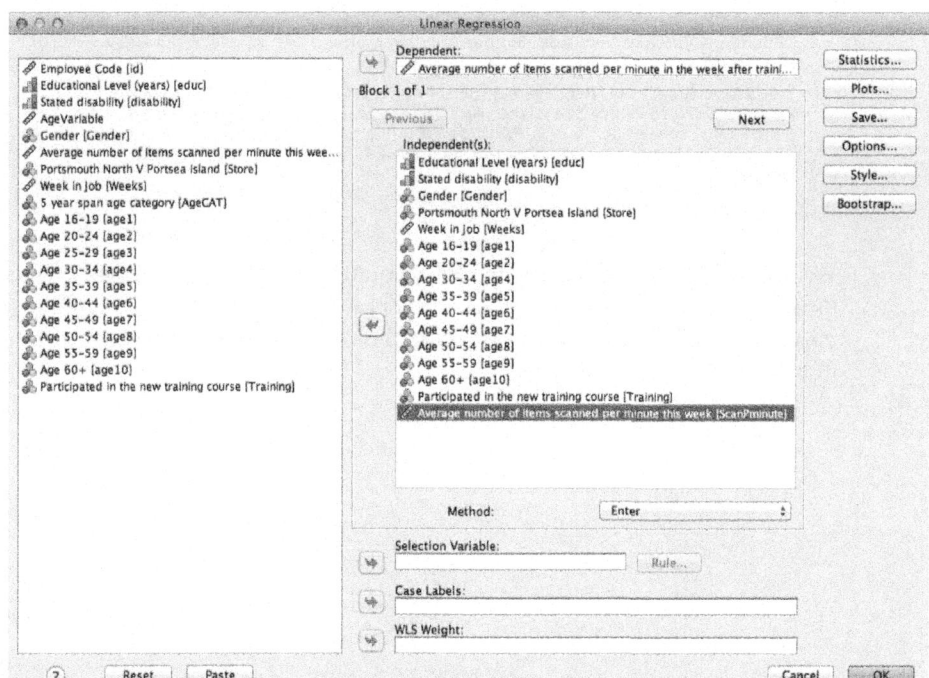

Notice here that the 'Scanspminute' (average number of items scanned per minute this week) variable was as an independent variable (this means we are actually predicting change in scan rate – see discussion on this in Chapter 9). Also note that the 'Training' variable included as an independent variable is the key intervention variable as it will tell us whether attending a training course accounts for Time 1 to Time 2 change in scan rate. The output for this model can be found in Figures 10.5 and 10.6.

## FIGURE 10.5

**Model Summary**

| Model | R | R-Square | Adjusted R-Square | Std. Error of the Estimate |
|---|---|---|---|---|
| 1 | .744[a] | .553 | .537 | 2.47558 |

a. Predictors: (Constant), Average number of items scanned per minute this week, Portsmouth North V Portsea Island, Age 55-59, Stated disability, Age 50-54, Age 35-39, Age 60+, Age 45-49, Participated in the new training course, Age 30-34, Age 16-19, Age 40-44, Week in job, Age 20-24, Educational Level (years), Gender

**ANOVA[a]**

| Model | | Sum of Squares | df | Mean Square | F | Sig. |
|---|---|---|---|---|---|---|
| 1 | Regression | 3304.106 | 16 | 206.507 | 33.696 | .000[b] |
| | Residual | 2665.894 | 435 | 6.128 | | |
| | Total | 5970.000 | 451 | | | |

a. Dependent Variable: Average number of items scanned per minute in the week after training

b. Predictors: (Constant), Average number of items scanned per minute this week, Portsmouth North V Portsea Island, Age 55-59, Stated disability, Age 50-54, Age 35-39, Age 60+, Age 45-49, Participated in the new training course, Age 30-34, Age 16-19, Age 40-44, Week in job, Age 20-24, Educational Level (years), Gender

We can see that the regression model accounted for 55.3 per cent of variance in our dependent variable and our model is highly significant ($F(16,435)= 33.696$, $p<0.001$). See Figure 10.6 for the statistics relating to each of our independent (driver) variables.

**FIGURE 10.6**

Coefficients[a]

| Model | | Unstandardized Coefficients | | Standardized Coefficients | t | Sig. |
|---|---|---|---|---|---|---|
| | | B | Std. Error | Beta | | |
| 1 | (Constant) | 7.586 | 1.201 | | 6.318 | .000 |
| | Educational Level (years) | -.077 | .049 | -.061 | -1.553 | .121 |
| | Stated disability | -.162 | .300 | -.018 | -.539 | .590 |
| | Gender | .991 | .312 | .136 | 3.176 | .002 |
| | Portsmouth North V Portsea Island | .033 | .237 | .005 | .140 | .889 |
| | Week in job | .007 | .005 | .054 | 1.471 | .142 |
| | Age 16-19 | -1.580 | .719 | -.083 | -2.196 | .029 |
| | Age 20-24 | -.109 | .354 | -.013 | -.309 | .758 |
| | Age 30-34 | .434 | .481 | .032 | .902 | .367 |
| | Age 35-39 | .786 | .495 | .055 | 1.590 | .113 |
| | Age 40-44 | 1.010 | .502 | .073 | 2.012 | .045 |
| | Age 45-49 | .123 | .561 | .008 | .220 | .826 |
| | Age 50-54 | -.116 | .548 | -.008 | -.213 | .832 |
| | Age 55-59 | -.353 | .520 | -.026 | -.679 | .497 |
| | Age 60+ | .675 | 1.315 | .017 | .513 | .608 |
| | Participated in the new training course | 1.600 | .260 | .206 | 6.146 | .000 |
| | Average number of items scanned per minute this week | .610 | .038 | .630 | 15.932 | .000 |

a. Dependent Variable: Average number of items scanned per minute in the week after training

From these model results, if we insert our coefficients into an unstandardized raw regression equation, we get the following:

Average (post-training) scan rate =
7.586
− 0.077 Education Level
− 0.162 stated disability
**+ 0.991 Gender**
+ 0.033 Portsmouth Location
+ 0.007 Week in job
− 1.570 **Age 16–19**
− 0.109 Age 20–24
+ 0.434 Age 30–34
+ 0.786 Age 35–39
**+ 1.010 Age 40–44**
+ 0.123 Age 45–49
− 0.116 Age 50–54

− 0.353 Age 55–59
+ 0.675 Age 60+
**+ 1.600 Participated in training**
+ 0.610 Pre-training scan rate

We can see that out of all 16 independent variables in the model, five are significant (these are highlighted in bold). What we are most interested in here is the impact of participation in the checkout training. We can see that the unstandardized beta coefficient for the variable that indicates participation in this training course is B=1.600 and this is highly significant ($p<0.001$). Before we move on to model the impact of participation in training on scan rate we need to consider some descriptive information. See Figure 10.7 where we obtain this descriptive information. Analyze→Descriptive Statistics→Descriptives.

The descriptive information for the variables in our model is presented in Figure 10.8.

There are two key values in Figure 10.8 that we could use to (very quickly) begin to model the impact on scan rates of the training programme. First, the mean value for participation in training = 0.32. This variable is coded 0 = not participated and 1 = participated. Therefore a mean of 0.32 indicates that about one-third of the organization participated in the training programme. The second useful value is average number of items scanned per minute after the training programme, which comes to 20.60. We can immediately see that the there is a difference in scan rate at the pre-training versus the post-training levels (pre-training average scan rate per minutes = 19.278). For a number of reasons, we cannot just take the difference in these two scan rates as the impact of the training. First, this increase happened across the board regardless of who went on the training; second, just looking at the increases overall does not tell us anything about what factors are linked to this increase. Thus to model the impact of our training course we need to look at the regression model output in Figure 10.6, which tells us the potential contribution that participation in the training course had, taking into account all other factors in the model. The unstandardized beta coefficient for the training participation was B=1.600. This suggests that all other things being equal, participation in training in our organization can have 1.6 item-per-minute scan-rate improvement. We can check this using the following set of calculations:

Average post-training scan rate =
(all other things being equal) + 1.6(average value for participation in the training course)

This is a variation on our raw regression equation without including all other factors in our model (we do not need to include each of these because we can calculate an estimate of their contribution to the equation, as follows) and inputting the average participation value as our actual variable data.

**FIGURE 10.7**

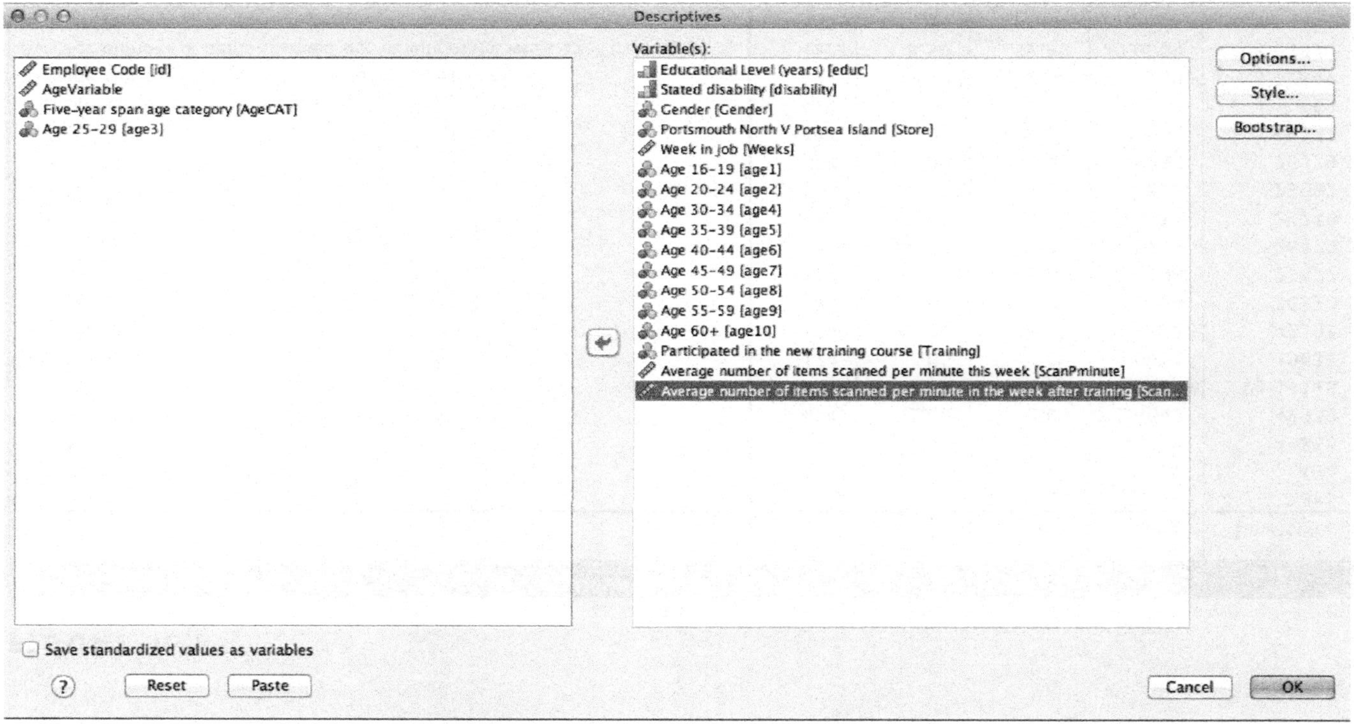
Descriptives
Employee Code [id]
AgeVariable
Five-year span age category [AgeCAT]
Age 25-29 [age3]
Variable(s):
Educational Level (years) [educ]
Stated disability [disability]
Gender [Gender]
Portsmouth North V Portsea Island [Store]
Week in job [Weeks]
Age 16-19 [age1]
Age 20-24 [age2]
Age 30-34 [age4]
Age 35-39 [age5]
Age 40-44 [age6]
Age 45-49 [age7]
Age 50-54 [age8]
Age 55-59 [age9]
Age 60+ [age10]
Participated in the new training course [Training]
Average number of items scanned per minute this week [ScanPminute]
Average number of items scanned per minute in the week after training [Scan...
Options...
Style...
Bootstrap...
Save standardized values as variables
?
Reset
Paste
Cancel
OK

## FIGURE 10.8

### Descriptive Statistics

| | N | Minimum | Maximum | Mean | Std. Deviation |
|---|---|---|---|---|---|
| Educational Level (years) | 474 | 8 | 21 | 13.49 | 2.885 |
| Stated disability | 474 | 0 | 1 | .22 | .414 |
| Gender | 474 | 1.00 | 2.00 | 1.4557 | .49856 |
| Portsmouth North versus Portsea Island | 474 | 1.00 | 2.00 | 1.4662 | .49939 |
| Week in job | 474 | 1.00 | 103.00 | 36.6561 | 29.14116 |
| Age 16–19 | 474 | .00 | 1.00 | .0401 | .19636 |
| Age 20–24 | 474 | .00 | 1.00 | .2342 | .42393 |
| Age 30–34 | 474 | .00 | 1.00 | .0759 | .26520 |
| Age 35–39 | 474 | .00 | 1.00 | .0696 | .25477 |
| Age 40–44 | 474 | .00 | 1.00 | .0738 | .26179 |
| Age 45–49 | 474 | .00 | 1.00 | .0654 | .24749 |
| Age 50–54 | 474 | .00 | 1.00 | .0612 | .23992 |
| Age 55–59 | 474 | .00 | 1.00 | .0738 | .26179 |
| Age 60+ | 474 | .00 | 1.00 | .0084 | .09157 |
| Participated in the new training course | 474 | 0 | 1 | .32 | .469 |
| Average number of items scanned per minute this week | 474 | 5.00 | 32.00 | 19.2789 | 3.77649 |
| Average number of items scanned per minute in the week after training | 452 | 5.50 | 32.50 | 20.6009 | 3.63830 |
| Valid N (listwise) | 452 | | | | |

As we know the average value for our training participation variable, we can set out the following:

Post-training scan rate = (all other things being equal)
+ 1.6(participated in training)

As we know the average post-training scan rate (20.60) and the training participation rate (0.32) we can also set out the following:

20.60 = (all other things being equal) + 1.6(0.32)

Because we know the 20.60 (mean post-training scan rate) and we know the coefficient contribution to training course (1.6) and the mean of the training participation variable (0.32), we can transpose the equation to calculate what we need to insert into our (all things being equal) part of the equation:

All other things being equal = 20.60 − 1.6(0.32)

Thus we can calculate:

20.088 = 20.60 − 1.6(0.32)

And if we retransform this back to our regression equation predicting post-training scan rate we get the following:

20.60 = (20.088) + 1.6(0.32)

With this we can conduct some modelling of what the impact would be on our scan rate with various levels of participation on the training course. If we assume that all of our staff participated in the training course then our mean level for our participation variable would be 1 rather than 0.32 (which indicates that about one-third of the organization participated). Thus our equation would read the following with 100 per cent participation:

21.688 = (20.088) + 1.6(1)

Furthermore, if no one participated our equation would read the following (our mean level for our participation variable would be 0 rather than 0.32):

20.088 = (20.088) + 1.6(0)

We could run variations of this with different levels of participation in training and see what the potential impact on scan rate would be. However, clearly, with all other things being equal, full versus no participation in the training course changes the scan rate by an average of 1.6 items per minute in our entire organization. This is extremely powerful information that we can then use to help evaluate and justify the impact of our training course in our organization – especially when we start to consider what impact this would have across all our employees.

If we assume that each of our 452 checkout operators works 35 hours per week on the checkouts and that these operators are working at full productivity, each employee works for 2,100 minutes scanning items per week (35 × 60). Working on the average scan-rate per minute of 20.6, at the moment if all employees participated in the training course this should lead to 43,260 items scanned per week (2,100 × 20.6) per employee.

Without the training programme, the average scan-rate per minute would be 20.088; this amounts to a total of 42,184.8 items scanned in an average week per employee (2100 × 20.088).

Compared to not running the training course, if full participation in the new training programme occurred, this should increase the average scan rate to 21.688 from 20.088, which amounts to an additional average scan potential of 3,360 scans per employee ((2100 × 21.688) – (2100 × 20.088)). Thus with 452 employees this increases the potential number of items scanned in a week by 1,518,720 items.

> **Snapshot hidden gem**
>
> Using our model, we can say that if all employees went on the customer service training programme, we predict the potential number of items scanned in a week could increase by over 1.5 million items.

This is just one example of the kind of predictive modelling that we can do with the results of our scan-rate regression modelling. Obviously here we are making a number of assumptions that would need consideration if we were to try to present the implications of our analysis to a board of directors (to justify the investment in our training programme). These assumptions would need nuanced modelling themselves (eg assumptions such as all operators work 35 hours a week at full scan-rate productivity). However, hopefully the reader can begin to see some of the potential of applying our analytic results to actual business scenarios.

# Obtaining individual values for the outcomes of our predictive models

In considering how else we might be able to use our regression models in an applied way to answer the 'So what?' question, there is a particularly useful feature of SPSS that we can use to help apply our regression results to create predictive models. SPSS has a very practical tool (that most statistical programs should also have) that can be used to review predicted model values for all individuals in our data set and to help translate your model findings into a truly predictive tool.

You can get SPSS to run your regression model and save the values of our outcome variable that our model predicts on the basis of: 1) our regression equation results; and 2) the actual values of each individual independent variable for each employee that we have in our data set (and that helped to produce 1) in the first place). The benefit of this tool is that (after you have saved the data file as a different name so that you don't mess with the original data) you can add new employees where you have data values for the predictor (independent) variables and run the analysis again, saving predicted values in our predicted dependent variable for the new cases. This is particularly useful when we want to use existing patterns with our organization to make predictions about new cases. This also allows you to enter as many 'what if' scenarios as you like (by adjusting various values of your independent variables with a particular individual) to get a (new) predicted value of our particular outcome. The opportunities to use this predictive modelling tool are considerable (we go on to show other examples of using this tool below).

The process for getting SPSS to apply a regression model and save a predicted value of our outcome variable is quite simple. We demonstrate this below in an application where we make predictions about future behaviour of graduate candidates on the basis of behaviour (performance and leaving behaviour) exhibited by previously hired graduates.

# Example 3: predicting the likelihood of leaving

For our next model we intend to apply our predictive models that we ran with employees in our Chapter 6 (prediction of turnover case study) to obtain data that tells us the likelihood of leaving for each employee within our organization. In the employee turnover case study, Chapter 6 (see page 217), we used binary logistic regression to predict individual turnover using gender of the employee and of the immediate manager, age, length-of-service, performance appraisal rating, country and leaver status. The model we tested is presented diagrammatically in Figure 10.9 and our data set used was 'Chapter 6 Individual Turnover.sav'.

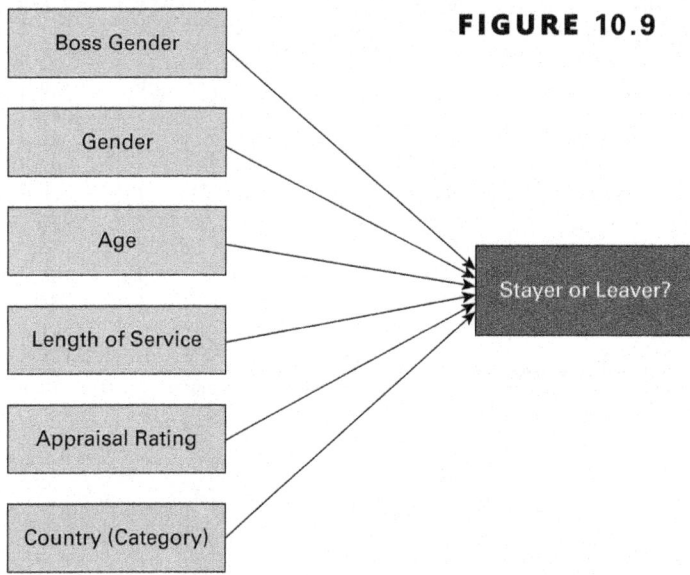

**FIGURE 10.9**

The output that this model produced can be found in Figure 10.10.

## FIGURE 10.10

**Omnibus Tests of Model Coefficients**

|        |       | Chi-square | df | Sig. |
|--------|-------|-----------|----|------|
| Step 1 | Step  | 49.799    | 14 | .000 |
|        | Block | 49.799    | 14 | .000 |
|        | Model | 49.799    | 14 | .000 |

**Model Summary**

| Step | -2 Log likelihood | Cox and Snell R-Square | Nagelkerke R-Square |
|------|-------------------|------------------------|---------------------|
| 1    | 1204.203[a]       | .030                   | .056                |

a. Estimation terminated at iteration number 5 because parameter estimates changed by less than .001.

**Classification Table[a]**

|        |                  |        | Predicted |        |                    |
|--------|------------------|--------|-----------|--------|--------------------|
|        |                  |        | Stayer or Leaver | | Percentage Correct |
|        | Observed         |        | Stayer    | Leaver |                    |
| Step 1 | Stayer or Leaver | Stayer | 1441      | 0      | 100.0              |
|        |                  | Leaver | 209       | 0      | .0                 |
|        | Overall Percentage |      |           |        | 87.3               |

a. The cut value is .500

**Variables in the Equation**

|         |                | B     | S.E. | Wald   | df | Sig. | Exp(B) |
|---------|----------------|-------|------|--------|----|------|--------|
| Step 1[a] | BossGender   | -.184 | .163 | 1.268  | 1  | .260 | .832   |
|         | Gender         | -.608 | .162 | 14.151 | 1  | .000 | .544   |
|         | Age            | -.001 | .009 | .021   | 1  | .886 | .999   |
|         | LengthOfService| -.017 | .011 | 2.488  | 1  | .115 | .983   |
|         | AppraisalRating| -.248 | .097 | 6.499  | 1  | .011 | .780   |
|         | Country        |       |      | 9.188  | 9  | .420 |        |
|         | Country(1)     | -.249 | .604 | .170   | 1  | .680 | .779   |
|         | Country(2)     | .002  | .594 | .000   | 1  | .998 | 1.002  |
|         | Country(3)     | -.059 | .516 | .013   | 1  | .909 | .943   |
|         | Country(4)     | -.455 | .624 | .532   | 1  | .466 | .634   |
|         | Country(5)     | -.734 | .649 | 1.281  | 1  | .258 | .480   |
|         | Country(6)     | -.415 | .597 | .485   | 1  | .486 | .660   |
|         | Country(7)     | -.572 | .535 | 1.141  | 1  | .285 | .565   |
|         | Country(8)     | -.506 | .471 | 1.154  | 1  | .283 | .603   |
|         | Country(9)     | -.698 | .434 | 2.592  | 1  | .107 | .497   |
|         | Constant       | .168  | .657 | .066   | 1  | .798 | 1.183  |

a. Variable(s) entered on step 1: BossGender, Gender, Age, LengthOfService, AppraisalRating, Country.

> FROM the 'Snapshot hidden gem' in Chapter 6 (page 226) we can tell the following:
>
> Country differences do not come out as significant in accounting for turnover in our model; however, women are more than twice as likely to leave than men and a higher appraisal rating will increase the chances of employees staying (thus women and employees who get low performance ratings are a 'higher risk of leaving' category than other employees).

Recall from Chapter 3 that the structure of the logistic regression model (those who find equations intimidating can read on without worrying too much about the mechanics of what is going on here; our application will begin to make sense as you read on) looks like this:

### Logistic regression model

$$Ln(p/(1-p)) = b_0 + b_1 x_{1i} + b_2 x_{2i} + b_n x_{ni}$$

where p is the probability that Y=1, or, put another way:

$$P(Y) = 1/(1+e^{-(b_0 + b_1 X_{1i} + b_2 X_{2i} + \ldots + b_n X_{ni})})$$

where 'e' is the base of natural logarithms, i is the instance of the variable, Y is the dependent variable, x(1 to n) are the n independent variables and b is the degree to which that independent variable impacts the dependent variable in the equation.

So, in other words, the regression model can calculate the probability that Y = 1 (whether someone is likely to be a leaver) and in a retention risk analysis project this is exactly what we want to know. In this example, Y = turnover, so the probability that Y = 1 is the probability that someone in our organization will leave. With SPSS, we can use our regression model (above) to determine the probability that any given individual will leave. This is particularly useful because we have no idea what the likelihood is of anyone leaving until we have run our turnover regression model. All we really knew about turnover before we created the model was whether employees have already left or whether they are still there.

By running our regression models, identifying drivers of turnover, we can then apply our regression equation to everyone's data values linked to these 'drivers' and we can get SPSS to make predictions as to the probability of each person leaving. We could, for example, determine that the likelihood of someone leaving was 20 per cent, or 40 per cent, or 60 per cent, or 80 per cent, etc. This would have extremely useful applications in talent management and succession planning.

Having a good idea of the risk of an individual resigning when having career discussions, reviewing top talent and planning succession for senior roles in the organization is critical. It may indeed flag when to take action that may turn things around for an individual to prevent them from resigning and, particularly for senior roles, save the organization a considerable amount of money.

With this example, we run the logistic regression model and save the regression model equation's predicted output for each individual in our organization; SPSS applies the regression equation to the data in the predictor variable columns in the data set and saves the solution of the regression equation (the probability that someone is going to be a leaver) in a new column.

To do this we run our binary logistic regression model (that we ran above) by selecting Analyze→Regression→Binary Logistic (See Figure 10.11).

**FIGURE 10.11**

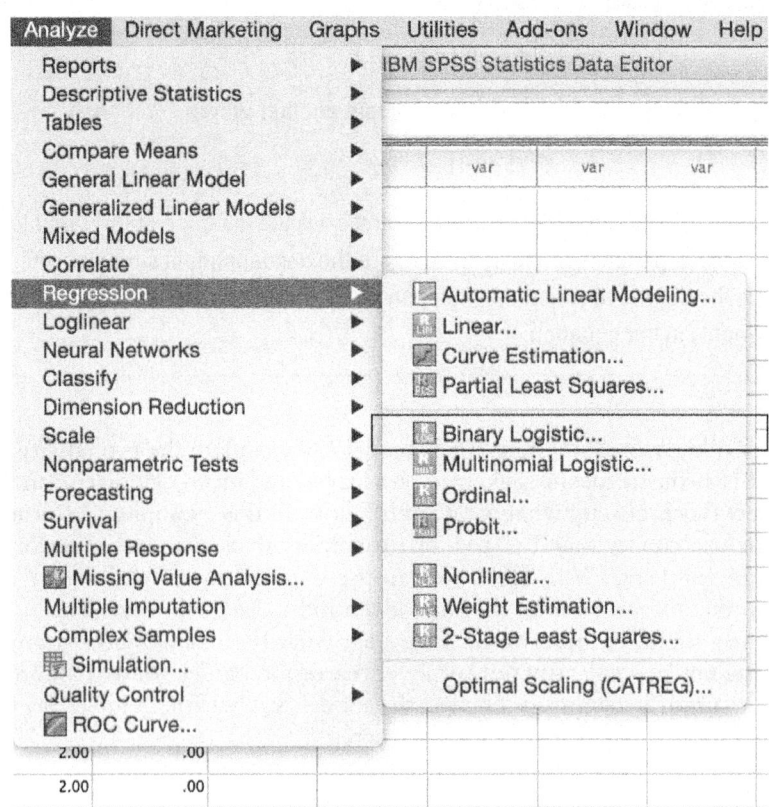

This then opens up the logistic regression window and we set up the model as we did in Chapter 6 (see Figure 10.12).

**FIGURE 10.12**

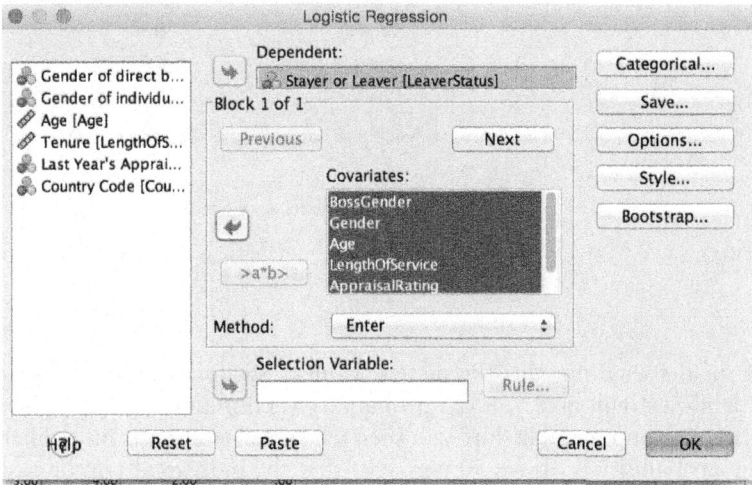

We make sure that we select the 'Country' variable as a categorical variable (see Chapter 6 and Figure 10.13).

**FIGURE 10.13**

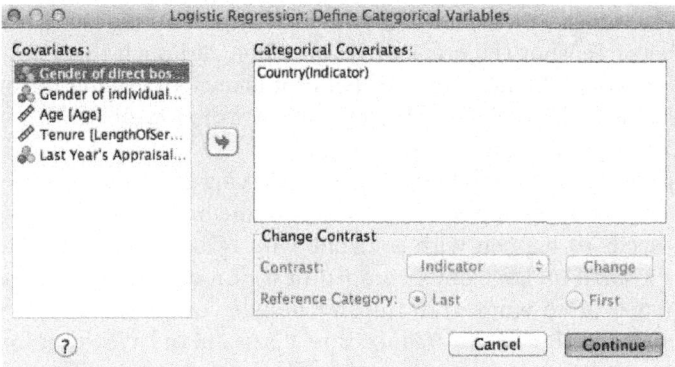

Select 'Continue' to return to the logistic regression window (Figure 10.12) and before clicking on OK we then select the 'Save...' button. Figure 10.14 will appear. This will give you some options around what additional information you may like to produce with the individual-level data. Here you select the 'Probabilities' and 'Group membership' option in the 'Predicted Values' selection box.

**FIGURE 10.14**

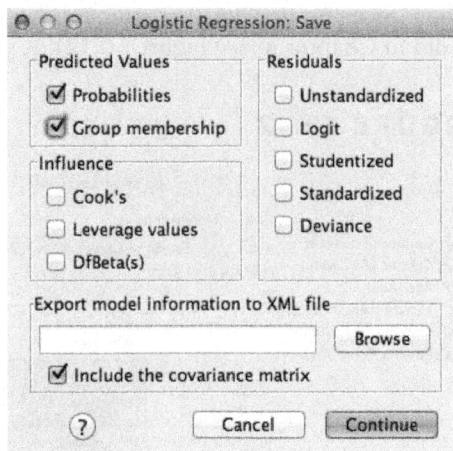

Let's just focus on the 'Predicted Values' section for now. Selecting 'Probabilities' will give you the probability each individual has of leaving. Selecting 'Group membership' will then tell you whether it is more likely (as in the probability is above 50 per cent) that the individual will be a stayer (0) or a leaver (1).

Click 'Continue' and then 'OK' once you return to the logistic regression window.

Let's now go straight to the data view in our data set and look at the new data columns as well as the content that has been created by our model prediction (see Figure 10.15).

In Figure 10.15 it is the column labelled 'PRE_1' that shows the probability of leaving. You can see that the highest probability of leaving in our particular screenshot (Figure 10.15) is 0.4564. Although this is closer to 0 than 1, many would agree that 46 per cent chance of leaving the organization is relatively high. Figure 10.16 shows that the lowest figure goes down to 0.03786, or 3.8 per cent.

Clearly the difference between someone having a risk of leaving of 46 per cent and a risk of leaving of 3.8 per cent is quite high. Indeed it may be that all that needs to happen with someone who is at 46 per cent before they resign is a small nudge from a competitor (or an unfair decision from their line manager or co-worker). If this individual is on the succession plan for the future leadership of the organization it is useful to have this information, which may help to prevent a resignation before it happens. The reader will see that in some cases the leaver status with each employee in our data set is .00 and in some cases 1. The employees who have a 1 in this column have already left. It is the people who are still in the organization (with .00 in the leaver column) that have a higher PRE_1 value who may need special attention to make sure that they don't leave.

## FIGURE 10.15

6 : LeaverStatus    .0

| | BossGender | Gender | Age | LengthOfService | AppraisalRating | Country | LeaverStatus | PRE_1 | PGR_1 |
|---|---|---|---|---|---|---|---|---|---|
| 1 | .00 | .00 | 27.00 | .00 | 1.00 | 3.00 | .00 | .45640 | .00 |
| 2 | .00 | .00 | 33.00 | .00 | 1.00 | 3.00 | .00 | .45440 | .00 |
| 3 | .00 | .00 | 26.00 | .00 | 1.00 | 4.00 | 1.00 | .36127 | .00 |
| 4 | .00 | .00 | 31.00 | .00 | 1.00 | 4.00 | .00 | .35972 | .00 |
| 5 | .00 | .00 | 33.00 | .00 | 1.00 | 4.00 | .00 | .35910 | .00 |
| 6 | .00 | .00 | 18.00 | .00 | 2.00 | 1.00 | .00 | .35409 | .00 |
| 7 | .00 | .00 | 23.00 | .00 | 2.00 | 1.00 | .00 | .35255 | .00 |
| 8 | 1.00 | .00 | 28.00 | .00 | 2.00 | 3.00 | 1.00 | .35250 | .00 |
| 9 | .00 | .00 | 28.00 | .00 | 2.00 | 1.00 | 1.00 | .35101 | .00 |
| 10 | .00 | .00 | 17.00 | 1.00 | 1.00 | 8.00 | .00 | .34858 | .00 |
| 11 | 1.00 | .00 | 41.00 | .00 | 2.00 | 3.00 | 1.00 | .34852 | .00 |
| 12 | .00 | .00 | 48.00 | .00 | 2.00 | 1.00 | 1.00 | .34490 | .00 |
| 13 | .00 | .00 | 49.00 | .00 | 2.00 | 1.00 | 1.00 | .34459 | .00 |
| 14 | .00 | .00 | 18.00 | 2.00 | 1.00 | 8.00 | .00 | .34439 | .00 |
| 15 | .00 | .00 | 19.00 | 2.00 | 1.00 | 8.00 | 1.00 | .34408 | .00 |
| 16 | .00 | .00 | 25.00 | .00 | 1.00 | 7.00 | 1.00 | .33518 | .00 |
| 17 | .00 | .00 | 39.00 | .00 | 3.00 | 3.00 | .00 | .33470 | .00 |
| 18 | .00 | .00 | 32.00 | .00 | 1.00 | 7.00 | .00 | .33308 | .00 |
| 19 | .00 | .00 | 38.00 | .00 | 1.00 | 7.00 | 1.00 | .33129 | .00 |
| 20 | .00 | .00 | 42.00 | .00 | 1.00 | 7.00 | .00 | .33009 | .00 |
| 21 | .00 | .00 | 43.00 | .00 | 1.00 | 7.00 | .00 | .32980 | .00 |
| 22 | .00 | .00 | 44.00 | .00 | 1.00 | 7.00 | 1.00 | .32950 | .00 |
| 23 | .00 | .00 | 19.00 | .00 | 2.00 | 6.00 | .00 | .31678 | .00 |
| 24 | 1.00 | .00 | 21.00 | .00 | 2.00 | 1.00 | 1.00 | .31238 | .00 |

Another really useful way of using this method to predict individual turnover is with new recruitment and selection contexts. Many organizations run very expensive and detailed assessment centres to assist in decisions when selecting new joiners into the organization. The application of our regression models that we use in the previous example can be applied to help selectors make some 'evidence-based' decisions on who to hire. For example, models could be developed to predict expected post-hire performance levels with new assessment-centre candidates as well as the likelihood that they will not leave within a short period after coming on board. These models could be run using assessment-centre data input as the independent variables. The information that these models produce could provide critical input into selection decisions (and associated courses of action required for hiring using the model to predict likely outcomes).

# Predictive HR Analytics

**FIGURE 10.16**

| | BossGender | Gender | Age | LengthOfService | AppraisalRating | Country | LeaverStatus | PRE_1 | PGR_1 |
|---|---|---|---|---|---|---|---|---|---|
| 1628 | 1.00 | 1.00 | 53.00 | 34.00 | 4.00 | 9.00 | .00 | .04879 | .00 |
| 1629 | 1.00 | 1.00 | 54.00 | 34.00 | 4.00 | 9.00 | .00 | .04873 | .00 |
| 1630 | 1.00 | 1.00 | 52.00 | 35.00 | 4.00 | 9.00 | .00 | .04806 | .00 |
| 1631 | 1.00 | 1.00 | 53.00 | 35.00 | 4.00 | 9.00 | .00 | .04800 | .00 |
| 1632 | 1.00 | 1.00 | 54.00 | 35.00 | 4.00 | 9.00 | .00 | .04794 | .00 |
| 1633 | 1.00 | 1.00 | 54.00 | 35.00 | 4.00 | 9.00 | .00 | .04794 | .00 |
| 1634 | 1.00 | 1.00 | 39.00 | 22.00 | 5.00 | 9.00 | .00 | .04774 | .00 |
| 1635 | .00 | 1.00 | 52.00 | 33.00 | 5.00 | 9.00 | .00 | .04672 | .00 |
| 1636 | 1.00 | 1.00 | 46.00 | 23.00 | 5.00 | 9.00 | .00 | .04655 | .00 |
| 1637 | 1.00 | 1.00 | 56.00 | 37.00 | 4.00 | 9.00 | .00 | .04627 | .00 |
| 1638 | 1.00 | 1.00 | 41.00 | 24.00 | 5.00 | 9.00 | .00 | .04609 | .00 |
| 1639 | 1.00 | 1.00 | 46.00 | 24.00 | 5.00 | 9.00 | .00 | .04579 | .00 |
| 1640 | 1.00 | 1.00 | 56.00 | 38.00 | 4.00 | 9.00 | .00 | .04552 | .00 |
| 1641 | 1.00 | 1.00 | 43.00 | 25.00 | 5.00 | 9.00 | .00 | .04522 | .00 |
| 1642 | 1.00 | 1.00 | 50.00 | 25.00 | 5.00 | 9.00 | .00 | .04481 | .00 |
| 1643 | 1.00 | 1.00 | 57.00 | 39.00 | 4.00 | 9.00 | .00 | .04472 | .00 |
| 1644 | 1.00 | 1.00 | 58.00 | 39.00 | 4.00 | 9.00 | .00 | .04466 | .00 |
| 1645 | 1.00 | 1.00 | 58.00 | 40.00 | 4.00 | 9.00 | .00 | .04394 | .00 |
| 1646 | 1.00 | 1.00 | 45.00 | 27.00 | 5.00 | 9.00 | .00 | .04364 | .00 |
| 1647 | 1.00 | 1.00 | 58.00 | 41.00 | 4.00 | 9.00 | .00 | .04322 | .00 |
| 1648 | 1.00 | 1.00 | 46.00 | 29.00 | 5.00 | 9.00 | .00 | .04218 | .00 |
| 1649 | 1.00 | 1.00 | 47.00 | 29.00 | 5.00 | 9.00 | .00 | .04212 | .00 |
| 1650 | 1.00 | 1.00 | 49.00 | 30.00 | 5.00 | 9.00 | .00 | .04133 | .00 |
| 1651 | 1.00 | 1.00 | 53.00 | 35.00 | 5.00 | 9.00 | .00 | .03786 | .00 |

# Making graduate selection decisions with evidence obtained from previous performance data

As discussed in previous sections of this book, decisions made about people are often subjective, relying on gut instinct and involving bias (that may or may not be unconscious). Although gut instinct can be extremely useful in technical and process-driven situations, we can never expect to know everything there is to know about an individual and hence using gut instinct when it comes to making decisions about people is not useful. Leaders do, however, often rely on instinct rather than evidence when making decisions about people (Ulrich, in Fitz-enz, 2010). Ulrich also suggests that 'most leaders would not make product decisions based on feelings alone; rather they use data based on how different product features meet or do not meet customer expectations. We should expect no less from people analytics.'

Recruitment and selection are one of the key areas of the employee process where the decisions we make have an enormous impact on the organization for years to come. In the recruitment and selection case study (Chapter 8), we discovered that key aspects of assessment-centre activities are found to predict post-joining performance. In this model, we also found that the onboarding activity of induction had a positive impact on first-year performance.

Specifically, we developed a complex model to predict performance after one year with newly recruited graduates. We constructed a model based on data available from a range of sources; our predictor variables (independent variables) included assessment-centre scores, gender, highest level of education reached, whether they had previous work experience, and which department of the organization they had joined. We also included onboarding factors such as whether graduates attended an induction day or induction week, and whether they had an onboarding buddy.

The reader may recall that we used the data file 'Chapter 8 Selection.sav': this file had a number of variables containing data linked to 360 graduates. The file contained the following variables:

| | | |
|---|---|---|
| 1 | GradID | Employee Identifier |
| 2 | Gender | Male (1) or Female (2) |
| 3 | EducationHighest | Education Category: BSc (1) MSc (2) Ph.D. (3) |
| 4 | BAMEYN | Black, Asian or Minority Ethnic: Yes (1) or No (2) |
| 5 | WorkExperience | Worked Before: Yes (1) No (2) |
| 6 | GradJOBfunction | Function Joined: (1) HR; (2) Finance; (3) Marketing; (4) Sales; (5) Risk; (6) Legal; (7) Operations |
| 7 | ACPersonalityO | Assessment C Personality Openness (percentage) |
| 8 | ACPersonalityC | Assessment C Personality Conscientious (percentage) |
| 9 | ACPersonalityE | Assessment C Personality Extraversion (percentage) |
| 10 | ACPersonalityA | Assessment C Personality Agreeable (percentage) |
| 11 | ACPersonalityN | Assessment C Personality Neuroticism (percentage) |
| 12 | ACRatingINTCOMPA | Assessment C Competency Technical (1-5) |
| 13 | ACRatingINTCOMPB | Assessment C Competency Team Player |

| 14 | ACRatingINTCOMPC | Assessment C Competency Critical Thought |
|---|---|---|
| 15 | ACRatingINTCOMPD | Assessment C Competency Business Aware |
| 16 | ACRatingINTCOMPE | Assessment C Competency Drive Innovation |
| 17 | ACRatingAPTnumerical | Numerical Aptitude Test Score |
| 18 | ACRatingAPTverbal | Verbal Reasoning Aptitude Test Score |
| 19 | InductionDay | Attend Induction Day: No (0) Yes (1) |
| 20 | InductionWeek | Attend Induction Week: No (0) Yes (1) |
| 21 | OnBoardingBuddy | Given Joining Buddy: No (0) Yes (1) |
| 22 | Year1performanceRating | Year 1 Performance Rating:<br>(1) Fails to Meet Expectations<br>(2) Just meets expectations<br>(3) Meets Expectations comfortably<br>(4) Exceeds Expectations<br>(5) A Star Performer |
| 23 | LeaverYr2 | Leaver in first 24 Months (0) No (1) Leaver |
| 24 | HRDummyV | HR Dummy Variable |
| 25 | FinanceDummyV | Finance Dummy Variable |
| 26 | MarketingDummyV | Marketing Dummy Variable |
| 27 | SalesDummyV | Sales Dummy Variable |
| 28 | RiskDummyV | Risk Management Dummy Variable |
| 29 | LegalDummyV | Legal Dummy Variable |
| 30 | OperationsDummyV | Operations Dummy Variable |

The complex model that we ran (see Chapter 8, Figure 8.19, page 307) was significant and confirmed that it is possible to predict graduates' 12-month performance ratings from the information held and collected during recruitment, selection and onboarding.

# Business Applications: Scenario Modelling and Business Cases

In Figure 10.17, we can recall the results of our model.

## FIGURE 10.17

**Model Summary**

| Model | R | R-Square | Adjusted R-Square | Std. Error of the Estimate |
|---|---|---|---|---|
| 1 | .815[a] | .664 | .635 | .69911 |

a. Predictors: (Constant), OperationsDummyV, Black Asian Minority Ethnic Yes or No, Openness Percentile, RiskDummyV, Assessment Centre Rating Core Competency C - Critical Thinking, Neuroticism Percentile, Worked Before, Did they attend the Induction Day, Aptitude Test % score Verbal Reasoning, SalesDummyV, Did they get an onboarding Buddy, Education Category, Aptitude Test % score Numeric Reasoning, Assessment Centre Rating Core Competency B - Team Player, Assessment Centre Rating Core Competency D - Business Awareness, Did they attend the Induction Week, Extroversion Percentile, Agreeableness Percentile, Conscientious Percentile, Male or Female, Assessment Centre Rating Core Competency E - Drive and Innovation, Assessment Centre Rating Core Competency A - Technical Capabilities, FinanceDummyV, MarketingDummyV, LegalDummyV

**ANOVA[a]**

| Model | | Sum of Squares | df | Mean Square | F | Sig. |
|---|---|---|---|---|---|---|
| 1 | Regression | 281.954 | 25 | 11.278 | 23.075 | .000[b] |
| | Residual | 142.716 | 292 | .489 | | |
| | Total | 424.670 | 317 | | | |

a. Dependent Variable: Performance rating 1 year in (1 fails to meet expectations- 5 A star performer)

b. Predictors: (Constant), OperationsDummyV, Black Asian Minority Ethnic Yes or No, Openness Percentile, RiskDummyV, Assessment Centre Rating Core Competency C - Critical Thinking, Neuroticism Percentile, Worked Before, Did they attend the Induction Day, Aptitude Test % score Verbal Reasoning, SalesDummyV, Did they get an onboarding Buddy, Education Category, Aptitude Test % score Numeric Reasoning, Assessment Centre Rating Core Competency B - Team Player, Assessment Centre Rating Core Competency D - Business Awareness, Did they attend the Induction Week, Extroversion Percentile, Agreeableness Percentile, Conscientious Percentile, Male or Female, Assessment Centre Rating Core Competency E - Drive and Innovation, Assessment Centre Rating Core Competency A - Technical Capabilities, FinanceDummyV, MarketingDummyV, LegalDummyV

**Coefficients[a]**

| Model | | Unstandardized Coefficients B | Std. Error | Standardized Coefficients Beta | t | Sig. |
|---|---|---|---|---|---|---|
| 1 | (Constant) | -4.823 | 1.202 | | -4.014 | .000 |
| | Male or Female | -.858 | .131 | -.362 | -6.567 | .000 |
| | Education Category | .138 | .083 | .064 | 1.677 | .095 |
| | Black Asian Minority Ethnic Yes or No | -.019 | .104 | -.007 | -.186 | .853 |
| | Worked Before | .061 | .089 | .024 | .679 | .497 |
| | Openness Percentile | -.003 | .004 | -.045 | -.930 | .353 |
| | Conscientious Percentile | .008 | .003 | .144 | 2.978 | .003 |
| | Extroversion Percentile | .010 | .004 | .179 | 2.785 | .006 |
| | Agreeableness Percentile | .001 | .003 | .018 | .317 | .751 |
| | Neuroticism Percentile | -.001 | .002 | -.016 | -.419 | .676 |
| | Assessment Centre Rating Core Competency A - Technical Capabilities | .364 | .138 | .155 | 2.633 | .009 |
| | Assessment Centre Rating Core Competency B - Team Player | .131 | .120 | .046 | 1.091 | .276 |
| | Assessment Centre Rating Core Competency C - Critical Thinking | .090 | .140 | .032 | .644 | .520 |
| | Assessment Centre Rating Core Competency D - Business Awareness | .359 | .113 | .150 | 3.193 | .002 |
| | Assessment Centre Rating Core Competency E - Drive and Innovation | .346 | .165 | .123 | 2.088 | .038 |
| | Aptitude Test % score Numeric Reasoning | .010 | .007 | .070 | 1.407 | .161 |
| | Aptitude Test % score Verbal Reasoning | .008 | .010 | .039 | .770 | .442 |
| | Did they attend the Induction Day | .357 | .141 | .102 | 2.526 | .012 |
| | Did they attend the Induction Week | .023 | .129 | .007 | .182 | .856 |
| | Did they get an onboarding Buddy | .232 | .252 | .035 | .919 | .359 |
| | FinanceDummyV | .154 | .254 | .051 | .607 | .544 |
| | MarketingDummyV | .624 | .219 | .224 | 2.842 | .005 |
| | SalesDummyV | -.064 | .296 | -.016 | -.215 | .830 |
| | RiskDummyV | .923 | .245 | .219 | 3.773 | .000 |
| | LegalDummyV | 1.151 | .255 | .357 | 4.517 | .000 |
| | OperationsDummyV | .402 | .233 | .115 | 1.722 | .086 |

a. Dependent Variable: Performance rating 1 year in (1 fails to meet expectations- 5 A star performer)

In terms of using the model to answer the 'So what?' question, two particular uses come to mind. One application is that this analysis may help us try to quantify the value of continuing with expensive onboarding activities whilst controlling for assessment-centre scores. The model could help to determine whether the return on the investment put into onboarding activity is worthwhile. The second is to assist with selection decisions. If we removed the onboarding piece from the model and looked at the pre-hiring information only, along with its impact on first-year performance, we could indeed use the model to help select new employees based on expected first-year performance (we outline this in examples 5 and 6 below). Before we do this, however, let's explore what impact the induction day might have on graduate performance and consider a model where we might be able to ascertain how important such an investment might be.

# Example 4: constructing the business case for investment in an induction day

Here we explore the above model to help us build a business case for continuing to invest in the organization's induction day. We follow a similar approach to evaluating the impact of the checkout scan rate training, as above. When we set out the raw regression equation based on the results of the regression model output presented in Figure 10.17, it looks like this (the significant drivers are highlighted in bold):

Performance rating year =
– 4.823
– **0.858 Gender**
+ 0.138 Education Category
-0.019 BAME
+ 0.061 Worked Before
– 0.003 Openness percentile score
+ **0.008 Conscientiousness percentile score**
+ **0.010 Extraversion percentile score**
+ 0.001 Agreeableness percentile score
– 0.001 Neuroticism percentile score
+ **0.364 Technical capabilities rating**
+ 0.131 Team player rating
+ 0.090 Critical thinking rating
+ **0.359 Business awareness rating**
+ **0.346 Drive and innovation rating**
+ 0.010 Numeric reasoning test score
+ 0.008 Verbal reasoning test score
+ **0.357 Induction day attendance Y/N**

\+ 0.023 Induction week attendance Y/N
\+ 0.232 Onboarding buddy Y/N
\+ 0.154 Finance dept Y/N
**+ 0.624 Marketing dept Y/N**
− 0.064 Sales dept Y/N
**+ 0.923 Risk dept Y/N**
**+ 1.151 Legal dept Y/N**
\+ 0.402 Operations

So how will we use this model to determine the return on investment in onboarding? We can do this simply by using 'what if' statements and asking questions. For example: if no one went on the induction day, what would be the impact on average year-one performance of the new graduates? What if everyone went on the induction day? The answer to this question is quite simple to estimate, because we are just looking at the difference on performance in scenarios where no one versus everyone went on the induction day. This means we just need to look at the unstandardized beta (B) coefficient. So, according to the model, individuals who attend the induction day are awarded, on average, a performance rating 0.357 points higher on the 1-to-5 scale than those who do not. This may be for a number of reasons that we might want to explore in another analytic research activity (we can only work with the data that we have here for now). Possible reasons for why induction-day presence could be important in predicting performance include: the induction helps ensure a quicker time to productivity due to 'knowing where everything is' or that it ensures a faster building of informal networks due to people met on the induction day, or many other things. According to Taylor (2010), benefits of an induction day include person–job fit, reducing intentions to leave and absenteeism, increasing employee commitment and job satisfaction.

Again here, it might be important to look at some descriptive statistics with our data-set context for our scenario. Let's take a look at the descriptive statistics again. Analyze → Descriptive Statistics → Descriptives (see Figure 10.18).

**FIGURE 10.18**

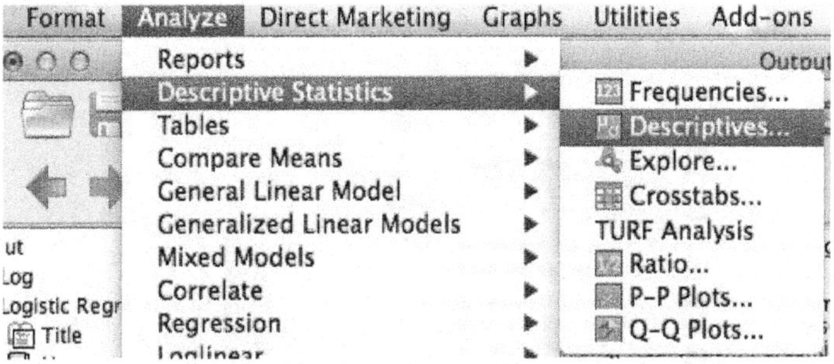

Here we can select the onboarding statistics-related variables and the performance rating variable (Figure 10.19).

**FIGURE 10.19**

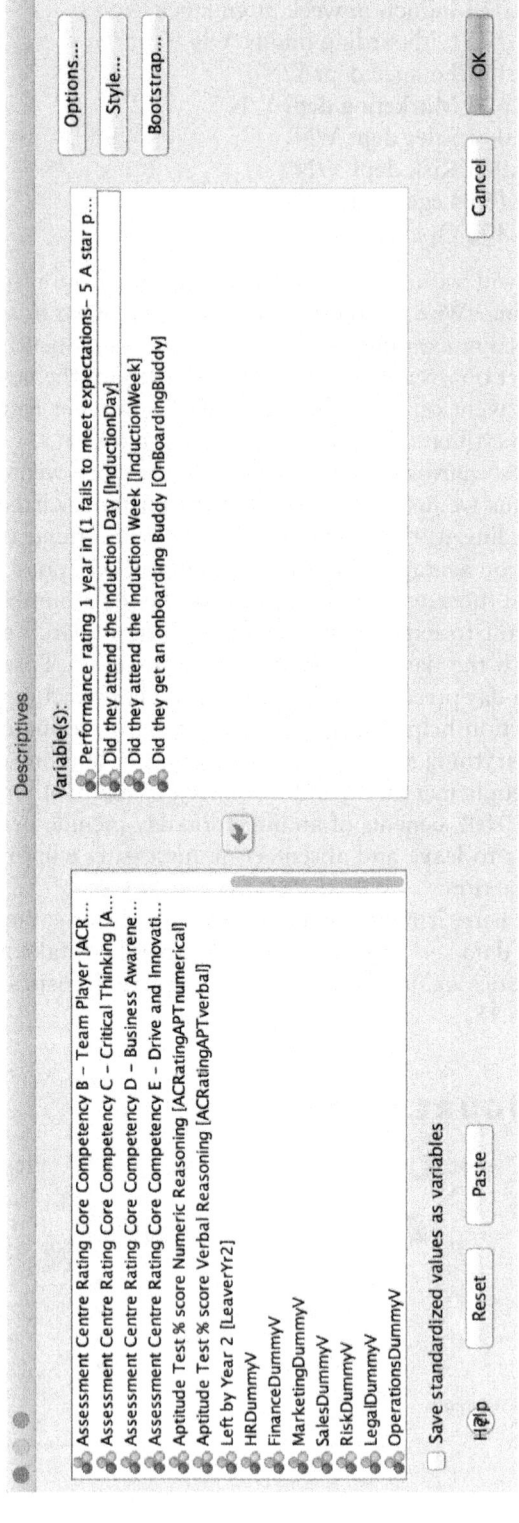

Selecting 'OK' here then produces the descriptive statistics set out in Figure 10.20.

### FIGURE 10.20

**Descriptive Statistics**

|  | N | Minimum | Maximum | Mean | Std. Deviation |
|---|---|---|---|---|---|
| Performance rating 1 year in (1 fails to meet expectations– 5 A star performer) | 318 | 1.00 | 5.00 | 3.4057 | 1.15743 |
| Did they attend the Induction Day | 360 | .00 | 1.00 | .8722 | .33431 |
| Did they attend the Induction Week | 360 | .00 | 1.00 | .7750 | .41816 |
| Did they get an onboarding Buddy | 360 | .00 | 1.00 | .9111 | .28498 |
| Valid N (listwise) | 318 | | | | |

From this output we know the current mean of graduates' first-year performance rating is 3.4057 with 87 per cent of new graduates attending induction day. If we were to increase this to 100 per cent, then we can model the resultant increase on the first-year performance rating.

The regression coefficient that our model produces in predicting performance for our graduates associated with induction day is unstandardized beta= 0.357 ($p<0.05$). We could use this to develop a model to assess the importance of the induction day.

All other things being equal, the first-year average performance rating = all other values (being equal) + 0.357 (average induction day attendance).

Currently, we have:

$$3.4057 = \text{all other values (being equal)} + 0.357 (0.8722)$$

We can transpose the equation to calculate what we need to insert into our (all other values being equal) part of the equation:

$$\text{All things being equal} = 3.4057 - 0.357 (0.8722)$$

Thus:

$$3.094 = 3.4057 - 0.357 (0.8722)$$

Now if we were able to update the attendance to 100 per cent, the predicted average performance would be:

$$3.094 + 0.357 (1) = 3.451$$

Or if we had no induction day, hence reducing the attendance to zero, the associated first-year performance would be:

$$3.094 + 0.357 (0) = 3.094$$

We have stored the value labels in the SPSS variable view for the first-year performance variable as:

1 = Fails to meet expectations by some margin.

2 = Just meets expectations.

3 = Meets expectations comfortably.

4 = Exceeds expectations.

5 = A star performer.

So we can say that the presence of an induction day improves the overall average performance from 3.094 to 3.451, significantly lifting performance towards the high-performer end. So a key part of evaluating a business case for investment into the induction day is that it can help improve employee performance.

### Snapshot hidden gem

Using our model, we can predict that attendance at induction day for new joiners improves their performance rating by more than one-third of a rating point.

# Example 5: using predictive models to help make a selection decision in graduate recruitment

The modelling scenario where we can use analytics to provide predictive information at selection stage involves the use of evidence from our regression model to help supply additional information that can help make a decision on who we should hire.

The above model included information on what features known at selection stage predicted future performance. This is very useful information that can be used by selectors. Of course, when making the selection decision, we have yet to carry out onboarding (as we have not yet hired any candidates), so let's look at our graduate performance regression model again without the induction variables included. We run the above model again (see Figure 8.19, page 307, in Chapter 8 for how we previously set this up); importantly this time we run it without the three onboarding variables and the following output is produced (Figure 10.21).

## FIGURE 10.21

**Model Summary**

| Model | R | R-Square | Adjusted R-Square | Std. Error of the Estimate |
|---|---|---|---|---|
| 1 | .809[a] | .654 | .628 | .70566 |

a. Predictors: (Constant), OperationsDummyV, Black Asian Minority Ethnic Yes or No, Openness Percentile, RiskDummyV, Assessment Centre Rating Core Competency C - Critical Thinking, Neuroticism Percentile, Worked Before, Aptitude Test % score Verbal Reasoning, SalesDummyV, Aptitude Test % score Numeric Reasoning, Education Category, Assessment Centre Rating Core Competency B - Team Player, MarketingDummyV, Assessment Centre Rating Core Competency D - Business Awareness, Male or Female, Agreeableness Percentile, Conscientious Percentile, Assessment Centre Rating Core Competency A - Technical Capabilities, Assessment Centre Rating Core Competency E - Drive and Innovation, LegalDummyV, Extroversion Percentile, FinanceDummyV

**ANOVA[a]**

| Model | | Sum of Squares | df | Mean Square | F | Sig. |
|---|---|---|---|---|---|---|
| 1 | Regression | 277.774 | 22 | 12.626 | 25.356 | .000[b] |
|   | Residual | 146.895 | 295 | .498 | | |
|   | Total | 424.670 | 317 | | | |

a. Dependent Variable: Performance rating 1 year in (1 fails to meet expectations- 5 A star performer)

b. Predictors: (Constant), OperationsDummyV, Black Asian Minority Ethnic Yes or No, Openness Percentile, RiskDummyV, Assessment Centre Rating Core Competency C - Critical Thinking, Neuroticism Percentile, Worked Before, Aptitude Test % score Verbal Reasoning, SalesDummyV, Aptitude Test % score Numeric Reasoning, Education Category, Assessment Centre Rating Core Competency B - Team Player, MarketingDummyV, Assessment Centre Rating Core Competency D - Business Awareness, Male or Female, Agreeableness Percentile, Conscientious Percentile, Assessment Centre Rating Core Competency A - Technical Capabilities, Assessment Centre Rating Core Competency E - Drive and Innovation, LegalDummyV, Extroversion Percentile, FinanceDummyV

**Coefficients[a]**

| Model | | Unstandardized Coefficients | | Standardized Coefficients | t | Sig. |
|---|---|---|---|---|---|---|
| | | B | Std. Error | Beta | | |
| 1 | (Constant) | -3.755 | 1.136 | | -3.315 | .001 |
| | Male or Female | -.910 | .129 | -.384 | -7.069 | .000 |
| | Education Category | .150 | .083 | .069 | 1.808 | .072 |
| | Black Asian Minority Ethnic Yes or No | -.017 | .105 | -.006 | -.163 | .871 |
| | Worked Before | .058 | .089 | .023 | .650 | .516 |
| | Openness Percentile | -.003 | .004 | -.040 | -.828 | .408 |
| | Conscientious Percentile | .008 | .003 | .146 | 3.009 | .003 |
| | Extroversion Percentile | .010 | .003 | .190 | 2.983 | .003 |
| | Agreeableness Percentile | .000 | .003 | -.007 | -.132 | .895 |
| | Neuroticism Percentile | -.002 | .002 | -.028 | -.748 | .455 |
| | Assessment Centre Rating Core Competency A - Technical Capabilities | .387 | .139 | .165 | 2.783 | .006 |
| | Assessment Centre Rating Core Competency B - Team Player | .133 | .120 | .047 | 1.107 | .269 |
| | Assessment Centre Rating Core Competency C - Critical Thinking | .084 | .141 | .030 | .594 | .553 |
| | Assessment Centre Rating Core Competency D - Business Awareness | .380 | .113 | .158 | 3.365 | .001 |
| | Assessment Centre Rating Core Competency E - Drive and Innovation | .327 | .167 | .116 | 1.963 | .051 |
| | Aptitude Test % score Numeric Reasoning | .007 | .007 | .046 | .931 | .352 |
| | Aptitude Test % score Verbal Reasoning | .006 | .010 | .029 | .563 | .574 |
| | FinanceDummyV | .145 | .255 | .048 | .568 | .571 |
| | MarketingDummyV | .508 | .217 | .182 | 2.345 | .020 |
| | SalesDummyV | -.104 | .295 | -.026 | -.353 | .724 |
| | RiskDummyV | .885 | .243 | .210 | 3.635 | .000 |
| | LegalDummyV | 1.138 | .255 | .353 | 4.467 | .000 |
| | OperationsDummyV | .387 | .234 | .111 | 1.657 | .099 |

a. Dependent Variable: Performance rating 1 year in (1 fails to meet expectations- 5 A star performer)

The model came out as significant with an R-square of 0.654. The new model results enable us to produce a regression equation predicting graduate performance with information known before onboarding. The raw regression model (with unstandardized coefficients) is outlined below:

Performance rating year =
− 3.765
− 0.910 Gender
+ 0.150 Education category
− 0.017 BAME
+ 0.058 Worked before
− 0.003 Openness percentile score
+ 0.008 Conscientiousness percentile score
+ 0.010 Extraversion percentile score
+ 0.000 Agreeableness percentile score
− 0.002 Neuroticism percentile score
+ 0.387 Technical capabilities rating
+ 0.133 Team player rating
+ 0.084 Critical-thinking rating
+ 0.380 Business awareness rating
+ 0.327 Drive and innovation rating
+ 0.007 Numeric reasoning test score
+ 0.006 Verbal reasoning test score
+ 0.145 Finance dept Y/N
+ 0.506 Marketing dept Y/N
− 0.104 Sales dept Y/N
+ 0.885 Risk dept Y/N
+ 1.138 Legal dept Y/N
+ 0.387 Operations

We can now use this model for subsequent recruitment exercises. So, say for the following year's graduate recruitment, we run the same assessment centre and gather the same information about candidates. This time, we can predict the first-year performance based on this information collected at the selection stage. For the purpose of this example, let's look at the candidates for the first assessment centre in the following year's graduate recruitment exercise, which took 10 candidates through the process to hire marketing graduates.

We open up the same data file we used in chapter 8 (Chapter 8 Selection. sav) and then click File → data → Save as we are going to add new details from the graduate candidates collected at this new assessment centre. All of the graduates are applying for a position in the Marketing department. The data view for the last few lines appears as follows once we have entered in these extra lines (see Figure 10.22). We have saved this new data file with new assessment-centre details entered of 10 new graduates as 'Chapter 10 Selection 10 NEW CANDIDATES.sav'.

**FIGURE 10.22** New selection data file with assessment centre data input for 10 new candidates

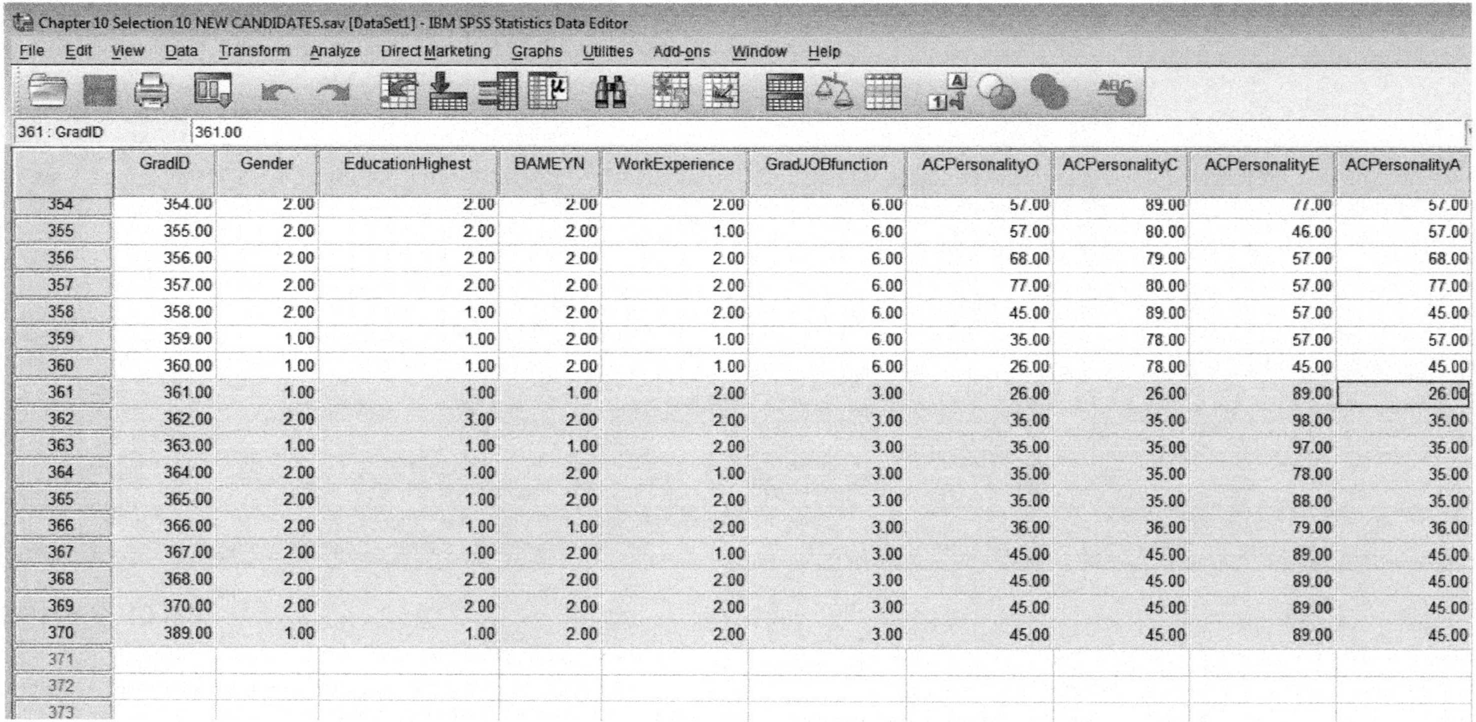


| | GradID | Gender | EducationHighest | BAMEYN | WorkExperience | GradJOBfunction | ACPersonalityO | ACPersonalityC | ACPersonalityE | ACPersonalityA |
|---|---|---|---|---|---|---|---|---|---|---|
| 354 | 354.00 | 2.00 | 2.00 | 2.00 | 2.00 | 6.00 | 57.00 | 89.00 | 77.00 | 57.00 |
| 355 | 355.00 | 2.00 | 2.00 | 2.00 | 1.00 | 6.00 | 57.00 | 80.00 | 46.00 | 57.00 |
| 356 | 356.00 | 2.00 | 2.00 | 2.00 | 2.00 | 6.00 | 68.00 | 79.00 | 57.00 | 68.00 |
| 357 | 357.00 | 2.00 | 2.00 | 2.00 | 2.00 | 6.00 | 77.00 | 80.00 | 57.00 | 77.00 |
| 358 | 358.00 | 2.00 | 1.00 | 2.00 | 2.00 | 6.00 | 45.00 | 89.00 | 57.00 | 45.00 |
| 359 | 359.00 | 1.00 | 1.00 | 2.00 | 1.00 | 6.00 | 35.00 | 78.00 | 57.00 | 57.00 |
| 360 | 360.00 | 1.00 | 1.00 | 2.00 | 1.00 | 6.00 | 26.00 | 78.00 | 45.00 | 45.00 |
| 361 | 361.00 | 1.00 | 1.00 | 1.00 | 2.00 | 3.00 | 26.00 | 26.00 | 89.00 | 26.00 |
| 362 | 362.00 | 2.00 | 3.00 | 2.00 | 2.00 | 3.00 | 35.00 | 35.00 | 98.00 | 35.00 |
| 363 | 363.00 | 1.00 | 1.00 | 1.00 | 2.00 | 3.00 | 35.00 | 35.00 | 97.00 | 35.00 |
| 364 | 364.00 | 2.00 | 1.00 | 2.00 | 1.00 | 3.00 | 35.00 | 35.00 | 78.00 | 35.00 |
| 365 | 365.00 | 2.00 | 1.00 | 2.00 | 2.00 | 3.00 | 35.00 | 35.00 | 88.00 | 35.00 |
| 366 | 366.00 | 2.00 | 1.00 | 1.00 | 2.00 | 3.00 | 36.00 | 36.00 | 79.00 | 36.00 |
| 367 | 367.00 | 2.00 | 1.00 | 2.00 | 1.00 | 3.00 | 45.00 | 45.00 | 89.00 | 45.00 |
| 368 | 368.00 | 2.00 | 2.00 | 2.00 | 2.00 | 3.00 | 45.00 | 45.00 | 89.00 | 45.00 |
| 369 | 370.00 | 2.00 | 2.00 | 2.00 | 2.00 | 3.00 | 45.00 | 45.00 | 89.00 | 45.00 |
| 370 | 389.00 | 1.00 | 1.00 | 2.00 | 2.00 | 3.00 | 45.00 | 45.00 | 89.00 | 45.00 |
| 371 | | | | | | | | | | |
| 372 | | | | | | | | | | |
| 373 | | | | | | | | | | |

You will see from Figure 10.22 that we entered new recruitment and selection data for the latest set of 10 graduates (rows 361–70); these graduates are all going into the Marketing function (see the 1.00 entries in the MarketingDummy column of Figure 10.23) and as yet we do not have onboarding information; there is also no 'Year1performanceRating' data in the data file associated with these potential graduates (because we have not yet hired them).

**FIGURE 10.23**

| | ACRatingAPTverbal | InductionDay | InductionWeek | OnBoardingBuddy | Year1perform anceRating | LeaverYr2 | HRDummyV | FinanceDummyV | MarketingDummyV |
|---|---|---|---|---|---|---|---|---|---|
| 354 | 97.00 | 1.00 | 1.00 | 1.00 | 5.00 | .00 | .00 | .00 | .00 |
| 355 | 97.00 | 1.00 | 1.00 | 1.00 | 5.00 | .00 | .00 | .00 | .00 |
| 356 | 96.00 | 1.00 | 1.00 | 1.00 | 5.00 | 1.00 | .00 | .00 | .00 |
| 357 | 89.00 | 1.00 | 1.00 | 1.00 | 5.00 | 1.00 | .00 | .00 | .00 |
| 358 | 97.00 | 1.00 | 1.00 | 1.00 | 5.00 | 1.00 | .00 | .00 | .00 |
| 359 | 96.00 | 1.00 | 1.00 | 1.00 | 5.00 | .00 | .00 | .00 | .00 |
| 360 | 92.00 | 1.00 | 1.00 | .00 | 5.00 | .00 | .00 | .00 | .00 |
| 361 | 82.00 | . | . | . | . | . | .00 | .00 | 1.00 |
| 362 | 83.00 | . | . | . | . | . | .00 | .00 | 1.00 |
| 363 | 84.00 | . | . | . | . | . | .00 | .00 | 1.00 |
| 364 | 82.00 | . | . | . | . | . | .00 | .00 | 1.00 |
| 365 | 78.00 | . | . | . | . | . | .00 | .00 | 1.00 |
| 366 | 78.00 | . | . | . | . | . | .00 | .00 | 1.00 |
| 367 | 84.00 | . | . | . | . | . | .00 | .00 | 1.00 |
| 368 | 78.00 | . | . | . | . | . | .00 | .00 | 1.00 |
| 369 | 84.00 | . | . | . | . | . | .00 | .00 | 1.00 |
| 370 | 83.00 | . | . | . | . | . | .00 | .00 | 1.00 |
| 371 | | | | | | | | | |

Now, to get information on which of these 10 candidates is most likely to perform best as a graduate we rerun the linear regression model, making sure we save the result. We run the linear regression model again just as we did in Chapter 8 using the Analyze → Regression → Linear options from the model (excluding the onboard variables).

We select the first-year performance as the dependent variable and the other variables selected above as the independent variables and then click on the Save... button on the right-hand side.

### FIGURE 10.24

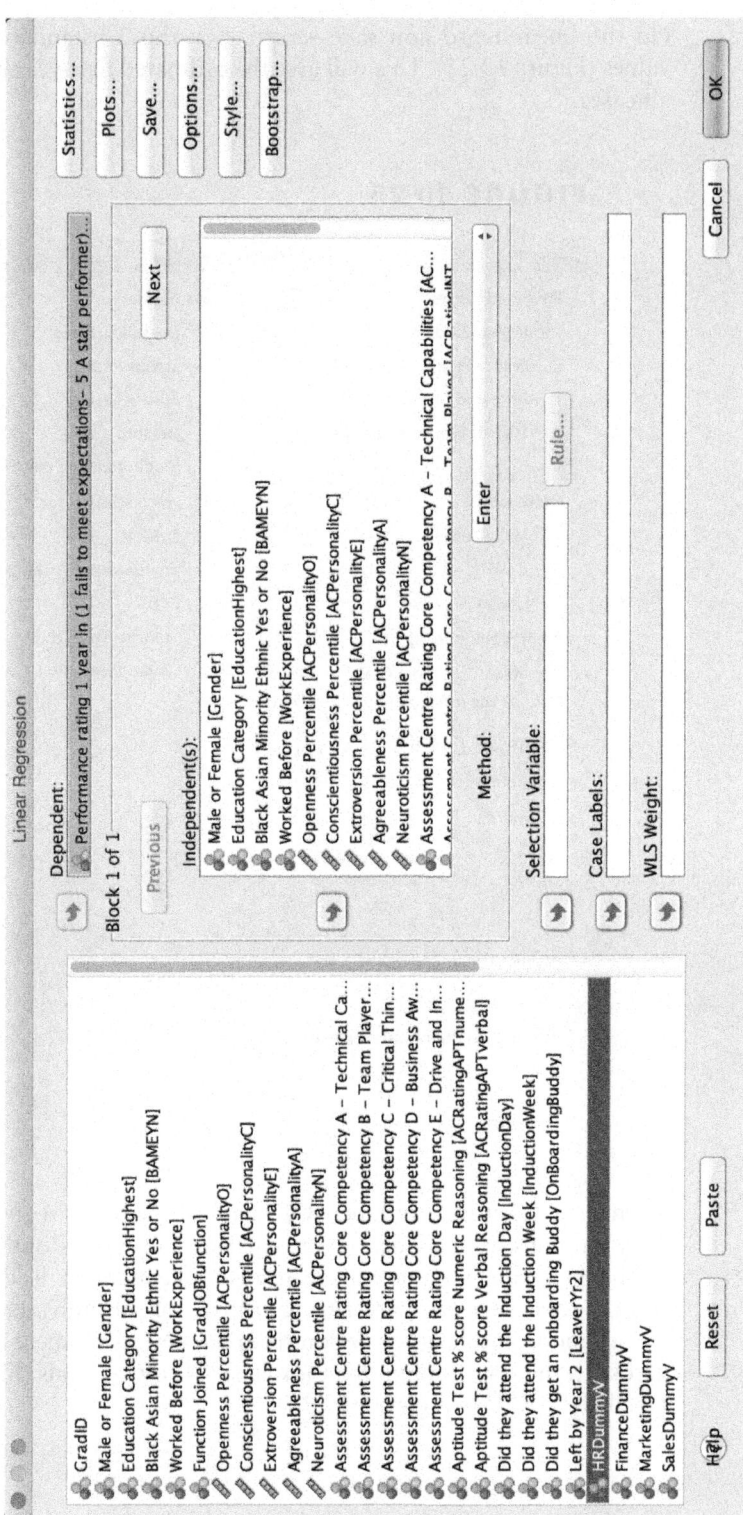

On the linear regression save screen, tick the 'Unstandardized' predicted values (Figure 10.25). This will give the estimated first-year performance for all cases.

**FIGURE 10.25**

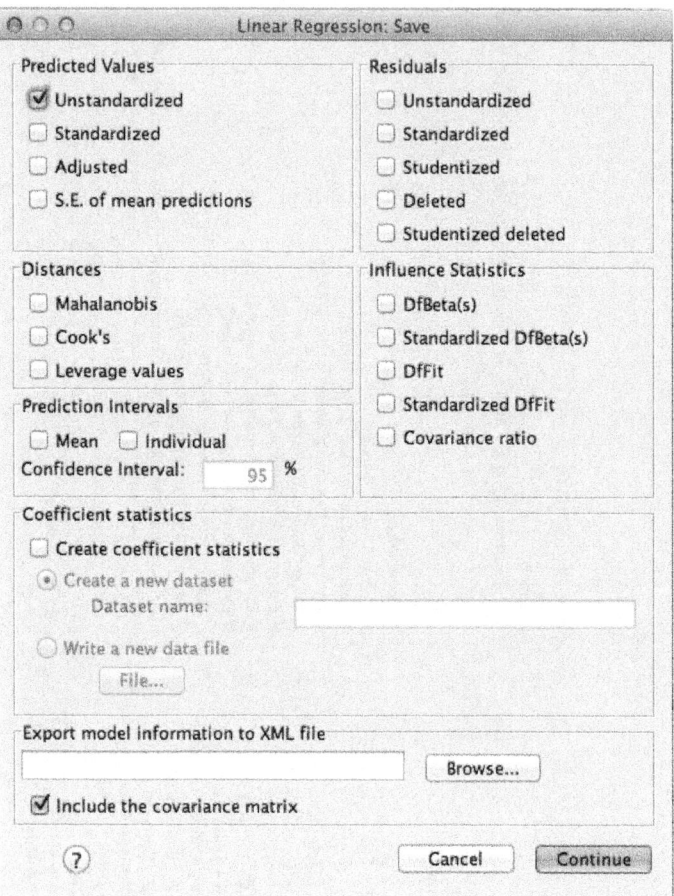

Then click 'Continue' and then 'OK' back at the linear regression page. This runs the regression model, giving the same results as outlined above, but saving the predicted value will create an extra column in the data file, showing the expected year-one performance rating for all individuals based on the model and using the information from the new assessment centre. Scrolling across to the final column for those last 10 rows reveals this in the column labelled 'PRE_1' (see Figure 10.26).

**FIGURE 10.26**

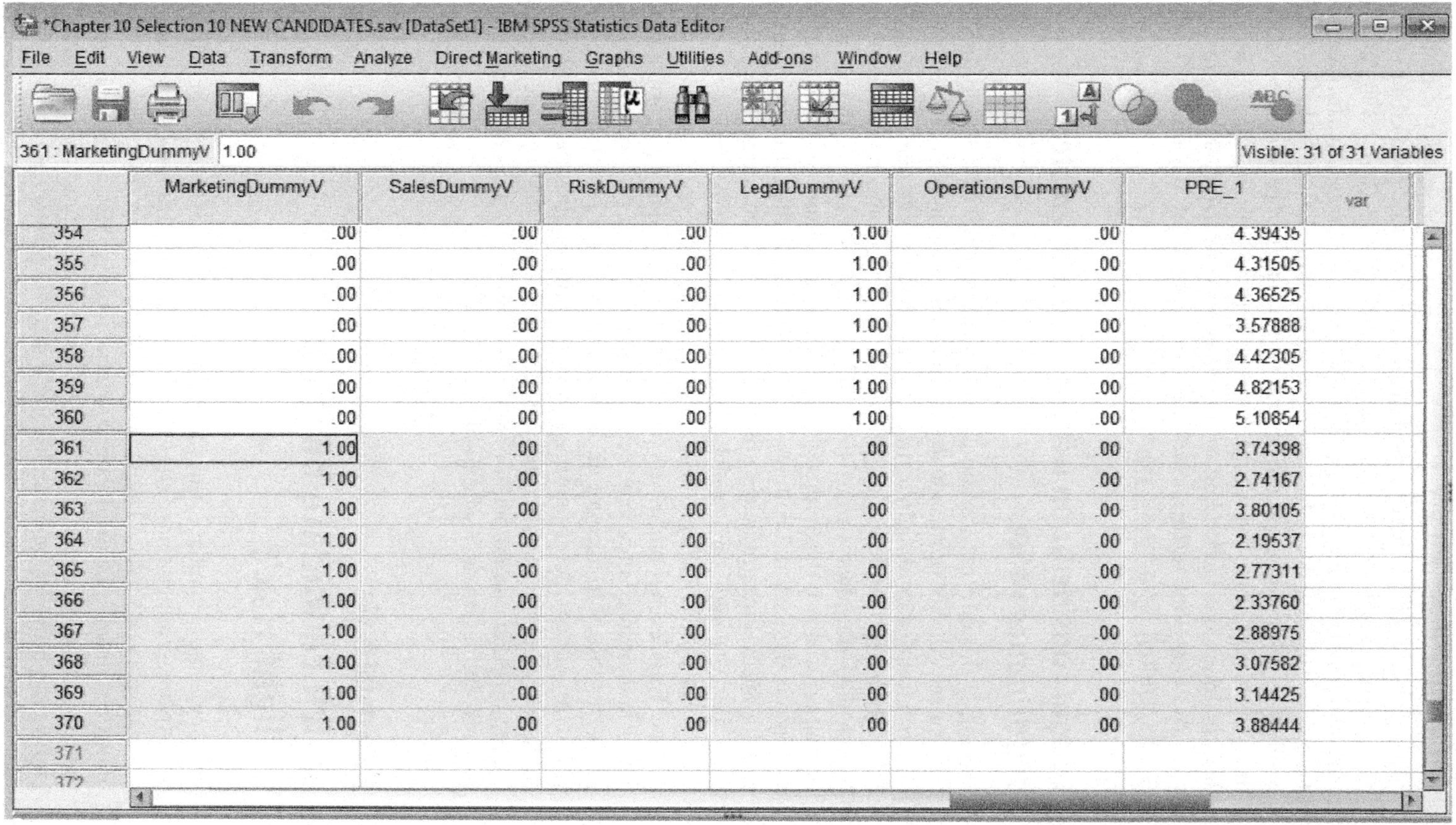

| | MarketingDummyV | SalesDummyV | RiskDummyV | LegalDummyV | OperationsDummyV | PRE_1 | var |
|---|---|---|---|---|---|---|---|
| 354 | .00 | .00 | .00 | 1.00 | .00 | 4.39435 | |
| 355 | .00 | .00 | .00 | 1.00 | .00 | 4.31505 | |
| 356 | .00 | .00 | .00 | 1.00 | .00 | 4.36525 | |
| 357 | .00 | .00 | .00 | 1.00 | .00 | 3.57888 | |
| 358 | .00 | .00 | .00 | 1.00 | .00 | 4.42305 | |
| 359 | .00 | .00 | .00 | 1.00 | .00 | 4.82153 | |
| 360 | .00 | .00 | .00 | 1.00 | .00 | 5.10854 | |
| 361 | 1.00 | .00 | .00 | .00 | .00 | 3.74398 | |
| 362 | 1.00 | .00 | .00 | .00 | .00 | 2.74167 | |
| 363 | 1.00 | .00 | .00 | .00 | .00 | 3.80105 | |
| 364 | 1.00 | .00 | .00 | .00 | .00 | 2.19537 | |
| 365 | 1.00 | .00 | .00 | .00 | .00 | 2.77311 | |
| 366 | 1.00 | .00 | .00 | .00 | .00 | 2.33760 | |
| 367 | 1.00 | .00 | .00 | .00 | .00 | 2.88975 | |
| 368 | 1.00 | .00 | .00 | .00 | .00 | 3.07582 | |
| 369 | 1.00 | .00 | .00 | .00 | .00 | 3.14425 | |
| 370 | 1.00 | .00 | .00 | .00 | .00 | 3.88444 | |
| 371 | | | | | | | |
| 372 | | | | | | | |

You can see, then, that many of the candidates are predicted to be low performers. There are three of the 10 candidates who are predicted to be high performers, gaining a score near 4, candidates 361, 363 and 370. We have two additional candidates who are expected to be average performers with a score very close to 3, candidates 368 and 369, with the rest of the candidates coming in with low expectations of performance. The recommendation, then, based on this model, would be to put forward candidates 361, 363 and 369 for interview. Depending on the resources available, the organization may also carry out further assessment on candidates 368 and 369 before recommending them for interview.

## Careful consideration with the use of predicted performance values

Obviously this information should not be used solely as the decision-making tool for selection of our graduates, as our regression models only ever work on probabilities (and significance of our predictors is determined on the basis of the probabilities) of patterns emerging from our historical data (which does not always translate to what happens today or in the future). If you peruse down the predicted values 'PRE_1' column for existing graduates in our data set and compare these values with the actual performance data for the existing graduates, you will see that the predictions are not always accurate. Although our model is significant in predicting performance, it does not predict 100 per cent of the variation in performance – it is not perfect. Thus, even if our model predicts that a candidate's performance will not be high, if hired they may well end up being a star performer (our model will never take into account all factors that account for performance). We should, of course, never assume that our model predictions would always come true… However, the analysis produces very useful evidence-based predictions that should help our selectors come to a decision (especially if they are vacillating over who to hire).

# Example 6: which candidate might be a 'flight risk'?

As discussed in Chapter 8, this same data set is also used to predict whether our existing graduates have chosen to leave the organization before completing two years of service. The same method can be used to determine which of our new marketing candidates are more likely to leave, although whether this should be used as a selection technique is a question of ethics. The model may, however, be better used to flag up any potential high performers we wish to hire but who are more at risk of leaving early – so that they may be managed accordingly.

Because leaving the organization or not leaving the organization is a binary decision, or a binary/categorical variable, we would use a binary logistic regression with 'left by year two' as the dependent variable, as we did in Chapter 8 (rather than a linear regression), and when we save the variables – as we have in this scenario example – we would select 'Probabilities' to give the probability of them leaving (see Figure 10.27). So again we are using the new graduate selection data set (Chapter 10 Selection 10 NEW CANDIDATES.sav) in which we have entered data for our 10 new marketing graduate candidates.

**FIGURE 10.27**

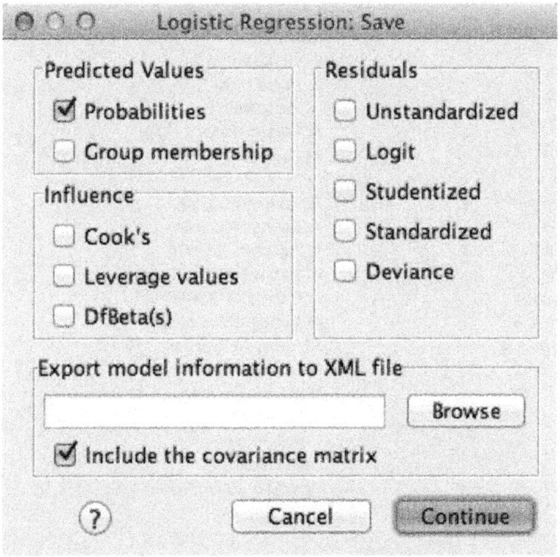

These predicted probabilities will then be saved in an additional column in exactly the same way as the predicted performance in example 5 here.

Figure 10.28 shows us setting up the logistic regression model predicting early leavers (notice again that we do not include onboarding/induction information or Year 1 performance rating as predictors because we have not yet hired these candidates).

## FIGURE 10.28

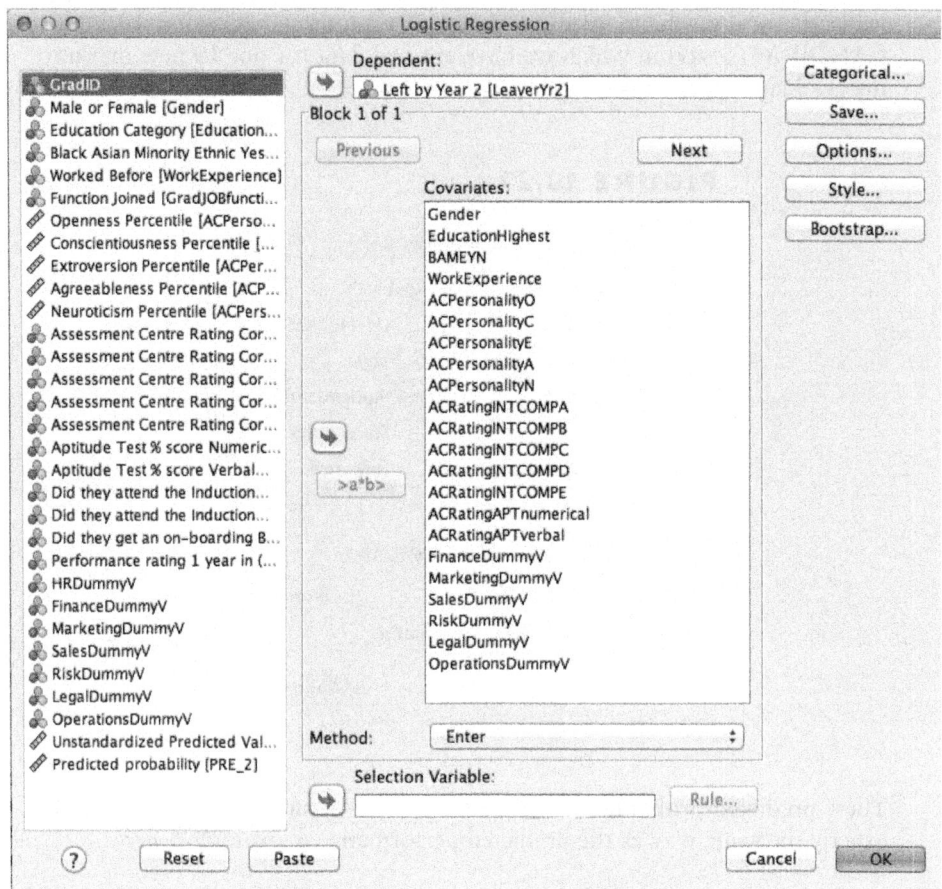

Before you click 'OK' to run the model you click on the 'Save...' button and select the 'Probabilities' in the predicted value selection box (Figure 10.27) and click 'Continue' and 'OK'. SPSS will now apply the regression model (predicting early leavers) to the 10 new candidates and give a probability of them being an early leaver. As we already have a PRE_1 column in our new data set (with predicted values of performance), SPSS saves the probabilities of leaving into a new column PRE_2 (see Figure 10.29).

**FIGURE 10.29** Sample screenshot of selection data set with performance and probability of leaving predictions calculated

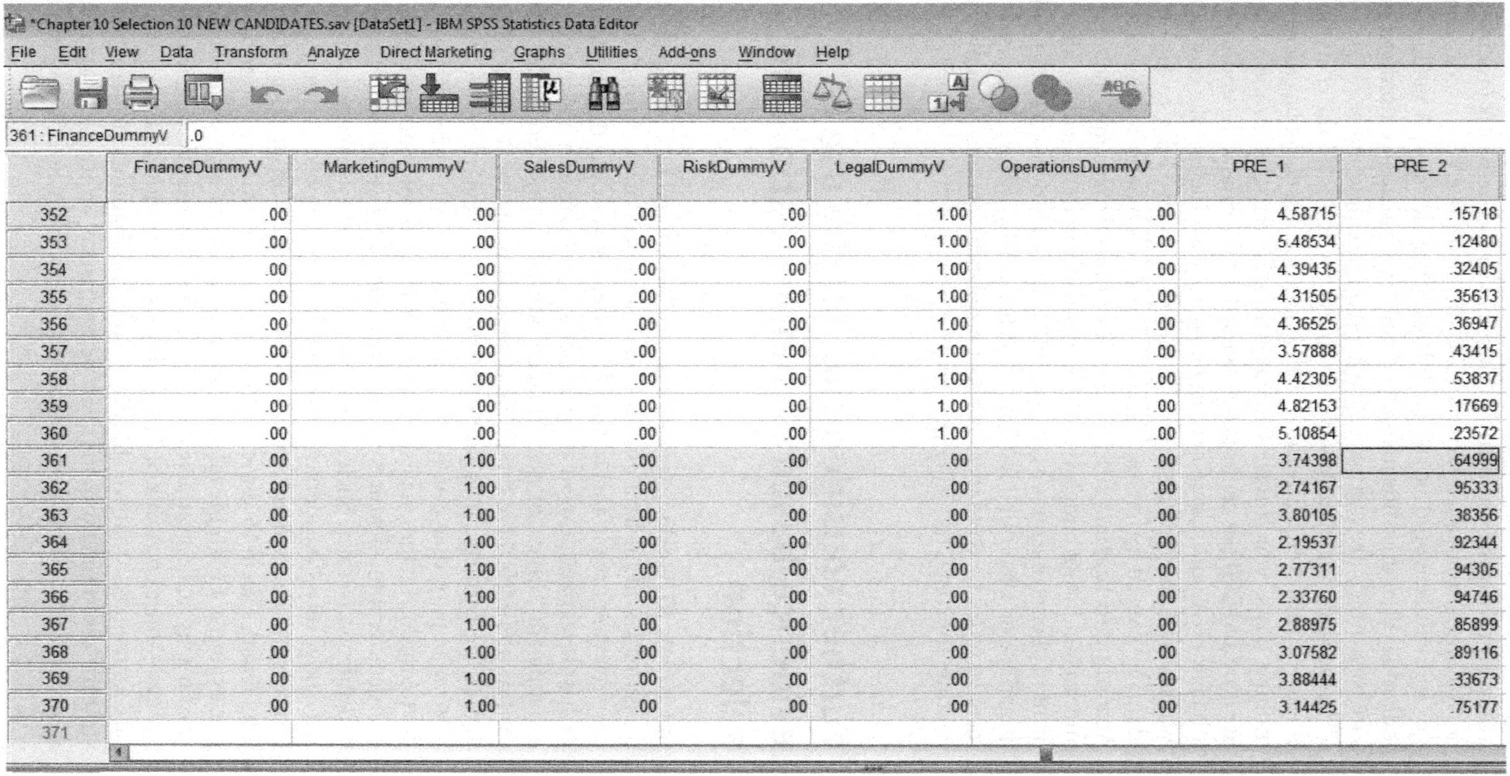

| | FinanceDummyV | MarketingDummyV | SalesDummyV | RiskDummyV | LegalDummyV | OperationsDummyV | PRE_1 | PRE_2 |
|---|---|---|---|---|---|---|---|---|
| 352 | .00 | .00 | .00 | .00 | 1.00 | .00 | 4.58715 | .15718 |
| 353 | .00 | .00 | .00 | .00 | 1.00 | .00 | 5.48534 | .12480 |
| 354 | .00 | .00 | .00 | .00 | 1.00 | .00 | 4.39435 | .32405 |
| 355 | .00 | .00 | .00 | .00 | 1.00 | .00 | 4.31505 | .35613 |
| 356 | .00 | .00 | .00 | .00 | 1.00 | .00 | 4.36525 | .36947 |
| 357 | .00 | .00 | .00 | .00 | 1.00 | .00 | 3.57888 | .43415 |
| 358 | .00 | .00 | .00 | .00 | 1.00 | .00 | 4.42305 | .53837 |
| 359 | .00 | .00 | .00 | .00 | 1.00 | .00 | 4.82153 | .17669 |
| 360 | .00 | .00 | .00 | .00 | 1.00 | .00 | 5.10854 | .23572 |
| 361 | .00 | 1.00 | .00 | .00 | .00 | .00 | 3.74398 | .64999 |
| 362 | .00 | 1.00 | .00 | .00 | .00 | .00 | 2.74167 | .95333 |
| 363 | .00 | 1.00 | .00 | .00 | .00 | .00 | 3.80105 | .38356 |
| 364 | .00 | 1.00 | .00 | .00 | .00 | .00 | 2.19537 | .92344 |
| 365 | .00 | 1.00 | .00 | .00 | .00 | .00 | 2.77311 | .94305 |
| 366 | .00 | 1.00 | .00 | .00 | .00 | .00 | 2.33760 | .94746 |
| 367 | .00 | 1.00 | .00 | .00 | .00 | .00 | 2.88975 | .85899 |
| 368 | .00 | 1.00 | .00 | .00 | .00 | .00 | 3.07582 | .89116 |
| 369 | .00 | 1.00 | .00 | .00 | .00 | .00 | 3.88444 | .33673 |
| 370 | .00 | 1.00 | .00 | .00 | .00 | .00 | 3.14425 | .75177 |
| 371 | | | | | | | | |

You will see (from Figure 10.29) that the candidate 361 is predicted to have fairly high performance rating (3.74) but there is a 65 per cent chance that this individual would be an early leaver. If a decision is made to hire this individual then their line manager should pay particular attention to making sure their needs are met in the early phase of employment.

In Chapter 6, the turnover case study, we discussed the costs involved in employee turnover. These included separation costs, replacement costs and training costs, which were estimated to cost the organization between 93 per cent and 200 per cent of each single leaver's salary, depending on certain job factors. A poor hiring decision may not only include the cost of turnover as discussed, but may also include the costs involved due to the operational 'damage' caused by having a person in position who is not suited to the role. According to Kiazim (2015), the types of problems could include: attrition and wasted hiring budgets; theft; embezzlement; damaged morale; endangerment of clients, business associates and other employees; loss of productivity; litigation; or even public scandal and negative publicity. It is, hence, recommended to try to avoid these types of problems by taking an analytic decision-making approach to hiring.

# Further consideration on the use of evidence-based recommendations in selection

In Chapter 12, we discuss ethical issues that should be considered in making decisions based on data and HR analysis; selection decisions are a particularly relevant area in this regard. So, although gender, ethnicity and even the highest level of education are part of the model created (indeed gender being a significant 'driver' of performance ratings), it does not mean that significant results with these should be used as a means for selecting the predicted highest performers. It is important to realize that there are always other factors at play that our models do not take into account; thus although demographic factors may show significance in some model it is almost never the demographic features themselves that directly cause variation in our dependent variables. Such a belief would be totally deterministic and would not show any consideration for the likely complex nature of behaviour. There could be so many reasons that we need to consider, for example, as to why females seem to show lower levels of performance in our models here. For example a high prevalence of male senior managers may be part of the reason why male graduates are more likely to receive higher performance ratings – due to possible biases at play. This does not mean that we shouldn't hire women, but that we should do something about our managers demonstrating discrimination in their performance appraisal judgements! The same is true for ethnicity and even higher levels of education, which are often linked to socio-economic background and not necessarily capability or aptitude/competencies – for which one may argue that the assessment-centre results are a better measure. So, when using a model for specific decision making and recommendations for action, it is worth considering what should and should not be included in our interpretations of what is going on in our organization.

# References

Fitz-enz, J (2010) *The New HR Analytics: Predicting the economic value of your company's human capital investment*, AMACOM, New York

Kiazim, O (2015) [accessed 20 November 2015] Cost of Poor Hiring Decisions, *HR Zone* [Online] http://www.hrzone.com/talent/acquisition/the-real-cost-of-a-bad-hiring-decision

Taylor, T S (2010) Resourcing and Talent Management, 5th edn, Chartered Institute of Personnel and Development, London

# More advanced HR analytic techniques

11

This book is designed to be an introduction for an HR professional who wants to add statistical competencies to their analytic capabilities. If this is indeed your first introduction to statistics, we would recommend putting this chapter to one side until you are confident with the techniques discussed in the rest of the book. Once you have had the opportunity to run the analyses yourselves again and again on your own data, the day-to-day basic techniques will become second nature and you may well want to understand more complex analyses procedures that have the power to do even more.

Up until this point, we have restricted the statistical modelling in this book to a range of statistical analyses that an HR analyst is most likely to conduct on a day-to-day basis. There is, however, a whole range of much more sophisticated statistical procedures that can be used to help answer a range of different and more complex HR analytic research questions. As you become more advanced, you will start to look beyond the basic techniques and realize that the possible analytic questions that could be explored go on and on.

The aim of this chapter is to provide an introduction to some of the more widely used advanced analytic techniques, so that you are aware of them, and to provide you with some recommendations for further reading. We will cover:

- Mediation processes: when the independent (predictor) variable has an indirect relationship with the dependent variable rather than a direct one. In other words, a serial (sequential) 'causal' process is occurring. We describe the analytic process to explore such a pattern of relationships.
- Moderation and interaction analysis: when two independent predictor variables combine or interact to account for variation in the dependent variable. In other words, the effect of a predictor variable on our dependent variable is contingent on another contextual factor.

- Multi-level linear modelling: when the data you are looking at is in a hierarchical structure of levels, for example individual → team → department.
- Curvilinear relationships: when a relationship exists between two variables that is not linear. For example, when a relationship between two variables drawn on a graph shows a curve rather than a straight line. The increase in an independent variable may initially be associated with an increase in a dependent variable, but as the independent variable continues to increase, we begin to see a decrease in the dependent variable (or vice versa).
- Structural equation models: a form of analysis that tests data against some form of theoretical predicted model generally involving a number of variables usually arranged in a predicted causal sequence; this analysis tends to involve the exploration of a number of regression equations simultaneously. These models can either be made up of observed variables or latent variables (or concepts) measured by multiple items (see Chapter 5 for a discussion of latent variables).
- Growth models: when analysis is conducted that predicts growth or change over time in the dependent variable by collecting data over a number of time points.
- Latent class analysis: a subset of structural equation modelling, its main purpose is to conduct analysis with a number of metrics in order to identify particular groups within a sample or population (on the basis of each individual's profile of scores across the range of metrics).
- Response surface methodology and polynomial regression analysis: polynomial regression explores the relationship between one or more independent variables and a dependent variable, taking into account the potential for curvilinear relationships between the independent variable(s) and the dependent variable. Polynomial analyses can be extended to explore curvilinear relationships and interactions between two independent variables and a dependent variable, taking into account the apparent level of the dependent variable expected at any particular level of one or more independent variables. Response surface methodology plots these relationships and interactions on 3D graphs.

Some of these statistical procedures could be very useful to HR analysts as they become more capable; for example, the moderation and interaction testing and the curvilinear relationship analysis. Some of the tests can be carried out with SPSS, some might require new menus to be added to SPSS (free of charge) and some of these might require additional statistical software. However, we explain these conceptually so that the analyst can begin to understand what some of these more sophisticated modelling techniques involve.

## Mediation processes

In many of the predictive analyses models presented in this book, it may appear that we often seem to look for evidence of a fairly straightforward cause-and-effect process where X is assumed to influence Y. However, in many cases a possible causal flow may involve a more complex serial process where one factor influences another only if it has an effect on a third factor, referred to as a mediator. With mediation, the effects of X on Y are expected to occur through an intervening causal process or a serial chain of causal reactions.

A simple example might be whether a challenging experience at work leads to someone leaving his or her job. Let's say for example that employees experience an increase in their workload. An increase in workload may only cause someone to look for work elsewhere when the increase in workload has led to some dissatisfaction with their job. An employee may not start looking for work at another organization if the increase in workload did not lead to dissatisfaction; importantly it is dissatisfaction that has a direct impact on people leaving, not the increased workload. The impact of an increase in workload (X) on people leaving (Y) is indirect through dissatisfaction (M) rather than direct. We could represent this possible causal flow in a diagram (see Figure 11.1).

**FIGURE 11.1**  Mediation process

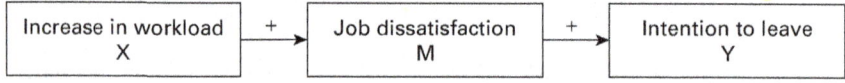

Recent decades have witnessed a shift in how mediation processes are tested analytically. For more than two decades, the Baron and Kenny (1986) method of mediation testing was the approach taken to examine the existence of mediation in the social science and management field. This involved conducting a series of three separate regression analyses. With the Baron and Kenny approach, to test for the above mediation model you needed to follow three steps:

- Step one
  We run a regression that predicts job dissatisfaction with increases in workloads. Thus the regression equation for this step looks like: job dissatisfaction = a + $b_1$ (increase in workload); and the standardized regression equation for this step looks like: job dissatisfaction = $Beta_1$ (increase in workload).
  
  If mediation exists as per Figure 11.1, increases in workload must be a significant predictor of job dissatisfaction.

- Step two
  We run a regression that predicts intention to leave with increases in workloads. Thus the regression equation for this step looks like: intention to leave = a + $b_1$ (increase in workload); and the standardized regression equation for this step looks like: intention to leave = $Beta_1$ (increase in workload).
  
  If mediation exists as per Figure 11.1, increase in workload must be a significant predictor of intention to leave.

- Step three
  We run a regression that predicts intention to leave with increases in workloads as well as job dissatisfaction as independent variables. Thus the regression equation for this step looks like: intention to leave = a + $b_1$ (increase in workload) + $b_2$ (job dissatisfaction); and the standardized regression equation for this step looks like: intention to leave = $Beta_1$ (increase in workload) + $Beta_2$ (job dissatisfaction).
  
  If mediation exists as per Figure 11.1, then:
  
  - Our mediator (job dissatisfaction) must be a significant predictor of Y (intention to leave) in step 3.
  - The increase in workload (X) Beta $(_1)$ in step 3 must be less than Beta $(_1)$ in step 2, so the (increase in workload) has less of an impact on (intention to leave) when we account for (job dissatisfaction).
  - If (increase in workload) is no longer significant in step 3, then we would say there is full mediation.
  - If there is no reduction in Beta $(_1)$ from step 2 to step 3 and the impact that an (increase in workload) has on (intention to leave) does not change across these two steps when we account for (job dissatisfaction), then we would say there is no mediation.
  - If (increase in workload) still has a significant impact on (intention to leave) but Beta $(_1)$ in step 3 is smaller than Beta $(_1)$ in step 2, we would say there is partial mediation.

The good thing about these steps is that they can be followed very easily and carried out with SPSS by running a few regressions.

There are, however, some challenges with this approach, some of which have been discussed in depth by Andrew Hayes (2009) in his paper 'Beyond Baron and Kenny: statistical mediation analysis in the new millennium'. One of the problems with the Baron and Kenny approach is that it requires a series of separate regression analysis to be conducted, which never actually give a robust statistic that can be used as an indicator of the extent of mediation. This has led to a new statistical approach often referred to as the Preacher and Hayes approach.

The Preacher and Hayes approach to analysing mediation involves creating a measure or coefficient of the degree of mediation (or indirect effects) to be produced and the significance of this coefficient to be tested using 'bootstrapped' confidence intervals. This new approach is actually very straightforward to carry out with SPSS once a new 'Process' menu (that runs additional SPSS macros) has been added to SPSS to enable this. For further details follow: **http://www.afhayes.com/introduction-to-mediation-moderation-and-conditional-process-analysis.html**.

Whilst it is very easy to run mediation models with the Preacher and Hayes approach (you literally insert the dependent variable into the relevant box on the menu, the mediator variable into the mediator box and the independent variable into the appropriate box and click 'OK') it takes some time familiarizing yourself with the different types of models that 'Process' can run in order to make sure that you have the correct set-up. The output is not always straightforward and takes a bit of getting used to; however, further discussion on this should be left for a more advanced HR analytics text.

Before finishing up on the discussion of mediation analysis, there is some debate within the organizational sciences about how the temporal element of mediation processes should be set up. As mediation models involve serial causal processes (ie X leads to M, which then leads to Y), there is an explicit assumption of causality implied with such models. One of the key challenges with such models is that often they are tested using correlation analysis or regression analyses, which whilst these approaches can identify the existence of the necessary relationships that should exist if the causal model were 'true', the existence of relationships between variables does not imply causality. As we know from our discussion on regression and correlation in Chapter 3, whilst regression and correlation do indicate a relationship, relationships do not necessarily imply causality (just as, as pointed out in Chapter 3, a high correlation between ice-cream consumption and skin cancer does not mean that ice cream gives you skin cancer – there may be other factors involved such as time spent in the sun, for example). It is often the case that an analyst conducting mediation testing is inferring causality from the pattern of data even despite this issue. The HR analyst should always bear this in mind.

## Moderation and interaction analysis

Most of the predictive models that we have explored in this book include examples where the analyst makes some kind of assumption that one or more factors may be influencing or driving a particular metric (such as performance or engagement, etc) in a linear or direct way (whilst taking into account how our collection of potential 'drivers' are related to each other). With the multiple regression and the binary logistic regression examples in this book, we are exploring the degree to which we can *directly* account for variance in our dependent variables by looking at our collection of potential 'drivers'. It is, however, sometimes the case that we can uncover really important patterns in our data by exploring how two potential drivers combine or interact to account for variation in our predicted metric. Thus, we might want to explore *interaction effects* in our predictive models.

A very straightforward example of an interaction effect that we do explore in the book (though with an ANOVA rather than a 'predictive regression model') is the differential impact that the introduction of a work–life balance (WLB) programme has on stress levels (across time) when males and females are compared. Whilst, from our example, there was evidence of a direct effect on stress levels from the WLB programme introduction (in that our organization showed a reduction in stress levels after the introduction of the WLB programme) and gender (in that women in our organization tended to report higher stress levels), the really important finding in accounting for stress levels was the interaction between gender and the WLB programme introduction. We found that the stress levels reduced to a greater extent following the WLB programme introduction for women compared to men. Thus, gender and WLB programme introduction interact as possible 'drivers' of stress levels.

A classic example of an interaction effect from the organizational psychology literature would be the demands-control 'stress' model presented by Karasek (1979). Karasek presented a model that aims to account for variation in occupational stress levels. The model tries to account for variation in employees' 'stress' levels (or psychological strain); so psychological strain can be considered to be our dependent variable. Karasek presented two main potential predictors of employee psychological strain: 1) the level of job demand (or pressure) that an employee experiences; and 2) the level of control (or autonomy) that an employee has over how they do their job. Both of these factors may indeed have *direct* effects on employees' psychological strain: the higher the job demands experienced then the more strain an employee feels; and the greater the level of job control a person has then the less psychological strain they will experience. However, Karasek argues that these two factors should interact in explaining possible positive or negative employee reactions. The negative impact of job demands may actually be dependent upon (or influenced by) how much job control they have.

One can infer from Karasek's model that if someone has a high level of job control, then they may generally be less stressed at work than if they have low control; one could also infer that people with high demands may generally be more stressed than people with low demands. Importantly, the model implies an interaction between these two factors, in that someone who experiences high job demands may not experience psychological strain if they have the decision latitude/ability to control how they respond to the high job demands. Thus job control interacts with job demands in accounting for employees' level of psychological strain. An indicative graphical representation of this interaction effect is presented in Figure 11.2.

Importantly, the interaction here indicates that the impact that job demands have on employees' levels of psychological strain is contingent on how much decision latitude or autonomy they have in their jobs. Thus, autonomy moderates the impact that job demands have on strain.

**FIGURE 11.2** Example impact of an interaction between job demands and job control on employees' level of psychological strain

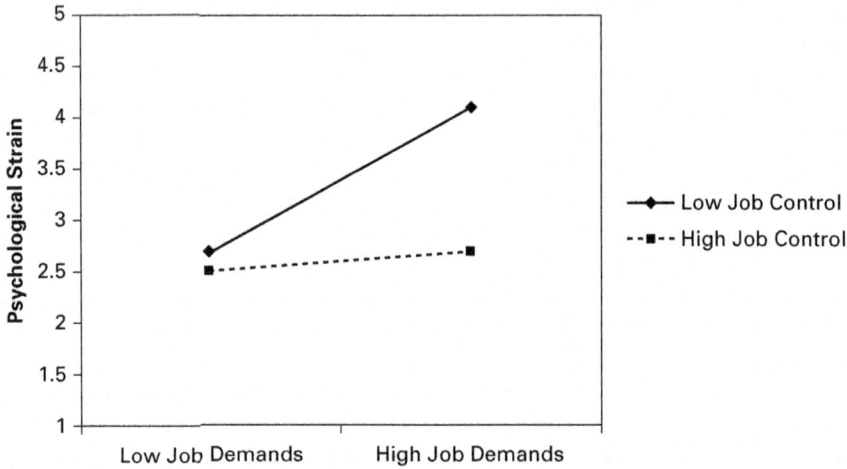

Calculating interaction effects with an ANOVA example has been discussed in Chapters 7 and 9. However, we have not outlined how to calculate interactions between independent variables in a multiple regression model. When two independent variables are continuous, where we believe that these factors may influence a particular dependent variable and furthermore we believe that the influence may involve an interaction effect, we can include such an analysis in our multiple regression predictive model.

An additional example of a possible interactional analysis, linking to a case study that we have presented, is our prediction of increases in performance ratings between 2014 and 2015. We presented this analysis in Chapter 7. In this example we were predicting increases in performance ratings that were given between 2014 and 2015; we included a measure of the degree to which individuals express that they experience work-related pressure and strain (to the point that they sometimes worry about work and lose sleep). We also included a measure of sickness absence in the model. Individual sickness absence and expressed levels of strain were both shown to be related to increases in performance rating; absence rates with a negative relationship and psychological strain with a positive relationship. We could easily conceive that there may be an interplay between pressure/strain and sickness absence and whether or not someone gets a higher performance rating than the previous year. Maybe people who are under strain but do not take time off sick are the ones who get the performance rating increase rather than those who are not under strain but take time off sick. This is easy to test with our regression. First, in accordance with the recommended approach to testing for moderation set out by Cohen and Cohen (1983),

**FIGURE 11.3**

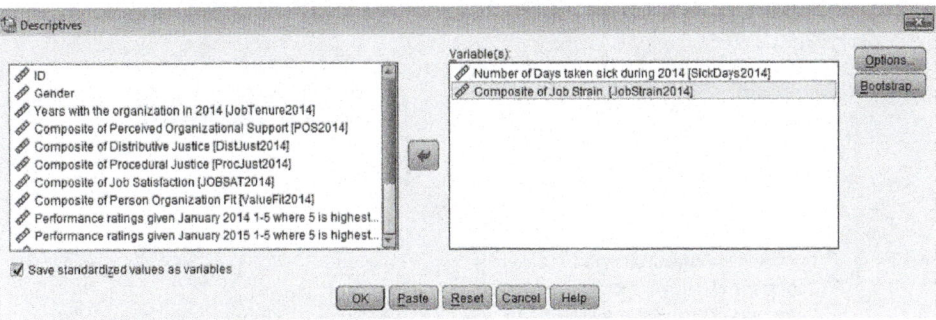

you need to standardize your two variables of strain and sickness absence. We recommend the approach of converting the data within the two metrics into z-scores, which equalizes the scale for both measures. This is very simple and SPSS has a tick-box option in its descriptive request menu to 'Save standardized values as variables' (see Figure 11.3). This transforms any variable selected into a z-score version of the variable (ie the measurement that shows the score's relationship to the mean, so a z-score of 0 would indicate that the score equals the mean, then the score will be positive or negative, indicating the number of standard deviations above or below the mean). Here, by selecting the 'JobStrain2014' and 'SickDays2014' variables and clicking the 'Save standardized values as variables' box (and clicking 'OK'), SPSS produces two new z-score versions of these variables.

To test an interaction between these two variables you then have to create a new interaction term variable, which is the product of these two z-score variables multiplied together. So here it would be:

Interaction-term = 'ZJobStrain2014' × 'ZSickDays2014'

You do this by using the Transform->Compute-> menu (see Figure 11.4), indicating 'InteractionTerm' as the name of the new 'Target Variable:' and setting out the 'ZJobStrain2014' × 'ZSickDays2014' formula by pulling these variables across into the 'Numeric Expression:' box and using the * as the multiply term.

Then once you have these three new variables (z-score of strain, z-score of sickness absence and the new interaction term), you include them as independent variables in a regression that predicts 2015 performance (whilst controlling for 2014 performance, which enables a prediction of change in performance – see discussion on this in Chapter 7, page 264). If the interaction term is significant ($p<0.05$) then we know that the two variables interact in their relationship with change in performance. See Figure 11.5, which has our interaction term at Beta=0.148, $p<0.05$.

## FIGURE 11.4

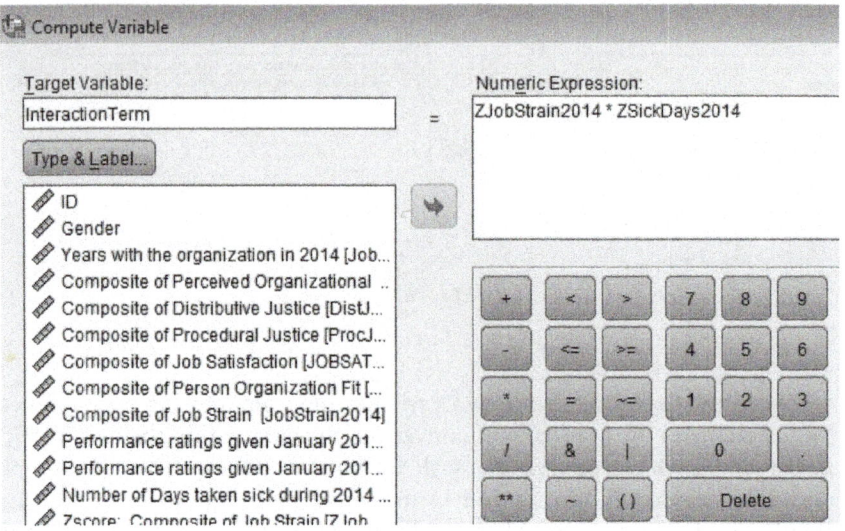

## FIGURE 11.5

Coefficients[a]

| Model | | Unstandardized Coefficients | | Standardized Coefficients | t | Sig. |
|---|---|---|---|---|---|---|
| | | B | Std. Error | Beta | | |
| 1 | (Constant) | 1.399 | .205 | | 6.839 | .000 |
| | Zscore: Composite of Job Strain | .156 | .055 | .172 | 2.826 | .005 |
| | Zscore: Number of Days taken sick during 2014 | -.274 | .096 | -.186 | -2.869 | .005 |
| | Performance ratings given January 2014 1–5 where 5 is highest | .399 | .057 | .419 | 6.940 | .000 |
| | InteractionTerm | .262 | .114 | .148 | 2.290 | .023 |

a. Dependent Variable: Performance ratings given January 2015 1–5 where 5 is highest

To further understand the interaction, the easiest thing to do is to plot the results on an interaction graph (such as that presented in Figure 11.2). For a thorough discussion of interaction and moderation effects, a comprehensive paper written by Dawson (2014) would be a good reference to follow up. For a discussion on how to plot the above interaction graphs as well as Excel spreadsheet templates for such plots see: **http://www.jeremydawson.co.uk/slopes.htm**.

The previous explanation outlines how to set up interaction analysis with a multiple regression that has a continuous dependent variable and two continuous independent variables. If the predictive model involves a binary variable such as that used with individual turnover analysis, and we are interested in whether two categorical variables might interact, we can very simply use the SPSS menu to run such an analysis. In Chapter 6 we have a predictive model that tries to account for individual leavers. So our dependent variable is a binary variable. Two of the predictor variables included are categorical (gender of employee and gender of boss). If we think that the genders of the employee and their boss may be important in predicting turnover patterns, the interaction between these two gender variables may be worth exploring. To check for this in a predictive model we can simply ask SPSS to check for the interaction between gender of individual by gender of boss. To do this you click on the two variables when setting up the regression and then click on the '>a*b>' button (see Figure 11.6), which transfers an interaction term into the regression model (into the 'Covariates:' box). Again, if this interaction term is significant in the model output then we can assume that the two variables interact.

**FIGURE 11.6**

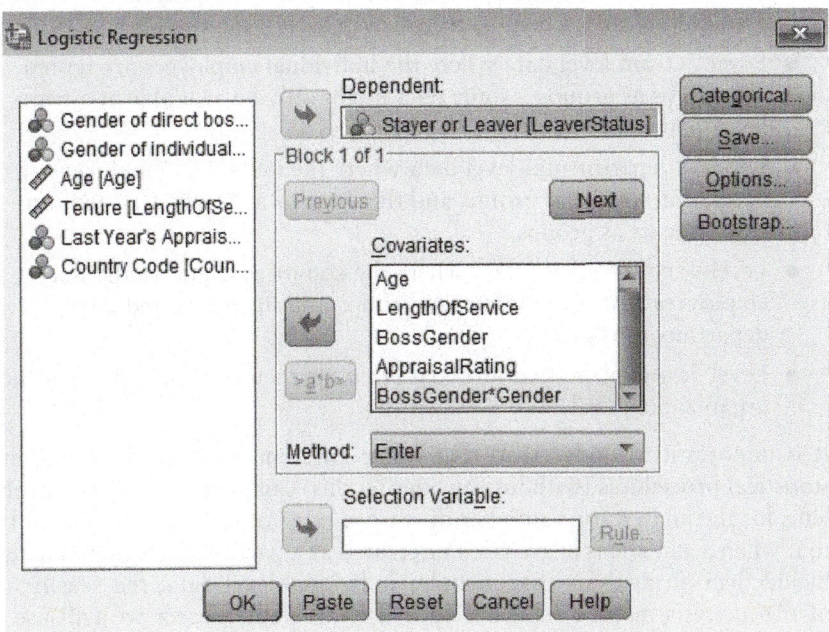

## Multi-level linear modelling

The very nature of HR data means that HR analysts will intuitively be aware of the fact that data can be presented at different levels. For example, data can be at the individual employee level, the team level, the department level, the function level, the country level and the organization level. Often with HR data, analysis at one level (eg the individual employee) has been or needs to be manipulated so that it can be analysed at another level (eg team). Employee engagement scores are a classic example of this – often when a survey company conducts an employee attitude/engagement survey where each employee is given a questionnaire to fill out, and given an 'engagement' score (as well as scores on measures for other constructs). However, due to issues of confidentiality, the data that they then provide to the organization is usually computed average (engagement) or percentage (engaged) scores aggregated to a higher level such as team, department or organization (which might be benchmarked against other organizations within the industry). This is why in the engagement case study in Chapter 5 we conduct analysis at the aggregate team level; often this is the lowest level of engagement data that is available to an HR analyst. In the engagement modelling and in various other analyses these team-level engagement scores are then used to predict other metrics (such as team turnover statistics and team diversity data). Below we make this level data structure a little clearer in a simplistic scenario of five levels:

- Level 1: individual data relating to a particular employee. This could be data held or recorded in an HR database.
- Level 2: team-level data where the individual employees are nested into teams as groups – some data might only be available at a team level (team sales figures).
- Level 3: departmental-level data where the individual employees are nested into teams as groups and these teams are further nested into departments as groups.
- Level 4: country-level data where the countries include individual employees nested into teams as groups and further nested into departments as groups.
- Level 5: organizational-level data that characterizes something at the organization level.

It is important to understand that using different levels of data in some statistical procedures (without considering this) can potentially create problems for the analyst for a number of reasons. One of these reasons might be that when a statistic is aggregated or created at a particular group level, and included in an analysis that includes individual-level data, the sensitivity of the analysis may be reduced. To make this point clearer we will use a hypothetical situation where we have 5,000 employees in an organization organized into 300 teams (of on average 16–17 team members) in 10 departments across 10 countries. If we had team-level statistics (eg percentage of engaged team members in each team) linked to each individual and we used this team engagement score as a possible factor to try to predict what made individual employees leave in the last 12 months, each team member would be given the same team engagement score when we try to predict why and whether they left. Probably, the analysis would be more sensitive if we had individual engagement scores, as it would take into account individual variation in engagement rather than use a blunt aggregated team figure for each individual. Playing this out, we might be trying to predict whether an individual will leave, but with a measure that has something to do with the team rather than the individual. It might be the case that the reason an individual left was because they were disengaged, even though their team was highly engaged; thus team-level engagement might not be likely to predict whether this individual was going to be a leaver.

A second reason why it might not always be sensible to use group-level statistics that have been aggregated or created at a particular group level, and include them in analysis that has involved working with individual-level data, is that many statistical procedures such as multiple linear regression may include some assumptions that the individual employees or objects of study (eg teams) are 'independent'. By this it means that the individual elements are free to vary at the individual level that is not explained as a function of some grouping. If people are actually organized into a group and this grouping could well explain the particular phenomenon that we are trying to predict, it would be quite important to take this grouping (or lack of independence) into account in the analysis.

In this book we do not discuss or present multi-level linear modelling, which is a form of predictive modelling that can take into account some of the complications associated with multi-level nested data. In short, multi-level analysis enables a researcher to predict particular outcomes at one level whilst taking into account the nesting within the data. For example, with multi-level analysis you could model individual turnover or engagement data by incorporating both the individual and the nested (eg team) nature of the data structure. The results would be able to identify the importance of individual versus group-level predictors of individual turnover or engagement data. As explained, however, we do not set out this type of analysis in this book. The main reason for this is that multi-level analysis is considered an advanced analytic method that is beyond the scope of this text. Once you open up a multi-level box with HR data, the statistical and mathematical foundations become really quite complex. The second reason for this is that there are so many possible multi-level nested data structures with HR-related data that this would take up too much of this introductory text. For a further discussion on multi-level modelling please refer to Tabachnick and Fidell (2013) and Field (2013) on multi-level linear modelling.

# Curvilinear relationships

Sometimes, we may test our data for relationships but not find any evidence of a significant statistical linear relationship. Testing for correlations and running regression analysis will, as a default, test for linear relationships between variables. Even if there is no evidence that there might be linear relationships in our HR data, it may be the case that a curvilinear relationship may exist. With linear relationships, as one variable increases then the values of a second variable will either increase (with a positive linear relationship) or decrease (negative linear relationship). The following situation may, however, exist: as we witness cases increase with one variable (A) we see a corresponding increase on a second variable (B) but after we find that our first variable (A) increases beyond a certain point we then see a decrease in our second variable (B). Or, alternatively, we witness an initial decrease in our variable (B) followed by an increase in (B) as (A) increases from the lowest point to the highest point. Either of these would be a curvilinear rather than a linear relationship.

A good HR-related example of a possible curvilinear relationship would be job pressure and performance: as pressure goes up people may begin to rise to the occasion and perform better, but their performance may well start to go down once the job pressure gets too high.

One of the challenges with curvilinear relationships is that with most predictive models, unless you specifically look for a curvilinear relationship, analysis output may suggest that either: 1) no relationship exists between two variables; or 2) the relationship that exists is linear in nature. As an example of 2), we can consider our team-level case study presented in Chapter 5. In this example we were predicting team-level engagement and one of the factors that seemed to predict team engagement was the percentage of the team who were male; the analysis indicated that the higher the percentage of males in the teams, then the lower the team engagement scores were found to be (Beta=–0.303, $p<0.001$). This clearly indicates that as the teams become more male dominated then team engagement seems to go down. However, if the analyst interrogated the relationship between the percentage of the teams that were made up of males and team engagement, he or she would have found that the relationship in this organization is curvilinear. Of the 928 teams in the data set, the lowest proportion of males is 1 per cent and the highest is 100 per cent. The Beta of –0.303 would suggest that the teams with the highest level of engagement would be with the almost all female teams, and engagement gradually goes down to its likely lowest level when we have all male teams. However, this is not the case with our data. As teams go from 1 per cent male to 40 per cent male there tends to be an increase in engagement, and as the percentage tips over towards 100 per cent the engagement levels tend to go down. How do we know this?

We ask SPSS to check for quadratic curve estimation in the relationship between male team percentage and team engagement.

To do this you select the Analyse→Regression→Curve Estimation option (see Figure 11.7).

Then you select the team engagement variable into the 'Dependent(s):' box and the 'Percentage of Team That Were Male' variable into the 'Independent: Variable' box (see Figure 11.8), whilst making sure that you select the 'Linear' and 'Quadratic' models tick-box options. Note that 'quadratic' is a type of curvilinear model.

## FIGURE 11.7

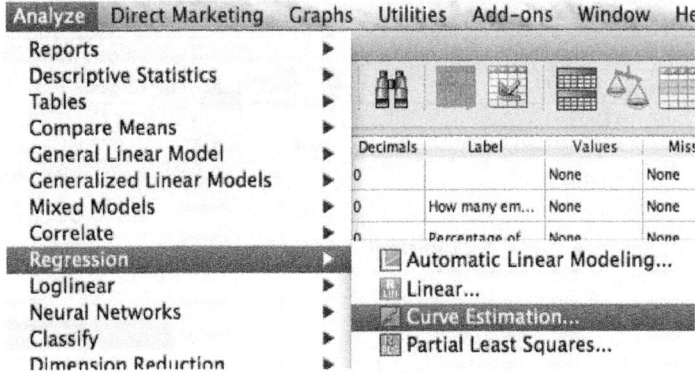

## FIGURE 11.8

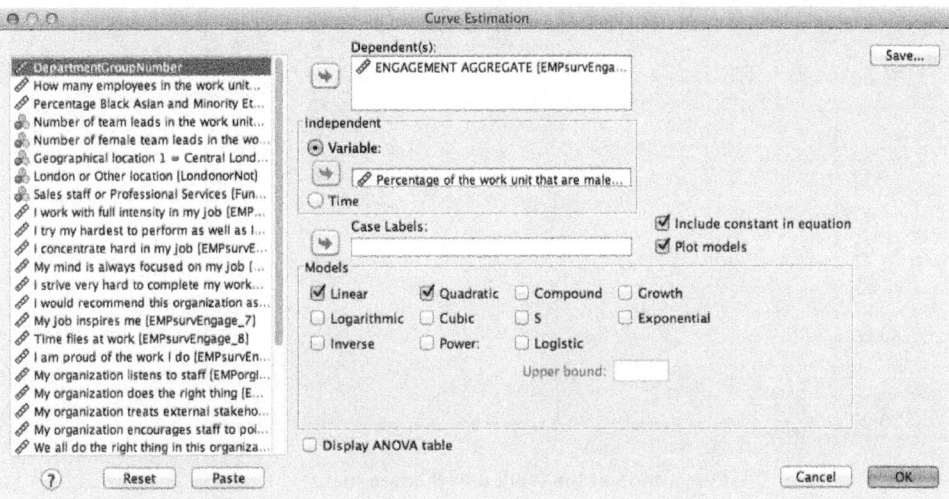

As you will see from the output (Figure 11.9) the linear regression term is significant (b1=−0.169, p<0.001) with an R-square of 0.141, but a quadratic regression term is also significant (b1=0.186, p<0.001, when controlling for the negative linear relationship) with an R-square of 0.189. As the scatter graph shows (which includes a dotted curvilinear line of best fit through the plots), engagement initially increases as the proportion of males in each team goes up from 1 per cent; then team engagement starts to go down after the percentage of males starts to go beyond 30 per cent or 40 per cent.

## FIGURE 11.9 Model summary and parameter estimates

Dependent Variable: ENGAGEMENT AGGREGATE

| Equation | Model Summary | | | | | Parameter Estimates | | |
|---|---|---|---|---|---|---|---|---|
| | R-Square | F | df1 | df2 | Sig. | Constant | b1 | b2 |
| Linear | .141 | 151.472 | 1 | 925 | .000 | 91.123 | −.169 | |
| Quadratic | .189 | 107.807 | 2 | 924 | .000 | 83.085 | .186 | −.003 |

The independent variable is Percentage of the work unit that are male.

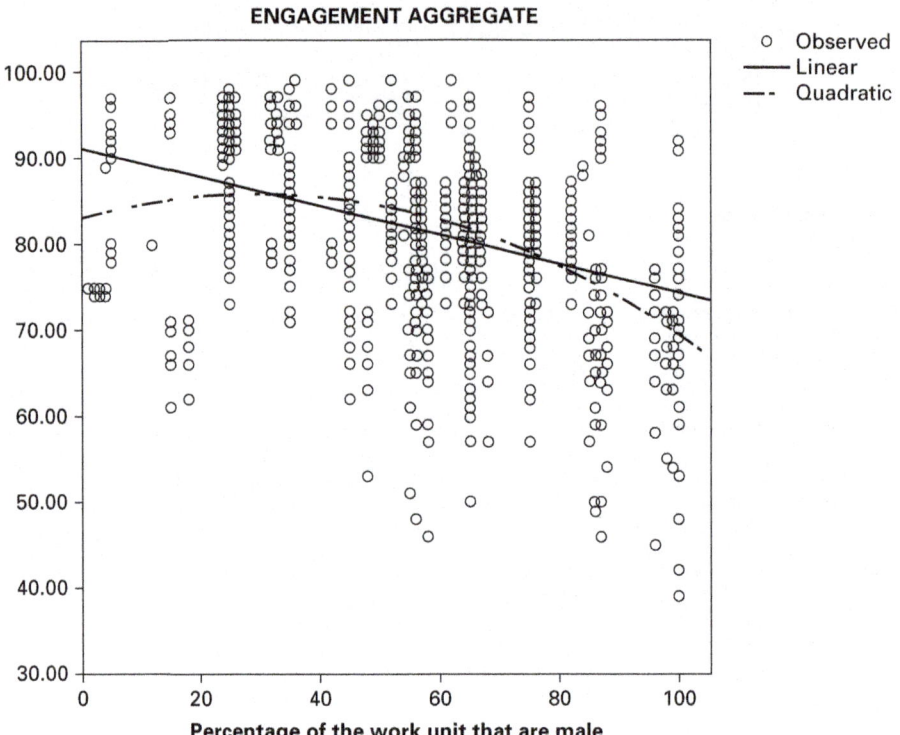

The above description demonstrates how to (very easily) test a curvilinear relationship between two variables with SPSS. However, if we wanted to include a curvilinear relationship in a model predicting team engagement with a broader collection of independent variables (such as the model we ran in Chapter 5, page 183) we would simply need to create a standardized version of the male percentage in team variable (as we did on page 419), create a squared form (a quadratic term) of this standardized variable (created using the Transform->Compute Variable) and include both of these as predictors. This will ensure that this curvilinear relationship is controlled for in the predictive model.

## Structural equation models

Structural equation modelling (SEM) is a form of analysis that tests data against some form of theoretical predicted model that generally involves a number of variables usually arranged in a predicted causal sequence. In its simplest form it involves a number of sequential regression analyses with multiple observed dependent variables, where the researcher indicates the expectation that particular predictive relationships should exist. The HR analyst also can conduct analysis that, in effect, takes into account the complexities and imperfections ('error' in measurement) of multi-item measurement metrics and model expected predictive relationships (referred to as 'structural' relationships) at the same time. Often with SEM the researcher is interested in testing a particular process of causality between a range of different variables. Imagine extending the simple mediated model presented in Figure 11.1 to include multiple independent variables, multiple mediators and multiple dependent variables. These models can incorporate interactions, mediation and multi-level structural relationships; the possible complexities of models that can be tested with SEM are considerable. Importantly, the researcher may have a number of different possible theoretical models that they may want to test for in order to identify which one 'fits the data' the best.

In order to carry out structural equation modelling, you need a specific SEM program because you cannot generally conduct this analysis with the standard statistical programs such as SPSS, Stata, SAS or Minitab. The main SEM programs are AMOS, LISREL, EQS and M-plus; with M-plus fast becoming the 'go-to' SEM program because of its versatility. The potential for variations and complications in the types of models that you can run with SEM programs is endless; discussing these is far beyond the remit of this book. Whilst it is useful for the analyst to be aware of SEM, it is quite unlikely that an HR analytics team would have much need to conduct this form of complex 'theory testing' analysis. For further reading, a good introductory book on SEM with M-plus is Geiser (2013); and Kelloway (2014) is also recommended.

## Growth models

Growth models are specifically designed to predict growth or change over time in particular variables and therefore require data to be collected over a number of time points with each individual or object (such as a team). In essence, growth models involve a sophisticated form of modelling change. In Chapter 9 (on monitoring the impact of interventions) we do look at some forms of change, indeed we see whether checkout scan rates change over two time points, whether employee commitment to the organization's values changes over three time points, and we also predict performance whilst controlling for an earlier performance rating (that in effect predicts change in performance). Some of these forms of analyses are really looking at average change linked to a particular sample. However, with growth models we specifically identify growth patterns with individual cases (eg with employees) and try to predict and account for these growth patterns. From an HR analytics point of view, some examples of how these types of models might be useful in analysis could include the prediction of individuals who show a constant growth or increase in a particular performance dimension (eg sales or general increase in performance appraisal ratings). Such a model could be very useful, for example, to identify factors in a recruitment and selection process that predict high achievers and people who show continual growth in their development (rather than trying to predict performance taken just at one time point). There is more than one method of exploring and analysing growth models. In general they involve more complex methods than we have presented in this book; however, two methods of growth analysis utilizing different analysis techniques are outlined below: multi-level modelling – individual growth models; and latent growth modelling.

## *Multi-level modelling: individual growth models*

One of the approaches that can be used for growth modelling is referred to as multi-level modelling: individual growth models. In effect, this utilizes multi-level linear modelling techniques mentioned above. This approach treats multiple waves of data collection linked to each individual (or entity such as a team) modelled as nested or grouped data in a multi-level model. If you think about it, if you have five or so data points collected for each employee, in a data set of a whole workforce that has these multiple waves of data collection the multiples waves will be linked across the individual employees. Thus, the analysis treats the five (or more) data points per employee as being 'nested' with that individual. The growth model then explores the degree to which the data set as a whole seems to find particular individual growth patterns (eg a linear increase or decrease) over the five waves, but it allows for (and models) the existence of variation in the growth patterns for each individual. Using this technique, the researcher can incorporate and identify various predictors of particular growth patterns (eg linear increases, linear decreases, curvilinear increases or decreases).

Translating this into an HR analytics example, to explain this further we could use an example of a workforce of financial sales staff who sell insurance products for a bank. With such a workforce we could monitor their quarterly sales in dollars ($), and let's say we have two years of quarterly sales figures amounting to eight data points per sales staff. If we had 200 sales staff where we tracked their sales figures from the day they started, we could have a data set of sales staff in their first two years. We could then model certain sales trajectories, eg they start high and show no increase over time, they show a linear increase over time, they show a linear decrease or they show a curvilinear growth in sales (where the sales person either starts off selling well but this flattens out or they take a while to get going but then they increase later on in the period (see the examples in Figure 11.10).

**FIGURE 11.10** Example sales trajectory profiles

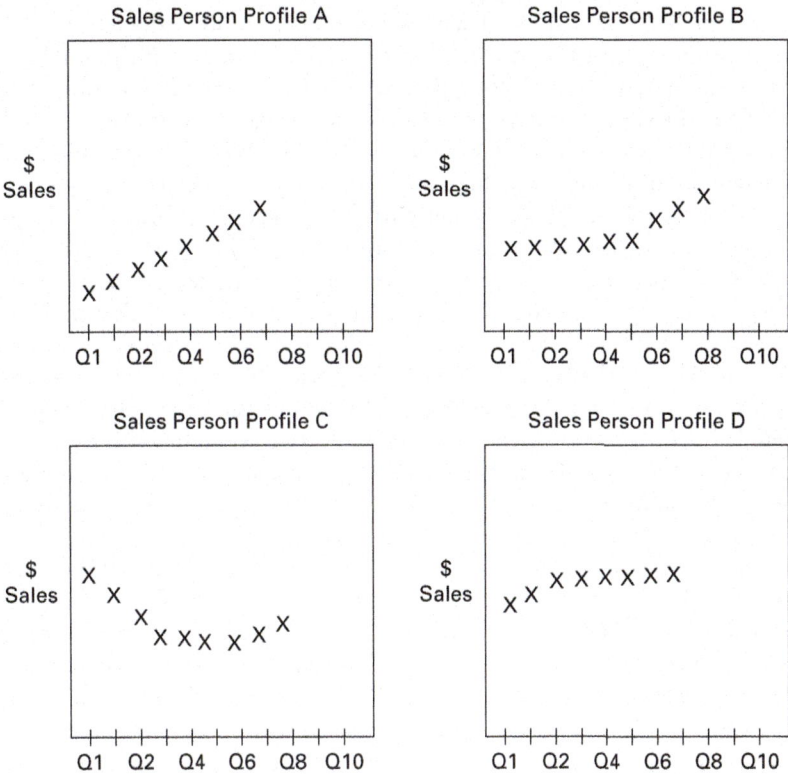

Once the researcher identifies these possible growth trajectories they could then look for possible predictors of the different profiles of performance. These predictors could be something like scores given on an assessment centre in recruitment (which could evaluate assessment-centre efficacy), education level, previous experience and induction training provision, amongst other possible factors. This kind of analysis is quite complicated to get to grips with; however, it can be conducted with SPSS. A good reference for this is Heck, Thomas and Tabata (2013: Chapter 5), although some familiarity with multi-level statistics is probably needed. The statistical reference book for this type of analysis is a seminal text by Singer and Willet (2003) – though the Heck, Thomas and Tabata (2013) book is more helpful as an SPSS guide. An additional reference for this form of analysis is Hoffman's (2015) *Longitudinal Analysis: Modelling within-person fluctuation and change*.

## Latent growth modelling

A second form of growth modelling involves the use of structural equation modelling and is referred to as latent growth modelling (LGM). Because this involves structural equation modelling analytics this cannot be carried out with most of the mainstream software packages (such as SPSS) and requires an SEM package such as M-plus. It also is only really feasible to use this with more than five waves of data (it can be done with fewer but the set-up becomes much more complicated). However, assuming that the analyst has SEM software and more than five waves of data, the opportunities that this analysis approach enables are considerable. It is similar to the above-mentioned multi-level modelling: individual growth model approach in that it enables the researcher to predict particular patterns of growth over time; however, the diagnostic sophistication of LGM is much greater. It can pretty much do all of the analysis that we set out with the multi-level modelling: individual growth modelling, but it can easily incorporate additional types of analysis that the previous type struggles with. For example, it can have multiple slopes with multiple growth trajectories. If we use our sales example again, you could model a scenario where commission payments were also modelled over time for each sales person. So you could have eight waves of data associated with sales and eight waves of data associated with commission paid each quarter. You could then explore the degree to which certain types or patterns of commission payments were associated with certain types of sales growth pattern. For example, you could test whether paying certain types of remuneration deal and growth trajectories of bonus payments were linked to certain trajectories of sales growth. For example, if you do not increase bonus payments over time does this tend to be followed by a flattening out of sales performance; or is the provision of a base salary (with no commission) linked to a high immediate sales performance and a flatter increase over time (assuming that the organization had such variation in their remuneration practices, of course)? Although the learning investment required to be able to understand and carry out LGM is quite considerable, the potential for the advanced analyst to identify really important patterns of behaviour is considerable.

## Latent class analysis

Latent class analysis is a powerful analytic tool that could potentially play a role in helping answer certain types of HR analytic questions. In essence, it helps an analyst to create employee profiles within a particular data set from a range of different metrics or indices. This analytic tool could be used with HR analytic activities that involve the imperative to identify particular groups of employees that behave in a particular way. Classic examples might be identifying talent pools using a range of different metrics. The HR analyst might be tasked to identify 'key talent' using a range of indices (eg performance ratings, ratings of potential, position in competency band, etc).

Latent class analysis enables the analyst to explore and produce a range of different classes within the organization based on how employees 'score' on a range of indices; for example, the analyst could produce and explore three or four different profiles within the organization to classify them (eg as 'key talent'; 'potential key talent', etc).

Another example could be with appraisals where a range of different performance material is collected across a number of dimensions; how the organization deals with multiple and varying appraisal information for each individual could be more complicated than one might think. If there were six different appraisal dimensions representing different competencies, the organization might want to have a particular matrix where people who get certain scores on different dimensions will be given particular performance ratings. Of course, the more dimensions that are involved the more complicated this gets. For example, if someone gets an above-average score on four of the six but below average on the remaining two, should they get a different rating than someone who got four average and two above-average ratings? The possible combinations represent a real complication to determining performance-rating classes with multiple indices. If, in the end, the organization wanted to create say four different classes of performance rating, it would be perfectly sensible to see if various performance clusters naturally occurred in the data across the six dimensions. Latent class analysis could well become a very useful tool in such situations. We will not, however, go into any more depth on this topic given the fact that specialist software is usually required to conduct such analysis (eg M-plus).

## Response surface methodology and polynomial regression analysis

Response surface methodology is an analysis tool that is specifically designed to explore the implications (in an outcome variable) of two particular independent variable measures matching at different levels on their dimensions; the analysis utilizes polynomial regression analysis. On the flip side of this, the analysis specifically enables the exploration of the implications if there are mismatches or gaps at different levels of two dimensions. In some ways this form of analysis is an extension to moderation or interaction testing mentioned earlier in this chapter, as the analysis explores what level employees (or teams) tend to have on a given dependent variable; given the levels that they have on two separate independent variables. Response surface analysis is, however, a much more sophisticated version of interaction testing as not only does it take into account the linear impact on a particular dependent variable that the interaction between two independent variables has, but it takes into account curvilinear relationships and interactions (hence the polynomial regression element) and the implications of a mismatch/gap or congruence between the two independent variables. If we use our earlier 'stress' and 'job demands' as an example – the suggestion by the Karasek model is that the interplay between job demands and decision latitude may be key in determining employees' psychological well-being.

**FIGURE 11.11** RSM surface plot of a hypothetical relationship between job demands and decision latitude that has psychological well-being as the dependent variable

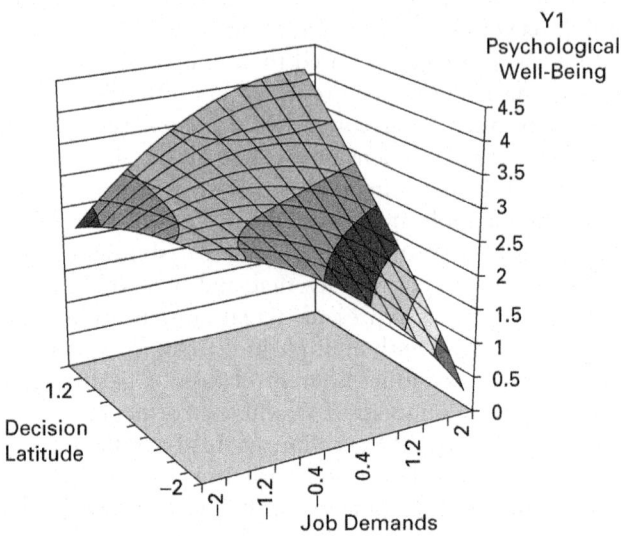

**NOTE:** the different shades in the 3D shape assist in determining the incremental position along the well-being scale.

Figure 11.11 shows an RSM surface plot of a hypothetical relationship between job demands and decision latitude (autonomy) at various levels in our organization. The two X axis scales are z-scores, hence we have a negative and positive, and the Y axis is psychological well-being. From this graph we can see that the optimal scenario of well-being is a scenario where employees have high demands but they also have higher-than-average levels of decision latitude; when the incongruence of demands and latitude levels is on the high demands and low latitude levels, we see lower levels of well-being.

With this particular example (Figure 11.11), the main interesting feature of the analysis is not necessarily the gap or mismatch between the two independent variables, but what happens to the well-being at different levels of the two independent variables. Because this example does not necessitate a 'match' between the two variables the power of this analysis is not fulfilled; it is not much more than a sophisticated interaction analysis that incorporates curvilinear relationships (that polynomial regression analysis enables). Where RSM really comes into its own is when the idea of congruence or incongruence becomes more important for our dependent variable.

To demonstrate our point further here we can present another hypothetical example where a match of some sort could be important. Organizations that place great emphasis on customer focus often have this as a key competency in performance appraisal ratings; where all employees are rated on the degree to which they demonstrate 'customer focus' when going about their everyday job. When it comes to performance appraisal

**FIGURE 11.12** Hypothetical RSM graph showing the importance of congruence/incongruence in employee versus supervisor customer focus (on employee performance ratings)

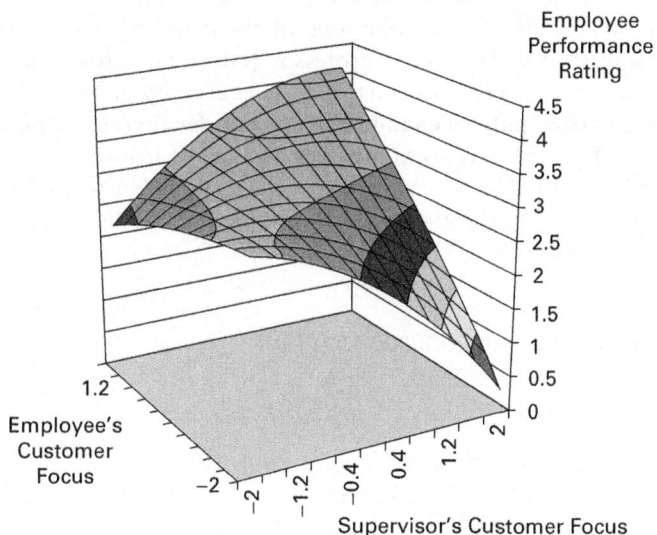

**NOTE:** the different shades in the 3D shape assist in determining the incremental position along the well-being scale.

time, employees' supervisors will rate their subordinates on customer focus and supervisors will also be rated themselves. Here we hypothesize that the degree to which the supervisor has a customer focus may have important consequences for employees in that this will determine the implications of the employee themselves getting rated as high or low customer focus. Figure 11.12 shows an RSM graph of the supervisor versus employee customer focus ratings being plotted together, along with the employees' performance ratings. As we can see, the consequences of incongruence between the employee and customer ratings seem quite important. If the employee is rated highly on customer focus but the supervisor is not so customer focused then the employee is not rewarded (with a high-performance appraisal) for their customer focus; the rewards for high levels of employee customer focus seem greater, however, when the supervisor is highly customer focused (the high point of the surface).

Interestingly, as shown in Figure 11.12, employees with a low level of customer focus seem to be punished to a much greater degree when the supervisor cares a lot about customer focus, especially when compared to employees who have supervisors who are not rated highly on customer focus. This pattern of results actually indicates a curvilinear pattern of incongruence effects on performance ratings. Interestingly, we do not witness any curvilinear effects where there tends to be congruence between the employee and the supervisor ratings of customer focus. Where employees and supervisors have low customer focus the employee does not get a particularly low rating.

The polynomial regression analysis and RSM graphs give us a range of statistical tests for congruence and incongruence effects; they tell us whether any congruence and incongruence effects are linear/curvilinear. The analysis gives us significance levels for these effects and a range of Excel tools exist that plot various effects. Probably one of the main experts in polynomial analytic and RSM techniques is Professor Jeffrey Edwards (no relation to either author) who is currently based at the University of North Carolina at Chapel Hill: **http://public.kenan-flagler.unc.edu/faculty/edwardsj/**.

Professor Edwards's website includes a range of instructions on how to conduct RSM with SPSS and how to plot the response surface graphs. Using his method, if we plot the above RSM example, we are shown the following incongruence graph $(Y=-X)$:

**FIGURE 11.13**   Incongruence graph

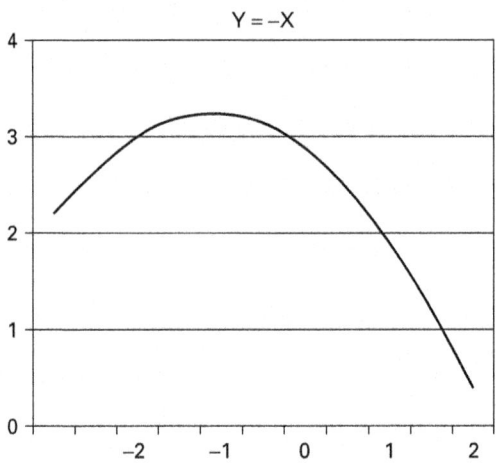

This graph demonstrates a curvilinear incongruence effect of employee versus supervisor customer focus on the employees' performance ratings. The plots also show that this is not the case where there is congruence between employee versus supervisor customer focus; though there is a slight positive relationship (linear increase) along the congruence line $(Y=X)$ (see Figure 11.14).

The potential for exposing some really interesting HR analytic insights with RSM are, we hope, quite obvious. Where congruence or incongruence of any particular two factors is expected to have an important impact on a particular metric, it is undoubtedly the ideal advanced form of analysis that can expose what is really going on in the organization.

One of the challenges for anyone interested in carrying out RSM at the moment is the fact that to carry out the analysis with SPSS the analyst needs to engage in the SPSS syntax interface (see below). This should not pose a huge problem for the advanced HR analyst (who will learn to love the SPSS syntax interface as she/he becomes more capable) but for the beginner this might seem daunting.

**FIGURE 11.14**  Congruence graph

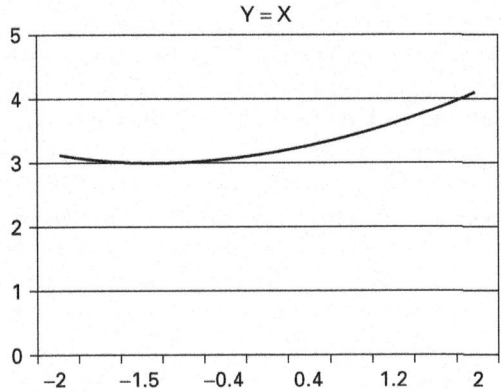

# The SPSS syntax interface

Every single statistical procedure that SPSS carries out after the analyst clicks various buttons has a set of SPSS syntax commands driving the procedure behind the scenes. Advanced SPSS users often tend to use, learn and interact with the syntax command language as their capabilities increase. They do this through a specific interface called the SPSS syntax interface. Almost without fail, at the bottom of any statistical procedure that an analyst has set up using windows, mouse clicks, buttons and pull-down menus, you will find a 'Paste' button. If you browse through the various screenshots of analysis windows throughout the case study chapters (eg on pages 199, 243, 326, 339) you will see a 'paste' button. Whenever these are pressed, the SPSS syntax command language for the analytic procedure is copied into a separate SPSS syntax interface screen. For example, pressing the 'Paste' button with the model analysed on page 243 in Chapter 7 produces the following syntax box (Figure 11.15):

**FIGURE 11.15**

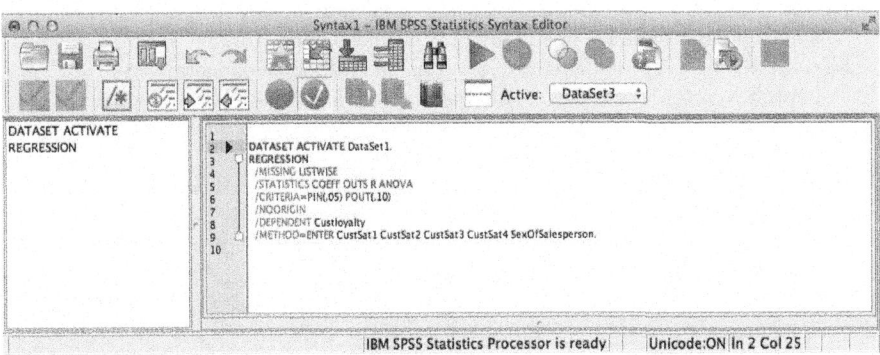

This interface box is known as the SPSS syntax interface and the text in the main box is the syntax command associated with the regression model being tested (in this case referring to the test we run on page 247 of Chapter 7). If the analyst wanted to run the analysis using this interface he or she could simply select the particular set of commands (drag the mouse over the text whilst left clicking) and click on the triangle ▶ button at the top of the screen. This would run the analysis that the analyst had previously set up using windows and buttons. This syntax box can be saved as a syntax command document with the .sps extension. We will not go into any depth in our discussion of the SPSS syntax interface here, however, as this would require an advanced course of instruction. The point of raising it is that some more complex analysis procedures actually require the analyst to use the command interface.

With all of the topics outlined above, we expect that once an analyst gets to a high degree of competence with predictive HR analytics, they will begin to really understand some of the real potential of applying sophisticated statistical analysis to HR data within their firm. This chapter can serve as a guide to just some of the more advanced analytic techniques that could really help the analyst to demonstrate their analytic capabilities to the full extent.

# References

Baron, R M and Kenny, D A (1986) The moderator-mediator variable distinction in social psychological research: conceptual, strategic and statistical considerations, *Journal of Personality and Social Psychology*, **51**, pp 1173–82

Cohen, J and Cohen, P (1983) Applied multiple regression/correlation analysis for the behavioral sciences, 2nd edn, Erlbaum, New Jersey

Dawson, J F (2014) Moderation in management research: what, why, when, and how, *Journal of Business Psychology*, **29**, pp 1–19

Field, A (2013) *Discovering Statistics Using IBM SPSS Statistics*, 4th edn, Sage, London

Geiser, C (2013) *Data Analysis with Mplus*, Guilford, New York

Hayes, A F (2009) Beyond Baron and Kenny: statistical mediation analysis in the new millennium, *Communication Monographs*, **76**, pp 408–20

Heck, Thomas and Tabata (2013) *Multilevel and Longitudinal Modeling with IBM SPSS*, 2nd edn, Routledge, New York

Hoffman, L (2015) *Longitudinal Analysis: Modelling Within-Person Fluctuation and Change*, Routledge Press (Taylor & Francis), New York

Karasek, R A (1979) Job demands, job decision latitude, and mental strain: implications for job redesign, *Administrative Science Quarterly*, **24**, pp 285–308

Kelloway, K E (2014) *Using Mplus for Structural Equation Modeling: A Researcher's Guide*, 2nd edn, Sage, California

Singer, J D and Willett, J B (2003) *Applied Longitudinal Data Analysis: Modelling change and event occurrence*, Oxford University Press, New York

Tabachnick, B G and Fidell, L S (2013) *Using Multivariate Statistics*, 6th edn, Pearson, Boston

# Reflection on HR analytics
## Usage, ethics and limitations

12

This chapter is intended to serve as a reflective seminar where key issues and challenges with the activity of predictive HR analytics are explored. Often, with texts, blogs and discussions on the subject of HR analytics, authors only focus on the promise and potential of the discipline. It is very rare that analytics experts discuss challenges and complexities associated with HR analytics. The HR analytics expert, however, needs to be as aware of the challenges that the activity might lead to as well as the potential for considerable business benefits. Some of these challenges are linked to practical difficulties that arise when attempting to conduct sophisticated HR analytics; some are important challenges linked to debates in research science; some involve management challenges and behavioural issues; and some involve important ethical challenges.

## HR analytics as a scientific discipline

Carrying out HR analytics is a scientific activity and the HR analyst is in effect acting as a research scientist. They are exploring aspects of the empirical world, attempting to answer research questions and using statistical techniques to interrogate data, test or check for patterns or causal factors that are apparent in the organizational world, with the intention of drawing conclusions from the analysis. A capability and area of expertise that a scientist will need to develop as they become more of an expert is the ability to understand what constitutes a good research design and what the limitations of particular types of research methods may be. In this regard the master HR analyst needs to be aware of the potential problems and methodological limitations inherent in the field of HR analytics. Some of the challenges in this regard include the following:

- Constraints on objectivity: as a representative of the organization, and ultimately representing the leadership within the organization, the analyst's 'objectivity' may not be guaranteed.

- Constraints on the analyst's ability to 'experiment' in order to discover possible and causal features of the environment.
- Constraints on data availability to discover possible and causal features of the environment.

## Constraints on objectivity

Ultimately the HR analyst will often be operating within certain constraints. They will be operating within a context where they are expected to carry out analysis that will identify factors that could potentially improve the bottom line of the organization. Also, as we discussed in Chapter 9 in our case studies exploring the impact of interventions, sometimes management decisions have been made and the investment might be so considerable that the organization's leaders may not want to hear that the investment has not led to the outcomes that were intended. This could put the analyst in a difficult position if they explore and find evidence that a decision made has cost the organization. A scientific approach to investigating workplace scenarios would actively involve looking for things that do not work; looking for evidence that decisions made have produced negative results. Also the analyst may be assigned to a particular research question that could necessitate (politically) a particular finding.

It may be the case that an analyst discovers, through exploratory analysis, that there is a problem with something fundamental that the organization has done or is doing.

## Constraints on the ability to experiment

As an HR analytics professional, you may find yourself wanting to test a hypothesis – such as the hypothesis that excessive levels of stress will increase employee turnover, or that a higher bonus payment will translate into higher employee performance. It is important in these circumstances to accept that you can only analyse the data you have in the organization. Indeed it is not ethical, even if it were possible, to experiment on employees. You cannot just give a bonus to a random sample of staff (but not give it to others, in order to create a control group) and then monitor their performance, for example. We talk later in the chapter about the data always being linked to human beings, so even if you did have a budget or leadership support to conduct experiments to test hypotheses, it is not ethical to do so. As we discussed in Chapter 9, however, there may be natural conditions that occur in the organization that enable a natural control group to exist, which can fundamentally strengthen the analyst's ability to infer causality from the analysis undertaken.

## Constraints on data availability

Often there will be problems with the availability of data, either that it has not been collected, or that there are missing groups or missing data, which we talk about later in this chapter. The management information (MI) function has a responsibility to ensure the integrity and completeness of the data, and indeed many MI functions will conduct regular data audits and 'amnesty' exercises to encourage completion of the data. Nevertheless it is rare for the data to be 100 per cent complete and you can only conduct analysis on those people for whom you have complete information (on whatever it is that you are testing).

# The metric becomes the behaviour driver: Institutionalized Metric-Oriented Behaviour (IMOB)

Chasing and monitoring certain numbers and performance metrics can become an automatic activity that the HR analyst will become engaged in. As discussed in Chapters 1 and 3, at the moment HR information and metrics teams spend considerable time producing descriptive reports and monitoring particular metrics (such as turnover or particular performance metrics across different parts of the organization). Once a particular metric has been identified as being an important metric to focus on, then managers and also the HR analyst may well focus on such a metric as an indicator of a key performance measure. However, when investigating a particular aspect of employee behaviour in the workplace, sometimes rather than the metric representing a factor of interest (eg performance) the metric *becomes* the performance measure that all involved focus on. There is a danger, however, that once a particular performance metric becomes institutionalized, the metric starts to drive a particular type of performance. Behaviour and management focus within the organization starts to become oriented towards the achievement of a particular metric. Thus the phenomenon of Institutionalized Metric-Oriented Behaviour (IMOB) occurs. The problem with such activities is that an inordinate amount of attention and people effort becomes oriented around such metrics. This has a number of implications:

1 Line managers have a tendency to manage and monitor the metrics rather than carry out proper people-management activities.
2 Employees become overly focused on ensuring that they perform well on this particular metric.
3 Behaviours important to overall broad good performance either tend to be ignored by employees and managers or, in the worst case scenario, are actively discouraged in favour of behaviours that will reflect well in the metrics.
4 Certain staff members may be more or less disadvantaged by their inability to reach full potential on achievement of particular metrics.

As a hypothetical example of how IMOB can lead to points 1, 2 and 3 above, we can consider the supermarket performance metric case study example discussed in Chapter 7. Many supermarkets monitor and manage scan rates of checkout operatives. Common sense might suggest that a key performance metric that can be applied to a checkout operator would be how fast they process products. The slower the scan rate, the longer the queues of shoppers and the slower the rate of income generation in a particular period. There is evidence that shoppers will be put off going to a shop if queues get too long (see Briggs, 2015).

It makes sense, therefore, that some supermarkets might focus on this particular metric. Certain supermarkets we have spoken to actively communicate weekly averages of scan rate per minute to staff as a performance management indicator. Presumably those who have low scan rates may be under pressure to speed up. When such a metric becomes the focus of IMOB, the line managers will place too much emphasis on each of their employees' scan rates and employees will become overly focused on increasing it, potentially at the expense of other behaviours. Obviously in a context such as a supermarket that has an IMOB of scan rate, the HR analyst may well spend some time predicting scan rates. As the HR analyst explores some predictive models and finds key trends and patterns, this reinforces the IMOB. The danger in such a situation is that one piece of knowledge (that customers do not like queues) leads to the monitoring of one particular metric at the expense of another piece of knowledge (for example, that customers might like a pleasant interaction at the checkout). Thinking through the possible implications of the IMOB of scan rate in supermarkets, the checkout operatives might be discouraged from engaging in a meaningful conversation with customers as this may inhibit fast scan rate. Thus the metric could actually be discouraging quality customer-oriented behaviour and be all about the quantity metric. It is also possible that some members of staff may be disadvantaged with this particular metric. It may be that some staff with disabilities, for example, may struggle to reach the full potential of extremely fast scan rate; it might also be the case that staff on certain shifts at certain times of day/certain times of the week (where there may be less customer flow-through) might also be disadvantaged. Some of these issues were mentioned as being instrumental in one particular supermarket that decided to remove the practice of monitoring checkout scan rate (*Yorkshire Post*, 2015).

Checkout scan rates at supermarkets are just one example where a performance measure can become an example of IMOB; many different examples could be presented. In academia, for example, some teaching quality metrics can become institutionalized (eg student evaluation scores). In environments where engagement surveys are conducted, the team engagement scores can become institutionalized. In call centres, incoming call rates, call lengths and percentage of time on the phone can become institutionalized. In consultancy or law firms, time reporting metrics and 'billable hours' are another example. Most readers may well be able to reflect on how their organization operates and whether there are examples of IMOB within their own work environment.

Because of the dangers of unintended consequences that can occur with IMOB, as an HR analyst you must always ask yourself 'Are there any unintended consequences that might occur with a particular focus on any one metric?' You also need to be highly sensitive to the potential for a particular focus on any metric to foster and indeed help create instances of IMOB.

## Balanced scorecard of metrics

One of the main reasons practitioners and theorists recommend a 'balanced scorecard' in performance management and performance metrics is to avoid problems associated with a mono-metric focus and target or metric-oriented behaviour. The problems associated with IMOB mentioned in the previous section will be inherent wherever performance is judged against one metric. Thus, it is recommended that any attempt to predict or model any metric or aspect of organizational performance should include a number of different indices or metrics in order to judge the full range of the particular performance, success of a function or employee behaviour.

Whenever the HR analytic expert is tasked with investigating a particular issue or factor, they should generally be on the lookout for more than one form of metric. As mentioned in the performance case study (Chapter 7), there are many ways to measure and monitor different types of performance. The HR analyst should always be thinking about different possibilities of data indicators that might provide information about different types of or aspects of performance. Similarly, if the phenomenon under investigation is diversity, then a range of different diversity indicators will need to be considered. For example, the analyst could consider the percentage of teams who are female, the BAME proportions in teams, the proportion of team leaders who are female and BAME, the proportion of team leavers who are female or BAME, the proportion of people promoted within teams over a recent period who are female or BAME, the engagement scores of females versus males and BAME within a team, etc. Ultimately the analyst should be on the lookout for as wide a range of different metrics on a particular measure as possible. Aside from the importance of avoiding the likelihood of institutionalizing metric-oriented behaviour, the sophistication of possible diagnostic and predictive modelling becomes much greater with an awareness of the potential differential meaning and implications of a range of different indicators and metrics of a phenomenon (eg diversity in this case).

## What is the analytic sample?

In many analytic models that the HR analyst might want to explore, the sample to be utilized may be the entire organization. If this were the case, one would assume that the data sets to be used for the analysis will represent the entire organization. Importantly, this may not always be the case either, because the analyst is only interested in a particular subsection of the organization or because the data available (or indeed unavailable) might end up meaning that the sample at hand is not the entire organization. An example of the former might be some analysis that has a specific focus on part of the organization: for example, predicting customer satisfaction of financial advisors within a bank (Chapter 7), in which only the financial advisors are considered. Another example might be checkout operators within one supermarket who were employed within a given period.

As employees are always joining and leaving organizations, even if we decided to try to utilize the whole organization we may need to restrict the sample to cover those employed within a certain time period; this decision may of course end up restricting the sample that the analyst used, and indeed the nature of the interpretations that can be drawn from analysis conducted with the HR data. Often, in designing models and analytic strategies, the HR analyst will have to make explicit choices around who to include in the analysis and who not to; however, deciding who is to be included in the analysis may not always be as simple as one might expect.

Ultimately the sample used in the analysis may end up being restricted by the fact that there may not always be a full set of data across all chosen measures for each employee. If we consider a potential model where we try to predict an increase in individual financial sales figures over a one-year period, the factors that we consider to predict these figures could include performance appraisal ratings of particular competencies as well as customer satisfaction ratings linked to each employee. The potential for some of the data required to not be available with some employees is quite high. To run these models, we would need two years of sales figures. So we can only analyse the data with employees who have been in the organization for two years or more; thus anyone who has not been employed in the organization for at least two years will not be included. Similarly, it may be the case that some information has not been collected for every employee, eg customer satisfaction surveys may not have been responded to by all customers; thus immediately these employees will not be included in the analysis. So this model will exclude employees who have been employed for less than two years and people who have not had customer satisfaction ratings taken. Immediately therefore, if the analyst wanted to make assumptions about the workforce they would have to recognize that the modelling is based on a particular sample in its foundation. When there has been a restriction of the sample, not only does this mean that there may be restrictions on whether the analyst can comfortably generalize the findings to the rest of the organization but this may also imply that there is some bias to the analysis. The analyst must always consider who has been excluded from the sample.

Whilst the analytic example mentioned here would exclude any employee who has been employed within the last 24 months, even if the analyst wanted to explore a cross-sectional (single time point of data collection) model with current data, some information may be missing depending on when each aspect of data is collected and whether an employee was employed at the time of data collection (eg if a performance appraisal is conducted annually, the timing of the analysis will be important – some people may not have had an appraisal yet if they had joined within the last 12 months).

Another example where an analyst needs to carefully consider the potential sample is when we explore some model that included team employee engagement. As most engagement surveys are voluntary and the employee does not have to complete the questionnaire, it may be the case that a team engagement score might only represent a portion of the team rather than the whole team. The team engagement scores, therefore, may have an inherent bias in that they only represent the people who wanted to complete the survey; this may well have been people who had higher levels of engagement. Importantly, this issue needs to be considered when the analyst tries to link team engagement scores with some other team figures (eg team sales that are compiled from all team members' sales figures); it may be the case that the two sets of data actually represent different groups or samples. The analyst needs to carefully consider these issues; such problems may well mean that the relationships between two sets of measures might not be found because the two sets of data are associated with fundamentally different groups.

To make this more complicated, it may be the case that there are country-specific differences in the data that is allowed to be stored for each employee. There may be a number of reasons why different countries collect and store information on employees in a different way. This could be due to differences in legislation regarding data that can be collected and stored on employees; it can also be due to differences in meaning and interpretation of a particular metric. As an example, the meaning and country norms of who might be considered an employee can have a profound impact on what any analysis of employees might mean. As a specific example, the governments of some countries have employment policies linked to immigration and dictate that all organizations above a certain size must employ a certain proportion of local nationals (rather than expats). This can have profound implications on who is considered an employee because many organizations employ local workers on a zero-hours contract so that they can comply with these legislative requirements. The implication might be that the organization appears to have many more employees that actually do work within the organization. Thus the analyst needs to be aware that what might be in the database – and the meaning of particular data – is likely to vary across countries.

# The missing group

Linked to the above issue of variations in what data is collected across countries is the issue that if a particular group does not have particular data that is to be included in some analysis, then this entire group could be excluded from the analysis. This could be problematic in terms of the legitimacy of whether the data and results actually represent a particular population. Thus the analyst always needs to look at what the final number (N) is that SPSS uses in a particular analysis. If it is lower than it should be then it might be the case that some groups have missing data on one of the metrics included in the analysis; an investigation may need to be carried out to explore who has the missing data and why.

An example might be in a multinational organization where the employee engagement survey asks a number of diversity-related questions, including sexual orientation. Whilst this is common practice in many countries in the West, in other countries, for example, homosexuality is considered a crime – hence it would not be appropriate to ask people to confirm their sexual orientation on an employee attitude survey. This, then, has repercussions in how you might choose to analyse the diversity data across countries in a multinational organization.

## The missing factor

Any research endeavour designed to determine the cause of events or the impact of a potential intervention will only be a worthwhile project if the measures and indices included in the project are valid, appropriate and (more importantly) comprehensive enough to sufficiently provide answers to the analytic research question. Something to watch out for when conducting statistical analysis utilizing predictive models with HR-related data is that some key factors could be missing in the analysis and this factor may actually explain some of the results that the analyst relies on. The analyst will need to be particularly sensitive to possible factors that are not included in the analysis, which could actually play a key role in influencing the results. In research methodology terminology, such a factor is referred to as an 'extraneous variable'. A straightforward example of such a factor could be analysis that looks at job satisfaction, pay levels or employee engagement across particular teams, without taking into account some fundamental differences (eg gender or occupational job role) that could be associated with or explain variation across the teams. To some extent, the issue of the missing factor is partially addressed when we include control variables in the analysis (see examples in Chapter 5); for example, when we try to predict team engagement we can include as many control variables that are available and that we think are appropriate (eg gender percentage in the team, average team age, average job tenure, etc). However, sometimes the missing factor may be the fact that two or more of our possible variables may interact or there are contingencies to the effect that any one factor may have on another. Thus the interaction may be the missing factor. Ultimately, any modelling will involve judgement on the part of the analyst, and as the person driving and testing the models becomes more experienced they may intuitively get a sense of what possible extraneous variables might be influencing the results.

## Carving time and space to be rigorous and thorough

Almost without fail, when providing HR analytics training to HR metrics/ HR information teams, there is often the response that the potential opportunities for enabling considerable insights are recognized but there is a concern or expectation that the analytics team will not be given the required amount of time and space to be able to conduct the analysis. Whilst it is very quick to actually run analysis with SPSS if you know what you are doing, the analyst will have to be given enough time and space to be able to thoughtfully set up data sets and explore and experiment with the various analytic models in order to get the most out of the data. Often when one runs some sophisticated models, in interrogating the data and results an analyst discovers that they should go back and test the data for problems (eg a lack of reliability, missing data, etc). Carrying out analysis and perfecting predictive models are not a linear process. It is very important that before any results are pulled together and presented, the predictive analyst is given space and time to:

1 explore and understand the data available;
2 consider the most appropriate research questions;
3 test and explore particular models;
4 run the analysis;
5 interrogate the analysis;
6 rerun the analysis;
7 subject the analysis and results to further interrogation.

As it stands at the moment, in most large organizations, MI teams have to be constantly producing descriptive report after descriptive report to support IMOB behaviour and often have very little time available to go offline and start exploring and conducting HR analytic models. Thus, in the management and culture of any developed HR analytics team, there must be an acceptance that in carrying out and conducting predictive HR analytics time needs to be given to the analyst to go through the seven steps mentioned above. In essence, creative space also needs to be provided for the analyst to be able to draw on their analytic imagination. Indeed, there will be little likelihood of determining the correct prescriptive action to address the reports if the analysis is not conducted properly and the bulk of the time is spent producing more and more descriptive reports.

## Be sceptical and interrogate the results

If one believes some of the highly optimistic claims made by proponents of HR analytics (about how predictive analytics can transform your organization) then there will be an expectation that the predictive models and analytic insights will produce ground-breaking information that can change how they do business and thus lead to enormous business benefits.

Whilst it is possible that highly experienced HR analytics experts could identify some important insights that could save the organization vast sums of money – or identify factors that, if the organization focused on them, would lead to higher performance – it is important that the analytics expert always looks at the results with a slightly sceptical eye. Before reporting on/ acting on any insights gained, the analyst needs to be extremely comfortable that the recommendations made have been carefully interrogated and that any assumptions made with the data (eg who is and is not represented by the numbers) are made very clear; transparency in the analysis approach is important in order to ensure that the audience of any recommendations is aware of any assumption made.

Importantly, whilst it will be important for the HR analytics expert to be an advocate of the benefits of careful statistical analysis, conducting predictive analytics is not an exact science and the insights that can be gained will often be limited to how good the available data is, and how rigorous the research exercise is that the analyst has undertaken. Importantly, the expert HR analyst will be just as aware of the limitations with predictive analytics as they are of the benefits. An example of particular limitations that the analyst should always be aware of includes the key adage that 'correlations do not imply causality'. Even when the models include the tracking of changes over time, it is often the case that the analysis used with the predictive models relies on the observation of correlations/relationships between data in the data set.

# The importance of quality data and measures

As any HR or MI analyst will understand, records within HR information databases are often incomplete and there are often gaps in information collected or stored in different regions and functions. One of the key things that the HR analytic team would need to do is to undertake an audit of the quality of information that is collected in different parts of the organization and identify any areas where there may be gaps or problems with the quality of data that is collected and stored. As discussed above, it may be the case that if particular data is missing in particular parts of the organization, this could end up excluding these groups from the analysis. Also, if the analyst is to rely on certain measures when designing and conducting particular predictive models, the measures need to be accurate measures of the concept at hand. With analytic techniques such as regression analysis, where we try to account for variation in a particular factor, some part of the variance in our dependent variable will be due to error in measurement. This issue was discussed in Chapter 5 in our discussion of measures of engagement. Aside from ensuring that the appropriate measures are used in the analysis conducted, which is an essential requirement of any good analytics model, the measures themselves need to be reliable and valid. As the maxim of 'garbage in, garbage out' implies, if the quality of the data being entered into the analysis is not at a required level, then what comes out of the analysis is likely to be of questionable quality.

# Taking ethical considerations seriously

## Employee confidentiality and willing participation

HR functions, as a norm, store and are privy to a huge amount of sensitive information on each employee. Some of this data involves the storage of personal information that the employee has voluntarily provided to the organization; some of this information, however, is collected and created by agents of the organization (eg a bonus payment or performance appraisal rating) but is often quite personal information about a particular individual nonetheless. Much of this data is theoretically 'owned' by the organization and often employees have contractually agreed that the organization can use this data in the course of its business.

## Big Brother concerns

In the very nature of available technology in today's workplace it is perfectly possible that data may well be collected and stored on employees that they were not even aware of. Where this may be the case there may be ethical concerns should the organization try to include this data in an HR analytics analysis. An example of an analytic project that employees may not have been aware of (and therefore they may not have been comfortable with) is modelling conducted at a global financial institution that linked food bought in the staff canteen and gym equipment used in the staff gym. This story was passed to one of the authors by the HR analytics director who helped to conduct the analysis. This particular organization used employee identity cards to enable employees to access various non-work-related facilities such as catering facilities and gym facilities. The information stored by this organization on each employee was so fine-grained that an HR analyst had access to what employees ate at the staff dining room during the day and what gym equipment they used (and for how long) when they went to the staff gym during the day.

The HR analytics team at this organization linked this data to the individual employee performance data within a call-centre function at the financial institution. They were able to model the ideal profile of meals, exercise period, workout pattern and ideal gym equipment that was associated with high performance at the call centre in the afternoon. Whilst there may be some potential for this information to be quite useful in terms of helping to identify the best profile of high performers, the Big Brother or surveillance implications of this kind of analysis are really quite profound. The implications of having bad health and dietary habits identified and used in a performance management discussion when someone is not performing in the call centre raises serious ethical concerns. One needs to question where the boundaries may lie as to what is information of a personal nature that the employer should not really be using for the purposes of HR analytics. It is quite normal for gym companies, canteens and shops to track and profile consumer behaviour, however. So some of this analysis is not particularly different from the activities that marketing analysts may conduct in terms of consumer behaviour; the difference is of course that there is a distinct power relationship present between the employer and employee that may not exist between service providers and customers.

Ultimately the analyst should always ask her- or himself: 'If this analysis was being conducted on me or a member of my family without my or their knowledge would there be a level of discomfort?' Ultimately, if there are potential questions around a particular type of analysis then the right thing to do is to communicate with the employee group and probably give them the opportunity to opt out of the analysis.

## *Who owns the data?*

In many cases, when an analyst is about to embark on an analytics activity, the legitimacy of the analysis in terms of invading employees' privacy is likely to be clear cut and well within managerial prerogative to carry out. However, where there is a possible challenge to this managerial prerogative, a source of this problem may be that the data might not really be owned by the organization.

Who owns the data being analysed? Often it is the case that when an employee starts work and signs a contract there may be a clear indication made in the contract that any HR information that the organization collects and stores is 'owned' by the organization. However, there is always the likelihood that some data collected falls outside that which has been agreed formally. When in doubt the HR analyst should communicate the intention to HR and potentially the workforce in general.

## *HR data security issues*

Even without considering HR information from an HR analytics perspective, the HR function will be highly aware of the importance of data security. As HR information systems become more sophisticated, the sheer amount of possible private information (eg salaries, bank account details, date-of-birth information, eating habits from the staff canteen...) that can be stored becomes massive. The responsibility that the HR analyst needs to take on board to ensure data security is of paramount importance – especially as one of the key things they will be doing is gathering considerable amounts of information from a variety of sources. The analyst may indeed be linking this information to an individual employee in order to draw conclusions about some aspect of their psychological state, behaviour or expected behaviour. We will not go into detail here about the importance of data security; many geographical regions have different legislative guidelines around the globe (eg the EU has quite strict data security guidelines) and it is the HR analytic expert's job to be aware of these regulatory frameworks and accord with them in conducting their HR analytic activity. Ultimately, taking data security seriously can be considered to be a key ethical standard that an HR analytics expert should abide by (see below).

## *Problems with using targeted demographic profiles – stereotyping, prejudice and discrimination*

In the performance case study (Chapter 7) we presented an analytic scenario where age categories were interrogated in order to explore the possible profiles of top performers with average checkout scan rates. It was found that women of a particular age and education profile were the fastest checkout scanners. If the organization conducted this analysis and identified a particular profile such as this, a big question that the analyst (and the managers) will face is what should be done with this information. One response would be to introduce a policy of only hiring women between the ages of 30 and 35 to work on the checkouts. Such an approach, whilst rational to some degree, may have a number of implications. It would, of course, end up exposing the organization to potential gender and age discrimination challenges.

Everybody is different and the basis of predictive analysis revolves around patterns in the data rather than definitive certainties. In a sense, predictive analysis risks creating a stereotyped picture of the workforce based on profiles and categories identified in the analysis. A grave danger that could occur with a reliance on stereotypes is the tendency of people to be lazy thinkers (or so-called 'cognitive misers': see Fiske and Taylor, 1984) and not try to challenge stereotypes. This stereotyping can often lead to outright prejudice and discrimination (Brown, 2010). As with any stereotype, the differences within a social category will almost always be as big as the differences between categories. As such, where a recognizable demographic pattern is exposed in predicting any particular type of behaviour such as performance, the analyst should, ethically, go out of their way to demonstrate that although certain profiles may be associated with the highest level of performance, there will always be cases within the 'ideal' profile that do not accord with the expectations that the modelling has produced. Similarly, there will always be cases where employees in a non-ideal profile perform particularly well. One of the challenges that an expert predictive HR analyst might be faced with is how to identify patterns within the workforce without actively stereotyping the organization; without creating evidence that might support a simplified view of the world that may lead to the creation of prejudicial perceptions and discriminatory mindsets. One possible way around such a dilemma is for the analyst to try always to explore the data to identify complexity on the data and to accept that there will always be exceptions to scenarios identified in any predictive model. The analyst should always try to identify contingencies, contextual moderators or boundary conditions (see the discussion on interactions and curvilinear relationships in Chapter 11) that challenge a simple view; in doing so, the analyst will be successfully identifying a more sophisticated model and will reduce the likelihood that any overly simplistic profiling ends up stereotyping the workplace.

# Ethical standards for the HR analytics team

Given that predictive HR analytics is an emerging but growing field, it will be important that some kind of ethical principles can be identified to potentially guide HR analytic activities. As one can consider any analytics team to be positioned under the umbrella of the HR function, any ethical guidelines and principles associated with HR in general can be applied to HR analytics experts. There are no specific agreed ethical guidelines that can be drawn on to help act as an ethical guide for HR; one could, however, consider the ethical standards set out by the UK CIPD as reasonable initial guiding principles (CIPD, 2012).

## UK's CIPD HR ethical standards and integrity commitment

In agreeing to be a member of the UK's CIPD, there is an expectation that HR practitioners must:

- Establish, maintain and develop business relationships based on confidence, trust and respect.
- Exhibit and defend professional and personal integrity and honesty at all times.
- Demonstrate sensitivity for the customs, practices, culture and personal beliefs of others.
- Advance employment and business practices that promote equality of opportunity, diversity and inclusion, and support human rights and dignity.
- Safeguard all confidential, commercially sensitive and personal data acquired as a result of business relationships and not use it for personal advantage or the benefit or detriment of third parties.

Whilst the CIPD standards are not specifically designed for HR analytics activities, there are some ethical standards that could be considered to govern the use of people and HR data exploration within the HR analytics team. Some of these are set out here, drawn from an article written by Professor Paul Schwartz (Berkeley Law, University of California) entitled 'Analyst ethical standards' (Schwartz, 2011):

1 Organizations should comply with legal requirements in conducting analytics.
2 Organizations should consider whether analytics activities reflect cultural and societal norms about what is acceptable; beyond just legal requirements, that is.
3 Organizations should consider the impact of the use of analytics activities and ensure that the trust of various stakeholders is not breached, violated or lost.
4 Clear accountability should be introduced into the HR analytics process, and the organization should develop policies that govern information management. An individual should be designated to oversee the appropriateness of analytics activities.
5 Appropriate safeguards need to be introduced to protect the security of information that is used in the analytic process.
6 Organizations should consider whether analytics activities involve sensitive areas and accompany the process with safeguards proportionate to the risk.

As a set of guiding principles for an analytics team to consider adopting, these six standards seem to be wholly appropriate.

# The metric and the data are linked to human beings

You must always remember that the data being analysed is actually information linked to living, breathing, feeling human beings and not just numbers and data sets. It is not unusual for HR information analysts, or indeed any quantitative analyst, to become so engrossed in the analytic activity in exploring data linked to people that the human aspect is forgotten or lost. People who are used to managing people projects and conducting workforce planning can very quickly start referring to people as 'heads' (as in headcount), 'resources' and 'capacity' reduction. The authors have both had anecdotal experience of HR professionals discussing employees as if there were no human beings involved and discussing the employees as 'heads' or 'resources' in a clinical fashion (eg 'underutilized heads'), such that the level of dehumanization was distasteful. Ultimately the HR analytic expert needs to try to be aware that whilst there may be ways of describing analytic activities using technical jargon – and this may give the appearance of the highly technical aspect of HR analytics, which may boost one's sense of technical expertise – almost every analytic activity will be linked to human beings.

Whilst not specifically related to HR analytics, Keenoy and Anthony (1992) wrote an interesting book chapter that reflected upon the tendency for language used in relation to redundancies to become dehumanized. Instead of job lay-offs/redundancies, the descriptions that are used by organizations might include terms such as 'delayering', 'rationalization', 'headcount reduction', 'rightsizing', 'workforce re-profiling' – and that because of the language used, the 'reality of job loss is banished from our language'. Whilst this is obviously not about HR analytics, the tendency for narratives linked to discussions of the workforce to lose some link with the human beings is something that the HR analytics expert needs to be aware of and be sensitive to. When predicting sickness absence rates, for example, there are real people behind the numbers that are being analysed; what may also be linked to sickness absence is some degree of human suffering.

Thus, HR analytics experts should try to ensure that that they do not lose sight of the fact that the data is data about people – and not forget the 'human' in HR analytics.

# References

Briggs, F (2015) [accessed 20 November 2015] Shopper Are Put Off by Queues More Than Seven People Deep, *Retail Times* [Online] http://www.retailtimes.co.uk/shoppers-put-off-queues-seven-people-deep-box-technologies-intel-research-shows/

Brown, R (2010) *Prejudice: It's social psychology*, 2nd edn, Wiley, Chichester

CIPD (2012) [accessed 20 November 2015] Code of Professional Conduct, *CIPD* [Online] http://www.cipd.co.uk/binaries/code-of-professional-conduct_july-2015.pdf

Fiske, S T and Taylor, S E (1984) *Social Cognition*, AddisonWesley, Massachusetts

Keenoy, T and Anthony, P (1992) HRM: metaphor, meaning and morality, in *Reassessing Human Resource Management*, pp 233–55, ed P Blyton and P Turnbull, Sage Publications, London

Schwartz, P M (2011) [accessed 20 November 2015] Privacy, Ethics and Analytics, *Privacy Interests*, May/June, pp 66–69 [Online] http://www.paulschwartz.net/pdf/pschwartz_privacy-eth-analytics%20IEEE%20P-%20Sec%20%282011%29.pdf

*Yorkshire Post* (2015) [accessed 20 November 2015] Morrisons Abandons High-Tech Checkout System [Online] http://www.yorkshirepost.co.uk/business/business-news/morrisons-abandons-high-tech-checkout-system-they-re-now-going-to-look-to-see-how-many-are-queuing-1-7170389

# INDEX

Note: *Italics* indicate a Figure or Table in the text.

advanced analytic techniques   412–36
   curvilinear relationships   423–26
   latent class analysis   430–31
   mediation processes   414–16
   moderation and interaction
      analysis   416–21
   multi-level linear modelling   421–23
   polynominal regression analysis   431–35
   response surface methodology   431–35
   SPSS syntax interface   435–36
   structured equation models (SEM)   427
analysis software   13–15

BAME (Black, Asian or Minority Ethnic)   124
   percentage in the UK workforce   *142*
Baron and Kenny method   414–15
Bersin, J   3
'big (HR) data'   3–4, 53–55
   value creation   55
Business Objects   54

case study examples
   comparing ethnicity and gender   128–35
   diversity   108–43
   employee attitude   144–89
   employee performance   237–84
   employee turnover   190–236
   gender and job grade analysis   111–22
   monitoring impact of interventions   319–64
   multiple linear regression   102–03, 135–41
   recruitment and selection analytics   285–318
   team diversity   123–28
categorical variables   62–64, 65, 69
   binary   63
   nominal   63
   ordinal   63–64
Chartered Institute of Personnel and Development (CIPD)   6, 192–93
   ethical standards   450–51
chi-square test
   cross-tabulation and   75–81
   example   77–79
   gender and job grade analysis   114–22

   purpose of   76
   regional differences in staff turnover   198–203
   SPSS and   *81*
Cognos   54
consumer panels   321–22
continuous variables   64–65, 66, 69–71
   interval   64–65
   ratio   65
Cronbach's alpha   105, 165
curvilinear relationships   413, 423–26, 431

*Daily Mail*   274
data/information systems   10–56
   country-level   422
   customer satisfaction survey data   12
   employee attitude survey data   11
   ethnicity   124
   group/team-level   66, 67, 422
   HR database   12
   human dimension   451–52
   individual-level   66 , 67, 422
   operational performance data   12
   organizational-level   422
   ownership   448
   parametric   68, 72
   sales performance data   12
   security   448–49
   types of   4, 62
   variables   62
   *see also* 'big (HR) data'
data integrity   61–62
databases   54–55, 57
   big data   54
   multidimensional   54
   object-oriented   54
   relational   54
dependent variables (DVs)   67
distributive justice perceptions   254
diversity analytics   108–43, 441
   benchmarking   110–11
   comparing ethnicity and gender example   128–35
   dashboards   109–10
   employment engagement survey variables   124–26

# Index

diversity analytics *continued*
  ethnic diversity across teams example 122–28
  gender and job grade analysis example 111–22
  multiple linear regression example 135–41
  predictive models 111
  problems with targeted demographic profiles 449–50
diversity and inclusion (D&I) 108–09, 122–28, 444
  business case 109
  indices 143
  social case 109

Edwards, Professor Jeffrey 434
employee attitude surveys 144–89
  analysis and outcomes 174–77
  ethics and 188, 447–49
  example questionnaire 154
  publishing results 188
  survey companies 174
  *see also* employee engagement
employee engagement 145–47, 443
  analysis and outcomes 174–77
  construct 155, 156
  definitions 145–46, 156
  differences in levels 177–83
  example 158–68
  factor analysis example 158–66
  independent samples t-test 177–83
  measuring 147–53
  performance and 146, 147
  predicting team-level 183–88
  reliability analysis example 166–69
  survey variables 175–76, 443
employee performance 237–84
  customer loyalty example 241–46, 249–53
  customer reinvestment example 246–49
  ethical considerations 282, 438
  growth trajectories 270–82
  high-performing age groups 279–82
  key drivers 263
  measures 238–39
  methods 239–40
  over time 264–68
  patterns in employee profile data 270–74
  predicting from selection data 307–10
  predicting individual 253–57
  sickness-absence 239, 255–57, 263, 268–70, 321
  stepwise multiple linear regression examples 258–64, 264–68

stress 325–36, 417–21
supermarket checkout scan rates 274–76, 276–79
using survey measures 255–57
employee turnover 190–236
  average rates by industry 197
  cost of 190, 191, 231–35, 410
  measuring 192–93
  predicting individual employee example 217–26, 406–10
  predicting the likelihood of leaving 383–90
  predicting team example 226–31
  predictors 192
  regional differences example 194–98, 198–203
  sampling 442–43
  team level by country example 203–17
  voluntary 191
ethics 437–52
  Big Brother concerns 447–48
  data ownership 448
  data security 448–49
  employee confidentiality 447
  standards 450–51

Facebook 54
factor analysis 104–05, 153–58
  exploratory example 158–66
  group-level engagement data example 170–74
Fitz-enz, J 1
frequency tables example 194–98

Gallup 144, 148, 149
Google 54
growth models 413, 427–31
  latent growth modelling (LGM) 429–30
  multi-level modelling 428–29
Guest, David 145

Hadoop 54, 55
Hawking, Stephen 223–24
'Hawthorne effect' 323–24, 358
Hay Group 144, 146
Hayes, Andrew 415
HR analyst 437–39
  data availability/quality 438–39, 446–47
  ethics and 438, 447–51
  objectivity 437–38
  rigour 446
  scepticism 445–46
HR interventions *see* interventions

HR professionals
  analytic literacy  8
  analytics as a scientific discipline
    437–39
  statistical competence  6
  training  5–7
Huselid, M  1, 3, 8

independent variables  68
information source examples  11–12
Institutionalized Metric-Oriented Behaviour
    (IMOB)  283, 439–41
interventions  319–64, 438
  embedded/sustainable impact  323–24
  isolating effects  324–25
  measures  320–21
  panels/pulses  321–22
  sampling  322–23
  simple change testing  321
  stress examples  325–30, 330–36
  supermarket checkout training examples
    352–59, 359–63
  value-change initiative examples
    336–44, 344–51

JASP  15
job satisfaction  254
job strain  254, 263

Kane, J  13, 14
Karasek, R A  417, 431
Kiazim, O  410

latent class analysis  413, 430–31
latent variable  104
Levene, Professor Howard  132
Levene's test  132–34, 180, 211, 213
Lewin, Kurt  150
LinkedIn  54
logistic regression analysis  81–85, 217–22,
    385, 416
  case study examples  84–85
  model chi square  82
  model chi-square p-value  82
  multiple  135–41, 183–88, 240
  Nagelkerke R-square  82–83
  odds ratio  83
  P-value (Sig.) for each independent
    variable  83

Mattox II, J R  1
Mauchly's 'Test of Sphericity'  341, 342,
    343, 349
Mayo, Elton  323
McKinsey  55

measures  4, 320–21
  balanced scorecard  441
  classical test theory  151–52
  combination  153
  employee engagement  147–53
  employee flows  193
  employee performance  237–84
  employee turnover  192–93
  factor analysis  153–68
  individual  238
  reliability analysis  165–66
  team  238
  validity  152–53
mediation processes  412, 414–16
  Baron and Kenny approach  414–15
  Preacher and Hayes approach
    415–16
Mercer  144, 146
Microsoft Excel  61
Minitab  13
moderation and interaction analysis
    412, 416–21
multi-level linear modelling  413, 421–23
multiple linear regression  135–41, 183–88,
    240, 360, 416
  dummy variables  24
  predicting employee turnover  240–82
  predicting performance from selection
    data  307–10
  stepwise  240, 254–64, 264–68

Nagelkerke R-square  82–83, 234, 235
null hypothesis  59, 60, 86

odds ratios  223–26
one-way independent analysis of variance
    (ANOVA) test  89–90
Oracle  55
organizational citizenship behaviour
    (OCB)  167

Paddy Power  223
perceived organizational support (POS)
    164, 254
performance management  237–84
person organization fit  254
polynominal regression analysis  413
predictive HR analytics
  analysis strategies  57–107
  benefits of  2–3, 58
  definition  2
  people strategy and  7–8
predictive modelling  4–5
  business applications  7,
    366–410

probability level (p-value)  60
procedural justice perceptions  254, 263
protected characteristics  108
'pulse' survey  322

R  14
recruitment and selection  285–318
   bias  285, 287–317
   cost  318
   ethical considerations  410–11
   gender/BAME applicants  287–90
   gender/BAME shortlisting and offers  290–302
   graduate selection decisions  390–94, 398–406
   gut instinct  390
   male–female employee ratio  285
   predicting performance from selection data  307–10
   predicting turnover from selection data  310–17
   reliability/validity of methods  286–87
   validating selection techniques as predictors of performance  302–06
reliability analysis  105–06, 165–66
   four-item engagement scale example  166–69
   group-level engagement data example  170–74
   multiple item indicators  166
   testing  166
research hypothesis  59, 86
response surface methodology  413

sampling  322–23, 441–43
SAP  54, 55
SAS  14
scenario modelling  365–411
   customer reinvestment example  367–73
   graduate selection  390–94, 398–406
   investment in an induction day  394–98
   likelihood of employee leaving  383–90
   training programme impact  373–82
Sesil, J C  1
sickness-absence  239, 255–57, 263, 268–70, 321
Smith, T  1
SPSS  13, 15–53, 61, 413
   chi-square and  80, *117*, *120*
   copying data from an Excel spreadsheet  30–33
   correlation option  97
   data view  15, *16*
   entering data into the data view  21–30
   factor analysis  *104*
   independent samples t-test  87
   joining two data sets using employee ID  46–53
   loading a data file from another source  33–46
   logistic regression analysis  84–85
   multiple linear regression analysis  101, *102*
   one-way ANOVA  *90*
   paired samples t-test  89
   preparing the data/data file  21–53
   reliability analysis  *106*
   setting up variables in the variable view  21–30
   syntax interface  435–36
   variable view  17, *18*, 19–21
Stata  14
statistical significance  59–61, 101
   confidence  60–61
   probability level  60–61
statistical tests
   by data type  *69–71*
   categorical data  75–85
   continuous/interval-level data  85–103
   Games-Howell  *212*, 213
   general liner model (GLM)  330–35, 337–44, 344–51
   Greenhouse- Guisser  341
   homogeneity of variances  211
   Huynh-Feldt  341, 350
   Levene's test  132–34, 180, 211, 213
   Mauchly's 'Test of Sphericity'  341, *342*, 343, *349*
   multiple linear regression analysis  98–103
   Nagelkerke R-square  82–83, 234, 235
   one-way independent analysis of variance (ANOVA)  89–90, 203–17
   one-way repeated measures analysis of variance (ANOVA)  93–96
   Pearson's correlation  96–98, 117
   post-hoc  90, *91–92*, *212*
   supermarket checkout training  352–59
   t-tests  85–89, 128–35, 177–83, 330
   within and between ANOVA  94–96
stress  325–36, 417–21
structural equation models (SEM)  413, 427
supermarket checkout
   scan rates  274–76, 276–79, 440
   training  352–63

test statistic  59, 60
Towers Watson  144, 146, 148, 149
t-tests  85–89, 330
   independent samples  85, 86–88, 128–35, 177–83

paired samples 85, 88–89
repeated/related 325

unique identifier 61
Utrecht Work Engagement Scale (UWES) 145

validity 152–53
   construct 152–53, 157
   criterion 153, 157
   discriminant 153, 157
   face 152, 157
   *see also* measures

values 336–44
variables 62
   categorical 62–64
   continuous 64–66
   dependent 67
   dummy 240
   independent 68
   latent 104
   *see also* data

Workday 54, 55
work–life balance (WLB) programme 325, 417